ENGLEWOOD CLIFFS, NEW JERSEY   Prentice-Hall, Inc.

edited by
NAOMI ROSENBAUM
York University

Readings
on the
International
Political
System

FOUNDATIONS OF MODERN POLITICAL SCIENCE SERIES

P9-APR-691

Acknowledgments

I am grateful to all the contributors to this volume who have so graciously allowed me to reprint their work. I am especially indebted to J. David Singer and Ole R. Holsti who have made new or revised manuscripts available, to Morton A. Kaplan and Anatol Rapoport who have helped me with copyright problems, and to Karl W. Deutsch who has advised and generally encouraged me. The readings in this book complement Professor Deutsch's illuminating discussion in *The Analysis of International Relations* (Prentice-Hall, Inc., 1968), but the collection as a whole is intended as a self-sufficient introduction to the contemporary study of international relations.

My editors, S. P. Rosenbaum and Robert A. Dahl, have done much to improve the style and clarity of this volume. Its shortcomings are, of course, my fault and not theirs.

FOUNDATIONS OF MODERN POLITICAL SCIENCE SERIES

Robert A. Dahl, Editor

Contents

Contents

v

Contents

vi

Contents

Introduction

This book is about international relations, understood as what makes
up the international political system of the title. But what are
"international relations"? Dutch uncles eating Turkish delight?
De Gaulle and his foreign policy? the war in Vietnam? As this book
will show, all of these are international relations. So is everything
else that goes on among and between nation states. This is the process
of international relations, and that process is, in turn, the subject
of the field of study called international relations. Different views
of the process create correspondingly different analyses by scholars.
The main purpose of this book is to illustrate a particular approach
to the subject; its other purpose is to present some of what has
recently been found out about the process.

The articles collected here are representative of the most recent work in the field of international relations. Their authors share a distinctive set of images, seldom stated but implicit in their work. What follows in this Introduction is an attempt to describe the theoretical assumptions that seem to be shared by the contributors to this volume, and by most of the scholars in the field today.

The central ideas are "international political behavior" and the "international political system." These together entail understanding international relations in terms of the political acts of individual human beings. *International political behavior* refers to the sum of these acts, including as acts such subjective elements as perception and opinion. The *international political system* is the pattern created by international political behavior. For even those modern scholars (some of them included here) who dislike the labels of behavioralism or systems analysis, the study of national interactions is increasingly the study of the network of political activity that extends across national boundaries.

Until recently the study of international relations tended to define its subject matter relatively, in terms of roles and activities that literally took place outside whatever country attention was focused on. War, diplomacy, and imperialism were all carried on somewhere "overseas," outside one's own territory, by people like soldiers and diplomats whose jobs took them "abroad." Understandably, the most common approach was through case studies of particular bilateral relationships. This made it possible to specify the contexts in which series of events could be considered part of "external" affairs. Such case studies provided the raw data of international relations, but they could not help missing a great deal. There was no sense of politics as a process, or of how the different sets of activities interact. For instance, the war in Vietnam has always been a happening in international relations. Yet in many ways the most important parts of the war have taken place away from Vietnam, inside the United States and the Soviet Union. The notions of international political behavior and the international political system make it possible to pull together more of the pieces, to identify and study their interactions.

II

International relations cannot help being an elusive subject. It is difficult to find the abstractions that will usefully focus the mass of potential subject matter. There are, after all, more than one hundred and thirty countries in the world, having between them over eight thousand two-way routes for possible relations. To narrow things even this far we must use the abstractions of "country" or "nation," simplifying ways of referring to the extremely complicated relationships between territories and groups of people. This is not very helpful when we are interested in what goes on *between* the nations. In trying to use the nations as the initiators of a process, we may end up personifying them or identifying them exclusively with their leaders. But only the individual human components of nations can actually *do* anything, either within or between nations. Leaders have the most influential roles in the process, but by themselves they can do little more than give orders or send messages. The study of international relations therefore needs abstractions that arise from the patterns created across boundaries by the acts of individual human beings. These patterns are the "systems of action" that are the central concern of the writers collected in this volume.

Not all systems of action are either political or international. A *political system,* within or between nations, can be loosely defined as activity related to the distribution of power. Of course, whether within or between nations, political activity coexists with economic, cultural, social, and doubtless many other systems. Internationally, however, the *political* strand of action is central. International systems can be defined only in relation to those political units—the nations. And all attempts to influence international systems must operate through the nations.

"Systems of action," as used here, are artificial and abstract. They represent only an analytical aspect of reality. This becomes clear as we look at an example of how international political behavior operates to build up a system of action between nations. Let us consider the assassination of a President of the United States. One single act, say the firing of a gun, means something, to take only a few of the most obvious groups, for the President's family, for the Vice-President, for the Stock Exchange, and for the leaders of the major powers. History suggests that the murderer's motive may be private revenge or simply a delusion, and that he probably has little idea of the likely consequences of his act. Yet, in its different, analytically separable aspects, the killing exists in the context of at least four different settings and affects groups of people of whom the assassin probably was not aware. The death of a President is part of at least four systems of action, two of them political. One of these political systems is international. So that from one point of view assassinating a President is international political behavior and therefore a component of the international political system.

Abstract, analytical systems of action can be useful tools of research. They make it possible, by selecting related aspects of reality, to pull together the elusive fragments of international relations and to find the meaningful parts of the overabundant material. We are able to delimit or "map" systems of action with a considerable degree of accuracy, and they have inner logics that help us to predict their course.

Not that it is obvious how to pick out the behavior or aspects of behavior of which the international political system is composed. It is comparatively easy to isolate the political system of a given nation or smaller political unit. Each of the human acts that make up political behavior begins in some identifiable physical location, which will have some political identity. Each act is performed by particular and—in principle—identifiable human beings. The formal location (jurisdiction) and the formal identity of the actor (role and affiliation) together provide a reasonably clear indication of what system is under consideration. For

3

instance, when a member of the House of Representatives, in Washington, D.C., questions a member of the Army Corps of Engineers, there is little doubt about what political system is operating. But what about when the Representative questions a spokesman for the Agency for International Development? It is still the American political system but in some way it also belongs to the international political system.

Where, after all, do international relations take place? And who is usually responsible for them? Only a few places are not part of at least one nation, and few individuals have international tasks independent of their national roles. The rules that serve to identify other political systems might lead us to say that international political behavior is no more and no less than what the Secretary-General does at United Nations headquarters. There does exist, of course, a small autonomous political system made up of the acts of international civil servants. Yet this is clearly not what we mean by international relations. The United Nations-centered "universal" system is above rather than between nations, and not yet very important for them. International relations, in the sense of the international political system, take place in some imaginary space *between* nations. International relations must be defined, not in terms of the boundaries they are enclosed by, but in terms of the boundaries they move across.

Boundaries are in fact the guides to identification of the international political system, for they mark the separate existence of nations. Within the political lines we call national borders, each nation is made up of a group of people sharing habits, attitudes, and a sense of being a community. The main function of the border is to mark the limits of the sense of familiarity and the power of exclusion. Beyond the border lie the foreigners, and we intend to keep them there. But even to draw a contrast between ourselves and the others, we have to look across the boundaries; to keep them out, we must build walls and fight battles across the line. Only through its relations with other nations can a nation be either identified or defended.

In short, the existence of even one nation implies the existence of others, and of interactions of the people of those nations. This is the system of action we call international relations—a system of action logically inseparable from the boundaries it moves across. It is a political system because the border lines in relation to which it exists are themselves so political.

III

The international political system, then, can be identified in the following way. We look at acts and actors, but not just in terms of a simple geographical or geopolitical location. A political act is international political behavior (and thus part of the international political system) if it is primarily a response to or an initiative toward conditions beyond the

4

boundaries of the national political system it originates in. This is true both of conscious decisions and of acts of other sorts. To the extent that an "actor's" role, public or private, consists of such international behavior, he is participating in the international political system. The presence of actors filling roles of this sort is usually an indicator of international political behavior.

Thus, the two primary concerns in the study of the international political system are to identify the sorts of acts that compose it and to delineate the roles that produce such acts. Related to this is the study of the influences on and the consequences of these acts. A few theories have also tried to map directly the configurations of the international political system.

The articles in this volume show the wide variety of thinking that can be based on interpreting international relations as the international political system. The pieces have been arranged according to the social structure within which each studies international political behavior—moving from the individual (the unorganized private individual) toward the whole international system. The first section of the book is about the international political behavior of individuals having no direct roles in the international system. The focus is on individual attitudes and perceptions. The second section is about individuals in national roles that are also international roles; these are the makers of foreign policy. The third and fourth sections are about group behavior that is possible only in an international context; these are conflict and cooperation among separate states. The final section is about characteristics of the developing supranational system whose roles and component acts would be directly international. This last section returns to individual behavior, which must be the source of any international system not made up of nations.

None of these articles has been simplified or cut in any way. They were selected for originality and, hopefully, for durability. These are the approaches and, in many cases, the actual findings that seem likely to be influential in the study of international relations. Theoretically and practically, this is where the action is.

PART ONE

THE PEOPLE: PERSONALITY, ATTITUDE, AND OPINION

In an important sense people, not nations, are the basic units of international relations. Nations provide the structure and rationale of the international political system; they mobilize the most important parts of the international behavior of individuals. Yet it is nationally and individually variable human behavior that provides the repertoire of international politics. A nation's acts depend on what its people can and will do. A nation made up entirely of children could not fight a war, nor could a nation of pacifists or agoraphobes. We can guess that a nation whose population included more than a certain proportion of children, pacifists, or phobiacs would be unlikely to do anything at all

7

internationally. It is not possible to say much about the international political system without knowing a good deal about the physical, psychological, and other characteristics of the population of the various nations.

Nations are not merely masses of individual people, however. The many definitions of *nation* have to take into account at least three elements: population, territory, and political authority. From a social psychological point of view, the most important thing is the national community. That is, a nation exists if, and only if, people's ways of thinking and feeling cluster within a geographical area to form distinctive shared habits and attitudes. Their common government is only one of many shared institutions. Yet it is clear that many nations consist of several such national communities, or of only a fragmented, incomplete one. For participation in the process of international relations, what matters is the existence of national political institutions that receive recognition and response from other nations. So that for the field of international relations, there are two interesting sets of problems about individuals: What do individual characteristics mean for the character and behavior of nations? How do groups of individuals come to interact as national units?

In the first article in this book, "Man and World Politics: The Psycho-Cultural Interface," J. David Singer suggests that it is helpful to think of some of the most important sorts of national characteristics as if they were the sums of individual psychological traits. National character, ideology, and the "climate of opinion" can be treated as equivalent to the totals of the individual personalities, characters, and attitudes of the people in a nation. Singer is thus able to discard metaphysical definitions for operational definitions based on the techniques of modern psychologists. He is well aware of the unequal impact that individuals have on society as a whole, but he argues convincingly that national behavior is not unpredictable or unpredictably different from the sum of individual behavior. There are no "emergent" characteristics that cannot be handled by the tools of modern social science. The transition from the individual to world politics becomes, in principle, easy to describe.

Using Singer's techniques, we would be able to describe what is distinctive about a nation's psychological makeup, but we would have no indication of how the nation got to be that way. In the second piece in this section, "Nation-Building in America: The Colonial Years," Richard Merritt focuses on how nations come into existence. He is interested in what the actual historical development of contemporary nations may suggest about the general process of building nations, and about the chances for new nations or supranational associations. The United States is his subject; it is significant as one of the few enduring nations built up from communities that previously had a considerable period of separate political existence. Merritt suggests that the development of a nation is characterized by the growth of shared political and social institutions, a constant widening of human interactions, and common ideological identifications. These three elements can also provide objective, quantifiable

The People

indicators of the levels and viability of national development. Merritt supports his notions with a series of accounts of what went on in the Thirteen Colonies in the years from 1735 to 1775, when the colonists were acquiring shared political institutions. This was a time of increasing frequency and range of interaction of the colonists, as is shown by statistical records of the increase of intercolonial road and water travel, and mail and newspaper traffic. At the same time communications and transactions with Britain remained the same or decreased. Merritt also traces an ideological shift in the editorials of colonial newspapers, which can be assumed to reflect elite opinions; here references to an American community increase and become increasingly favorable, while identification with Britain diminishes.

Merritt's ideas about the nature of national communities are based on theories about group learning and communication. Shared experience in a common environment is thought to have a reinforcing "feedback" effect that tends to bring with it an awareness of and a further strengthening of the community. Karl Deutsch (who first formulated these ideas about community development) and Ronald Inglehart apply the same theories to the task of measuring and predicting supranational integration (Part Five, Chapters 19 and 20). Ernst Haas uses similar notions in his study of the International Labor Organization (Part Four, Chapter 17). Merritt uses persuasively three of the techniques typical of recent work on nations: comparative and systematic study of historical material, derivation of national characteristics and behavior patterns from aggregated statistical data, and content analysis of mass media to find elite and mass attitudes.

With "Knowledge and Foreign Policy Opinions: Some Models for Consideration" by William Gamson and Andre Modigliani, we shift to a direct and recognized connection between individuals and international relations. Opinion about foreign affairs is an explicit reaction to the external world and at the very least a potential source of international political behavior. It is known that most people, perhaps more than ninety per cent of the population in many countries, are ordinarily indifferent to foreign affairs. Even when they are concerned, most people remain startlingly ignorant about what goes on in the world. This has led to the notion that democratic control of foreign policy is dangerous but may be made less so by an increase in the level of public information about foreign affairs. Informed opinion would be both more attentive and more enlightened. Gamson and Modigliani conclude that the main effect of increased knowledge, about foreign affairs or about most other things, is to increase the strength and consistency of opinions previously held. The better informed people are, the better they are able to coordinate their general political orientations, beliefs, and ideologies to support their opinions. Researchers seem to have been misled by the correlation between higher levels of information about the world and certain attitudes toward foreign policy, such as a rejection of militarism. Rejection of militarism is characteristic of social scientists, but this does not necessarily mean

9

that it is good policy. The difficulty presumably comes from the wide range of plausible opinions possible about any issue in foreign policy. Gamson and Modigliani's findings undercut the optimistic assumptions of many programs for education in current events. At the same time, a moderately high level of information does seem to be a necessary, if not a sufficient, condition for "enlightened" policy choices.

In "The President, the Polls, and Vietnam," Seymour Martin Lipset considers how public opinion becomes more than just a potential part of the international political system. He is concerned with public opinion as an element of foreign policy. The classic democratic model makes popular views the source of policy; Lipset is interested in how opinion may be manipulated to become a support for policy selected on quite other grounds. Opinion is an individual thing, but it is mediated and shaped by national leaders. Gamson and Modigliani were interested in the content of opinion, but Lipset is more concerned with its effects. In a careful examination of a series of polls on the war in Vietnam, Lipset shows the American people so divided in their grounds for both approval and disapproval that the sum of their opinion is ambiguous and malleable. The polltakers, and even more so the government, can with some justification read several interpretations from the data. Selecting and publicizing one of these interpretations is a very effective way to influence both future opinion and future policy options.

Lipset leaves us face to face with the central problems of the study of international political behavior. Will increased understanding of the international political system make the system more or less tolerable for the human beings that create it? Individuals, the basic components of the system, are both the most easily understood and—it would seem partly for this reason—the most easily manipulated.

The People

Man and World Politics: The Psycho-Cultural Interface

J. David Singer

Reprinted with permission from the *Journal of Social Issues,* Vol. 24, No. 3 (1968),
127–56. Mr. Singer is Professor of Political Science and Research Political Scientist
in the Mental Health Research Institute at the University of Michigan.

In every discipline, the would-be theorizer must eventually come to grips with the age-old issue of the parts-versus-the-whole, or the components-versus-the-system. This issue divides, in turn, into two fairly distinguishable subissues. First, what is the relative importance of each for explanatory purposes? Can we develop a satisfactory general theory without any regard for the parts, the particles, the particular? Is inclusion of them desirable, necessary, sufficient? How much attention can we pay to micro-level entities and phenomena without invading an unfamiliar discipline, without becoming extreme reductionists? These questions cannot, of course, be answered in even the most tentative fashion until we devise an acceptable solution to the second subissue: what sort of conceptual scheme permits us to embrace parts as well as whole, or allows us to explicitly ignore one or the other? Can we develop a paradigm which gets at the interplay between micro- and macro-level phenomena? How is the interface between them best formulated and described?

For the social scientist, the issue—in one way or another—is that of relating the individual to all those social groups of which he is a member, as well as understanding the relationship between the smaller of these groups and the larger. In sociology and psychology, the hybrid discipline of social psychology has largely emerged in response to this set of questions. In anthropology, the personality-and-culture approach represented a serious, if not fully successful, effort to cope with the matter (Cohen, 1961; Hsu, 1961; Kluckhohn and Murray, 1953). In economics, the impression is that all but a handful of brave, but nonempirical, theorists have preferred to ignore the problem for the present, with the consumer, the firm and the market generally serving to identify the separate fields of interest. In political science, it has indeed been a traditional preoccupation, with man-versus-the-state and individual freedom-versus-public order very much on our minds. But as we have shifted from prescientific to more rigorous methodologies, we seem to have suffered from the same sorts of separatist tendencies as the economists, even to the extent that the philosophical issues in the discipline have been defined in so irrelevant a fashion as that of the "behaviorists" (usually at the individual level) versus the "institutionalists."

In the world politics field, the picture is much the same. Some of us

The organization of this paper and the development of its argument have benefited from the comments and criticism of Fred I. Greenstein, Karl W. Deutsch, Guy E. Swanson, Harry Gollob and Michael Wallace; the final revision is, of course, my responsibility and not theirs.

The People

concentrate on individuals (or at least their attitudes and opinions) and others concentrate on the foreign policies of the nations, with a smaller third group focussing upon the international system.[1] Even the psychologists and sociologists who have lately ventured into the world politics field, despite their many valuable and promising contributions, have tended to shy away from any systematic effort to integrate psychological and societal phenomena.[2]

Rejoining Men with Their Political System

In order to get on with theory building and hypothesis testing it is necessary to bring the parts and the whole together, but in a more rigorous fashion than has been evident in the past. This need for rejoining men and their political systems is essential for at least two reasons. First, without paradigms that embrace both the micro- and macro-levels, we cannot advance very far in answering the question: how much latitude do individual citizens and decision-making elites enjoy in world politics? Or to put it another way, what is the relative potency of men vis-a-vis their institutions?[3] Second, we can seldom get very far in answering more specific theoretical and policy questions if we work with paradigms that leave out either the individual or the larger environment. By definition, any paradigm which ignores one or the other remains woefully incomplete.[4]

While the behavior of men or of social systems may be *described,* and perhaps even *predicted,* without recourse to such variables, no satisfactory *explanation* is possible until we understand the psychological link which joins man to his sociopolitical environment, and through which each impinges on the other. In the absence of a judicious and well-balanced conceptual scheme, moreover, we will continue to suffer from two extremes of misinterpretation. On the one hand, there is the traditional view which sees individuals—be they members of an elite or of a mass public—as more or less irrelevant to an understanding of world politics. On the

---

[1] Among those who *have* concerned themselves with the micro-macro issue, either explicitly or implicitly, there seems to be the familiar division into two schools of thought; one might be called the ecological determinist school, exemplified in the thoughtful analysis developed by Waltz (1959), and the other might be called the individual autonomy viewpoint. Among the handful of explicit but pre-operational efforts to synthesize these viewpoints are Sprout and Sprout (1965), Wolfers (1959), and Singer (1961).

[2] Two exceptions come to mind. One is an early article by Angell (1955) and the other is the recent anthology edited by Kelman (1965), especially his own opening and closing chapters. See also Stratton (1929), Murphy (1945), and Klineberg (1964).

[3] An important study on this issue is Rosenau's research into the relative potency of role constraints versus "personal preference" in the foreign policy behavior of U.S. Senators in the Acheson and Dulles eras (1968).

[4] I am certainly not urging that all research must come to a halt until we have solved these problems, or that inquiries which sidestep them are of no value. I am merely urging that anything approximating a coherent and complete theory must ultimately be sufficiently molecular to embrace the behavior of men and sufficiently molar to embrace their environment.

13

other, there is the tendency to anthropomorphize and to describe nations in such personal terms as aggressive, intro-punitive, sadistic, narcissistic, ego-defensive and the like. Closely related to this is the tendency to assume that any character trait which is widely distributed within the population provides a sufficient basis for understanding that nation's foreign policies.

The purpose of this paper, then, is to examine the interface between individual man and the larger societal environment, from a world politics point of view, and at the same time avoid both types of pitfall. My intent is to do this via a concentration on those variables which join man to that environment: psychological variables. Given the centrality of this problem to any potential theory of world politics, and the relative inattention to it to date, my hope here is to address it in a fashion which may clarify some of the conceptual problems and at the same time increase our capacity to move toward such theory in a more operational and data-based fashion. With these objectives in mind, let me first outline a general taxonomy of world politics which hopefully is not only quite susceptible to operational treatment, but is also neutral regarding the inclusion of variables which would bias it toward either the individual autonomy or ecological determinist point of view.

What is offered here is not a theory, but a taxonomy within which a range of theories might be developed. Moreover, it is only a static taxonomy, since space limitations preclude any attention to the dynamic interaction of the variables which are discussed. That is, all I can hope to do in this paper is describe certain components of the "global machine" in a state of rest; in a forthcoming study, I hope to describe what occurs when they are combined with other components and the entire apparatus is set in motion. As a further concession to spatial limitations, I summarize in only the briefest fashion those nonpsychological variables, which, while essential to the completeness of the scheme, have already been elaborated elsewhere (Singer, 1968).

A General Framework

In addition to the above specific requirements for any taxonomy which is addressed to the individual-versus-society issue, a framework for the understanding of global politics must also satisfy at least four other criteria: first, it must embrace both institutional and behavioral classes of variables; second, it must be a developmental scheme in the sense that it can handle a wide range of historical periods in the evolution of the global system; third, it must be sufficiently a-theoretical (or multi-theoretical) to permit the sort of integration and synthesis most appropriate to the present state of our discipline; and fourth, it must be stated in terms that permit operational definition and measurement. Elsewhere, I hope to spell out a fairly complete scheme (Singer, 1968) but here let me

The People

merely sketch in the outlines of that framework, and indicate that it relies heavily upon a general systems approach.[5]

Entities and Their Attributes

Whereas most laymen and most foreign policy practitioners tend to organize their ideas on world politics around a variety of social *entities,* many social scientists increasingly tend to build their schemes around *roles and relationships.*[6] In my judgment, this represents a regressive step, moving us away from conceptual clarity and operational measurement with no trade-off in the form of enhanced explanatory power. To the contrary, by subdividing an entity's roles into those appropriate to the economy, the polity or the society, we reduce the probability of ever seeing the entity in anything approximating its entirety. By focussing on only one portion of the relationships of these multipurpose entities, how can we expect to describe and understand their behavior in that isolated role, no less in their other roles? While many of the notions in common use are indeed theoretically misleading and scientifically non-operational, a fair number may easily be refined and salvaged; therefore, the burden of proof ought to be on those who would reject the more familiar concepts and intellectual frameworks.

Thus, let me begin by specifying the classes or levels of entity around which the present paradigm is organized. These are: (a) national states; (b) such subnational entities as: political parties, pressure groups (latent as well as manifest), labor and professional associations, and family, tribal, religious and ethnic groups; and (c) such extranational entities as associations of the above sorts of subnational groups, international intergovernmental organizations, and international nongovernmental organizations.

Once the social entities are specified—and the paradigm permits selection of those most appropriate to a given researcher's theoretical interests—we find that all relevant entities may be identified, measured and compared according to three sets of attributes. First, there are the obvious *physical* attributes, including elements of geography, demography and technology; for the purposes of this paper, no further elaboration of

5 That approach is best exemplified in the articles found in the Yearbook of the Society for General Systems Research, published annually since 1956, and the most integrated single effort is James Miller's forthcoming *Living Systems* (1968). In my judgment we have not yet developed a general systems theory; hence the word "approach."

6 Perhaps most instrumental in this movement is Talcott Parsons, whose theoretical views are synthesized for a political science audience in Mitchell (1967). For those who think I misinterpret Parsons, there is this quote: "the unit of a partial social system is a role, and not the individual. . . . A social system is a behavioral system. It is an organized set of behaviors of persons interacting with each other: a pattern of roles. The roles are the units of a social system" Grinker (1956, 328). Two compelling discussions from the entity-oriented viewpoint are Cattell (1955) and Campbell (1958), both of which are reprinted in Singer (1965).

these attributes is necessary. The second set of attributes falls into the *structural* class, and may be conventionally (if not readily) divided into the formal and the informal, or better still, placed on a formal-informal continuum. Toward the formal end are those attributes based on observation and description of what political scientists usually refer to as institutions, and would include such phenomena as the types and powers of legitimate political and economic institutions handling legislative, administrative, judicial, banking, commercial-industrial regulation, social welfare, military, information control and related functions. Toward the informal end are those structural attributes based on the observation of: urban-rural distribution; social mobility, kinship and marriage patterns; citizen access to and influence over the decision-making process; size, centralization and scope of political parties and other unofficial or quasi-official associations (including pressure groups); number, power and role of religious, ethnic and linguistic groupings and the like. Also relevant as aspects of informal structure might be the extent of pluralistic cross-cutting ties, and the general coalition configurations which develop among the system's many component subsystems.

The final attributes are what might be called the *cultural* ones; being central to this paper, they will be developed in more detail in later sections. Here, let me merely point out that I use culture in a much narrower sense than do those anthropologists who permit it to embrace everything from belief in an after-life to technological artifacts, often including social structure as well. The usage here is similar to that found in some of the recent comparative politics literature (Almond and Verba, 1963; Pye and Verba, 1965; Banks and Textor, 1963). Note further that these cultural attributes are all strictly nonbehavioral, or more accurately, both post-behavioral and prebehavioral in the sequential or causal sense. We will return to them in due course.

Relationships Among Entities

Before moving from the identification of entities and their attributes to their behavior and interaction, an intermediate set of variables needs to be delineated. Reference is to the relationships that exist between and among our relevant entities, and in addition to describing some illustrative types of relationships it is necessary to clarify two definitional points. First, relationships exist not only among entities at the *same* level of analysis (i.e., among pressure groups, among nations, among international organizations) but also among those at *different* levels of analysis. Second, relationships are of two types. One type deals with the *similarity* or dissimilarity of attributes while the other deals with degrees of *interdependence* and connectedness. On the similarity side, we first decide on the attributes which interest us, next measure or scale each entity's rank or interval score on that attribute dimension, and then compute the discrepancy or "distance" between the two. And while such distances are

16

usually measured on only one attribute dimension at a time, it is quite feasible to locate nations or other entities within a certain conceptual space on the basis of multidimensional distances, as in Rummel (1965). On the interdependence side, we are again concerned with the concept of closeness and distance, but in terms of interdependence, interpenetration, connectedness, dominance and the like. Needless to say, there is no necessary correlation between the similarity and the interdependence of a given pair of entities.

Behavior and Interaction Among Entities

A final aspect of our taxonomy is the distinction between relationship (in the sense of interdependence) and *interaction*. In brief, whenever a nation[7] *behaves* vis-a-vis another nation (or any other entity) and the second nation responds to that behavior, we may speak of an interaction. Of course, we require evidence that the two behavioral events or acts are somehow linked causally if we are to identify them as an interaction; if not, we merely have two isolated acts. When we observe a fairly long series of causally connected acts and responses, we may speak of an interaction sequence.

It should be noted, then, that two or more entities may display both relationships and interactions, and despite the tendency in our literature to use relationship and interaction interchangeably, it seems imperative to differentiate between an essentially static pairwise phenomenon and a highly dynamic one. To put it differently, relationships change slowly and are described in highly spatial terms, whereas interactions occur in a brief interval and are highly temporal in nature. Obviously, relationships affect interactions, and vice versa, and are causally quite connected; one often *observes* a sequence of interactions in order to infer a relationship. Thus, after observing a large number of behavioral events and interactions, such as the exchange of many threatening diplomatic messages, we may infer the existence of a hostile relationship.

Conversely, one may often predict an interaction sequence or a single behavioral event on the basis of a recognized relationship. For example, if we infer a relationship such as high economic interdependence, we may predict a continuing succession of direct or indirect cargo shipments between the two nations under consideration. But since all these export and import actions happen to leave a relatively reliable trace, via standard bookkeeping procedures, it is more efficient to measure the economic interdependence between these entities by examining periodic records of aggregate shipments and transfers; we need not dispatch research assistants to all the ports of entry and departure. On the other hand, there are a great many relationships which can be inferred only by direct

---

[7] To keep an already complex paper somewhat simpler, I will often refer only to national entities from now on, but it is understood that the reference could always be to subnational and extranational ones as well.

observation of interaction sequences, especially interactions between individuals and between less formal social entities. And there are, likewise, many interactions which cannot be readily observed—especially in diplomacy—and these must be inferred by observing changes in relationship.

Psychological Attributes: The Individual Level

Given this fairly general framework, the next step in articulating the role of psychological variables in world politics is to direct our attention to the individual level of analysis and to certain psychological attributes of the single human being, both normal and deviant. My effort here will be to impose some order on a bewildering melange of constructs such that the political scientist or other macro-social scientist can put them to greater use. I recognize that others, in and out of psychology (Smith *et al.*, 1956), have tried before with only moderate success, but the possible payoffs seem worth the effort, and I therefore trust that our behavioral science colleagues will be understanding in their appraisal, and if necessary, gentle in their disapproval of this intruder's temerity.

In the view outlined here, there are three basic and differentiable psychological properties of individuals which are of interest to the societal scientist. These properties or constructs may be labeled: (a) personality, (b) attitude and (c) opinion. Further, they may be roughly scaled on three different dimensions. First, there is the generality dimension; second, there is durability; and third, there is the observability dimension. In the verbal descriptions of these three types of psychological attributes, these ranges will become more apparent, but the ordering may be graphically summarized here.

Dimensions / Attributes	Generality	Durability	Observability
Personality Attitude Opinion	High Medium Low	High Medium Low	Low Medium High

FIGURE 1   *Postulated Ordering of Psychological Attitudes on Three Descriptive Dimensions*

Perhaps more critical than the hypothesized ways in which personality, attitude and opinion may scale on the above dimensions is the nature of the subject matter with which all intrapsychic activities are concerned. There would seem to be three very general substantive areas. The first of these concerns beliefs about reality in the individual's life space: how he responds, cognitively and affectively, to the way "things

18

The People

are done" or used to be done. The second concerns the way things *should* be done, in both the present and future, as well as the way they should have been done in the past; this category is quite similar to what we often refer to as values. The third concerns the way things *will* be done in the future or *might* have been done in the past. These may be thought of as the perceptual, the preferential and the predictive dimensions. These three dimensions, it would seem, are largely undifferentiated at the personality level, moderately differentiated at the attitudinal level, and rather clearly differentiated at the opinion level. Thus, if we treat personality as a reservoir of predispositions, we need not expect that any sharp distinctions between present and future, or between "is" and "ought," will be found. That is, we look to general personality traits and their configurations as a major *source* of (and perhaps predictor of) preconscious and unverbalized attitudes and opinions, rather than as the *location* of these more specific and differentiated psychic attributes. When we move to attitudes, the distinctions between and among what is, what ought, and what will, should be expected to take on greater clarity. And at the level of opinions, the distinctions may well be quite clear and perhaps might even become specific enough to be stated by the individual in relatively operational terms.

Given these general remarks on the relationships among personality, attitude and opinion, we may now turn to a more detailed consideration of each in turn. Note again that whereas most social psychologists tend to treat attitudes and / or opinions as components, aspects or levels of personality, the approach here is to treat all three as separate—but causally interdependent—psychological attributes of the individual.

Personality

Of all the terms used in the psychological literature, none causes more difficulty than personality, and at least two reasons come to mind. First, and on this there seems to be a strong consensus, personality is the most inclusive and all-embracing psychological property attributed to the human being.[8] Second, there is an overwhelmingly long list of schemata and taxonomies by which an individual's personality may be compared with another's, or with itself over time.[9] One's choice of scheme here is

---

[8] A useful compendium, albeit a decade in age, is McCary's *Psychology of Personality: Six Modern Approaches* (1956).

[9] Over thirty years ago, Allport and Odbert (1936) pointed out that over 17,000 personality trait names could be identified in Western literature. A more recent scanning of the personality literature reveals such dimensions as: high or low on the need for achievement, affiliation or power (McClelland, 1958, and Atkinson, 1958); authoritarian (Adorno, *et al.,* 1950); conservative (McCloskey, 1953); open- or closed-minded (Rokeach, 1960); misanthropic (Rosenberg, 1957); intolerant of ambiguity (Frenkel-Brunswik, 1949); provincial or cosmopolitan (Levinson, 1957); introverted (Jung, 1923); narcissistic and/or egoistic (Freud, 1922); optimistic or pessimistic; altruistic; exhibitionist; apathetic; dominant; dependent; sadistic or masochistic; manic-depressive; inner-directed or other-directed and so on.

less important than the fact that these (and other) formulations are attempts to classify and measure fairly basic internal predispositions toward action of normal, as well as mentally ill, people. As Cattell (1950, 2) puts it, "personality is that which permits a prediction of what a person will do in a given situation." And typically, these predispositions are thought of as a consequence of biological inheritance, the near-universal infancy experience, and the varying experiences of puberty and adulthood. A paraphrase of Allport's view is illustrative:

> The newborn babe lacks the characteristic organization of psychological systems, and has a *potential* personality that develops within the skin. The givens of personality are an idiographic complex of physique, temperament and intelligence, motivated in infancy by essentially biological and nutritional drives. As the infant matures and interacts with the social and physical environment, he develops a personality. Once beyond the infantile stage, this personality cannot be understood in terms of biological motives alone (Bertocci, 1965, 302).

An equally important aspect of personality is that we generally see it as the organizing and integrating framework within which all other intrapsychic attributes are embraced. In addition to its generality, post-adolescent personality is thought of as showing only the most gradual change over time, at least in the "normal" individual who has essentially "normal" experiences during a lifetime. Finally, despite the availability, demonstrated reliability, and apparent validity of many of the tests (projective and otherwise) by which we observe and measure personality, the inferential leap between the measuring instrument and the intellectual construct is so great that personality must be treated as the least observable of our three psychological variables.[10] In short, personality is defined here as a hypothetical construct embracing and structuring the individual's total reservoir of behavioral predispositions.

Attitudes

Shifting to a somewhat more restricted, malleable and observable cluster of individual attributes, we come next to what will be called *attitudes*.[11] While attitudes are largely shaped by the personality which organizes and embraces them, they are also seen as responsive to and modifiable by immediate (or even moderately distal) experience; more particularly, an

[10] Two possible paths to improvement in the measurement of personality come to mind. First, the clinical psychology and psychiatry subcultures could profitably borrow and adapt the more rigorous and operational methods already in use in other social sciences; there seems to be room for considerable modification in coding, classifying and scaling procedures. Second, some tentative evidence seems to be emerging that we might find occasional correlations between mental state or personality and certain biochemical or electro-physiological indicators.

[11] A fairly complete survey of the measures for those which are most relevant to political science is in Rieselbach (1964).

The People

individual's attitude on any matter may best be viewed as resulting from the interplay of personality and experience (Brim and Wheeler, 1966).

In the taxonomy employed here, attitudes (as well as personality and opinion) fall into the three subclasses outlined earlier: the individual's perceptions of the way things *are* done in his "life space," his preferences for the way things *should* be done, and his predictions as to the way things probably *will* be done. Attitudes, then, are defined here in a literal —if broad—sense to mean the partially structured disposition to act in a certain way; the meaning is highly analogous to that used when we describe the attitude of an astronaut's capsule moving in space, or that of a dancer prior to or during a single routine or even that of the Leaning Tower of Pisa. The notion may be further conveyed by terms such as posture or stance. That is, an entity's attitude markedly affects its probability of acting or moving in a given, and—depending on the state of our theory—predictable direction.

An individual's attitudes may differ from his neighbor's not only in their content, but in their degree of generality, in their durability, in the amount of affective loading with which their holder invests them, and in the extent of their structure, integration and coherence (Converse, 1964). The interdependence between personality and attitudes will be explored further, but a more orderly procedure would be to move on next to our third and final set of psychological attributes: opinions.

Opinions

While much of the literature tends to treat opinions and attitudes as more or less interchangeable, it seems worthwhile to preserve the distinction, even at the risk of raising some difficult problems of operationalization. Thus, I would define opinions as considerably more specific than attitudes, markedly more transitory and appreciably more susceptible to systematic observation and measurement. At the same time, they may be divided into the same subclasses as attitudes: perceptions, preferences and predictions. To illustrate in regard to specificity (durability and observability will be discussed below), we can classify a person's *general* approval or disapproval of strong supranational organizations—for instance—as *attitudinal*. He may perceive those organizations now in existence as weak, may prefer that they become stronger and may (for example) predict that they will not become stronger in some relevant future. This attitudinal cluster should, of course, predict fairly well to his *opinions* on a particular aspect of the general problem. Thus, during the Congo crises of 1960, this individual might hold the opinions that the Secretary General was not exploiting the full latitude voted him by the General Assembly, that he should have assumed wider powers and that, if certain governments acquiesced in the original range of assumed authority, Mr. Hammarskjold would gradually try to expand that range. Whether the problem was sufficiently salient to the individual to convert the general attitude into a specific set of opinions is, of course, in doubt, as is the extent to which the attitudinal and opinion clusters were each internally consistent as well as logically compatible with one another.[12]

The Interplay of Psychological Attributes

Let me now return to a somewhat more detailed consideration of the interplay between and among all three of these psychological attributes. More particularly, what are the ways in which personality relates to both attitude and opinion? There would seem to be two different types of relationship here. First, there is the generally understood notion that a certain personality type will hold attitudes and opinions whose content is largely predictable from, and shaped by, his personality. For example, the parochial or provincial *personality* is associated with negative *attitudes* toward outsiders and with *opinions* which favor policies designed to keep such groups in a distant, if not subordinate, position.

But there is a second type of interrelationship at work here, and it tends to get less attention. Reference is to the way in which personality affects the structuring and the durability of attitudes and opinions, regardless of their substantive *content*. Of course, the personality syndrome as defined here is such that its content will not be independent of its structure and durability, but these qualities may be, for analytical convenience, treated separately. At the attitudinal level, if we look at perceptions, preferences and predictions, it should immediately be evident that there is a fair degree of interdependence among them. Perceptions and preferences will both affect predictions; perceptions and predictions will affect preferences, and preferences and predictions will affect perceptions; all three attitudinal components are highly interconnected. Moreover, the way in which any two of these combine in order to affect the third is very much a function of the more fundamental personality traits.

Let me illustrate each of these three combinational effects. For example, a normal and concerned individual who perceives his nation to be following a given diplomatic strategy and who prefers that it be reversed, will—depending upon the strength of the preference—be more likely to predict such reversal than will his counterpart who prefers continuation of the present strategy. But most of the variance in the prediction will probably be a function of the personality dimension which embraces optimism and pessimism. The optimistic personality might even

---

[12] It has become something of a ritual for political scientists to note how uninterested and/or uninformed the bulk of the world's citizens are in regard to politics, and while the evidence seems compelling, it may be somewhat beside the point for students of foreign policy. Overlooking, for the moment, the ways in which elite foreign policy articulations and arguments may easily lead to public cynicism and indifference, the fact is that those members of the public who *are* attentive and/or informed are generally those whose opinions do exercise some impact on the policy making process.

22

The People

be defined operationally by the extent to which his predictions coincide with his preferences; the extreme optimist might be called the "wishful thinker," and the person whose preferences and predictions are usually far apart appears in the role of Cassandra.

In the second and more interesting case, when perceptions and predictions combine to shape preferences, the effect of personality becomes more striking. The inner-directedness dimension or trait is central here, with strongly inner-directed personalities tending to hold onto their preferences even though they see little chance of those preferences being realized. To put it in different language, certain personality types can tolerate a much greater degree of dissonance or incongruence between the way they *expect* things to be and the way they *prefer* them to be. Those who are (a) less inner-directed, or (b) have a lower tolerance for such dissonance, find a fairly convenient solution; they tailor their preferences so as to make them more "realistic."[13] Turning to the third case—preference and prediction combining to shape perceptions—this is probably the sector which most social psychologists have emphasized when examining international politics. They are, quite rightly, struck by the frequency with which citizens and elites either construct, or accept, the most outrageous distortions of past or present reality. Here, again, a personality typical of many societies takes its toll. Whether we call it other-directedness or something else, these attitudinal misperceptions just could not be so universal and so pronounced were it not for the prevalence in America and elsewhere of the socially acquiescent personality. While I know of no hard evidence to this effect, every indication is that—and this is almost definitional—very few citizens are deviant enough to resist the cumulative distortion of perception (Livant, 1963) and perpetuation of arbitrary judgments (Jacobs and Campbell, 1961) which social pressures are able to generate.[14]

Personality may be thought of not only as a predictor of the way in which attitudes are structured and modified, but also as a predictor of the way in which opinions will combine and change. Again, we will merely scratch the surface here, as the intent is only to demonstrate that all three attributes are highly interdependent, and that from the observation of an individual's opinion, we may make some reasonable inferences about his personality. In the most obvious sense, we generally expect that a so-called authoritarian personality would tend to correlate with opinions that perceive relationships very much in terms of superior-subordinate, and

---

13 This normative flexibility—because it is a widespread personality trait in the industrial societies of today—may well account for (i.e., acquiesce in) a great deal of the incompetence and inhumanity found in modern foreign policies. Seeing no feasible way of changing things, many citizens merely revise their notions as to what constitutes acceptable (or justifiable) diplomacy or strategy.

14 Such manipulability could be expected to vary from one society to another, and one study (Milgram, 1961) found that a French sample was significantly more resistant to such pressures than a matched Norwegian sample. We must be careful, however, not to confuse that "decent respect for the opinions of mankind" which might be more prevalent in a society characterized by high mutual trust, with high suggestibility; conversely, the distrust of others may not be equivalent to inner-directedness.

that prefer clearcut lines of authority, well-defined roles and boundaries, and vigorous law enforcement, for example. Similarly, closed-minded personality types will find it difficult to change their opinions in the face of new evidence, but might nevertheless be expected to change such opinions when authority figures express an opinion contrary to the one originally held by the subject. To put it another way, many of the personality measures and classifications used today are based on the kind of opinions and attitudes expressed or admitted to by the respondent or subject, and we should therefore not be surprised that those constructs which we call personality traits would correlate strongly with opinions and attitudes. Further, the way in which an individual structures and integrates his opinions and attitudes will also provide important indicators of, and be responsive to, the basic personality traits.

Cultural Attributes: The Societal Level

Having summarized and / or hypothesized the general relationships among personality, attitude and opinion at the individual level, let me now shift to the societal level, be it a subnational, national or extra-national entity which concerns us. The central thesis here is that, even though no social group can be properly thought of as having a personality, an attitude or an opinion, we may nevertheless attribute certain properties to a group on the basis of the distribution and configuration of these psychological properties. In other words, I would hold that the aggregation of individual *psychological* properties provides a quite sufficient base for describing the *cultural* properties of the larger social entity which is comprised of those individuals.

The Aggregative-Emergent Argument

This position brings me face to face with the ancient, and still open, issue of aggregative versus emergent properties. If the issue can still arouse controversy between the defenders of "organismic" and "mechanistic" approaches in disciplines ranging from biology to astonomy, we need not be surprised by its durability in the social sciences.[15] In my view, however, there is a relatively straightforward solution to the problem, such that the reductionist or aggregative position taken here need not appear as foolish and simplistic as it is often made out by advocates of the "emergent properties" school. That solution requires, however, a somewhat more refined taxonomy and more self-conscious epistemology than is often found among the occasionally mystical "gestaltists" in sociology, political science and anthropology.

First, it requires that we define levels of analysis along only one

[15] Perhaps the most balanced and thorough treatment of the issue, from a physical science point of view, is in Nagel (1961) 336–397.

The People

dimension, or at least, only one at a time. If we want to treat the economic, the political and the social *sectors* of society, and the cultural and the structural *attributes* of society as different "levels of analysis" (as does Smelser in *Journal of Social Issues,* Vol. 24, No. 3, for example) there may be no serious harm, but to shift from a horizontal back to a vertical axis and to also include the physiological and the psychological in the scheme (as do many, including Smelser) is to court conceptual chaos. It would seem more in keeping with the symbolism associated with "levels" and with conceptual clarity were we to adhere to the vertical axis alone and base our levels of analysis on the size and complexity of the entities which we are considering at the moment; e.g., from cell to organ to organism, or individual to family to nation. This and closely related points are made succinctly by Coleman (1964, 84):

> One important measurement problem in sociology concerns the two levels on which sociologists must work: the level of the individual and that of the group. We have observations at two levels, concepts at two levels, and relationships at two levels. Furthermore, it is necessary to shift back and forth: measuring group-level concepts from individual data, or inferring individual relationships from group-level relations.

A second distinction of importance in this epistemological issue is that between structure and culture. Even though the structure and the culture of a social system are causally linked in a most intimate fashion, they are by no means identical; nor does it enhance our clarity to ignore the boundary between them. In the taxonomy proposed here, the *structure* of a system is defined as that set of properties which we attribute to it on the basis of the observed *relationships* among the entities (individuals or groups) which comprise the system. *Culture,* on the other hand, is defined as the set of properties we attribute to the system by observing the distribution of *psychological attributes* among the individuals who comprise the system. The problem is one of distinguishing between the construct or verbal representation which we use for descriptive and explanatory purposes and the operations by which we ascertain that construct's presence or absence, strength or direction of change. While there are many exceptions, a large number of system properties can only be defined and measured by observing subsystem phenomena, and on that basis, the distinction between structure and culture should not be too difficult to observe.

The third and equally critical clarification that is required is that between behavioral phenomena and essentially static phenomena of a pre- or post-behavioral nature. For example, much of the social science literature concurs that the *structure* of a social system is a property we attribute to the system on the basis of observing relationships among its subsystems. But since little of the literature distinguishes between *relationship* (marital, friendly, hierarchical, alliance, etc.) and *interaction* (embrace, fight, speak, exchange, etc.) we end up by confusing the formal or informal *structure of* a system with the behavioral and interactional regularities which *occur within* that system. To be sure, we may infer

25

relationships by observing interactions, and we often predict interactions from known relationships, but they are—and deserve to be treated as—quite distinct classes of phenomena.

The Linkage Between Subsystems

A final distinction of importance, and one which appears to lie at the heart of the aggregative versus emergent confrontation, is that between the procedures we use to *describe* a social system and those we use to *explain* how it "got that way." We may, quite legitimately, observe the distribution of subsystem attributes, the relationships among the subsystems, and the interactions among them, and on the basis of these offer a fairly full *description* of that system.[16] But until we have observed and demonstrated the linkage between and among subsystem attributes, relationships, and interactions, we can not *explain* and account for the properties, behavior or relationships of the system itself. Admittedly the line between scientific explanation and description begins to blur as that description becomes more complete, but the intellectual operations are sufficiently different to merit explicit demarcation.

As one reads the philosophers of science as well as the critics of the position taken here, it turns out that the ancient argument against reductionism and in favor of organic or holistic epistemologies rests largely on the inability of a reductionist model to *account for* the system's properties or behavior; we cannot, they remind us, explain or predict the behavior or future states of the system solely on the basis of the properties of its constituent elements. But even here, knowledge of the components' properties can carry us a fair part of the way from description to explanation. To illustrate, we can pour pellets of steel into a container until it is full, with little qualitative change in the aggregate; it merely becomes larger. But if we do the same thing with pellets of enriched uranium under appropriate conditions, we will eventually arrive at the "critical mass" threshold, with important qualitative change in the aggregate as a result. In such a case, the emergent properties of the system are largely explicable in terms of the properties of its component parts. In the same vein, observation of the placement or relationships among components may enhance our understanding of the system's behavior. For example, a society which becomes involved in a limited war and has a large number of citizens who are intolerant of ambiguity may move quickly into all-out war in the "drive for closure." The same result could come

16 My impression is that this view does not run afoul of the stricture which Wallace (1961, 43) and others keep returning to. He inveighs against the "statistical fallacy, which offers an enumeration of the properties of individual persons as if it were a description of a social or cultural system...." Given the context, he is presumably concerned about those "personality and culutre" authors who treat psychological factors as all, and nearly ignore the structural attributes of the society. Nor do we seem to be committing Robinson's (1950) "ecological fallacy" in which one infers individual attributes from group attributes for which only the marginals are known.

The People

about, even if such a personality trait were infrequent in that society, but typical of its elites or only of its chief of state. My point, then, is that while knowledge of subsystem or component properties, or relations or interactions among these components, may not always suffice for explanatory, or even predictive, purposes, such knowledge constitutes a major basis for *describing* the larger system. And while explanation and operational description must be distinguished, the latter is not so plentiful in social science that we can afford to dismiss it as trivial.

Once any of these four distinctions becomes blurred, we are much more likely to reject the view outlined here and retreat into some sort of metaphorical and pre-operational formulation. That is, unless levels are arranged on one set of dimensions only, unless structure and culture are distinguished, unless behavioral and nonbehavioral phenomena are differentiated and unless the needs of explanation kept distinct from those of description, we have almost no choice but to accept the organic-emergent position. By explicitly recognizing these distinctions, however, it becomes possible to devise social science taxonomies within which data may be gathered and the testing of alternative theories may go forward.

Having digressed for this unavoidable epistemological-ontological excursion, let me now return to the psycho-cultural interface by which we might better comprehend the relationships between man and world politics. To reiterate, the position taken here is that the cultural properties of any subnational, national or extranational system may be described in a strictly aggregative fashion, by observing the distribution and configuration of individual psychological properties.[17]

National Character, Ideology and Climate of Opinion

The most straightfoward, if not the only, way to convert the distribution of individual properties into social system properties is to let each of the three *psychological* variables serve as the basis for a distinct *cultural* variable. Choosing that path, let us treat *personality* as the basis for national (or any other social system's) *character, attitude* as the basis for *ideology,* and *opinion* as the basis for *climate*. That is, when we have ascertained which individuals score where on one or more personality, attitude or opinion scales, we have the basis for descriptive statements about the culture (or portions thereof) of the entity which they constitute. In this manner, then, the three societal "equivalents" would rank the same way as their psychological "counterparts" on the three dimensions used earlier. National character (or basic personality, as it is often called) would be the most general of the three cultural variables, most durable,

---

[17] As suggested earlier, my definition of cultural properties is considerably narrower than that used by most anthropologists, whose consensus is approximated in Kroeber and Kluckhohn (1952); the classical and global definition is Taylor's: "That complex whole which includes knowledge, belief, art, morals, law, custom, and any other capabilities and habits acquired by man as a member of society."

and least accessible to direct observation and measurement.[18] At the other end, climate of opinion would be most specific, most transitory, and most observable; ideology would fall in the middle range on all three dimensions. Let me now say a few words about each of these cultural attributes of national, subnational and extranational entities and then go on to a discussion of their measurement and statistical description.

There are many approaches to the study of national character, but two stand out in the literature; one tends toward the *organismic* and the other toward the aggregative and *statistical*. The former often attributes certain individual personality traits to the society as a whole, usually anthropomorphizing to some extent. This approach usually rests either on the assumption that there is near-uniformity of personalities within the social system or that the social structure impinges upon and molds diverse personalities in such a way as to produce highly uniform attitudes, opinions or behavior. The statistical approach is obviously the one taken here, and it coincides with the definition offered by Inkeles and Levinson (1954, 983): "national character refers to relatively enduring personality characteristics and patterns that are modal among the adult members of a society." Whether we speak of national character or of basic personality, the theme is almost always an aggregative and additive one, in which we look for the ways in which certain personality traits are distributed throughout a given population. There is, of course, no assurance that we will find only one modal personality in a given entity; the possibility of bi- or multi-modal types is always present (Levinson, 1957).

Moving from personality and national character to attitude and its societal counterpart, *ideology,* we come to that cultural attribute which is perhaps most central in understanding a nation's foreign policy. Neither as remote from policy concerns as personality, nor as evanescent as opinion, attitudinal configurations provide the most salient nonmaterial incentives and constraints within which nations decide upon their behavior in world politics. When we speak of ideology, it is important to distinguish among the various ways in which it is defined. A formal institution such as political party, pressure group or government usually has both an official or articulated ideology, as reflected in speeches and documents, and an operative ideology, which actually guides the group's behavior. The latter may not even be fully known to the group's own members, but it inevitably differs from the official ideology, especially as the time lag since the articulation or revision of the official ideology increases. There are few more serious errors in science, or in policy, than to assume that the official and the operative ideologies are identical; yet it occurs with

18 It is certainly not my intention to suggest that ease of direct observation necessarily guarantees that our measures will be high on both reliability and validity. As Campbell and Fiske (1959), as well as others, have pointed out, it is difficult to actually *achieve* construct validity but easy to believe that it has been achieved. Reliability is, however, an essential precondition for validity and while it may often be necessary to make trade-offs between the two, our selection of variables cannot be insensitive to the observation and measurement problem. These issues are discussed more fully in the next section.

The People

alarming frequency.[19] Not only is it crucial to distinguish between the formal and the operative ideology of an elite group, but to distinguish between both of these and the ideology of the larger social entity for which the elite claims to act. This distinction is often most evident when we contrast opinions to attitudes. That is, the elite may hold, or merely express, a given set of attitudes, and may try to bring the general public's attitudes into line with either of these. Unfortunately, there has been little research on the congruence between elite and mass ideology, but the impression is that the effort is not always successful. The several publics may well express, and even hold, *opinions* which coincide with those urged by the elite, but never internalize them sufficiently to qualify as attitudes.[20]

Ideology is crucial in foreign policy not only because it provides the matrix within which the present is interpreted, the past recalled, and the future anticipated, but because it provides the boundaries within which the climate or distribution of opinion can range. Within that range, opinion distributions for given sectors of a society will respond to behavioral events and information about them.

On the basis of what we now know about the malleability of most people's *opinions*, it is safe to say that political elites and / or mass media can—if they have a fairly accurate picture of the attitudinal configuration or ideology within their society—generate an impressively wide range of opinion changes. There are important constraints on such manipulation, including the climate of opinion at the moment, the ideology of the period, and the more slow-moving national character, but the degree of malleability is remarkable as well as alarming. More specifically, the would-be engineer of opinion change needs to know how many individuals in what particular classes (from mass to elite, from indifferent to attentive, etc.) hold what attitudes and opinions with what tenacity on what issues. In other words, he must know in some detail what the ideology and the climate of opinion look like at some particular point in time. This consideration leads us, then, to the problems of observation, measurement and description by which such distributions and configurations may be ascertained.

The Observation and Description Problem

The statistical description of a nation's character, ideology or climate of opinion—all combining to constitute its cultural attributes—are not only

[19] A particularly distressing example is Leites' *Operational Code of the Politburo* (1951), based largely on the "holy scriptures" of Marxism-Leninism. The saving grace of the study is its open-endedness, in which an extremely wide range of behavioral patterns is predicted from a given cluster of formal articulations.

[20] Highly suggestive in this context is Kelman's "Compliance, Identification, and Internalization: Three Processes of Attitude Change" (1958). Despite the fact that he does not distinguish among attitude, opinion and behavior, his scheme meshes in a general way with the one proposed here. The "compliance" process may be thought of as producing opinion change but little more, with identification and internalization both affecting attitudes and internalization perhaps even impinging on personality.

of interest to those who would modify or exploit that state of affairs. Until we have progressed further along this road, social scientists will also have a most incomplete understanding of the dynamic processes which occur within and between those entities, from small groups to the global system, which constitute our major theoretical focus.

In the sections above, I contended that opinions were most susceptible to observation, that personality traits were least susceptible, and that attitudes would fall somewhere between. Such a statement may misleadingly suggest that all three phenomena can—or must be—measured via direct observation alone. If we bear in mind that all psychological, and therefore, all cultural (in the restricted sense used here) phenomena are literally intrapsychic, it is evident that we must *always* make an inferential leap from those events which can be observed directly to the variable which we seek to measure. To return to an epistemological theme which is central to the whole scheme developed here, we need to be ingenious in looking for the traces and indicators of our variables, but we must remember that the traces, and the variables they reflect, are seldom the same thing. If this were not so, the problem of validity in social science measurement would be considerably less vexatious; that is, we would be less concerned with the question of whether we are measuring that which we claim to be measuring. As difficult as the problem is in other sectors of social science, it is even more troubling at the intrapsychic level, where few of our observations are made in the natural setting and most occur in the artificial and contrived laboratory or interview setting. In addition to this type of danger, validity is also threatened by the rather standard practice whereby we not only observe such behavioral events as verbal response in order to tap opinion, for example, but move back and forth (or up and down) among all three variables by inferring attitudes from opinions and personality from attitudes, and by predicting opinions from attitudes and attitudes from personality.[21]

To continue at the individual level, it seems to me that social scientists have all too often tended to assume that directly elicited verbal behavior represents the major—or even the only—avenue to understanding and measuring individual traits. Thus, in order to get a personality, we generally ask for written or oral responses to such stimuli as Rorschach blots, TAT pictures or incompleted sentences. To get at attitudes, we present our subjects with rather lengthy questionnaires, many of whose items seem to have little face validity, and then tote up the responses. To get at opinions, we usually organize a survey, replete with its myriad costs and problems of sampling, fielding an interview team, and then laboriously coding the alleged responses.[22]

[21] This inferential strategy is particularly risky in a cross-cultural research setting, inasmuch as variations in social structure—or differential rates of change therein—may impinge upon essentially similar modal personalities and "produce" appreciably different ideologies.

[22] For a valuable discussion of the many problems involved in the opinion survey approach, see Kahn and Cannell (1957), Kish (1965), and Maccoby (1954). An early study which concentrates on the sources of error is Hyman *et al.* (1954).

The People

It is certainly not my intention to reject these observational methods, but it is worth emphasizing their several shortcomings and suggesting the availability of alternative strategies. First of all, it cannot be emphasized too often that the assumed directness of these methods is generally over-stated. The inferential leap from verbal response back to imputed trait is a long and elusive one at best. As to projective tests, there is the subjectivity of the coding criteria, illustrated by the amount of training and experience required before the interpreter is considered qualified and before we get any satisfactory degree of inter-coder agreement. Whereas a cardinal rule in the search for reliability is to reduce coding procedures to a highly routinized algorithm, the projective tests are of limited value except in the hands of an insightful, artistic and trained expert. And even as the personality scales gradually reach satisfactory levels of reliability across time and across subjects, they still leave unanswered a number of serious questions on the validity side. On too many occasions we hear the assertion of the hyper-operationalist: "The_____syndrome is what this scale is designed to measure, and what it measures is, therefore, the _____syndrome!" Worth consideration, too, in both the paper-and-pencil and the face-to-face situations are the dangers of systematic error resulting from interviewer or experimenter induced bias, the unnatural setting, the low salience of the questions, respondent indifference and faulty recording (Remmers, 1954). Whether we are interrogating publics or elites, whether we seek to measure something as deep and general as a personality trait or as close to the surface and specific as an opinion, the inferential leap is a long one, marked by a variety of hurdles, only some of which we fully understand.

An Alternative . . .

Are there any alternatives to the direct verbal expression route, and are they any less problematical? One option which political scientists are now using with some regularity is the search for behavioral rather than prebehavioral or merely verbal indicators. Thus, we ask respondents—or find out through informants or public records—which political party they belong to, how they have voted or plan to vote, which pressure groups and professional associations they belong to and in what capacity, whether they write to their newspapers or legislators, and so forth. By and large, these provide somewhat more reliable information, but they too pose certain problems of validity. If we want to tap psychological attributes it is usually in order to use such data for predicting to *behavior,* and it may be risky to observe behavior, infer back to alleged psychological predis-positions and then predict to the very behavior which has been observed. The danger of tautological explanations is very much with us in this sort of research design, but as more varied psychological and behavioral data become available, the opportunities for cross-validation will inevitably increase. The same problems remain even if we shift from interrogation

31

to behavior-inducing experiments, or if we observe more natural or field-setting behavior, since we must still infer personality, attitude and opinion phenomena from the more directly observable—but not easily codeable —behavioral phenomena.

Having emphasized the pitfalls, let me now retreat somewhat and recognize that often we have no alternative other than direct interrogation or experimentally induced behavior, and that social scientists have shown remarkable ingenuity and rigor in seeking to minimize the misleading effects of these methods. Moreover, it is worth reiterating that there really is no such thing as a *directly observable* variable in social science; we always have an inferential leap of some magnitude between the event or condition on the one hand and the repertorial representation on the other. Thus, despite the danger to validity and reliability, any serious research on personality, attitude and opinion will continue to depend on the resourcefulness and precision with which we apply and develop the basic research strategies already in use. The only place where dramatic improvement seems both necessary and possible is at the personality level, where much of our knowledge depends upon the psychiatrist's protocols and reports, and the clinical psychologist's investigations. The consensus, which I largely share, is that the intrapsychic probings of these researchers (especially the former) leave a great deal to be desired when it comes to the operationalization of their variables; intuition is absolutely essential to scientific discovery, but it is seldom sufficient.[23]

Despite the central argument here—that we can and should employ the distribution and aggregation of individual attributes in order to measure certain social attributes—it does not necessarily follow that we can *only* do so by *observing* individual responses. That is, we seem to have underestimated the extent to which the distribution of intrapsychic phenomena within a population may be inferred via observation of *collective* phenomena.[24] Not only does this strategy avoid the artificialities of many interview and experimental situations, but it even provides an economical route for getting at macrophenomena in a more direct fashion. Thus, we may follow the anthropological approach and merely observe a great deal of social interaction and, on the basis of the way things are done and discussed, infer the nature of the personalities, attitudes and opinions of those who constitute the entity under investigation. Another tack widely used in anthropology is to examine the physical or artistic artifacts of the entity and treat them as indicators of these same phenomena; whether pottery or poetry, conference chambers or constitutions, and whether recent or ancient, these products may serve as manifestations

[23] Interestingly enough, some of the most rigorous research on personality variables is that of the anthropologists. Some imaginative and persuasive methods of data-acquisition and analysis via Rorschach blots are reported in Wallace (1952) and in the anthology compiled by Kaplan (1961). On the cross-cultural use of Rorschach see Adcock and Ritchie (1958).

[24] An excellent discussion, with examples, of alternative methods for getting at such social phenomena is in the volume of *Unobtrusive Measures* (Webb *et al.*, 1966).

32

The People

or traces of the way in which a population views or did view many phenomena of interest to us.[25] Likewise, such phenomena as elections, mass movements, migration, market behavior, social mobility, and so forth may all provide the empirical base from which we might infer back to the underlying culture.

When we observe societal and collective phenomena in order to tap the distribution of individual psychological attributes, however, there is again the danger of circularity in our reasoning. Thus, unless we have sufficient understanding of the social structure (roles and relationships) within which these interactions occur, and unless the state of our theory is relatively advanced, inferences about national character, ideology and opinion distributions can be quite wide of the mark. Another way to avoid unwitting circularity is to opt, quite consciously, for the cyclical model in which feedback is explicitly introduced; in such models, each set of variables serves the dependent, the independent, and the intervening role, in turn. Moreover, with some of the more recent tools of path analysis, and causal inference (Blalock, 1964), we can discover which particular sequence offers the most powerful explanation in the process, thus settling many of the old issues as to which is cause and which is consequence in sequences that can only be understood within a feedback framework (Deutsch, 1963).

Turning from problems of observation to the ways in which we might report and describe our observations, the standard tools of descriptive statistics seem quite appropriate to the task at hand. What are the familiar ways in which a frequency (or probability) distribution is portrayed so that the dominant characteristics of the configuration are best illuminated? First of all, we generally want to know something about the central tendency of a set of observed frequencies; and the median, mode and mean all have their uses in this regard. Beyond these, important aspects of an aggregate can be graphically portrayed via the histogram (bar graph), the frequency polygon (line graph), or the cumulative frequency curve, especially if individual scores on a given psychological dimension are collapsed into grouped frequency distributions. Nor should the factor analysis approach be overlooked (Cattell, 1955). While these graphic representations offer an economical overall picture of the dispersion, as well as the central tendency, of an aggregative distribution, we can get a more precise indication of the former by computing the variance or the standard deviation. Going a step further, the asymmetry of the distribution is precisely measured by computing the magnitude and direction of its skewness, and another measure of the curve's deviation from normality is found in its kurtosis (peakedness). To demonstrate the application of these familiar statistical descriptors is neither necessary

---

[25] One approach is represented in the McGranahan and Wayne (1948) analysis comparing popular drama in Germany and the United States during the late 1920's. And despite certain acknowledged inadequacies in his methods, David McClelland has demonstrated the possibilities of systematic examination of such cultural artifacts as textbooks and tapestry for generating politically relevant data (1961).

nor appropriate here, but their relevance to the many empirical studies (many of which are cross-cultural) of personality, attitude and opinion distributions should be self-evident. Nor is this the place to suggest the theoretical purposes to which such descriptions might be put.[26]

The Individual . . .

Up to this point, I have tended to treat every individual's personality traits, attitudes and opinions in an undifferentiated fashion, ignoring the obvious fact that some individuals exercise a far greater impact on world politics than others. Let me now recognize, if not rectify, that omission by way of a brief digression. While research on the strength and direction of differences between elites and others has not yet led to many universal generalizations, the evidence does point to the regular existence of certain mass-versus-elite discrepancies. In the work of Lasswell (1948), Dicks (1950), and others, we find suggestions of data which would permit the construction of cultural profiles which take explicit account of such discrepancies.[27] One might, for example, superimpose on the histogram for some trait or cluster of traits in the general population, similar profiles of the groups from which foreign policy or military elites are drawn. It might well turn out that the isomorphism or lack thereof between the two configurations would predict to that nation's behavioral tendencies or correlate strongly with the types of relationships it forms. Or, in line with the "two-step flow" hypothesis (Katz, 1957), a useful inquiry into the identity and potency of community influentials could be mounted. That is, if the foreign policy opinion profile for a general population sample and for several alternative reference groups could be assertained on perhaps a weekly basis, and the various media could be content analyzed, one might be able to trace the path along which information and influence tend to move. Space limitations preclude further pursuit of these research possibilities, but the options are many and the need is great.

In Conclusion . . .

Between the familiar regions of individual behavior and the dimly perceived ones of world politics lies a terra incognita into which few social

[26] A few possibilities, might, however, merit a footnote. We could, for example, search for the amount of symmetry in the way two populations perceive one another as well as themselves, in order to ascertain which of the many combinations of these four attitude configurations best predicts to the relations and interactions between the entities which they comprise. Some basis data can be found in Cantril and Buchanan (1953) and in Singer (1964). Another possibility might be a longitudinal analysis, in which any observed convergence or divergence in cultural profile could be examined to ascertain whether cultural differences and similarities associate with various types of interdependence, friendly or hostile, in any regular fashion.

[27] A systematic and carefully coded survey of much of the literature on the social background and personality traits of modern political elites is in Raser (1966).

34

scientists have yet begun to venture. Given the inadequacy of our maps, it is little wonder that we have given those regions a wide berth. My purpose here was to draw up a tentative map, preliminary to more thorough exploration. The map is largely conjectural, but may possibly have profited from the missteps and false starts of those who have explored comparable regions in other disciplines.

On the basis of those not dissimilar experiences, certain caveats seem justified. First, the map should identify the entities which exist in the region, and next, provide operational descriptions of their major attributes. Once these entities are recognized and described, we may safely inquire into their various roles and relationships vis-a-vis one another. Then, if we can resist the temptation to assign them all sorts of goals, purposes and functions, and treat the whole matter as an empirical question, we might get on to the next item on our agenda. That item, of course, is not explanation, but description. Until we have described a range of phenomena, we cannot explain it, and the main purpose of the map drawn here is to help us describe and measure now that which we hope to explain later.

Leaving the map-making metaphor behind, the scheme proposed explicitly rejects the need for an "'emergent properties" concept when the description of social entities is the matter at hand. Conversely, it urges that we can be both operational and relevant by defining and measuring the *cultural* properties of a subnational, national, or extranational entity strictly in terms of the *psychological* properties of those individuals who constitute that particular system. It does not deny the possibility that the interaction of individual properties (both within and among single humans) may produce emergent effects, but it insists that: (a) those effects are either structural or behavioral, and (b) if they are not in either of these two classes, but are indeed themselves cultural, then the effects can be observed in the form of individual psychological properties.

In sum, while the nature of the man-society conjunction has been debated and discussed for years, no satisfactory formulation has yet emerged. I have, therefore, taken not only a very explicit, but fairly extreme, aggregative position here, in the hope that if it accomplishes little more, this paper will have served to clarify and sharpen the methodological and theoretical issues. In the interim, I should like to believe that this type of formulation will carry us some distance toward a fuller understanding of the psycho-cultural interface by which man's role in world politics might be more fully comprehended.

References

Adcock, C. J. and Ritchie, J. E. Intercultural use of Rorschach. *American Anthropologist*, 1958, **60**, 881–892.

Adorno, T. W. *et al. Authoritarian personality.* New York: Harper & Row, 1950.

Allport, G. W. and Odbert, H. S. Trait-names: a psycho-lexical study. *Psychological Monographs* No. 211, 1936.

Almond, Gabriel and Verba, Sidney. *The civic culture*. Princeton: Princeton University Press, 1963.

Angell, Robert C. Governments and peoples as foci for peace-oriented research. *Journal of Social Issues,* 1955, **11**, (1), 36–41.

Atkinson, John. *Motives in fantasy, action, and society*. Princeton: Van Nostrand, 1958.

Banks, Arthur S. and Textor, Robert B. *A cross-polity survey*. Cambridge, Mass.: M.I.T. Press, 1963.

Bertocci, Peter A. Foundations of personalistic psychology. In Benjamin Wolman (Ed.), *Scientific psychology*. New York: Basic Books, 1965.

Blalock, Hubert M. *Causal inference in nonexperimental research*. Chapel Hill, N.C.: University of North Carolina Press, 1964.

Brim, Orville G., and Wheeler, Stanton. *Socialization after childhood*. New York: John Wiley, 1966.

Campbell, Donald T. Common fate, similarity and other indices of the status of aggregates of persons as social entities. *Behavioral Science,* 1958, **3**,(1), 14–25. Reprinted in J. David Singer (Ed.), *Human behavior and international politics*. Chicago: Rand McNally, 1965.

Campbell, Donald T., and Fiske, D. W. Convergent and discriminant validation by the multitrait-multimethod matrix. *Psychological Bulletin,* 1959, **56**, 81–105.

Cantril, Hadley, and Buchanan, William. *How nations see each other: a study in public opinion*. Urbana, Ill.: University of Illinois Press, 1953.

Cattell, Raymond B. *Personality: a systematic theoretical and factual study*. New York: McGraw-Hill, 1950.

Cattell, Raymond B. Concepts and methods in the measurement of group syntality. *Psychological Review,* 1955, **48**,(1), 48–63. Reprinted in J. David Singer (Ed.), *Human behavior and international politics*. Chicago: Rand McNally, 1965.

Cohen, Yehudi A. (Ed.), *Social structure and personality*. New York: Holt, Rinehart & Winston, 1961.

Coleman, James S. *Introduction to mathematical sociology*. New York: Free Press, 1964.

Converse, Philip E. The nature of belief systems in mass publics. In David Apter (Ed.), *Ideology and discontent*. New York: Free Press, 1964.

Deutsch, Karl W. *The nerves of government*. New York: The Free Press, 1963.

Dicks, Henry V. Personality traits and national socialist ideology. *Human Relations,* 1950, **3**, 111–154.

Frenkel-Brunswik, Else. Intolerance of ambiguity as an emotional and perceptual personality variable. *Journal of Personality,* 1949, **18**, 108–143.

Freud, Sigmund. *Introductory lectures on psychoanalysis,* trans., Ivan Riviere. London: Allen and Unwin, 1922.

Grinker, Roy (Ed.), *Toward a unified theory of human behavior*. New York: Basic Books, 1956.

Hsu, Francis L. K. (Ed.), *Psychological anthropology*. Homewood, Illinois: Richard D. Irwin, Inc., 1961.

Hyman, Herbert. *et al. Interviewing in social research*. Chicago, Illinois: University of Chicago Press, 1954.

The People

Inkeles, Alex, and Levinson, Daniel J. National character: the study of modal personality and sociocultural systems. In Gardner Lindzey (Ed.), *Handbook of social psychology.* Cambridge, Mass.: Addison-Wesley, 1954.

Jacobs, Robert C., and Campbell, Donald T. The perpetuation of an arbitrary tradition through several generations of a laboratory microculture. *Journal of Abnormal and Social Psychology,* 1961, **62**, 649–58. Reprinted in J. David Singer (Ed.), *Human behavior and international politics.* Chicago: Rand McNally, 1965.

Jung, Carl G. *Psychological types.* New York: Harcourt, Brace, 1923.

Kahn, Robert, and Cannell, Charles. *The dynamics of interviewing: theory, techniques, and cases.* New York: John Wiley, 1957.

Kaplan, Bert (Ed.), *Studying personality cross-culturally.* Evanston, Ill.: Harper, Row, 1961.

Katz, Elihu. The two-step flow of communications. *Public Opinion Quarterly,* 1957, **21**, 61–78.

Kelman, Herbert C. Compliance, identification, and internalization: three processes of attitude change. *Journal of Conflict Resolution,* 1958, **2**, (1), 51–60.

Kelman, Herbert C., (Ed.), *International behavior: a social-psychological analysis.* New York: Holt, Rinehart & Winston, 1965.

Kish, Leslie. *Survey sampling.* New York: John Wiley, 1965.

Klineberg, Otto. *Human dimension in international relations.* New York: Holt, Rinehart & Winston, 1964.

Kluckhohn, Clyde and Murray, Henry (Eds.). *Personality in nature, society, and culture.* New York: Alfred A. Knopf, Inc., 1953.

Kroeber, Alfred L., and Kluckhohn, Clyde. Culture: a critical review of concepts and definitions. *Papers of the Peabody Museum,* 1952, **47**,(1a), 643–56.

Lasswell, Harold D. *Power and personality.* New York: W. W. Norton, 1948.

Leites, Nathan C. *Operational code of the politburo.* New York: McGraw-Hill, 1951.

Levinson, Daniel J. Authoritarian personality and foreign politics. *Journal of Conflict Resolution,* 1957, **1**,(1), 37–47.

Livant, William P. Cumulative distortion of judgment. *Perceptual and Motor Skills,* 1963, **16**, 741–745.

Maccoby, Eleanor and Maccoby, Nathan. The interview: a tool of social science. In Gardner Lindzey (Ed.), *Handbook of social psychology.* Cambridge, Mass.: Addison-Wesley, 1954.

McCary, J. L. (Ed.), *Psychology of personality: six modern approaches.* New York: Logos Press, 1956.

McClelland, David. *The achievement motive.* New York: Appleton-Century-Crofts, 1958.

McClelland, David. *The achieving society.* Princeton: Van Nostrand, 1961.

McCloskey, Herbert. Conservatism and personality. *American Political Science Review,* 1958, **52**, 27–45.

McGranahan, Donald, and Wayne, Ivor. German and American traits reflected in popular drama. *Human Relations,* 1948, **1**, 429–455. Reprinted in J. David Singer (Ed.), *Human behavior and international politics.* Chicago: Rand McNally, 1965.

Milgram, Stanley. Nationality and conformity. *Scientific American,* Dec. 1961, **205**,(6), 45–51.

Miller, James G. *Living systems.* New York: John Wiley [forthcoming in 1969].

Mitchell, William. *Sociological analysis and politics: the theories of Talcott Parsons.* Englewood Cliffs, N.J.: Prentice-Hall, 1967.

Murphy, Gardner (Ed.), *Human nature and enduring peace.* Boston: Houghton Mifflin, 1945.

Nagel, Ernest. *The structure of science.* New York: Harcourt, Brace, 1961.

Pye, Lucian, and Verba, Sidney (Eds.), *Political culture and political development.* Princeton: Princeton University Press, 1965.

Raser, John R. Personal characteristics of political decision makers: a literature review. *Peace Research Society Papers,* 1966, **5,** 161–181.

Remmers, H. H. *Introduction to opinion and attitude measurement.* New York: Harper & Row, 1954.

Rieselbach, Leroy. Personality and political attitudes: available questionnaire measures. Ann Arbor: University of Michigan, 1964. Mimeo.

Robinson, W. S. Ecological correlations and the behavior of individuals. *American Sociological Review,* 1950, **15,** 351–357.

Rokeach, Milton. *The open and closed mind.* New York: Basic Books, 1960.

Rosenau, James N. Private preferences and political responsibilities: the relative potency of individual and role variables in the behavior of U.S. Senators. In J. David Singer (Ed.), *Quantitative international politics: insights and evidence.* New York: Free Press, 1968.

Rosenberg, Morris. Misanthropy and attitudes toward international affairs. *Journal of Conflict Resolution,* 1957, **1,**(4), 340–345.

Rummel, Rudolph J. A social field theory of foreign conflict. New Haven: Yale University, 1965. Mimeo

Singer, J. David. The level-of-analysis problem in international relations. *World Politics,* 1961, **14,**(1), 77–92.

Singer, J. David. Soviet and American foreign policy attitudes: a content analysis of elite articulations. *Journal of Conflict Resolution,* 1964, **8,**(4), 424–485.

Singer, J. David. (Ed.) *Human behavior and international politics: contributions from the social-psychological sciences.* Chicago: Rand McNally, 1965.

Singer, J. David. The global system and its sub-systems: a developmental view. In James N. Rosenau (Ed.), *Linkage politics: essays on the convergence of national and international systems.* New York: Free Press, 1969.

Singer, J. David. *Behavior and interaction in the global system.* Englewood Cliffs, New Jersey: Prentice-Hall, Inc. [forthcoming].

Smith, M. B., Bruner, J. S., and White, R. W. *Opinions and personality.* New York: John Wiley, 1956.

Sprout, Harold, and Sprout, Margaret. *The ecological perspective on human affairs with special reference to international politics.* Princeton: Princeton University Press, 1965.

Stratton, George M. *Social psychology of international conduct.* New York: Appleton-Century-Crofts, 1929.

Wallace, Anthony, F. C. *The modal personality structure of the Tuscarora Indians.* Washington, D.C.: Government Printing Office, 1952.

Wallace, Anthony, F. C. *Culture and personality.* New York: Random House, 1961.

Waltz, Kenneth. *Man, the state, and war.* New York: Columbia University Press, 1959.

The People

Webb, Eugene, *et al. Unobtrusive measures: nonreactive research in the social sciences.* Chicago: Rand McNally, 1966.

Wolfers, Arnold. The actors in international politics. In William T. R. Fox (Ed.), *Theoretical aspects of international relations.* Notre Dame, Indiana: University of Notre Dame Press, 1959.

Nation-Building in America: The Colonial Years

C H A P T E R   T W O

Richard L. Merritt

Reprinted with permission of the publishers from K. W. Deutsch and W. J. Foltz (eds.), *Nation Building* (New York: Atherton Press, 1966), pp. 56–72. Copyright © 1966 by Atherton Press. Mr. Merritt is Associate Professor of Political Science at the University of Illinois.

The seventeenth-century American colonies existed in a state of semi-isolation, separated from one another, in many cases, by stretches of uninhabited wilderness and, more generally, by inadequate systems of intercolonial transportation and communication.[1] Contacts with the mother country were often easier to maintain and, perhaps, more fruitful than those with neighboring colonies. To the extent that there was any coordination among separate colonial administrations, it was the result not of the colonists' cooperation, but of the efforts of His Majesty's Government in England. Even as late as the middle of the eighteenth century, the colonists were unable to organize an effective intercolonial defense against marauding Indians on the western frontiers, and some voices expressed fears of armed conflict among certain colonies.

By the early nineteenth century, however, the United States of America comprised an integrated political community. The American people possessed a sense of national community and a set of political structures sufficient to maintain a high degree of mobility, as well as a large volume of mutual transactions, to ensure expectations of peaceful relations within the American union, and to enable the achievement or at least the satisfactory pursuit of common national interests. The national government successfully protected those common interests, battling the world's most important maritime power (1812–1815) and resisting attacks upon the national unity by northern secessionists (1815). The American republic was unified by 1820 and, with the voluntary and often enthusiastic support of its population of almost ten million, was master in its own house.[2]

In considering this dramatic change in the fabric of American society, this chapter will concentrate upon nation-building during the colonial years. Three elements of change deserve particular attention. The first is the development of political structures formally amalgamating the colonies. The second is the pattern of informal communication transactions among the colonists. And the third is the growth of common or at least mutually compatible perceptions and attitudes in pre-Revolutionary America.

[1] I would like to thank Prof. Karl W. Deutsch and Prof. Edmund S. Morgan of Yale University and Prof. Louis P. Galambos of Rice University for their helpful comments on earlier versions of this chapter; Prof. Leonard W. Labaree of Yale University for many kind favors; and the Carnegie Corporation for its generous support of this project.
[2] 1820 was also a milestone—perhaps the first overt manifestation—of a sectional rivalry that was to divide the Union four decades later.

41

Functional Amalgamation

In theory, obedience to the Crown and the British Parliament united the colonies politically, while the supervision, after 1696, of the Board of Trade united them administratively. With the passage of time, however, royal and Parliamentary politics reduced the Board's importance as a decision-making body. It remained primarily to investigate and channel colonial problems to the fragmented but authoritative decision-makers and to provide a gloss of administrative uniformity to all decisions affecting the colonies. Vetoes by the Crown and colonial control of the purse added to the political decentralization of the New World—a decentralization mitigated by little more than cooperation resulting from royal instructions issued to colonial governors.

This is not to say that there were no efforts to unite the varied political structures of the colonies. King James II's attempt to form a single New England Confederation in the 1680's collapsed with his own deposition; efforts to coordinate strategies in King William's War were similarly unsuccessful; and Benjamin Franklin's plan of union, adopted by the Albany Congress in 1754, met speedy defeat at the hands of both the Crown and the colonial assemblies. The most successful joint effort of this sort was the Stamp Act Congress of 1765; this time, however, representatives of several colonies met together not to plan long-term common policies or to create common political structures, but to raise their voices in a united protest against the Stamp Act.

Throughout the colonial period, there were only two more or less enduring structures performing governmental functions on an inter-colonial basis. The first of these was the post office. Although founded as early as 1692, it was not until 1753 (when Benjamin Franklin and his fellow publisher, William Hunter of Virginia, assumed the posts of joint deputy postmasters general for North America) that the colonial post office system became an efficient and effective means of intercolonial communication. The second structure, neither so formal nor so closely coordinated as the post office system, was a network of committees of correspondence that sprang up periodically after 1764. By means of the committees, patriots throughout the colonies sought to maintain contact with one another and keep each other apprised of the latest British maneuvers.[3]

---

[3] To these might be added a third institution providing a measure of coordination in America—the British Army. This was particularly true during the French and Indian War, when the army centralized commissaries and other departments. For a short period, in fact, a colonist, Philip Schuyler of New York, acted as commissary general. The coordination provided by the army, however, came from London; it did not represent a colonial effort to secure intercolonial cooperation. Indeed, even though British-sponsored, such measures often came to nought in the face of colonial apathy or opposition. Cf., Stanley McCrory Pargellis, *Lord Loudoun in America* (New Haven: Yale University Press, 1933), pp. 67, 102, 184, 354; Edward E. Curtis, *The Organiza-*

The People

Together the post office system and the committees of correspondence performed only minor governmental functions. They did not constitute an attempt at over-all amalgamation and at a comprehensive set of institutions and processes to carry on such major tasks as the distribution of power and income, the establishment of principles of legitimacy, the allocation of resources, and the use of force on an intercolonial scale.

Even the First Continental Congress, which met at Carpenter's Hall in Philadelphia, September 5, 1774, was not originally intended to be a permanent structure to legislate for all the colonies. Just as the Stamp Act Congress had met almost nine years earlier to present a united front of opposition to specific Parliamentary measures, so, too, did the delegates of twelve colonies gather in the City of Brotherly Love to coordinate colonial opposition to the so-called Intolerable Acts.

It was this conference, however, that broke the bonds committing the colonies to independent and uncoordinated (if often parallel) courses of action. In lieu of accepting Joseph Galloway's plan of union, which gave coequal control over colonial affairs to the British Parliament and an intercolonial legislature, the First Continental Congress drafted petitions of rights to be sent to the people of Great Britain and to King George III and passed a series of resolutions enjoining colonial merchants to refrain from trade with the mother country. These resolves, termed the "Association" by the delegates, called for committees of inspection in every town or county. Thus, based on a claim to legitimacy that was intercolonial in extent, the Association was in fact an effort to coordinate enforcement functions based on local but parallel activity throughout the continent. The rush of events during the next half year did not give the colonists sufficient time to test fully the effectiveness of their Association in practice, but its psychological significance—the first major breakthrough in the formation of amalgamated intercolonial structures—should not be dismissed.

The ensuing months saw the proliferation of structures seeking to perform governmental functions on an intercolonial basis. The Second Continental Congress, which met some three weeks after Major Pitcairn's skirmish with the Minutemen, soon began to assume more than mere consultative powers. On June 15, 1775, two days before the Battle of Bunker Hill, the Congress elected George Washington commander-in-chief of a unified "Continental Army," and a week later it began to issue paper currency. On July 26, Congress established a national post office system, with the venerable Benjamin Franklin as postmaster general. And, before the year was out, not only had Congress created a navy (with only one ship) and a marine corps, but it had also undertaken, through its Committee of Secret Correspondence, to open diplomatic relations with France and other European powers. Thus, during the course of a single year, the net of intercolonial structures, which had been of only marginal importance, had grown much stronger and much more complex; by the end of 1775,

tion of the British Army in the American Revolution (New Haven: Yale University Press, 1926).

these structures were performing a significant number of the wartime and peacetime functions of a national government.

That the degree of integration was not perfect is less important than the fact that an intercolonial form of central government, albeit temporary, had been established. During the first years of the Revolutionary War, the colonies carried on certain functions in a manner not too dissimilar from the operation of a military alliance. To be sure, a Continental Army with a commander-in-chief existed. But George Washington's influence in the decision-making circles of the individual colonies—especially with respect to such matters as recruitment and war financing—seems to have been less than that exerted on alliance partners by the Supreme Allied Commanders in the two world wars of our century, nor did the Continental Congress of 1775 have any more power to lay and collect taxes than does the NATO Council today. In fact, it could be argued that the colonists, in unifying certain governmental structures during the year before the Declaration of Independence, took only the first step along the road that led, by 1791, to over-all amalgamation. But it was an important first step. From both a functional and a psychological point of view, the colonists crossed the threshold of political amalgamation in that year of decision, 1775.

Communications and Colonial Integration

This brief description of the manner in which links formally binding the colonies to one another developed during the first three-quarters of the eighteenth century touches on one important aspect of nation-building in colonial America. A second aspect comprises informal contacts—commercial, intellectual, and communications ties that expanded rapidly, if by leaps and bounds, among the colonists during these years.

Illustrative of this expansion is the growth of intercolonial trade. The number of ships plying between the ports of New York, Philadelphia, Hampton, and Charleston, on the one hand, and harbors in Great Britain or Ireland, on the other hand, doubled from 1734 to 1772 (increasing from 264 to 556), but the number of ships engaged in the coasting trade quadrupled (from 402 to 1,750) during the same period. Comparable figures for the port of Boston are even more dramatic: the number of ships sailing from Boston to the mother country rose from an average of forty-eight a year in the 1714–1717 period to fifty-nine a year in the four years from 1769 to 1772 (an increase of 23 per cent); the number of coastal vessels jumped from 117 to 451 (an increase of 286 per cent). Of the total annual tonnage shipped from Boston, 19 per cent (3,985 tons) went to Great Britain or Ireland in 1714–1717, whereas 16 per cent (6,171 tons) of the yearly tonnage did so in 1769–1772. The share of the total tonnage shipped each year from Boston to other colonial ports rose from 17 per cent (3,583 tons) in 1714–1717 to 43 per cent (16,766 tons) in

The People

1769–1772.[4] In short, although the shipping facilities of the colonies generally expanded during the course of the eighteenth century, coastal shipping grew at a much more rapid rate than did trade with the mother country.

Population expansion accompanied the growing intercolonial commercial ties. From 1700 to 1775, the American population multiplied tenfold. Along with a general movement west, people began to fill in the gaps separating the urban clusters scattered along the Atlantic seaboard. By the middle of the 1770's, according to census data currently available, a fairly continuous line of settlement ran from Penobscot Bay in the north to Savannah in the south.[5]

With the expansion of the population came the construction of post roads, ferries, and other means to facilitate intercolonial travel and communication. This is not to say that the transportation system was complete or ideal, for some of the roads were almost impassable in bad weather. But two facts stand out. First, the roads multiplied and were considerably improved during the eighteenth century. (A good indication of this fact is the amount of time it took to travel between two cities: post office records report that a letter required three days to go from Philadelphia to New York in 1720, but only one day in 1764.[6]) Second, travel between colonies was often faster and cheaper than that between coastal and inland population clusters in the same colony.

Intercolonial mobility made increasingly possible the exchange of ideas among the colonists. Among the many colonial travelers, one of the more notable was the evangelist George Whitefield. From 1738 until his death in 1770, he made seven journeys throughout the colonies, five of them extending from Georgia to New England. The religious revival that he occasioned, termed the "Great Awakening," was perhaps the first mass movement to sweep America. It was the spirit engendered in this movement that helped Whitefield to collect money throughout the colonies (and even in England) for such worthy causes as an orphanage in Georgia, the construction of Dartmouth and Princeton colleges, and the reconstruction of the Harvard College library after a fire in 1764.

Religion provided a number of other opportunities for intercolonial contacts. There was often correspondence, for example, among co-religionists in different colonies. Some church organizations, such as the Baptists, the Friends, and the Methodists, held intercolonial synods to

---

[4] The remainder went to the Caribbean and other colonies in the New World (58 per cent in 1714–1717 and 38 per cent in 1769–1772) and to Europe and Africa (6 per cent in 1714–1717 and 3 per cent in 1769–1772). Computed from data given in U.S. Bureau of the Census, *Historical Statistics of the United States, Colonial Times to 1957* ([Series Z 56–75] [Washington, D.C.: U.S. Government Printing Office, 1960]), pp. 759–760. The earlier figure for the port of Hampton is from 1733, rather than 1734.

[5] Stella H. Sutherland, *Population Distribution in Colonial Amercia* (New York: Columbia University Press, 1936).

[6] Seymour Dunbar, *A History of Travel in America* (Indianapolis: The Bobbs-Merrill Company, 1915), I, 177, note 2.

coordinate church policy and doctrine. Although it is true that a few of the larger church organizations were located mainly in particular regions (all but seven of the 668 Congregational churches were in New England, and more than one-half of the Episcopalian churches were in the southern colonies[7]), most churches had local parishes scattered throughout the colonies. To a considerable extent, the diversity of religions in America produced a common norm of religious toleration among Americans—a norm that eventually served to remove the religious question from the political arena. And, during the later colonial years, church organizations contributed to that vital flow of ideas and contacts that created a framework for American nation-building.

Another indication of the expanding facilities of intercolonial communication in eighteenth-century America is the press. The number of newspapers multiplied in the decades between 1735 and 1775. At the time of John Peter Zenger's trial for seditious libel, there were only nine newspapers in all America; by the end of the French and Indian War, their number had more than doubled, and thirty-eight were in existence on the eve of the Revolution. Then, too, the size and news coverage of the journals kept pace with their numbers: the newspaper of 1775 was generally three or four times as large as that of 1735, and the number of lines in the average journal doubled.

Nor were the colonial newspapers entirely for local consumption. In one of the first issues of his *Virginia Gazette,* William Parks encouraged his readers to place advertisements in his journal, arguing that, "as these Papers will circulate (as speedily as possible) not only all over This, but also the Neighboring Colonies, and will probably be read by some Thousands of people, it is very likely that they may have the desir'd Effect. . . ."[8] Some two dozen years later, also seeking advertising revenue, Hugh Gaine wrote in the masthead of his *New-York Mercury:*

> For the Benefit of those that advertise in this Paper: It may not be amiss to inform them, That it is conveyed to every Town and Country Village in the Provinces of New-Jersey, Connecticut, Rhode-Island and New-York; to all the Capital Places on the Continent of America, from Georgia to Halifax; to every English Island in the West-Indies, and to all the Sea Port Towns and Cities in England, Scotland, Ireland and Holland.[9]

Influenced by the huckstering spirit of colonial times, Parks and Gaine undoubtedly exaggerated somewhat, but nonetheless it is true that many of the colonial newspapers did enjoy wide circulation throughout the colonies and, occasionally, abroad. And, increasingly, the printers found newsworthy items in the affairs of their colonial neighbors: in 1738, about

---

[7] Charles O. Paullin, *Atlas of the Historical Geography of the United States* (Washington, D.C., and New York: Carnegie Institution and American Geographical Society, 1932), p. 50 and Plate 82.

[8] Cited in Lawrence C. Wroth, *The Colonial Printer* (New York: The Grolier Club, 1931), p. 203. The date of the *Virginia Gazette* was October 8, 1736.

[9] *New-York Mercury.* August 2, 1762, p. 1.

The People

one-fifth of their news was datelined in other colonies, and, by 1768, this proportion had risen to one-quarter.[10]

In many respects, the colonial printer exemplified the growth of an interlocking, national elite. When Samuel Green set up shop in Cambridge in the 1640's not only did he become America's second printer, but he also founded a printing dynasty that endured for five generations and included no less than a score of colonial America's printers in Massachusetts, Connecticut, Maryland, Virginia, and elsewhere. Benjamin Franklin, whose fine hand one sees in practically all aspects of the life and thought of colonial America, was clearly the giant of the American printing profession in the middle of the eighteenth century. In addition to turning his *Pennsylvania Gazette* into one of the more influential colonial newspapers, Franklin manufactured and sold materials for making ink (and even an occasional keg of the fluid itself) to colleagues in other colonies; he collected rags and sold newsprint throughout the colonies; and he lent money to and formed partnerships with his former journeymen (including a couple of nephews) to set up shop in other colonies. Franklin's account books reveal that copies of his almanacs were sold in wholesale lots to merchants and printers from Boston to Charleston, South Carolina, and even in Jamaica.[11] His *Poor Richard's Almanack* was popular enough to warrant special editions for New England and the southern colonies, as well as the regular edition for the middle colonies.[12]

A similar intercolonial elite developed in other professions. Colonial merchants, for example, normally had extensive familial and business connections in several colonies; lawyers, doctors, and men of science often visited or corresponded with their colleagues in other parts of America.[13]

In emphasizing the importance of informal ties among the colonists in eighteenth-century America, I do not mean to suggest that there were no clashes or divisive factors at work. To the contrary, the path leading toward a dense net of informal transactions of all sorts, toward an informal division of labor on an intercolonial basis, was strewn with many a rocky barrier. Diverse and often unstable colonial currencies, as well as the virtual absence of intercolonial credit facilities, hampered trade and commercial relations. Conflicting territorial claims led to harsh words and, occasionally, even to bloodshed. Religious factionalism and regional jealousies sowed the seeds of mutual antagonism. Perhaps the most

---

10 The percentage of the news lines reprinted from other colonial newspapers is based upon an analysis of sixteen newspapers for each year, four each from Boston, New York, Philadelphia, and Williamsburg. See footnote 15 below.

11 George Simpson Eddy, *Account Books Kept by Benjamin Franklin: Ledger "D," 1739–1747* (New York: Columbia University Press, 1929), *passim*.

12 Leonard W. Labaree, ed., *The Papers of Benjamin Franklin* (New Haven: Yale University Press, 1959–), III, 262n.

13 Michael Kraus, *Intercolonial Aspects of American Culture on the Eve of the Revolution, with Special Reference to the Northern Towns* (New York: Columbia University Press, 1928), p. 90; Robert K. Lamb's discussion of interlocking colonial elites in Karl W. Deutsch, *Nationalism and Social Communication: An Inquiry into the Foundations of Nationality* (Cambridge, Mass., and New York: Massachusetts Institute of Technology Press and John Wiley and Sons, 1953), pp. 18–20.

dramatic elaboration of such intercolonial hostilities came in a sermon delivered on the eve of the Revolution by the Loyalist Jonathan Boucher of Philadelphia. After describing the New Englanders as "the Goths and Vandals of America," Boucher declaimed: "O 'tis a monstrous and an unnatural coalition; and we should as soon expect to see the greatest contrarieties in Nature to meet in harmony, and the wolf and the lamb to feed together, as Virginians to form a cordial union with the saints of New England."[14]

More to the point, however, is the fact that such a union *was* formed. It may seem truistic to note that the expanding range and strength of intercolonial contacts throughout the eighteenth century indicate something of the extent to which colonists sought such contacts or considered them worthwhile. But—and this is the important point—when the time of decision arrived, mutual interests among the colonists predominated over material antagonisms.

Images of an American Community

But what about the colonists themselves during the pre-Revolutionary years? Did they perceive themselves as members of a peculiarly American political community or as a part of a British, or perhaps Anglo-American, community? Were the colonies divided by walls of indifference, more interested in their connections with the mother country than in one another's concerns and problems, more interested in local happenings than in events affecting the colonies as a whole?

One way of finding answers to such questions is to examine the focus of attention of one the more popular and enduring media of colonial communication. It is not unreasonable to expect that the content of a communication medium reflects the interests and tastes of its audience, particularly if its continued publication rests upon popular subscription. Such was the case with the colonial press. The following remarks on colonial perceptions are based upon a tabulation of place-name symbols (such as "the Carolinas," "Warwickshire," or "Livorno") appearing in a fairly substantial sample of newspapers, published in four American urban centers between 1735 and 1775.[15]

The symbols used in the colonial press indicate that, in the years prior to the Revolution, the colonists increasingly substituted self-awareness for their early absorption in European wars and other events outside the Anglo-American political community. Meanwhile, they maintained a

[14] Jonathan Boucher, *Reminiscences of an American Loyalist,* pp. 132–134, cited in Max Savelle, *Seeds of Liberty: The Genesis of the American Mind* (New York: Alfred A. Knopf, 1948), pp. 563–564.

[15] The entire contents of four issues a year of the *Massachusetts Gazette* (from 1735 to 1775), the *Boston Gazette, and Country Journal* (1762–1775), the *New-York Weekly Journal* (1735–1751), the *New-York Mercury* (1752–1775), the *Pennsylvania Gazette* (1735–1775), and the *Virginia Gazette* (1736–1775) were systematically analyzed. For further details, see Richard L. Merritt, *Symbols of American Community, 1735–1775* (New Haven: Yale University Press, 1966).

The People

fairly steady interest in the mother country. Although symbols of place names located in the British Isles generally occupied about one-fifth of the newspapers' symbol space throughout the forty-one years, their share declined sharply relative to the space given over to American symbols. In the decade from 1735 to 1744, one symbol in three referred to a place name in the Anglo-American community, that is, in Britain or America; in the last colonial decade, the same amount of space was spent on American symbols alone. The years 1774 and 1775 found the colonial printers devoting more than one-half of their total symbol space to news of America.

A more detailed analysis of American symbols in the colonial press,[16] that is, symbols referring to American place names, reveals an interesting and, I believe, significant shift in the intercolonial focus of attention— a shift away from purely local interests to an awareness of events affecting the colonies as a whole, with attention paid by the newspapers to symbols of colonies other than their own remaining essentially unchanged over the long run. Although news of the home colony remained important in each newspaper from 1735 to 1775, it declined in significance relative to intercolonial news. In the decade from 1735 to 1744 about three-eighths of the American symbols pertained to local news, whereas only one-quarter did so in the last pre-Revolutionary decade. The colony that gave itself the greatest amount of attention (an interest shared by the newspapers of other colonies as well) was Massachusetts Bay; in contrast, symbols of Pennsylvania and New York place names were prominent mainly during the years of the French and Indian War, and Virginia was important only in the eyes of Virginians. The saliency of the collective concept in the colonial press remained low, however, until 1763. After that date, symbols referring to the colonies as a single unit comprised about one-quarter of the total number of American symbols in the newspapers.

But increases in mutual attention, however well balanced, do not always result in a heightened sense of community. That America during the 1930's devoted an increasing share of its attention to Nazi Germany is hardly an indication that the two countries were drawing closer together. Indeed, in most respects the opposite was the case. This fact emphasizes the need to consider another facet of the intercolonial pattern of communication—the contexts in which the symbols occurred in the newspapers. Did all or most southerners, for example, look upon New Englanders as "the Goths and Vandals of America"? Were all or most of the references to England in a eulogistic context?

The fact that few place-name symbols appeared in contexts clearly approving or disapproving the place names represented by the symbols makes it difficult to give final answers to such questions. But a brief test

---

16 In tabulating the distribution of American symbols only, direct place-name symbols ("Virginia" or "Boston") as well as indirect references to such symbols ("this colony" or "this city") were included. In the comparison of the total number of American place-name symbols with the number of British place-name symbols, such indirect symbols were not tabulated.

applied to place-name symbols appearing in samples of colonial newspapers for 1738 and 1768 indicates that American symbols appeared in more favorable contexts in 1768 than in 1738, whereas the reverse was true for British symbols.[17] Such a finding accords well with a commonplace discoverable in many studies of American history—the commonplace that, on the whole, the colonies did not grow more hostile toward one another during the decades prior to 1775, particularly in contrast to an emerging sense of alienation from England.

An even better indication of a growing sense of community among the colonists is to be found in their use of self-referent symbols. When did they begin to consider the land they inhabited as "America" rather than as the "British colonies"? When did they begin to think, or at least to speak, of themselves as "Americans" rather than as "His Majesty's subjects"?

Three significant points emerge from an analysis of such self-referent symbols appearing in the colonial press from 1735 to 1775. First, the territorial differentiation of the Anglo-American political community was perceived and made symbolically evident before the distinction between Englishmen and Americans appeared in the newspapers. The predominant image of the 1750's and early 1760's pictured the colonists as Englishmen transplanted in American soil. Second, in both of these changes, British writers and journalists (as mirrored in the colonial press) were quicker than were colonists to make the symbolic distinctions. Articles with British datelines in the colonial newspapers identified the colonies as American throughout the years after 1735, and by 1768 they termed the inhabitants of that continent "Americans" more often than "His Majesty's subjects" or even "colonists"; the corresponding shifts in articles of American origin did not take place until, respectively, 1763 and 1773. And, third, these changes in symbolic identification were neither revolutionary nor evolutionary in the strictest sense of the terms. Rather, like other learning situations, they were both gradual and fitful, with a few periods of extremely rapid advances and other periods of more or less mild relapse.

By way of a final note on colonial perceptions and attitudes, it must be added that the newspapers of different colonies followed rather similar patterns in their usage of place-name and self-referent symbols. There were, to be sure, variations, but even these grew smaller as the years went by.

[17] Using the method described by Ithiel de Sola Pool with the collaboration of Harold D. Lasswell, Daniel Lerner, *et al., Symbols of Democracy* ("Hoover Institute Studies" Ser. C, No. 4, [The Hoover Institute and Library on War, Revolution, and Peace, Stanford, Calif.: Stanford University Press, 1952]), p. 14, I subtracted the number of American symbols appearing in unfavorable contexts from the number of such symbols appearing in favorable contexts and divided the remainder by the sum of all American symbols appearing in the sample of newspapers for each year. For American symbols in 1738, the quality of symbol usage was $-.013$; by 1768 it had gone up to $\pm.000$. I then performed the same test for British symbols used in the two years. The change in the quality of British symbol usage was from $+.079$ in 1738 to $+.004$ in 1768. The low scores result primarily from the large number of symbols appearing in neutral contexts.

The People

Students of international political communities have found eighteenth-century American history particularly rich in parallels to the modern multistate world. In emphasizing the colonial years, it must be borne in mind that they by no means present a complete picture; the process of nation-building in America continued for years and even decades after the outbreak of the Revolution in 1775. At the very least, however, the evidence provided by the American experience is useful in testing current ideas about nation-building and large-scale political integration on the international level. What, then, are some of the general lessons of the American experience?

First, it seems clear that the growth of a rich community life in the colonies, resting upon common perceptions and experiences as well as a high degree of mutual interaction, was slow, with rapid advances interspersed with years of decline. By the end of the French and Indian War, however, the colonists possessed communication habits and facilities considerably better than those of the seventeenth century or, indeed, of the early 1750's. The politically relevant strata of colonial society had a much wider range of opportunities to learn about events and attitudes that influenced their fellow colonists than had been available before then. And, judging from symbol usage in the colonial press, with these changes in communication habits and facilities came a new set of perceptions and focuses of attention. American events became increasingly more important in the colonists' attention patterns. The idea of referring to the colonies as a single unit was gaining favor. The newspapers began separating the colonies from the mother country through their symbol usage instead of identifying the colonies as a part of a British political community. In short, the trends toward increased American community awareness and an enhanced sense of American community developed slowly, to be sure, but were well under way long before the outbreak of revolution.

Through the lens provided by their changing self-images and attention patterns, the colonists began to perceive new interests that they held in common. Events that may have seemed unimportant in earlier years took on a new aura of significance. The grumbling responses that the Molasses Act and the Iron Bill elicited from the colonists in the 1730's and 1750's were isolated and thus, to a great extent, ineffective. As facilities for and habits of intercolonial communications improved, however, such tones of dissatisfaction could find echoes throughout the continent. An Indian uprising in 1763, less threatening than other attacks upon the colonists during the course of the previous two decades, could become a major topic of discussion in the press. Then, too, the rapidly expanding newspapers could spend a larger amount of space on differences between the perspectives and interests of the colonists and those of the mother country.

The Stamp Act crisis of 1765 presents an interesting case in point. **51**

As with similar events in colonial history, judging again from symbol usage in the colonial press, the "crisis" came at a time of important breakthroughs in American self-awareness and images of American separatism. It neither precipitated nor preceded the beginnings of such trends. It seems less likely that the crisis itself generated bonds of community awareness among the colonists than that the rapidly growing ties of communication and community enabled the colonists to voice the effective opposition that has come to be called the "Stamp Act crisis"—an event that then made a further contribution to the developing sense of American community. Later British policies emphasizing divergent American and British interests met a similar combination of changing identification and attention patterns in a context of improved intercolonial communication facilities. And, as in the case of the Stamp Act crisis, an increasing sensitivity among the colonists to perceived threats to their rights contributed to the magnitude of the response triggered by specific British actions.

It is significant that the growing ties of communication and community preceded any widespread functional amalgamation of colonial political institutions. Thus, the American experience in nation-building runs directly counter to the arguments of those who would form nations, or even world governments, out of various groups of peoples simply by gathering their leaders at one table to draft a binding constitution.

In the American experience, gradual processes of integration—shared focuses of attention, common perceptions of the community and its inhabitants, complementary habits and facilities of communication and decision-making—had to cross a certain threshold before such formative events as the Stamp Act and similar British measures were perceived by the participants in a common or mutually compatible manner. And both rewarding mutual transactions and common perceptions of important events proceeded some distance before common political institutions, whether limited to minor functions or performing the most important functions of government, became acceptable to or actively desired by the politically relevant strata of the colonial population.

The People

Knowledge and Foreign Policy Opinions: Some Models for Consideration

CHAPTER THREE

William A. Gamson

Andre Modigliani

Reprinted with permission from the *Public Opinion Quarterly*, Vol. 30 (Summer, 1966) 187–99. Mr. Gamson is Professor of Sociology at the University of Michigan. Mr. Modigliani is Assistant Professor of Social Relations at Harvard University.

There is a seldom cited but widely shared and appealing law of public opinion, which can be stated very simply: "The more knowledgeable people are, the more likely they are to agree with me." This law would appear to be particularly applicable when one is concerned with public opinion on foreign policy, since these matters of state are far from most people's daily lives and highly complex. Unenlightened thinking will surely be more prevalent among those who have little information and understanding; those who are sophisticated and aware will tend to share the opinions of the prototype of these characteristics, oneself.

The Enlightenment Model

Many social scientists are strongly convinced of the inadequacy of military force or the threat of force as a means of influence in international relations. For such people, this "enlightenment" model leads to the expectation that, with increasing knowledge and sophistication, people are more likely to reject belligerent policies. An examination of public opinion data does not immediately disabuse one of this view. In one study, for example, the better-informed people were, the less likely they were to support the statement, "We should never compromise with Russia but just continue to demand what we think is right."[1] In a 1953 poll, 70 per cent of the college-educated favored United Nations atomic energy control, while 61 per cent of the high school-educated and only 52 per cent of the grade school-educated favored such an alternative.[2] Or, in a 1954 poll, only 9 per cent of the college-educated, against 16 per cent of the grade school-educated, felt we should give up trying to reach agreements with Russia on outlawing atomic weapons.[3]

On the other hand, certain results which show that more knowledgeable people are more likely to support a militaristic policy tend to come as a surprise to those who believe in the enlightenment model. Back and Gergen report some examples of such greater willingness to engage in

An earlier version of this paper was presented at the Montreal meetings of the American Sociological Association, September 1964, under the title, "Competing Images of Soviet Behavior."

[1] Previously unreported data from Andre Modigliani, "The Public and the Cold War," Cambridge, Harvard University, 1962, unpublished undergraduate honors thesis.

[2] AIPO, May 24, 1953, reported in *Public Opinion Quarterly,* Vol. 27, 1963, p. 167.

[3] AIPO, Apr. 28, 1954, reported in *ibid.,* p. 168.

The People

war on the part of the more knowledgeable.[4] Of those who had opinions, 29 per cent who scored low on a measure of political knowledge, and only 9 per cent who scored high, favored decreasing the war effort in Korea. In a 1958 poll, 42 per cent of those who were poorly informed and only 18 per cent of those who were highly informed felt Berlin was not worth fighting over.[5]

The Mainstream Model

Such results give rise to a second explanation, more defensible than the enlightenment model. In this second explanation, education brings with it, not so much better understanding of the world as greater participation in it and attachment to the mainstream. The politically educated are not better analysts of complex situations but are simply more aware of what official U.S. policy is. Being more integrated into their society, and more susceptible to the influence of its institutions, their opinions are more likely to fall within the narrow boundaries of open official discussion. This occurs at the expense of either more conservative *or* more liberal alternatives that are not legitimized by the support of major political officials. The two models are summarized in Chart 1.

Note that both of the above explanations of the effect of knowledge are *consensus* theories, i.e. they predict that increasing knowledge will move all groups toward the same point. Either because they gain better understanding (the enlightenment model) or because they are more subject to social influence (the mainstream model), people are similarly affected by increased knowledge. In these theories, there is a single pole toward which knowledge impels people regardless of their starting point.

The above issue is vital, because we intend to present some data that appear to support the mainstream argument. However, on closer analysis they reveal a contradictory result—a polarization of opinion with increased knowledge. The data are drawn from a probability sample of 558 residents of the Detroit Metropolitan Area and are part of the Detroit Area Study data for 1963–64.[6] The questionnaire included a sixteen-item measure of knowledge of foreign relations. The questions were straightforward and factual but required considerable knowledge. Respondents were asked to state which among the following countries are located in Africa: Ecuador, Ghana, Afghanistan, Mongolia, and Morocco; which among West Germany, Algeria, France, Japan, England, and Russia have developed and

4 Kurt W. Back and Kenneth Gergen, "Public Opinion and International Relations," *Social Problems*, Vol. 11, Summer 1963, pp. 77–87, report on Gallup Survey 474, April 1951.

5 Previously unreported data from Modigliani, *op. cit.* The exact wording of the Berlin item was; "We should try talking to Russia (about Berlin) but avoid fighting no matter what since it's not worth it to get into a war over Berlin."

6 We are indebted to John C. Scott, Director of the Detroit Area Study, and Robert Hefner and Sheldon Levy, principal investigators for the 1963–1964 study, for allowing us to include several of our items in the questionnaire and making the data freely available to us.

CHART 1   SUMMARY OF ENLIGHTENMENT AND MAINSTREAM MODELS

Enlightenment Model

Independent variable: The degree of enlightened understanding of the true and complex nature of foreign affairs. Such enlightenment tends to be a product of education and is reflected in sophisticated knowledge of foreign affairs.

Dependent variable: Willingness to use military force to influence international affairs.

Central hypothesis: The greater the understanding and knowledge of foreign affairs, the less belligerence in one's foreign policy opinions.

Mainstream Model

Independent variable: The boundaries and clarity of official government foreign policy.

Intervening variable: One's attachment to the mainstream and the resultant exposure to influences such as the mass media. Such attachment and exposure are highly related to education and are reflected in factual information about foreign affairs and knowledge of the nature of, and rationale for, official policies.

Dependent variable: The degree of conformity of one's foreign policy opinions to official government policy.

Central hypothesis: The greater the attachment to the mainstream, the greater the degree of conformity of one's foreign policy opinions to official policy.

tested their own atomic weapons; and which among Egypt, Poland, Spain, Mainland China, and India have Communist governments. They were scored for number right minus number wrong on the sixteen items and are here divided into high, medium, and low knowledge groups.

Respondents were also asked a number of items on particular policies toward the United Nations, trade with Communist countries, disarmament, and so forth. We have singled out for consideration here those with particular relevance for the mainstream theory. They are items in which respondents are asked to choose one among three alternative policies, one of which had official government sanction at the time the survey was conducted.

According to the mainstream argument, we should expect that, with increasing knowledge, individuals will tend to reject both of the alternatives that are not officially endorsed and accept the one that is. With this in mind, we can examine the data in Table 1. On all three policy items, there is a pronounced increase in the percentage picking the official "mainstream," or middle, alternative as knowledge increases. This is at the expense of *both* more liberal and more conservative alternatives on China and on trade. However, on the question of military strength there seems to be some shift from right to left, as one might expect from the enlightenment theory.

The most striking feature of Table 1, though, is still the dramatic and consistent increase in support for government policy with increased knowledge. One might argue that, where there has been no policy shift, as in our policy toward China, increased knowledge will bring equal defections from both poles; where policy has recently shifted (as it did

The People

TABLE 1   RELATION OF FOREIGN AFFAIRS KNOWLEDGE TO SELECTED POLICIES

(in per cent)

Policy	Knowledge		
	Low	Medium	High
China:[a]			
The United States should withdraw some of its support of the UN if other nations admit Communist China	24	16	12
The United States should oppose letting Communist China into the UN but should continue to support the UN if other nations admit Communist China	46	60	66
The United States should not oppose letting Communist China into the UN	30	24	22
	100	100	100
(N)	(152)	(202)	(159)
$\chi^2 = 13.9$, $p < .05$			
Trade:[b]			
The United States should not sell anything to Russia	29	16	14
The United States should only sell surplus food to Russia	33	45	50
The United States should be willing to sell anything except military weapons to Russia	38	39	35
	100	100	100
(N)	(159)	(203)	(161)
$\chi^2 = 19.9$, $p < .05$			
Military strength:[c]			
Should be built up	40	28	17
About right	55	65	70
Should be cut back	5	7	13
	100	100	100
(N)	(153)	(198)	(151)
$\chi^2 = 22.8$, $p < .05$			

[a] The question read: "Which do you think would be the best United States policy toward admitting Red China to the UN?"
[b] The question read: "Some discussion concerning trade with Russia has been in the news recently. Which of these positions is closest to what you think about the matter?"
[c] The question read: "There are a number of different opinions about how much military strength the U.S. should have. How do you feel? Do you think that the present military strength of the U.S. should be cut back, built up, or is it about right?"

with trade with the Soviet Union and to some degree with the arms race), increased knowledge will exert its *dominant* pull on those who advocate the old official policy. By this reasoning, those low in knowledge are, because of their diminished contact with mainstream influences, more likely to lag behind in policy shifts. In this instance, the shift represents a liberalization. This would suggest that, where administration policy shifts to the right, the move to the official alternative that accompanies increased knowledge will be greatest among those who favor the more liberal rather than the more conservative alternative. While we cannot test this hypothesis here, Table 1 does seem to offer some encouragement.

Knowledge and Foreign Policy Opinions

The Cognitive Consistency Model

However, we must consider still another theory relating knowledge of foreign affairs to policy opinions, the cognitive consistency model. This final model contrasts with earlier consensus models in its implication that increasing knowledge will change people in *different* directions leading to a greater polarization of opinion among the more knowledgeable. This model argues that endorsement of a specific policy position stems from more general attitudes and assumptions that are being applied to a specific case. Knowledge of foreign affairs is important not because it reflects enlightenment or exposure to mainstream influences but because it reflects conceptual sophistication. Such sophistication reflects the ability to integrate specific policies with more general attitudes and assumptions one holds.

Clearly, the cognitive consistency model implies a polarization of opinion among the more knowledgeable. Poorly informed individuals, even with different ideological orientations, will have difficulty relating their orientation to specific policies. The result is a good deal of randomness and inconsistency in the choices of such individuals and no clear differentiation among those members with different predispositions. However, among the sophisticated, those with different predispositions will rally around different specific policies, creating sharper differentiation among those with different ideological orientations. This model is summarized in Chart 2.

To explore the cognitive consistency model, we need some measure of general attitudes and assumptions; since we are considering policies relevant to the Cold War, attitudes and assumptions about the Soviet Union seem appropriate. In a separate study, the authors have been attempting to evaluate three coherent sets of assumptions or "belief systems" about the Soviet Union by examining, through an analysis of historical data, the predictions they imply about Soviet-Western interaction. The assumptions these belief systems make about long-range Soviet goals, Soviet risk-taking behavior, and the Soviet view of the West have

CHART 2   SUMMARY OF THE COGNITIVE CONSISTENCY MODEL

Independent variable: One's general political orientation, ideology, and beliefs. For example, assumptions about the nature of the Soviet Union and the nature of the Cold War.

Intervening variable: One's conceptual sophistication and the ability to integrate general attitudes and assumptions with specific policy opinions. Such sophistication is likely to be a product of education and will be reflected in knowledge of foreign affairs.

Dependent variable: The degree of relationship between one's specific foreign policy opinions and one's general attitudes and assumptions.

Central hypothesis: The greater the conceptual sophistication, the greater the relationship between general assumptions and specific policy opinions.

The People

been outlined elsewhere.[7] Using this earlier formulation as a guideline, we wrote three items to assess each respondent's assumptions about these aspects of the Soviet Union.

Each respondent was classified into one of three belief systems, which we shall refer to as Positions A, B, and C. Briefly, Position A states that the Soviet Union is actively pursuing the goal of world domination and is willing to incur high risks to achieve this goal. It views Western resistance as so sporadic that the Soviet Union can achieve its goals through continual pressure short of war. Position B states that the Soviet Union is actively interested in achieving a *limited* expansion of influence and is willing to incur only moderate risks in the achievement of its goals. It views the West as both susceptible to limited encroachments and as attempting such encroachments on the Soviet Union—much like an opponent in a game. Position C states that the Soviet Union is actively interested only in holding on to what it has and is unwilling to incur risks except in self-defense. The West is viewed as actively seeking to undermine Soviet influence and control in the world.

Each respondent was asked to make a first and a second choice among the following sets of statements:

I. *On Soviet goals:* Many people are concerned about what the Russian government is really trying to do. Which of these do you think is closest to what their aims really are?

a. When all is said and done, Russia is determined to conquer the United States. (Position A)

b. Russia is trying to get the most it can from the United States but it isn't really trying to conquer us. (Position B)

c. Russia is more interested in increasing its own security and standard of living than it is in getting the most it can from the United States. (Position C)

II. *On Soviet risk-taking behavior:* How willing do you think the Russians are to take chances to get what they want?

a. Russia is cautious and will try to avoid starting any trouble which could lead to a serious crisis. (Position C)

b. Russia is even willing to risk starting a serious crisis in order to get what it wants. (Position A)

c. Russia is willing to stir up quite a bit of trouble to get what it wants, but it will try to avoid causing any really serious crisis. (Position B)

III. *On Soviet view of the West:* Which of these best describes what the Russians believe about the United States—even if they are wrong in what they believe:

a. Russia almost always seems to believe that they can take advantage of us and get away with it. (Position A)

b. Russia almost always seems to be afraid that we are trying to take advantage of them. (Position C)

[7] See William A. Gamson, "Evaluating Beliefs about International Conflict," in Roger Fisher, ed., *International Conflict and Behavioral Science,* New York, Basic Books, 1964, pp. 27–40; William A. Gamson and Andre Modigliani, "Tensions and Concessions: The Empirical Confirmation of Beliefs about Soviet Behavior," *Social Problems,* Vol. 11, 1963, pp. 34–48; and William A. Gamson and Andre Modigliani, "The Carrot and/or the Stick: Soviet Responses to Western Foreign Policy, 1946–1953," Center for Research on Conflict Resolution, Carnegie Project No. 4, Working Document 10, paper presented at meetings of International Peace Research Society, Chicago, November 1964, mimeographed.

c. Russia seems to believe both that they can take advantage of us and that we try to take advantage of them. (Position B)

We neither expected nor found a consistency across items that matched our ideal or a priori statement of the three belief systems. However, there was sufficient relationship among answers to the three items to identify each respondent with the belief system he most nearly approximated.

It is a central premise of the cognitive consistency model that specific policy opinions flow from more general attitudes and assumptions. If this is correct, then we should expect some relation between assumptions about the Soviet Union and the sort of policy items included in Table 1. Table 2 indicates that the expected relationship exists.

TABLE 2   BELIEF SYSTEMS BY SELECTED POLICIES

(*in per cent*)

	Belief System		
Policy	*A*	*B*	*C*
China:[a]			
Withdraw from the UN if China enters	24	16	16
Oppose entry but don't withdraw from the UN	56	62	48
Do not oppose Chinese entry to the UN	20	22	36
	100	100	100
(N)	(114)	(293)	(107)
$\chi^2 = 13.1, \ p < .05, \ C = .19$			
Trade:[a]			
Trade nothing with Russia	32	17	11
Trade surplus food only	39	47	36
Trade anything but weapons	29	36	54
	100	100	100
(N)	(117)	(297)	(109)
$\chi^2 = 20.5, \ p < .05, \ C = .24$			
Military strength:[a]			
Should be built up more	38	29	17
About right	57	64	70
Should be cut back	5	7	13
	100	100	100
(N)	(111)	(287)	(105)
$\chi^2 = 14.5, \ p < .05, \ C = .21$			

[a] See Table 1 for the exact wording of the items and alternative answers.

On policy toward China, Position A people are the most likely of the three groups to be for withdrawing from the UN; Position B people to oppose Chinese entry but not withdraw; and Position C people not to oppose Chinese entry into the UN. The other two items show a similar pattern. However, the degree of relationship is quite small. Using as a measure of degree the contingency coefficient, corrected so that it has an

The People

upper limit of 1, the three items show C's of only .19, .24, and .21, respectively.

The slimness of the relation between belief system and specific policy opinion is easily accounted for by the cognitive consistency model. Such a relationship, it suggests, will be pronounced only among respondents high in conceptual sophistication and knowledge. Those low in knowledge will be unable to relate their general assumptions to the specific situation in a consistent manner. By controlling for knowledge of foreign affairs in Table 3, we see that the predicted pattern emerges. The relationship between belief system and policy for those high in knowledge has coefficients of .46, .51, and .31 as against coefficients of .14, .19, and .14 for those low in knowledge. Clearly, belief systems are connected with policy opinions primarily for the knowledgeable.

TABLE 3   BELIEF SYSTEMS BY SELECTED POLICES, CONTROLLING FOR KNOWLEDGE

(*in per cent*)

| | Knowledge/Belief System | | | | | | | | |
| | Low | | | Medium | | | High | | |
Policy	A	B	C	A	B	C	A	B	C
China:[a]									
Withdraw	25	22	32	16	17	15	28	8	3
Oppose	45	50	35	58	63	51	67	71	54
Do not oppose	30	28	32	26	20	33	5	21	43
	100	100	100	100	100	100	100	100	100
(N)	(44)	(78)	(31)	(31)	(132)	(39)	(39)	(83)	(37)
		$C = .14$			$C = .15$			$C = .46$	
Trade:[a]									
Nothing	34	29	18	28	14	13	31	12	3
Surplus food	33	34	30	34	46	46	51	60	30
Anything	33	37	52	38	39	41	18	28	67
	100	100	100	100	100	100	100	100	100
(N)	(46)	(80)	(33)	(32)	(132)	(39)	(39)	(85)	(37)
		$C = .19$			$C = .18$			$C = .51$	
Military strength:[a]									
Build up	48	38	36	36	31	10	27	16	8
About right	48	57	61	61	61	80	65	75	66
Cut back	4	5	3	4	8	10	8	9	26
	100	100	100	100	100	100	100	100	100
N	(46)	(77)	(31)	(28)	(131)	(39)	(37)	(79)	(35)
		$C = .14$			$C = .24$			$C = .31$	

[a]See Table 1 for the exact wording of the items and alternative answers.

One of the striking implications of the cognitive consistency model is that increases in knowledge should have a polarizing effect on the opinions of a set of persons. Knowledge has the effect of allowing one to understand more clearly the policy most consistent with his predispositions.

Knowledge and Foreign Policy Opinions

This means that subsets of persons who share different belief systems will tend to deviate from one another with increases in knowledge, each moving toward the policy most consistent with its underlying assumptions. Thus, Position A advocates, with more knowledge, will be more sharply in favor of withdrawing from the UN, trading nothing with Russia, and building up arms. Position C people will move in exactly the opposite direction, becoming *less* favorable on all these alternatives, while Position B people will show larger percentages for the official government policy on all these items.

Note how such an interpretation is possible in the results of Table 1. If Position A and Position C people are moving[8] in opposite and offsetting directions and Position B people are moving toward the center from the more extreme alternatives, then the over-all effect will be an increase in

TABLE 4   KNOWLEDGE BY SELECTED POLICIES, CONTROLLING FOR BELIEF SYSTEMS

(*in per cent*)

Policy	Belief System/Knowledge								
	A			B			C		
	Low	Med.	High	Low	Med.	High	Low	Med.	High
China:[a]									
Withdraw	25	16	28	22	17	8	32	15	3
Oppose	45	58	67	50	63	71	35	51	54
Do not oppose	30	26	5	28	20	21	32	33	43
	100	100	100	100	100	100	100	100	100
(N)	(44)	(31)	(39)	(78)	(132)	(83)	(31)	(39)	(37)
		$C = .34$			$C = .22$			$C = .38$	
Trade:[a]									
Nothing	34	28	31	29	14	12	18	13	3
Surplus food	33	34	51	34	46	60	30	46	30
Anything	33	38	18	37	39	28	52	41	67
	100	100	100	100	100	100	100	100	100
(N)	(46)	(32)	(39)	(80)	(132)	(85)	(33)	(39)	(37)
		$C = .25$			$C = .28$			$C = .33$	
Military strength:[a]									
Build up	48	36	27	38	31	16	36	10	9
About right	48	61	65	57	61	75	61	80	66
Cut back	4	4	8	5	8	9	3	10	26
	100	100	100	100	100	100	100	100	100
(N)	(46)	(28)	(37)	(77)	(131)	(79)	(31)	(39)	(35)
		$C = .24$			$C = .22$			$C = .45$	

[a] See Table 1 for the exact wording of the items and alternative answers.

[8] We ask the reader's indulgence in the use of such process language to describe differences among individuals with different knowledge. Our data, of course, show nothing about process, but since the models we are contrasting are talking about the effects of knowledge on opinion formation, it is stultifying to make use of elaborate circumlocutions whenever we discuss interpretations of this data. We hope that this general reminder will be sufficient to allow us the convenience of such language in interpreting static results.

The People

the support for the official policy. Combining advocates of all three positions may conceal the fact that knowledge has a different relationship for those with different images of the Soviet Union.

Table 4 (which is simply a rearrangement of Table 3, controlling for belief systems) shows the polarizing effect we have been discussing.[9] While the pattern is least clear with Position A people, by and large increases in knowledge tend to increase agreement with the policy that Table 2 showed to be associated with the belief system in question. Thus, Position A people are less likely to favor admitting China to the United Nations as knowledge increases, while Position C people are more likely to favor this alternative as knowledge increases. Similarly, on the question of trade with Russia, increasing knowledge moves Position A people away from free trade, Position C people toward more liberal trade, and Position B people away from the extremes of trading nothing or anything.

Conclusion

The over-all pattern of results in Table 4 is not without its aberrations. We are inclined to feel that they are best illuminated by a combination of the mainstream and cognitive consistency models. We would suggest that two primary forces are operating, both of which tend to correlate with education and knowledge. On the one hand, *there is a strain toward attitudinal consistency that increases with knowledge*; this produces a higher relationship between belief system and policy among the more knowledgeable and an increasing polarization around different policy alternatives for those who start with different premises. At the same time, *there is greater attachment to society and susceptibility to social influences* —a force that produces support for official government policies.

If we can interpret our measure of knowledge as reflecting both these forces, then some of the aberrations in Table 4 make sense. Let us consider the question concerning policy toward UN admittance of China. Among advocates of Position A, the strain toward consistency would impel them toward the extreme right,[10] or "withdrawal from the UN," position with increased knowledge, while the strain toward conformity would impel

---

[9] Our belief systems show only the slightest relationship to our measure of knowledge of foreign relations. Advocates of Position C are equally represented in all three knowldege groups; however, Position A people are slightly overrepresented at the expense of Position B people in the highest and in the lowest knowledge groups. The over-all relationship, however, is so slight and irregular that we will treat the two measures as independent.

[10] Our use of the terms "extreme right" and "extreme left" does not represent any judgment on our part about the true place of such alternatives in the political spectrum. We do not wish to imply, for example, that agreement wtih the proposition, "The United States should not oppose letting Communist China into the UN," reflects any kind of extremist position as that term is sometimes used; this opinion clearly may be held by moderates. We use the term "extreme left" *only* to refer to its position in the set of three alternatives offered. In fact, we attempted to word the items so that none of the policy alternatives would appear extreme in the absolute sense—that is, we wished to ensure some variance in our respondents' choices.

them toward the middle, or "opposition without withdrawal," position. Hence, with increasing knowledge there are two forces pushing Position A advocates away from the left, or "acceptance of China," position, but only one force pushing them into the extreme right position. The data, in fact, show that defection from the left position is much more pronounced than increased endorsement of the right position (see Table 4, China question, under Position A: endorsement of the "withdrawal" position increases only from 25 to 28 per cent, while endorsement of the "do not oppose" position drops from 30 to 5 per cent).

Conversely, for advocates of Position C we have two forces pushing them away from the extreme right position and only one pushing them into the extreme left position. Again the data show that increased knowledge brings greater defection from the right position than increased endorsement of the left position (see Table 4, China question, under Position C: endorsement of the "do not oppose" position increases only from 32 to 43 per cent, while endorsement of the "withdrawal" position drops from 32 to 3 per cent).

For Position B advocates *both* forces act to push them out of the extreme right *and* left positions and into the middle, and the data show defections from both extremes with increasing knowledge (see Table 4, China question, under Position B: endorsement of the "do not oppose" position decreases from 28 to 21 per cent, and endorsement of the "withdrawal" position also decreases from 22 to 8 per cent).

As a final complication, we would suggest that in cases where government policy has recently shifted, the pure direction of such a shift may be an important variable. Specifically, a shift to the left in government policy (as had recently occurred on trade with the Soviet Union and perhaps on arms build-up) may act as added reinforcement for leftward shifts, and deterrent to rightward shifts. And, indeed, on these two policy questions the data show that increased knowledge brings a much greater increase for the left alternative among Position C advocates than increase for the right alternative among Position A advocates.

We cannot disentangle the contribution of these hypothesized forces in our own results. But with a careful selection of policy questions and with independent measures of conceptual sophistication and conformity to official doctrine, it should be possible to parcel out the effects of each.

The President, the Polls, and Vietnam

the Polls,

and

Vietnam

C H A P T E R   F O U R

Seymour Martin Lipset

Reprinted with permission from *TRANS-ACTION* Magazine, Vol. 3 (September/
October 1966), 19–24. Copyright © 1966 by Washington University, St. Louis, Mo.
Mr. Lipset is Professor of Government and Social Relations at Harvard University.

Never before in the annals of American political history has a President exhibited such an obvious and intense concern over his public image as indicated by the public opinion polls. President Johnson's well-reported attention to the rise and fall of percentage points raises the question: what are the uses and abuses of polls in affecting the actions of political leaders.

There is a very great difference in the reliability of responses with respect to domestic and foreign affairs. Domestically, the polls indicate that we are dealing with relatively stable attitudes on issues such as the welfare state, race relations, etc. In addition, when new issues arise, such as how to deal with inflation, unemployment, or Medicare, people can react to them in terms of direct personal experience or liberal-conservative predispositions.

Conversely, in the area of foreign policy most Americans know very little, and are only indirectly involved. They have no way of checking on often conflicting reports from countries and regions under contention, nor on public sentiments elsewhere in the world. Consequently, the press and political leaders can have much more influence in determining public opinion on foreign issues than on domestic issues. Whether Tshombe is a villain or a hero, whether the downfall of Nkrumah is good or bad, is defined *for* the average American rather than *by* the average American. If we trace the poll popularity of a single leader, say Tito of Yugoslavia or de Gaulle of France, it becomes clear that the poll variations in the United States follow policy decisions made about him on the basis of whether his actions further or hamper American concerns. In other words, polls do not make policy so much as follow policy in most areas of international affairs.

When it comes to Vietnam, basically the opinion data indicate that national policy-makers, particularly the President, have an almost free hand to pursue any policy they think correct and get public support for it. They can escalate under the justification that this is the only way to prevent a "Communist take-over" in Southeast Asia; they can negotiate with the Viet Cong for a coalition goevrnment if this policy is presented as one which will gain peace while avoiding such a presumed take-over. These conclusions do not mean that most people are fickle, but rather that they agree on certain larger objectives, peace without the expansion (or contraction) of communism, and find it necessary to trust the judgment of national leaders as to what is possible given these purposes.

The highly publicized efforts by the President and other foreign policy advocates to interpret the various poll results dealing with the Vietnam conflict—with both hawks and doves claiming that the American people agree with them—point up the need to clarify the meaning of the polls. Some months ago, a faculty group at various San Francisco Bay Area colleges actually dug down in their own pockets to pay the National Opinion Research Center (NORC) of the University of Chicago to conduct a survey which might clear up some of the confusion. Unfortunately, this survey was no more conclusive than others which have been conducted over the years by other pollsters such as George Gallup, Louis Harris, National Analysts, and the Opinion Research Corporation. The results of most surveys can still be interpreted by both extremes in the foreign policy debate to fit their own preconceptions.

No Pigeonholes for Hawks and Doves

The truth is that the American people as a whole, and many, if not most, individuals cannot be placed in the category of dove or hawk. Two sets of attitudes stand out among the various responses. The great majority of the American people desire peace in Vietnam, do not want war with China, are prepared to accept some sort of compromise truce with the enemy, and, in fact, anticipate a negotiated peace rather than a victory which will see the defeat of the Viet Cong. On the other hand, a substantial majority is strongly hostile to communism and all the Communist countries, including Soviet Russia, Cuba, and China. Almost nobody interviewed by NORC (5 per cent or less) believed that our foreign policy toward any one of these countries is "too tough"; a large majority agree with statements that the US is "too soft" in dealing with China and Cuba; almost half think we are "too soft" in our relations with the Russians. Most of those who do not think the policy is "too soft" say it is right.

Most Americans are, in fact, both doves *and* hawks; the more thorough and detailed the querying of opinions, the more clearly this appears. Early in March of this year, the Gallup Poll asked, "Would you favor or oppose bombing big cities in North Vietnam?" Sixty percent voiced opposition, while only 28 per cent favored it. (The NORC study used a similar question and reported 55 per cent against bombing cities in North Vietnam and 39 per cent in support.) These results would seem to clearly indicate a dove majority against bombing North Vietnam. Yet in the same survey, Gallup also inquired, "Would you favor or oppose *bombing industrial plants and factories* in North Vietnam?" The response distribution was almost precisely opposite to the "bomb North Vietnamese cities" question. Sixty-one per cent said they were for the bombing of factories and 26 per cent were against. In other words, three-fifths of the American public were for bombing the North Vietnamese factories, but three-fifths (not all the same people) were also against bombing their cities, in March and April. This means that the policy of "strategic" bombing and avoiding "civilian" targets is generally approved. Thus, when Louis Harris asked about US resumption of bombing in January ("Do you think President Johnson was right or wrong to resume bombing in North Vietnam after the recent pause?") 73 per cent said he was right; only 10 per cent were opposed. And two months later a National Analysts survey conducted for NBC which inquired, "Should the US continue bombing North Vietnam?" reported almost identical results, 78 per cent for continuing; 14 per cent for stopping the attacks.

The American public shows a similar general propensity to discriminate among the methods which should be used in fighting the war. Almost the same size majority (68 per cent) told National Analysts interviewers that they *opposed* the US using "any nuclear weapons in Vietnam," as *approved* US use of "gas that does not kill people."

Are these illogical or inconsistent responses? No, as in the case of the answers to the bombing questions, they reflect a national mood to do as little as possible to stop Communist expansion. The dominant attitude seems to be not to let Vietnam "go Communist" coupled with a desire to end the war as soon as possible, on the most minimal conditions which include a willingness to negotiate directly with the National Liberation Front (NLF).

Peace—yes; Communism—no

The various surveys point up this mixed pattern of responses. Peace sentiments are strong. Almost everyone (88 per cent) polled by NORC would favor "American negotiations with the Viet Cong if they were willing to negotiate," and a majority (52 per cent for, 36 per cent against) would be willing to approve "forming a new government in which the Viet Cong took some part" in order to "end the fighting."

But the *same sample* of respondents who gave these dove answers turned into veritable militant hawks when asked, "If President Johnson were to announce tomorrow that we were going to withdraw from Vietnam and let the Communists take over, would you approve or disapprove?" Four-fifths of the NORC sample, 81 per cent, disapproved, as compared with but 15 per cent favoring getting out. A goodly majority (56 per cent for, 39 per cent against) would *not* agree to "gradually withdrawing our troops and letting the South Vietnamese work out their own problems" even though the possibility of a Communist victory was not mentioned in the question.

The willingness of the Americans to fight the war was expressed in the response to a NORC question which first asked respondents to choose among three alternative courses of action: continuing the present situation indefinitely; fighting a major war with hundreds of thousands of casualties; or supporting a withdrawal of American troops which leads to an eventual Communist take-over. Almost half (49 per cent) would continue the present situation; 23 per cent favored escalation to a major war; and 19 per cent would support getting out. However, when the choice was narrowed to either support of escalation to a major war or withdrawal, twice as many (60 per cent) chose major war as favored withdrawal. The same aggressive posture is reflected in the answers to an NBC-National Analysts poll, in March, which asked respondents to choose whether we should "pursue a more offensive ground war in Vietnam than we are presently doing, or should we establish defensive positions around the cities we now control?" Over half (55 per cent) chose to escalate as compared to 28 per cent who favored holding our present lines.

The People

When pollsters' questions remind respondents of the cost of the war in lives and do not mention communism, Americans often support the more pacific alternative; when they are faced with fighting or agreeing to a Communist victory, they opt for continuing the war, and even with escalating if necessary.

Yet, though most Americans ruefully are willing to keep fighting in Vietnam if this is necessary to prevent a complete take-over, or expansion to neighboring countries, they clearly would much prefer not to be there, and are anxious and willing to turn over responsibility to someone else. Back in June 1954, when it first appeared as if the US might send troops to Indo-China, only 20 per cent told Gallup interviewers that they would approve sending US soldiers "to help the French fight the Communists in Indo-China." And much more recently, on various occasions, clear majorities have reported to Gallup, Harris, and NORC alike that they would like to see the United Nations take over from the United States, either to fight or settle the war. Thus in the first few months of this year, 70 per cent told NORC they would approve the UN or some neutral countries negotiating a peace "with each side holding the territory it now holds"; 74 per cent indicated to Gallup interviewers they would approve the UN working out "its own formula for peace in Vietnam"; more people (49 per cent) said that the US should submit the Vietnam question to the UN and abide by the UN's decision, *no matter what it is,* than opposed the idea (37 per cent); and a UN army for Vietnam and Southeast Asia was approved by a three to one majority (almost identical to the results obtained by Gallup to a similar question a year earlier).

Peace Hopes and the UN

The strength of the sentiment to turn the war over to the United Nations may be seen in the fact that this is the only issue on which poll results indicated that negative judgments of President Johnson far outweighed his support. In September 1965, the Harris Survey reported that 42 per cent agreed with the statement, the President was "more wrong than right" in not asking the UN to take over in Vietnam, while only 25 per cent thought he was "more right than wrong," and the rest were not sure. A more recent Harris Survey released in early April of this year reports that Americans favor by nearly two to one (50 per cent to 27 per cent) "turning over the entire Vietnam war to a special three-man United Nations committee for arbitration and a decision binding on all parties."

These attitudes not only reflect ambivalent sentiments about US participation in Vietnam, they also indicate the very strong positive feeling of the overwhelming majority of the American people toward the United Nations. All the surveys have consistently indicated widespread popular support for the UN. (The vociferous rightist critics of American membership in the international body can hardly find more than a small minority to support their views among the general public. Most Americans

69

seem to identify the UN with prospects for world peace, and are willing to do anything to endorse it, including criticizing American foreign policy if a question is worded in such a way as to make the pro-UN response involve such criticism.)

In evaluating the poll responses, it is important to keep in mind that the proportion of Americans who can be considered soft on communism is insignificantly small. Those who approve forming a new government in which the NLF takes part are almost as hard in their attitudes toward Castro, Communist China, and Russia as those who oppose NLF participation. In other words "hard line" anti-Communists are almost as prone to favor dealing with the Viet Cong directly, as those who are generally more favorable to the expansion of relations with Communist countries. For example, 60 per cent of those favorable to a coalition with the Viet Cong think our policy toward Castro is "too soft," as compared with 70 per cent among those who would not admit the Viet Cong to the government. The response pattern with respect to attitudes toward Communist China and Russia is similar.

What the polls show is that the anti-communism of Americans has little to do with their opinions about how the war in Vietnam should be handled at the tactical level. But, the belief in the need to defeat the Communist enemy, serves to support any actions which the President can argue need to be taken to defeat this enemy. Such attitudes provide a strong reservoir of support for the hawks, and an equally significant impediment for the doves.

These mixed "hawk-dove" sentiments in large measure underlie the general state of opinion concerning President Johnson's handling of the Vietnamese situation. Polls taken before the spring 1966 Buddhist crisis, by Gallup and Harris over the previous year, had indicated approval for the President in the ratio of two to one. The last such precrisis survey, Gallup's of late March, indicated that 56 per cent approved, while 26 per cent disapproved. (The NORC survey taken a little earlier found a comparable division, 61 per cent approving and 29 per cent disapproving, almost identical to the results reported by the NBC- National Analysts poll, also taken in March.)

Who Are the President's Critics?

It is difficult to tell from the available reports of the various surveys whether the critics of President Johnson are disproportionately hawks or doves. It is clear that a large majority both of the extreme hawks, those who favor "carrying the war more into North Vietnam," and of the more pacific doves, those who would "pull our troops out now," tell pollsters they oppose the President's Vietnamese policies. The President, on a number of occasions, has stated that most of those who disapprove of his Vietnamese policies are hawks, rather than doves. And he has interpreted increases in the proportions voicing criticism, such as occurred in

May and June of 1966, as reflecting a growth in sentiment to escalate. This may be so, but the President has not presented figures comparing the attitudes of his supporters and opponents on a variety of specific policy issues. This would be the only way to reach a conclusion on this point.

The NORC survey tried to do so, but the findings are indecisive and incomplete. Those who "disapprove the way the Johnson administration is handling the situation in Vietnam" are slightly more likely to give dove rather than hawk responses on a few policy questions. However, these data derive from those questions which produced large dove responses among the sample generally, such as negotiate with Viet Cong, form a new government with them.

Most recently, a Gallup survey taken in early June reports that among those who disapprove of Johnson's handling of the situation in Vietnam, 10 per cent gave answers which could be categorized under the heading "we should be more aggressive," while 13 per cent said that "we should get out." My own interpretation of the data presented by various pollsters is that the proportions of hawks and doves among the President's critics, reported recently by Gallup, has tended to be a relatively stable pattern. That is, the critics have usually contained slightly more doves than hawks. It should be stressed, however, that there is always a third group present among the President's critics whose responses cannot be classified in either category.

Clearly, the American people are worried about the Vietnam war. Indeed, they are, according to recent reports, at least twice as concerned over the war as they are over the next leading "issue"—the Negro civil rights issue. When Gallup asked a national sample in December what headline they would most like to see in "tomorrow's paper," almost nine out of ten respondents spontaneously mentioned peace. Almost half (46 per cent) specifically said "peace in Vietnam," while another 41 per cent stated peace in general. These findings were reiterated in the NORC study which found that more voters (62 per cent) said they "worried a great deal" about the war in Vietnam than about any other issue. Only 7 per cent said the issue of the war did not worry them at all.

The anxiety and serious thought which Americans devote to the Vietnamese war does not mean that they see any quick or simple way to gain the peace they so ardently desire. They know that we have not been doing well. A CBS-Opinion Research Corporation survey reported in December that when asked which side controlled "most of the land area of South Vietnam," more people said the Viet Cong. *Only 24 per cent* thought the US was "making progress toward victory." The bulk of those interviewed also had a reasonably accurate estimate of the numbers of American troops in Vietnam and the casualties suffered by them. Last December, when asked by Gallup, how long they think the war will last, less than 20 per cent thought it would end in a year or less; 26 per cent guessed at two or three more years; while 36 per cent said at least four more years. And when asked by Gallup in January of this year: "Do you think the war will end in a clear-cut victory in Vietnam, or will it end in some sort of compromise settlement?" only 7 per cent foresaw a clear-cut victory; 69 per cent predicted a compromise ending. This anticipation of a compromise settlement is reflected in the large majorities favoring a negotiated settlement as reported by both Gallup and Harris.

The fact that the government of South Vietnam became involved in serious troubles with its own people in the late spring should not have been too surprising to many Americans. The CBS-National Analysts survey reported in December 1965 that only 22 per cent of Americans thought most South Vietnamese are loyal to their present leaders, i.e., the Ky regime. In spite of this lack of belief in popular support for the South Vietnamese government, when this same sample was asked: "Do you think we should have pulled out before American fighting units became involved, or do you think that staying there was the right thing to do?" only 20 per cent said we should have pulled out, 65 per cent thought staying in Vietnam was right. The ability of people to hold these contradictory beliefs is based on an overriding belief that supporting the war is not specific to Vietnam, but a necessity to stop Communist expansion.

Confusing, but Consistent

The data presented by the various pollsters make it possible for one to argue that the American people are tough, soft, informed, confused, decisive, and indecisive, depending on the case one wants to make. To interpret them in any of these ways, however, would be wrong. These attitudes reflect certain consistent underlying beliefs about peace and communism which most of the American public, like those who hold office, find difficult to reconcile. Very few are willing to approve actions which they perceive would increase the chances for a larger war, reduce the possibilities for early peace, or encourage Communist expansion into non-Communist areas, inside or outside of Vietnam. And the survey data suggest that most Americans share with their leaders the sense that they are in a morass from which they do not yet see a way out.

The findings of the surveys clearly indicate that the President, while having a relatively free hand in the actual decision-making to escalate or to de-escalate the war, is more restricted when considering the generic issues of action or inaction. He must give the appearance of a man *engagé*, of being certain of what he is doing, i.e., that the anticipated consequences do in fact come about.

The President seems to present his program along two parameters:

as part of a plan to secure the peace, particularly if the action involved is actually escalation;
pacific actions are presented as ways to contain communism, or even to weaken it.

The President knows that in order to get the support of the American people for a war they wish they never were in, he must continually put his "best peace foot" forward—he continually talks and offers peace, so that he may have public endorsement for war.

And conversely, any effort to make peace, to reach agreement with any Communist state, would best be presented as a way to "contain" communism, to weaken it by facilitating splits among the various Communist states, or to help change it internally so that it will be less totalitarian, more humane, and less expansionist.

There are, of course, important limits, real limits, on the ability of the President to determine public response. During 1966, his personal popularity and endorsement for the Vietnamese policy dropped sharply— to a point where the percentage indicating support fell to less than 50 per cent. A Gallup survey in May indicated only 41 per cent of the general public approved "the way Johnson is handling the situation in Vietnam," as against 37 per cent who disapproved. This general decline in support was a result of the internal turmoil among the South Vietnamese, and a feeling that the President had become indecisive in his handling of the war. Clearly, there was no way that the President could have prevented the American people from learning of the opposition in the streets to General Ky's government. These events, according to Gallup, led to a sizable increase in the proportion who felt that continued fighting is useless, who viewed the war as lost. Gallup reported as of early June, before the facilities at Haiphong and Hanoi were bombed, that for the first time since the US became heavily engaged in Vietnam less than half the population, 48 per cent, supported continuing the war, as compared with 35 per cent who were in favor of taking our troops out.

Yet according to the Harris Survey, another effect of the despair over the South Vietnamese turmoil was to increase sharply the numbers of Americans who favored sharp escalation in tactics as a means of ending the war. Thus, *before* the decision was made to bomb installations at Hanoi and Haiphong in June, Harris reported that those in favor of bombing the two cities had increased from 20 per cent as of September 1965, to 34 per cent in May 1966, while opposition to such bombings had dropped from 47 to 34 per cent. Support for blockading North Vietnamese ports, a step not yet taken, jumped from 38 per cent in September to 53 per cent in May. Those willing to "carry the ground war into North Vietnam at the risk of bringing Red China into the fighting" went up from 28 per cent in December 1965 to 38 per cent in May.

Once the religious strife was terminated, the President could regain his hold on public opinion by the twin tactics of escalating the bombing raids and emphasizing the military defeats suffered by the Viet Cong, and the presumed demoralization of the Ho government in Hanoi. Gallup reports as of July 1966 show that between early June and mid-July general support for the President jumped from 46 per cent to 56 per cent and specific endorsement of his role in the Vietnam conflict rose from 41 per cent to 49 per cent. As of August, Harris found that "more than 80 per cent favor the bombings of military targets at Hanoi and Haiphong. . . ." Those in favor of intensifying the war effort rose from 47 per cent in May

73

to 60 per cent in August. These changes underscore the need for Presidential action as a basis of continuing support.

Democratic 'War Losses'

These results do not mean, however, that any course of decisive action is without great political risks. The deeply felt general anxiety over the continuation and escalation of the war may result in considerable loss of support to the Democrats in the 1966 Congressional elections. A minority, but one large enough to affect the outcome in many districts, is increasingly unhappy. The fact that some of the critics are hawks and others doves does not change the fact that they may vote for the opposition, or not vote at all as a means of protest. A Harris Survey early in the year reports that "those who disagree with the Administration conduct in Vietnam today say they are likely to vote 52–48 per cent Republican next fall."

There are other indications of the diverse ways which the continuation of the war may aid the Republicans and even stimulate right-wing sentiment in the country. On one hand, in July of this year for the first time in many years, a larger group (30 per cent) told Gallup interviewers that the Republicans are more likely than the Democrats (22 per cent) to keep the US out of World War III. Contrast this result with the finding in October 1964 that 45 per cent saw the Democrats as the more pacific party, with 22 per cent for the Republicans. But the survey data also suggests that the social base for a new wave of McCarthyism may be emerging. In March of this year when asked by national analysts: "Do you agree with the right of an American citizen to demonstrate against the war in Vietnam?" only 34.5 per cent agreed, 62 per cent opposed. Two earlier surveys, by the Opinion Research Corporation and Gallup in November and December, also yielded results which suggest that the large majority of the public do not view opposition to the war as legitimate, seeing the bulk of the protesters as "communists" or "draft dodgers."

To sum up the implications of the polls, it seems clear that the President holds the trump cards in dealing with the public on foreign policy matters. The public knows they do not know, and feel they must trust the President, for there is no one else on whom they can rely in the international field. There is no equivalent to Dwight Eisenhower around today—an opposition leader with sufficient personal status and international experience to become a counter-center of foreign policy confidence.

If this is so, why does Lyndon Johnson pay so much attention to survey results. Not, I would suspect, to convince himself that he is doing right, or that he is following the wishes of the people. *The President makes opinion, he does not follow it.* His interest in the opinion polls, therefore, reflects his desire to be sure that his approach is reaching the American public in the way he wants them affected. The polls tell him how good a politician he is. They are also a weapon against his critics. He feels he

74

is under no obligation to make public politically unpalatable information. And, as we have seen, there is enough in the surveys for the President to find justification for whatever policy he wants to pursue in Vietnam, and to tell his political critics that the people are behind him.

The poll data can also enable the President, and other politicians as well, to ignore opposition demonstrations, which are organized by relatively small minorities. Thus, opinion surveys of university student populations, who have provided the main source of organized disagreement, indicate that the overwhelming majority of American students are behind the war. There have been four national surveys of campus opinion, two in 1965 by Louis Harris and *Playboy,* and two in 1966 by Samuel Lubell and Gallup, the latter in June. All of these indicate that a large majority of American students (between two-thirds and three-quarters) support the war in Vietnam. Faculty opinion, according to a *Playboy* poll, is also behind the war, although by a smaller majority than the students.

As a final point, it may be noted that the opposition to the Vietnamese war is far less than that voiced to the Korean war. As of January 1951, Gallup reported that 66 per cent said: "Pull our troops out of Korea as fast as possible" as contrasted with 25 per cent who said, "Stay and fight." If the evidence of the polls is to be believed, the American public are far more willing to fight in Asia today than 15 years ago.

The findings presented in this effort to sum up the results of opinion surveys on the Vietnam war may depress many who hope to modify American foreign policy through mobilizing segments of the public in support of various peace movements. It is obvious that such efforts face considerable obstacles, particularly during an on-going war. But ignorance of difficulties is not a virtue, even if knowledge may not suggest a path to influence or victory.

The President, the Polls, and Vietnam

THE GOVERNMENTS: THE MAKING OF FOREIGN POLICY

In each nation only a very few people are consciously involved in the international political system. Central among these are the official makers of foreign policy. The second section of this book is concerned with the making of foreign policy as a process that is the central professional activity of a relatively small and self-aware group of individuals. It seems reasonable to assume that in addition to personal idiosyncrasies and the general psychological and social characteristics of their country as a whole, the makers of foreign policy are influenced by elements created by or enhanced by their jobs. The articles in this section look for what is unique about the making of foreign policy, how this process may vary, and the probable results.

The making of foreign policy fits logically into general theories about the making of rational choices. For such theorizing, it is generally convenient to disregard unpredictable choices based on irrationality. As James A. Robinson shows in "The Concept of Crisis in Decision-Making," social psychological theories about rational decision-making attribute considerable importance to the conditions under which choices must be made. It seems to make a difference if a decision has to be made under conditions of "stress" or "crisis"—conditions characterized by unfamiliarity, dangerous threats, inadequate skills, rapid shifts of cues, and lack of information: the typical circumstances of foreign policy. Robinson outlines a research program for studying foreign policy decisions in times of crisis; the next two articles give examples of research that follow up Robinson's suggestions and, in general, confirm his hypotheses.

Ithiel de Sola Pool and Allan Kessler show the effects of crisis on the psychological responses of leading decision-makers in "The Kaiser, The Tsar, and The Computer: Information Processing in a Crisis." Personal qualities of the "actors" may be particularly influential on foreign policy decisions. The organizational machinery allows considerable latitude to tsars, kaisers, and other leaders whose freedom of action is often especially great in external affairs. During crises they have even more freedom; they are also subject to the kind of stress that seems to further heighten the impact of individual personalities. Pool and Kessler test and seem to confirm psychologists' notions that, under pressure, people narrow their attention in certain ways. In the midst of a crisis, less is taken into account. In this experiment, a computer was used to replay messages received by the Tsar and the Kaiser in the period just before the outbreak of World War I. The actual communications were edited to correspond to psychological hypotheses about what the two men would in fact have noticed. The involvement in war occurred, or re-occurred, much as it did in 1914.

In the article by Pool and Kessler the technique of computer simulation is described in considerable detail, including a reproduction of part of the "flow chart" that gave instructions to the computer. Although the conclusions of the study are very tentative, they do confirm the usefulness of the method. Students of the international political system cannot do laboratory experiments, but with high-speed calculating machines they can use large quantities of data in the repeated reproductions that make it possible to use history as a sort of laboratory.

The 1914 crisis has been extensively studied from different viewpoints in the last few years. Here is a genuine crisis, typical of the kind of event we would like to be able to predict and, thereby, prevent. All the official information has now been made public, in most cases under hostile auspices that are relevant to its authenticity. One series of studies, concentrating like Pool and Kessler's on messages exchanged between heads of state, has traced out the patterns of mutual attitudes of the leaders. These studies were able to confirm the long-suspected pattern of spiraling hostility, in which each decision-maker overestimated the hostility of the

The Governments

other and responded by defensive measures that, in turn, were seen as hostile and were overreacted to—the pattern of tensions underlying the classic arms race. The studies were carried out by a method of content analysis based on word counts, very like that used by Merritt in his piece in Part One and by Deutsch in Part Five.

The article by Ole Holsti and Robert North reprinted here is a follow-up to these studies of leaders' attitudes. It is a novel and interesting attempt to confirm content analysis by "hard" or objectively verifiable data. The results of content analysis are always open to dispute when they move away from general statements; tracing a general growth of hostility between Germany and Russia in 1914 is easier than mapping the pattern in sufficient detail to show in advance when the declaration of war was to be expected. In "Perceptions of Hostility and Financial Indices During the 1914 Crisis: An Experiment in Validating Content Analysis Data," Holsti and North report on a study of the few months immediately preceding the outbreak of war. They trace the rise and fall of the sale of gold and of stocks and bonds in the main markets of the West, assuming that the financiers were responding in some way either to their governments' actions or to some underlying factors of which the governments were also aware. The financial indicators, in fact, predicted war and validated the findings of the earlier content analyses. Holsti and North feel that such financial changes are, nevertheless, too remote from the causes of war to serve as adequate indicators of the imminence of battle. Leaders' perceptions, on the other hand, are related to the social conditions that explain wars. And content analysis, which has in recent years been almost entirely automated, provides a reliable means of finding the leaders' perceptions.

These three articles are all explicitly within the theoretical framework of the social psychological study of crisis decision-making. Arnold Wolfers' piece, "The Goals of Foreign Policy," has a broader context, the general study of foreign policy. The goals or intentions of foreign policy are one among the many sets of factors that students of decision-making find important. Other theorizers about international relations have attempted to explain the whole process in terms of the different ways nations seek the single goal of power. These are the "power school," or "realists," who follow Hans Morgenthau. The "realists" see goals as dictated by permanent, objective national interests. These national interests are necessarily incompatible, the source of international conflict and inevitable wars. In contrast, the study of decision-making stresses the formulation of goals. Wolfers gives a careful analysis of the notion of "goals," and suggests that nations in fact pursue goals that in some cases are complementary rather than competitive. This is the "non-zero-sum game" of Anatol Rapoport's article in Part Three. National interests are made up of intricate mixtures of private and public, national and international, and ideological and status, goals. Wolfers' six-fold analysis gives us a start toward understanding the ways national interests may interact and helps us to avoid the sort of surprises that cause crises, wars, and scholarly confusion. Implicit in Wolfers' discussion is the inadequacy of theories of inter- 79 national politics that rely on monocausal explanations, like the pursuit of power or mutual perceptions of world leaders. Analysts of crisis behavior, of course, are artificially narrowing their explanations in order to focus on one factor that seems both important and amenable to systematic study. Members of the power school probably have policy rather than analysis in mind when they simplify. In any case, the important thing is not to forget what has temporarily been put aside. Wolfers reminds us again how rich and complex is the bank of data from which we hope to abstract explanations and policy imperatives.

In the concluding chapter David McLellan presents another historical case study, "The Role of Political Style: A Study of Dean Acheson." He gives an example of the idiosyncratic element in decision-making, which the generalizing social scientist must put aside as, at present, too complex to be assimilated into his models. It is from studies such as McLellan's that hypotheses will come for more general speculation on the role of the unique individual in choosing policy. Studying the relevance of Dean Acheson's personality for his successes and occasional failures as Secretary of State, McLellan also suggests something of the effects of institutional arrangements for making policy. Acheson was effective in the United States after World War II. The outcome of his activities depended in part on institutional and personal relationships between and within the executive and legislative branches of the government. McLellan's approach makes the case study of a policy-maker into something far more than biographical chitchat or the anecdotage of conventional diplomatic history.

The study of diplomatic history was the earliest version of the study of foreign policy and the oldest approach to the study of international relations. Confining the study of international relations to the study of governmental relations made the subject at least seem able to be handled. The articles in this section show how such an approach may, in its own way, widen the field of consideration almost indefinitely. But the focus on the making of foreign policy is still justified by the peculiar importance of foreign policies. They are, after all, the channel for those who wish to influence what goes on between nations. And, as this section shows, if the interest is long standing, the ways of analyzing foreign policy are new.

The Governments

The Concept

of Crisis

in

Decision-Making

CHAPTER FIVE

James A. Robinson

Reprinted with permission from *Symposia Series Studies,* National Institute of Social
and Behavioral Sciences, No. 11 (1962), 6–9. Mr. Robinson is Professor
of Political Science at the Ohio State University.

The concept *crisis* presently lacks a technical meaning. It is not the subject of a large body of scholarly and scientific literature; indexes to political, psychological, and sociological sources contain few references to the term. The first dictionary definition is the medical one; no special political or social science usage is listed. Nevertheless, the word appears with non-technical or undefined meaning in a number of political titles (e.g., 23, 30, 33, 40, 47, 49). On the basis of one's personal contacts and interviews with policy-makers, one is inclined to hold that decision-makers experience something called crisis (34a). Commentators contend that crisis is an enduring characteristic of the present epoch: E. H. Carr wrote about the twenty years' crisis (7); General Marshall thought the crisis with the Soviet Union would last a generation; Professor Morgenthau has sum-marized the last half-century of United States foreign policy in terms of a series of long crises (34). In short, the word is ubiquitous; a technical, operational, and agreed-upon usage is absent. Does this paradox suggest that greater clarity might now be appropriate for the concept, or that it is not after all appropriate for technical usage, or that present concepts of stress, disaster, risk, decision time, extremity, e.g., are sufficient ana-logues?

Whether crisis is a useful concept in theories of decision-making partly depends on one's theory or model of the decision process. It may be helpful to conceive of the decision process as the interaction between the *occasion* for decision, *individual* characteristics of the decision-makers, and the *organizational* context in which decision-makers act. This is not to over-look the point that other factors or variables affect the outcome of any decision; for example, the resources or capabilities of society, state, or province are likely to be partial determinants of its public policy (10, 46). But assuming that the political analyst can hold constant resource factors (wealth, geography, etc.), he may wish to study how the decision process affects public policy. The intensive increase in the study of decision-making during the last twenty-five years has produced numerous studies of individual decision-making and of organizational decision-making. There are fewer studies of the interaction of individual and organizational charac-teristics in decision situations, but attention seems to be increasing (1, 2,

The author acknowledges the assistance of William Welsh of Northwestern Uni-versity and Robert Eichelman now of Stanford University in planning research on crisis decision-making. We have received support from a Ford Foundation Public Affairs grant to Northwestern University.

82

43, pp. 55–91), and we may expect that one of the next major trends in decision analysis will be in this direction.

Individual factors may be classified (and oversimplified) as *personality characteristics, personal values,* and *personal experience.* Psychological research is identifying a number of characteristics of personality structure which are relevant to decision-making and to international relations. The recent publication of David C. McClelland's *The Achieving Society* (29) highlights the relation between individual needs for achievement and the economic development of nations. The instrument which measures "need achievement" is also being used, although with somewhat less success, to measure "need for power," a subject long of interest to students of political science, especially of international relations. Alexander and Juliette George have revealed how President Wilson's childhood deprivation of affection, esteem, and love led to his intense compensation through craving for power and dominance over others, to the point that United States policy, including joining the League of Nations, was affected (14).

In addition to personality characteristics, personal values are among the individual factors which may affect decision-making and public policy. William A. Scott's current study of the structure of individual attitudes toward other nations is relevant to the role of public opinion in foreign policy-making (41, 42). Philip Jacob is undertaking a study of the role of values of elite groups in foreign policy-making in Thailand, Egypt, and Iran (18). Although these studies are in their formative and inconclusive stages, they represent interest in the hypothesis that personal values affect the outcome of a decision process.

Personality characteristics and individual values are supplemented by the personal background and experience of individual policy-makers. Donald R. Matthews has demonstrated that United States Senators with certain kinds of previous experience perform differently in the Senate than Senators with other kinds of personal and social backgrounds. Prior experience, as it interacts with the dominant organizational characteristics of the Senate, makes a difference in the legislative effectiveness (and therefore policy) of individual Senators (31, chap. 5). Ithiel Pool and colleagues have described how foreign travel affects the attitudes of businessmen to tariff policy (36a).

Individual factors (personality, values, experience) can be shown to have some significant (in the statistical sense) effect on decisions of public policy. But the correlations or connections between individual factors and decisional outcomes are rarely, if ever, one to one. The understanding, explanation, and prediction of policy decisions can be increased by adding knowledge of organizational factors to knowledge of individual factors. Although studies of organizations, including public and business administration, are also experiencing greater attention, they also remain incomplete. But if we consider two classical types of organizations (centralized and decentralized), hypotheses linking individual characteristics to organizational ones may be readily formulated for further research and

The Concept of Crisis in Decision-Making

investigation (11). For example, one would predict that individuals who have high needs for achievement or power would perform more effectively and with greater satisfaction at the top of centralized organizations, but that if they can not be at the top their optimal performance will occur in relatively decentralized organizations in which they can bargain and "politic." This is only an hypothesis, but it illustrates the possible interaction of individual and organizational factors.

Let us turn now to the third element in the decision process, the occasion or situation calling for a decision. This factor also interacts with individual and organizational characteristics. It brings us back to the subject of crisis. By the occasion or situation, we mean the circumstances under which decision-makers come to feel that a decision is required. Although no typology of decision situations is readily available for standard use, we may list some general categories and illustrate them with actual cases.

> I. Origin of the decision situation.
> A. External to the decisional unit (e.g., the Korean decision [36, 44]).
> B. From within the decisional unit (e.g., the Suez decision [12, 13]).
> II. Decision time.
> A. Short (e.g., the Korean decision).
> B. Long (e.g., the Japanese Peace Settlement [8]).
> C. Intermediate (e.g., the Marshall Plan [19, 37]).
> III. Relative importance of the values at stake.
> A. High (e.g., violence vs. non-violence, as in the Korean decision).
> B. Low (e.g., apparently small differences in consequences of acting or not acting or between different action alternatives, as in the Monroney Resolution or the Fulbright Resolution [39, chap. 2]).

The utility of any typology such as this is to be determined by its use in research. Two criteria eventually should be applied to it: (1) does it help in predicting decisional outcomes when used in combination (either as a constant or a variable) with other aspects of the decision process, individual and organizational factors? and (2) are these three characteristics—origin, time, and values—independent of each other or are they interdependent and parts of the same factor? The answer to the first question can be found by correlational techniques when applied to enough cases, and the answer to the second may depend on the application of some form of factor analysis. We are not, however, quite to that stage of research.

As Charles McClelland's inventory of the use of the term in international relations shows, crisis is often synonymous with conflict (28). Although such a conceptualization opens a wide range of research possibilities because of the generalized nature of conflict, it still requires further specification and scaling of crisis or conflict situations. Similarly the use of the term in one of the rare laboratory experiments devoted to crisis does not differentiate crisis from non-crisis or scale degrees of crisis. Hamblin (15, 16, 17) defines a crisis as "an urgent situation in which all group members face a common threat." This definition begs the question,

The Governments

what is urgent? And are there degrees of common threat? On the other hand, Bettelheim's notion of extreme situation (5, 6, pp. 108–9), i.e., one in which concentration camp prisoners "did not know exactly why they were imprisoned, and never knew for how long," does not include as many characteristics of decision situations as research on decision-making seems to reveal. Likewise, Lasswell seems more restrictive than necessary by defining crisis in terms of potentially violent situations (24, pp. 79–93; 25, pp. 242–5 and 250–84).

The concept *stress* as used by Torrance seems close to our notion of crisis. Torrance writes "...the distinctive element in stress is...the lack of structure or loss of anchor in reality experienced by the individual or group as a result of the condition labeled 'stressful'. In the group situation, this lack of structure or loss of anchor in reality makes it difficult or impossible for the group to cope with the requirements of the situation..." (48, p. 101). Stressful situations are said to include unfamiliar situations, rapid shifts in customary activity, dangerous threats to central values, instability and confusion, either paucity or plethora of cues, and inadequate skills. Several of these characteristics are incorporated in our typology of occasions. While our types still require sharper measures to distinguish among them, they do suggest possibilities for scales and continua.

Therefore, at present we are inclined to define crisis in terms of this typology of decision occasions. A situation of the greatest severity (most crisis-like) would be one in which the occasion for decision arose from without the decisional unit, required a prompt decision, and involved very high stakes. In this sense, the United States decision to employ ground and air forces in defense of South Korea in 1950 was a high crisis situation. The North Korean attack was unanticipated and unplanned for; no previously determined rules-for-action had been formulated to be applied if such a situation occurred. The reaction time was less than a week; one of the consequences of further delay was to lose some alternatives and pay the price of the loss of South Korea. The values at stake included not only the independence of South Korea but also the integrity of the United Nations, and also increased the possibility of large-scale violence.

Contrast the Korean decision with the British intervention in Suez in the fall of 1956. The Government planned this policy and cooperated with France and Israel in its timing and execution. In one sense, the occasion for the use of force was external, i.e., Nasser and Egypt's policies, but the Suez decision seems different from the Korean decision in this respect. It may be, however, that the difference is more sharply drawn by the time available for response. Britain did not define the situation as one requiring a reaction so quickly as the United States policy-makers perceived in the Korean outbreak. Moreover, it is questionable whether the values at stake were quite as high in the Suez as in the Korean case. The Government overrode resistance from within the Conservative Party as well as among the Labor Party. Although Britain confronted the opposition of the United States and the United Nations, it is doubtful that its decision carried as high a risk of World War III as the United States decision in Korea. Although it has become customary to refer to the British Middle East decision of November 1956 as the "Suez Crisis," a crude comparison of that decision with other "crisis decisions" indicates some difference in severity.

Let us compare the Korean and Suez cases to the Marshall Plan of 1947. Like Suez, the Marshall Plan was a response to events in another part of the world, but a longer time for planning and responding was available than in the case of Korea. Further, the values at stake were not immediate violence or the immediate possibility of World War III. The values were very important economic ones, however, which in fact would eventually affect political independence and integration of Western Europe. It is not unlikely that without some kind of sustained, external assistance in 1947 and 1948 Western Europe might have confronted a situation which could have eventuated in violence. In any event, comparison suggests that the Marshall Plan was a less severe occasion for decision than either Suez or Korea.

If we continue to think of occasions for decision as being on a scale running from most to least crisis-like, we should call attention to important foreign policy decisions with little crisis overtones. The peace treaty with Japan was planned from within and between decisional units of the war-time allies, matured over a long period of time, and while it involved important economic and political values, it seems to have been somewhat lower in the importance of values at stake than the Marshall Plan, the Suez or Korean decisions. Still lower on the scale of crisis-likeness were such policies as the Fulbright Resolution endorsing participation in postwar international organizations or the Monroney Resolution of 1958 which led to the formation of an International Development Association with a modest amount of capital for long-term loans at low rates of interest to underdeveloped countries.

These few, brief summaries of the occasions for certain recent foreign policy decisions must suffice [for the present] to illustrate the variations in the degree of crisis in decision situations.

Assuming some kind of scale could be constructed for typing the degree of crisis of a decision, what would be its use in studies of decision-making? First, one might ask whether some kinds of persons or decision-makers (i.e., those with certain personality characteristics, values, or previous experience) perform differently in crises than in non-crises? Second, do some kinds of organizations (highly centralized as opposed to decentralized) respond differently to different kinds of decisional situations? Much has been written about the comparative efficiency of American and Soviet institutions for making foreign policy decisions (e.g., 3, 22). It has been hypothesized that the Soviet Union, owing to the closed character of its political system, can plan for long-range contingencies with more flexibility and reveal its decisions with greater surprise than the United States can. It is argued both that the Soviet Union can respond to crisis more quickly and less quickly than can the United States: more quickly because of the centralized character of its decision process; no more quickly because of the high value consensus in the United States which impels opposition to close ranks with the executive in the face of great crisis. Third, do some combinations of individual and organizational factors perform differently in crisis than in non-crisis, while other combinations perform similarly regardless of the situation for a decision? Assuming one possesses agreed-upon *and* operational indicators of *effective* performance, are some combinations of individual and organizational factors more effective in one kind of situation than the other; are there any combinations which perform most effectively regardless of the occasion?

Our conception of the decision process is the interaction of occasion, individual characteristics, and organizational arrangements. What really interests us is whether variations in combinations of these factors produce differences in the *outcomes* or *consequences* of the decision. That is, we are interested in knowing whether differences within the decision process lead to differences in the substance or content of the decision.

The decision itself may be considered in terms of the subject-matter of the policy field, e.g., international relations (violent or non-violent alternatives), public welfare ("liberal" or "conservative" social programs), public expenditures (high or low), and so on. Ultimately we should like to confront the question whether different decision processes might make a difference in the likelihood of peace or war, more or less governmental programs, and other differences in the content of public policy.

The decision may also be considered in terms of such characteristics as the number of alternatives available, the satisfaction (legitimacy) the decision-makers and their constituents have with the decision, the amount of time spent in reaching a decision, and so on. As students of the decision process, we are interested in whether certain combinations of occasion, individual, and organizational factors are more likely to consider a large rather than a small number of alternatives, to do so with more or less satisfaction, and within longer or shorter periods of time.

Thus, the question whether crisis is a useful concept in decision theory and research depends on its role in constructing a typology of occasions for decisions. If differences in decision situations can then be shown to interact with differences in individual and organizational factors with predictable effects on decision outcome, the concept *crisis* may prove to be useful theoretically.

References

1. For discussion, see C. Argyris, "The individual and organization: some problems of mutual adjustment," *Administrative Science Quarterly* 2, 1–24 (1957).
2. C. Argyris, *Personality and Organization* (Harper, New York, 1957).
3. M. Beloff, *Foreign Policy and the Democratic Process* (Johns Hopkins University Press, Baltimore, 1955).

4. M. Beloff, *New Dimensions in Foreign Policy: A Study in British Administrative Experience, 1947–1959* (Macmillan, New York, 1961).

5. For discussion, see B. Bettelheim, "Individual and mass behavior in extreme situations," *Journal of Abnormal and Social Psychology* **38**, 417–52 (1943).

6. B. Bettelheim, *The Informed Heart: Autonomy in a Mass Age* (Free Press, Glencoe, Ill., 1960).

7. E. H. Carr, *The Twenty Years' Crisis, 1919–1939* (Macmillan, New York, 1939).

8. B. C. Cohen, *The Political Process and Foreign Policy: The Making of the Japanese Peace Settlement* (Princeton University Press, 1957).

9. E. A. Cohen, *Human Behavior in the Concentration Camp* (W. W. Norton, New York, 1953).

10. R. E. Dawson and J. A. Robinson, "Interparty Competition, Economic Resources, and Welfare Policies in the American States," unpublished manuscript (Midwest Conference of Political Scientists, South Bend, Ind., 26–28 April 1962).

11. R. Eichelman, "Personality Variables and Organizational Structure: Their Effect on Personal Satisfaction and Contribution," unpublished manuscript (1961).

12. For discussion, see L. D. Epstein, "British M.P.s and their local parties: the Suez crisis," *American Political Science Review* **54**, 374–90 (1960).

13. For discussion, see L. D. Epstein, "Partisan foreign policy: Britain in the Suez crisis," *World Politics* **12**, 201–24 (1960).

14. A. George and J. George, *Woodrow Wilson and Colonel House* (John Day, New York, 1956).

15. For discussion, see R. L. Hamblin, "Group integration during a crisis," *Human Relations* **11**, 67–76 (1958).

16. For discussion, see R. L. Hamblin, "Leadership and crises," *Sociometry* **21**, 322–35 (1958).

17. For discussion, see R. L. Hamblin and J. A. Wiggins, "Suggestibility, imitation and recall during a crisis," *Midwest Sociologist* **20**, 26–32 (1957).

18. P. E. Jacob and J. Flink, "Toward an Operational Definition of Values and Their Function in Decision-Making," mimeographed (September, 1961).

19. J. M. Jones, *The Fifteen Weeks: February 21–June 5, 1947* (Viking, New York, 1955).

20. P. Kecskemeti, *The Unexpected Revolution: Social Forces in the Hungarian Uprising* (Stanford University Press, 1961).

21. L. M. Killian, "The significance of multiple-group membership in disaster," *American Journal of Sociology* **62**, 309–314 (1952).

22. H. A. Kissinger, *The Necessity for Choice: Prospects of American Foreign Policy* (Harper, New York, 1961).

23. For discussion, see J. LaPalombara, "Political party systems and crisis governments: French and Italian contrasts," *Midwest Journal of Political Science* **2**, 117–42 (1958).

24. H. D. Lasswell, *World Politics and Personal Insecurity* (University of Chicago Press, 1934).

25. H. D. Lasswell and A. Kaplan, *Power and Society: A Framework for Political Inquiry* (Yale University Press, New Haven, 1950).

26. P. Levi, *Survival in Auschwitz: The Nazi Assault on Humanity* (Collier Books, New York, 1961).

The Governments

27. S. M. Lipset, "Opinion formation in a crisis situation," *Public Opinion Quarterly* **17**, 20–46 (1953).

28. For discussion, see C. A. McClelland, "The acute international crisis," *World Politics* **14**, 182–204 (1961).

29. D. C. McClelland, *The Achieving Society* (D. Van Nostrand, Princeton, 1961).

30. W. Manger, *Pan America in Crisis: The Future of the OAS* (Public Affairs Press, Washington, 1961).

31. D. R. Matthews, *United States Senators and Their World* (University of North Carolina Press, Chapel Hill, 1960).

32. R. L. Meier, *Social Change in Communications-Oriented Institutions,* Report No. 10 (Mental Health Research Institute, University of Michigan, Ann Arbor, March, 1961).

33. R. I. Miller, *Dag Hammarskjold and Crisis Diplomacy* (Oceana Publications, New York, 1961).

34. H. J. Morgenthau, *The Purpose of American Politics* (Alfred A. Knopf, New York, 1960).

34a. R. M. Nixon, *Six Crises* (Doubleday, Garden City, N.Y., 1962).

35. R. C. North, "International Conflict and Integration: Problems of Research," unpublished manuscript (Symposium on Inter-Group Relations and Leadership, University of Oklahoma, 6–8 April, 1961).

36. G. D. Paige, *The Korean Decision: June 24–30, 1950* (Program of Graduate Training and Research in International Relations, Northwestern University, Evanston, Ill., 1959).

36a. For discussion, see I. de S. Pool, S. Keller, and R. A. Bauer, "The influence of foreign travel on political attitudes of American businessmen," *Public Opinion Quarterly* **20**, 161–175 (1956).

37. H. B. Price, *The Marshall Plan and Its Meaning* (Cornell University Press, Ithaca, 1955).

38. D. Robinson, *The Face of Disaster* (Doubleday, Garden City, N.Y., 1959).

39. J. A. Robinson, *Congress and Foreign Policy-Making: A Study of Legislative Influence and Initiative* (Dorsey Press, Homewood, Ill., 1962).

40. A. M. Schlesinger, Jr., *The Crisis of the Old Order* (Houghton Mifflin, Boston, 1956).

41. For discussion, see W. A. Scott, "Empirical assessment of values and ideology," *American Sociological Review* **24**, 299–310 (1959).

42. For discussion, see W. A. Scott, "Rationality and non-rationality of international attitudes," *Journal of Conflict Resolution* **2**, 8–16 (1958).

43. H. A. Simon, D. Smithburg, and V. Thompson, *Public Administration* (Alfred A. Knopf, New York, 1956).

44. For discussion, see R. C. Snyder and G. D. Paige, "The United States decision to resist aggression in Korea," *Administrative Science Quarterly* **3**, 341–78 (1958).

45. W. J. H. Sprott, *Human Groups* (Penguin Books, Baltimore, 1958).

46. For discussion, see H. Sprout and M. Sprout, "Environmental factors in the study of international politics," *Journal of Conflict Resolution* **1**, 309–28 (1957).

47. A. H. Stanton and S. E. Perry, *Personality and Political Crisis: New Perspectives from Social Science and Psychiatry for the Study of War and Politics* (Free Press, Glencoe, Ill., 1951).

48. For discussion, see E. P. Torrance, "A theory of leadership and interper-

sonal behavior under stress," *Leadership and Interpersonal Behavior*, eds. L. Petrullo and B. M. Bass (Holt, Rinehart and Winston, New York, 1961), pp. 100–117.

49. For discussion, see D. B. Truman, "The American system in crisis," *Political Science Quarterly* **74**, 481–97 (1959).

The Governments

The Kaiser,
the Tsar,
and the Computer:
Information
Processing
in a Crisis

Ithiel de Sola Pool

Allan Kessler

Reprinted with permission from *The American Behavioral Scientist,* Vol. 8 (May, 1965), 31–38. Dr. Pool is Professor of Political Science at the Massachusetts Institute of Technology. Mr. Kessler is at the Institute of Public Administration at Indiana University.

Summary

Crisiscom is a computer simulation of national decision makers processing information during a crisis. The project has several purposes:

1. It is designed to increase our understanding of the process of deterrence by exploring how far the behavior of political decision makers in crisis can be explained by psychological mechanisms. This is done by comparing the output of the highly simplified computer model based on principles of individual psychology with records of actual political behavior.

2. It is designed to put together a good deal of what we know about the psychology of deterrence into a rigorous and formal system and thus to serve as an integrating device for that body of knowledge.

3. It is designed to be used in human games of the type represented by Bloomfield's DETEX political-military games to provide inputs for teams that cannot be staffed with humans and to represent aspects of the environment that are not played out by the human players. (1.)

4. It is designed perhaps ultimately to provide a way of simulating a variety of possible crises. It will be some time before we have enough confidence in the model to use it in such a semi-predictive fashion, but that cannot be ruled out.

In the Crisiscom computer model two human decision makers are represented (the number is easily expanded). Each of them receives a large number of messages which enter into his cognitive system.

The elements of the cognitive system of each simulated decision maker are messages that represent interpersonal relationships among international actors. For example, "President Johnson" (an actor, A_1) "visits with" (a relation, R_x) "The Prime Minister of Great Britain" (an actor, A_2). The set of relations, R, is at present limited to two—affect and salience. Affect refers to the attitude or feelings which an actor, A_i, has toward another actor, A_j, or toward an interpersonal relationship. Salience describes the importance of an actor or interpersonal relationship or another actor. The cognitive system of A_n (the world he knows) is thus comprised

This is a corrected version, specially prepared for this volume, of the paper that appeared initially in *The American Behavioral Scientist,* Vol. 8 (May, 1965).

This work was supported by the Naval Research Laboratory under a contract to the Simulmatics Corporation and by the Advanced Research Projects Agency of the Department of Defense under Contract 920F-9717 with the Center for International Studies, M.I.T. This contract is monitored by the Air Force Office of Scientific Research. We have made use of the computer time sharing system of Project MAC, an M.I.T. research project sponsored by the Advanced Research Project Agency, Department of Defense, under Office of Naval Research contract Nonr. —4102(01).

of elements A_1, A_2, ..., A_m, and affects or saliences which relate them *as perceived by* A_n.

A_n came to perceive these relationships as a result of receiving messages about the actors and their interpersonal relationships. However, the total information conveyed in these messages is too great for any one human to handle. Not all the information is absorbed by A_n. Psychological mechanisms restrict has input and distort it. As a result each decision maker has an incomplete and imperfect picture of the relationships among all actors. As the simulation has been run recently, both actors have been fed the same set of messages about the world but by the end of a week's crisis they have quite different perceptions.

In the present program the cognitive systems of only two of twenty-four actors are completely represented, namely the cognitive systems of decision makers J and K. J and K receive information about themselves and about the other actors in the form of messages written by a scenario writer. Each message has the format A_n, R_a, A_m. For example: The King of Ethiopia confers with President Nasser of Egypt. These messages are written in natural English and as long as the sentence order is A_n, R_a, A_m, the computer accepts them.

The scenario consists of a large number of messages of the kind just described about interpersonal relationships among the actors. The decision maker does not pay attention to all messages. In accordance with well established psychological principles, he is "selectively exposed" to a subset of them. He pays attention to some, ignores others.

These incoming messages that are selected not only enter into the decision maker's attention space; they also change his basic image of the world with which he started the simulation. This basic image is represented by an affect matrix which tells how each actor feels about each other actor. New messages alter slightly this continuing perception of the relationships in the world.

In our present simulation the following hypotheses about selective perception operate on the messages in the scenario:

1. People pay more attention to news that deals with them.
2. People pay less attention to facts that contradict their previous views.
3. People pay more attention to news from trusted, liked sources.
4. People pay more attention to facts that they will have to act upon or discuss because of attention by others.
5. People pay more attention to facts bearing on actions they are already involved in, i.e., action creates commitment.

In its present stage the model is thus a rather simple representation of a number of the major mechanisms that come into play in crisis, but clearly not of all of them. In the future a number of additional mechanisms of decision making will be grafted onto the model. The model is modular permitting continued growth and refinement.

We have been utilizing historical crisis events to test our simulation,

The Kaiser, the Tsar, and the Computer

even in its present simple form. We have written a scenario of messages representing the week of the outbreak of World War I. This week was chosen because it is extensively written up by historians and has also been replicated by gaming procedures. Thus comparison is possible between what seemed important to national decision makers as described by historians, as played by game players, and as put out by the simulation.

The scenario messages were written by going through historical documents about the week, but most of all from the newspapers of that week. The two key decision makers we have represented are the Kaiser and the Tsar. Appended to this report are a sample of the list of messages they received, a sample of the list of messages that went into the attention space of each one on each day, and part of the final affect matrix (representing their basic picture of the world).

The results are intuitively very satisfactory. The Kaiser and Tsar behave as we think they would. Each pays attention to those events that affect him particularly. They each miss some key cues that if they had been mutually perceived might have prevented war. Instead each sees the overt military acts of the other unmitigated by his moderating intents, while remaining conscious of his own moderate intentions that he must have (wrongly) assumed equally obvious to the other.

Readers not interested in the computer processes can turn to the next to the last section headed, A Test of the Crisiscom Model Against A Real World Crisis. It deals with the World War I experiment.

Purpose of the Project

Crisiscom is a computer simulation of the behavior of national decision makers in international crisis. More specifically it is designed to represent the ways in which psychological mechanisms enter into their processing of the information they receive. It is designed to simulate the process whereby two different decision makers acquire in their own minds quite different pictures of the world in which they are interacting. A flow of messages representing the real world comes to the decision makers. They selectively attend to different messages in this flow leaving each decision maker with a quite different image of the world from that of the other. This in a nutshell is the process simulated by the Crisiscom program.

There were several reasons for developing such a simulation. First among them is the desire to explore how far a limited set of psychological relations can take us in understanding the behavior of national decision makers in a crisis. We are attempting by the simulation to push to the limits the hypothesis that the basic principles of individual psychology which describe how individuals behave in personal crises also account for the behavior of national decision makers in a world political crisis. We do this not because we believe this proposition to be true. On the contrary, it is perfectly clear that individual psychology accounts for only a small part of international politics. However, the best way to ascertain what part, if any, individual psychology plays in the determination of political behavior is to postulate the truth of the extreme proposition and then see what conclusions it leads us to. We can then compare those conclusions with reality. We are, in short, engaged in a kind of experiment—the kind sometimes called a Gedanken experiment—in which we press an idea to see where it breaks down.

Our procedure corresponds to the ideas of the philosopher Hans Vaihinger in his book *The Philosophy of As If.* (2.) We model a hypothetical world based on certain propositions to ascertain just what the consequences of these propositions would be; we look at the world *as if* they were true.

Various devices have been developed to explore hypothetical futures of which computer simulation is only one. Gaming is at present an increasingly popular and effective tool for answering that "what if" question. It is effective because it forces each player to specialize on thinking about a particular set of roles and particular aspects of the situation. The same player trying to write an essay predicting how things would be in some specified hypothetical future would miss many of the eventualities which other players force onto his attention as they play out their own required roles.

Human gaming, however, has certain limitations as well as some enormous advantages. One of its limitations is that it is expensive and time consuming. For the results to be useful the players should be experts on the roles they are representing. There are limits to the numbers of experts one can collect and to the periods of time for which one can commandeer them. Furthermore, in the time available it is usually possible to play out only one alternative out of the many branches that history could follow depending on eventualities.

Computer simulation gets around both these disadvantages of human gaming though at its own price. The computer runs fast and can run the same game over many times with minor variations. However, in all candor, it is necessary to recognize that no computer program ever written contains as much expertise as is stored in the heads of a group of specialists.

Thus an intelligent approach to the problem of exploring strategic futures is to use both human gaming and computer simulation and also combinations of them. Computer simulation should be developed to assess how far it can approximate the results achieved in human games. It should be used to play out many variants of situations that one can game with experts only once. Finally, the two procedures can be linked. A computer can be used to produce the results of minor teams or of nature or other factors for which players themselves cannot be provided.

With these considerations in mind, we can now summarize the purposes that the Crisiscom project has set out to achieve. It set out to explore how realistic a simulation could be produced with a relatively constricted and simple model arising entirely from the propositions of social psychology about human behavior in crisis. Secondly, it set out to produce a program that would provide messages that could be used in mixed human-machine games. Thirdly, in the process of achieving these objectives it served to advance our understanding of the psychological system known as deterrence by working out the interactions of various propositions about behavior in a crisis. Finally, perhaps, it advanced us a few steps toward the point where such computer simulations might have some predictive value.

The Model

We now proceed to describe the Crisiscom model by three successive elaborations, each covering the same ground, but each more fully and accurately than the last.

1. THE CRISISCOM MODEL IN SKETCHY FORM

The Crisiscom simulation represents the interaction of national commanders in a crisis in which they confront each other.

a) Each receives information about the world.
b) Each handles this information in ways which are determined by his own background and by the principles of psychology.
c) Each then reacts by originating new messages.

This happens each time period, so the model cycles through those three steps over and over. The messages put out by the commanders become part of the input of messages at the next period.

A skeleton basic flow chart is presented in Figure 1. The two commanders are designated $DM(J)$ = decision-maker J, and $DM(K)$ = decision-maker K. In the present version of the model this is a man-machine simulation rather than a pure machine simulation. The decision-making portion of the model is done by human simulation, the bias and distortion portion by the computer.

We now describe the model in greater detail.

2. THE CRISISCOM MODEL SOMEWHAT ELABORATED

In the real world decision makers receive information about their world from various sources and through various media. In most cases the volume of information they receive is too large for them to attend to, so they use a variety of techniques of selective attention, forgetting and distortion, in order to limit this information to proportions they can handle.

Let us consider the selective attention and distortion processes. Two decision makers, J (let's say for Mr. Johnson) and K (let's say for Mr. Kosygin) receive messages from a human scenario writer as to the events and relationships occurring among 24 countries or country blocks. For example, associated with the recent Guantanamo affair, messages of the following nature would come to J and K.

The Governments

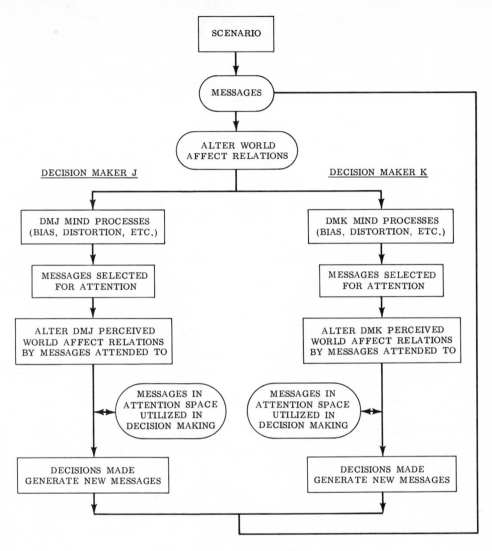

FIGURE 1   *Crisiscom General Flow Chart*

Guantanamo affair. USA arrests Cuba's fishermen. Each message is a statement related to some event having two actors and a relationship between them. Another message related to Guantanamo would be: *Cuba cuts water supply to USA military base.*

The importance of the message to each decision maker, their feelings about the reliability of the source of the message, their attitudes toward the particular countries' relationship, and the importance of the relationship to the countries involved all are important in determining the probable nature and extent of distortion of the message before it reaches J or K.

97

The Kaiser, the Tsar, and the Computer

Underlying the distortion processes is the decision maker's perception of the world, his perception of the attitudes and feelings—or affect—existing between each pair of countries. For example, J may perceive that the Soviet Union has negative feelings toward Communist China while France has a more positive affect toward Communist China. A decision maker's perceptions tend to remain stable and change significantly only

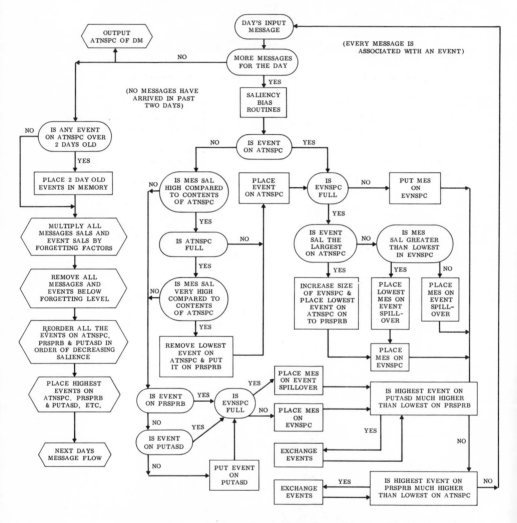

FIGURE 2   *Message Input Flow for a Decision Maker on a Decision Day (Third Approximation)*

ABBREVIATIONS:
PRSPRB — Pressing Problems
PUTASD — Put Aside; SAL — Saliency
ATNSPC — Attention space; MES — Message
EVNSPC — List of Most Salient Messages Associated with an Event
SPILLOVER — List of Least Salient Messages Associated with an Event

The Governments

when new information about countries' relationships is greatly at variance with his present perception. Similarly, a decision maker will pay less attention to messages that differ from his present perception of the relationship between the countries involved. However, relationships *that do come to his attention,* and that differ from his present perception, will alter that perception. (Emphasis has been placed on "relationships that do come to his attention" because, on a given day, the decision maker cannot attend to all messages: some must be put aside as pressing problems, some are ignored and some forgotten.) The most important events are attended to, that is, are placed in the decision maker's attention space. On some days, a decision maker who is concerned with very important events may put aside events that would have come into attention space of they occurred on another day. What the decision maker attends to is a function of the importance of the messages in his present attention space and this importance or salience itself altered by the distortion processes. Thus, what J attends to may differ from what K attends to. In turn, the information to which K and J attend differentially alters their perception of the world. Once events have been attended to they are placed in the decision maker's memory where they are subject to forgetting. This classification and ordering of messages and events is illustrated in detail in Figure 2.

At present, decisions based on the information in J's and K's attention spaces are made by humans who receive this information at the end of a decision day. Later, this output will be the input to simulated decision processes which will generate messages to be placed in the environment.

3. THE CRISISCOM MODEL MORE FULLY ELABORATED

Figure 2 is a flow chart of the computerized portion of the simulation for a single time period.

Crisiscom Input

Messages from a scenario writer are the input for Crisiscom. Every message is a combination of two countries and a relationship between them.

Messages are associated with a unique event. At present the scenario writer must specify the following values for each message.

AFFT — The affect (-1 to $+1$) of the (REL) between CONE and CTWO
SLCONE — The salience (0 to $+1$) of (REL) for CONE
SLCTWO — The salience (0 to $+1$) of (REL) for CTWO
SALJ — The salience (0 to $+1$) of the message for DM(J)
SALK — The salience (0 to $+1$) of the message for DM(K)
SALPOJ — The salience (0 to $+1$) of the message for DM(J)'s Public Opinion
SALPOK — The salience (0 to $+1$) of the message for DM(K)'s Public Opinion
ASOURJ — J's affect (-1 to $+1$) toward the message source
ASOURK — K's affect (-1 to $+1$) toward the message source

Examples of messages can be found in the Appendix.

Several sociopsychological hypotheses relate the perception processes with the attention space structure. These hypotheses provide mechanisms for biasing the salience and affect evaluations. Since the criteria for entrance to attention space is a function of salience of the messages, these biases influence the possibility of a message entering the attention space.

1) *People pay more attention to information that deals with them.* When the actor, or ego, is one of the elements in the structural configuration under evaluation, salience is weighted more heavily.

2) *People pay less attention to facts that contradict their views.* This hypothesis interacts with both semantic and affect relations. A message can be found to be completely incredible, or in some degree semantically explicable but having an affect relations which is unbalanced. Rather than attempt to balance the relations, the actor may avoid or ignore the message.

3) *People pay more attention to information from trusted, liked sources.* Whenever the source of a message is identified in the scenario it is included in the structural configuration under evaluation. In addition to testing the credibility of the source generating such a message, the actor's affect toward the source alters the salience of the message—positive affect increases salience.

4) *People pay more attention to information that they will have to act on or discuss because of attention by others.* Ego considers in his evaluation not only the actors in the message, but also other actors whom he thinks show interest in the relationship. He even considers the attitudes of actors who might attend to the information because of their relations to ego or to the actors in the message. As an example, the low salience of the uprising in Zanzibar for the President may have become increased because Communist decision makers might have and then did demonstrate their attention to the event.

5) *People pay more attention to information bearing on actions they have already taken, i.e., action creates commitment.* When information is being fed back to the actor about information he has previously generated, he evaluates this information higher. The consequences of his actions which he learns through messages from others may involve him to a greater degree.

Decision makers are concerned with events that occur in their world. George Miller has hypothesized that a person can attend to 7 ± 2 things at a time. (3.) Decision makers can attend to 7 ± 2 events, i.e., his attention space has 7 ± 2 events in it. Associated with each event the decision maker can attend to 7 ± 2 messages. An event space has these 7 ± 2 messages in it. Other associated messages are placed on the event spillover. The selection of input events and messages for attention is a function of the number and importance of the events and messages presently in the decision maker's attention space. In the long run the decision maker will attempt to attend to the messages and events he perceives as most salient to him. However, in the short run this may not be feasible as there is a certain amount of inertia which tends to give precedence to the events the decision maker is presently attending to over the new events that arrive.

The decision maker keeps his attention space and event spaces as full as possible, and continually seeks information to keep them full. He may attend to few very important events, many unimportant events, or some number in between these extremes depending on the salience of the messages he is receiving as he perceives them. If an event is very important to him, he will seek as many messages as he can attend to. If an event is unimportant to him, he will not attend to a large number of messages. The decision maker's attention space holds up to 9 unimportant events. Unimportant events have up to 5 messages in their event spaces. The decision maker will attend to up to 5 very important events. Normally an important event may hold up to 9 messages. However, very important events may hold many more messages at the expense of attending to fewer events. It is possible for the decision maker to attend to only one extremely important event having a large number of messages in its event space. Therefore a continuum of few events with many messages, to many events (9) with few messages is specified for the selection of information for the attention space.

Events not attended to immediately are placed aside as pressing problems or put aside according to their importance.

When a very important message compared to the contents of attention space arrives, and its event is not in attention space, the event associated with this message may displace an event in attention space.

At the end of the day the attention space of each decision maker is made available to the programmer.

To bypass the decision processes, any event which has its most recent message over two days old is placed in memory. The salience of an event is exponentially reduced over time until it is below the forgetting level at which time it is deleted.

Each day the mind spaces are reorganized by placing the events and messages in the hierarchy of the mind spaces in order of importance ignoring all inertia factors.

A Consideration of the Psychological Principles

The decision maker's "mind" represented in the Crisiscom simulation consists of two main parts: one representing the kind of stable backlog of experience that each person carries with him into any new situation; the other representing the flow of new messages and information which the decision maker processes. The first of these is represented by the affect matrix (and in principle in later versions of the model in the matrices representing other relationships besides affect.) The affect matrix is part of the initial condition of the simulation at t_0. It states how the decision maker perceives each actor (in the present runs actors are countries) in relation to each other actor. Not all cells in the affect matrix need be filled out. In some instances the decision maker may have no idea how two actors feel about each other. The matrix is not symmetric. Actor One may have an affect of $-.3$ toward Actor Two while Actor Two has an affect of $+.1$ to Actor One. Such sharp differences are, of course, unusual. The affect matrix summarizes the way in which each decision maker views the world. It thus provides the base line against which he tests incoming messages.

The other part of the decision maker's mind is a hierarchical set of list structures, the items on the lists being messages. This hierarchy is composed of: 1) an attention space, 2) a pressing problems list, 3) a put-aside list, and 4) memory. The put-aside list acts as a buffer for the memory. Onto it go the messages that are hardly considered and it is from the bottom of memory that forgetting deletions occur. The pressing problems list is used for important messages that could not be considered on the day of their arrival, important things that have to be put off until tomorrow. At the beginning of the day some pressing problems may go immediately into the attention space. The attention space is for those things being considered on the given day.

In memory are stored all messages that have been considered and have managed to avoid being deleted by the forgetting deletion operations.

It is in this framework that the selective process of retention takes place and in which in turn the affect matrix gets modified by the flow of new information.

This model conforms rather closely to what we know about the actual characteristics of human information handling. It has to be a rather complex model to do so. Powerful as the pleasure principle may be in guiding human behavior, the algorithm people use in conforming to it is a complex one.

The simple algorithm, that people pay attention to what they like to hear and disregard what they do not like to hear, does not work. There are contradictory experimental results as to whether people are more likely to see good news or bad news. Sometimes it is one; sometimes it is the other. So this is *not* one of the determinants of bias in our model. The process is a more purposeful one. The determinant seems to be an unconscious pleasure maximizing calculation that takes into account the consequences of inattention. An unpleasant story that has no action consequences for the hearer may be disregarded because that way pain is minimized. But a "danger, live wire" sign will get high attention because, by taking note of that unpleasant fact, the pain can be minimized. Experiments show that most people do not read newspaper stories that contradict their political views, but debaters read carefully statements that disagree with their stand because they thereby increase the probability of a pleasant outcome, winning the debate.

Our model handles information in ways that conform to this complexity of human rationality. It does pay less attention to facts that contradict prior views, but more attention to action relevant facts.

The Governments

A Test of the Crisiscom Model Against a Real World Crisis

We have run the seven days from 25 July through 31 July, 1914, through the Crisiscom simulation. A seven-day crisis will do very little to the basic image of the world that a decision maker holds. The affect matrix which represents that image of the world should remain quite stable. When the events are as world shaking as those of 1914 there may indeed be deeper effects drastically changing his views in the future, i.e., a sleeper effect. That could be the case even if nothing else happened, but it takes time for such attitude changes to occur. Nonetheless in a crisis of any intensity some perceptible shift in the image of who is good and who is bad and who loves whom should be visible, even if not large. That is what happens if one compares the affect matrices from beginning to end of the week.

The place where big changes may be expected in a short period is in what the decision maker is attending to.

Both the changes in attention and the changes in the affect matrices are recorded in the computer output describing our major test of the Crisiscom simulation so far. That test is a replication of the minds of the Kaiser and the Tsar in the seven days of the outbreak of World War I. We picked that crisis because it has been widely used in other kinds of gaming and other kinds of research. It has been the subject of a Project Michelson study by Professor Robert North of Stanford University (4.) and of human gaming using the device of Harold Guetzkow's internation simulation. (5.) At the end of this article the reader will find a sample of the messages that were fed into and the calculations performed by the computer. There are approximately 1400 of them, 200 per each day of the crisis. To the reader of ordinary history books what is fascinating is the amount of chaff in the communications channel which the historians forget. We collected our messages from the daily newspapers of that time plus the North collection of documents which includes later revelations that at that time were secret to the public. (About one per cent of the message input was secret.) These were the messages that might normally have come to the attention of the decision maker as he lived and worked in that particular week. They included vast numbers of casual events in the sporting world, in the business world, progress in the development of airplanes, crime, etc. A volcano erupted in the USA, the English bought a Rembrandt, suffragettes pawned their jewels for funds, there were riots in Russia, strikes in the USA, a mutiny in Mexico, etc. The historian filters out these irrelevancies before he reports to the reader on the subject of his essay. But in the real decision process competition for attention is an important fact. It is handled in our computer simulation. With its speed and large memory a computer can do what an essay writer cannot, i.e., it can analyze the interaction between the crisis that interests us and the rest of what was going on. This is a unique advantage the full significance of which we did not realize until we actually became invoved in this sample simulation.

The Kaiser, the Tsar, and the Computer

But needless to say as war was breaking out the Tsar and the Kaiser did not give much of their energies to the trial run through the Panama Canal or terrorism in Ireland. They selected a few events to which they gave attention. The attention space, it will be recalled, contains material on 7 ± 2 events with each having the capability of having 7 ± 2 messages considered. However, it will also be recalled that terribly important events reduce the number of things to which attention is paid (a psychological proposition that is well confirmed). That is what happened in the period with which we are concerned. It was normally the case that less than 49 messages were in the heart of the attention space.

The computer also has stored other messages on a pressing problems list, a set-aside list and memory. We save the reader the tedium of reproducing this vast mass of data.

It is clear that the computer has selected for the attention space a reasonable set of the most important messages. The reader should recognize that this is partly but not wholly a reflection of the initial coding of saliency. That coding is subsequently modified by reactions to the salience of the message to the other side; by its salience to public opinion; and by the passage of time. The reasonableness of the output is therefore by no means guaranteed. In our simulation we sent each decision maker J and K almost the same set of messages. This need not have been done but we chose to do it that way for experimental purposes.

The way in which the psychological processes in our model work may be well illustrated by looking at the difference in the messages accorded attention in the course of Day One. Both the Tsar and the Kaiser gave more attention to Austria's ultimatum to Serbia. The fact of the ultimatum was the primary message for both men. For the Kaiser, however, almost as important was the fact that Germany's mobs rallied for war. For the Kaiser, Serbian reaction was the *third* ranking message closely followed by Germany's fears that Austria's ultimatum was too harsh. The Tsar ranked the messages in a somewhat different order. Behind the bald fact of the ultimatum, the *second* most significant fact for him was the reaction to the ultimatum in Serbia. That Germany's mobs rallied for war was also important although *third,* but that Germany feared that Austria's ultimatum was too harsh was a much less credible and therefore less salient news event. The fourth most important event was Russia's own reaction.

The event of the Austrian ultimatum to Serbia was one that both men could not dismiss from attention, but much of the rest of what they saw in the world was quite different. The Tsar preoccupied himself with the visit of the French President to Russia and with Russia's alliance with France. He worried about England's possible noncommitment to what later became the Allied cause and requested a show of England's support.

The Kaiser did not concern himself with the Tsar's alliance problems but rather with some of his own. He attempted to localize the Serbian conflict and paid a lot of attention to that. He concerned himself with

The Governments

Belgian neutrality and also with a purely domestic financial matter, ordering banks to hold 10 per cent of their assets.

By the end of the seven days J and K are not looking at the same world although reality impinges itself on each. Three events, Russia's mobilization, Germany's mobilization and the secret treaties, are in the attention space of both men. But two events, the collapse of Europe's stock markets and Germany's military precautions, are also in the attention of the Kaiser, while two other events, Serbia's Balkan allies and the Russian press, are in the attention of the Tsar.

Even when the same event is in both men's mind, the picture of it differs. Let us look at Russia's mobilization. The Kaiser is primarily concerned with the facts: "Russia orders complete mobilization," "Russia's Tsar declares war is inevitable," "Russia calls up reserve troops," "Russia's troops are near Germany's border." The Tsar, on the other hand, who has administrative responsibility for the mobilization is, in addition, concerned with various political aspects of it. Most notably included in his list is the message "England confers with Russia on mobilization measures." Also included is that "France advises Russians to speed up military preparations" and that he as "Tsar orders general mobilization." (The last is a different message from the fact that Russia as a country had ordered complete mobilization. It identifies the Tsar's personal role.) The relation to France is particularly interesting. The Kaiser reflecting wishful thinking pays attention to the message that "France asks Russia to cut down mobilization." He neglects the message which the Tsar retains that "France asks Russia to speed up preparations." Here is the kind of reversed perceptions that causes the breakdown of international discourse.

The differences in the material in attention space devoted to German mobilization is in some respects a mirror image of that just noted for the Russians. Here we find the Russians paying attention merely to the bald fact "Germany mobilizes." (Note that this is repeated as three different messages. The program permits this for messages of truly extraordinary importance; they thus fill much of the attention space.) The Kaiser, on the other hand, also pays attention to such administrative aspects as "Germany's war chiefs confer on mobilization" and "Germany's officers press for mobilization." The Kaiser also thinks about his justification that Germany has threatened to mobilize if Russia continues arming. Here again we find the expectable psychological aspects of the situation well represented in the simulation. The Tsar gives no thought to the process which justifies German mobilization in the mind of the Kaiser, only to the fact.

Further Development of the Crisiscom Simulation

The Crisiscom simulation is now a working model. It has been used on the gaming of one crisis and can be used on others, but it is not at the

The Kaiser, the Tsar, and the Computer

TABLE 1   A PARTIAL LISTING OF THE INITIAL (I) AND FINAL (F) AFFECT MATRIX VALUES OF THE KAISER

(Both Decision Makers Have Same Initial Matrix in this Example)

	Austria		England		France		Germany		Russia		Serbia	
	I	F	I	F	I	F	I	F	I	F	I	F
Austria	0/0		−0.31/	−0.330	−0.38/	−0.399	0.65/	0.670	−0.48/	−0.480	−0.69/	−0.820
England	−0.21/	−0.264	0/0		0.63/	0.630	0.34/	0.321	0.36/	0.363	0.12/	0.159
France	−0.47/	−0.504	0.66/	0.657	0/0		−0.38/	0.380	0.68/	0.677	0.28/	0.318
Germany	0.68/	0.682	0.38/	0.395	−0.33/	−0.330	0/0		−0.36/	−0.295	−0.41/	−0.299
Russia	−0.67/	−0.839	0.39/	0.426	0.69/	0.690	−0.38/	−0.615	0/0		0.63/	0.729
Serbia	−0.70/	−0.738	0.13/	0.13	0.31/	0.310	−0.46/	−0.46	0.71/	0.742	0/0	

A PARTIAL LISTING OF THE INITIAL (I) AND FINAL (F) AFFECT MATRIX VALUES OF THE TSAR

	Austria		England		France		Germany		Russia		Serbia	
	I	F	I	F	I	F	I	F	I	F	I	F
Austria	0/0		−0.31/	−0.326	−0.38/	−0.396	0.65/	0.65	−0.48/	−0.48	−0.69/	−0.869
England	−0.21/	−0.257	0/0		0.63/	0.613	0.34/	0.352	0.36/	0.337	0.12/	0.133
France	−0.47/	−0.491	0.66/	0.663	0/0		−0.38/	−0.38	0.68/	0.68+*	0.28/	0.307
Germany	0.68/	0.671	0.38/	0.378	−0.33/	−0.33	0/0		−0.36/	−0.30	−0.41/	−0.398
Russia	−0.67/	−0.968	0.39/	0.466	0.69/	0.742	−0.38/	−0.763	0/0		0.63/	0.810
Serbia	−0.70/	−0.729	0.13/	0.13	0.31/	0.310	−0.46/	−0.460	0.71/	0.754	0/0	

* Error in scenario

end of development. We would like to see it further developed, further tested, and further used.

The development of a model of this sort is partly an open-ended matter. More and more aspects of reality can be built into it. Right now we have a very small model representing a limited range of the psychological mechanisms that are relevant to crisis. Specifically, we represent the processes of selective attention and very little more.

There are a number of obvious next steps. One of them is to introduce distortion processes. Right now a message that is received can be rejected or accepted. It cannot be changed by the receiver. We know that receivers do distort messages. We wish to introduce balancing processes whereby, though the message sent to J and K might be the same, the message that appeared in attention space could be different.

Another important direction of development is to introduce more relations than just affect. Some specific relations of military and naval reference would be useful, i.e., mobilizing forces. A relatively small dictionary of relational terms would give the model greatly enhanced flexibility and perhaps some predictive power.

Another important development permits J and K themselves to generate messages as well as receive them. In the process of generating messages they would be programmed to reflect the character of their countries and perspectives. These messages would then become part of the message flow, making Crisiscom a truly dynamic model whose ultimate play of a game would be hard to predict *a priori*.

Finally, we plan to replace much of the initial coding of saliency now done by a human with computer operations based on Robert Abelson's Hot Cognition model. (6.)

The Kaiser, the Tsar, and the Computer

```
THE ATNSPC OF DM 1 AT THE END      OF DAY   1
---- ---- ---- ---- ---- ---- ---- ---- ---- ---- ---- ---- ---- ---- ----

---- ---- ---- ---- ---- ---- ---- ---- ---- ---- ---- ---- ---- ---- ----
LOCALIZATION HOPES .

GERMANY ASSERTS NEED FOR LOCALIZATION OF SERBIA'S CONFLICT .
----+---- --0.67195---- --0.24999---- 1$---- ----+---- ---- ---- ---- ----
ENGLAND REQUESTS LOCALIZATION OF CONFLICT IN SERBIA .
----+---- --0.42719---- --0.27999---- 1$---- ----+---- ---- ---- ---- ----

---- ---- ---- ---- ---- ---- ---- ---- ---- ---- ---- ---- ---- ---- ----
AUSTRIA 'S ULTIMATUM TO SERBIA .

AUSTRIA SENDS ULTIMATUM TO SERBIA .
----+---- --0.66989---- --0.67999---- 1$---- ----+---- ---- ---- ---- ----
GERMANY 'S MOBS RALLY FOR WAR .
----+---- 0.66759---- 0$---- ---- ---- 1$---- ----+
ULTIMATUM AROUSES ALARM IN SERBIA'S CAPITAL .
----+---- --0.58053---- --0$---- ---- 1$---- ----+---- ---- ---- ---- ----
GERMANY FEARS AUSTRIA 'S ULTIMATUM TOO HARSH .
----+---- --0.35165---- --0.10999---- 1$---- ----+---- ---- ---- ---- ----
RUSSIA'S COUNCIL MEETS TO DISCUSS AUSTRIA 'S ULTIMATUM .
----+---- 0.34117---- --0.12999---- 1$---- ----+
FRANCE DENOUNCES SEVERITY OF AUSTRIA 'S ULTIMATUM .
----+---- --0.34065---- --0.41999---- 1$---- ----+---- ---- ---- ---- ----
RUSSIA DENOUNCES SEVERITY OF AUSTRIA 'S ULTIMATUM .
----+---- --0.33717---- --0.42999---- 1$---- ----+---- ---- ---- ---- ----
ENGLAND DENOUNCES SEVERITY OF AUSTRIA ' SULTIMATUM .
----+---- 0.26801---- --0.37999---- 1$---- ----+
RUSSIA ACCUSES AUSTRIA OF PLOTTING INTERNATIONAL WAR .
----+---- --0.21981---- --0.50999---- 1$---- ----+---- ---- ---- ---- ----
GERMANY DENIES FOREKNOWLEDGE OF AUS 'S ULTIMATUM .
----+---- --0.20505---- --0.26999---- 1$---- ----+---- ---- ---- ---- ----
USA FEARS WAR IMMINENT IN SERBIA .
----+---- 0.13231---- --0.09999---- 1$---- ----+

---- ---- ---- ---- ---- ---- ---- ---- ---- ---- ---- ---- ---- ---- ----
BELGIUM 'S NEUTRALITY .

BELGIUM REASSERTS NEUTRALITY STATUS .
----+---- 0.65695---- 0$---- ---- 1$---- ----+

---- ---- ---- ---- ---- ---- ---- ---- ---- ---- ---- ---- ---- ---- ----
GERMANY 'S BANKS .

GERMANY ORDERS BANKS TO HOLD TEN PERCENT OF ASSETS .
----+---- 0.65637---- 0$---- ---- 1$---- ----+

---- ---- ---- ---- ---- ---- ---- ---- ---- ---- ---- ---- ---- ---- ----
RUSSIA'S ALLIANCE WITH SERBIA .

RUSSIA ASSURES SERBIA FULL SUPPORT .
----+---- 0.63795---- 0.71999---- 1$---- ----+
SERBIA ASKS RUSSIA FOR FULL SUPPORT .
----+---- --0.58353---- --0.31999---- 1$---- ----+---- ---- ---- ---- ----

---- ---- ---- ---- ---- ---- ---- ---- ---- ---- ---- ---- ---- ---- ----
```

The Governments

```
DATE JULY 25 1914 ..                                              COC1O
( 14 )                                                            000020
ENGLAND'S MUSEUM .. ENGLAND OPENS NEW MEMORIAL MUSEUM ..          COC30
( .OC .18 .OC .05 .C3 .04 .03 .75 .68 0 )                         COC4O
USA TREATY WITH JAPAN .. USA SENATE DELAYS SIGNING JAPAN LAND TREATY ..  COC5O
(-.18 .18 .25 .11 .18 .06 .08 .57 .65 0 )                         COC6O
CANADA'S RAILROAD .. CANADA MEETS WITH USA TO DISCUSS RAILROAD LOANS ..  COC7O
( .31 .35 .21 .09 .08 .07 .06 .71 .48 C )                         COC8O
USA HYDROPLANE .. USA HYDROPLANE PREPARES FOR TRIAL RUN ..        COC9O
( .00 .21 .CO .13 .13 .15 .15 .82 .64 C )                         00100
HAITI'S REVOLUTION .. USA SENDS WARSHIPS TO HAITI ..              00110
(-.41 .48 .52 .28 .20 .23 .18 .76 .72 0 )                         00120
AUSTRIA'S ULTIMATUM TO SERBIA .. AUSTRIA SENDS ULTIMATUM TO SERBIA ..  00130
(-.68 .73 .75 .68 .70 .58 .58 .91 .88 C )                         00140
RUSSIA'S ALLIANCE WITH FRANCE .. FRANCE'S MINISTER GOES TO RUSSIA TC STR  CO150
ENGTHEN ALLIANCE ..                                               00160
( .57 .53 .68 .49 .68 .24 .39 .59 .81 0 )                         CO170
CRISIS IN IRELAND .. ENGLAND FEARS CIVIL WAR IN IRELAND ..        CO180
(-.48 .67 .63 .23 .22 .20 .19 .48 .36 0 )                         CO190
PROHIBITION .. USA WITNESSES MORE PROHIBITION DEMONSTRATIONS ..   CO20O
( .00 .29 .00 .C7 .06 .06 .43 .45 0 )                             CO210
DEATH OF LORD WEMYSS .. ENGLAND'S LORD WEMYSS DIES ..             CO22O
( .00 .37 .00 .12 .10 .08 .08 .81 .89 C )                         CO230
AUSTRIA'S ULTIMATUM TO SERBIA .. ENGLAND DENOUNCES SEVERITY OF AUSTRIA'S  CO240
ULTIMATUM ..                                                      CO250
(-.38 .36 .40 .31 .42 .24 .21 .63 .71 C )                         CO26O
RUSSIA'S ALLIANCE WITH FRANCE .. FRANCE GIVES RUSSIA FULL DIPLOMATIC SUP  CO270
PORT ..                                                           CU28O
( .63 .51 .61 .41 .61 .28 .45 .61 .90 0 )                         CO290
PRINCE OF WALES .. ENGLAND'S PRINCE INHERITS FOUR MILLION POUNDS ..  CO30O
( .00 .19 .00 .C5 .04 .07 .08 .56 .58 C )                         CO310
BICYCLE RACES .. ITALY BEATS USA IN BICYCLE RACE ..              CO32O
( .08 .11 .08 .C4 .03 .06 .C7 .41 .31 0 )                         00330
USA IMMIGRATION .. USA RAISES QUOTA FOR RUSSIA'S IMMIGRANTS ..    CO34O
( .39 .21 .32 .12 .32 .25 .34 .32 .75 C )                         00350
MEXICO'S CIVIL WAR .. PEASANT MOBS STORM MEXICO'S CAPITAL ..      CO36O
( .00 .63 .00 .26 .20 .21 .14 .51-.20 0 )                         00370
AUSTRIA'S ULTIMATUM TO SERBIA .. GERMANY DENIES FOREKNOWLEDGE OF AUS  CO38O
'S ULTIMATUM ..                                                   CO390
(-.27 .45 .38 .45 .31 .41 .25-.73-.56 0 )                         CO40O
AUSTRIA'S ULTIMATUM TO SERBIA .. RUSSIA ACCUSES AUSTRIA OF PLOTTING INTE  CO410
RNATIONAL WAR ..                                                  CO42O
(-.51 .46 .48 .38 .46 .40 .32-.14 .42 0 )                         CO430
RUSSIA'S ALLIANCE WITH SERBIA .. SERBIA ASKS RUSSIA FOR FULL SUPPORT ..  CO44O
( .32 .62 .53 .49 .53 .55 .39 .43 .82 0 )                         CO45O
SERBIA'S REPLY .. AUSTRIA ALLOWS TWO-CAY TIME LIMIT FOR SERBIA'S REPLY ..  CO46O
(-.29 .44 .51 .42 .48 .28 .31 .73 .75 0 )                         CO48O
AUSTRIA'S ULTIMATUM TO SERBIA .. FRANCE DENOUNCES SEVERITY OF AUSTRIA'S  CO49O
ULTIMATUM ..                                                      CO50O
(-.42 .39 .41 .40 .43 .32 .38 .55 .51 C )                         00510
MEXICO'S CIVIL WAR .. MEXICO'S LEADERS SIGN ARMISTICE ..          CO52O
( .00 .73 .CO .28 .22 .23 .21-.31-.42 0 )                         CO53O
HAITI'S REVOLUTION .. NEW VIOLENCE BREAKS IN HAITI'S CAPITAL ..   CO54O
( .00 .68 .00 .31 .30 .26 .66 .43 0 )                             CO55O
JEWEL ROBBERY .. THIEVES STEAL JEWELS FROM GERMANY'S DUTCHESS ..  CO56O
( .00 .11 .00 .11 .06 .27 .09 .81 .35 0 )                         CO57O
GERMANY'S STEAMSHIP LINES .. GERMANY'S STEAMSHIP LINES RAISE PRICES TO U  CO58O
SA ..                                                             CO59O
```

The Kaiser, the Tsar, and the Computer

A PARTIAL LISTING OF THE FINAL AFFECT MATRIX OF THE KAISER.

THE AFFECT MATRIX OF DECISION MAKER 1 AT THE START OF DAY 7

	ALASKA	AUSTRA	AUSTRI	BELGIU	CANADA	COLOMB	DENMAR	ENGLAN
ALASKA	0.	-0.220	-0.140	0.160	0.480	0.	0.210	0.330
AUSTRA	0.190	0.	0.100	0.210	0.370	0.	0.220	0.670
AUSTRI	-0.100	0.060	0.	-0.130	-0.200	0.	0.130	-0.329
BELGIU	0.200	0.210	-0.210	0.	0.230	0.	0.470	0.580
CANADA	0.370	-0.380	-0.230	0.160	0.	-0.140	0.230	0.520
COLOMB	0.	0.130	0.	0.	0.230	0.	0.190	0.210
DENMAR	0.130	0.200	0.310	0.430	0.200	0.	0.	0.480
ENGLAN	0.180	0.480	-0.264	0.590	0.610	0.140	0.390	0.
FRANCE	-0.110	-0.200	-0.595	-0.380	-0.360	-0.210	-0.280	-0.657
GERMAN	0.150	-0.120	0.682	-0.310	0.240	0.	0.290	0.395
GREECE	0.	-0.160	-0.380	0.240	0.	0.	-0.120	-0.140
HAITI	0.120	-0.130	0.	0.	0.230	0.330	0.	0.310
IRELAN	0.140	-0.210	-0.210	0.410	-0.160	0.	0.360	0.490
ITALY	0.	0.130	-0.170	0.230	0.130	0.	0.280	-0.310
JAPAN	-0.150	-0.120	0.130	0.200	0.270	0.	-0.130	-0.310
LUXEMB	0.	0.140	0.210	0.480	0.130	0.	0.410	0.400
MEXICO	-0.100	0.	0.	0.	0.210	-0.380	-0.080	-0.210
MONTEN	0.	0.	-0.450	0.210	0.	0.	0.270	0.210
PERU	0.	0.140	0.120	0.180	0.230	0.560	0.	0.210
RUSSIA	0.380	-0.100	-0.839	0.130	0.310	0.	0.240	0.426
SERBIA	0.	0.	-0.738	0.130	0.	0.	-0.210	0.130
TURKEY	-0.140	0.100	0.390	-0.100	0.110	0.	-0.140	-0.380
USA	-0.610	-0.300	-0.140	-0.310	-0.680	-0.320	-0.200	-0.540
VENEZU	0.140	0.	0.	0.	0.210	0.410	0.	0.270

	FRANCE	GERMAN	GREECE	HAITI	IRELAN	ITALY	JAPAN	LUXEMB
ALASKA	0.310	-0.100	0.	0.130	0.	0.100	0.200	0.
AUSTRA	-0.280	-0.170	-0.110	0.	-0.160	-0.190	0.210	-0.080
AUSTRI	-0.399	0.670	-0.300	0.	-0.070	-0.235	-0.090	-0.120
BELGIU	0.550	-0.290	0.	0.	-0.130	0.120	0.	0.390
CANADA	0.370	-0.260	-0.110	-0.160	-0.130	-0.060	0.	-0.230
COLOMB	0.130	-0.130	0.	0.320	0.	0.100	0.	0.
DENMAR	0.460	0.320	-0.110	0.	0.230	0.260	-0.080	0.330
ENGLAN	0.630	0.321	0.210	-0.130	-0.360	-0.280	0.260	0.290
FRANCE	0.	-0.380	0.260	0.	-0.190	-0.290	-0.110	0.430
GERMAN	-0.330	0.	-0.220	-0.300	0.	0.400	0.310	-0.280
GREECE	0.240	-0.380	0.	0.	0.	-0.380	0.	0.200
HAITI	0.150	-0.310	0.	0.	0.	0.120	0.	0.
IRELAN	0.220	0.160	0.100	0.	0.	0.190	0.	0.240
ITALY	0.260	0.320	-0.280	0.	0.	0.	0.230	0.310
JAPAN	0.210	-0.340	0.100	0.	0.	-0.170	0.	0.
LUXEMB	0.510	0.230	0.210	0.	0.	0.130	0.	0.
MEXICO	-0.100	-0.290	0.	0.340	0.	-0.120	0.	0.
MONTEN	0.310	-0.330	0.400	0.	0.	0.100	0.	0.200
PERU	0.160	-0.180	0.	0.380	0.	0.	0.	0.
RUSSIA	0.690	-0.615	0.310	0.120	-0.110	-0.200	-0.260	0.240
SERBIA	-0.310	-0.460	-0.431	0.	0.	-0.330	0.	0.200
TURKEY	-0.400	0.370	-0.280	0.	0.	-0.400	0.	0.110
USA	-0.500	-0.530	0.140	-0.400	-0.130	-0.120	-0.270	0.
VENEZU	0.130	0.180	0.	0.230	0.	0.	0.	0.

The Governments

References

1. L. Bloomfield and B. Whaley, "The political-military exercise: a progress report," *Orbis,* Vol. 8, 854–70, 1965.
2. H. Vaihinger, *The Philosophy of As If,* New York: Barnes & Noble, Inc., 1952.
3. G. Miller, "The magical number seven plus or minus two: some limits on our capacity for processing information," *Psychological Review,* Vol. 63, 81–97, 1963.
4. R. North, et al., *Content Analysis: A Handbook with Application for the Study of International Crisis.* Evanston, Ill.: Northwestern University Press, 1963.
5. H. Guetzkow, et al., *Simulation in International Relations: Developments for Research and Teaching.* Englewood Cliffs, N.J.: Prentice-Hall, Inc., 1963.
6. R. Abelson, "Computer simulation of hot cognition," in *Computer Simulation of Personality,* S. Tomkins and S. Messick, Eds. New York: John Wiley & Sons, Inc., 1963, p. 282.

Explanatory Notes

1) In the affect matrix the row label is the country which feels a certain way about the country named in the column label.
2) In the listing of messages in attention space:
   a) The first number under each message is a current saliency measurement.
   b) The second number under each message is an affective significance measure relating to the subject's treatment of the object.
   c) The third number under each message indicates the day the message first appeared.
   d) Lines without numbers label an event. The messages about that event follow it.

Perceptions of
Hostility and
Financial Indices
During the
1914 Crisis:

An Experiment in Validating Content Analysis Data

Ole R. Holsti

Robert C. North

Reprinted by permission of the publisher from Richard L. Merritt and Stein Rokkan (eds.), *Comparing Nations* (New Haven: Yale University Press, 1966), pp. 169–90. Copyright © 1966 by Yale University. Mr. Holsti is Associate Professor of Political Science at the University of British Columbia. Mr. North is Professor of Political Science at Stanford University.

Critics of content analysis have justifiably pointed to the lack of studies in which inferences based on content data are tested against independent material.[1] For example, is there any significant relationship between what policy makers say and write and the actual decisions they make? If there is not, then the value of content analysis for decision-making studies is placed in serious doubt. This paper reports on an experiment to test the validity of content data being used in a study of decision making during the 1914 crisis.

The summer of 1914 and events leading to the outbreak of World War I have provided the "laboratory" for the current study. This particular crisis period was chosen because the archives of the participating powers are relatively open, providing more decision data than are frequently available, and because the events constitute an almost classic case of an incident leading to a "localized" war, which then got out of hand and escalated into a major conflict.

The basic content unit was the "perception" abstracted from the documents in terms of the following elements: the perceiving party or actor; the perceived party or actor; the asserted action or attitude; and the target party or actor.[2] The 1914 documents provided more than 5,000 cognitive and affective perceptions of four variables—hostility, friendship, frustration, and satisfaction—of which hostility has emerged clearly as the best predictor of state behavior. This finding is supported by a multiple

This is a revised version, specially prepared for this volume, of a paper that appeared initially as "Comparative Data from Content Analysis: Perceptions of Hostility and Economic Variables in the 1914 Crisis," in Richard Merritt and Stein Rokkan (eds.), *Comparing Nations* (New Haven: Yale University Press, 1966).

[1] See, for example, Bernard Berelson, *Content Analysis in Communication Research* (Glencoe: The Free Press, 1952), pp. 74–75.

[2] For a more complete discussion of the content analysis techniques used in this paper, see Robert C. North, Ole R. Holsti, George Zaninovich, and Dina A. Zinnes, *Content Analysis: A Handbook with Application to the Study of International Crisis* (Evanston, Northwestern University Press, 1963). For other studies which have employed these data, see Dina A. Zinnes, Robert C. North, and Howard E. Koch, "Capability, Threat and the Outbreak of War," in James N. Rosenau, ed., *International Politics and Foreign Policy* (New York, Free Press, 1961); Dina A. Zinnes, "Expression and Perception of Hostility in International Relations" (Ph.D. dissertation, Stanford University, 1963); Ole R. Holsti and Robert C. North, "History as a 'Laboratory' of Conflict," in Elton B. McNeil, ed., *The Nature of Human Conflict* (Englewood Cliffs, N.J., Prentice-Hall, 1965); Ole R. Holsti, "The 1914 Case," *American Political Science Review*, LIX (1965), 365–378; and Ole R. Holsti, Robert C. North, and Richard A. Brody, "Perception and Action in the 1914 Case," in J. D. Singer, ed., *Quantitative International Politics* (New York: The Free Press, 1968).

Perceptions of Hostility and Financial Indices

regression analysis (including the variable change of *status quo*), which produced the following beta weights for each variable:

Hostility	9.66
Friendship	−2.11
Frustration	1.90
Satisfaction	1.39
Change of *status quo*	0.27

The question of how valid these data are remains: when the purpose of content analysis is merely to describe systematically certain attributes of documents, the problem of validity would be of relatively little concern, except insofar as it may be adversely affected by systematic rather than random sampling and error and by coding error. Because data drawn from these documents are also to be used for drawing inferences about the attitudes, perceptions, and values of their authors, the question of validity becomes a critical one. That is, in order to draw valid inferences about authors from the messages they produce, the content data must be validated, *directly* or *indirectly*, with independent behavioral indices. Owing to possible differences in encoding habits, conscious efforts to deceive, and the like, inferences as to the antecedent causes of messages drawn solely from content data cannot be considered self-validating.[3]

Direct and systematic methods of validation—for example, interviewing or observing decision-makers during the crisis—cannot be used when the events under analysis took place some half century ago. Alternatively, one can search for eyewitness reports which might tend to confirm or disconfirm inferences drawn from the content analysis data. Such reports, drawn from diaries and memoirs of those who took part in the 1914 decisions, are in fact consistent with the content data. For example, we may infer, from an analysis of the Kaiser's messages and the comments he wrote on many other documents, that he was under considerable stress during the final days prior to the outbreak of war. This inference receives support from the observations of those who saw him frequently. Admiral Tirpitz wrote of the Kaiser during the critical phase of the crisis: "I have never seen a more tragic, more ravaged face than that of our Emperor during those days." But at best, such eyewitness evidence is anecdotal and unsystematic; at times it may even be highly suspect, as in the case of memoirs written years after the actual events. In short, while it would be desirable to have direct, systematic, and reliable evidence regarding the attitudes, perceptions, and values of decision-makers in the various capitals of Europe during the summer of 1914, such data are not in fact available.

The indirect approach to validation taken in the present analysis involves comparing the content analysis data with a series of indices which

---

[3] For an elaboration of this point, see Ole R. Holsti *et al.*, "Content Analysis," in Gardner Lindzey and Elliot Aronson (eds.), *The Handbook of Social Psychology*, 2nd ed., (Reading, Mass: Addison-Wesley, in press), and Ole R. Holsti, *Content Analysis for the Social Sciences and Humanities* (Reading, Mass: Addison-Wesley, in press).

The Governments

meet several criteria. They must be available in quantitative form in sources of unquestioned authenticity. They must be reported on a daily basis; hence, such otherwise useful data as trade statistics, which are usually reported annually, quarterly, or monthly, are of little use. And, most importantly, they must be indices whose sensitivity to changes in the international political climate can be demonstrated. Figures on the flow of gold, the price of securities, commodities, currency, and the like satisfy each of these requirements. These data were collected from sources quite separate from the diplomatic documents which had been subjected to content analysis, including major daily and financial newspapers.[4]

The logic of this analysis is illustrated in Figure 1. Elites for whom international events are salient include not only political decision-makers. Members of the financial community must also be sensitive to international developments because virtually all forms of investment will be affected by them. The attitudes of political leaders have been measured by content analysis of documents, but we wish to know whether data thus derived are valid. The attitudes of financial elites can be measured directly with a high degree of precision and reliability by changes in various financial indices. We may then compare the results. If we find a high correlation between the financial and content data, our confidence in the latter is enhanced. If such a relationship is not found to exist, the value of content analysis data is open to serious question.

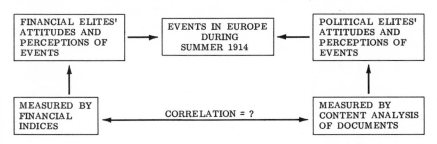

FIGURE 1   *Design to Test the Validity of Content Analysis Data*

The Flow of Gold

Any study of the flow of gold involving the major actors in the 1914 crisis must center on London—"the financial center and the free market for gold."[5] Whereas notes could be redeemed for gold to an unlimited

---

[4] For example, *The Times* (London), *The Economist* (London), *The Wall Street Journal*, *Le Temps* (Paris), and F. W. Hirst, *The Political Economy of War* (New York: E. P. Dutton and Co., 1915).

[5] Ruth M. Jaeger, *Stabilization of the Foreign Exchange* (New York: Isaac Goldman Co., 1922).

TABLE 1   INFLUX (+) OR EXFLUX (−) OF GOLD FROM LONDON—DAILY AVERAGE (IN £ THOUSANDS)

	Average June 20–26	June 27–July 2	July 3–16	July 17–20	July 21–25	July 26	July 27	July 28	July 29	July 30	July 31	Aug. 1
	+120.33	+92.0	+71.0	+9.8	+6.0	0.0	+269.0	−22.0	−911.0	−1034.0	−1204.0	−60.0
Intensity level of perceived hostility*		3.46	3.66	3.79	4.17	4.92	4.46	5.10	5.18	5.48	5.70	6.42

Spearman rank order correlation: Rising Hostility—Exflux of Gold

$$n = 11 \qquad r_s = +0.850 \qquad P < .01$$

* Scaled by Q-Sort; mean of all statements is 5.00.

extent in the Bank of England, the government banks of Berlin, St. Petersburg, and Paris had been hoarding gold for a considerable period of time prior to the assassination of Francis Ferdinand.[6] As late as July 25, the influential London *Economist* opposed demands from some British bankers that England take official steps to prevent a run on gold in times of panic.[7] Thus fluctuations in the influx or outflow of gold from London took place in a market free—until July 31—of any governmental interference.

Table 1 shows the daily average net flow of gold in and out of London. As the crisis developed there was first a marked decrease in the influx of gold followed by a wave of withdrawals when war broke out on the *Continent*. Only on August 1 was there any abatement. Late in the previous day the bank rate had been raised to an almost unprecedented 8 per cent; on August 1 the rate was increased again to 10 per cent. Thus the drop in net outflow from £1,204,000 on July 31 to £60,000 was less the result of a restoration of confidence than of a consciously adopted policy on the part of the British to take remedial steps by abolishing the free market in gold.

When the movement of gold is compared to the fluctuations in the intensity of perceived hostility[8] (Figure 2), there is a significant correlation ($r_s = .85$). It is interesting to note, for example, that the marked drop in the hostility curve on Monday, July 27 was matched by a sharp rise in the influx of gold. During the preceding weekend many observers and participants, including the Kaiser and Winston Churchill, had felt that the Serbian reply to the ultimatum marked the end of the crisis.[9] Similarly the steady rise in hostility starting on July 28 corresponds to the withdrawal, in panic proportions, of gold. The reported correlation coefficient between gold flow and perceived hostility is actually conservative. It includes data from August 1 when, as shown above, the outflow of gold was reduced by artificial means. If this period were not included, the correlation would be .88.

As stated earlier, and inferences regarding the value of content

[6] Hirst, pp. 281, 290. By the law of July 3, 1913, the Bank of Germany was authorized to build up a gold-silver war reserve of 240 million marks. At the same time the French were building up a counterpart to the German fund. *The Economist,* July 25, 1914, p. 169; August 15, 1914, pp. 316, 321.

[7] *The Economist,* July 25, 1914, p. 169.

[8] By all perceivers (decision-makers of France, England, Russia, Germany, and Austria-Hungary).

[9] On the text of the Serbian reply, the Kaiser wrote, "A brilliant performance for a time limit of only forty-eight hours. This is more than one could have expected! A great moral victory for Vienna; but with it every reason for war drops away, and Giesel might have remained quietly in Belgrade! On the strength of this I should never have ordered mobilization." Max Montgelas and Walther Schücking, eds., *Outbreak of the World War, German Documents Collected by Karl Kautsky* (New York: Oxford University Press, 1924), p. 254. Churchill wrote, "On Saturday afternoon the news came in that Serbia had accepted the ultimatum. I went to bed with a feeling things might blow over...we were still a long way, as it seemed, from any danger of war. Serbia had accepted the ultimatum, could Austria demand more?" Winston S. Churchill, *The World Crisis, 1911–1914* (New York: Charles Scribner's Sons, 1928), p. 208.

117

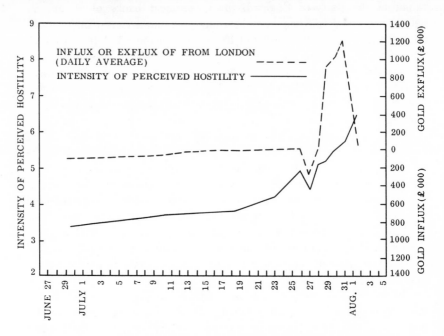

FIGURE 2   *Fluctuations in the Intensity of Perceived Hostility: Gold Flow*

analysis data through comparisons with economic indices is greatly strengthened if evidence can be introduced to show that the latter are in fact sensitive barometers of the course of international politics. That is, if a financial index such as the flow of gold from London—or any of the others considered in this paper—is to serve as a criterion against which content data may be compared for purposes of validation, it is necessary to determine whether the criterion itself is valid. Is there any evidence that the outflow of gold was related to the European crisis? Table 2 reveals that the great bulk of outbound gold was in fact shipped to the Continent. The net outflow for the period was £1,440,000; included, however, are British purchases of £1,703,000 in bars and the receipt of £803,000 from various nations in South America. The net direct outflow (June 27-August 1) to continental Europe, excluding neutral Switzerland, was £3,011,000; the net outflow to the Continent from July 27 to August 1, a period encompassing the outbreak of war, was £3,018,000. Thus, gold shipments to the Continent for the entire period account for 75.0 per cent of all *gross* outflow and for 211 per cent of *net* outflow. During the period of July 27-August 1, gold shipments to Europe account for 75.7 per cent of *gross* outflow and for 102 per cent of *net* gold exports. Again these figures may be conservative; the final destination of gold shipped to Switzerland, for example, might well have been one of the continental belligerents.

Finally, there is strong, although indirect, evidence that much of the gold was recalled by the governments of the major powers involved in

The Governments

TABLE 2 GOLD INFLUX (+) AND EXFLUX (−) FROM LONDON
(IN £ THOUSANDS)

Source or Destination	June 27–July 2	July 3–16	July 17–20	July 21–25	July 26	July 27	July 28	July 29	July 30	July 31	Aug. 1	Net
France			− 6				− 22	− 380	− 971	− 143	− 16	− 1538
"Continent"		− 7						− 275		− 572		− 854
Belgium						− 50		− 41		− 548		− 639
Within empire				− 280					− 150	− 80	− 100	− 610
Egypt	+ 185		+ 45					− 465	− 100			− 335
Switzerland									− 60			− 60
Germany		+ 20										+ 20
United States	+ 70											+ 70
South America	+ 128	+ 165		+ 124		+ 118			+ 73	+ 139	+ 56	+ 803
Bars purchased	+ 77	+ 815		+ 186		+ 201		+ 250	+ 174			+ 1703
NET	+ 460	+ 993	+ 39	+ 30	0	+ 269	− 22	− 911	− 1034	− 1204	− 60	− 1440
DAILY AVERAGE	+ 92.0	+ 71.0	+ 9.8	+ 6.0	0	+ 269.0	− 22.0	− 911.0	− 1034.0	− 1204.0	− 60.0	——

the crisis. An examination of the weekly statements of the European national banks (Table 3) reveals sharp increases in gold reserves during the crisis period. While the figures in Table 3 undoubtedly reflect internal stockpiling of gold—the German Bank, for example, was relieved of the necessity to honor withdrawals in gold after the outbreak of war[10]—they also suggest that major financial institutions on the Continent had been in large part responsible for the run on gold in London.

TABLE 3   GOLD RESERVES OF NATIONAL BANKS*

Bank of	Gold Reserves	On	Gold Reserves	On	Net Change
France	£159,028,000	June 25	£165,654,000	July 30	+£ 6,626,000
Belgium	£ 13,451,000	June 25	£ 15,980,000	August 6	+£ 2,529,000
Germany	£ 63,712,200**	July 2	£ 75,426,000	August 15	+£11,713,800
Russia	£159,575,000	June 29	£160,204,000	August 4	+£ 629,000

* No figures are available for the Austro–Hungarian Bank after July 23, 1914.
** 1,306.1 million Marks, converted in pounds at the rate of 20.50 M/£.

The Prices of Stocks and Bonds

The analysis of the price of securities, unlike that of gold, can be undertaken in many places. Securities exchanges operated in the capitals of the major European powers. The data analyzed here consist of 20 stocks and bonds for Serbia, Russia, France, Germany, Austria, Hungary, England, and Belgium, traded on the London, St. Petersburg, Paris, Berlin, Vienna, and Brussels exchanges (Table 4).

Selection of stocks and bonds for analysis from among the many issues traded on various exchanges was somewhat arbitrary. None of the European exchanges had a standard index, comparable to the Dow-Jones Industrial average on the New York Stock Exchange, which was designed to reflect price movements of all issues. Hence it was necessary to devise a substitute. Twenty stocks and bonds issued in Serbia, Russia, Austria-Hungary, Germany, France, Great Britain, and Belgium were selected. While Belgium was not directly involved in the crisis, one Belgian security —Bank of Brussels stock—was included because it was common knowledge that, in case of war between France and Germany, the Schlieffen Plan called for a sweep of the German army through Belgium. An effort was made to select widely owned "blue chip" issues, the prices which would be more likely to reflect widespread attitudes in the financial community toward the future, rather than more speculative issues, whose prices might be responding to events other than international ones. To facilitate inter-

10 For some days prior to the outbreak of war German banks paid out only 20 per cent of demands in gold; on the declaration of "The State of Threatening Danger of War" (July 31), payments in gold were stopped altogether. On August 5 the Austro-Hungarian Bank Act, which required 2/5 gold backing for currency, was suspended. *The Economist*, August 1, 1914, p. 229; August 14, 1914, p. 320; December 19, 1914 (Special War Supplement), p. 13.

The Governments

TABLE 4. SECURITIES OF PROSPECTIVE BELLIGERENTS
(JUNE 20–26=100)

Security	June 27–July 2	July 3–16	July 17–20	July 21–25	July 26	July 27	July 28	July 29	July 30
Serbia: 4% Bonds	99.0	96.2	92.0	89.8	87.2	89.7	87.6	83.5	83.5
Serbia: Monopoles	98.8	98.0	98.9	97.3	96.6	95.5	93.6	92.5	92.5
Banque Internationale	98.8	97.8	95.6	91.2	89.0	89.0	85.8		
Baku	100.2	100.1	99.0	96.0	94.4	94.4	92.0		
Moscow: Kazan	97.2	96.0	93.3	92.6	93.1	93.1	88.6		
Russian 4½% 1909	99.8	99.9	98.0	95.8	91.5	94.0			
Russia: 4% Bonds	100.1	98.3	97.5	96.5	93.8	91.5	90.2	89.1	89.1
Austria: Credit Shares	99.5	97.8	97.2	95.5	92.8	94.5	93.5	94.3	92.7
Austria: 4% Gold	99.8	99.9	99.7	99.0	98.1				
Hungary: 4% Gold	99.6	98.5	98.0	97.5	94.3				
Hungarian Bonds	101.0	97.2	97.0	94.7	91.4	90.1	89.0	89.0	89.0
Germany: 3% Imperial	99.7	99.2	98.8	97.8	96.5	95.9	95.8	94.8	94.8
3% Prussian Consols	99.7	99.2	98.8	97.7	96.4	97.0	96.9	94.7	
General Electric	99.9	99.8	98.1	94.7	91.2	92.1	91.2	88.9	86.9
France: 3% Loan	99.0	98.9	97.8	96.5	93.8	93.7	92.9	92.9	
3½% French Loan	100.0	99.9	99.7	97.0	93.6	94.4	94.4	93.1	
Bank of France	100.0	99.4	98.7	98.0	97.5	97.5	97.5	94.8	
British Consols: 2½%	99.8	101.1	101.3	100.3	98.4	96.8	95.8	94.8	93.1
Port of London B 4%	100.3	100.8	99.0	98.9	98.5	97.9	97.9	95.9	95.9
Bank of Brussels	99.9	99.5	98.5	97.6	97.0	97.0			
INDEX	99.6	98.9	97.8	96.2	94.2	94.3	93.3	92.5	92.1

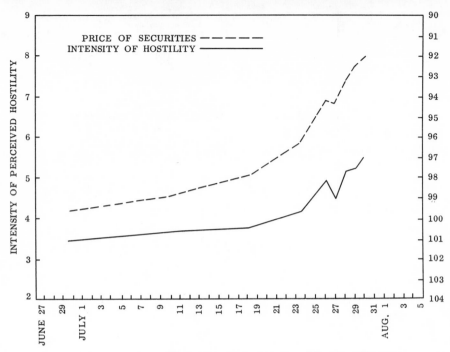

FIGURE 3   *Fluctuations in the Intensity of Perceived Hostility: Security Prices*

pretation, the price of each security is given as a percentage of its value during the pre-crisis week (June 20–26). The index is the average value for the twenty securities. When the composite index is compared to the fluctuations in the intensity of perceived hostility (Figure 3), there is again a striking similarity. The drop in hostility on July 27 was matched by a slight rise in the value of securities. Some individual shares of nations most intimately involved in the Austro-Serbian dispute rose quite markedly —Serbian Bonds (2.5%), Russian Bonds (2.5%) and Austrian Credit shares (1.7%). Subsequently there was a virtual collapse in prices, corresponding to the rise in perceived hostility. The figures on the extent of the collapse in the last few days of the crisis are actually stated conservatively. In the first place, many of the quoted prices were, according to observers, nominal and thus higher than the actual price for which one could sell his securities.[11] Second, for the purpose of the index, the price of a security which was no longer traded—usually due to the closing of various exchanges[12]—is carried through July 30 at the last quoted price.

[11] *The Economist*, August 1, 1914, p. 231.
[12] The closing dates of the various European exchanges are: Vienna (July 27), Budapest (July 27), Brussels (July 27), Berlin (July 29), St. Petersburg (July 30), Paris (July 30), London (July 31). The closing of the Barcelona Bourse on July 28, however, was attributed to "free fighting between members." *The Economist*, August 1, 1914, p. 220.

The Governments

Again one might raise a question regarding the relationship between the falling price of securities and the European crisis. For purposes of comparison the price movements of the securities of traditionally neutral nations, Sweden and Switzerland, were analyzed (Table 5). The values of these stocks and bonds were unusually stable, falling less than one per cent during the crisis.

In contrast, the paper losses in values of the stocks and bonds of the major participants in the crisis were staggering. In the ten-day period ending with July 30, the value of 387 representative British stocks fell by £188,000,000. By July 25, the value of the securities of 23 German industrial firms had dropped from £79,000,000 to £65,900,000—and the worst was yet to come! In one sense the "cost" of the war reached catastrophic proportions even before the first shot was fired.[13] Thus the comparison with the securities of belligerents and neutrals during the crisis strongly suggests that security prices during July 1914 were in fact reacting to events in the European international system.

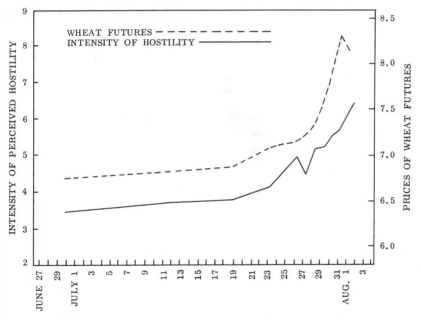

FIGURE 4   *Fluctuations in the Intensity of Perceived Hostility: Wheat Prices*

[13] *The Economist,* August 1, 1914, p. 229; August 29, p. 383. Some contemporary accounts of the various exchanges describe something of the atmosphere in which trading took place: Price losses "exceed anything that has happened in the past." "The market has become completely demoralized, the chief factors being the Eastern situation." "A panic on the Bourse, on which prices fell below any recorded since 1895." *The Economist,* July 18, 1914, p. 126; July 25, 1914, p. 173; December 19, 1914, p. 13.

TABLE 5 SECURITIES OF PROSPECTIVE NEUTRALS
(JUNE 20–26=100)

Security	June 27–July 2	July 3–16	July 17–20	July 21–25	July 26	July 27	July 28	July 29	July 30	July 31
Sweden 3%	100.0	100.0	100.0	100.0	100.0	100.0	100.0	100.0	100.0	100.0
Sweden 3½%	99.7	97.9	98.4	98.5	99.2	98.3	98.0	98.0	98.0	98.2
Switzerland Chemin de Fer	100.3	99.6	99.5	99.5	99.5	99.5	99.5	99.5	99.5	99.5
INDEX	100.00	99.17	99.30	99.33	99.57	99.27	99.17	99.17	99.17	99.23

Spearman rank order correlation: Rising Hostility—Falling Securities Prices

	n	r_s	P
Securities Index (Neutrals)	10	+0.520	n.s.
Securities Index (Belligerents)	9	+1.000	<.01

Average Loss in Value—Securities of:

Serbia	12.0%
Hungary	8.4%
Russia	10.1%
France	6.4%
Great Britain	5.5%
Germany	7.9%
Austria	4.6%
Belgium	3.0%
Sweden	0.9%
Switzerland	0.5%

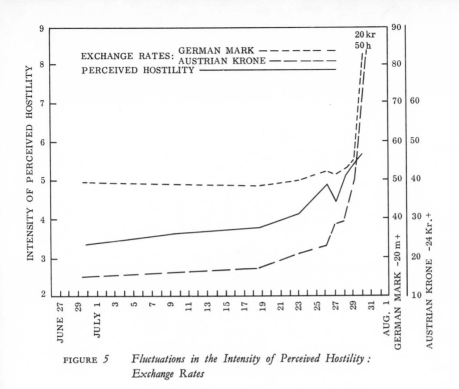

FIGURE *5*   *Fluctuations in the Intensity of Perceived Hostility :*
Exchange Rates

Wheat Futures

The development of a major international crisis often brings about wide-spread hoarding of various commodities. Speculators—anticipating panic buying, hoarding, and diminished supplies—would be expected to bid the price of commodity futures up as the crisis deepened. Table 6 reveals that, during the month of July, wheat futures in London rose more than 20 per cent. Moreover, the pattern of rising prices corresponds almost exactly to that of increasing hostility. Similar increases in prices took place on the Continent. In Berlin, for example, the price of rye rose from 172.5 reichsmarks per sack to 176 rm between July 27 and July 29; wheat rose from 202.25 to 207 rm, and oats rose from 167.25 to 169.75 rm during the same period.[14]

Exchange Rates

The standard against which all currencies were measured in 1914 was the British pound sterling; the value of any currency fluctuated in terms

14 *The Economist*, pp. 230, 231.

Perceptions of Hostility and Financial Indices

TABLE 6 DECEMBER WHEAT FUTURES IN LONDON—DAILY AVERAGE (IN SHILLINGS)

	Average June 20–26	June 27–July 2	July 3–16	July 17–20	July 21–25	July 26	July 27	July 28	July 29	July 30	July 31	Aug. 1
	6.90	6.74	6.81	6.87	7.08	7.15	7.21	7.30	7.56	8.02	8.29	8.13
Intensity level of perceived hostility		3.46	3.66	3.79	4.17	4.92	4.46	5.10	5.18	5.48	5.70	6.42

Spearman rank order correlation: Rising Hostility—Rising Wheat Prices

n	r_s	P
11	+0.983	<.01

of how much sterling one could buy with it. An analysis of the exchange rates of the German mark and the Austrian krone during the 1914 crisis reveals an unprecedented rise in the exchange rates of these currencies (and thus a drop in value) vis-à-vis the pound (Table 7). Figure 5 shows that once again the fluctuation of the economic variable correlated closely with changes in perceived hostility. Although day-to-day figures on the Russian ruble are less readily available, the trend is the same. According to one source, the ruble, which was quoted at 95.6 to the ten-pound note on July 27, was quoted at 110–120 only three days later.[15]

The extent of the collapse of continental currencies is illustrated by the fact that the mark lost 1.6 per cent of its normal value; the krone fell 9.7 per cent and the ruble fell 24.5 per cent during the short span of the crisis.

Interest Rates

Table 8 reveals that both official bank rates and free market money rates are also highly correlated with changes in perceived hostility during the crisis. Although official rates are usually a highly stable figure—many of the rates at the outbreak of the crisis had not been changed since 1913 or earlier—every one of the major participants for which figures are available increased rates at least once during the six-week period. Three increases in as many days brought the British figures from 3 per cent on July 29 to 10 per cent on August 1; during a similar period the French rate rose from 3½ to 6 per cent, the Vienna rate from 4 to 8 per cent, and the Brussels rate from 4 to 7 per cent. In each case the action on interest rates was a direct outgrowth of the European crisis; a primary reason was to insure that gold would not flow out of the country.[16]

The market money rate, unlike the official rate, fluctuates from day to day much as the price of securities or exchange rates. Although figures were not quoted in Paris, London, or Berlin after July 29, the rates on that day were almost double what they had been earlier in the month. As with the official rate, the market rate fluctuated in concert with the level of hostility perceived by key decision-makers.

One by-product of this analysis is a picture, albeit sketchy, of the collapse of an international economic system. That system, which Lenin had prophesied would lead to war and which many early twentieth-century liberals had predicted would make future wars impossible, was, in the words of *The Economist*, "staggering under a series of blows such as the delicate system of international credit has never before witnessed, or even

15 Hirst, p. 283.
16 "The rise to 8 per cent (in England) marked a real panic. Almost the whole continent, from Paris to St. Petersburg, and from Amsterdam to Vienna and Rome, wants to convert paper into cash; and the great banks even in Paris and Berlin are, of course, hoarding gold against an emergency." *The Economist*, August 1, 1914, p. 219.

Perceptions of Hostility and Financial Indices

TABLE 7   EXCHANGE RATES: GERMAN MARK AND AUSTRIAN KRONE
(IN RELATION TO £ STERLING)

	June 20–26	June 27–July 2	July 3–16	July 17–20	July 21–25	July 26	July 27	July 28	July 29	July 30
German Mark										
Mark	20	20	20	20	20	20	20	20	20	20
Pfennig	49.6	49.7	49.3	48.9	50.1	52.5	·52.0	53.0	55.0	82.0
Austrian Krone										
Krone	24	24	24	24	24	24	24	24	24	26
Heller	16.3	15.2	16.6	17.3	21.2	23.5	29.0	30.0	40.0	50.0
Level of perceived hostility	3.46	3.46	3.66	3.79	4.17	4.92	4.46	5.10	5.46	5.70

Spearman rank order correlation: Rising Hostility——Falling Currency Values

	n	r_s	P
German Mark	9	.933	<.01
Austrian Krone	9	.983	<.01

TABLE 8 OFFICIAL AND MARKET MONEY RATES

	June 20–26	June 27–July 2	July 3–16	July 17–20	July 21–25	July 26	July 27	July 28	July 29	July 30	July 31	Aug. 1–2	Aug. 3–5
Official money rates*	3.92%	3.92%	3.92%	3.92%	3.92%	4.08%	4.25%	4.58%	4.58%	4.92%	5.92%	6.33%	7.17%
Market money rates**	2.63%	2.48%	2.27%	2.31%	2.47%	2.71%	3.17%	4.00%	4.17%	—	—	—	—
Intensity of perceived hostility	3.46	3.66	3.79	4.17	4.46	4.92	5.10	5.18	5.48	5.70	6.42	6.30	

Spearman rank order correlation: Rising Hostility—Rising Money Rates

	n	r_s	P
Official rate	12	+.967	<.01
Market rate	8	+.834	.01

* Average rates in London, Paris, Berlin, Vienna, St. Petersburg, and Brussels.
** Average rates in London, Paris, and Berlin.

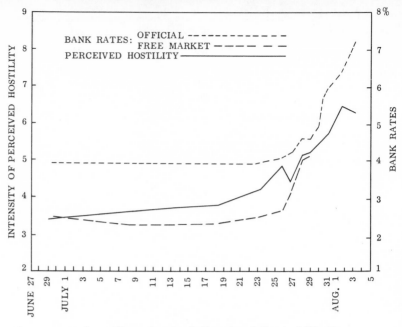

FIGURE 6   *Fluctuations in the Intensity of Perceived Hostility :*
Bank Rates

imagined."[17] Hence, "In a single moment all this wonderful machinery was broken or thrown out of gear."[18] Gold became a weapon of war, and as a result the free movement of gold was in effect abolished as an expedient of war. Major securities exchanges were closed to prevent a more ruinous panic; not even the New York Stock Exchange escaped the effects of war in Europe. The price of commodities came to depend on the rate of merchant ship sinkings rather than on the free market. Exchange rates reflected the outcomes of battles rather than the finely tuned system of international credit. The effects of the crisis on the shipping insurance business were characteristic of the inability of the old system to cope with the strains that had developed. Insurance rates for the last week of the crisis and the first week of the war are given in Table 9. It was only the establishment of the government War Risks Office on August 7, in effect replacing the old system with a new one, which broke the virtual paralysis in the shipping insurance industry. In the final days prior to the outbreak of general war, one observer, reflecting upon the closing of the London Stock Exchange, noted the inability of the international system to cope with the situation which was developing:

17 *The Economist,* August 1, 1914, p. 219.
18 *The Economist,* August 15, 1914, p. 302.

The Governments

Nothing, indeed, could have given a more dramatic touch, and nothing could have testified more clearly to the impossibility of running modern civilization and war together than this closing of the London Stock Exchange owing to a collapse of prices, produced not by the actual outbreak of a small war, but by the fear of war between some of the great powers of Europe.[19]

TABLE 9   SHIPPING INSURANCE RATES

Date	Rate per £100 value	Rate as % of value
July 28	5 shillings	0.25
July 31	60–80 shillings	3.0–4.0
August 4	10–15 guineas	10.5–15.8
August 6	20 giuneas	21.0
August 7	10 guineas	10.5
August 9	8 guineas	8.4
August 12	4 guineas	4.2
August 14	3 guineas	3.1

Source: *The Economist,* August 15, 1914, p. 304.

Conclusion

The analysis in this chapter has sought to determine whether we can have confidence in the validity of the content analysis data as a measure of decision-makers' attitudes and perceptions. In the absence of any feasible method of establishing validity directly, we have taken an indirect approach. Multiple indicators of the behavior of various financial elites revealed a pattern of responses to developments in Europe almost identical to that found through content analysis of the diplomatic documents. Moreover, there is clear evidence that when gold moved from London to the Continent, when stocks were sold at a loss, or when commodity futures were purchased, it was done in response to increasing apprehension about war in Europe. This analysis cannot, of course, establish beyond all possible doubt that the content analysis data provide a valid measure of decision-makers' attitudes and perceptions for every event, but it does buttress our confidence in the data on the 1914 crisis.

One further question may appear to emerge from this analysis. If there is a close correspondence between the attitudes of political elites (as revealed through content analysis of their messages) and various financial elites (as revealed in their behavior on the stock exchange and elsewhere), why not rely on the latter indices and forego the rather arduous task of content analyzing diplomatic documents?[20] In the first

[19] *The Economist,* August 1, 1914, p. 219.

[20] Such a suggestion has in fact been made, apparently in all seriousness, by a poiltical scientist. See Richard L. Merritt, "The Representational Model in Cross-National Content Analysis," in Joseph L. Bernd (ed.), *Mathematical Applications in Political Science* (Dallas: Southern Methodist Univ. Press, 1966).

place, financial indices of the type examined in this chapter respond to a variety of stimuli—some economic, some social, and some political. The stock market collapses of 1929, 1962, and 1966 in the United States, for example, were probably more closely related to internal than to international factors, and recent sales of gold by the Soviet Union are largely a response to agricultural difficulties. The evidence strongly suggests that, during the summer of 1914, financial indices reflected the state of international tensions, but such is not always the case. Moreover, while prices on the New York Stock Exchange or the value of the Swiss franc may still respond to dramatic international developments,[21] such data can no longer be gathered in many major world capitals—for example, in Moscow and Peking.

In summary, then, the findings reported in this chapter were intended to serve only a limited purpose—to serve as partial and indirect validators for the content analysis data from the 1914 documents. They are clearly *not* intended to provide a general purpose index of tensions in the international system which can be used in all situations.

[21] See, for example, the analysis of such financial indices during the Cuban missile crisis in, Ole R. Holsti, Richard A. Brody, and Robert C. North, "Measuring Affect and Action in International Reaction Models," *Peace Research Papers, II* (1965), 170–190.

The Governments

The
Goals
of
Foreign Policy

C H A P T E R   E I G H T

Arnold Wolfers

Reprinted with permission of the publishers from Arnold Wolfers, *Discord and Collaboration: Essays on International Politics* (Baltimore: The Johns Hopkins Press, 1963). pp. 67–80. The late Dr. Wolfers was Director of the Washington Center of Foreign Policy Research of the Johns Hopkins University.

It might seem that the mere existence of a multitude of nation-states, each capable of independent decision and action, would suffice to explain the peaceless state of the world and the power struggles that fill the international arena. Undoubtedly, the anarchical condition inherent in any system of multiple sovereignty constitutes one of the prerequisites of international conflict; without it, there could be no international relations, peaceful or nonpeaceful. Yet, in the last analysis, it is the goals pursued by the actors and the way they go about pursuing them that determine whether and to what extent the potentialities for power struggle and war are realized. This can be seen by imagining two extreme sets of conditions, both theoretically compatible with a multistate system, in which, as a consequence of the wide differences in the objectives pursued by the states in question as well as in the means they are willing to employ, the chances of peace would stand at opposite poles.

Starting at one pole, one can postulate a situation in which all actors are entirely satisfied with the established state of international affairs, and are content, therefore, to concern themselves exclusively with domestic matters. In this case, they would have no incentive to make or press demands on others. As a consequence, there would be no rational cause for conflict or for disturbances of the peace. Needless to say, this is a utopia. In some historical instances, however, conditions so nearly approached this extreme that to some observers the utopia appeared within reach, while in other times various schools of thought held it up as at least a goal toward which policy should be directed.

Thus, since the days of Cobden, free-traders have argued that if governments ceased to interfere with commercial activities across borders the chief source of international conflict would be removed. Others have pleaded insteal for economic autarchy which, by eliminating the need for international economic intercourse altogether, would make economic demands on others unnecessary. Then again, the satisfaction of demands for national self-determination, one of the cornerstones of Woodrow Wilson's peace strategy, was expected to eliminate a potent cause of international conflict. If every nation had the government of its choice and if every ethnic group were united within the boundaries of a single state, demands for more territory or for independence, objectives most conducive to war, would lose their *raison d'être*. It might be added that some have advocated policies of isolation and neutrality on the same grounds: a condition of dissociation among nations would reduce their interdependence and thus minimize the occasions for conflict. My purpose here is not to determine whether such policies are practical or desirable, but to draw attention to the close relationship between foreign policy objectives and the incidence of tension that might lead to a resort to violence.

This close relationship appears confirmed if one moves to the other pole and postulates that nations are engaged in making exacting demands on one another and are prepared to fight rather than give in. Actually, to be able to predict very serious threats to the peace, one need only assume that a single powerful actor within a multistate system is bent on attaining goals of territorial expansion or dominion over others, because resistance to any drive toward acquisitive goals of this nature is almost certain to materialize. The stage is thus set for clashes that justify a high expectation of violence.

Before looking into the kinds of goals or objectives that nations tend to pursue in their external activities, one semantic hurdle must be taken. It is customary to distinguish between goals and means, a custom I intend to follow to a certain extent; yet it is impossible to draw a sharp line of demarcation between the two ideas. All means can be said to constitute intermediary or proximate goals, and few goals if any can be considered ultimate, in the sense of being sought as ends in themselves. Even when a nation aims for a goal as highly valued as national independence, it can be argued that the nation is seeking such independence as a means of providing its citizens with benefits other than national independence itself.[1]

To make things more complicated, what constitutes a means or intermediate goal in one context may be a remote if not ultimate goal in another, with specific objectives changing places from one instance to another. Thus, enhanced power may be sought as a means of obtaining more territory, while the acquisition of more territory in turn may be desired as a means of enhancing national power. In the case of Europe prior to the establishment of NATO, the question was whether what was needed most was higher productivity as a means of increasing defensive strength or conversely whether more defensive strength providing a greater sense of security was not a prerequisite of greater efforts toward higher productivity.

Because the objectives a nation seeks to reach can range from the most immediate means to the most remote or ultimate ends, all goals will be taken to fall within the scope of this chapter with the single exception of power and influence. The justification for this exception should become clear when the unique position of these two values as the means *par excellence* for the attainment of all other foreign policy goals is discussed.[2]

[1] Percy Corbett, for instance, points out that "for democratic purposes it seems worthwhile to insist that the prime object of foreign policy...is the welfare of the individuals and groups organized as a national society" and goes on to conclude that "insofar as territorial integrity and political independence are judged to minister to that welfare, they may well be described as the mediate and instrumental objective to which foreign policy is especially directed." "National Interest, International Organization, and American Foreign Policy," *World Politics,* Vol. V, No. 1 (October, 1952), p. 51.

[2] Arnold Wolfers, *Discord and Collaboration* (Baltimore: The Johns Hopkins Press, 1962), Chap. 7, "Power and Influence: The Means of Foreign Policy."

The Goals of Foreign Policy

The fact that power may be turned into an end in itself will be taken into consideration in that connection.

Despite the difficulties and complications arising out of the way ends can serve one another as means, it often becomes necessary to inquire whether a nation is seeking certain results from its policy primarily for the results' own sake or merely as means of reaching more remote goals. If a nation is helping others through economic aid to raise their standard of living, it may make a great deal of difference for the chances that such aid will be continued or extended whether the nation extending the aid considers economic improvement abroad as being desirable in itself, or promotes it merely for the sake of cementing its alliance with the assisted country or of drawing that country over to its own side. To take another example, there has been uncertainty in Europe whether American support for European integration implies that the United States believes such integration to be a good thing in itself—worthy therefore of continued support, cold war or no cold war—or whether greater European unity is valued solely as a means of strengthening Western defenses. Then again, the importance of aim or purpose may be illustrated by a question that has led to much controversy. Some see the Soviet Union supporting revolutionary movements abroad because world revolution *per se* is the goal of Soviet policy; others maintain that the aim is to bolster the security of the Soviet Union as a nation-state, and the revolutions can count on Soviet support only when and where they are expected to enhance the power of the Soviet Union and its alliances. Frequently, of course, a single means can serve to promote two or more concurrent ends. The Soviet leaders being both the rulers of Russia and the leaders of world communism may be unable themselves to distinguish between their national and world revolutionary goals and interests.

As soon as one seeks to discover the place of goals in the means-end chain of relationships, almost inevitably one is led to probe into the dark labyrinth of human motives, those internal springs of conscious and unconscious actions which Morgenthau calls "the most illusive of psychological data."[3] Yet if one fails to inquire why actors choose their goals, one is forced to operate in an atmosphere of such abstraction that nothing is revealed but the barest skeleton of the real world of international politics.

It is understandable that historians have devoted so much time to probing the motives of actors. Although the success of an act such as an effort to pacify an area does not depend on the nature of the motivation, overt behavior remains unintelligible except in relation to motivation. An act of intervention may be the same in its outward appearance whether it is motivated by imperialist design or by the desire to help a people throw off the yoke of a tyrannical government. However, when other governments are making up their minds how to react to such intervention or deciding what to expect from the intervening nation in future con-

[3] Hans J. Morgenthau, *Politics Among Nations: The Struggle for Power and Peace,* 3rd ed., (New York: Alfred A. Knopf, Inc., 1960), p. 6.

The Governments

tingencies, they cannot avoid seeking to discover what it was that prompted the particular action.

If nations are seen to desire a wide variety of accomplishments and gains ranging all the way from such ambitious ends as empire or predominance to mere trade advantages, opportunities for cultural exchanges, or voting rights in international organizations, one might expect that whatever a nation values and can attain only from other nations will automatically be transformed into a foreign policy objective. This is not the case. Leading statesmen may give expression to hopes or ideals of their people, but these hopes do not, thereby, become what properly can be called policy goals. They will become goals only if the decision is reached that some national effort involving sacrifices, or the risk of sacrifices, is to be made for their realization. All goals are costly. Therefore an aspiration will not be turned into a policy goal unless it is sufficiently cherished by those who make and influence policy to justify the costs that its attainment is expected to require in terms of sacrifices. The American people, or influential Americans, may place high value on the liberation of satellite peoples; the question is whether such liberation is valued highly enough to turn it into an American foreign policy goal for which a high price possibly would be paid.

Picturing aspirations and goals at opposite poles is not accurate. One might better regard them as the two ends of a continuum that runs from mere hopes to goals of vital interest. "Liberation," declared a goal of American policy at the beginning of the Eisenhower Administration, is more than a mere hope as long as it is promoted by propaganda that risks enhancing East-West tension; when one speaks of peaceful liberation one implies that the goal is not considered vital enough to justify a resort to force. World revolution is not merely a hope, but a goal of Soviet foreign policy. Yet, while it may be close to the pole of vital goals usually assumed to justify the resort to violence, it may be sufficiently removed from this pole to keep Soviet policy-makers from initiating a war for the sake of its promotion. Statesmen are well advised to keep in mind that threats to the peace may arise if other nations are left uncertain whether or not national spokesmen who proclaim national aspirations have actually decided to turn a particular aspiration into a policy goal, possibly a goal deemed vital enough to warrant risking or sacrificing the peace.

In analyzing international politics, there would be no need to concern oneself with the problem of goals if nation-states were single-purpose organizations. If they were, states would never consent to make sacrifices for purposes—such as the promotion of peace—that obviously do not constitute their sole objective. It should be added, however, that even if foreign policy were directed predominantly toward a single goal, such a goal would not monopolize the entire activity of states, except in the extreme emergency of a war. Always there would remain the many domestic goals which no government can ignore and which compete for resources with whatever external purposes the nation may be pursuing. Often these domestic objectives place the severest restraints on external

137

The Goals of Foreign Policy

aspirations, as one can gather from any parliamentary debate in which the demand for financial appropriations to meet the needs of external pursuits runs up against demands to increase social benefits or to reduce taxes.

Appearances to the contrary, there is no division of opinion among analysts of international politics about the fact that the policy of nations aims at a multitude of goals. Some exponents of realist thought have been misunderstood to hold that power or even maximum power represents the only significant goal. Authors like Nicholas Spykman and Hans Morgenthau have contributed to this misapprehension, the first by stating on one occasion that "the improvement of the relative power position becomes the primary objective of the internal and the external policy of states,"[4] the latter by his statement that "the aspiration for power is the distinguishing element of international politics."[5] However, Morgenthau also stresses that power is only an immediate aim or chief means of foreign policy,[6] while Spykman, relating the quest for power to the task of survival, mentions the existence of other objectives that are "geographic, demographic, racial, ethnic, economic, social and ideological in nature."[7]

The goals of national independence, territorial integrity, and national survival which figure so large in the foreign policy of all nation-states are not uniform in scope or character and must, therefore, be treated as significant variables. Governments conceive of these cherished values in more or less moderate and in more or less ambitious and exacting terms. A good illustration is offered by colonial powers. Only those among them who insist that their "colonies"—or some of them—are not colonies at all but an integral part of their national territory are led to treat the preservation of these areas as a requirement of national survival and thus as a vital goal that justifies almost any sacrifice. The new postcolonial states present another illustration of differences in outlook among different actors. Some insist that any continuing ties with the mother country are unacceptable because such ties would defeat the goal of sovereign independence; others favor "union" or commonwealth types of association in the interest of economic welfare, provided the goal of sovereign equality is attained.

The goal of national survival itself is given a wide variety of interpretations by different countries or countries facing different conditions. Nations intent upon keeping their involvement in international conflicts at a minimum are inclined to consider their survival at stake only when their own territory comes under the threat of attack or actually is attacked. The idea of "indivisible peace" which would require them to participate in collective action against any aggressor anywhere has little appeal to them. In contrast, a nation engaged in a global struggle, as the United

[4] Nicholas John Spykman, *America's Strategy in World Politics: The United States and the Balance of Power* (New York: Harcourt, Brace & World, 1942), p. 18.
[5] Morgenthau, *op. cit.*, p. 31.
[6] *Ibid.*, p. 27.
[7] Spykman, *op. cit.*, p. 17.

The Governments

States is today, will tend to regard any shift in the balance of power that favors its adversary as at least an indirect threat to its own survival. As a consequence, it may consider its survival at stake in a conflict over remote and intrinsically unimportant islands such as Quemoy and Matsu or over legal rights in West Berlin on the ground that, by an assumed domino effect or chain reaction, defeat at any one point will lead to defeat at every other point, until in the end all chances of survival are nullified.

No attempt will be made here to identify and classify all the many goals that nations set for themselves or may set for themselves in the framework of their foreign policy. Instead, I shall limit myself to a discussion of what appear to be particularly significant and persistent groups of contrasting goals. Most of them are in the nature of dichotomies; in the case of the goals pertaining to the national "sell" and its accepted limits, however, a distinction into three categories has suggested itself. These will be treated in a later chapter as goals of national self-extension, national self-preservation, and national self-abnegation.[8]

One can distinguish goals pertaining, respectively, to national possessions and to the shape of the environment in which the nation operates. I call the former "possession goals," the latter "milieu goals." In directing its foreign policy toward the attainment of its possession goals, a nation is aiming at the enhancement or the preservation of one or more of the things to which it attaches value. The aim may apply to such values as a stretch of territory, membership in the Security Council of the United Nations, or tariff preferences. Here a nation finds itself competing with others for a share in values of limited supply; it is demanding that its share be left intact or be increased. Because of the possessive nature of these goals, they are apt to be praised by some for being truly in the national interest, while condemned by others as indicating a reprehensible spirit of national selfishness or acquisitiveness.

Milieu goals are of a different character. Nations pursuing them are out not to defend or increase possessions they hold to the exclusion of others, but aim instead at shaping conditions beyond their national boundaries. If it were not for the existence of such goals, peace could never become an objective of national policy. By its very nature, peace cannot be the possession of any one nation; it takes at least two to make and have peace. Similarly, efforts to promote international law or to establish international organizations, undertaken consistently by many nations, are addressed to the milieu in which nations operate and indeed such efforts make sense only if nations have reason to concern themselves with things other than their own possessions.[9]

[8] Wolfers, *op. cit.*, Chap. 6, "The Pole of Power and the Pole of Indifference."
[9] Dean Acheson expresses approval of the pursuit of such goals by the United States "so as to maintain an environment favorable to our interests" (*A Democrat Looks at His Party*, Harper & Bros., New York, 1955, p. 62). Writing in the same vein, Paul A. Nitze says that the United States "can no longer look merely to its narrow competitive interests within whatever structure happens, from time to time, to exist as a result of the policy and will of others or as a result of the chance operations of impersonal forces. If this is so, it follows that a basic objective of U.S.

The Goals of Foreign Policy

Milieu goals often may turn out to be nothing but a means or a way station toward some possession goal. A nation may hope to increase its prestige or its security by making sacrifices for the establishment and maintenance of international organizations. But this need not be its exclusive aim. Instead, the nation in question may be seriously concerned about the milieu within which it operates and may expect such organizations to improve the environment by making it more peaceful or more conducive to social or economic progress. Here for once the analogy with the behavior and interests of individuals should not be misleading. A man is rightly considered not merely selfish but shortsighted in terms of his own interests if he puts all his efforts into the accumulation and protection of his possessions while remaining indifferent to the peace and order, the public health and well-being of the community in which he resides or works. These are aspects of his milieu, as the term is used here. It is one thing to be in good physical or financial condition within an orderly and prosperous community, but quite another thing to be privileged by the wealth of one's possessions in surroundings of misery, ill health, lack of public order, and widespread resentment. The difference need not be one only of greater or lesser security of acquired possessions; it may also signify a difference in happiness, in future opportunities, and perhaps in moral satisfaction.

Nations also face these differences in their milieu, although it is up to them to decide to what extent they wish to devote their resources to the benefits they may hope to derive from helping to preserve or improve conditions prevailing beyond their borders. There is bound to be competition here with the demands that their goals of possession, some of them pressing and vital, make on the limited national resources. Statesmen and peoples called upon to allot priorities among goals that belong to these two categories often face trying dilemmas. Recent debates on aid to underdeveloped countries supply ample material to illustrate these dilemmas. Is it desirable to divert, to the promotion of a more friendly environment or to the satisfaction of a generous public impulse to help underprivileged peoples, funds that otherwise might go into the build-up of military forces?

In considering this question, one might be tempted to substitute for "milieu goals" the term international goals. There is, however, danger in using the word international here because it might suggest either that these goals are not in the national interest or that governments can and should pursue goals other than those concerning the national interest.[10]

---

foreign policy is the creation and maintenance of a system of world order within which U.S. interests and U.S. security can find their satisfaction." (Annex A, "The Purpose of United States Military and Economic Assistance," from the *Study* submitted to the President's Committee to Study the United States Military Assistance Program, March, 1959).

[10] Thomas Cook and Malcolm Moos (*Power Through Purpose: The Realism of Idealism as a Basis for Foreign Policy,* The Johns Hopkins Press, Baltimore, 1954, p. 138), declaring that nations should substitute "international interests" for the traditional interests, claim that the American people's "root concern" and "ultimate

The Governments

The likelihood of milieu goals being also in the national interest of other countries does not make them less valuable; it only points up that nations find themselves sharing common interests. If some critics of milieu goals expect their country always to be the loser if it engages in costly efforts by which others benefit, they fail to realize that any promotion of peace or international lawfulness, any fight against the trade in narcotics or the spread of epidemics, to cite only a few examples, depends on concerted efforts by many nations—and such efforts are not likely to be forthcoming unless they are in the common interest.

Not all criticism of efforts directed toward milieu goals can, however, be discounted in this fashion. Frequently enthusiasm for such goals stems from an inclination to downgrade certain values that nations cherish highly—and need not be ashamed to cherish—such as adequate national security and its military prerequisites. Thus, nations have been advised to act on the principle of collective security, in the strict sense of the term, in order to help create a milieu in which threats to national possessions will cease to arise. But even assuming that such a milieu would be created, it is at best a long-run goal. In the meantime much can happen to a nation that diverts its limited military power from the task of protecting itself against immediate and specific threats to the task of "police action" in places where its survival is not at stake.

Another case of what may turn out often to be excessive zeal for a milieu goal takes the form of advice to wealthy countries to concentrate on lessening mass poverty and economic maldistribution throughout the world. Here again, immediate needs of self-preservation, which include the need for internal unity and public support of the government, place limits on the extent to which the pursuit of this goal is rational under given circumstances.

It has been argued that it is incompatible with the essence of national statehood to devote efforts to the creation of a "better world for all to live in." There is nothing, however, in the functions the nation-state performs to prevent it from engaging in acts of altruism if its people or its rulers so desire and if in the judgment of its leaders it can afford to do so. A government that had assured its country of adequate security would not be violating its duties if it extended help to friendly nations without concern for the advantages its own country might expect to gain in return. Whether such altruistic acts are likely to occur, or whether, if a government claimed credit for them, its motives would be found to have been as pure as one were asked to believe, is another question. Acts of national foreign policy expressing a generous and sympathetic impulse— as was surely the case when the United States launched the Marshall

---

concept" is the "spreading and sharing...of its societal blessing." They are pleading, in other words, for "milieu goals" as a substitute for national possession goals on the ground that the latter consist exclusively of the goals of national glory and aggrandizement, values alien to the American people. They disregard the fact that no nation could hope to survive if it failed to be concerned about its own independence and territorial integrity, core possession of all nation-states.

The Goals of Foreign Policy

Plan—usually will be found to have served the national security interest or economic interest of the donor as well. The same is true, too, of many acts of individual generosity and charity which may pay high "dividends" to the donor and yet be a moral credit to him. But while an altruistic act by an individual is likely to benefit the actor more if he is not conscious of serving his own interests too, usually when nations are involved suspicion of hypocrisy will be easily aroused; self-righteous claims of pure benevolence, by hurting the pride of others, will diminish the desirable effect of greater amity. For this reason it is wise for governments and peoples to be aware of—and in fact to stress—the element of national self-interest, however farsighted, that leads nations to improve the milieu by rendering services to others.

Another distinction between contrasting goals has been touched upon earlier: the distinction between goals arising from interests of the citizens as private individuals and from state interests, respectively.[11] While it was denied that state interests were the interests of a nonhuman Leviathan, nevertheless a significant difference exists between goals meant primarily to serve the nation as a state or territorial entity and goals that are of prime interest to individual citizens or groups of citizens in their private capacity. If the latter benefit the nation as a whole, this can only be in an indirect fashion. Therefore, I call the first "direct national goals," the second, "indirect national goals."

Some goals like national independence or national security unmistakably are direct national goals. They have no meaning for men as private individuals except as these individuals identify themselves with their nation-state. The erection of tariff barriers, on the contrary, is of interest primarily to those private groups that expect to profit from tariff protection and it may or may not be advantageous to the nation as a whole. When tariff protection is made the objective of national policy, it becomes an indirect national goal.

There is no yardstick by which to decide whether the promotion of any particular interest of larger or smaller groups of citizens deserves to be turned into a national goal, but it would be absurd to maintain that no goal can be in the national interest unless it is of the direct type. In a democratic society the state is not regarded as an end in itself or as an absolute good. We assume that the state must justify itself by its ability to insure such values as liberty, welfare, and happiness to its citizens. Although in promoting such values the nation usually will benefit some people more than others and frequently even serve some at the expense of others—as in the case of tariffs, subsidies, or bars to immigration—this inequity does not in itself militate against such promotion. It greatly increases the difficulty, however, of deciding what is and what is not in the interest of the nation as a whole. Not everything that is good for General Motors—or for the auto workers—is good for the nation, but it can be.

[11] Wolfers, *op. cit.*, Chap. 1, "The Actors in International Politics."

It should be pointed out that indirect national goals are not a peculiarity of democratic foreign policy although they are alien to Communist countries in which private interests have no place at all. But a difference between democratic and autocratic countries may show up in the kind of private interests believed worthy of becoming an object of national concern. While in modern mass democracies the interests assumed to be those of the general public (or the common man) are likely to qualify for national support, in more stratified societies it is the interests of certain minorities, ruling groups, or economic elites that will tend to be identified with the interests of the nation.[12]

Indirect national goals present a problem similar to the milieu goals. They, too, can absorb more of a nation's efforts and resources than is compatible with the vital needs of national security or power. The danger is particularly serious in the case of indirect goals because of the influence that subnational pressure groups are capable of exerting on their behalf.

There is bound to be controversy in instances in which, in the absence of a clear-cut national emergency, the question of priority arises with respect to possession and milieu goals or to direct and indirect national goals. Such controversy reflects differences in value patterns as well as in estimates of what the situation requires. Nowhere more than here does it become evident how little guidance policy-makers can gain simply from being referred to the "national interest." Countries presently partitioned offer a striking illustration of the dilemmas governments and nations face when setting these priorities. Reunification has become a pressing possession goal for these partitioned countries. The core value of territorial integrity is at stake. Yet most Germans seem to agree with the official view of the West German government according to which the goal of preserving the freedoms West Germans enjoy under a democratic constitution—an indirect national goal—should be given precedence over German reunification. If the restoration of the former territorial integrity of the country enjoyed top priority among German national goals, West Germany could bring it about at the price of turning Communist and joining the Soviet camp.

There come to mind other circumstances in which an indirect national goal might gain precedence even over what were formerly regarded as national core values. In the case of a threat of nuclear devastation some governments might be led to decide—or be forced by public opinion to decide—that surrender rather than defense offers the only chance for the nation to survive in any meaningful sense of the term. Here, then, the indirect national goal of keeping citizens alive and their possessions intact would have won over the goal of national self-preservation in the traditional sense.

---

[12] Charles Beard in *The Open Door At Home: A Trial Philosophy of National Interest* (Macmillan Co., New York, 1935) discusses under the labels "industrialist statecraft" and "agrarian statecraft" the way powerful sections of the population succeed in making the promotion of their special interests the goal of a policy parading as a policy of the national interest.

One further pair of contrasting categories of goals deserves attention. It makes sense, especially in our era, to distinguish between ideological or revolutionary goals on the one hand and traditional national goals on the other. The example that comes to mind is that of Communist governments which, it is widely assumed, engage their countries in efforts to promote the universalist goal of worldwide victory for communism whether or not their countries as nation-states with a territorial base and with distinct security interests stand to gain by such efforts. There is no way of proving, however, that the Soviet Union while claiming to promote the cause of international communism actually consents to sacrifices that would not be justified by the way in which its leaders interpret the Soviet national interest. In assisting "wars of liberation," for instance, the Soviet Union may hope to gain friends or allies for itself while simultaneously helping history along its predestined path toward a Communist world. The Soviet leaders themselves may not be able to distinguish between their national goals and their revolutionary or universalist goals because ever since Lenin declared Russia to be the "Fatherland of the Revolution" they have been able to claim, sometimes to the dismay of Communists abroad, that what was good for Russia—and only what was good for Russia—was good for communism. It seems evident however, that Communist doctrine colors Soviet thinking so strongly that the interpretation of what constitutes a Soviet national interest, as well as the Soviet image of the outside world, is strongly affected by the doctrine.

The Communist governments are not the only governments that are influenced by universalist ideological causes and are therefore ready to engage in efforts unappealing to nation-states of nineteenth-century European vintage. Some of the more revolutionary neutralist leaders, as will be discussed in a later chapter,[13] carry on their fight against colonialism even after their own countries have gained independence. When this happens these leaders place their states in the service of the transnational cause of abolishing Western colonial rule everywhere. Similarly, and even prior to Woodrow Wilson, the United States has engaged in policies directed toward spreading democracy abroad, especially by promoting the institution of free elections in other countries.[14] While much of the declaratory policy by which governments claim to be pursuing such lofty ends as self-determination for all peoples, or a world safe for democracy, may be either hypocritical or a matter of self-delusion, it would be as difficult to argue that Woodrow Wilson was acting in behalf of specific American interests when he struggled to get the Covenant of the League of Nations into the Versailles Treaty as it would be to assert that Lenin after becoming head of the Russian government placed its power and prestige exclusively in the service of national as against world revolutionary objectives. However, although men like Lenin and Wilson, who were motivated to an exceptional

13 Wolfers, *op. cit.*, Chap. 14, "Allies, Neutrals, and Neutralists."
14 See Theodore Wright's discussion of this policy in his article on "Free Elections in the Latin American Policy of the United States," *Political Science Quarterly*, Vol. LXXIV, No. 1 (March, 1959).

The Governments

degree by revolutionary or ideological fervor, were able to inject a universalist element into the policy of their respective countries, events in their own lifetimes demonstrated the persistent predominance of the concern with strictly national interests: it was not long before the Soviet Union, following its Czarist predecessors, was to struggle to keep the Dardanelles open to Soviet shipping and before the United States was to refuse to join the League of Nations.

The Role

of

Political

Style:

A Study of

Dean Acheson

C H A P T E R   N I N E

David S. McLellan

Reprinted with permission of the publishers from Roger Hilsman and Robert C. Good (eds.), *Foreign Policy in the Sixties* (Baltimore: The Johns Hopkins Press, 1965), pp. 229–56. Mr. McLellan is Professor of Political Science at the University of California, Riverside.

If we are to judge a Secretary of State in the performance of the responsibilities of the office it is first essential to stipulate the criteria by which we propose to do so.[1] There have been many biographies of diplomats and Secretaries of State, but few if any have attempted a systematic assessment of the individual's performance in the light of the scope and functions of the office. Furthermore while most such biographies probe into the actor's childhood, education, and career-line experience, very rarely do they undertake a systematic examination of the actor's mode of leadership, decision-making, and configuration of policy in the light of such biographical factors. And yet foreknowledge of an actor's personality in its public dimension ought to help illuminate the character of his leadership and decisions.

What then are some of the elements by which we may examine and distinguish Dean Acheson's performance from that of other Secretaries of State? Here we are on thin ice, indeed.

According to Alexander de Conde the principal functions of the American Secretary of State are two in number. First, it is his responsibility to seek the attainment of ends generally understood under the rubric of the national interest. Secondly, in the process of defining and maintaining the national interest, the Secretary of State must act within the limitations of a definite number of roles—as chief adviser to the President, as the advocate of the President's policies before the Congress and before other executive officers, as administrator of the Department of State, and as the figure principally responsible for the conduct of United States relations with foreign countries.

The choices that a statesman makes from among the alternative modes of political behavior and perspective available to him will determine how he defines the national interest, mobilizes support, and fulfills the functions of the office. For example, the manner in which a Secretary of State views the office and the function of government will generally exercise a subtle influence upon his performance. Similarly a statesman's concept of leadership accounts for much. He may either act upon the principle that a statesman's task is to provide leadership based upon understanding the requirements of correct and effective action, or he may assume that the statesman's function is to reflect the views of his constituents.

The character of a statesman's performance will also be shaped by the

[1] I am indebted to Deane E. Neubauer for intellectual assistance and to Bette Forest for her aid in editing the manuscript.

The Role of Political Style

manner in which he reacts to problems. A Secretary of State may either respond by attempting to maintain the *status quo* by the application of legalistic formulae, as James Byrnes attempted to do in dealing with the Soviets, or his performance may be characterized by a willingness to innovate when faced by new and challenging problems. This in turn will depend to a great degree upon his confidence in organized social intelligence to produce answers and to resolve or control problems. Finally, the Secretary of State's performance will depend upon the degree to which his assumptions about international politics correspond to reality. A statesman who deduces the national interest and the line of policy from a priori principles will differ fundamentally from one who eschews abstract principle in favor of a pragmatic approach. Neither view is capable of full implementation because the moralist is, by necessity, bound to bump up against conflicting principles and the pragmatist operates with some sense of an ultimate goal which implies moral purpose; nevertheless each perspective colors and may fundamentally alter the conduct of foreign relations.

In summary the statesman's attitude toward the sphere of politics and toward government, his conception of leadership, his capacity for innovation, his confidence in organized social intelligence, and his view of international politics are the elements which energize a statesman's performance and determine his definition of the national interest. They also help the Secretary of State define the role of the office and inform the choices he makes in mobilizing support and choosing among alternative policies. To govern is to choose and each Secretary of State's performance is characteristically a configuration of the way in which his perspectives and attitudes about government, leadership, innovation, reason, and the nature of world politics contribute to his choices from among alternative modes. The manner of performance that a statesman assumes and which imparts a distinctiveness to his handling of the office I shall call "style."

Since the standards and modes of performance that a leader relies upon in public office are generally those which he has acquired as he moves out of his family circle into the wider arena to build the reputation which has made him eligible for high public office, the statesman's social class, education, and career-line experience hold important clues to his later performance. Let us now examine Acheson's performance in the light of the choices that his personality characteristically led him to make from among the alternative modes of political behavior and leadership.

I. Government

There are few extant expressions of Acheson's conception of government, but one in particular fits in with what we know of his career. In a letter discussing why young men might be encouraged to choose a career in government service, Acheson wrote, "A career in public service is rewarding because there is no better or fuller life for a man of spirit. The old

148

Greek conception of happiness is relevant here: 'The exercise of vital powers along lines of excellence, in a life affording them scope.' "[2] Far from regarding government as a rather second rate career Acheson seems to have had a higher regard for it than for his lucrative career as a corporation lawyer. Acheson took to Groton a lively social conscience inherited from his father, the Episcopal Bishop of Connecticut. His youthful admiration for "Teddy" Roosevelt and Woodrow Wilson opened his eyes to government as a career worthy of a young gentleman's ambitions. Somewhere in those early years he appears to have established the relationship between individual excellence, which he had always sought, and active participation in political life. This is to be seen in his persistent willingness to serve in government posts despite the frustrations and hazards which such service involved, especially during the 1930's and 1940's. Even when he was forced to resign as Under Secretary of the Treasury in 1934 as the result of a clash with Roosevelt over monetary policy (FDR's decision to drop the gold standard), Acheson did not let the incident destroy his respect for government. Unlike Raymond Moley, Lewis Douglas, Walter Lippmann, and others who broke with FDR in the early years of the New Deal, Acheson continued to view the creative role of government as essential to the well-being of society.

Out of Acheson's difficulties with Roosevelt in 1934 came his extremely close relationship with Truman. Subsequent to his resignation as Under Secretary of the Treasury Acheson regretted very deeply his behavior in the gold episode.

I wasn't particularly well satisfied with my performance in it. It wasn't that what I had done was wrong...[but] I did not have enough consideration for the problems of the President....Whether I was all right or not it warned me that there are terrible problems that an assistant to the President can get into by allowing things to get to the point where trouble occurs, and that therefore one ought to be very alert and watchful to consider his position and interests twice as much as one's own.[3]

As a result of this chastising experience Acheson approached the Truman relationship with a keen sense of the President's problems and the delicacy of his prestige. "My troubles with F.D.R. had a very deep and very lasting effect on my judgment in many things."[4] Among other things Acheson's respect for the Presidency led him to discourage James Forrestal from surreptitiously establishing a role for the cabinet outside the purview of the President.

Acheson speaks now with considerable regret of the years from 1934 to 1940 when he was obliged to stand on the sidelines while others played the great game of politics. He eagerly returned to government in 1941 when Roosevelt appointed him Assistant Secretary of State for Economic Affairs. It is characteristic of Acheson's zealous regard for governmental

[2] Paul Nitze, "The Role of the Learned Man in Government," *Review of Politics*, Vol. 20, p. 282.
[3] Princeton Seminar: transcript of a seminar held at Princeton University, 1953–54, with Mr. Dean Acheson participating.
[4] *Ibid.*

service that during the war years he labored unflaggingly in a post far removed from the center of high diplomacy then being conducted from the White House. Instead of drama, his post called for unremitting efforts to maintain America's wartime economic operations amidst a miasma of conflicting authority and red tape. Acheson only began to emerge into the public limelight in connection with the Bretton Woods Agreements which he helped to shape and negotiate.

If one were to try to account for Acheson's high regard for government, his legal career in Washington would need to be given considerable weight. If Acheson's respect for government was not already in bloom by the time he arrived in Washington to become Justice Brandeis' law clerk (1919–21), it undoubtedly blossomed under the influence of that champion of the public interest against the claims of unconfined and irresponsible economic power. One finds in Acheson's writings—as in Brandeis'—the view that government is an indispensable agent for helping men maintain an open society in which all may participate in defining the ends for which society exists. In fact Acheson goes a step further than Brandeis. Recognizing the complexity of modern society Acheson accepts the possibility that government must actively intervene to provide men with the knowledge of the means to attain social ends which are unattainable by private means. This must be done in such a way as to avoid giving government unrestrained and arbitrary power so that it, in turn, becomes a menace to the ends which it exists to serve. It is precisely the challenge of coping with these questions that seems to have motivated Acheson's enduring interest in government.

Oliver Wendell Holmes was another influence on Acheson during the twenties, and no one familiar with Acheson's mind and writings can doubt the influence of that worldly skeptic. But unlike Holmes, Acheson refused to withdraw to the Olympian heights of the bench. When Roosevelt told Acheson he was sending his name up to the Senate for appointment to the Washington Circuit Court of Appeals, Acheson was indignant. "Would you like to be a judge?" he queried Roosevelt. Whatever FDR answered, Acheson retorted, "Well neither would I," and with that made clear his commitment to the life of political action.[5]

Acheson's fierce pride in government and respect for its intrinsic worth and distinction is nowhere better revealed than in a speech attacking Wendell Willkie's quest for the Presidency in 1940. To Willkie's claim that the war required a production engineer in the White House, Acheson replied: "Government is not a branch of manufacturing. The leadership of a people is not learned by designing an assembly line. Churchill has never produced anything, if by 'anything' Mr. Willkie means electric current or business deals. . . . We are not voting for a production manager, we are voting for a President."[6] Acheson expressed the view more than once during the pre-Pearl Harbor years that the disaster which overtook

[5] Personal interview, Sept. 8, 1959.
[6] Speech in support of re-election of President Roosevelt, Radio Station WBAL, Baltimore, Md., Nov. 1, 1940.

The Governments

the West could have been averted had the democratic governments really been leading instead of following public opinion.

Acheson then possesses a lofty notion of government. To demonstrate how that influence was a significant factor in Acheson's style, we must provide evidence of the policy consequences of his view of government.

It is generally accepted that the years from 1946 to 1952 witnessed a revolution in American foreign policy. Less than ten years after a probable majority of Americans could still support the isolationist side in the debate over events leading up to World War II, the United States was the center of history's most far-reaching set of alliances. Almost overnight it had become the leader of the non-Communist world, which it endeavored to support by costly policies of economic and military assistance. It is doubtful if such a transformation could have been carried out had there not been leaders such as Acheson whose profound regard for government enabled them to use its capacity for ordering and stabilizing international politics.

Many of Acheson's "difficulties" with Congress also derived from his lofty conception of government. Acheson is convinced that the Congress is neither organized nor inspired to participate in the making of foreign policy as a fully responsible partner. Acheson sensed all too keenly that its collective and individual attitudes, conditioned as they were by the defense of local and parochial interests or by an anti-governmental philosophy, were out of phase with requirements for the sane and sensible conduct of foreign affairs. Furthermore, the power of Congress is farmed out to a score of congressional committees. Acheson quickly perceived that because of the excessive dependence in Congress upon committees, the Secretary of State need only concentrate upon a few key members of a few key committees to secure enactment of foreign policy. Contemptuous of the parochialism and petty politicking of its rank and file and knowing that he could secure passage of what he wanted by even a hostile Congress, Acheson took little care to hide his sentiments behind the mask of artifice and false good fellowship.

In this regard Acheson was extremely sensitive to the efforts of some congressmen to reduce the issues of international relations to the personal and parochial. During the hearings on the Bretton Woods Agreements when he was confronted by a series of utterances deprecating the honesty and good faith of the other signatories, Acheson burst out: "Who are we to sit around and suspect the motives of countries with whom we agree we must cooperate."[7] Whenever senators queried him about what America's allies were contributing toward mutual security, Acheson always reminded them that relations among sovereign states and allies could not be carried on in a bargain basement spirit, that governments conducted their policies with something in mind other than getting a return on their money. He goaded congressmen, not always successfully it must be added, to raise their sights to the level of statecraft. He lacked the indispensable political

[7] U.S., Congress, House, Committee on Banking and Currency, *Bretton Woods Agreement Act,* 79th Cong., 1st Sess., p. 63.

gift for believing that every argument has an equally legitimate intellectual background.[8]

This did not endear him to men whose political behavior was conditioned by the defense of local and parochial interests or by an anti-governmental philosophy. Senator Taft and his cohorts were irritated by the singular vehemence with which Acheson dismissed their argument that the main line of American security lay with a balanced budget. Since any efforts to explain the political and strategic "facts of life" to them always met with incredulity and doctrinaire resistance, he finally gave up even the pretense of trying to discuss the issues rationally. These men preferred to deal with a man like Louis Johnson who was willing to cut the military budget if he thought it would advance his presidential aspirations. Although Acheson was hardly a New Deal "braintruster" (his confirmation as Under Secretary of the Treasury had been opposed because of his alleged connections with reactionary Wall Street interests), his zealous regard for the integrity of government policy made him the symbol of excessive governmental authority or, in the words of one conservative senator, "the very heart of the octopus itself."[9]

Similarly members of the Fourth Estate (especially the columnists) were offended by Acheson's refusal to let them plunder the State Department at will for news stories. As Reston put it, Mr. Acheson had "an exceedingly high conception of the office of Secretary of State,"[10] meaning that he wasn't willing to take Reston into his confidence.

Again, Acheson's refusal to hand up sacrificial victims to the House Un-American Activities Committee reflected a regard for the integrity of government service not always shared even by his illustrious successor. All in all Acheson's conception of government and his style of conduct resembled too much Plato's "selfless instrument" to please this array of powerful interests.

Acheson's conception of government led him to value the advice of the expert over that of the legislator. It seems clear that Mr. Acheson's determination to be guided by the expertise and intelligence available to him in the Department of State created the impression, according to Senator Knowland, of a "Poppa knows best" attitude that many senators resented. In his determination to conduct foreign policy according to the highest canons of excellence, Mr. Acheson ignored Woodrow Wilson's prophetic words that the man of excellence can succeed in politics only if he possesses the power of persuasion. "Men are not led," declared Wilson, "by being told what they don't know. Persuasion is a force, but not information; and persuasion is accomplished by creeping into the confidence of those you would lead."[11] Obviously Dean Acheson was not

8 Personal interview with Lord Franks, Worcester College, Oxford, Eng., June 27, 1964.

9 James Rosenau, *The Senate and Dean Acheson: A Case Study in Legislative Attitudes* (Ph.D. thesis, Princeton University, May, 1957).

10 Personal interview, June 16, 1960.

11 Woodrow Wilson, *Leaders of Men,* edited with an introduction and notes by T. H. Vail Motter (Princeton: Princeton University Press, 1959), p. 39.

The Governments

interested in creeping into anyone's confidence. He chose to command by the force of his logic. In other times and perhaps with a different President, Acheson might have been able to succeed in his relations with the Senate. Truman's failure, however, to fully perform the presidential function of mobilizing public support behind his administration's foreign policy left Acheson terribly exposed in his relations with the Congress. What surprises us is that in the face of a hostile Congress Acheson accomplished as much as he did.

Acheson's sensitivity to the importance and distinctiveness of government found its most successful outlet in international affairs. It is reflected most characteristically in his belief that international relations is a sphere of human intercourse in which only governments can come to any stable, lasting argreements. Acheson always supported the United Nations as an institution, but he never felt that it embodied those attributes of sovereignty and power which alone afford the basis for any real agreement in international politics. In accordance with the same principle he never allowed such notions as the conscience of mankind or the pressure for an ideological crusade to blind him to the reality that governments were, after all, still the final and effective expression of their people's consciences and interests and that until something occurred to alter that relationship the United States had better rely upon governments rather than abstract principles for the adjustment of its interests. Where he departed from this principle as, for example, in his refusal to recognize the Chinese People's Republic, it was no doubt reluctantly and under the extreme political pressure of the times.

While his energies were constantly directed toward encouraging Europeans as well as Americans to transcend the limitations of parochial nationalism, he recognized that the only stable basis for such advances lay in the hard currency of governmental agreements. The skill with which Acheson wove the lines of diplomacy into an effective system of Western security is accounted for by his sensitivity to the realities upon which government and international politics are based. As we shall see at a later point, Acheson's superb understanding of the creative potentialities of government contributed immensely to the confident and authoritative style with which he inspired other statesmen and secured their cooperation in delicate and trying diplomatic ventures.

II. Leadership

Every leader operates according to some principle of leadership. In evaluating situations, making policy choices, and in carrying them out, each leader consciously or unconsciously expresses a characteristic mode of leadership. He may believe that his best prospects for success are to be found in keeping his policies in harmony with the prevailing desires of his constituents; or he may feel more at ease when he is molding public opinion to accept policies based upon knowledge and intelligence; or he may assume that there is no problem connected with leadership, that the "office" itself provides the necessary support for whatever needs to be accomplished.

A life dedicated to the pursuit of excellence and to respect for intellect and reason as crucial to the affairs of men engendered in Acheson a conception of leadership strikingly adapted to deal with problems of foreign policy, but peculiarly at odds with American political institutions and mores. We can most readily grasp Acheson's conception of leadership if we recall Plato's classic model of political leadership. In a discussion marked by a bitterness of tone rarely found elsewhere in the dialogues, Plato demands of Callicles if the ruler is merely to reflect the views of his constituents and practice such arts as will enable him to persuade them of the wisdom of whatever legislation or action best serves his own ends, or whether it is not the function of the ruler to cultivate the pursuit of knowledge and to act solely with regard to the requirements of correct and just action. "Does it seem to you," Plato has Socrates ask of Callicles,

> that orators always speak with an eye on what is best and aim at this: that their fellow citizens may receive the maximum improvement through their words? Or do they, like poets, strive to gratify their fellows, and in seeking their own private interests, do they neglect the common good, dealing with public assemblies as though the constituents were children, trying only to gratify them, and caring not at all whether this procedure makes them better or makes them worse.

Acheson shared Plato's belief that it is the task of the statesman to discover the best possible policy and not merely to carry out the mandate of the people. Unlike Plato, however, he did not shrink from competition in the political arena to establish and maintain the loftier view.

Time and again in his pre-1949 utterances Acheson revealed a marked contempt and aversion for the principle that leadership involves representing the lowest common denominator of constituency desires. In an address given at Yale University, November 28, 1939, Acheson decried the American lack of will to resist the totalitarian powers (including Russia): "We should stop analyzing ourselves—stop Gallup polling ourselves—and start analyzing the needs of our situation and the potentialities of our power."[12] In the spring of 1946 he deplored the tendency of Americans to ascertain their convictions by "this mass temperature taking [polling]" and expressed the conviction that only leadership possessed of will and courage could meet the crisis that Americans faced in international affairs.[13]

About this same time Acheson gave a startling demonstration of what he meant. General MacArthur made an unauthorized statement to the effect that the occupation of Japan could be greatly curtailed in view of the docility with which the Japanese were accepting their defeat. The circumstances at the time were such that every congressman was under

---

[12] "An American Attitude Toward Foreign Affairs," speech to Annual Dinner of Davenport College, Yale University, Nov. 28, 1939.

[13] "Random Harvest," speech to Associated Harvard Clubs, Boston, Mass., 1946.

The Governments

pressure to bring the boys home. MacArthur's statement had the effect of contributing to this pressure and thereby undermining the policy of the government in a very delicate and crucial area. The Pentagon prudently avoided rebuking MacArthur publicly and even President Truman was cautious in his public criticism of the hero. By contrast, Under Secretary of State Dean Acheson blasted the impropriety of MacArthur's statement. When Senator Wherry endeavored to make Acheson retract his criticism of MacArthur, Acheson curtly rebuffed him. Wherry never forgot nor forgave Acheson's forthright rejection of his defense of MacArthur.

It is not surprising, therefore, that once he had become Secretary of State, Acheson acted upon the assumption that the guideline to foreign policy is not public opinion, or even congressional opinion, but the relatively objective knowledge of the expert and that his task was to make that knowledge the basis of action. At best, this is a difficult principle to uphold under the conditions of American society. It was rendered even more difficult because Acheson was not equipped, either by temperament or by conviction, to employ the techniques of public relations which had served FDR so successfully. His first few press conferences were brilliant affairs, but Acheson soon lost his zest for a function in which he sensed an inherent conflict between maintaining the integrity of political action and the type of information which the press wanted. In a revealing interview with James Reston on his last day in office Acheson explained why he and Reston had not enjoyed better working relations. Reston expressed the conviction that had Acheson been more willing to confide in the press, some of the rip tides of adverse publicity which had swirled around him could have been avoided and a greater effectiveness of communications achieved. Secretary Acheson explained that "what Reston suggested would have been impossible since there was a basic conflict of purpose between the two." "A Secretary of State," Acheson said, "has to germinate new policies and to nurse them along until they have reached the stage of development where they can withstand the battering assault of the political arena. The reporter's primary purpose, on the other hand, is to get news for his paper, no matter what the effect on policy."[14]

So great was Acheson's contempt for pandering to public opinion that it pained him to have to seem to justify policy to the public. Here is a strikingly characteristic expression of this attitude:

The United States, in my judgment, acts in regard to a foreign nation strictly in regard to American interests or those wider interests which affect American interests. And if it is to American interests or those wider interests which affect it, to do one thing in one country and another thing in another then that is the consistency upon which I propose to advise the President, and I am not in the slightest bit worried because somebody can say: "Well you said so and so about Greece, why isn't this true about China?" I will be patient, and I will try to explain why Greece is not China, but my heart will not be in that battle.[15]

[14] Douglas Cater, *The Fourth Branch of Government* (Boston: Houghton Mifflin Co., 1959), p. 20.

[15] Quoted in Norman Graebner, "Dean G. Acheson," in *An Uncertain Tradition*, ed. Norman Graebner (New York: McGraw-Hill Book Co., 1961), p. 281.

Attitudes such as these cut Acheson off from many of the channels that are normally open to the decision maker in the process of eliciting support for his policies.

Acheson's relations with Congress present us with much the same dilemma. Did Acheson fail to permit the Senate to participate effectively in the policy process, or were the attacks upon him inspired solely by partisanship and personal malice? Findings by James Rosenau on the basis of a content analysis of everything said about Acheson on the floor of the Senate during his four years in office point to the latter as the cardinal explanation. Rosenau found that of some 121 senators who occupied office between 1949 and 1953 only 21 were actively hostile to Acheson, and of these only 13 were indiscriminating in their hostility. These 13 mounted a campaign against Mr. Acheson based upon alleged communism and treachery which under the circumstances of the time other senators were either unable or unwilling, out of fear, to refute. Rosenau concludes that their image of Acheson was so irrational and distorted (and one might add vicious) "that it is apparent that he could have engaged in no actions which would have met with their approval."[16]

Confronted by such people, Acheson was probably wise in acting upon the premise that only leadership of the strongest intellectual and moral force could succeed. He perceived all too clearly that if the loyalty of our allies, the professional development of the foreign service, and rationality in our international behavior were to be protected, foreign policy must not be allowed to become a hostage to pathological or partisan elements in Congress. Therefore, rather than curry favor with such elements or allow them to prolong America's fitful slumber in an isolationist torpor, Acheson gambled on the premise that leadership based upon knowledge and skill would be its own best advocate and our only long-run salvation in the cold war.

When we examine the success of Acheson's style of leadership in specific policy arenas we discover a more mixed situation. The remarkable consensus upon which the administration's European policies (Marshall Plan, NATO) rested enabled Acheson to conduct policy based upon the logic and expertise of the State Department and its sister services. Thus troops to Europe and the principle of German rearmament easily met the challenge of the "Great Debate" and were quickly accepted as an established part of our foreign policy.

The same was not true of Far Eastern policy, and here we may discover the Achilles' heel of Acheson's style of leadership. Many administration critics asserted, but few offered any proof, that prior to the fall of Nationalist China the administration's policy was not accepted by the Republican Party in Congress. Senator Vandenberg admitted privately and publicly that Republicans were consulted about China policy continuously over the post-war period and that, while they did not participate as directly in China policy as in the formulation of European policy, they

16 Rosenau, *The Senate and Dean Acheson,* p. 343.

The Governments

never came up with any better alternative to that pursued by the administration. Where the State Department let itself in for more trouble than necessary was in not sufficiently committing the Congress to a policy position *after* the fall of Chiang Kai-shek. It was not enough for Acheson to announce that the department was in search of a policy, and until it found one it could only wait until the dust settled.

In a democracy this puts the cart before the horse. Under the circumstances what was needed above all was public confidence that the State Department knew what it was doing, and the only way to achieve that was by associating with it the appropriate committees of the Senate in the search for a new terrain from which to view the monumental events occurring in Asia. Acheson's principle of leadership seems to have inhibited him from doing this. Instead he had the department publish the China *White Paper*, and a conference of China experts was held in the autumn of 1949. But neither of these actions produced beneficent results where they were most needed. It was not Acheson's style to let the Senate mess around with policy until the departmental experts had arrived at a clear decision. Unfortunately, since it was likely to be some time before the dust settled enough to get a clear decision, it would have been the better part of wisdom for Acheson to have sought to minimize the mistrust and suspicion of the department in connection with the fall of China. And this depended upon securing senatorial endorsement while public opinion was still open minded on the subject.

A similar ingenuousness characterizes Acheson's explanation for not urging the President to secure congressional sanction for the decision to go into Korea.

The question of congressional consultation was raised by Senator Kenneth Wherry (R-Neb.) at a Blair House meeting on June 30. Senator Alexander Smith (R-N.J.) asked Acheson informally whether it would not be a good idea to have a resolution in Congress approving the dispatch of United States ground forces to the Pusan bridgehead. It was the subject of full-scale discussion at a meeting of the President and his staff with Senate Majority Leader Scott Lucas (D-Ill.) on July 3. In each instance Acheson rejected so advising the President because by-and-large Congress acquiesced in the President's action and Acheson felt that it would be dangerous to gild a lily—"if you start gilding it, you may get into some trouble." This is how Acheson explains a decision fraught with terrible consequences. Among the senators who spoke in support of the President's constitutional authority to commit ground forces to Korea was Senator William F. Knowland (R-Calif.): "I believe that he has been authorized to do it under the terms of our obligations to the United Nations Charter... [and] under his constitutional power as Commander-in-Chief..." When disaster overtook the expedition Knowland referred to the Blair House meetings as those which "led this country into war, but without a declaration of the Congress of the United States."[17]

---

[17] Hearings, *Military Situation in the Far East*, p. 765.

The Role of Political Style

What is the lesson to be drawn from the bitter fruit of these two policies? In his study, *A Citizen Looks at Congress*, Acheson views the administration's conflict with its congressional foes as nothing but partisan "power striking against power," which the people could understand as the efforts of the Executive to maintain the integrity of policy against the irrational forces gathered in Congress.[18] If Acheson understood that by the end of 1949 public confidence in the State Department's Far Eastern policies had been shattered, he failed to appreciate that the most urgent need was not a better or wiser policy but rather to restore public confidence in the department's activities. This was helped by appointing Dean Rusk Assistant Secretary of State for the Far East, but an even larger public effort at restoring confidence and consensus was needed, and until it succeeded rationality and knowledge would be at a discount in effectively determining policy. American foreign policy is often akin to a ship on a storm-tossed sea. No amount of competence on the part of the navigator can hope to avail against the natural forces of tempest raging in the public mind. Acheson may have failed to adequately appreciate that in a democracy like the American, public opinion is more than an obstacle, it is a natural force; and it is no shame for the statesman to reckon with it accordingly.

III. Intellect and Innovation[19]

Logically, the impulse and capacity to innovate on the part of a decision maker derives from his belief that the existing situation is not being satisfactorily met, and from his willingness to do something about it. This in turn presupposes that the decision maker has certain standards of knowledge by which he judges the adequacy or inadequacy with which the situation is being met. It also assumes that he is willing to act because he believes that by acting he can improve his control over the situation. It stands to reason, therefore, that a decision maker who views the importance of his relationship to the decision-making process self-consciously, who possesses a well-developed sense of the standards and criteria for judging whether a situation is satisfactory or not, and whose social philosophy supports him in the belief that by acting he can improve the situation, will be more likely to accept the value of innovation than a decision maker who lacks such qualities. Dean Acheson's capacity for innovation rested upon such qualities.

In Dean Acheson's life there is a long history of identification with

18 Dean Acheson, *A Citizen Looks at Congress* (New York: Harper & Row, Publishers, 1956).

19 Gordon A. Craig has testified to the importance of innovative capacity in an essay on Otto von Bismarck. According to Bismarck's associates, Craig writes, he had "the quality that Thucydides admired in Themistocles: the ability, by some hidden force of mind or character, to fasten immediately, after short deliberation, upon what was needed in a given situation." Gordon A. Craig, *From Bismarck to Adenauer: Aspects of German Statecraft* (Baltimore: The Johns Hopkins Press, 1958), pp. 14–15.

The Governments

that social philosophy which expresses the belief that by the steady application of intelligence and self-discipline man has a fighting chance to avoid the worst disasters of an unpredictable future. This is the same philosophy that nurtured Holmes, Brandeis, and FDR. A liberal, Acheson is neither wedded to an egotistic psychology, nor beguiled by a formal individualism into denying that man's problems are social or collective in nature, and that government affords an engine whereby man's intellect can be pitted against those collective problems. Like Brandeis, Holmes, and FDR, Acheson developed a deep aversion to all attempts to shackle human behavior with immutable laws, "...whether they are the laws expounded in the *Social Statics* of Herbert Spencer or those in *Das Kapital* of Karl Marx."[20] Dean Acheson was one of the very few men who broke with FDR in the early years of the New Deal who could look back twenty years later and declare that the New Deal "not only produced economic but spiritual results of great importance. The people were no longer called upon to bear their fate with courageous resignation and to learn the lessons which it taught. They had a leader who told them that by their own organized effort they could end their miseries and they had a government which could lead the way and mobilize the means."[21]

Acheson's confidence in man's capacity to manage his social existence is all the more striking because he does not believe in the innate reasonableness and perfectibility of man. He is too close to the Old Testament and too much of a New England skeptic to believe in notions about man's goodness and rationality. Speaking in 1946 of the problems that the world faced, Acheson remarked that "they come pretty directly from the medium with which one works, the human animal himself."[22] Acheson stresses the importance of will and self-discipline if men are to overcome their difficulties. Intelligence alone is neither sufficient nor easily come by. Whatever threads of wisdom man achieves must be spun from his "own innards." "Most of us," he continues, "can only splice those odd fragments of conclusion which this unaccustomed effort produces."[23] Nor does Acheson believe that man can exorcise the Old Adam by recourse to agents outside himself. Moral salvation is a matter of the individual soul, not of society.

Acheson's view of the human prospect is redeemed by his knowledge that the problems men face in their social life are not all the direct consequence of man's fall from grace; they are problems created by the working or non-working of human intelligence and as such they are susceptible to human control. The implications of this outlook for Acheson's conduct of foreign policy were immense. It meant that he understood that the evil of power in international relations was rooted not so much in the sinfulness of man but in the context, the constellations, the situation,

---

[20] Dean Acheson, *A Democrat Looks at His Party* (New York: Harper & Row, Publishers, 1955).

[21] *Ibid.*

[22] "Random Harvest."

[23] *Ibid.*

The Role of Political Style

in which even good men are forced to act selfishly or immorally. In the conduct of foreign policy Acheson was *not* wedded to the so-called laws of power politics and man's *animus dominandi,* but acted in the knowledge that it was within his power to modify and influence the configuration of events. The chief thing that Acheson shares in common with Machiavelli is the belief that "a certain region of historical event which contemporaries were content to accept as the province of chance, could be brought under human control by systematic and self-conscious statesmanship."[24]

Long before the atomic bomb had rendered nugatory the easy assumption that civilization could survive the blind play of man-made forces, Acheson expressed the growing sense of man's need for a way out of his blind bondage to so-called natural laws. In a speech at the Annual Dinner of Davenport College, Yale University, November 28, 1939, Acheson called upon his listeners to recognize that the old European order was passing and that there was a need for vigorous reconstruction "from which we cannot stand aloof if we are alive to our interest." He rejected the idea of armed isolation as the solution, on the grounds that without Europe the democratic values of the United States would die. He argued that for the future America should devise a realistic policy consisting of a therapeutic and a prophylactic side. Among other remedies Acheson proposed that darkening winter evening in 1939 was one that came to life a decade later—that America join with other financially strong nations in making capital available to economically needy areas of the world. "Man," he concluded, "is an ingenious creature once he possesses understanding and the will."

Understanding and will sum up the ingredients essential to innovate action, but they do not give adequate weight to the temper of mind and intellectual power necessary to overcome popular apathy and the force of events. In order to act in drastically new ways the decision maker must be supported by a powerful sense of the mutability of history and by a most profound personal self-confidence. Finally to be effective the decision maker's predisposition to act must also be accompanied by a knowledge of how to act. The one without the other is useless. We can best explore the significance of the innovative temper of mind if we compare Acheson's crucial role in the development of the Truman Doctrine and the Marshall Plan with the policy alternatives and criticisms of opponents such as Henry Wallace and Senator Robert Taft.

It is hard to imagine now just how new and radical these policies appeared at their conception and just how persuasive were many of the criticisms directed against them. Taft assumed that there was nothing the United States could or should do to preserve the European balance of power. His position was essentially the product of a static conception of the environment. It was also a recipe for disaster because it held that there were uncontrollable forces afoot in the world which rendered all human action unfeasible except the final desperate resort to war. The Wallace

[24] Herbert Butterfield, *The Statecraft of Machiavelli* (London: Macmillan & Co. Ltd., 1955), p. 18.

The Governments

alternative was equally rigid and equally dangerous. It demanded that leadership put faith in pure, untarnished principle. It rested upon the assumption that only steadfast adherence to faith in the Soviet Union and to acts of generosity and trust unsullied by policy considerations could serve to avert a catastrophic breakdown of Soviet-American relations. Wallace made no allowance for the possibility that if his approach failed the resulting disillusionment might pitch Americans in the direction of a military showdown with the Soviet Union. Wallace assumed that the relationship between the Soviet Union and the U.S. was so fragile that the least deviation would have catastrophic consequences. Wallace, like Taft, ignored the possibility that resistance to Soviet expansionism need not result in a "hot" war.

To Acheson post-war Europe was a potential vacuum. Should its economic and political structure collapse, it would suddenly become a raging vortex into which both the United States and the Soviet Union would be sucked. While Europe survived, the deadliness of the Taft and Wallace positions were obscured, but once it fell into anarchy or under Soviet domination it would be too late. The trick was to re-establish Europe as a community capable of controlling its own destiny and by so doing reduce the Soviet threat to what Acheson likes to call "manageable proportions."

Acheson's superb confidence that the United States could by the application of collective social intelligence steady the tottering European edifice explains the decisive style with which he was able to act. Drawing upon the intellectual resources of the State Department, Acheson produced the Truman Doctrine in less than a month. The Truman Doctrine, contrary to the criticism made at the time, was molded almost entirely by a sensitive intellectual probing for that policy which would supply the "missing component." It is also characteristic of Acheson's innovative style that in the midst of preparing the Truman Doctrine for presentation to the Congress, he assigned the State–Army–Navy Coordinating Committee the task of preparing the studies which eventually led to the Marshall Plan. It was also Acheson who encouraged the Planning Staff to proceed with the formulation of the Marshall Plan in anticipation of its eventual necessity.

Only a mind accustomed to believing that by one's own action one can help to create alternatives, as well as define the framework within which man operates, could have envisaged the potential for change present in the European situation. No one of the policies adopted under Acheson's guidance was an end in itself, any more than FDR viewed the New Deal as an end in itself. Each was part of an effort to restore the European community by contributing to the European's sense of security and self-confidence and to his belief that Europe still had a substance worth preserving. Beyond that, Acheson, like Roosevelt, recognized that even the quest for community is not a static end in itself so much as a means for enabling men to control the potentially disruptive influences in their lives. Just as Roosevelt viewed the New Deal as a means of bringing the

161

The Role of Political Style

American economy into an equilibrium that was manageable, so Acheson conceived of the Marshall Plan, NATO, and Point IV as means for making the international equilibrium manageable. By restoring the European and world communities, the sphere for the play of uncontrolled forces would be that much reduced and man would be enabled to struggle against his fate in a real match, not a mismatch. It is doubtful if innovation on the scale and style attained by post-war American foreign policy would have been forthcoming without such a profound belief in the mutability of history and in man's ability to influence his destiny by acting upon it rather than passively accepting it. His social philosophy predisposed Acheson to see in a desperate situation the potential for change which in turn encouraged and supported him in his determination to act.

Acheson likes to quote Dwight Morrow's words that "there are two classes of people: Those who talked about things, and those who did things. Competition in the second group was not keen." This statement epitomizes Acheson's pride in knowing how to get things done, in being able to take hold of a problem situation and mold it to his will. In this regard it is illuminating to compare Acheson's and Kennan's approach to the Marshall Plan. Joseph Whelan, a biographer of Kennan, has written:

In many respects the nature and purposes of the Marshall Plan seemed to fit perfectly into Kennan's general conception of the proper way in which to meet the Soviet challenge...the "containment" involved was subtle and indirect. It posed no overt threat to Soviet Russia. To this humanitarian appeal to reason and thoroughly "liberal," "positive" approach to the great problems of European recovery George Kennan had no objections. It, apparently, epitomized the kind of "mystical" containment-by-internal-virtue that he had in mind.[25]

Acheson's contribution to the Marshall Plan lay in his capacity to recognize in the European crisis a political problem susceptible of solution in relatively concrete economic terms. Acheson's readiness to act, to undertake a new departure, was supported by a sense of precisely what could be done to remedy the European economic crisis. Once he knew that the United States could reasonably supply the "missing component" that would make Europe a secure and viable entity, he experienced no hesitation in putting his plans into action.

Acheson invariably began policy-making with a searching appraisal of what was existentially desirable and what was humanly possible. He recognized that no policy is a universal solution or cure-all; no policy devised by men, no matter how morally satisfying, could hope to resolve the cold war overnight. Since the power that policy can call upon is always limited, Acheson's mind was on how to maximize its efficiency. The art of devising such policy lay in mastering a knoweldge of all the elements present and potential in a situation and determining what new increment, if added, would make a difference. The trick was to produce a policy which by its form and substance would transform a hopeless

[25] Joseph G. Whelan, "George Kennan and His Influence on American Foreign Policy," *The Virginia Quarterly Review,* Spring, 1959, p. 206.

The Governments

situation into a viable one. Policy for Acheson began with knowledge of the problem, not with some a priori moral abstraction to which policy had to conform.

There is further testimony to and evidence of the powerful role of social intelligence in guiding and supporting Acheson's innovative and decision-making style. As Under Secretary and as Secretary, Acheson made the fullest use of the resources available to him in the State Department. It takes nothing away from General Marshall to recognize that it was Acheson who provided the inspiration for the brilliant staff work upon which the Truman Doctrine and the Marshall Plan ultimately rested. Marshall could and did weigh the alternatives, but he was skeptical, if not unappreciative, of the value of extended intellectual palaver. "Most discussions were largely 'hot air' anyway, he thought, and no way for a Secretary to spend his time."[26] Acheson, by contrast, valued those sessions in which he met with the working staffs to explore the problems, to bring his logic to bear, and to infuse the thinking of the participants with purpose and direction. "Meeting with members of his own staff," Joseph Jones writes,

Acheson never stated an opinion or conclusion until everyone present had an opportunity to give his own ideas about the subject and suggest a remedy. By questions he stimulated others to talk, while he listened and took occasional notes. When every aspect of the matter had been carefully and fully understood, he would summarize what he had heard, point out conflicts in points of view, attempt to reconcile them, introduce facts and reasoning that might not have appeared and finally suggest a solution. It was as though he were aware that this logic and facility for expression might, if brought into play too early, intimidate full expression.[27]

No individual would have taken the staff work as seriously as Acheson did nor have exercised such care in bringing it to bear upon the formulation of policy had he not possessed a conscious respect for the value of collective organized intelligence.

Acheson has summed up the ingredients of sound policy-making in the following terms: "...information, carefully prepared; then a discussion of its meaning, conducted with spirit, criticism, and relevance; and an indication of the course of action.... To the staff this practice is a constant demonstration both that their contribution is important and that it is fairly heard and considered."[28]

Acheson built his relationship with Truman upon the same intellectual foundation. Far from deprecating Truman's intellectual abilities, Acheson insisted that the President know as fully as time and circumstances permitted what the problems were and what alternatives existed. While such an approach required that the President do an enormous amount of homework, it was precisely the relationship that Truman wished to achieve. As the result of the complete intellectual and policy rapport that

---

[26] Joseph Jones, *The Fifteen Weeks* (New York: The Viking Press, Inc., 1955), p. 111.

[27] *Ibid.*, p. 101.

[28] Dean Acheson, as quoted in *The New York Times,* Oct. 11, 1959.

The Role of Political Style

Acheson established with Truman, it was possible for the President to step into the foreign policy picture without the least awkwardness or straining for contrived effects. At the same time Acheson enjoyed great freedom of action because he knew that he had the President's confidence and support. Such a relationship favored the realization of policies based upon inquiry and the most complete intellectual understanding.

Acheson's domination of the late years of the Truman administration is not unrelated to the advantage that the use of collective intelligence gave him in proposing new policies or influencing events crowding in on the administration. The National Security Council recommendation to increase the military budget ceiling from $15 billion to somewhere between $18 and $20 billion (N.S.C. 68), was essentially an outcome of Acheson's staffwork designed to enable the United States to cope with the deepening cold war crisis and the loss of our atomic monopoly. Whatever the fate of N.S.C. 68 would have been, the Korean aggression clearly demonstrated its urgency.

It was also the essential logic of Acheson's staffwork that determined the sequence of Blair House decisions that put the United States at war with North Korea. On Saturday night, acting on the advice of his own counselors, Acheson took the initiative in presenting the President with a plan for handling the Korean situation within the framework of the United Nations. Acting on the request of the President, Acheson, on Sunday evening, laid before the conference a set of additional recommendations for our representative in the Security Council. Twenty-four hours later on his own initiative, he presented the Blair House conference with proposals for American military intervention.[29]

By the same token, major responsibility falls to Acheson for the decision or lack of decision that permitted MacArthur to take his ill-fated plunge across the 38th parallel. This is true on two counts, the political and the military. Politically, Acheson failed to adequately assess the likely Chinese reaction to MacArthur's advance to the Yalu. Militarily, there was no one except Acheson in the government, and least of all in the military with enough determination to pass judgment on the military logic of what MacArthur was doing. We all know that MacArthur disregarded or interpreted orders to suit his own purposes. What is frightening is that for a variety of reasons no one in the Pentagon, least of all General Marshall, felt that he could interfere with the right of the local commander to exercise his discretion, even if it meant enlarging the war. Having let MacArthur slip the leash, Acheson, the only strong figure besides the President who might have put MacArthur back on the leash, felt constrained not to do so for fear of being charged with interference in military affairs. This "hands off" posture stood Acheson in good stead in refuting the charges—made against him in the course of the MacArthur hearings—that he had influenced military judgment against MacArthur's

[29] Glenn D. Paige, *The Korean Decision* [June 24–30, 1950] (unpublished manuscript, Northwestern University, 1959).

The Governments

strategy. But it is frightening to know that civilian control of the government was at the mercy of such a rigid demarcation of functions as to inhibit the Pentagon from interfering with a local commander and the Secretary of State from making decisive use of his judgment.

No one knows how close to demoralization the Truman administration came in that disastrous winter of 1950–51. In Washington the Republicans were plotting to destroy Acheson, if not to impeach the President. The American people were demoralized and incensed by the failure of their government to act decisively in the face of provocation. At the United Nations the State Department knew that it had to sweat out a series of agonizing resolutions designed to mollify Communist China, before our allies, exhausted by appeasement, would return to the fold. Only by going through this nerve-racking process could the United States hope to regain the diplomatic initiative and leadership. Meanwhile in bloody Korea, MacArthur was clamoring for another Dunkirk, while 8,000 miles away the Pentagon struggled to regroup his shattered armies in a desperate holding action. The imperturbable style with which Acheson kept a steady flow of decisions and policies going out to all fronts is eloquent testimony not only of his nerves but also of his belief in the ultimate triumph of human will and collective human effort.

In short, the imprint of the Acheson style is on most of the foreign policy achievements and failures of the Truman administration, and these are substantially a reflection of the intellectual power that Acheson generated during his years as Secretary of State. This intellectual power derived in turn from Acheson's pragmatic commitment to the liberal principle that problems exist to be solved and that man can better his condition substantially if not infinitely by the application of intelligence to his affairs.

IV. Style of International Relations

Acheson was the architect of most of the policies which still constitute the main elements in the struggle against the Soviet Union. Ineluctably many of his policies contributed to the deepening of the cold war. Yet few of them created the uneasiness among thoughtful people that those of his successor did—policies such as "massive retaliation" and "brinkmanship."

I believe that this quality of reasonableness and sanity is attributable to the conscious and unconscious restraint with which Acheson handled power. In part his handling of power was tempered by a tremendous respect for the contingencies and inscrutability of foreign affairs.

What is occurring in that vast external realm is so complex, so complicated, and so voluminous that [the statesman] cannot fully comprehend it; nor until much time has elapsed grasp its full significance. This is not wholly, or even principally, because of man-made impediments to knowledge—iron curtains, censorship, and the like—

165

The Role of Political Style

but because of the obscurity and complexity of the molecular changes which combine to bring about the growth or decay of power, will, and purpose in foreign lands.[30]

Secondly, Acheson's style of handling power was tempered by a confidence born of humility and an awareness of the human capacity for error and for personal opportunism in evading the responsibility for one's acts.

"International politics," writes one scholar, "offers opportunities and temptations for immoral action on a vast and destructive scale which tend to present themselves in the guise of necessity of State."[31] Acheson expressed it with simpler elegance: "We are a moral people, but like others fall from grace and too often take an immodest view of our capacity to act morally."

How are we to assess the quality of moral responsibility which expressed itself in Acheson's style of international dealings? There are a number of points at which Acheson has gone on record with explicit or implicit denials of the tenets or canons of *Realpolitik*. To the pessimistic and amoral notion that in serving politics one is inevitably wedded to "the ethics of doing evil," Acheson opposes the assertion that the political process affords scope for human excellence and courage. To the claim that "the very act of acting destroys our moral integrity,"[32] Acheson opposes the Holmesian dictum that "man is born a predestined idealist, for he is born to act. To act is to affirm the worth of an end and to persist in affirming the worth of an end is to make an ideal."[33] I believe that Acheson's faith in the efficacy of human will and reason to overcome threatening situations sets him apart from the "realist" for whom power exercises a fatal attraction toward resignation, expedience, irresponsibility, and the glorification of amorality and war.

It is illuminating in this regard to examine Acheson's attitude toward the Soviet Union and the cold war. A great many of his difficulties could have been solved had he acquiesced in the popular clamor for a moral crusade against the Soviet Union. There were any number of occasions on which Acheson could have quietly let the tiller of responsibility slip from his hands and in the wake of an upsurge of xenophobia emerged as a national hero. This Acheson steadfastly refused to do. "I hear almost every day someone say that the real aim of the United States is to stop the spread of communism. Nothing seems to put the cart more completely before the horse than that. The thing to oppose is Russian imperialism," of which communism is but "the most subtle instrument . . . the spearhead."

---

[30] Dean Acheson, "The President and the Secretary of State," in *The Secretary of State.* ed. Don K. Price, © 1960 by the American Assembly. (Englewood Cliffs: Prentice-Hall, Inc.) p. 35.

[31] *The Anglo-American Tradition in Foreign Affairs,* ed. Arnold Wolfers and Laurence Martin (New Haven, Conn.: Yale Univ. Press, 1956).

[32] Hans J. Morgenthau, *In Defense of the National Interest* (New York: Alfred A. Knopf, Inc., 1952).

[33] Oliver Wendell Holmes as quoted in Dean Acheson, "Morality, Moralism, and Diplomacy," *The Yale Review,* XLVII (1958), 492.

The Governments

By refusing to place the Soviet-American conflict on an ideological footing, Acheson denied Americans that release from moral restraint for which so many yearned in the late forties and fifties.

I think it is safe to say that Acheson's greatest safeguard against irresponsibility in the conduct of foreign policy lay in his willingness to act upon the assumption that nothing was ever hopeless and that by planning and making sacrifices the worst possible alternatives or contingencies could be avoided. "We live in dangerous times," he remarked not long before assuming the office of Secretary of State in January, 1949, "because of the decisions of another power which are beyond the control of any or all of us. There is no formula which will exorcise these dangers. The decisions which create them will be affected by the facts which we are helping, and successfully helping, to forge from the unfolding future."[34]

Upon assuming office in 1949 Acheson had occasion to make some profoundly serious decisions affecting the whole future of our lives for many years to come. The establishment of the North Atlantic Treaty Organization involved the decision, in Acheson's mind at least, to push ahead with the restoration of Europe, including West Germany, without treating Soviet offers of negotiation with any great seriousness.

When Acheson went to the Paris Foreign Ministers' Conference following the lifting of the Berlin blockade, for the first time an American diplomat had no intention of playing the Soviet game of seeking compromise for the sake of compromise. For the first time, refusal to accept Soviet domination of Eastern Europe was an explicit tenet of American diplomacy. In a sense Acheson was saying: "Not even a united Germany is an end in itself—our basic policy and aim is to push freedom as far east as possible."[35]

No one will deny that there is a disturbing note of aggressiveness in that attitude; but the policy to which it gave rise—situations of strength —aimed at changing the Kremlin's outlook, not a physical roll-back and liberation. Acheson always recognized that any relaxation of the Soviet grip on Eastern Europe could only be brought about by modifying the expectations of the Soviet leaders.

We get a clearer view of Acheson's responsible temper in connection with the Korean War, although here Acheson cannot be fully absolved from the dreadful negligence which led to MacArthur's crossing of the 38th parallel. Amidst the disarray and panic which attended our defeat in Korea, Acheson stood out as a bulwark of sanity if not serenity. There was plenty of clamor for repeating the horror of Hiroshima and Nagasaki in the winter of 1951, but this time the world would not have forgiven us had Acheson or Truman acquiesced in such a course. Something of the restraint with which Acheson viewed the Korean operation even before it degenerated into MacArthur's *Götterdämmerung* is to be gleaned from a memorandum Acheson sent Philip Jessup concerning President Truman's speech to be given at San Francisco following his Wake Island Conference

[34] Dean Acheson, address to Michigan State Bar Association, 1948.
[35] Princeton Seminar.

The Role of Political Style

with the victorious MacArthur. In his memo criticizing a draft of the speech, Acheson ordered deleted all reference to Korean events as a victory.

...the whole idea of victory should be taken out. We should not be talking about victory. This is out of keeping in the U.N. There are no victors or vanquished in this kind of situation, only an adjudication. The only victor is peace.... To talk in terms of victory makes this too much of a U.S.–U.S.S.R. conflict. This part of the speech should be done with great restraint, should be sober, somber, with a sense of responsibility.[36]

Acheson also objected to the speech's "hammering away at the theme of communist imperialism in this way. Not only stale and uninteresting but dangerous in the present situation."[37]

In assaying the sources of Acheson's style of handing these matters, a large place must be given to the temper of mind induced by the law. Take for example the following three passages of which the first two are from Holmes, the third from Acheson: "When I emphasize the difference between law and *morals* I do so with reference to a single end, that of understanding and learning the law.... It is for that I ask you for the moment to imagine yourself indifferent to other and greater things." Holmes continues:

For my own part, I often doubt whether it would not be a gain if every word of moral significance could be banished from the law altogether, and other words adopted which should convey legal ideas uncolored by anything outside the law... by ridding ourselves of an unnecessary confusion we should gain very much in the clearness of our thought.[38]

Now listen to Acheson saying the same thing. In discussing questions of foreign policy, "I would not, for the most part, use the language of moral discourse or invoke moral authority," but would "state principles in terms of their purpose and effect without characterizing them as moral or immoral...not because moral principles can, or should be, excluded from the relations of states to one another.... It is rather because to characterize conduct between nations as moral or immoral will involve us in confusions of vocabulary and of thought, with which, despite their importance, we need not struggle....."[39]

From his position on the bench Holmes could work out the logic of this cosmic skepticism to its utmost limits, upholding legislation which he personally considered foolish or in error. "We need," he declared, "to transcend our own convictions," to permit much that "we hold dear to be done away with short of revolution by the orderly change of law."[40]

[36] Memo: Schulman to Jessup in the files of Charles Murphy, Truman Library, Independence, Mo.

[37] *Ibid.*

[38] Oliver Wendell Holmes, Jr., "The Path of the Law," quoted from *The Mind and Faith of Justice Holmes,* ed. Max Lerner (New York: Modern Library, Inc., 1964), pp. 78–79.

[39] Acheson, "Morality, Moralism, and Diplomacy," p. 481.

[40] Holmes, Jr., "The Path of the Law."

The Governments

It was far harder for Acheson, caught in the maelstrom of political events, to adhere to such a philosophy. Yet Holmes provided the lodestar by which Acheson navigated. "To those," Acheson writes, "who have any appreciation of the perils which surround us, of the lightning speed with which relative (indeed absolute) positions can change, of the effect which popular attitudes, so easily and often unworthily stimulated can have in forcing governments to foolish action or restraining them from wise action, a moralistic approach to foreign relations and by this I mean one which attempts to apply the maxixms or ideology of moral teaching seems ill-adapted to the complexity of the task."[41] What approach then is adapted to the task? The method of the common law by which principle evolves out of the adjustment of conflicting claims in particular cases, a method by which the lines of principle are etched out a bit at a time by the process of inclusion and exclusion. It combines a deep skepticism of the wisdom of attempts to remold the social system at a single stroke or in accordance with any a priori doctrine, with an optimistic view of the ability of rational men to find what is fair and reasonable in particular problems or cases.

Transferring this approach to international relations, we find the following contrast. Hans Morgenthau, the arch realist, believes it possible to start with something called the national interest, which is known and definable in advance. To Morgenthau international politics is like a very special map on which the expert, by use of special glasses, can plot and read off the national interest; Acheson believes leaders are dealing always with an incomplete map and each problem requires that the statesman take pen in hand and draw in the reasonable connections to the national interest. The virtues of this approach are seen again and again in Acheson's style of dealing with allies like Britain and France. Instead of going to a conference with an a priori definition of the national interest, which was likely to divide the participants, Acheson went with the idea of solving a common problem, a course that had the advantage of orienting the participants toward areas of consensus rather than areas of conflict. When progress on NATO and E.D.C. became stymied by political and economic deadlocks in 1951, Acheson proposed the creation of a Temporary (NATO) Council Committee (presided over by Harriman, Plowden, and Monnet). The writ of this committee was so extensive that it practically rewrote the budgets of the member states. In this fashion NATO served as an instrument for overcoming the limitations of national sovereignty. In doing NATO business the United States could quite properly intervene in French internal affairs, and British and French attitudes toward Germany were adjusted to meet the common needs of NATO.[42]

Thanks to the reasonableness and tolerance of Acheson's style, old nationalistic bogies were allayed: France was persuaded to forego her claims against Germany, Germany was encouraged to link her destiny to the democratic West, and Britain was persuaded to accept the Coal and

41 Acheson, "Morality, Moralism, and Diplomacy," p. 485.
42 Princeton Seminar.

The Role of Political Style

Steel Community. And through it all emerged little or none of the rancor that developed against his successor. By a curious irony Acheson was more of a hero in the eyes of the Europeans than he was in the minds of his own countrymen.

Acheson did not come to his test of truth by imposing the a priori assumption and tenets of *Realpolitik* upon reality. Rather he seems to have found in the verification and validation of each preceding act "clues and 'leadings'," as William James would say, to the next policy with which we feel all the while—such feeling being among our potentialities— that the original ideas remain in agreement. The connection and transitions come to us from point to point as "being progressive, harmonious, satisfactory."

This does not mean that Acheson's decisions were always right, but they had a certain reasonableness and proportion about them which they certainly would not have had, had they been derived from the a priori postulates of doctrinaire realism. They had about them the spirit of life and reason and hope, which engaged the response and will power of the sorely divided nations of Western Europe and beyond. In the midst of their suffering and anxiety Acheson neither preached to them nor did he scare them by insisting upon rigid moral "principles, categories, supposed necessities"; rather he encouraged in them a spirit of hope and confidence by "looking towards last things, fruits, consequences, facts." He acted in terms of problems and solutions, of real and immediate dangers, and of ways of overcoming them. By so doing he contributed to freeing the mind and will of Europeans.

The political value of such a pragmatically determined decision-making was immense. It bred in Europe a sense of purpose and confidence that Europeans had not felt for twenty years. It created movements in the European experience that were worthwhile because they led toward "other movements which it will be worthwhile to have been led to" such as European cooperation and federation. The breath of life was pumped into the spectral vision of an economically and politically federated Europe. The powerful appeal of communism and neutralism were countered by rekindling the vision of the role an independent and united Europe might once again play in world politics. These moves may have been made in reaction to moves taken on the initiative of the Communist world, but we now know that because of them Europe is a healthy, revitalized, and prosperous weight in the balance of world affairs.

By undertaking to solve their problems in terms that Europeans could understand rather than in terms of narrow national interest, Acheson established the moral and political ascendancy of America in Europe in a way that force and browbeating could never achieve. By the style of his actions Acheson became the guarantor if not the *auctor* of the European and North Atlantic communities. By resisting the course of expediency at home and of pseudomorality and cynicism abroad he was able to inspire confidence in the Europeans and others of the rightness of American

The Governments

action. By setting them the example, by answering "for the rightness of the action" and "for the certainty that it will yield good fruit to the man who undertakes it," Acheson became the inspiration for taking action, if not freely, at least in the knowledge that any other alternative was hopeless.

PART THREE

INTERNATIONAL CONFLICT: WAR, WEAPONS, AND STRATEGY

The activity known as war can take place only between nations.
Among individuals there are debates, quarrels, and fights; within nations
there are riots, revolutions, and civil wars; but wars, by definition,
occur only when individuals are mobilized to do battle by and on behalf
of their nations. It has long been argued that war is not only an
unavoidable consequence of the coexistence of nations but the most
typical of international relations. Such a notion is implicit in Clausewitz's
description of war as the continuation of politics by other means.
In a nuclear age we see more and more clearly that war could be
at the same time the most characteristic and most self-destructive

aspect of the international political system. Recent work, however, has tried to draw a distinction between the unavoidably conflicting desires and needs of nation states, and war—seen as the least desirable way of managing international conflict. The enduring interest in war has produced the modern studies of conflict resolution and deterrence strategy which are the subjects of this section.

In "Peaceful Settlements and the Dysfunctions of Secrecy," Lewis Coser speculates about interstate relations in the light of social psychological studies of the functions and functioning of inter-personal conflict. He points out that under conditions of divergent purposes and mutual fear, conflict might seem to nations—as it does to individuals—the only way to test an uncertain balance of strength. In the past the ability to keep the enemy guessing has been considered an element of national strength, but mistaken calculations about adversaries were partly responsible for such destructive combats as the Second World War.

Even statesmen are beginning to reassess the value of truthful communication between potential combatants; Kennedy and Khrushchev used it to avert battle in the Cuba Missile Crisis of 1962. Coser argues that any secrecy at all is dangerous and unproductive national policy today. He discusses ways to ensure a mutual exchange of information: by scientists, for example, who could be licensed to freely travel and gossip among hostile powers. Coser's article shows a use of social psychological research different from the studies of individual psychology utilized by Singer (Part One, Chapter 1) and Pool and Kessler (Part Two, Chapter 6). In his article studies of small group behavior are extrapolated into the much larger international context. The study of conflict holds considerable promise for such a transfer; it examines conditions of tension which seem to be psychologically similar in committees and between nations.

Clinton F. Fink reports on a project directly focused on the international system. His article, "More Calculations about Deterrence," is about the prevention of military aggression by means of military threats. Deterrence, in the general sense of the word, occurs whenever one individual uses threats to stop another from doing something. Recently, deterrence in the military sense has become an important part of nuclear strategy. Fink's study is about a series of historical cases in which a major power tried, by military threats, to inhibit another major power's threatened attack on a third smaller power. In six of the cases the agression was called off, in eleven it took place as announced. Fink is re-examining an earlier study by Bruce M. Russett, and makes some methodological comments which have far-reaching implications. In each case the cancellation of an attack followed a deterrent threat, but that it was caused by the threat, or by the threat alone, is difficult to establish. The reasons for the change of plans could only be inferred in a general way from what was known of the characteristics of attacker, victim, and would-be defender. Fink suggests that specific attempts at deterrence may have been successful only in the context of much more broadly inhibiting

174

relationships among the three parties to the possible conflict. For instance, all of the successful cases of deterrence were in the postwar period and involved major powers armed with nuclear weapons. The problem, a common one in the study of international relations, is to move from correlations to causal relationships when the data are neither random nor representative, but dependent on availability.

Some students of international relations have attempted to solve the problems of data by turning to limited and abstract models of human behavior, such as the theory of games. Games theory comes from the study of how the choice of strategies in games like chess is based on a calculation of the probable strategies of an opponent. The most common kinds of games are "zero-sum games," in which each player gains only at the other's expense, but there are also "nonzero-sum games" which allow for a degree of shared interest or benefit. Military policy, in particular, deterrence policy as developed in the United States under Secretary McNamara, has been strongly influenced by the assumptions of the theory of games. In his article "Critique of Strategic Thinking," Anatol Rapoport argues with passion that such assumptions put aside the values that distinguish real life from "games." The deliberate discard of distinctions is acceptable only in the realm of abstract theory; it eliminates consideration of the goals that are the only justification for what we call defense policy.

Herman Kahn, of the Hudson Institute, is Rapoport's principal object of attack here. It is Kahn's work he has chiefly in mind when he writes of the bloody-minded unreality of games theorists, and of their unawareness of the psychological elements in decision-making and the moral components of government. Rapport overstates his case, as Kahn's article, "The Arms Race and World Order," shows. Kahn leads a study of the nuclear arms race to the surprising conclusion of a plea for world government. He feels that world government is likely to become possible only after a nuclear catastrophe. Writing in 1962, Kahn anticipated a nuclear confrontation that would frighten both sides into a realization, if only temporary one, that something must be done to lengthen the odds against recurrence. He suggests advance plans that will enable nations to be ready for such a *rapprochement*—plans similar to some of Coser's suggestions (Part Three, Chapter 1).

Karl Deutsch has written that if the international system is like a game, it is less like chess than like the croquet game in *Alice in Wonderland,* where the balls are hedgehogs, the hoops are soldiers, and the mallets are flamingos—all of them ready to interfere in the game. Kahn's version of the theory of games is not a rigorous one, but it provides insight into the refracted world of today. The theory has contributed to international politics by suggesting alternatives to the apocalyptic futility of "Red or Dead." Along with techniques of conflict management, the theory of games has enlarged the repertoire of defense strategies, but—and this is Rapoport's point—it cannot provide goals.

Peaceful Settlements and the Dysfunctions of Secrecy

CHAPTER TEN

Lewis Coser

Reprinted by permission of the publisher from the *Journal of Conflict Resolution,*
Vol. 7 (September, 1963), 246–53. Mr. Coser is Professor
of Sociology at Brandeis University.

Indices of Strength

One of the most startling paradoxes advanced by that master of the sociological paradox, Georg Simmel, runs as follows:

> The most effective prerequisite for preventing struggle, the exact knowledge of the comparative strength of the two parties, is very often attainable only by the actual fighting out of the conflict [Simmel, 1904; Coser, 1956, pp. 133–37].

In other words, the most effective deterrent to violent conflict is the revelation of comparative strength; however, relative strength can often be ascertained only through such conflict.

This paradox arises from the fact that in contentions for national or international power, as distinct from, say, economic competition, no clear-cut index of strength is readily available; it is therefore difficult to appraise the relative power of the contenders before a conflict has actually settled the issue. In economic transactions, money functions as a measure of available resources; in contrast, for power contentions

> ...no medium of exchange could be devised which would bear the same relation to estimates of fighting power as monetary metals [bear] to estimates of economic value [Lasswell, 1930, p. 148].

Money can serve as a common denominator to express many dimensions of economic values e.g., quality, quantity, scarcity. But millitary strength is multidimensional and there is no common denominator to measure it. Military power consists not only of the number of men in the armed forces and those who can be devoted to war indirectly; it is also dependent on military equipment presently available as well as on the potentialities for future production of such equipment. It depends on the totality of economic resources that can be mobilized. Furthermore, the relative strength of the contenders can hardly be measured by such objective factors alone; the number of military personnel and the quantity of military hardware is given value only by the willingness to fight and the willingness to utilize resources.

Thus, not only do we deal here with multimensional factors, but with motivations and attitudes that are difficult to measure and assess before they have been converted into actions. Under such conditions the contenders will be strongly tempted to engage in violent conflict to test their strength. In other words, relations in which unambiguous measures of relative strength are not available contain a higher probability of the use of violent trial through battle than of the use of other mechanisms of conflict resolution. This fact seems independent of the causes and conditions that define the substance of the conflict, such as contentions for power or resources, or ideological dispute. The manifest issues over which conflict arises can in principle be resolved by a variety of means ranging from violence to mediation or bargaining. I wish to claim, however, that, no matter what the specific causes of the conflict, indeterminacy in the assessment of the strength of opponents increases the likelihood that violence rather than other means of resolution will be resorted to by the opponents.

Of course, a state will not be likely to go to war if it perceives its power to be disproportionately smaller than that of its enemy. Even though power cannot be accurately assessed, very large discrepancies of power can be readily perceived. This is why the chances of attack of the United States by, say, Mexico, are exceedingly small in the twentieth century. But when contenders feel that their power is more or less evenly matched, given their common inability to gauge their relative strength more precisely, then the temptation is strong to engage in trial through battle.

When prospective antagonists make estimates of their respective power, it is clearly the perceived power, not the actual power, that is important in shaping their policy. Therefore, misperceptions of the power of the other side may seriously contribute to faulty policy decisions. One may *overestimate* the adversary's powers. S. F. Huntington has noted, for example, that:

> The armed services inevitably overstate the military capabilities of the opponent: in 1914, for instance, the Germans estimated the French army to have 121,000 more men than the German army, the French estimated the German army to have 134,000 more men than the French army, but both parties agreed in their estimates of the military forces of third powers [Huntington, 1958].

The recent clamor about an alleged "missile gap" between Russia and the United States provides another example in point. But one may also *underestimate* the power of the antagonist, as did Hitler with respect to Russia and England. In such cases, the lack of accurate knowledge, the discrepancy between perceived and real power, has profoundly destabilizing effects on the relationship and leads to disastrous policy decisions. In most of these cases, the actual power of the contenders in relation to each other becomes clear only during and after the fight.

A high measure of pluralistic ignorance is built into any conflict situation in which there do not exist single indices of strength, such as monetary values. Such indeterminacy spurs the readiness to engage in violent conflict. But the reverse must be considered also: If it is felt that only violent conflict can resolve the indeterminacy, each party in the preparation for the conflict will tend to maximize secrecy about its own strength, thus further increasing the indeterminacy and making the out-

179

break of violent conflict even more likely. Thus, built-in ignorance of the strength of the antagonist is not the only factor to be considered; the adversaries also deliberately increase the ignorance of their antagonists.

The withholding of information about one's power and capability is one of the most frequent and effective defenses available to power holders. To the extent that the outsider can be prevented from gaining full knowledge of one's real strength, to that extent one maximizes one's power over him. Secrecy has been traditionally one of the major instruments of the men of power. According to Max Weber:

> Everywhere that the power interests of the domination structure toward *the outside* are at stake, whether it is an economic competitor of a private enterprise, or a foreign, potentially hostile, polity, we find secrecy.

Secrecy protects from observation and shields the power holder, and this ability to keep the adversary guessing is a major weapon in his armory. But this very secrecy also contributes to lack of stability insofar as it makes relative appraisal of power more hazardous.

There seems to be no way out from the impasse. In order to avoid violent action it is necessary that the parties to the conflict have at their disposal adequate information about their relative strength; yet very lack of adequate indices for measurement of such strength and the tendency of the contenders to use secrecy as a weapon seem to make it impossible for them to resolve the conflict in a peaceful way. If there is to be bargaining, the cards must be on the table, but in the situation which I have sketched, both sides always have some of the cards up their sleeves.

Now let us imagine that both contenders have become aware of the fact that any conceivable outcome of a violent conflict between them will without doubt redound to their mutual disadvantage. Suppose that both are aware that their struggle, far from being a zero-sum game in which one wins what the other loses, is in fact one in which there is no payoff at all for either party. In such struggles the very notion of winning and losing is no longer applicable. In all previous wars the situation was essentially the same as that in the westerns we can see on TV screens every night. The "equalizer" of the Old West made it possible for *either* man to kill the other; it did not assure that *both* would be killed.[1] But this is precisely the outcome which both adversaries have to envisage now. If any result of the conflict can only be a situation in which the survivors envy the dead, strategies which applied to other types of conflict have ceased to be applicable.

In situations in which the most probable outcome of violent conflict is destructive of the very values and aims of *both* contenders, rational and prudent strategy would seem to require that both turn toward the search for solutions which maximize their common chances of survival. In other words, in such situations both have a common interest in the avoidance

---

[1] This example is borrowed from Thomas C. Schelling (1960).

International Conflict

of violent conflict, and such avoidance becomes a problem to be solved by each of them. Their common interest in avoiding the struggle must lead them to search for means of falsifying Simmel's prediction. They are thus mutually dependent in the very pursuit of their otherwise antagonistic goals.

This situation seems to have something in common with what mathematical economists refer to as the Pareto point. This point represents the optimum output of a pair of competitors in the sense that their *joint* utility (the sum of the two) will be greatest at that point. In other words, the two do better collectively if they adjust their production at the Pareto point. This point cannot be reached if both parties simply attempt to maximize their own utilities but only if they develop a set of norms specifying that the utility of one is to some extent dependent on the utility of the other. In other words, maximum joint utility in such situations can only be reached if both develop an ethics in which the concern for self and for other are of equal weight.[2] This is approximately the case in a situation in which both contenders are aware that the outcome of a struggle between them will be disastrous for both of them so that they need to cooperate in order to avoid it. The joint utility of refraining from struggle must take primacy over the pursuit of individual utilities which, in this case, are simply unattainable.

In situations in which the respective parties conduct a conflict to maximize their individual utilities, they have a powerful incentive to hide their capabilities from potential adversaries. The problem is very different, however, if the joint utility of avoiding violent action is to be pursued. Since the probability is high that indeterminacy of power relations will lead to a trial through battle, only the overcoming of this indeterminacy can insure against the outbreak of violent conflict. Therefore both sides must be concerned with keeping the potential adversary fully informed of their respective strength so that the indeterminacy of the system is reduced as far as possible. This means that all factors which shroud one's strength in secrecy, whether these result from deliberate design or the force of circumstance, must be considered highly dysfunctional with respect to the avoidance of violent conflict. If both sides want to avoid violent action, they must both be strongly motivated to replace the strategy of secrecy by a strategy of disclosure. Their common interest now leads them to accept rules allowing them to assess their relative strength without engaging in violent struggle. Their joint interests require that their power positions be communicated unequivocally so that trial through battle is no longer necessary. Full disclosure of one's own strength allows the adversary better to assess relative strength, and hence increases the chances that adjustments can be made through bargaining rather than through violence.

It might still be objected that if A is informed of an Achilles' heel in the position of B, this will be an incentive for A to strike. My counterargument would be that if both are convinced that violent conflict is a

---

[2] Cf. Anatol Rapoport (1960, pp. 71 ff.).

Peaceful Settlements and Dysfunctions of Secrecy

joint disutility to be avoided, then if B knows that A knows his weakness, this will be an incentive for B to come to a peaceful settlement which corresponds to their relative strength. In such a situation B will consider it most rational to concede a point to the adversary while proceeding to prepare for elimination of the present Achilles' heel in order to be in a better situation in future bargaining.

Yet the assessment of relative power is not complete when the adversaries are provided with certified knowledge of their respective military strength. They also need to know under what circumstances the adversary is willing to fight. They need to know, in other words, which symbolic events would induce the other party to transform his war-making potentialities into warlike action. The potential antagonists must be able to ascertain which types of events have a symbolic value that releases the will-to-fight on the other side. The signposts for violent action are likely to differ according to the social structure of the antagonistic camps. While in one social system the crossing of a particular line of demarcation or the erection of a missile base near its borders may be sufficient to activate a warlike response, in another system very different sets of circumstances, say an attack against the political system of an allied nation, may set off the will-to-fight. If this is so, it stands to reason that both parties must engage in a cooperative effort to disclose to the other as fully as possible those events which would move them to violent action. Here again the main problem is to make the statements as creditable as possible. Both sides must bend their efforts to persuade the other that they are not merely bluffing. How can this be attained?

It would seem that disclosure to the potential enemy of variant plans of action which decision-makers habitually prepare for various contingencies would constitute the best means of conveying to the adversary the extent of the commitment to risk a war. If in the recent Cuban events the Russians had had access to the advance plans of America with respect to Russian missile bases in Cuba, if they had known that such missile bases were not acceptable to American decision-makers, be it because of their real or their symbolic value, there would have been no need to go to the brink of war through drastic demonstrations of our will-to-fight. In this area also, just as in the cases discussed earlier, full disclosure will help decrease the uncertainties which might lead antagonists to attempt a trial through battle.

New Structures of Communication

A strategy of disclosure involves more than a different way of doing things; it involves a different structure of communication. If we are to find means that serve to relay information to an adversary in reliable fashion, we must maximize the chances that the messages he receives will be taken by him to be creditable. Statements made by A about this strength

International Conflict

and capability must be communicated to B in such a way that they are believed.

A strategy of disclosure depends on opening channels of information as widely as possible, on unblocking lines of communication between the antagonists; above all, it depends on the quality of the messages sent and on the state of mind of the recipient. It is of central importance to devise special means of relaying communication about one's strength, means which are so convincing to the receiver that he will not fail to act upon them. How then can one maxmize creditable knowledge?

A few years ago, Leo Szilard suggested that

...in a state of virtually complete disarmament, neither the United States nor the Soviet Union would have any military secrets. In these circumstances America and the Soviet Union might choose to permit each other to employ plainclothes inspectors, whose identities are not known, as the simplest way to convince each other that there are no evasions [Szilard, 1955, p. 302].

This suggestion to transform the traditional spy system into a mutually accepted reciprocal "spy" network has considerable merit even before complete disarmament has been reached. Suppose that each side has indeed arrived at a decision to abandon its previous strategy of secrecy and to engage instead in a strategy of disclosure. There would still remain the problem of making this creditable to the other side. Here such a mutual "spy" network can make a significant contribution.

The employment of spies to pierce the cover of secrecy with which the adversary surrounded himself has been an age-old tactic in the strategy of warfare. However, the creditability of the messages received through such spy systems has been a perennial problem for intelligence officers. As any reader of spy stories knows, many of the messages transmitted by spies, though they contained most valuable information, had little if any effect because they were simply not believed by the receiving party. Before receiving a message, a person is in a certain state of mind, with sets of beliefs based on prior experience. If the message clashes sharply with this prior state of belief, it is very likely that it will be disregarded and hence will fail to influence future courses of action. Only those messages that seem creditable to the receiver have meaningful consequences. In other words, the receiver will rank-order incoming messages and act only upon those which seem to him to contain a high degree of probability.[3] Yet, in the world of spies and counterspies, with conflicting messages crisscrossing each other, much that is objectively correct information will nevertheless be discarded as improbable. Spy systems, then, have a relatively low capacity to communicate information that can be acted upon.

Following Szilard it may now be suggested that in the new situation which has been sketched, the adversary's "spy" should be highly welcome to his antagonist and the information he conveys should therefore carry much higher creditability. To again quote Szilard (1955):

[3] Cf. Colin Cherry (1957, pp. 245–50).

Peaceful Settlements and Dysfunctions of Secrecy

Today an American agent operating in Russia is a spy who serves the interests of America as well as his own interest; he does not serve the interest of Russia. But when the proper agreement has been concluded, the plainclothes inspector operating on behalf of America on Russian territory serves the interest of Russia, as well as of America, for he is but the means chosen by Russia to convince America that it is indeed disclosing all its capability.

Karl Deutsch recently suggested a related measure in a somewhat different context when he urged an agreement for the mutual or international registration of all scientific and technical personnel. He writes:

Professional inspectors might then be able to make sure...of the whereabouts and the accessibility of scientific personnel. The agreement might then explicitly protect the scientist's freedom to travel and gossip—two propensities which have long been the despair of security officers—and any attempt on the part of any country to conceal the whereabouts of its scientists, to keep them inaccessible to inspectors, or to interfere with their freedom of travel and communication, might serve as prima facie evidence of bad faith...[Deutsch, 1962, p. 68].

The more freely the scientists talk and gossip the more creditable the contention of their government that no valuable information is being withheld.

An invitation to representatives from the opposing camp to participate in key meetings of military and political decision-makers would be another means conducive to making knowledge about one's intentions creditable. Military attachés of the opposing power should be given full access to hitherto "top secret" files so as to facilitate to the utmost their ability to gauge correctly the other side's intentions. When the uncertain and contradictory knowledge hitherto gathered through spy systems and by military attachés is replaced by certified knowledge and a strategy of full disclosure, one moves from a highly unstable system of interaction to one in which the antagonists, to be sure, are still hostile to each other, but are predisposed to engage in bargaining rather than in trial through battle in order to achieve their differing goals.

This is not the place to enumerate in detail the great varieties of proposals for the reduction of pluralistic ignorance between potential enemies which have been advanced in recent years. These range from the monitoring of troop movements or suspicious explosions to systems of inspection by specialized personnel or by ordinary people. My concern here is only to stress that any and all of such measures, to the extent that they serve to make available creditable information to the antagonists, will serve to reduce the area of uncertainty in their dealings with each other and will allow accumulation of reliable information about relative strength—which is the precondition for rational bargaining.

Bargaining under Conditions of Full Disclosure

Let us assume that both parties approach a condition of full knowledge about their respective power. Perceived power now approximates actual power. The "cards are on the table." This still does not resolve the conflict between the two sides; they are still contending for power, territory, influence, or ideas, but it provides a setting in which the conflict is divested of anxiety-provoking features, that is, of the collective anxiety that arises in both camps from guessing—instead of knowing—about the relative balance of power. Once stripped of these unrealistic features the conflict is reduced to the real issues at hand and hence can be carried out by other than violent means.

In realistic conflicts, the weighing of the cost of alternative means of action is a major component of the decision-making process.[4] If disclosure of the adversary's capabilities reveals that the costs of engaging in violent action are likely to be prohibitive, such means will be abandoned and replaced by other means of conflict resolution. Furthermore, if it is realized that there can be *no* payoff for *any* of the participants in an outbreak of violence, there is all the more reason to seek for functional equivalents to war. If this is the case, the atomic age may paradoxically present a most hopeful feature. In no other age was it likely that *both* parties would under *all* circumstances feel that going to war would maximize disutilities for *both* of them. In other words, the very power of the weapons now at the disposal of the antagonists has become so frightful that their very existence is a major deterrent to their employment. The atomic age maximizes the chances that bargaining rather than violent conflict will be the mode of adjustment engaged in by both adversaries.

In collective bargaining, the common interest of both parties leads them to accept rules which enhance their mutual dependence in the very pursuit of their antagonistic goals.[5] Collective bargaining requires that *some* agreement be reached between the parties. Hence, no party is independent of the other since it cannot attain its goals without the other. Each side is dependent for the achievement of its own goals upon the maintenance of a working relationship with the other. A student of the bargaining process in labor management relations, Neil W. Chamberlain, describes this process in terms which seem applicable here and bear quoting:

> The coming together of union and management...arises not because of any sympathetic regard for the other, or because of a voluntary choice of the other as a partner; it arises from the absolute requirement that some agreement—*any* agreement—be reached, so that the operations on which both are dependent and which give both their functional significance may proceed.

This

> ...represents the striking of a working relationship in which both agree, explicitly or impliedly, to provide certain requisite services, to recognize certain seats of authority,

[4] This is not necessarily so in nonrealistic conflicts, but these will not be considered here since it is felt that in international conflicts, though a great deal of affect and emotion is likely to be mobilized, the realistic goals of maximizing power, interests, or values are likely to predominate. On the distinction between realistic and nonrealistic conflicts cf. Coser (1956, pp. 48–55).

[5] Cf. Coser (1961).

Peaceful Settlements and Dysfunctions of Secrecy

and to accept certain responsibilities toward the other. Without such an agreement there could be no operation [Chamberlain, 1951, pp. 445–46].

In the bargaining relation, both attempt to maximize their own interests and each party secures its interest in the measure of its bargaining power. Each party wrests from the other the maximum advantage possible, yet both parties have an overarching interest in maintaining the relation and in coming to *some* agreement.

Compromise is the very stuff of bargaining relations. In a compromise, each party agrees to scale down some of its initial demands and modifies its initial perceptions of what would constitute "victory" or "defeat" in terms of what it can attain within the bargaining relationship.[6] Bargaining and compromise may never in themselves permanently settle the terms of the relationship. Whenever there is a change in the relative power position of either contender, they will have to enter into new bargains to settle their accounts. Bargaining, in other words, is a resolution mechanism, but it can only help to solve problems as they appear within the constellation of forces given at any particular moment. Yet it may be suggested that a continued bargaining relation is likely to broaden in the long run the area of common values and common sentiments. The more habitual the recourse to bargaining and compromise, the higher the chances that both parties slowly move toward a measure of integration. In integration, "new alternatives are accepted of such a kind as to render it extremely difficult to discern the balance between concessions made and concessions received" (Lasswell, 1930). The true integration of two desires—in contrast to their compromise—signifies

...that a solution has been found in which both desires have found a place, that neither side has had to sacrifice anything [North *et al.*, 1960, p. 371].

The world powers are very far indeed from such a condition, yet we can dimly discern it in the future providing they follow the road of bargaining and compromise in the settlement of disputes.

[6] Cf. Coser (1961), Lasswell (1930), and Robert C. North *et al.* (1960).

International Conflict

More
Calculations
About
Deterrence

C H A P T E R   E L E V E N

Clinton F. Fink

Reprinted by permission of the publisher from the *Journal of Conflict Resolution,*
Vol. 9 (March, 1965), 54–65. Mr. Fink is Associate Research Psychologist in the
Center for Research on Conflict Resolution at the University of Michigan.

A central problem in post-World War II discussions of defensive military policies has been that of "deterrence," defined as "the discouragement of military aggression by the threat (implicit or explicit) of applying military force in response to the aggression" (Snyder, 1960, p. 167). Thus defined, the notion of deterrence involves the notion of behavioral influence by communicative means; a deterrent threat is a conditional threat of punishment for an action, where both the specified action and the carrying out of the punishment are undesirable to the one who makes the threat. The purpose of the threat is to prevent the undesired action without actually fighting. Deterrence is problematic because deterrent threats are not always successful; many instances have been recorded in which such a threat has been followed by the very action it was designed to prevent. This is simply a special case of the more general statement that no communicative means for influencing human behavior is uniformly effective under all conditions. The practical problem which arises in this situation is: How can a government make its deterrent threats more effective? The scientific question which must be answered in order to solve the problem is: What are the factors which determine the effectiveness of a deterrent threat?

Common sense has a ready answer: A threat cannot be effective unless it is believed by the recipient, and it will not be believed unless it is credible; therefore, to be effective, a threat must be credible. This conclusion is one of the basic assumptions in much of the literature on deterrence during the past decade. The problem of deterrence thus becomes the problem of credibility: To make a deterrent threat more effective, it must be made more credible. But this only pushes the inquiry one step back. We must now ask: How can a government make its deterrent threats more credible? And the prerequisite scientific question now becomes: What are the factors which determine the credibility of a deterrent threat?

Once again, common sense has an answer: A threat will be credible if there is reason to believe that the one who makes the threat is both *able* and *willing* to carry it out. This is similar to the conditions for credibility of any statement of intentions, for example, the government's promise to exchange metal money for each piece of legal paper money. Thus, in order for a deterrent threat to be credible, it must be imbedded in a context

This article was written during my tenure as a USPHS Postdoctoral Fellow at the Mental Health Research Institute. I am especially grateful to Karl W. Deutsch and George Levinger for their extensive comments on an earlier draft.

of information concerning the threatener's ability and willingness to carry it out. These are the main factors cited in the literature which discusses the determinants of credibility (e.g., Schelling, 1960; Kaufmann, 1954; Snyder, 1960).

Most of the literature on deterrence has not been based on systematic empirical investigation, but has remained analytic, speculative, or normative. Recently, however, Russett (1963) presented the results of a comparative study of six historical cases of successful deterrence and eleven unsuccessful deterrence attempts, in which he explored the question of what makes a threat credible. The deterrence situations he examined were a special class defined as "all the cases during the last three decades where a major power 'attacker' overtly threatened a (minor power) pawn with military force, and where a (major power) defender either had given, prior to the crisis, some indication of an intent to protect the pawn or made a commitment in time to prevent the threatened attack" (p. 98). Thus, instead of ordinary self-defense, these cases involved the defense of a third party.

By comparing data on cases where the deterrent threat succeeded with data on cases where it failed, Russett arrived at a number of conclusions concerning factors which determine the credibility of such threats. In the present paper, I will argue that Russett's data do not compel assent to his conclusions, first because the observed dependent variable is not a satisfactory index of the *credibility* of the threat, and second because it is not a satisfactory index of the *effectiveness* of the threat. Furthermore, the assumption that the threat is a significant deterrent factor is not required in order to provide at least two equally plausible alternative explanations of the data. This situation calls for further empirical research in order to choose among alternative interpretations of Russett's findings and in order to gain more knowledge about the determinants of national nonagression.

Summary of Russett's Study

The sample consisted of 17 historical (1935–1961) deterrence situations, having in common the following elements:

(1) The "attacker" (A) and the "defender" (D) were both major powers—e.g., US, USSR, China, Germany (in several cases, D was a coalition of major powers).

(2) The "pawn" (P) was a minor power—e.g., Iran, Egypt, Cuba, West Berlin.

(3) At a particular time (t), A threatened to attack P militarily.

(4) At some other time, either before or after t but before A could carry out the attack, D overtly expressed an intention to defend P militarily (i.e., to counterattack A if A attacked P). This expressed intention is referred to below as "D's deterrent threat."

Russett stated the problem as follows:

...Propositions about factors which determine the credibility of a given threat need

More Calculations about Deterrence

to be tested systematically on a comparative basis. . . . We shall explore the question of what makes a threat credible by asking which threats in the past have been believed and which disregarded [p. 98].

This implies that the 17 cases were to be subdivided into two groups according to whether or not A *believed* D's deterrent threat, and then compared in order to see what factors are differentially associated with belief and disbelief. In fact, however, the cases were subdivided according to whether or not A subsequently *attacked* P. The implicit assumption involved here was that if A believes D's threat, A will not attack P, but that if A does not believe D's threat, A will attack P. On the basis of this assumption, the observed *effectiveness* of D's threat (success = A does not attack P, failure = A attacks P) was used as an index of its *crediblity* (high credibility = A believes that D is likely to carry out his threat, low credibility = A believes that D is unlikely to carry out his threat). In six cases, the observed outcome was success, while in the remaining eleven cases, the observed outcome was failure.

Nine independent variables were observed, each of which was thought to be a determinant of credibility:

(1) Relative importance of P, defined in terms of population size.

(2) Relative importance of P, defined in terms of gross national product.

(3) Existence, prior to the crisis, of a formal commitment by D to defend P.

(4) Relationship between the overall strategic military capabilities of D and A.

(5) Relationship between the local (in P's territory) military capabilities of D and A.

(6) The type of political system possessed by D (dictatorship vs. democracy).

(7) Military cooperation between D and P, in the form of arms and advisers sent to P.

(8) Political interdependence between D and P.

(9) Economic interdependence between D and P, defined in terms of the amount of trade between them relative to the average amount of trade each has with all other countries.

Although Russett did not specify which component of credibility would be affected by each of these variables, it appears that the first three and the last three are relevant to D's *willingness* to carry out the deterrent threat, while variables 4, 5, and 6 are relevant to D's *ability* carry it out. It was assumed that A would take these factors into account in deciding whether or not to believe the threat. Each variable was dichotomized, and one of the two values was hypothesized to be associated with high credibility. The success and failure cases were then compared in order to test these nine hypotheses. The data for each case were presented in the appendix to Russett's paper (p. 109).

Russett concluded that none of the nine factors is a sufficient condition for high credibility, and that the specified values of variables 1, 2, 3, 4, 5, 6 and 8 are not necessary conditions for high credibility. The crucial conclusions were that the *necessary conditions for high credibility* are: (a) equality of military strength between D and A (on either variable 4 or 5), and (b) presence of military and economic interdependence between D and P (variables 7 and 9). This led to the following hypothesis: "If other factors are equal, an attacker will regard a military response by the defender as more probable the greater the number of military, political, and economic ties between pawn and defender" (p. 107). On the basis of these findings, a practical recommendation was made, to the effect that if the US wants to make more credible its promise to defend third areas, such as Europe, from Soviet attack, it can do so by increasing its economic dependence on those areas.

Credibility vs. Effectiveness

A crucial difficulty in Russett's argument arises from his use of the (observed) effectiveness of D's threat as a measure of its (unobserved) credibility. This assumes that in all cases of successful deterrence, D's threat was credible, and in all cases of unsuccessful deterrence, D's threat was not credible. Unless this assumption is correct, no valid inferences about the determinants of high credibility can be drawn from the data.

Clearly, the equation of effectiveness and credibility is not simply a matter of definition. Effectiveness is the *behavioral outcome* of D's threat, defined in terms of A's subsequent action toward P (attack or no attack). Credibility, however, refers to A's *cognitive reaction* (belief or disbelief) to D's threat. Since these two variables are not identical, there is no strictly logical justification for assuming a one-to-one correspondence between them.

One might rely on the empirical assumption that in order to be effective a threat must be highly credible; i.e., that high credibility of D's threat is a *necessary* condition for successful deterrence. If this is true, then it is legitimate to infer from observed success that the threat was believed by A. However, one cannot also infer from observed failure that the threat was *not* believed by A. This can be maintained only if high credibility is also a *sufficient* condition for success. In other words, the general empirical assumption required as justification for using success and failure as an index of credibility is that: "A believes D's threat" is a necessary *and* sufficient condition for "A does not attack P."

But this assumption, in unqualified form, contradicts Russett's explicit theory for predicting A's response to the deterrent threat. Using the probability-utility model which is currently popular in the analysis of national decision-making (cf. Snyder, 1960; Singer, 1962), Russett specified four variables that jointly determine A's behavior:

(1) Va = the utility to A of an attack on P which *is not* countered by D;
(2) Vw = the utility to A of an attack on P which *is* countered by D;
(3) Vo = the utility to A of not attacking P and consequently not being attacked by D;
(4) s = A's subjective probability that an attack on P would not be countered by D.

More Calculations about Deterrence

The conditions under which D's deterrent threat will fail were then stated in the following formula:

Precisely, he (A) will press the attack only if: Va(s) + Vw(1 − s) > Vo [Russett, p. 107].

Va (*s*) represents the *expected utility* (to A) of an attack on P which is not countered by D, while *Vw* (1 − *s*) represents the expected utility (to A) of an attack which is countered by D. (It is important to note that the term *1* − *s* represents credibility, or A's subjective probability that D *would* counter an attack on P.) The algebraic sum of these two expected utility terms represents the *total expected utility of attacking (EUa)*. Thus, the theory states that A will attack R (and therefore, by definition, D's threat will fail) whenever *EUa* > *Vo*. By implication, it also states that A will not attack P (i.e., D's threat will succeed) whenever *EUa* ⩽ *Vo*. Thus, the statement that high credibility is a necessary and sufficient condition for success is equivalent to the statement that a high value of 1 − *s* (e.g., between 0.5 and 1.0) is a necessary and sufficient condition for *EUa* ⩽ *Vo*. That this is false can be shown by analysis of the formula.

First, note that the value of *EUa* must always fall within the range defined by the values of *Va* and *Vw*. This is so because *EUa* is actually a weighted average of *Va* and *Vw*, where the weights are provided by the complementary probabilities, *s* and 1 − *s*. By formula, *EUa* = *Va*(*s*) + *Vw*(1 − *s*). If *s* = 1, then 1 − *s* = 0, and *EUa* = *Va*. As *s* decreases, 1 − *s* increases, and the value of *EUa* shifts proportionately, reaching the arithmetic mean of *Va* and *Vw* when *s* = 0.5 = 1 − *s*. As *s* decreases further, 1 − *s* increases further, and the value of *EUa* moves closer and closer to the value of *Vw*, until *s* = 0, 1 − *s* = 1, and *EUa* = *Vw*.

Since *EUa* must fall between *Va* and *Vw* for all values of 1 − *s*, it follows that *EUa* < *Vo* for any value of *Vo* which is greater than both *Va* and *Vw*, regardless of the value of 1 − *s*. Therefore, no value of 1 − *s* is a necessary condition for *EUa* ⩽ *Vo*. Furthermore, *EUa* > *Vo* for any value of *Vo* which is smaller than both *Va* and *Vw*, regardless of the value of 1 − *s*. Therefore, no value of 1 − *s* is a sufficient condition for *EUa* ⩽ *Vo*. This implies that high credibility is neither necessary nor sufficient for success, according to Russett's own formula. Therefore, his predictive model does not justify the use of effectiveness as an index of credibility.

However, the formula does allow us to specify a set of conditions under which high credibility will be both necessary and sufficient for success. This will be the case whenever *Va* > *Vw* and *Vo* = ½(*Va* + *Vw*). Under these conditions, *EUa* will be less than *Vo* if, and only if, credibility is high (1 − *s* > 0.5). Since *Vo* falls exactly at the midpoint between *Va* and *Vw*, *EUa* can be less than *Va* only if *Vw* is weighted more heavily than *Va*, and this can occur only if *s* < 0.5 and 1 − *s* > 0.5, since these are the respective weights of *Va* and *Vw*. It can easily be seen that if *Vo* is not equal to the arithmetic mean of Va and Vw, then the minimum value of $1 - s$ that is required in order to make $EUa \leqslant Vo$ will be different from 0.5. If Vo is greater than the mean, then the minimum required value of $1 - s$ is proportionately reduced, since EUa will not have to come as close to Vw in order to be less than Vo. Conversely, if Vo is less than the mean, then the minimum required value of $1 - s$ is proportionately increased, since EUa will have to come closer to Vw in order to be less than Vo. For example, consider all cases in which $Va = +1$ and $Vw = -1$. If $Vo = 0$, then any value of $1 - s > 0.5$ will lead to $EUa < Vo$. But if $Vo = -0.2$, then any value of $1 - s > 0.6$ will lead to $EUa < Vo$. And if $Vo = -0.5$, then any value of $1 - s > 0.75$ will lead to $EUa < Vo$.

In general, for all values of Vo which lie between Va and Vw, where $Va > Vw$, the minimum magnitude of $1 - s$ (degree of credibility) which is required in order to predict that A will not attack P (successful deterrence) is directly proportional to $Va - Vo$, or in other words, is inversely proportional to $Vo - Vw$. Thus, as Vo varies from Va to Vw, the minimum degree of credibility which will be associated with success varies from 0 to 1. If one does not wish to define high credibility as $1 - s > 0.5$, it is possible to give a more general rule. High credibility will be both necessary and sufficient for successful deterrence whenever: (a) $Va > Vo > Vw$, and (b) high credibility is defined as any value of $1 - s$ which is greater than $(Va - Vo)/(Va - Vw)$. Under these conditions, if the formula for predicting A's behavior is true, it is legitimate to infer from observed success that D's threat was credible, and to infer from observed failure that D's threat was not credible.

The above analysis reveals the precise points at which Russett's study needs to be strengthened. First, the meaning of high credibility and low credibility needs to be more clearly defined. This is essential if the inference from outcome to credibility is to mean the same thing in each of the 17 empirical cases. But let us make the reasonable assumption that the less exact terms "likely" and "unlikely" imply a cutting point somewhere near $1 - s = 0.5$. Now, since credibility is only one determinant of behavioral outcome, one cannot infer the degree of credibiity directly from outcome except under specified boundary conditions. In order for success to be a valid indicator of high credibility, and failure a valid indicator of low credibility, Va must be greater than Vw, and $Va - Vo$ must equal approximately $\frac{1}{2}(Va - Vw)$, for all observed cases. It is not necessary that the absolute values of Va, Vo, and Vw be identical across all 17 cases, but only that their relative values be the same for all cases. The critical weakness lies in the fact that Russett presented no evidence or argument to support the assumption that, in each case, $Va - Vo = \frac{1}{2}(Va - Vw)$. If we wish to accept this assumption, then we can accept conclusions about credibility based on observations of the effectiveness of D's threat. But if there is no reason to accept this assumption, then there is no reason to accept any conclusions about the determinants of credibility.

More Calculations about Deterrence

Apparent vs. Actual Effectiveness

A second major difficulty arises from the fact that effectiveness itself was not actually observed. In summarizing Russett's study, I stated that he defined success as the behavioral outcome "A does not attack P," and failure as the outcome "A attacks P." Strictly speaking, this was an oversimplification. Russett's explicit definition of success was "an instance when an attack on the pawn is prevented or repulsed without conflict between the attacking forces and regular combat units of the major power 'defender'" (p. 98). The crucial element in this definition is that D's threat *prevents* A from attacking P. But prevention implies more than the simple observation that A does not attack; it also implies that D's threat is crucial in producing that outcome, i.e., that the threat was an *effective inhibitor of an action that otherwise would have occurred.* According to this meaning of effectiveness, D's threat can be considered successful only if: (a) in the absence of the threat, A would have attacked P; (b) nothing else besides D's threat acted as an effective deterrent; and (c) A did not attack P. If A would not have attacked anyway, then the same behavioral outcome only gives the *illusion* that D's threat was effective; this case can be called *apparent* effectiveness. Unless both conditions *a* and *b* can be assumed to hold, then conclusions about the determinants of actual effectiveness cannot confidently be derived from the data.

The crucial assumption is that in the absence of D's threat (or some other deterrent factor), A would have attacked P. This was assumed to be true for each of the six "success" cases. Apparently, the only basis for this assumption is the fact that in each case, A had threatened to attack P. But to infer from A's threat that A will attack P unless prevented by some deterrent is to attribute perfect credibility to A's threat. One cannot ignore the possibility that A might threaten P, not because A actually intends to attack P, but rather as a means to some other end. For example, it might be simply a tactical move on the part of A in order to distract D's attention or in order to win a concession on some other point. Possibly the only factor which is needed in order to differentiate the "success" and "failure" cases is that in the former, A did not intend to attack P, while in the latter, A did intend to attack.

Even if it is granted that A would have attacked, it still must be shown that it was D's deterrent threat and not some other input which made the difference. Suppose, for example, that D's deterrent threat was only one of several world social forces that were brought to bear on A in response to A's threat to attack P. Various countries, international organizations, or even factions within A may have tried, by various means (including threats of nonmilitary retaliation, promises, and suasion), to deter A from such aggression. The total pattern of such forces might have to be considered the effective deterrent in this case,

194

and it is conceivable that D's threat alone would not have been sufficient.

The implication of the above argument is that before one can accept Russett's data as evidence regarding the determinants of threat effectiveness, evidence must be obtained on the six "success" cases to show that they are in fact cases of actual success.

Alternative Interpretations of the Data

If the preceding arguments are correct, it follows that Russett's data can, by themselves, tell us nothing about the determinants of either the credibility or the effectiveness of D's deterrent threat. However, the data are not meaningless, since the observed dependent variable is itself interesting. There were, in fact, two different behavioral outcomes (attack vs. no attack) within the set of 17 deterrence situations studied. If one admits the possibility that D's threat had little or no causal relevance to the outcome, then the data can be reexamined in an effort to develop hypotheses about the determinants of A's final response.

To facilitate the analysis, the findings can be summarized by means of a series of 2 × 2 contingency tables. This can be done readily from Russett's appendix (p. 109), since all variables there were dichotomized. Table 1 shows the number of "attack" (failure) cases and the number of "no attack" (success) cases for each value of the nine independent variables. To provide a rough measure of the degree of association between the independent variables and behavioral outcome, phi coefficients have been computed, and the variables are listed in descending order according to their corresponding phi values.

One may have some reservations about applying a statistical test to these data, on grounds that historical connections among many of the cases contradict the assumptions of independence required by the test. For example, three of the "success" cases involved the US in the role of defender against the USSR, all within a two-year period; and four of the failure cases involved Great Britain and France in the role of defender against Germany, again within a two-year period. It can be argued that these seven cases are not really seven independent cases, but rather only two, and that the sample is therefore artificially inflated from the point of view of statistical inference. However, the effect of reducing sample size would be to reduce the degree of confidence one could have that any of the correlations are different from zero. Recognizing that the purpose of the present analysis is not to test hypotheses, but rather to suggest them, it does not seem necessary to apply the most rigorous statistical criteria. Thus, for each 2 × 2 table, the chance probability of obtaining the given array of data (or a more extreme array) has been computed by means of Fisher's exact test, simply as a basis for comparing the obtained correlations.

Among the nine independent variables, economic interdependence between D and P is most highly associated with outcome. On the basis

Situational variable		Number of cases for each outcome		Phi coeffi-cient	Probability by Fisher's Exact Test
		Attack	No attack		
(9) P–D Econ. Interdependence:	Present	2	5	0.63	0.076
	Absent	9	1		
(7) P–D Military Cooperation:	Present	7	6	0.41	0.140
	Absent	4	0		
(8) P–D Polit. Interdependence:	Present	4	4	0.28	>0.200
	Absent	7	2		
(4) Strategic Superiority, D/A:	Present	5	4	0.20	>0.200
	Absent	6	2		
(6) D's Political System:	Dictatorship	2	2	0.17	>0.200
	Democracy	9	4		
(5) Local Superiority, D/A:	Present	2	0	−0.27	>0.200
	Absent	9	6		
(3) Precrisis Commitment by D:	Present	6	1	−0.37	0.160
	Absent	5	5		
(1) Population Ratio, P/D:	20%+	5	0	−0.48	0.075
	20%−	6	6		
(2) GNP Ratio, P/D:	5%+	5	0	−0.48	0.075
	5%−	6	6		

of this finding, Russett argued that the credibility of D's threat is positively associated with D—P interdependence. But the obtained correlation can be interpreted in quite a different way. Perhaps in most cases A threatened to attack a pawn which was known to be important to D *in order to harass D* and perhaps win some other point in another arena of A—D interaction. If so, then A's threat and D's deterrent threat set up an apparent deterrence situation, which was bound to result in no attack because A had no intention of doing so. Thus, D—P economic interdependence may be associated with no attack, not because it influenced A's decision about attacking *following* D's threat, but rather because it influenced A's decision to make a false threat against P *prior* to D's deterrent threat.

Although military cooperation between D and P was more weakly associated with outcome, it was nevertheless present in all cases of no attack. This may be accounted for in the same way as the previous correlation. The fact that D sent arms and advisers to P may have been treated by A as evidence that D was interested enough in P to be affected by a threat against P. This objective fact of D—P cooperation may have been the trigger for a false threat by A rather than a cue enhancing the credibility and effectiveness of D's deterrent threat. This same line of argument is consistent with the fact that the relative military strength of A and D was not associated with outcome: If A did not really intend to attack P, then it would not be necessary for D to be militarily superior to A in order for the outcome to be "no attack."

It is more difficult to account for the unexpected finding that the

196

TABLE 2   BEHAVIORAL OUTCOME OF 17 DETERRENCE SITUATIONS AS A FUNCTION OF DATE OF OCCURRENCE OF THE CRISIS

Date of crisis	Number of cases for each outcome		Phi coefficient	Probability by Fisher's Exact Test
	Attack	No attack		
Post-1945	4	6	0.62	0.017
Pre-1940	7	0		

relative size of P and D was negatively correlated with outcome. Neither the "credibility" interpretation nor the "false threat by A" interpretation is consistent with this result, since a P that is relatively unimportant should neither be selected as a special target by A nor produce a highly credible threat by D. Perhaps this merely reflects the fact that the size of P relative to the defender does not function as a sign of the importance of P in D's value hierarchy. But if this is true, why shouldn't the correlation be near zero rather than near − 0.50? One answer might be that the sample is so small that one cannot attribute much significance to the obtained correlation. However, this would remove the necessity for interpreting any of the obtained correlations, since the statistical significance level obtained by Fisher's exact test is 0.075 for both the most positive and the most negative correlations in the table. A second possible answer is that the P/D ratio varies mainly because of variations in the size of D rather than because of variation in the size of P. A glance at Russett's list of cases (1963, p. 99) shows that in all six "success" (no attack) cases, D was either the US or the USSR, which are much larger than other major powers, while in the failure (attack) cases, more than half involved Great Britain and France as defenders. When D is very large, P is more likely to be relatively small. This difference alone can account for the obtained negative correlation between relative size of P and behavioral outcome.

Differences in the size of D are coupled to another fact which may be of significance. One can also see from Russett's list of cases that all of the "no attack" outcomes occurred during the post-World War II era, while most of the "attack" outcomes occurred prior to the war. Table 2 shows the relationship between behavioral outcome and date of occurrence of the crisis.

The striking fact about these data is that the historical period is as strongly associated with outcome as is D—P economic interdependence. But the correlation between date and outcome permits an entirely different interpretation. It is conceivable that a crucial change has taken place in the total international situation, sharply increasing the total pattern of deterrent pressures which can be brought to bear on a potential attacker. Perhaps the focusing of world political pressures through the United Nations exerts a great restraining force, a general downward pressure on EU_a, even without explicit deterrent threats by D. It is

More Calculations about Deterrence

quite plausible that such extra pressures were far weaker during the prewar period, so that the total deterrent environment has changed. Under this interpretation, the association between outcome and D—P economic or military interdependence may be merely a reflection of the fact that the postwar policies of both the US and the USSR have led to an increase in the number of satellites for each. In this case, P—D interdependence can be seen as a cause for D's deterrent threat, but as causally irrelevant to the behavioral outcome.

A different mode of analysis of the data, which Russett apparently used in ariving at several of his conclusions, is to look for factors which may be necessary conditions for the occurrence of the preferred outcome (no attack). Since a necessary condition is one which must be present in order for the desired event to take place, it follows that in order to claim that a factor may be necessary, it must be present in all cases with that outcome. From Tables 1 and 2, it can be seen that the following conditions were present in all six cases where the outcome was "no attack": (1) there was military cooperation between D and P; (2) D did not possess local military superiority over A; (3) the population ratio of P/D was less than 20 percent; (4) the GNP ratio of P/D was less than 5 percent; (5) the crisis occurred after 1945. It is also true, although not shown in these tables, that in each case: (6) D was either the US or the USSR; (7) D possessed nuclear weapons at the time of the crisis.

Thus it is possible that any one of these conditions, or any combination of two or more of them, is a necessary condition for the outcome to be "no attack." There are probably many other factors which were also present in each of these cases, so that a decision as to which, if any, are necessary to the outcome is not possible on the basis of the limited data which have been presented.

Implications for Further Research

The alternative interpretations which I have given for Russett's data reflect a theoretical approach to the study of deterrence which is generally similar to his. The differences seem to lie mainly in which factual assumptions we are willing to make or which potentially relevant variable we are willing to ignore for purposes of a particular study. Thus, the general theory which we both use postulates that if there are factors motivating A to attack P, then some inhibiting factors must be present in order to prevent that attack. Russett's study concentrated on a specific subset of all possible inhibiting factors, while assuming that other inhibiting factors as well as the motivating factors were constant or else could be ignored. My thesis is simply that greater attention must be paid to the latter two sets of factors if valid conclusions are to be drawn about the first set.

The model I have been using predicts behavioral outcome from the relative strength of two motives: A's motive to attack P (Ma) and A's motive not to attack P (Mo). It states that A will attack if $Ma - Mo > 0$, and that A will not attack if $Ma - Mo \leqslant 0$. Further, Mo is broken down into at least two components: the motivation not to attack which arises from D's deterrent threat (Dd), and the motivation not to attack which arises from other deterrent factors (Od). $Mo = Dd + Od$. Thus, A will attack if $Ma - Dd - Od > 0$, but will not attack if $Ma - Dd - Od \leqslant 0$. The magnitude of Dd will make a difference to the outcome only if $Ma - Od > 0$, because the predicted outcome will always be "no attack" when $Ma - Od \leqslant 0$.

The "other inhibiting factors" which contribute to the strength of Od need not be restricted to threats of military retaliation by nations other than D. It is possible to broaden the concept of deterrence to include other methods of influencing A, such as threats of economic retaliation or promises (by D or by other nations) of reward for doing something else (cf. Milburn, 1959, p. 139). In addition, inhibiting factors need not all arise in A's social environment, but may come partly from politically active groups within A. Thus, one may consider both negative and positive pressures against attacking, arising from various sources.

Future empirical research on the determinants of effective deterrence must deal explicitly with these various classes of variables, since it cannot be assumed a priori that they are negligible in any historical case. If the problem is to determine whether some particular variable influences the magnitude of Dd, and if the behavioral outcome of the deterrence situation is to be used as an index of the magnitude of Dd, then ideally the cases would be selected so that they all have the same magnitude, greater than zero, of $Ma - Od$. If it is not possible to find a sufficient number of such cases on record, then it may be possible to do the next best thing, which is to measure the strengths of the various component motivational forces and make empirical predictions by plugging the obtained values into one or more predictive formulas in order to see whether predictions are improved by including the variable in question. If the problem of measuring the motivational forces appears insurmountable for the present, it may be necessary to give up the motivational model as a basis for designing the study, or even to redefine the problem.

One approach which does not depend so directly on the motivational model starts with the postulate that the behavioral outcome of the deterrence siutation is determined by the total pattern of communicative influence attempts (threats, promises, and suasion) directed at A's decision-makers after A threatened to attack P. It can be assumed that some of these messages will be favorable to the attack, and that others will oppose it; it can also be assumed that some countries will not attempt to influence A in a particular case, thus by default communicating permissiveness. It can also be assumed that the impact of each message will be a function of the power of its sender; thus each message can be weighted according to some index of the sender's power, and a weighted sum of favorable, unfavorable, and permissive messages can be obtained. A's response can be predicted from the ratio of the total strength of unfavorable messages to the total strength of favorable messages, perhaps modified by the total amount of permissiveness present in the situation. The link between these factors and the motivational model is contained in the assumption that Mo is positively correlated with the total strength of unfavorable messages, and that Ma is increased by the occurrence of favorable messages and perhaps by the presence of permissiveness. Whether it is easier to gather data on the matrix of influence attempts impinging on A, or directly on the motivational state of A, will have to be answered in the process of trying to gather both kinds of data.

An important implication of the present discussion is this: The question of whether deterrent threats of military retaliation are *ever* effective in preventing aggression is prior to the question of what determines the effectiveness of such threats. Can one find evidence to refute the null hypothesis that the incidence of military attacks by one nation on another, following a threat by the attacker, is the same whether or not a deterrent threat is made? Perhaps this hypothesis can be tested by broadening the empirical base beyond deterrence situations involving only the defense of small third parties by large defenders against large attackers. By including self-defense situations as well and by taking all cases regardless of the size of the principal participant nations, a much larger sample of deterrence situations can be obtained. With a larger sample, the chances will be greater of finding cases in which there was no deterrent threat (remember that there apparently was such a threat in every case in Russett's sample); unless such cases can be found, it will not be possible to test the hypothesis in question.

Russett's study was an effort to apply *ex post facto* experimental logic to the empirical investigation of deterrence. I have tried to show some of the difficulties encountered in such studies. But despite these difficulties, I believe that this kind of systematic analysis of historical cases can lead to an advance in knowledge about international relations. If nothing more, it can at least help clarify the nature of and the reasons for our ignorance of general laws governing the behavior of nations.

References

Kaufmann, William W. *The Requirements of Deterrence.* (Memo No. 7.) Princeton, N.J.: Center for International Studies, 1954.

Milburn, Thomas W. "What constitutes effective deterrence?" *Journal of Conflict Resolution,* 3, 2 (June 1959), 138–45.

Russett, Bruce M. "The calculus of deterrence," *Journal of Conflict Resolution,* 7, 2 (June 1963), 97–109.

Schelling, T. C. *The Strategy of Conflict.* Cambridge: Harvard University Press, 1960.

Singer, J. David. *Deterrence, Arms Control and Disarmament: Toward a Synthesis in National Security Policy.* Columbus, Ohio: Ohio State University Press, 1962.

Snyder, Glenn H. "Deterrence and power," *Journal of Conflict Resolution,* 4, 2 (June 1960), 163–78.

Critique
of
Strategic
Thinking

Anatol Rapoport

Reprinted with permission of the publishers from Roger Fisher (ed.), *International Conflict and Behavioral Science* (New York: Basic Books, Inc., 1964), pp. 211–37. Copyright © 1964 by The American Academy of Arts and Sciences. Mr. Rapoport is Professor of Mathematical Biology and Senior Research Mathematician at the Mental Health Research Institute, University of Michigan.

Instead of defining "strategic thinking" at the outset, we shall rely on the entire discussion to convey its essential features and flavor. Moreover, we shall not be concerned with the merits of specific policy recommendations dominated by strategic thinking. Critical analyses of such recommendations are undertaken elsewhere in this volume and in other writings of the authors represented here. Our concern will be with the general framework in which strategic thinking occurs. Specifically we have in mind the underlying, frequently implicit but sometimes helpfully explicit, assumptions on which rest the arguments of the numerous proponents of various deterrence policies in the present global conflict. The output of the RAND Corporation contains a wealth of examples of this approach. An especially revealing specimen, in which the emotional as well as the intellectual props of the strategic orientation are alarmingly apparent, is Herman Kahn's much-discussed volume, *On Thermonuclear War*.[1]

We shall be referring to the exponents of strategic thinking as "the strategists," and it will appear at times that "the strategists" are being accused of shortsightedness, callousness, and other faults. It should be clear that these accusations are leveled not at individuals but at idealized representatives of a mode of thought. In practice it would be impossible to point out "the strategists" as a sharply defined group. All of us at times think strategically. Indeed, strategic thinking is only a variant of rational thinking, and so is a part of the heritage of science. We could easily resign ourselves to the conclusion that the evil by-products of strategic thinking represent a part of the price we pay for being civilized. On the other hand, we could accept the responsibility placed on us by civilization to apply the methods of analytical critique to self-appraisal. If, as some strategists maintain, thinking in strategic terms is no more than a dispassionate appraisal of realities and potentialities, the same is true of the critique of strategic thinking. Of necessity, however, such a critique, being a critique of *thinking* rather than an appraisal of military or poltical situations, must depend to some extent on intuitive and introspective methods and so must bring in concepts foreign to strategic thinking.

Our critique will be made from two points of view. From one, it will appear that there is an inherent tendency in strategic thinking to simplify the analysis of a situation in order to make a decision problem more tractable. Decision problems can be cast into several models, which

[1] Herman Kahn, *On Thermonuclear War* (Princeton: Princeton University Press, 1960).

International Conflict

can be arranged in an ascending order of complexity. The more complex the model, the more problematic becomes the estimation of data required to solve the associated decision problem. Accordingly, pressure is constantly operating on the strategist to simplify the situation, either by casting it into a simpler model or by skirting around the estimation problem. The concomitant danger is in the omission of possibly the most essential features of the problem.

From the other point of view, the dangers inherent in strategic thinking are even more serious. They lie in the tendency not merely to oversimplify problems but to misrepresent them. This happens when a decision problem cannot be solved at all within the framework of strategic thinking, even if exact data are available. We shall give examples of such problems, which have no "best" solutions in the context of strategic decisions. Such problems can be solved only if we invoke extra-strategic considerations, which must of necessity be couched in terms foreign to strategic thinking, such as social norms, trust, empathy, and so forth. Ironically, it is rigorous strategic analysis that has brought these extra-strategic concepts to the forefront. Nevertheless, when we assume the role of strategists, we tend to avoid introducing these concepts into our analysis. We shall offer conjectures on why this is so and will argue the necessity of overcoming this blindspot.

Theory of Rational Decision

We shall begin by examining the elements of the theory of rational decision, which serves as the alleged rigorous basis of strategic thinking. In particular, the theory of games, in many ways the most advanced and sophisticated branch of decision theory, has had a pronounced influence on strategic thinking.

As strategists, we do not, of course, always or even frequently represent situations as formal decision problems or as schematized games. Our expositions and recommendations rest, for the most part, on verbal arguments, frequently spiked with rhetoric. To the extent, however, that strategic thinking can lay claim to a "scientific" foundation (a claim often made in various guises), the support for this claim must come from an analysis of situations and problems in the methodological framework of rational decision theory.

It will be useful to distinguish three kinds of decision theory: formal, prescriptive (or normative), and descriptive (or empirical). The formal theory is purely deductive. Like mathematics, of which it frequently appears as a branch, formal decision theory does not depend on data. The axioms of the theory, as well as all the pertinent variables in any problem, are always assumed given. The task of the theory is confined to constructing a deductive apparatus to derive logically necessary conclusions from the given assumptions.

Prescriptive theory, on the other hand, is concerned with the determination of *optimizing* decisions. The existence of such "best" decisions does not by any means imply that real people are always or predominantly guided by them. Thus discrepancies between the prescriptive theory and observed behavior do not refute a prescriptive theory. Such a theory says how people ought to act, not how they do act.

A descriptive theory seeks to find principles that guide real people's decisions. It must therefore rely on behavioral data. Such a theory accomplishes its aims if it can say (and support the statement with empirical evidence) something like this: "People make decisions *as if* they were guided by the following decision rules. . . ." Since the decision patterns of different people may be different, the descriptive theory will rely in part on classifications, typologies, and other groupings of decision-makers.

It follows that formal decision theory (which includes the mathematical theory of games) is most closely related to the deductive disciplines (logic and mathematics), prescriptive decision theory to applied science (engineering and operations research), and descriptive theory to the behavioral sciences. Obviously, recommendations based on the deductions of the formal theory imply the application of prescriptive theory. But as we shall see, applications are often powerless without the knowledge of actual decision processes. Thus rational decision theory can provide a useful guide to action only if all three of its sources are drawn upon.

Decision Under Certainty

The simplest example of a decision problem involves the choice of one of several courses of action, where the outcome of each course is uniquely determined. If the choice is between actions A_1, A_2, . . . A_n, leading respectively to outcomes O_1, O_2, . . . O_n, and if O_i is the most preferred outcome, then the decision to choose A_i is called a rational decision.

Already in this simplest problem we can see the distinctive features of the formal, prescriptive, and descriptive approaches. The formal theory does no more in this context than *define* the rational decision. Prescriptive theory must prescribe. It can therefore be applied only after the most preferred outcome has been determined, which may require no more than an introspective "scanning" on the part of the decision-maker. Descriptive theory, on the other hand, must relate many people's preferences to their decisions, which requires the examination of many preference schemes and many decision schemes. It is by no means certain that such comparisons will immediately enable the investigator to organize his data into a theory, that is, a set of general propositions consistent with observed facts. In short, it is not certain that a descriptive theory of rational decisions is at all possible. To assume that it is possible is to affirm the basic faith inherent in the scientific enterprise.

The "minimal axioms" of a rational decision theory (whether formal, prescriptive, or descriptive) can be illustrated in the context of our example. They are generally taken to be

(1) *Consistency:* If O_i is preferred to O_j, then O_j is not preferred to O_i.

(2) *Transitivity:* If O_i is preferred to O_j, and O_j to O_k, then O_i is preferred to O_k.

(3) *Instrumentality:* If A_i leads to O_i, and A_j to O_j, and if O_i is preferred to O_j, then A_i is chosen in preference to A_j.

In the context of formal theory, these "axioms" are no more than definitions. In the context of prescriptive theory, they are rules for ordering preferences and choosing actions. What role do the axioms play in descriptive theory? Clearly they cannot be general descriptions of our gross observations of how people order preferences and choose actions. Violations of these principles are all too common, as the following examples show.

(1) A man prefers meat to fish at one time and fish to meat at another, apparently violating the consistency axiom.

(2) Among three oranges, a man prefers O_1 when he must choose between O_1 and O_2; O_2 when the choice is between O_2 and O_3; O_3 when confronted with O_3 and O_1. Here the transitivity axiom appears to be violated.

(3) A man knows that A_1 will lead to O_1 and A_2 to O_2 and prefers O_1 to O_2 but nevertheless chooses A_2, apparently violating instrumentality.

One possible conclusion is that such behavior is not "rational." But of course we can do better than that. We can often redefine the situation so as to remove the violations of the axioms. For example, it may appear on closer examination that the man prefers fish to meat only on Fridays. We can then list four choices instead of two: (1) meat on any day but Friday, (2) meat on Friday, (3) fish on any day but Friday, (4) fish on Friday. In this context, consistency is not violated.

In the second example, we may discover that the man compares oranges according to three criteria—price, appearance, and flavor—and that in each paired comparison a different criterion dominates the choice.

In the third example, the man may have realized after comparing O_1 and O_2 that not only O_1 would be the consequence of choosing A_1, but also some cost associated with A_1 itself, which was not compensated by the difference between O_1 and O_2.

Such investigations belong to descriptive decision theory. They are undertaken with a view to establishing a consistent and transitive preference ordering among a set of outcomes. Prescriptive theory, on the other hand, assumes such an ordering already established. Thus if each action leads to a certain outcome, application of the instrumetality principle makes the decision problem trivial.

Decisions Under Risk and Uncertainty

Choices of action cease to be trivial in situations in which actions do not lead to unique outcomes. The simplest possible case of this sort is that of two actions, A_1 and A_2, of which A_1 may lead either to O_1 or to O_1', while A_2 leads to O_2. A real decision problem arises if O_1 is preferred O_2, which, in turn is preferred to O_1'. Does (or should) the "rational man" prefer the certainty of O_2 to the risky choice between O_1, which is better, and O_1', which is worse?

Common sense dictates the relevant considerations. What are the relative likelihoods of O_1 and O_1'? How much is O_1 preferred to O_1'? In short, how big is the risk, and is it worth taking? We note that two new elements have been introduced into our view of rational decisions—degree of preference and likelihood of occurrence. In the context of *certain* outcomes, likelihood of occurrence was clearly irrelevant. Nor was it necessary to assume degrees of preference. Only an *ordering* of preferences was required. With the introduction of outcomes whose likelihoods influence decisions, both of the above-mentioned new concepts enter *per force*.

If the outcomes are uncertain, we can distinguish two limiting cases: (1) the likelihoods can be assigned as numerical probabilities; (2) nothing is known about the likelihoods. (Intermediate cases involving partial knowledge of the likelihoods will not be discussed here.)

The notion of a calculated risk (to the extent that this phrase is not simply a label used to justify a dangerous policy) depends essentially on the possibility of attaching numerical values to likelihoods of events, as is done in the theory of probability.

In our example, suppose the probabilities of O_1 and O_1' are known— p and p' ($p + p' = 1$)—and suppose the worth (utilities) of the three outcomes can be expressed *numerically* as u_1, u_1', and u_2 respectively. Then if the optimization principle is to maximize the expected utility, the decision-maker is told to choose the risky action A_1 provided $pu_1 + p'u_1' > u_2$, and the certain action A_2 otherwise.

On what basis is such a decision called rational? The most convincing rationale usually offered is that based on the law of large numbers proved in the theory of probability. The law applies if the utilities are additive; that is, the utility of N outcomes O_1 is Nu_1. Then the law states (roughly) that if the risky choice is made many times, the odds become so overwhelmingly large that the average gain *per choice* will be very nearly $pu_1 + p'u_1'$. Thus the situation is reduced to one where the choice is between (nearly) certain outcomes, namely between $pu_1 + p'u_1'$ and u_2 per choice. For instance, if a man rolls a die many times in succession and receives two dollars every time a 4 appears and pays one dollar when it does not, he can expect after 1,000 throws to lose very nearly fifty cents per throw ($\frac{1}{6} \times 2 + \frac{5}{6} \times (-1) = -\frac{1}{2}$). His choice is between this amount and nothing per throw, which results if he refuses to play. The gamble clearly does not pay. It pays, however, to the gambling house, which operates on precisely this principle, as do insurance companies and all businesses that base their policies on actuarial calculations.

If the expected gain principle is a rational one, at least where money gambles are involved, why do people make risky choices that do not pay? In particular, why do people gamble in casinos? The usual common-sense answers are either that gambling addicts are stupid or that they derive other satisfactions from the gambling situation, which compensate them for the monetary losses.

Neither of these explanations is satisfactory in the context of buying insurance. Clearly, the buyer of insurance (say fire insurance) accepts a risky choice with a negative expected money gain (positive to the insurance company). But few people would call him stupid on that account or guess that he gets a thrill from the gamble. A possible explanation is that people buy insurance because "this is the thing to do." This may very well be. It is easy, however, to construct an example removed from customary practice, in which the acceptance of a risky choice with even a large positive expected money gain will seem exceedingly unwise.

Suppose a man is asked to stake his life savings ($10,000) on a draw of a single card from a well-shuffled deck. If the deuce of spades is drawn, he gets a million dollars; otherwise he loses his $10,000. The probability of drawing a particular card is $\frac{1}{52}$. The expected gain is therefore $(\frac{1}{52} \times 1{,}000{,}000) - (\frac{51}{52} \times 10{,}000) = \$9{,}423.08$, a very substantial positive expected gain. Yet most would agree that the man would be foolhardy to accept this offer.

Utility theory was originally invented to circumvent this difficulty. James Bernoulli argued in effect that to most people a million dollars is by no means "worth" one hundred times more than $10,000. It might, for example, be worth only ten times as much. If utility values of money amounts instead of the money amounts themselves were used in the calculation of expected gains, it would turn out that many gambles with positive expected money gains have negative expected utility gains and vice versa. Thus the expected gain principle would be saved as a rational decision principle.

Let us now see how our risky decision rule reads: In risky situations assign numerical utilities to outcomes (whose probabilities are presumed known). Choose the action that leads to the greatest expected utility return. As always, we must keep in mind that a decision theory may be viewed as either prescriptive or descriptive. The rule as stated is a prescriptive rule. The verbs are in the imperative mood. In a corresponding proposition of descriptive theory, the verbs would have to be in the indicative mood: "For every person, each of a set of outcomes has a numerical utility, whose expected gain the person seeks to maximize." To validate this proposition, one should actually exhibit a "utility function," which governs each person's decision.

If the theory is prescriptive, the problem arises of how to apply the rule. For example, the decision-maker might ask, "How do I assign (my own) utilities to outcomes? I have a good idea about my order of preferences, but I am at a loss how to assign *numerical* values to the outcomes."

If the theory is neither prescriptive nor descriptive but only formal, these problems do not arise. The utilities, like the probabilities, are simply assumed given. The translation of the general principle (of maximizing expected utility gains) into specific cases involves nothing more than calculations of these expected gains. Since the calculations are sometimes difficult, the problems associated with risky outcomes may be by no means trivial (as they are in the case of certain outcomes where only an inspection and a comparison of magnitudes is involved). Still these problems remain, in the context of formal theory, straightforward problems (*problèmes bien posés,* to use Henri Poincaré's expression). One always knows how to solve them in principle. The problems associated with prescriptive and descriptive decision theories, on the other hand, become serious methodological problems as soon as risky outcomes are introduced. Whereas the determination of a simple preference order could reasonably be considered a simple task (at least in simple contexts), a method of determining utilities (introduced to preserve the expected gain principle) is by no means a straightforward problem.[2]

To summarize, the introduction of risky choices into a decision problem complicates the task of a formal decision theory only moderately, in that it necessitates a numerical calculation instead of a simple comparison of magnitudes. But it complicates the task of a prescriptive theory substantially, because it poses the problem of how to assign utilities to events. It complicates descriptive theory severely, because it poses the problem of determining how *other* people assign utilities to events (especially since different people may do so in different ways). This uneven rate of increasing complexity in the three types of theory persists as the decision situations become more and more complex.

Our next step is to pass from choices among risky outcomes to those among uncertain ones. These are outcomes whose probabilities are unknown. In addition to assigning utilities, the decision-maker must now also assign probabilities to events. The behavioral scientists correspondingly must ascertain how people assign probabilities to uncertain events (if they do). Formal decision theory bypasses this problem. Indeed, if probabilities were assumed as given, the problem would be reduced to the risky

---

[2] The theory of utility we have just outlined is based on ideas introduced by Bernoulli in the eighteenth century. Later this theory lost most of its appeal, mainly because there seemed to be no way to determine utilities either objectively or introspectively. In their *Theory of Games and Economic Behavior* (Princeton: Princeton University Press, 1955 [rev. ed.]), Oskar Morgenstern and John von Neumann reintroduced utility theory on a different basis. In their formulation, the utilities of outcomes of any decision-maker can, in principle, he determined if the decision-maker has consistent and transitive preferences among all risky choices. The utilities so assigned are then automatically such that the choices reflect decisions to maximize expected utility, and this optimization principle need not be introduced as an additional principle of rational decision [cf. R. D. Luce and H. Raiffa, *Games and Decisions* (New York: John Wiley & Sons, Inc., 1957), Chapter 2]. This stratagem virtually reduces decisions under risk to decisions under *certainty,* since each choice now leads certainly to a (possibly risky) outcome, which is not distinguished from any other kind of outcome. In this way, the prescriptive theory of decision under risk is reduced to triviality. The problems of descriptive theory remain (and possibly become aggravated), because of the difficulty of determining consistent and transitive choices among risky outcomes. Formal theory, however, is helped immensely by this "tautological" definition of utility, since the maximization of expected utility now becomes a logical consequence of its definition and so prescriptive aspects can be sidestepped. This solution has enabled Morgenstern and von Neumann to build their *formal* theory (decisions in conflict situations) on logically sound foundations.

choice problem. To distinguish the uncertain choice problems, formal decision theory has introduced assumptions not based on probability considerations and has thus continued the line of development that links elementary decision theory with the more advanced theory of games.[3] We shall not pursue this development here, although we shall examine the theory of games in its own characteristic context—the conflict situation.

Probabilities of Events

Let us now look at the problem of assigning a probability to an event. Such assignments can be made on three kinds of grounds—empirical, logical, or intuitive. To illustrate the first, suppose we are given a coin that is said to be biased and are asked to estimate the bias. A reasonable way to proceed is to toss the coin many (say 1,000) times. The observed frequency of heads is a good estimate of its probability. If such repeated experiments cannot be performed, we cannot estimate probabilities on empirical grounds.

Early workers in probability theory argued that probabilities can be assigned on logical grounds. In order to do so, it must be possible to list a set of events among which "there is no reason" to suppose any one is "more likely" than another. For instance, in the case of a perfectly symmetrical die, it is argued that since "there is no reason" to suppose that the appearance of any of the six faces is any more likely than another, we must assign equal probabilities to all the faces. The probabilities of complex events (for example, that at least one appearance of either 1 or 4 will occur in three successive throws) can be then computed according to the calculus of probabilities (also a purely logical procedure).

The "logical" assignment of probabilities raises the problem of listing the basic "equiprobable" events. In the case of the die, such events readily suggest themselves. But not all situations are so simple. A classical paradox illustrates the difficulty. Suppose Robinson Crusoe catches two turtles on the beach and contemplates the chances that he can start a turtle farm. (Assume that he cannot determine the sex of turtles by inspection.) He could assume that the three equiprobable possibilities are (1) two males; (2) two females; and (3) male and female. According to this assumption, his chances are $33\frac{1}{3}$ per cent. But he could assume with equal reason that there are four equiprobable cases: (1) male, male; (2) male, female; (3) female, male; (4) female, female. In this case his chances are 50 per cent.

The more nearly correct probability could be determined if Crusoe could get more evidence, for example, catch many pairs of turtles. But this would be an empirical, not a logical, determination of probability. It is clear that the assignment of a probability on "logical" grounds cannot

[3] For thorough and illuminating discussions of these matters, see L. J. Savage, *The Foundations of Statistics* (New York: John Wiley & Sons, Inc., 1954).

Critique of Strategic Thinking

also be "verified" logically. Such an assignment is made *arbitrarily*, depending on which events one has singled out as equiprobable. In some cases, to be sure, the choice of one set of equiprobable events seems obviously "natural" (as in the case of the symmetrical die), and so the assignment of numerical probabilities on logical grounds can be defended.

When the event under consideration is *unique*, and there is no natural list of equiprobable alternatives, there is no objective basis either on empirical or on logical grounds for assigning a numerical probability to it. An example of such an event is the outbreak of a thermonuclear war in a given time period. An assignment of a numerical probability to this event can be made only on intuitive grounds. This probability can represent a degree of belief of the person who assigns it, but there is no compelling reason to prefer one man's degree of belief to another's.

Decisions in Conflict Situations

So far we have been dealing with problems in which the decision-maker needs to consider only his own preferences and the possible "states of nature." Whatever explicit assumption he makes about nature, the tacit assumption of a rational decision-maker is that nature is neutral with regard to his preferences and ambitions. She does not guide *her* choices by what he does, striving to frustrate (or to help) him. The situation changes drastically as soon as an *opponent* appears on the scene—to wit, another decision-maker whose interests are wholly or partially opposed to those of the first decision-maker and who is, moreover, also "rational."

The extension of decision theory to this situation (and more generally to situations with more than two "players," as the decision-makers are now called) is known as the theory of games.

A crucial difference between decision problems involving one decision-maker (sometimes called games against nature) and a bona fide two-person game is that in the latter the other player is not neutral. The decision-maker, who finds himself on one end of the decision process, as it were, cannot assume that the other end is determined by a "state of nature" and so depends on chance. In certain special cases, when the decision-maker knows that the interests of the other player are diametrically opposed to his own (the situation known as the zero-sum game),[4] the decision-maker can assume that the opponent will do his utmost to thwart him. The problem of assigning probabilities to the moves of the other does not arise in this context. In fact, in the so-called "games with perfect information," like chess, the moves of the other are in principle certain

---

[4] The name "zero-sum" derives from the circumstance that in such games, whatever the outcome, the sum of the payoffs (in utility units) to the two players is zero. Thus whatever one wins, the other necessarily loses. The situation is the same if the sum of the payoffs is any amount, provided it is the same for all outcomes. Thus constant-sum games are not essentially distinguishable from zero-sum games. "Zero-sum" is the more customary designation and will be used here.

and would be actually certain if the game were played perfectly.[5] In a way, therefore, such games can be classed with decision problems under certainty, except that the outcomes are now arranged not in a one-dimensional array but in a two-dimensional one, since each outcome now depends on a *pair* of decisions (choices of action).

Such an array is called a strategy matrix. It is shown in game theory that the outcome of a play of any two-person game can be formalized as a single choice of a strategy[6] by each player. The rows and columns of the strategy matrix are accordingly the strategies available to the respective players; the entries are the outcomes.

We have seen that the problem of assigning probabilities to the possible states of nature (i.e., what is likely to happen and is not under the control of the decision-maker) does not arise in the theory of the two-person game. However, another problem of equal or greater difficulty does arise in prescriptive theory. The outcomes, we have seen, are the entries in the strategy matrix. The decision-maker must assign at least a preference ordering to these outcomes. He can in principle assign his own preferences by "introspective scanning." But how about the preferences of the other? In formal theory this is not a problem, because both players' utilities are presumed given. But it is a serious problem in prescriptive theory, because what the "best" strategy is depends on what strategy the other will choose, and this, in turn, depends on his preference order of the outcomes. Without knowledge of the others' preferences, the decision-maker does not know what game he is playing and so cannot choose the "best" strategy, no matter how rational he is and how rational he can assume his opponent to be.

If the game is known to be zero-sum, this difficulty is obviated. By definition, the utilities assigned to the opponent are one's own utilities with the opposite sign. However, even in this situation, two cases can be distinguished—games with saddle points and games without. A saddle point is an outcome that is both the worst for self *in its row* and the best for the opponent *in its column*.[7] All games of perfect information have such outcomes. In this case, an intuitively acceptable "best" strategy choice can be prescribed. This is the row (column) that contains a saddle point. This choice is best, because neither player can do better for himself *under the constraints of the situation* (namely, the partial control exercised by the opponent).

---

[5] More precisely, the moves are certain to be selected from a *set* of best moves, but the certainty of the outcome is not affected thereby. The structure of games of perfect information is such that once the rules have been stated, the outcome of the game is determined. For example, the outcome of a perfectly played game of tic-tac-toe is always a draw. Variations in the outcomes of chess games are due entirely to the fact that chess is not played perfectly. If it were, then either White would always win, or Black would always win, or every game would end in a draw (we still do not know which).

[6] For a rigorous definition of strategy, see, for example, R. D. Luce and H. Raiffa, *Games and Decisions* (New York: John Wiley & Sons, Inc., 1957).

[7] By convention "self" in a two-person games chooses a row of the strategy matrix; the opponent chooses a column.

Critique of Strategic Thinking

There are, however, also games without saddle points. Here there is no best single strategy for either player. But game theory shows that each player can choose a "mixed" strategy, which is best in a certain sense. A mixed strategy is a decision to choose each of the available strategies with a certain *probability*. It is best in the sense that it maximizes the *expected* utility gain for each player under the same constraints noted above.[8]

Thus the prescriptive problem is solved in the context of the two-person, zero-sum game. In real life, however, the problem remains of determining whether the game being played is indeed a zero-sum game. More generally, before a decision is calculated, the decision-maker must ascertain what the situation is. If the situation can be represented as a game, he must ascertain the other's utilities of outcomes. This problem falls outside the scope of both formal and prescriptive theory. It belongs to descriptive theory, which, in turn, is anchored in the behavioral sciences, whose methods depart widely from those characteristic of formal and prescriptive theories of rational decision.

Limits of Prescriptive Theory in Conflict Situations

So far, the limitations of rational decision theory we have discussed were *cognitive* ones. If probabilities could somehow be determined (in a one-person game), and if the utilities of outcomes, one's own and the opponent's (in a two-person, zero-sum game) could be correctly ascribed, the methods of prescriptive theory could determine a rational decision.

Once the limits of the two-person, zero-sum game have been transgressed, game theory cannot be unambiguously prescriptive even if the cognitive problem is solved. Examples of games without intuitively acceptable solutions are numerous; they appear already in the fundamental treatise on games,[9] together with the recognition of the limitations of the theory of games as a prescriptive theory. (The theory never claimed descriptive status.) We shall next examine two of the best known such examples.

PRISONER'S DILEMMA[10]

In this nonzero-sum game,[11] each player has a choice of two strategies— C (co-operating) and D (defecting). The choice of C by both (CC)

---

[8] See the final remarks of footnote 2.

[9] John von Neumann and Oskar Morgenstern, *Theory of Games and Economic Behavior* (Princeton: Princeton University Press, 1955, rev. ed.).

[10] Game theoreticians have adorned certain games with nicknames which stem from anecdotes used to illustrate their structure. For the stories of the "Prisoner's Dilemma" and the "Battle of the Sexes," see Luce and Raiffa, op. cit. "Chicken" is described in Quincy Wright, William M. Evan and Morton Deutsch, eds., *Preventing World War III: Some Proposals* (New York: Simon & Schuster, 1962), p. 253.

[11] In a nonzero-sum game, the sums of the payoffs are not constant. Hence some payoffs may be better for both players than others.

International Conflict

results in positive payoffs to both. The choice of D by both (DD) results in negative payoffs to both. However, a *single* defector gets a larger gain than that won by each of two co-operators, and a single co-operator suffers a loss larger than that suffered by each of two defectors. It follows that the temptation to defect is re-enforced by the fear of being the single co-operator. On the other hand, if both players defect, both lose, whereas they might both have won had they co-operated. Hence the dilemma. The game is illustrated in Figure 1.

	C	D
C	1, 1	−2, 2
D	2, −2	−1, −1

FIGURE 1   *Prisoner's Dilemma*[12]

Another example of a game that poses a dilemma for a prescriptive theory involves three players who are to divide a dollar by a majority vote. The game allows bargaining, coalitions, and side payments (bribes). If A and B tentatively agree to take fifty cents each (freezing C out), C may offer one of them (for example, B), a better deal. Suppose C offers B sixty cents, if B deserts A. The 60-40 split is clearly to the advantage of both B and C, compared to the previous arrangement. Nevertheless, if B accepts C's offer, he is in danger of losing everything, since in that case it will be of advantage to both A and C to freeze B out and split 50-50. But if this happens, we are back where we started. No matter what arrangement is proposed, it is always possible for *two* of the players to think of a better arrangement (for them); and being a majority, they can defeat the previous proposal. There is no *stable* solution. Hence no solution can be prescribed *without appealing to principles outside of the theory of games.*

Some of these principles have been mentioned already by Morgenstern and Von Neumann, who speak of "social norms" governing bargaining procedures. The application of social norms involves either traditional or moral considerations and falls outside the scope of strategic thinking. A social-norm solution is not an "optimum within the constraints imposed," because the social norm is not a "rule of the game," and hence is not one of the original constraints.

For instance, if A, B, and C decide to take thirty-three cents each and to donate one cent to charity, it is clear that each of the three pairs is actually refraining from "optimizing," since any pair could get the whole

---

12 The first of each pair of payoffs is to the row chooser.

213

dollar. Rather, the players are acting in accordance with some equity principle, not defensible on strategic grounds.

Similar considerations apply to the Prisoner's Dilemma. Suppose the players come from a society in which the following behavior norm (Kant's ethical formula) has become internalized: "When faced with a choice of action, choose the one that would benefit you if every one chose the same way." Two players subscribing to this principle will choose CC even in the absence of formal collusion. Now it is fallacious to argue that these players are also "optimizing rationally" because they have arrived at the best outcome on the basis of their knowledge of how people in their society behave. *On the basis of this knowledge,* a player who has not internalized the norm still might decide to defect and get the biggest payoff as the single defection. *This* would be the "rational" strategic choice. But then we are forced to the conclusion that two "rational" players (choosing DD) will do worse than two "irrational" ones (choosing CC). The hard fact remains that there is no solution of the Prisoner's Dilemma that is both strategic and intuitively acceptable. We can only conclude that decisions based on strategic thinking fail to "optimize" not because of cognitive errors, but because of the very nature of strategic thinking itself.[13]

The Lure of Strategic Thinking

What is the attraction of strategic thinking? What makes it the predominant mode in decision-making purporting to be "rational"? To understand the prestige of strategic thinking, we should first look at its successes, not at its failures. We must look also at the success of the entire orientation into which the mode represented by strategic thinking naturally fits. This is the "scientific" or "rational," orientation. Specifically,

(1) Rational thinking is realistic. It takes into account verifiable facts. It guards against mistaking our wishes for facts. It separates questions about *what is* from questions about *what ought to be.*

(2) Rational thinking is deductive. It uses all the available techniques of reasoning, including calculations and mathematical inference.

(3) Rational thinking is predictive and therefore productive. On the basis of established facts, reasonable valid inductions, and rigorous deductions, rational think-

[13] Some game theoreticians argue that if "social norms" influence decisions, then the utilities associated with adhering to such norms should be included in calculating the entries in the strategy matrix. Thus our two "socialized" individuals should not be considered to be playing a Prisoner's Dilemma game. From the point of view of formal theory, this is correct, and we have seen that such an interpretation amounts to defining utilities tautologically (cf. footnote a). It is clear, however, that this conception of utility is useless in many decision problems, for it is doubtful where a single utility measure exists for anything that may happen. Typically decision difficulties arise when one does not know how to compare utilities of outcomes, for example, the utility with a possible disutility of misplaced distrust (Othello's tragedy). Real-life situations structured like the Prisoner's Dilemma are genuine dilemmas.

International Conflict

ing provides us with the most reliable estimates and expectations of future events, thereby giving us a measure of control over our environment.

(4) Rational thinking is unencumbered not only by sentiments (in which we usually find strong admixtures of wishful thinking), but also by awe of authority, by superstitious and neurotic fears, and other compulsions. It is therefore essentially free and courageous thinking.

(5) Rational thinking is indicative of sanity, because mentally disturbed people are the ones who violate the principles of rational thinking most conspicuously.

Since the strategic mode derives from a dispassionate pursuit of rational considerations, it appears akin to the scientific mode and so shares in the superlative prestige which scientific thinking enjoys. In short, strategic thinking appears today as thinking in the problem-solving mode, therefore as *mature* thinking.

The problem-solving orientation is usually juxtaposed to more archaic orientations when cultures are compared or to less mature ones when personalities are compared. Examples of the former are the "traditional" decision modes of preliterate societies; examples of the latter are the neurotic reactions of compulsive individuals in the face of difficulties. The Nazi slogan "The true German thinks with his blood" is a characteristic example of a regression affecting a whole nation.

Similar comparisons are used to bolster the strategic mode in matters of international policy. "Realistic" is the label most frequently attached to strategic thinking in this context. The implication is that the alternative is the "idealistic" (that is "unrealistic") mode, dominated by sentiment or wishful fantasy, neglectful of realities, devoid of technical knowledge, and generally irresponsible. In international affairs, the "realist" is scornful both of the ravings of the hate groups and of the pleadings of the pacifists. His own voice appears as the voice of reason, the voice of science in an area where dispassionate scientific standards are especially difficult to apply. In short, the "realist's" accusation against the "idealist," who is presumably dominated by hate or love impulses, is that the idealist, unwilling or unable to conduct an objective analysis, ignores problems instead of facing them. One of the idealist's cardinal sins, according to the realist, is oversimplification. The accusation is not unfounded. But it can be turned with equal force against the theorizing realist.

The tendency to simplify is endemic to all theorizing, because the aim of theory is to pose and solve tractable problems. The most successful scientific theories are those that have identified those features of phenomena that turned out to be both essential and tractable. The theoretician is thus understandably biased to seek out tractable problems, hoping to come to grips with the salient features of the phenomenon he is investigating. This bias underlies the unwillingness to restructure theoretical approaches that have been "paying off."

While we cannot claim that strategic thinking has been particularly successful in international affairs (in the absence of either meaningful comparisons or criteria of success), the forces of intellectual inertia in

Critique of Strategic Thinking

this area are nevertheless very strong. These forces may derive from persisting traditions or from a natural selection of power-oriented personalities into influential political positions. They may also derive from the close link between political and military problems in our era or, specifically in the United States, from the dominant role of the business orientation in policy-forming bodies. (Rational business decisions in a private-enterprise society are predominantly strategic.) The forces of intellectual inertia exert a pressure to cast the problems of foreign policy into strictly strategic terms. Foreign policy becomes intellectually indistinguishable from military policy, which, by its very nature, is essentially strategic. The paradigm of a policy "problem" becomes: (1) the setting of goals, which are expressed predominantly in terms of power relations; (2) an appraisal of means—that is, predominantly of power resources; (3) an appraisal of the opponent's goals and means (conceived in similar terms); and (4) the design of some optimization procedure under the given constraints—that is, allocating power resources and implementing power policies in pursuit of our goals.

Given this framework, there is a strong tendency to *select* problems that can be made to seem tractable. This tendency is clearly discernible in those who think professionally about foreign and military policy, those who are given credence by virtue of their claims to pertinent expertise. The nature of this expertise is determined by the nature of the problems singled out for attention—that is, strategic problems. The cycle is thus closed: The problems determine the selection of the experts, and the experts determine the selection of the problems.

The underlying intellectual framework in which policy decisions are made remains based on the "theory of rational decision." This is particularly true in the context of conflict, where power relations are the most clearly perceived variables. If a recommended decision is supported by calculations involving the accepted "realities" (which may be tangible, like weapons, or intangible, like some vaguely perceived interplays of pressure), and if the projected goals of a policy and the means at the disposal of the decision-maker are expressed in power terms, the recommendations are considered seriously (whether they are accepted or rejected). If, on the other hand, the goals, the means, the estimates, the motives are made in terms other than the accepted currencies, the recommendations are not taken seriously. They appear to be not merely poor recommendations, but irrelevant to the problems.

Calculation (explicit or implicit) is the dominant mode in strategic thinking. Being also the explicit deductive tool of the exact sciences, calculation confers the prestige of science on strategic thinking in international affairs. As strategists, we are most comfortable in the role of engineers or of operations researchers. We would like to regard the independent variables (the payoffs and constraints) as given so we can get on with the job to which our expertise is geared. The facetious sign said to adorn an office at the RAND Corporation speaks for our cynical recognition of this bias. "DON'T THINK," the sign reads, "COMPUTE!"

216

Let us now see what "givens" must be fed into the machinery of rational decision, particularly in the context of international conflict.

In the simplest case, where actions are assumed to lead to unique outcomes, all that is needed is a preference ordering of the outcomes. If this can be done without ambivalence, the problem is solved. But human experience indicates that unambivalent ordering can be effected only in very special circumstances—for example, where some quantity of which one cannot have too much can be singled out. Such quantities readily suggest themselves in the familiar contexts of business, technology, sports, and so forth. More profit, greater efficiency, higher scores can always be assumed as preferred. Where outcomes are complex, preference orderings are by no means obvious, since undesirable side effects often ride on desirable goals. In *principle,* as strategists, we are not supposed to weigh one against the other. This is the business of the decision-maker. He is supposed to have done this weighing in advance so as to present the strategist with an ordering. However, the very presence of the strategist (who may himself be the decision-maker in certain cases) creates a pressure to formulate the problem so that it can be solved. This pressure tends to focus attention on comparable variables and to call attention away from noncomparable ones. Accordingly, the pressure is to structure situations in the language of one-dimensional value scales.

Dramatic illustrations of this mentality are provided by the arguments offered by strategists in support of large-scale civil defense measures. Typically, such decision problems are formulated in terms of simple arithmetic. If a civil defense program can assure a reduction of immediate fatalities in a thermonuclear attack from 100 million to 50 million, the result is held to be without question an argument in favor of the program. It is admitted that the "gain" should be weighed against other considerations, for example, the money costs of the program. Or, in response to vigorous protests against this too obvious oversimplification, it is also admitted that the gain should be weighed against the possibility of increased likelihood of war. But these are characteristically presented as separate problems—that is, problems of estimating and comparing costs or the respective likelihoods of war. *Aside* from "costs" it seems to the computing strategist that the choice between 100 million and 50 million casualties is a perfectly obvious one.

Without challenging this particular judgment, I should like to challenge the principle that such choices can be made on quantitative bases alone. Assume the following farfetched but not unthinkable situation. The United States is currently suffering 40,000 traffic fatalities per year. Assume an invention that could reduce fatalities to 20,000 per year, of which 10,000 would die on the highways, and 10,000 more would die in some unspecified but painless manner (in connection with the operation

217

of the invention). The identities of these 10,000 would be determined by lot and announced twenty-four hours before their deaths. My guess would be that this "improvement" would not be acceptable to the majority of Americans. The example may seem fantastic, but a somewhat analogous situation is said to have occurred during World War II. At a certain bomber plane base in the South Pacific, it was known that a pilot had a 25 per cent chance of surviving his tour of duty (thirty missions). A computation was made showing that the chance could be raised to 50 per cent if one-way missions were flown. A selection procedure could be instituted in which each pilot had even odds to draw a black or a white ball. If he drew a white ball, he would be rotated to the States. If he drew a black one, he would have to go on a one-way mission. Neither the commanders nor the pilots ever considered this alternative seriously.

It can be argued that the crucial feature in these examples is the foreknowledge of the doomed individuals. Certain death may be harder to accept than the original situation, even if the odds of dying are reduced. However, in the following example, this feature does not occur. In a conversation shortly after the end of World War II, Zhukov and Eisenhower were reported to have compared Soviet and American infantry tactics. According to Zhukov, Soviet infantry advances through a mine field "as if it were not there." American practice involves extensive preliminary mine-clearing operations. Zhukov is said to have argued that the Soviet tactics meant fewer total casualties. Whether Eisenhower was convinced of this or not, Soviet tactics seemed to him unacceptably callous.

Many more examples can be marshaled to show that the utility of saved human lives or the disutility of lost ones is not calculated primarily in numbers. The magnitude of effort to save five trapped miners exceeds by far the magnitude of effort that could be, but is not, undertaken to save many more lives in less dramatic circumstances. We are horrified when people burn in plane crashes, but are not so much affected when they burn in their own homes. Miscarriages of justice leading to the execution of innocent persons arouse indignation entirely out of proportion to the number of lives lost. In our roles as strategists we often phrase our arguments to imply that any but quantitative comparisons of lives lost or endangered are "irrational." Thus we dismiss the preoccupation with nuclear testing fall-out on the grounds that the number of lives endangered and the genetic hazards are small compared with natural hazards (cosmic radiation, X rays). "War is terrible," writes Herman Kahn, "but so is peace."

In pointing out seemingly "irrational" preference orderings ("irrational" because they cannot be neatly reduced to numerical terms), we depart from the role that, in other contexts, we rigorously defend—the role of ethically neutral scientists who presumably seek the most efficient means to each *given* goal. But we can never avoid postulating certain preferences (goals) and eschewing others. Whatever the source of this bias, it is consistent with the inclination to simplify the "givens." The bias

218

inhibits examination of preference orderings that may be actually operating in the population.[14]

Compared with the simple, quantitative utility assignments postulated in strategy problems, the values held by real people often seem to violate the axioms of rational decision. They seem at times inconsistent, at times intransitive, at times anti-instrumental. It may be that, by a proper redefinition of context, the observed value preferences can be shown to be rational in the framework of some consistent value system. But this investigation is beyond the competence of the strategists and therefore beyond their inclination to pursue it.

The most obvious shortcoming of strategic thinking appears when decisions must be made under uncertainty. Here the drive to simplify leads to a reduction of the problem to a more definite one: that of decision under risk where the probabilities of outcomes are known. Recall that the solution of a risky choice problem consists of maximizing expected utility. The determination of the maximizing strategy is possible only if both the utilities and the probabilities of outcomes are known. We have already discussed our propensity to simplify the assignment of utilities. In addition to the same propensity, another one is revealed in the context of uncertain outcomes—the propensity to assign probabilities to unique events, for example, to an outbreak of thermonuclear war. Obviously, such assignments cannot be made on empirical grounds, since one cannot speak of a "frequency" of such wars. Nor can such assignments be made on logical grounds because no universe of equiprobable events is available as a starting point. It follows that such assignments can be made only on intuitive grounds. The "probabilities" represent no more than degrees of belief for which, in the case of a thermonuclear war, no basis in experience exists. Nor can such estimates ever be verified. A nuclear war either will occur or it will not. *Neither* event will provide evidence either for or against a degree of belief. There is therefore nothing (not even a concern for future vindication) to prevent the advocate of a policy from assigning probabilities to events at pleasure, in particular, in a way that makes the recommended policy the optimizing one.

The simplifying assumptions inherent in strategic thinking not only reduce uncertainty choices to risky ones, but also reduce two-person games to one-person games. It is by no means our contention that international conflicts can be exhaustively studied as two-person games. Still, we should expect that a two-person game model more closely approximates a conflict situation than a simple optimization problem (game against

---

[14] Herman Kahn (See Reference 1) bases his estimate of ten to sixty million "acceptable" deaths in a thermonuclear war on a "poll." It should be unnecessary to point out the superficiality of such a procedure. Given different phrasings of questions, different descriptions of possible outcomes, different lists of alternatives, the results of such polls might be quite different and inconsistent. It is naïve in the extreme to interpret such results as indicators of value preferences. The procedure can be explained only by the investigator's impatience to get on with the problems which really interest him, namely the strategic problems.

Critique of Strategic Thinking

nature). Nevertheless, policy recommendations are frequently made in the latter context. This simplification is especially evident in civil defense planning, in which nuclear wars are implicitly identified with natural disasters of various magnitudes instead of with *responses* of an opponent who has taken our plans into account.

From the point of view of strategic calculations, game-against-nature models are preferable to two-person game models. In the latter, not only must one's own utilities be assigned, but also the opponent's must be estimated. Further, two-person game models with saddle points are preferable to those without saddle points. In the latter, not only preference orderings (one's own and the opponent's) but also numerical utilities are required Moreover, the solution of a two-person, zero-sum game without a saddle point is a "mixed strategy solution." Translated into a recommendation, such a solution might read: "Spin a roulette wheel. If 1 through 10 comes up, build ICBM's; if 11 through 18 comes up, concentrate on medium-range missiles; otherwise strengthen conventional forces." It would take considerable effort to convince a decision-maker ignorant of game theory that such a recommendation might really represent a "rational" decision in a situation that can be represented as a zero-sum game without a saddle point.

Finally and most significantly, situations that should be represented as nonzero-sum games are frequently cast (tacitly) into zero-sum models.

Misrepresentation of Conflict Situations

When a nonzero-sum game is represented as a zero-sum game, the problem is not merely oversimplified but actually misrepresented. The zero-sum game has a unique solution, at least in formal theory, but many nonzero-sum games have not, at least not in the conventional framework of optimization procedures. Nonzero-sum games, as we have seen, introduce *perforce* concepts alien to rational decision theory. These concepts include negotiation, social norms, even "trust"—that is, recognition that the opponent is not entirely an enemy in the sense that his interests partially coincide with one's own. The Prisoner's Dilemma is a case in point. If collusion is allowed, the dilemma disappears, since the mutually beneficial outcome CC (cf. Figure 1) can be agreed upon. In the context of the balance of terror, this outcome can be taken to represent bilateral disarmament; the other outcomes represent unilateral disarmament (CD and DC) and status quo (DD). Admittedly, this model is as much an oversimplification as any of the models proposed by the strategists. However, the model does capture the essential nonzero-sum feature of the situation. The strategists' arguments against disarmament, on the other hand, reveal their zero-sum bias in the way they circumscribe their repertoire of assumptions. For example, their refusal to consider "trust" seriously in the formulation of strategy reflects a tendency to keep the image of the enemy as the opponent in a zero-sum game. Whatever the enemy gains, we necessarily lose. In a zero-sum game, it is sufficient to examine only one set of payoffs (one's own). The Prisoner's Dilemma then appears as in Figure 2.

	C	D
C	1	−2
D	2	−1

FIGURE 2   *"Self's" Payoffs in the Prisoner's Dilemma*

This is a zero-sum game with a saddle point, DD. It leads to the outcome that harms both players.

An explicit criticism of this tendency to cast conflict situations into zero-sum games was made by T. C. Schelling. Schelling's critique focused on the absence of psychological components in game theory. Undoubtedly Schelling had in mind not the formal (i.e., mathematical) game theory, but rather the sort of theory one could use in application, either descriptively or prescriptively. His failure to make this point explicit stimulated vigorous rebuttals from game theoreticians, who demonstrated that Schelling's critical appraisal was irrelevant to formal game theory. Since Schelling and the game theoreticians were talking about different things, the rebuttals also missed their mark. It will be instructive to examine and to analyze a sample of Schelling's suggestions for modifying and extending game theory because of the way they reveal the limitations of strategic thinking.

Consider the following nonzero-sum game (Figure 3).

	B_1	B_2
A_1	1, 2	0, 0
A_2	0, 0	2, 1

FIGURE 3   *The Battle of the Sexes* [15]

From the point of view of formal game theory, this game has no "solution." Neither player can guarantee himself a maximum payoff under the constraints of the situation. For example, if both players randomize their choices, each gets an expected payoff of $\frac{3}{4}$. But this is not the best that either can do. In a negotiated settlement, either of the players can guarantee himself 1 if he is willing to let the other have 2. The question is: Who gets the bigger payoff? This question is relegated to negotiation, which is beyond the scope of game theory.

Theories of negotiation, arbitration, bargaining, and so forth have

[15] Cf. Luce and Raiffa, *op. cit.*, p. 90.

Critique of Strategic Thinking

enjoyed a vigorous development since game theory appeared on the scene. These theories were doubtless inspired by the problems posed in nonzerosum games and, to a large extent, by the relevance of these procedures to corresponding conflict situations. In particular, there have been attempts to construct formal bargaining theories in the spirit of rigor that characterizes the mathematical theory of games. (Compare the works of Braithwaite, Nash, Raiffa.) In formal bargaining theory, the solution of the Battle of the Sexes game awards $1\frac{1}{2}$ to each of the players. The solution is intuitively acceptable because of the perfect symmetry of the situation: the bargaining positions of the two players are exactly the same. Thus a certain equity principle (analogous to a social norm) is introduced into bargaining theory. This equity principle can be extended to asymmetrical games, in which the bargaining positions of the players are not the same. In that case, the equity principle is supposed somehow to reflect the difference in the bargaining positions—for example, the threat opportunities open to each player (emphasized by "power-oriented" investigators) or the possibility of increasing substantially the utility payoff to one of the players at only a slight expense to the other (emphasized by "ethically oriented" authors).

These are, no doubt, psychological components. A particular psychological component, closely related to that of "threat credibility," is pre-emption. The concept of pre-emption destroys the symmetry of the Battle of the Sexes game. Suppose that in the process of negotiation, A "pre-empts" by announcing that he will choose Row 2 regardless of what B does. If B believes him, argue the proponents of pre-emption, he has no choice but to choose Column 2. The resulting payoffs are 2 to A and 1 to B, and "equity" based on symmetry goes by the wayside.

Now from the point of view of formal game theory, this solution is irrelevant to the game as it is represented in the strategy matrix. The matrix of strategies is a formal representation of a game in which all the allowed moves have *already* been defined in terms of strategies which must be chosen *simultaneously* and *independently*. If we assume that one player can choose a strategy and announce his choice to the other, this means that a different game is being examined. In the "pre-empted" Battle of the Sexes game the strategies would be schematically presented thus:

A's STRATEGIES	B's STRATEGIES
A_1: Choose Row 1	B_1: Choose Column 1, whatever A does
A_2: Choose Row 2	B_2: Choose Column 2, whatever A does
	B_3: Choose strategy analogous to A's
	B_4: Choose strategy opposite to A's

The resulting (2×4) game is then the following:

	B_1	B_2	B_3	B_4
A_1	1, 2	0, 0	1, 2	0, 0
A_2	0, 0	2, 1	2, 1	0, 0

We see that B_3 dominates B's other three strategies. That is to say, by choosing B_3, B can do at least as well (and possibly better) than by choosing any of the other three strategies. Thus there is no need to consider the other three (*N. B.*: within the framework of rational decision theory!). The game now reduces to the following:

	B
	B
A_1	1, 2
A_2	2, 1

Only A has a choice, so the "game" has disappeared in any significant sense. We are back to the most primitive decision problem: a single decision-maker choosing under certainty.

So it appears that the introduction of pre-emption simply trivializes the game (when pre-emption is examined in the framework of formal game theory). In justice to the strategists, we should point out that they do not view pre-emption in this simple-minded way. They seem well aware of the real psychological problems involved in pre-emption. At least they allude to these problems when they refer to the "credible threat" with the emphasis on "credible." A dramatic model of the credible-threat situation is shown in Figure 4.

	SERVE	STAND FIRM
Swerve	1, 1	$-2, 2$
Stand Firm	2, -2	$-100, -100$

FIGURE 4   *The Game of Chicken*

"Chicken" differs from Prisoner's Dilemma in that neither strategy dominates the other for either players. As in the case of Prisoner's Dilemma, game theory cannot prescribe definitively here. A pre-emption by A would be the announcement, "I choose Row 2, regardless!" (Or, in the case of the two cars speeding toward each other, an announcement to drive straight ahead, regardless.) Now the real game of Chicken (like the game of Brinksmanship in international relations) is played in real time. Suppose the driver of one car signals his "pre-emption" to the other. Unless one is committed to the assumption that "our side always wins," one is forced to concede the possibility of counter-pre-emption in the remaining time. One might, if one wished, construct a game in which both pre-emptions are announced and in which the choices open to each player are now to believe or not to believe the other's determination. The probability that the opponent means business increases with the shortening distance between the two cars. This complicates the game but does not change its character. A further complication can be added by allowing "communications of the second order": that is, an announcement to the effect that one does not believe the other's intentions and a reply to the effect that he in turn does not believe that the other does not believe, and so on.

223

Critique of Strategic Thinking

Now it would seem that posing a psychological problem to strategists would either lead them to instigate psychological investigations or to examine current psychological knowledge for possible guidance. However, to the extent that we have become engrossed in strategic thinking, we tend to shy away from either seeking or making use of psychological knowledge. The reason is easy to discern. Psychology studies man, his real behavior, his motivations, and underlying values. As strategists, we study (or purport to study) the logic of conflict in which the values are given "utilities." We are most comfortable in situations in which the constraints are imposed either by neutral nature or by a *deus ex machina,* the enemy. In both cases, the constraints are fixed. Those imposed by nature can be studied with reasonable assurance that the very act of studying them will not change them. Those imposed by the enemy are circumscribed by power, which is always seen as directed against one's own power. Once the conflict is formulated strategically, it is not necessary to ask what the enemy *wants* to do, but only what the enemy *can* do. If he can blackmail us, he will. If he can do us in, he will. A genuinely psychological approach is a threat to the strategic view of conflict. This is why psychological problems are as a rule bypassed in strategically-oriented writings. These writings give hardly any thought to the actual psychological or cultural constraints imposed on decision-makers in real society, let alone to the value systems of these societies.

The strategist's idea of making a conflict more realistic is simply to make strategic considerations more complex. We have accordingly accumulated a vast collection of Rube Goldbergian contraptions, whose paramount attractiveness to virtuoso strategists is "ingenuity." In spite of our hopeless entanglements in this monstrous maze, most of us are quick to accuse those who would reformulate the issues and problems in human terms of muddleheadedness and naïveté. We have translated the game of strategy (where men may engage in ruthlessness and cunning to their heart's content *because* it is only a game) into a plan of genocidal orgies, and we call the resulting nightmare "realism." (In a pure power conflict, it is always "realistic" to expect the worst from the other, who is always the "enemy.") But even this tacit assumption is abandoned when we must make a strategy appear reasonable. At crucial points, the enemy is usually pictured as rational, that is, trying to maximize expected returns on the basis of utilities and probability estimates ascribed to him. This seems far from "expecting the worst." In the balance of terror, an irrational enemy may be far more dangerous than a rational one. But it suits us to assume the nuclear-age analogue of the Marquis of Queensberry rules.

The "realism" inherent in strategic thinking appears to be a curious mixture of cynicism and naïveté. One looks in vain for the sort of realism that preserves a connection, or at least a distinction, between data and

224

assumptions, between facts and inferences. This lack is especially glaring in the failure to face the fundamental distinction between natural and behavioral science. As a rule, the assumptions made in natural science do not affect the material under study; in behavioral science they do. If strategic thinking is to be realistic, it must deal with human behavior and must recognize this peculiar feature of assumptions about human behavior. This is particularly true of the assumption inherent in decision problems. We have seen that the calculation of expected gain involves the assignment of utilities and probabilities to events. Typically, the events are unique, and consequently, only subjective probabilities can be assigned to them. But such a probability is in no way a property of the events. It is an *attitude* of the one who assigns the probability. Even more obviously, the utility of an event is an attitude. So are the estimates of others' assignments of utilities and probabilities. Thus the solution of a decision problem of this sort depends primarily not on an act of cognition, but rather on a choice of attitudes. The situation that results from such a formulation of a decision problem is a situation of *our own making*. That is, in "solving" such a problem we do not *discover* a portion of reality and act upon knowledge so obtained; we *make* a portion of reality. The enemy may be cunning and ruthless, but we have played an important part in making him so (just as he has helped to make us cunning and ruthless). This principle of self-fulfilling assumption in human affairs has been pointed out so frequently that it is embarrassing to be obliged to restate it. Nevertheless, the fact remains that, although many strategists mention this principle as a serious difficulty in international relations, they have neither incorporated it into their theories nor refuted its relevance. In strategic thinking, the constraints remain fixed; in real life they are fluid and essentially affected by the operating assumptions of the decision-maker.

Summary

We have listed what seem to us some gross inadequacies of strategic thinking, having in mind at all times the context of international conflict, in which the inadequacies become, in our opinion, most flagrant and most dangerous. To begin with, we have described the tendency in strategic thinking to oversimplify problems in order to make them more tractable by methods of rational decision. Indeed, we have pointed out that when thinking strategically we often bypass the difficult problems of assigning utilities according to actually prevalent values (one's own and those of others) when simple numerical criteria are available; that we "objectify" subjective probabilities; that we leave the "rational opponent" out of the picture when the problem seems more tractable as a game against nature; that we tend to depict (usually tacitly) nonzero-sum games as zero-sum games. We could go on to touch on other questionable simplifications— for example, in the Nth-nation problem in nuclear deterrence, which is usually neglected in our preoccupation with bilateral deterrence.

225

We have said also that the psychological components of decision-making, being elusive, tend to be de-emphasized or left out altogether from strategic considerations.

Finally, we have pointed out that strategic thinking tends to ignore the dynamics of human interaction. In order to be solved, a strategic problem, once formulated, has to stay put. But *the formulation of the problem itself* is an "event" in the context of conflict, which may radically change the situation. Typically, the self-fulfilling assumption, although frequently mentioned in the writings of the strategists, does not function as a substantial factor in their formulations.

We might surmise on the basis of what has just been said that our critique of strategic thinking rests primarily on a contention that it is not sufficiently sophisticated, with the implication that strategic thinking could be "improved" by further development: One could be more careful in estimating probabilities and utilities, one's own and the opponent's in foreseeing possible deviation from rational behavior; one could introduce "dynamics"into the game matrices by making the payoffs variable instead of constant, and so on.

I have no quarrel with these conclusions in principle. But it was not the purpose of my argument to elicit such conclusions. I do not believe that the formulation of problems in the strategic mode can be made sufficiently realistic sufficiently soon to warrant the giant investment of effort required. Moreover, such an investment of effort would not be made in a vacuum but in the present atmosphere of global conflict. The pressures inherent in strategic thinking would therefore continue to operate and to drive our conceptions of the conflict into the same dangerous channels.

The main trouble with strategic thinking is that its power can be applied (if at all) only in the solution of problems, not in their formulation. But it appears (once we free ourselves from the compulsion to solve ready-made problems) that one of the most important problems of our age is to formulate our problems. Not "How can we get what we want?" but "What do we want?" is often the important question. We take for granted that we want to "win" the hot war if it occurs, and at any rate to win the cold one. Everyone knows what it means to win a basketball game. It is even fairly clear what it meant to win or lose past wars. We go on calling thermonuclear war "war," in spite of the fact that the actual events it comprises may have no resemblance whatsoever to the events we have known as "war." Because we call a thermonuclear war "war," we think we know or can imagine what it means to "win it." One simple-minded definition was actually offered: The winner of the war will be the one who writes the peace treaty. Is this what we want, "to write the peace treaty"? What does it mean to win the Cold War in terms of actual events, not phrases? Do we want to win it? How do we know we do? How do the Russians know that they want (if they do) a "Communist government" in every country? What kind of a government would it be in fact, not in cliché-ridden description?

One hundred and fifty years ago all Republicans were Democrats and vice versa. Republicans identified democracy with the republican form of government, which, in turn was pictured primarily as a government without a hereditary monarchy. Is it true today that all monarchies are less democratic than all republics? If not, why not? What reason is there to suppose that in another generation or so (history moves much more rapidly in our days) all free enterprise countries will be more democratic than all Communist countries or, for that matter, the other way around? Three hundred years ago the two "Isms," locked in mortal combat were Catholicism and Protestantism. One thousand years ago they were Christianity and Islam. Who won? And how do these struggles appear to us now?

These questions are of much more fundamental importance to humanity than the strategic ones, to which by far the greater effort (in terms of money and talent) is presently directed. Nor is it simply a question of priorities, that is of assigning more effort in one direction or less in the other. Strategic and human ways of thinking do not merely compete for money and talent. They compete for the mind and soul of man.

The
Arms Race
and
World Order

Herman Kahn

Reprinted with permission of the publishers from Morton A. Kaplan (ed.), *The Revolution in World Politics* (New York: John Wiley & Sons, Inc., 1962), pp. 332–51. Mr. Kahn is Director of the Hudson Institute.

Many sober people believe that the current international order, with its emphasis on anarchy, national egoism, and deterrence, is not going to last to the year 2000; that it will not, in fact, last more than a decade or two. One can hold this estimate even after recognizing that many successful adjustments have already been made to modern technology, and that the current arms race is not as uncontrolled as it would be if narrow military, technological, and economic factors were the sole determinants of military research, development, procurement, and operations.

Actually, as compared to the inherent technological possibilities, the current arms race is more of a walk than a race. It is rather severely limited by political, social, moral, economic, and doctrinal constraints on the participants. These constraints and adjustments doubtless "buy time," but many believe that they do not buy enough time for the system to adjust satisfactorily by gradual evolution. It still seems likely either that the system must be changed drastically in the near future, *or* that it will "blow up"—that is, change itself in a violent explosive manner. It is the main purpose of this paper to discuss the implications of this either-or view for the revolution in world politics.

If a blowup does occur, it is somewhat unlikely, perhaps most unlikely, that it will result in an "end of history." More likely it will be a very serious crisis that will produce major structural changes in the international scene. It may be a "small" thermonuclear war followed by a viable peace; it may even be a large thermonuclear war, but not an Armageddon. At least in the 60's, it is difficult to visualize a likely sequence of events that would set back either the population or the wealth of the world by more than a generation or so. This would be catastrophic, but it would not be "an end to history" nor even, necessarily, an end to modern civilization. We should make every effort to avoid such a catastrophe but, if this proves impossible, we should be prepared to prevent a second and more serious catastrophe that might mean an end to history or, alternatively, to modern civilization.

It is also possible that even the above rather cautious (as opposed to the apocalyptic or millennial) either-or viewpoint will be wrong, that the international order will not change dramatically at all—even though we

I would like to acknowledge my indebtedness to Morton Halperin, Morton Kaplan, and Max Singer for the many suggestions that have influenced or modified this paper and my appreciation to the Princeton University Press for allowing me to use some material from my book *On Thermonuclear War* (abbreviated *OTW* in the text).

The Arms Race and World Order

experience both war and crisis—or conversely, that it will change gradually and develop in such a way that the system will never be subjected to the strains which so many are predicting.

The no-change position can almost surely be ruled out. This 500-year old system which has by and large been very satisfactory and has seen an almost incredible amount of progress now seems obsolete. Indeed, even those "conservatives" who believe that relatively small changes and slow evolution will be sufficient to prevent a blowup also still tend to believe that the advent of nuclear weapons and modern technology will cause changes greater in their effect on the current social and international order than the introduction of cavalry, printing, and longbow, artillery, steam engine, rifles, telegraphy, etc. did in their respective eras. Indeed, it is most likely that the changes produced by modern nuclear technology will come on an accelerated time scale. Although the last fifteen years have set the stage, few believe that the necessary adjustments have been made.

This kind of either-or thinking, or even the more extreme kind which equates every kind of a blowup with an end of history, could and maybe even should lead to hysteria. However, it has been accepted with amazing calmness in the recent past, except by fringe groups. This calmness may not continue in the future. There is now a growing awareness and concern about the implications of the current and future arms race. This concern is expressed dramatically through the activities of the informal and formal "peace," "arms-control," and "international-order" groups. It also has a major impact on both policy and practical politics here and abroad. In addition to the spontaneous (and often perfectly proper) pressures that are building up, there is a good deal of evidence that the Soviet Union has in the past and hopes, even more in the future, to use that widespread fear of arms and the arms race to manipulate the West for purposes of its own. It is, therefore, of the utmost value to examine the different varieties of either-or thinking in some detail and with some care.

It may be helpful to start with a rather extreme example of either-or thinking. The following excerpt is from a well-known speech by Sir Charles Snow,[1] which attracted much favorable comment and little or no unfavorable comment:

> We are faced with an either-or, and we haven't much time. The *either* is acceptance of a restriction of nuclear armaments. This is going to begin, just as a token, with an agreement on the stopping of nuclear tests. The United States is not going to get the 99.9 per cent 'security' that it has been asking for. This is unobtainable, though there are other bargains that the United States could probably secure. I am not going to conceal from you that this course involves certain risks. They are quite obvious, and no honest man is going to blink them. That is the *either*. The *or* is not a risk but a certainty. It is this. There is no agreement on tests. The nuclear arms race between the United States and the U.S.S.R. not only continues but accelerates. Other countries join in. Within, at the most, six years, China and several other states have a stock of nuclear bombs. Within, at the most, ten years, some of those bombs are

[1] C. P. Snow, "The Moral Un-Neutrality of Science," *Science* (January 27, 1961).

International Conflict

going off. I am saying this as responsibly as I can. That is the certainty. On the one side, therefore, we have a finite risk. On the other side, we have a certainty of disaster. Between a risk and a certainty, a sane man does not hesitate.

In spite of the rather widespread acclaim with which the preceding statement was received, and in spite of the fact that the author has achieved distinction in both science and letters, the statement is neither accurate nor responsible. The United States is *not* asking for 99.9 per cent security via the arms control routes. In fact, we seem to be willing to accept agreements of a much lower reliability than almost anybody (even the passionate arms controllers) would have been willing to accept a few years ago when they did not know how difficult it was to get reliably enforceable and controllable agreements. Much more important, the "or" described above is not a certainty. Unless Sir Charles Snow has information denied to the rest of us, he cannot know that within ten years some of these bombs are going off. And more important, he cannot know that if some of these bombs go off there is a *certainty* of disaster. Whether any more bombs will go off depends on the situations and the decisions that are made.

It is likely that the reason for the rather widespread acceptance of the attitude expressed by Sir Charles is given in his last sentence. It would be nice indeed if all we had to do was to choose between a certainty and a risk of disaster. In that case, a sane man need not hesitate. Unfortunately for the peace of mind of responsible decision-makers, it is by no means clear on which side the certainties and the risks lie. It might be true that there is a certainty of disaster. It is even conceivable that a detached observer, say from Mars, with infinite wisdom would conclude that it was impossible for us poor creatures on earth to get out of the difficulties we are in; we have discovered weapons of mass destruction and sooner or later we are going to use them—and maybe more than once—until the peace of utter destruction prevents us from using them any more. On the other hand, it might be true that a number of different policies are possible and that these may give rise to varying degrees of risk and different historical outcomes. The latter position seems much more reasonable. The choices open to the human race would also be so unfortunate if the former view were correct, that it is impossible to imagine it as being the basis of policy.

In discussing policy alternatives it is crucial to recognize that the balancing of risks is a difficult job. It cannot be done rigorously, though analysis should help. It will involve, at best, judicious guesses, informed acts of faith, and careful steps in the dark; it is essential to recognize them for what they are. Some new and appealing paths might be even more risky than the perilous one we are now trodding.

In summary, one reason why people like to believe that the current system must inevitably end in total annihilation is that they want to stop thinking. They want to make the choice one between a risk and the certainty of disaster. If they can simplify the choices in this way, as moral men, they need no longer hesitate. Unfortunately, intelligent men cannot pose the problem in that fashion. A moderate form of the either-or position would seem preferable—more moderate in that it does not hold categorically that there really is an either-or situation, and more moderate in that it does not assign quite the same cataclysmic quality to a failure on the "or" side. But although the failure could clearly be catastrophic enough, it need not be so catastrophic as to mean that we ought to be willing to give up all other values to arrest it assuming—almost undoubtedly inaccurately—that such a choice could realistically be made.

It would be helpful at this point to discuss a "hypothetical" situation. What might the world look like in the year 2000 if current technological trends were to continue without any startling change in the international, social, and political order? It is the purpose of this exercise to make plausible the modified either-or view that an extrapolation of the current international order is simply incompatible with plausible technological developments. If one is convinced that the strains on the system are large enough to force large changes, whether one wishes them or not, then one is intellectually and psychologically prepared to think hard about the next set of problems—when and how these changes are likely to occur;[2] what we can do to guide them; and so on. It is a startling experience to examine the literature and find that, until recently, relatively little thought has been given to proposals concerning such problems. Most of this recent thought has been directed to relatively narrow and technical arms control and "legalistic" world government proposals.

Let us start by extrapolating one aspect of this current order. There are about twenty-five nations today which spend between a hundred million and a billion dollars a year on national defense. One can certainly believe, if current growth rates and attitudes toward national defense continue, that before the twentieth century ends, there will be something like fifty nations spending between a hundred million and a billion a year on national defense. Since progress in both the weaponry and the technical ability of these nations would accompany this increase in the number of nations, there would be at least half a hundred "small" nations able, within only a fraction of their customary defense budget, to acquire rather impressive strategic forces.[3] It is most unlikely that these forces would

---

[2] In fact it seems likely that technological progress, almost by itself, would make the situation critical much before the year 2000, unless there are compensating controls or other changes. However, by picking the year 2000 as a sort of outermost limit for the viability of the current system, almost all of the objections of more conservative colleagues are eliminated.

[3] Although current ICBM's are expensive to procure and maintain, it is quite likely that future models will be much less expensive. This is obvious from looking at the technology of the very next generation of solid-fueled or storable-propellant missiles. There is another reason why some models of ICBM's may reverse the normal trend of weapons systems to greater complexity and cost. Looking at the history of bombers, for example, one notes that the early bombers had inadequate performance, even for the minimum mission—improvements in speed, range, and altitude were of the greatest importance. This meant that technological improvements were applied to solving these problems with a consequent increase in cost. In the absence (and possibly in the presence) of active and passive defense, even the "model T" ICBM has a very impressive performance. This means that technological improvements may be used to

be comparable to the capabilities of the larger powers, and they might or might not serve effectively as "second strike" forces, but they are still likely to be potentially very destructive.

Many of these nations will also have the capability to procure weapons systems that, in the absence of adequate control, can launch missiles anonymously. The delivery vehicle could be, for example, a space platform in outer space, or more likely, a Polaris-type submarine. If the nation has good internal security, it can use even simpler techniques such as unmarked planes or "suitcase" bombs delivered clandestinely.

In addition to the twenty-five nations which today spend between a hundred million and a billion dollars annually on national defense, there are about ten nations spending over a billion dollars a year. By the year 2000, there could be about twenty nations spending more than a billion dollars a year on defense. It is, therefore, quite possible that there will be about twenty or more nations capable of achieving more than a modest strategic capability. These could obtain more than a few Polaris-type submarines or space-bombardment platforms in addition to military systems based in their national territories. By amortizing the cost over ten years, any of these nations will be able to build a nuclear doomsday machine, or its near equivalent, within its regular defense budget. (A near-doomsday machine can be defined as a device or a set of devices which when exploded will destroy all unprotected life in an area of at least continental proportions and also have major world-wide effects.)

The "strategic theory" of such machines has been discussed in *On Thermonuclear War*.[4] The conclusion reached at that time was that although it was most unlikely that any nation would build such devices in the next ten to twenty years, there were circumstances in which a nation might wish it had built such a device. If such circumstances occur often enough, then at least one or two nations may actually construct such machines. It is perhaps as likely as not that such devices will be built in the next thirty or forty years—if one assumes a continuation of the current anarchy. Of course, even if doomsday machines are built, it is unlikely that they will be used. However, almost all agree that the mere existence of a doomsday machine is a vast and totally unacceptable danger. If the present anarchy were to continue for a century or so, then, even

---

reduce the procurement and operating costs, rather than to improve the performance. If one accepts this last remark, then one can almost confidently predict that, in the next few decades, it will be possible for advanced nations to maintain large forces of some models of ICBM's for systems costs of less than $1,000,000 a year per missile and for less advanced nations to fabricate and maintain a force for systems costs less than five times this figure. In addition to being able to get simple strategic systems, many nations will be able to procure systems capable of disguised warfare, either because the weapons are fired from hidden sites (from seaborne or spaceborne platforms, for example) or because the weapon is so subtle either in its effect or its operation that the attacked nation is not aware—perhaps until too late—that it is being attacked. For example, the possibility of using some concealed form of bacteriological or chemical warfare to debilitate a nation's population over some years, to reduce its competitive capabilities, should not be out of the question by the year 2000 or perhaps earlier.

4 Pp. 144–51.

The Arms Race and World Order

though the probability that a doomsday machine will be constructed and used is unknown and unknowable, it seems (or should seem) too high to even the most optimistic prophets.

It is most likely that the international order will change before a doomsday machine is built. It will change partly because of the general and specific political impact of the advancing military and non-military technology, partly as a continuation of current political, legal, and moral trends (the revolution in world politics), and partly as a direct result of the actual or potential diffusion of "normal" weapons. It is difficult to believe that the world will go unchanged if there are fifty independent, sovereign, small and medium nations with the capability to acquire small amounts of reasonably destructive modern weapon systems and ten or twenty nations with the capability to acquire large amounts. This is true even if many of these nations are not strongly motivated to acquire such systems. Even a weak motivation is likely to be motivation enough—particularly in an unstable competitive situation.

Many nations may obtain nuclear weapons systems without producing cataclysmic instability. For example, the situation might turn out to be similar to that of the old American West. In these societies many people went armed; every now and then a quarrel broke out and somebody was either wounded or killed, but life went on.

The situation might turn out to be even more peaceful than the dueling analogy would suggest. Even before dueling became outlawed, there was a strong tendency in some of the dueling societies to minimize the role of duels. Individuals learned that force was not a proper way of settling personal disputes. And it might indeed turn out that the war system will wither away by itself.

Both of the preceding possibilities, a viable dueling system or an evolutionary withering away of the war system without any "special controls," seem somewhat remote. There are[5] ten problems which would either occur, or be greatly aggravated if there were a widespread diffusion of nuclear weapons. That list is repeated here and each of the problems is discussed very briefly.

1. *Greater Opportunities for Blackmail, Revenge, Terrorism, and Other Mischief-Making.* In a world armed to its teeth in nuclear weapons, every time there is a quarrel or a difference of opinion, there will always be, in the background, a possibility of violence of a kind and degree and speed that is quite different from what is possible today. This could occur even in relatively innocuous quarrels, for example, over fishing rights, as well as over obvious trouble-making irredentist movements or quarrels over prestige. There will be pressures not only to threaten all-out war, but also to use single nuclear weapons to show resolve, to commit oneself irrevocably, or to demonstrate recklessness. In other words, there is likely to be both encouragement and opportunity for playing the game of

[5] See Herman Kahn, *Thinking About the Unthinkable* (New York: Horizon Press, 1962).

International Conflict

chicken. This is particularly true because of the previously mentioned possibility for the anonymous delivery of weapons.

2. *Greater Proneness to Inadvertent War.* An inadvertent (unpremeditated) war is one which occurs without the considered intention of any of the governments that wage it. The possibility of inadvertent war could go up not only because there are many more weapons and missiles around, but also because—and even more important—there will be many more organizations around, each with a different standard of training, organization, and operational code. An inadvertent war could be caused by accidents such as a switch failing, a false radar return, or some other statistically possible event. It could also occur because of an unauthorized behavior, irresponsible behavior, a misunderstanding of orders, a generally lax discipline, or any one of a thousand ways in which something can go wrong. It is not inevitable that any particular provocation or accident will set off a large-scale chain reaction. However, every time there is a small war or accident, there will be great pressure to reform the system. This is, in fact, one likely mechanism for the creation of a crisis which causes a relatively peaceful evolution out of the current system of relative anarchy. Nations will refuse to live with a situation in which nuclear accidents actually do occur. If at all possible, they will do something to correct a system which makes such things likely or inevitable.

3. *Increased Capabilities for "Local" Munichs, Pearl Harbors, and Blitzkriegs.* The tendency to play the game of chicken has already been mentioned. A slightly more reckless, irresponsible, desperate, or decisive decision-maker might simply go ahead and attack another nation, saying, in effect, to the other nations, "what will you do about it?" Even if the attacked nation has a nuclear capability, in many cases it may not have much effective second-strike capability. The other nations, on the other hand, are going to be loath to start a nuclear war to avenge a *fait accompli*. The attacker might even use the attacked nation as a hostage to prevent effective reprisals.

The aggressor may not actually need to launch his attack. He might merely threaten to do so with explicit ultimatums, thus forcing the other side either to back down, or to attack with all the political and military dangers such an attack might bring. In other words, in a situation where there are opportunities for large payoffs through extremely aggressive behavior, we should not be surprised if some nations indulge in such behavior. There are golden opportunities here for both paranoiacs and megalomaniacs.

4. *Pressures to Pre-empt Because of Points One, Two, and Three.* To the extent that the behavior described above actually occurs, as opposed to being an academic possibility, one could expect decision-makers to note that it could happen to them and, therefore, to note also the importance of doing it first. Although few wish to be either executioners or victims, many would prefer the first role to the second if they believed they must choose. A world in which "reciprocal fear of surprise attack" is everpresent is a world which is going to be very unstable. There will also be pressure

The Arms Race and World Order

toward psychological and political pre-emption. In any situation in which there is an important gain to be made by saying something like, "One of us has to be responsible, and since it isn't going to be me, it has to be you," there is a tendency to overuse committal strategies—to say it first and firmly.

5. *Tendency to Neglect Conventional Military Capabilities.* Because of an overreliance on one's own nuclear capabilities, or fear of the other side's nuclear capabilities, it is likely to be extremely difficult for most nations to take the concept of limited conventional war seriously enough actually to allocate money, manpower, thought, and other scarce commodities into conventional or other limited capabilities. It will be difficult for them to do this, even though they realize abstractly that in a crisis they may find themselves unwilling to rely on their nuclear capabilities. This is likely to create all kinds of instabilities and opportunities for bluff, counterbluff, or actual attack that result in either defeat or escalation.

6. *Internal (Civil War, Coup d'Etat, Irresponsibility, etc.) and External (Arms Race, Fear of Fear, etc.) Political Problems.* It is difficult to believe that in a world as armed to the teeth and as dangerous looking as the one just pictured there will not be both responsible and irresponsible peace and accommodation movements. If every time a difficult decision is being made, a major portion of the country is being risked; if every time a country's diplomats walk into a hostile conference room, every woman and child feels threatened; if every time a nation stands firm against aggressive probes, panic seizes the hearts of many of its citizens, then many citizens will simply adopt an attitude of denial or apathetic fatalism while others call for "peace" with great intensity. The trouble with this kind of poiltical situation is that it is not likely, to put it mildly, to produce thoughtful and considered decisions or programs. In any case, as a result of a combination of apathy, denial, and hysteria, responsible political life is likely to suffer disastrously. And this may encourage or alternatively force other nations to play the game of "chicken."

If some of these "peace" movements are accompanied by violence, or even large-scale illegal non-violence, organized political life in the nation may be threatened even more gravely. In addition, the necessity for reliable internal control of nuclear weapons could force or encourage many governments to practice a rigid authoritarianism or despotism to prevent even small military or political groups from obtaining and using weapons for protest or revolutionary purposes. And eventually, the best of safeguards will occasionally fail.

7. *Facilitate Diffusion of Nuclear Weapons to Really Irresponsible Organizations.* To the extent that advanced nuclear weapons or components are treated as articles of commerce (perhaps for peaceful uses as in the Plowshare program), their cost will be well within the resources available to many large organizations. In fact, if we get them down to $100,000 or so, and this is not at all implausible, they are, in some sense, available to any dedicated middle-income individual who is willing to save a major fraction of his income for ten or twenty years. Exactly what this could

236

mean is hard to picture without detailed consideration of the various "scenarios" that are possible; but, somehow, few will feel comfortable in a world in which the Malayan guerrillas, Cuban rebels, Algerian terrorists (or the Right-Wing counterterrorists), the Puerto Rican Independence Party, or even gangsters could have access to nuclear weapons or other means of mass destruction. It should be realized that even if nuclear weapons and their delivery systems are not articles of commerce, almost all of their components will have peaceable "relatives." These will be articles of commerce. Thus, only a few special parts or assemblies will have to be manufactured by those organizations or individuals who wish to obtain some sort of weapons capability.

8. *Complicates Future Problems of Control.* If weapons are diffused widely, then even if an incident or a crisis occurs and even if such an event increases the willingness of most nations to control the situation, such control is likely to be more difficult to achieve because the small powers are now being asked to accept a reduction in their current capability rather than to abstain from the acquisition of weapons. Of course, if the control measures that are envisaged are sufficiently thorough-going and complete, all nations may be treated equally. Even then, it is going to be difficult, if not impossible, to get all of them to junk their nuclear-weapons systems peacefully and not just acquiesce to controls that prevent them from acquiring such systems, though, as France has shown, the last may be difficult.

9. *Creates and Intensifies Agent-Provocateur Problems.* It should be clear that one restraint on the behavior of "respectable" large nations in this super-armed world—and perhaps in any world—is that they do not want a reputation for being blatantly aggressive. Therefore, when a nation does want to be aggressive, it often needs an excuse to make its aggression seem defensive, or at least very special and limited. In the absence of a special situation (such as Berlin), it may be difficult to do this. It is usually almost impossible for a small power to be made to look so provocative against a large power to justify, for example, nuclear retaliation by the large power. But if the small power happens to have nuclear weapons, then many kinds of "accidental" incidents or provocations could be arranged or made use of. They could be used to justify all kinds of ultimatums or actual reprisals up to and including the forcible disarming of the small power which showed itself to be irresponsible enough to nearly cause a holocaust.

10. *Catalytic War or Escalation.* The widespread diffusion of nuclear weapons could give many nations the capability, and in some cases, would also create a pressure, to aggravate an on-going crisis or even to touch off a war between two other powers for purposes of their own. Here again the situation is so complicated that one must think through many scenarios to get a feeling for the possibilities. However, in advance of such systematic exploration, and without discussing our present knowledge of the problem, it should be clear that there are many possibilities for mischief-making by third parties.

The preceding comments should make it plausible that the diffusion of nuclear and other modern weapons can and probably will result in the creation of many more ways in which things can go wrong, and that under current programs, this increase in possibilities is unlikely to be compensated for. Therefore, there should be an automatic increase in the probability that things will go wrong. In short, the diffusion of nuclear weapons will probably increase the number of misunderstandings or crises, their seriousness, and their grim potentialities. This will tend to increase enormously the importance of having responsible and competent governments everywhere. It is likely that some governments will fail inadvertently to take the proper precautions, and that others will deliberately try to exploit the common dangers for unilateral advantages. These "failures" will probably occur too frequently for the system to exist unchanged.

This last statement is likely to be true even if the situation looks superficially stable. The widespread possession of nuclear weapons and delivery systems is likely to be similar to a situation that the physicist would describe as "quasi-stable equilibrium." Imagine, for example, a ball balanced on top of a small cup so that small movements of the ball can be tolerated, but not large ones. If this ball and the cup are isolated, it might sit on top of its cup forever; but if it is submitted to the vagaries and chances of a sufficiently uncontrolled environment, one can guarantee that sooner or later it will fall. This can be true even though every "reasonable" analysis of the situation looking at probable or plausible disturbances shows that the forces are in close enough balance so that the ball should stay where it is. It takes an improbable and implausible force to topple the ball. But some improbable and implausible events will occur. Barring a secular change in the situation, they will occur almost with certainty, and the ball will eventually fall. However, depending on the relationship of the degree of stability to the frequency and violence of the perturbing force, the metastable state might be expected to last for only seconds, or for centuries. My own admittedly undocumented estimate is that a nuclear war is likely to be avoided only for a few decades. After all, it is most unlikely that all the actors in the international scene will be cautious, prosperous bourgeois nations. In fact, as Kaplan states in his introduction, many will be "conscious antagonists of a system of domestic and international order they regard as bad or immoral." When they get weapons, they may seek to change this bad and immoral international system for one more to their liking.

Although the ball and cup analogy may simultaneously be both apt and misleading, many who have thought about this problem have come to the conclusion that reliable stability can come only through an international agency with an effective monopoly of force, total disarmament, or a permanent stabilization of something like the current system with two or three main blocs and with most non-bloc powers not having modern weapons systems. This last is likely to be stable only if the blocs are both monolithic in their external relations, cooperate on most issues, and act with a great deal of restraint when competitive. (See Kaplan's paper on

238

bipolar system models.) In the long run (or perhaps in the medium run), only some variant of "world government" seems plausible to this writer. Both the bloc solution and total disarmament seem too unstable in the presence of disturbances or the absence of saints in the role of decision-makers.

If this attitude toward the future availability of nuclear weapons, their delivery systems (from the technological and economic points of view), and the instability that would ensue if these technological and economic factors were exploited to the point where there was a widespread diffusion of those weapons is accepted, then the only questions remaining are the following: Under current and future conditions, how much motivation will there be to acquire these systems? If there is enough to create a problem, then how much change is required to handle the situation? How will these changes come about? Can we do much to influence these changes, or will most of them occur in a natural and unguided (but not necessarily peaceful) fashion?

It might be worthwhile at this point to comment on why it might take as long as thirty or forty years before the current system would reach the breaking point. One reason is obvious: Nations like the United States, the Soviet Union, members of the Western European Union, and so on are extremely cautious about resorting to the use of modern arms or formal threats to do so. In addition to being cautious themselves, they restrain those who are not. In other words, deterrence is likely to work on at least 99.99 per cent of the days (which would imply that with average luck, it would work for about thirty years). The only trouble is that even one failure is likely to be very destructive and might be catastrophic. However, the unsatisfactoriness of a world system based on current deterrence concepts, with their ever present possibility of failure, is no reason for us unwisely to weaken our deterrence. We can easily worsen the situation, not only as judged from a narrow national point of view, but also as judged from the viewpoint of developing a satisfactory world order.

The other important reasons for believing that the current deterrent system will probably be more stable than a superficial examination would indicate have already been mentioned. There are all kinds of constraints on the arms race and military postures and operations. For example, imagine that this paper had been written about five years ago and that there was convincing evidence that the Communist Chinese would openly prepare to test nuclear weapons at some point in the early sixties. (Many people now seem to believe that this is likely.) It would have seemed quite reasonable under those circumstances to assume that the Japanese and Indians would be working hard on their own bombs by now. Since these nations had (and probably still have) an intrinsically greater independent capability for achieving a nuclear explosion than have the Chinese, it would have seemed likely that the early 60's would see three Asian nuclear powers. In fact, one might easily have imagined four or five.

Well, it doesn't seem to be like that. As far as is generally known, neither the Indians nor the Japanese have programs for developing nuclear

The Arms Race and World Order

weapons. Although both Nehru and Bhabba (head of the Indian AEC) have stated that India could have nuclear weapons within two years after a decision to produce them, they have also stated that India will not make that decision. Citizens and leaders of India and other Asian nations now seem (though they may change their minds) to believe that the Chinese will use self-restraint, or that the Americans or Soviets or other nations will protect them from the Chinese; or they have some sophisticated (and probably incorrect) reason for not worrying. Some, of course, just refuse to face the problem.

A similar situation exists in Europe. Five years ago many would have assumed that once the French had achieved a nuclear explosion, the Germans, the Italians, and even the Swiss and the Swedes would also try to procure nuclear weapons. Well, once more, it isn't like that. The last two countries, it is true, have authorized their departments of defense to look into the problem of obtaining nuclear weapons, but in both cases, the legislatures have refused to appropriate substantial sums for this activity. These two nations have merely tried to establish the principle that they are entitled to get nuclear weapons if they want them, but they are not taking any serious actions in a direction that might rock the boat.

Similarly, in the late 40's, it would have seemed reasonable to many technologists that by 1965, or even 1960, some nation such as South Africa would have a gaseous diffusion plant of its own designed and financed by Europeans, whose major output would be fuel for reactors, but which as a by-product, would sell uranium to countries which might divert the material to bombs. One could have imagined such a munitions maker engaging in the manufacture and sale of bombs to "carefully" selected customers. It is true that there would be much pressure exerted on the South Africans not to do this, but they are already receiving much criticism and might feel that they could afford to ignore additional criticism. It is also true that South Africa, intensely hated for its apartheid policies, should, above all other nations, be interested in controlling the diffusion of nuclear weapons to small countries or clandestine groups. However, they might not realize that the sale of weapons to medium and advanced countries could speed the day when revolutionists, blackmailers, or neighboring countries would get nuclear weapons. They could also feel (and possibly correctly) that if they did not engage in this business other nations would, and that, by engaging in the nuclear weapons business, they could exert some control over the distribution in addition to making some profits.

None of these things has occurred or seems likely to occur in the near future. Because of technological and economic reasons, the development of power reactors (another source of fissionable material) has been much slower than expected. Another potential cause of the diffusion of weapons, the AEC's project Plowshare (peaceful uses of nuclear explosives), is being fiercely opposed—mainly because it may facilitate such diffusion. Further-more, there seems to have been very little interest in some of the latest

240

developments (such as the ultra high-speed centrifuge) which could be used even by small nations to acquire nuclear fuel for weapons.

There are grave constraints on other research and development programs in the United States and, we rather suspect, in the Soviet Union as well. We need only notice how little work has been done on bacteriological and chemical warfare in the United States, both during the Second World War and in the subsequent fifteen years. Although there is now great interest in these subjects, much or almost all of this interest is directed toward incapacitating agents rather than killing agents. By and large, scientists have been unwilling to work in this area, and the government has been loath to appropriate funds. Similar statements can be made about other areas of research or production that might cause—or that might be thought to cause—an undue or undesirable acceleration in the arms race. Fear of the arms race, rather than budgetary considerations or inadequate effectiveness, is probably the main reason for the current neglect of civil defense and de-emphasis on active defense. (See *OTW*, pp. 515–18 for the kinds of civil defense and other programs we might have with a "modest" increase in defense expenditures. "Modest" here implies allocating, 14 per cent or even less of the GNP to national security as we did in the immediate post-Korea years.) In addition, if public discussion is any guide, the emphasis in our nuclear-weapons laboratories has recently been on smaller and cleaner, rather than larger and dirtier weapons. And, finally, one of the reasons for the interest in mobile systems is that they seem to be able to achieve certain kinds of deterrence with many times smaller total yield deployed than is true of the systems available today.

Not only in the United States, but throughout the world, there are important unilateral constraints on the arms race. In addition, there are outlets for both energies and competition in economic development, in the propaganda and political war, and even in technological progress (for example, the space race). These constraints and "peaceful" alternatives may succeed in deferring the day of reckoning for some years, or possibly even for decades. But it is hard for members of even the moderate either-or school to believe that it will be deferred for more than a very few decades. Even if the arms race is controlled, both modern technology and modern morality create pressures and capabilities for a new world order. And if the arms race is not controlled, then any day may see a spectacular and revolutionary weapons development to make all nations equal in potential for violence in much the same way that the six-gun became the great equalizer in the American West. Differences in skill, morality, nerve, and recklessness could still be decisive, but mere physical size or wealth could become either irrelevant or a handicap.[6]

Although the breakdown of the current world order by a war or crisis need not lead to an end of history, it could be the most momentous

6 See Chaps. 9 and 10 of *OTW* for a reasonably detailed description of the current arms race.

The Arms Race and World Order

catastrophe to occur in historical time. We would all, of course, prefer to escape from this situation peacefully. How can we go about this?

First of all, we can try to buy time by increasing the safety of the current system while encouraging natural developments. Perhaps we can aid these natural developments by negotiation on *relatively* simple and apolitical[7] technical matters such as a nuclear-test ban or control of surprise attack. Such action would be taken in the hope that the "war system" would gradually wither away to be replaced by another system, perhaps by a more or less satisfactory world government, or, perhaps by some other more sophisticated arrangement whose character is not now clear.

We might try to facilitate the peaceful evolution of the new system by trying to negotiate major structural changes in the international order. There seem to be few significant feasible suggestions, though one will be mentioned later—(a condominium between the United States and the Soviet Union on the use of nuclear weapons). Many experts believe that it is almost impossible to negotiate a comprehensive arms-control agreement without a general political settlement, except as a reaction to a very dramatic event (such as a war or a crisis which is intense enough to have resulted in the evacuation of cities). Yet, in the absence of war or crisis, a general political settlement seems most unlikely. One can hope that the above will turn out to be a self-defeating prophecy, but it may not. One can, of course, accept the preceding view and still be willing to negotiate—partly because there are many political and social reasons for going through the motions of negotiating and partly because one's judgment may be wrong. The negotiations may succeed.

There is another possibly overwhelming reason for the study and preliminary negotiation of comprehensive agreements. It is precisely the point of the preceding argument that if one does not believe in a relatively peaceful evolution, then one believes that a war or crisis will occur and that presumably we should be prepared to exploit whatever constructive things could be obtained from the event. Such a war or crisis is much more likely to result in a satisfactory comprehensive agreement if there are political and military plans and preparations to exploit them—in particular, if an agreement exists ready to be initialled, or there is enough common understanding of what is needed to make it easy to arrive at agreement under pressure.

Consider some of the preceding possibilities. The simplest and perhaps the most important available short-term actions are unilateral measures. To take a most important example, we can make our command and control system so reliable that the possibility of an accident, unauthorized behavior, or miscalculation is very small. We can make our strategic forces

---

[7] Simple and apolitical as compared to agreements on important changes in the structure of the present international system. Some of the seemingly apolitical measures, however, may involve presently unforeseen political complications of a structural nature. If sufficiently unforeseen or long range, the prospect of such change may not handicap the negotiations excessively.

International Conflict

so invulnerable that we do not have to respond to an accident or a small attack by launching a major nuclear counterattack.[8] If we carry through both of these measures we are unlikely to be the victim of an accident or even of a deliberate attempt by a third party to set off a war. We will be able and prepared to wait and to analyze what happened rather than react hastily and wrongly. A nation that has invulnerable forces with adequate command and control deters the enemy from attacking *and* minimizes such specially dangerous situations as "reciprocal fear of surprise attack,"[9] "self-fulfilling prophecy,"[10] and "catalytic war."[11] We need such measures even if they are costly or handicap the operations of our forces. In addition, we must, on our own, design our strategic systems to be able to accept whatever implicit or explicit arrangements can be made; in particular, we must neither develop nor procure systems that needlessly accelerate or exacerbate the arms race. This last is not just a formal remark without content. In many influential quarters the most pertinent question that can be asked about a new weapons system is, "How will its procurement affect the arms race?"

The preceding question is sometimes allowed to dominate the issue to the point where analysts and others have refused to consider otherwise reasonable active and passive defense measures for fear of touching off an offense-defense race. Although an undue degree of unilateral disarmament seems inadvisable, there is much to be said for the concept of the limited use of unilateral measures, both in the hope of influencing others to do likewise and even more because there are limits to what we are willing to do in order to protect ourselves and further our policies. The following chart may help to clarify this point:

Where Do *You* Draw the Line?
1. Insecticides
2. Eating meat
3. Any violence
4. Police force
5. Conventional warfare
6. Kiloton weapons
7. Megaton weapons
8. Begaton weapons
9. Doomsday machines
10. Galaxy destroying machines

[8] For a detailed discussion of the problems see Chaps. 4, 5, and 6 of *OTW*. I mention there that I expect both the Soviets and Americans to procure such stable systems that under normal circumstances even a number of ICBM's landing and exploding would not touch off an all-out war—though the system is not likely to be so reliable that either side would deliberately test it.

[9] A crisis in which the enemy fears that we will feel so insecure as to be trigger-happy and that he must therefore pre-empt our possible attack.

[10] Signals being generated by defensive actions by one side, which touch off actions by the other side, which in turn generate signals that cause the first side to take additional precautions, and so on.

[11] An attempt by a third nation to try to touch off a mutually undesired war between the two largest powers for purposes of its own.

The Arms Race and World Order

It is the purpose of the chart to make it clear to both the pacifist, who generally draws the line somewhere between (3) and (5), and the more resolute militarist, who draws the line somewhere between (7) and (9), that they both believe in some degree of unilateral disarmament, and that there are things neither would procure nor plan to do, no matter what military risk might result from their failure to act.

Of course, we have to worry about the Soviets. Will they exercise similar restraint? It has been suggested that we might give them the knowledge and even the tools for decreasing their own vulnerability and for improving their safety practices. Bizarre as it seems today, the idea is not inconceivable; something like this may happen. There is, however, a possible asymmetry between us and the Soviets. Many Marxists seem to be dedicated to a deterministic theory of history in which the so-called permanent operating and other basic factors play the major role. It may be difficult for them to believe that a switch's failing or a fuse's melting could change the course of history. Most Americans have no great difficulty in believing this, since we tend to have a fairly shallow view of history. On the other hand, the Soviets worry a great deal about unauthorized behavior. As a result, in many cases, they will take the same precautions we do, though with different motivation.

It is also possible that the Soviets will systematically exploit the fear of the arms race to corrode the will of the West. They may see only opportunities where we see dangers. However, it is likely that the Soviets will recognize at least the need for highly protected, slow reacting, reliable forces and will procure them almost irrespective of their other policies.

The next thing we can do to stabilize the situation is to negotiate those technical agreements that have little or no political effect but may do much to decrease the immediate risk of war. For example, one might install communication systems between the Soviet and United States head-quarters. Then, if any unexpected events occur, the two countries can communicate directly with each other. There is a possibility (though nobody seems to have made any practical proposals)[12] that we can arrange not only to pass information on to the enemy, but also to establish reliable procedures that would allow him to verify its validity. If a complicated accident occurred, or if there were a crisis, each nation could then explain its view of what was happening and try to reassure the other that it was not in danger from a surprise attack or from other aggressive moves. Even if the verification procedures cannot be worked out, just being able to transmit information and proposals quickly and reliably may be valuable.

Another possibility is the systematic (probably for free rather than

---

12 The problem is that if the crisis is so serious that we are really concerned that the enemy might attack, then we are likely to be unwilling to initiate any kind of unilateral disarmament of other than the strictly offensive forces. By and large the practical measures that can be taken seem to be almost negligible in their effect on the offensive forces unless they also seriously weaken the defensive forces. The point needs further research, but a suprficial initial look has not turned up promising ideas. However, see Thomas C. Schelling, "Arms Control: A Proposal for a Special Surveil-lance Force," *World Politics*, Vol. 13 (October 1960), pp. 1–18, for some possibilities.

on a *quid pro quo* basis) exchange of information in peacetime to reassure each other of the safety of our operating practice; in that way each side would understand the nature of certain types of operations and not erroneously think of them as threatening. This exchange of information could be done formally or informally, explicitly or implicitly, officially or unofficially, openly or surreptitiously. There are many possibilities, and we ought to study systematically how to exploit them. We might even exchange observers to facilitate, on a controlled basis, this exchange of information.

One could also imagine operating warning networks jointly, particularly in outer space, or making agreements to prevent the tracking of mobile Polaris weapons (or, conversely, agreements which facilitate the tracking of third-power Polaris submarines), the spoofing and jamming of warning networks, the shooting down of satellites, and so forth. We may even be willing to cooperate in the operation of a world-wide monitoring and control system designed to prevent anonymous attacks by third powers.

The next class of measures could be implicit rather than explicit or, even if explicit, they could be negotiated on an informal basis, without having the binding character of the usual treaty. For example, we could simply tell the Soviets that if they don't shoot down our reconnaissance satellites, we will not shoot down theirs. Or that if they do not build an AICBM system, we will not build one. Similarly, for civil defense.[13] In all of these and in many other cases, detection is very simple. The projects are either so large that it is impossible to conceal them, or the nature of the acts themselves makes concealment most unlikely.

If the agreements are implicit, there may be some ambiguity. For example, is a warning radar part of an AICBM system? What about an advanced Nike-Hercules designed against antiaircraft, but which has some small capability against missiles? Is the construction of basements that might be used as shelters, or the decentralization of industry for "man-

[13] It is often said that we have today an implicit agreement not to initiate large-scale civil-defense programs. There may be some operational content to this belief. If the United States Government ever seriously considered spending, say, five billion dollars annually on civil defense, one of the most persuasive arguments that would be brought against the proposal would be the high probability of touching off an offense-defense arms race. That is, not only would the Soviets be stimulated into considering such civil defense programs for themselves, but they would also consider buying more and larger missiles, etc. While we might be able to "win" this arms race in the sense of increasing our objective military position *vis-à-vis* the Soviets, the resulting increase over the next five to ten years in the number and quality of weapons on both sides might represent an increase in the mutual danger that could swamp the competitive aspects. Insofar as the above considerations are both correct and symmetrical, one can say that we have an implicit agreement not to go into civil defense. I believe that they can be exaggerated. In particular, I do not believe that small civil-defense programs—say, of the billion-dollar-a-year level—have such an impact on the arms race. In any case, the Soviets seem to have such a small program, and we do not. Even the effect of large programs can be exaggerated. After all, the ability to kill millions of people, to destroy hundreds of billions of dollars of property, and to leave the environment more hostile to human life might be almost as deterring as the ability to kill tens or hundreds of millions of people.

The Arms Race and World Order

agerial purposes," the initial phase of a civil-defense program? The ambiguity is not likely to be very important, and in many cases, some ambiguity may be a valuable asset in facilitating agreement and in keeping the agreement flexible. Such implicit agreements between nations are actually traditional; they were almost common in the nineteenth century. They have gone out of fashion in recent years. Reinstituting them could be one of those simple measures that has vast importance for controlling current and future possibilities. Although particularly important as short-term interim measures, they may also have much direct influence on the medium- and long-term situations, particularly if age and custom tend to legitimate them.

It is often relatively easy to reach implicit agreements precisely because there is less difficulty in breaking them—at least in the short term. Neither nation is committed if it changes its mind. If time or experience modifies a country's views about the seriousness, consequences, or asymmetries of the agreement, it can simply inform its opponent that it has changed its mind. In most cases, there should be only the mildest exacerbation of tensions on the resumption of the forbidden practice or project.

Of course, such agreements have dangers. The policies involved in implementing implicit agreements must be examined carefully. These policies may tend in varying degrees to weaken our resolve. They also may discourage our friends and encourage our enemies in the satellite nations. They may have a similar effect on our allies. This last is especially likely to occur if the actions constituting the implicit agreements cause critics or anxious observers to believe that we are thinking of repudiating or modifying our more onerous obligations or that we are planning a private deal in which our allies' interests will not be fully recognized. By decreasing the risk of United States nuclear reaction, some implicit agreements could actually create or increase the opportunity for Soviet or Chinese nuclear blackmail. There can also be deleterious effects on the neutrals. Finally, there is the possibility that wishful thinking may cause us to slight control and inspection in such agreements—the recent moratorium on nuclear tests was, to put it mildly, inadequately inspected. And even if, as seems likely, the Soviets did not cheat by clandestine testing, they certainly used the agreement to slow our program down while pursuing a vigorous theoretical and practical pre-test program that seems to have been definitely aimed at procuring a lead by putting them in a position maximally to exploit their ending of the agreement. It is also worth noting that, although implicit agreements are not as binding as explicit treaties, at least as far as the West is concerned, the longer the agreement is kept in force, the harder it is to break the precedents and customs that have been established.

Even if all of the above general shortcomings are admitted, each proposal should be examined on its merits. Unless their costs are immoderately high, possible implicit agreements ought not to be dismissed out of hand. Almost any constructive action involves costs. Even doing

246

nothing can bring fearful risks. It may even be worthwhile to accept small competitive losses now, not only to increase stability, but also to head off the catastrophic loss in the morale of the West that is likely to occur should an increasingly dangerous arms race ever make our weapons seem more dangerous than an undue accommodation or a surrender.

As part and parcel of such a program, we could institute informal but regular confidential and open dialogues between the Soviets and the Americans to the end that we will understand each other and our problems better. Our ambassador or military attachés, for instance, might ask their opposite numbers such questions as "What do you think your country would do if my country did so and so?" Such dialogues would have to be held in complete confidence and would not commit either government. There are also possibilities for more open dialogues—for example, the recent proposals by D. G. Brennan or R. Leghorn for bilateral or multi-lateral "World Security Institutes." One could even make more ambitious proposals for international or multi-national research and study that could play an important role in generating and improving the efficiency of the dialogue.

The next type of agreement, the explicitly negotiated binding treaty on other than a minor technical issue, will almost inevitably have major political impact of far-reaching consequences. For this reason, such agreements are much less likely to be negotiated—unless there is at least a partial political settlement. However, they provide some of the major possibilities for big changes and so must be considered even in the absence of such a settlement. The proposed agreement for a nuclear-test suspension is a case in point. It also may be typical of the way in which we are likely to run into all kinds of unexpected difficulties and to find out, in a very costly fashion, that we had not considered the consequences of the agreement until late in the game.

However, it still seems desirable to sign such an agreement on roughly the terms that are currently being considered if no better alternatives can be worked out. Conceding all of the uncertainties and risks, not signing the agreement, if the Soviets are willing to sign, probably would be an enormous step backward. It is hard to see how we can turn our attention and energies to the control of the development and diffusion of nuclear weapons in other nations, if the three major powers cannot agree on self-restraint among themselves. There are other benefits that can be derived from such an agreement. For one thing, we can test future Soviet "sincerity" and the ability of the two countries to work together in the construction and operation of a control system. We shall educate both ourselves and the Soviets in the setting up and operation of one class of arms-control agreements. If nothing else, this should create in both the Soviet Union and the United States a bureaucracy with a vested interest in understanding and maybe even in promoting arms-control agreements. We may even build up pressures—hopefully in both countries—for additional measures. And although the consequences of Soviet or Chinese

The Arms Race and World Order

cheating could be much more serious than many proponents of the treaty are willing to concede, it seems—perhaps wrongly—that this is one of those uncalculated "calculated risks" that is worth accepting.

Of course, since the negotiations in Geneva have failed, perhaps we should turn our attention to acceptable "substitutes" that might be even better. One possible alternative (or complement) that probably would be of great importance, is the negotiation of a "Hague" convention against the use of nuclear weapons in warfare. This convention could simply set up a condominium on world affairs between the United States and the Soviet Union to the effect that they will refrain from the first military use of nuclear weapons under any circumstances and, in addition, that they will jointly constrain any third power which uses nuclear weapons in a military operation.[14] Other nations should be encouraged to adhere to the convention, thus making it a truly international accord. If effective, such a convention might be more useful than a test suspension in discouraging the diffusion and in controlling the use of nuclear weapons. It also would be a major precedent for the creation of a very limited but possibly adequate "world government."

In any case, the search for a solution less makeshift than the current one must go on. The time available probably is to be measured in one or two decades, rather than one or two centuries. This seems to indicate that our old concepts of national sovereignty are either obsolete or soon will be. To many this last remark implies that we should be unwilling to risk or fight a war solely to preserve the nation state as an independent sovereign entity. That seems reasonable. But it does not mean that we should not be willing to risk or fight a war to influence or to vote on the system which replaces national sovereignty and independence. However, it is difficult to decide what one should be willing to risk unless the alternatives are spelled out.

It would, therefore, be useful to touch on the most important possibility of all, the comprehensive agreement. Included in this are many of the suggestions for international police forces, world governments, and near world governments.

Probably the most detailed and comprehensive proposal has been worked out by Grenville Clark and Louis B. Sohn.[15] It is difficult for practical politicians, hard-headed statesmen, or professional planners to take such proposals seriously—except as manifestations or symptoms of the impracticality of the "do-gooders." As a result, such studies are rarely read by critics except from the viewpoint of content analysis; their substantive audience tends to be restricted to "friends and relatives." As a result, the Clark-Sohn proposals have not had the benefit of as much hostile informed criticism as they deserve. This is singularly unfortunate

---

[14] See OTW, pp. 240–43, for some discussion of this suggestion. Although many will believe it favors the Soviets more than us, in the medium and long run the joint benefits probably outweigh any asymmetries.

[15] *World Peace Through World Law* (Cambridge: Harvard University Press, 1958).

International Conflict

because their book is not only an extraordinarily worthwhile basis for continued work but it also may succeed in influencing history, even in its current, relatively unfinished state.

Consider, for example, the following hypothetical scenario of what could happen. The United States and the Soviet Union are today each supposed to have a handful of missiles. Imagine some of these missiles being shot off accidentally. Imagine also that this accident touches off a reprisal by the other side and, possibly, further exchanges on both sides until most or all of the ready and reliable missiles are launched. Imagine further that the accidental nature of the strike is soon discovered (since there is no immediate follow-up bomber attack and since the pattern and timing of the missile launchings do not conform to a reasonable surprise attack, this should become clear to both sides quite rapidly). Imagine finally that communications between the two countries are established soon enough so that both sides (today miraculously) succeed in calling off or preventing massive bomber strikes.

With current missile forces, it is most likely that at this point in history possibly five or ten or even more cities on one side or the other, or both, might have been destroyed. But both countries would survive this blow. One could confidently predict that the morning after this event there would be a deeply felt conviction among all the nations, but particularly the two antagonists, that deterrence and anarchy were not a good way to run affairs, that we simply could not go back to the old precarious balance of terror and assume the same risks over again. Under these circumstances, it would not be at all surprising to find the United States and the Soviet Union ready to sign something resembling the Clark-Sohn proposals within a few days. It would be realized that unless an agreement were made within days, that is, before the dead were buried, one side or the other would quite likely try to exploit the common danger for unilateral advantage. In this case the negotiations would probably degenerate into the usual unproductive Cold-War jockeying.

The proposals of Professors Clark and Sohn are enormously valuable. They constitute an alternative preferable to the current arms race. However, their proposals do seem to have serious defects. Therefore, in the absence of an immediate war or crisis, they have given us only a foundation on which to work. Much better proposals can be devised. But the improvement will come about only if hard-headed and realistic people take such proposals seriously and either work on them, or criticize the labor of others. Although much is being done now, more can be done. This is one place where the lone scholar, working without either an inter-disciplinary team or access to classified information, can hope to make a major contribution. However, the big inter-disciplinary studies will also play an important role. Let us, therefore, make a conscious attempt to encourage the design and analysis of "utopias" or other alternatives that might be brought about through the agency of a war or crisis. Bleak as this prospect is, a war or crisis is the most likely route by which we shall achieve a more stable international order.

INTERNATIONAL COOPERATION: INTERNATIONAL ORGANIZATION

Three centuries ago Thomas Hobbes cited the relations of states
as an example of the anarchic war of all against all in the State of
Nature. More than one contemporary theorist has suggested that the
most characteristic and important quality of the international political
system is the absence of any binding political authority. Yet, as
Hobbesian theory recognized, even units in a State of Nature may find
it safe and profitable to cooperate. And in the real world, nations
have increasingly coordinated their actions, even to the point of creating
permanent international organizations. These organizations were designed
to serve national interests rather than international or supranational

ones. They provide the setting for joint action in an unfriendly world. The United Nations original title gave a precise indication of what is our main concern here: the United Nations Organization. The articles in this section are concerned with the problem of what in fact such associations do for member nations, any why they are or should be valued.

In "Collective Legitimization as a Political Function of the United Nations," Inis L. Claude, Jr., applies to the United Nations the sort of functional analysis widely used in studying national politics. He suggests that the political sections of the UN, especially the General Assembly, provide a source of authority for certain sorts of collective decisions of the nations. The new nations which were formerly colonies of European powers have used the organization to certify and protect their nationhood. This is why the African and Asian states refused to join their usual allies, the Arabs, in the extreme demands that would has destroyed Israel, also a former colony and a member of the UN. The organization also continues to focus an ever-strengthening consensus on the eradication of colonialism. Claude suggests that such "legitimized consensuses" may also be emerging in the areas of the control of outer space and the regulation of Antarctica. He reminds us that the General Assembly, in spite of its legislative procedure, is not a parliament. The inadequacies of the Assembly's formal resolutions should not blind us to the real usefulness of this institution. International organization is useful as a place national interests coincide because of, rather than in spite of, the separateness of the nations.

Chadwick Alger writes about "Non-resolution Consequences of the United Nations and their Effect on International Conflict." "Non-resolution consequences" are the "latent functions" that are unintended and largely unnoticed side effects of the process of formulating, passing, and enforcing formal Assembly resolutions. Social psychology suggests a number of ways in which the interaction of small groups of people may lessen conflict among them. Many of the same activities seem to go on in the United Nations and Alger feels that this may have a mitigating effect on potential international conflict. For instance, national leaders who participate as delegates in the formal negotiating process of the Committees may be more likely to prefer a similar discussion procedure in other international situations. Delegates may develop friendships, or at least professional relationships based on mutual respect. Also verbal confrontations in the United Nations may be a substitute for military confrontations, releasing tensions or at worst giving sufficient advance warning for defensive measures. Since writing this article, Alger has been able to confirm some, though not all, of his hypotheses.

The third piece, "Discovering Voting Groups in the United Nations," is again about the General Assembly. Bruce M. Russett concentrates on the deliberate—and deliberately political—act of voting. Assembly votes have often been studied in connection with the groups of nations known to caucus in order to coordinate their policies before voting. Instead of

International Cooperation

looking for voting patterns of selected states, Russett used a computer to analyze the mass of recorded roll-call votes during several Assembly sessions; in the article reprinted here he reports on the 1963 session. He searched out the states whose voting patterns were similar, assuming that such resemblances would correspond to shared needs and desires. The nations, indeed, fall into large groups whose members, while not voting in exactly the same way, show approximately the same voting patterns in certain identifiable groups of issues. Attitudes toward the Cold War, toward intervention in Africa, and toward what Russett calls "supranationalism" are roughly the same within five groups and differ noticeably among them. The alignments do not correspond to those of the caucusing groups or to Cold War cliché groups of East, West, and neutralist. The similarities of voting behavior direct our attention to similarities of need and policy, which are by no means obvious.

The final article on international organization is Ernst Haas's "System and Process in the International Labor Organization: A Statistical Afterthought." The theoretical basis of the piece is the "functional" approach to international integration. This is the logic of the contemporary movements for European unity. They hope that nations will first cooperate and then merge for limited functional purposes. Then a series of such mergers might follow, each providing momentum for the next until a sort of snowball effect leads to the all-purpose merger that is political union— the furthest reach of international integration and the end of the nation state.

Since 1919 the International Labor Organization has survived, even flourished. Although a single-function organization, it has close to universal membership and it includes representatives of subnational groups (labor and employers) as well as of governments. Here, if anywhere, we should be able to see the integrative effects of functional cooperation. Cross-national interest groups based on occupation also seem likely, and we would expect them to contribute to the erosion of national boundaries.

Haas has long been interested in this functional approach to international integration. In this article he examines the voting of the representatives of different groups and concludes that cross-national occupational or class solidarity has little impact on national differences. The relevance for the study by Alger (Part Four, Chapter 15) is obvious. Haas also attempts to correlate general characteristics of the member nations with the sorts of agreements about labor they are willing to enter into. Here his findings support Russett's suggestions about the consistency of international behavior on the part of certain groups of states having common characteristics rather than deliberately coordinated policies.

All these articles show how very far the nations are from any deliberate or even inadvertent movement towards merging their separate identities. The pieces also suggest that nations will often find reason—enduring reason—to coordinate certain aspects of activity or to act as if they had merged certain functions. But the mergers will, it seems, be temporary or contingent. Because of shared national conditions nations will often act in ways that resemble, *but only* resemble, cooperation or even integration. The encouraging thing is that parallel, though not merged, national activities seem likely to remain indefinitely concerted through international organizations.

Collective Legitimization as a Political Function of the United Nations

C H A P T E R   F O U R T E E N

Inis L. Claude, Jr.

Reprinted by permission of the publishers from Inis L. Claude, Jr., *The Changing United Nations* (New York: Random House, Inc., 1966) pp. 73–103. © Copyright 1966, 1967 by Random House, Inc. Mr. Claude is Professor of Political Science at the University of Virginia.

As the United Nations has developed and as its role in world affairs has been adapted to the necessities and possibilities created and the limitations established by the changing realities of international politics, collective legitimization has emerged as one of its major political functions. By this, I mean to suggest that the world organization has come to be regarded, and used, as a dispenser of politically significant approval and disapproval of the claims, policies, and actions of states. In this chapter, I shall undertake to refine and elaborate this rough definition of collective legitimization and to discuss the performance of this role by the United Nations. It is essential in the beginning, however, to provide a foundation by offering some observations about the general problem of political legitimacy.

The Problem of Political Legitimacy

The history of political theory offers ample evidence of the perennial interest of philosophers in the problem of legitimacy, an interest which, more often than not, has been intimately linked with the highly practical concerns of rulers or rebels, intent upon maintaining or challenging the political status quo. The urge for formally declared and generally acknowledged legitimacy approaches the status of a constant feature of political life. This urge requires that power be converted into authority, competence be supported by jurisdiction, and possession be validated as ownership. Conversely, if we look at it from the viewpoint of those who attack the status quo, it demands that the *de facto* be denied or deprived of *de jure* status, that the might of their antagonists not be sanctified as right. The principle is the same, whether we are dealing with those who want the *is* to be recognized as the *ought,* or those who are setting out to convert their *ought* into a newly established *is.* Politics is not merely a struggle for power, but also a contest over legitimacy, a competition in which the conferment or denial, the confirmation or revocation, of legitimacy is an important stake.

To assert this is in some sense to deny the proposition that the behavior of political leaders, on either the domestic or the international plane, must be interpreted as a purely power-oriented phenomenon. This ancient viewpoint, which flourished in modern Europe as *Realpolitik* and has achieved great influence in contemporary America under the label of political realism, is always easier to entertain in the abstract than in the particular instance. The American "realist" who likes the ring of the generalization is not likely to insist that it rings true in the case of a national hero like Abraham Lincoln, or of a contemporary whose human characteristics are readily visible—Dwight Eisenhower or Lyndon Johnson, for instance. When one turns from generalization about rulers to consideration of individual cases, one is struck by the observation that the urge to possess and exercise power is usually qualified by concern about the justification of such possession and exercise. Among statesmen, the lovers of naked power are far less typical than those who aspire to clothe themselves in the mantle of legitimate authority; emperors may be nude, but they do not like to be so, to think themselves so, or to be so regarded.

In part, this reflects the fact that power holders are burdened, like other human beings, by the necessity of satisfying their own consciences. By and large, they cannot comfortably regard themselves as usurpers or tyrants, but require some basis for convincing themselves of the rightness of their position. In 1960, John F. Kennedy did not wish simply to become the most powerful man in the United States; he aspired to become the duly elected President of the United States—and the same held for his opponent. Respect for the rules of a democratic electoral system is admittedly far from universal, but most wielders of political power nevertheless express in some fashion the need to justify to themselves their acquisition, retention, and utilization of power.

In a larger sense, however, this argument confirms rather than denies the power-oriented character of politics. Power and legitimacy are not antithetical but complementary. The obverse of the legitimacy of power is the power of legitimacy; rulers seek legitimization not only to satisfy their consciences but also to buttress their positions. From one point of view, Kennedy's quest for power was restricted by his respect for the rules defining the legitimate means of getting and using power in the American political system. From another point of view, his attainment of power was a consequence of the operation of the legitimizing procedures of that system. He was a more powerful man than Richard M. Nixon from 1961 until his death, precisely because he, rather than Nixon, had been inaugurated as President—that is, had been certified and acknowledged as the legitimate possessor of supreme executive authority in the United States. Even if Kennedy had been a man without a conscience, he would have sought legitimization for the power that it would have conferred upon him. Legitimacy, in short, not only makes most rulers more comfortable but makes all rulers more effective—more secure in the possession of power and more successful in its exercise. Considerations of political morality combine with more hardheaded power considerations to explain the persistence of concern about legitimacy in the political sphere.

A cursory glance at the history of politics reveals a considerable number of alternative principles and processes of legitimization. Authority has sometimes been held to flow from *above*—from God, or from His earthly representative, or from natural or divine law. Under this heading we find, for instance, the divine right of kings, papal investiture, the attribution of civilizing missions to peculiarly enlightened peoples, and the obligation of ordinary men to respect and obey their natural betters. One might even make a case that Karl Marx, for all his repudiation of religion, was actually a preacher of the doctrine that the international proletariat constituted a Chosen People, with a cosmic if not a divine commission to rule and transform the world. While divinely appointed monarchs are rare in our time, every society is familiar with the official who derives his authority from a political superior, in whose name he acts. Conversely, legitimacy may be conferred from *below,* by the democratic expression of the consent of the governed, or the traditional conventions of the community, or some other alleged manifestation of the general will.

Legitimacy is sometimes tied to *antiquity.* In this connection, we find the principles of hereditary succession, seniority, and prescription; immemorial custom, long established tenure, and settled acquiescence spell authority. Finders are keepers, those who come first are served first, and "first families" and graybeards have acknowledged status. By contrast, the *freshness* of a mandate is sometimes taken as decisive; the man who won the most recent election or can cite the results of the latest public opinion poll can lay claim to the most authentic authorization of his position or policy.

In practice, most societies mix various patterns of legitimization. In constitutional monarchies, governments effectively win power by appeal to the electorate below, but have it formally conferred upon themselves from above, by the royal will. In the United States, the Constitution serves as the higher law and the venerable element in the political situation while the democratic process provides recurrent expressions of the power-giving will of the electorate. Thus, an American politician seeking to establish the legitimacy of a proposal or an action has a number of options: he can declare that it is constitutional, that it conforms to the American tradition, that it comports with supreme and eternal principles of justice and righteousness, or that it is demanded or approved by the most recent expression of the will of the people. He can invoke the wisdom of the founding fathers, the line of precedents established by the Supreme Court, the spirit of the times, or the results of the latest election or Gallup Poll.

Two fundamental concepts figure prominently and persistently in the history of the problem of political legitimacy: law and morality. Lawyers tend simply to translate legitimacy as *legality,* capitalizing upon the derivation and literal meaning of the word. Similarly, moralists are inclined to claim a monopoly, treating political legitimacy as a problem of moral justification. Law and morality are both well established and important legitimizing principles, but neither singly nor in combination do they exhaust the field. Each of them requires its own legitimization; the legitimacy of the positive law, or of the prevailing moral code, is sometimes the precise issue at stake in a political controversy. Moreover, relations between law and morality are variable. They sometimes reinforce each other, as when morality enjoins obedience to law, or law codifies and sanctions the demands of morality. However, they may also come into conflict, as when morality condones disobedience to an unjust law, or the law commands citizens to fulfill their public duty rather than follow the dictates of their private moral convictions. In the final analysis, the problem of legitimacy has a political dimension that goes beyond its legal and moral aspects. Judges, priests, and philosophers usually make themselves heard, but they do not necessarily have the last word; the process of legitimization is ultimately a political phenomenon, a crystallization of judgment that may be influenced but is unlikely to be wholly determined by legal norms and moral principles.

While, as I have suggested, different principles of legitimacy and agents of legitimization may be simultaneously operative within a given political unit and among the constituent units of the global political system, there is, nevertheless, a tendency for a single concept of legitimacy to become generally dominant in a particular era, to achieve widespread acceptance as the decisive standard. Indeed, the existence of such a consensus may be regarded as the essential characteristic of a cohesive and stable political system, at either the national or the international level. Like most fashions, fashions in legitimization change from time to time, and the crucial periods in political history are those transitional years of conflict between old and new concepts of legitimacy, the historical interstices between the initial challenge to the established concept and the general acceptance of its replacement. Thus, the era of modern European politics was ushered in by the substitution of the Voice of the People for the Voice of God (a change thinly concealed by the myth that the Voice of the People *is* the Voice of God) as the determinant of political legitimacy. The democratic principle has achieved widespread acceptance as the criterion of legitimate government within the state, however far short of general applicability it may have fallen as an operative political principle; the democratic pretensions of undemocratic regimes do not detract from, but lend support to, the proposition that popular consent is broadly acknowledged as the legitimizing principle in contemporary political life. The modern era has also seen the establishment of national self-determination as the basis of legitimate statehood, and the global extension of the reach of this legitimizing principle has been one of the most significant developments of recent decades.

At any given time, the operative significance of the dominant principle of legitimacy tends to be less than that of the agency of legitimization. This means that the crucial question is not *what* principle is acknowledged, but *who* is accepted as the authoritative interpreter of the principle or, to put it in institutional terms, *how* the process of legitimization works. There is, of course, a correlation between the nature of the legitimizing principle and the identity of its applicator. For instance, the principle of divine right tends to call for an ecclesiastical spokesman, and the consent theory implies reliance upon a democratic electoral process. In the long run, perhaps, the principle may be decisive; a secular change in the ideology of legitimacy can be expected utlimately to bring about the repudiation of the old and the recognition of a new agency or process of

Collective Legitimization

legitimization. Thus, over time, papal decrees have lost, and plebiscite results and public opinion surveys have gained, influence in the legitimizing process. Nevertheless, in the short run, a paraphrase of the maxim that "the Constitution means what the judges say it means" can be generalized. Principles of legitimacy are necessarily rather vague and uncertain in their applicability, and the nature of the process by which their application is decided, or the means by which legitimacy is dispensed, can be of the greatest importance.

Legitimization in International Relations

Against this background, I should like to discuss these two propositions: (1) that the function of legitimization in the international realm has tended in recent years to be increasingly conferred upon international political institutions, and (2) that the exercise of this function is, and probably will continue to be, a highly significant part of the political role of the United Nations.

The first proposition implies that the current fashion of legitimization of the status and behavior of states in the international arena emphasizes the *collective* and the *political* aspects of the process. While statesmen have their own ways of justifying their foreign policies to themselves and their peoples, independently of external judgments, they are well aware that such unilateral determinations do not suffice. They are keenly conscious of the need for approval by as large and impressive a body of other states as may be possible, for multilateral endorsement of their positions—in short, for collective legitimization. Moreover, it is a political judgment by their fellow practitioners of international politics that they primarily seek, not a legal judgment rendered by an international judicial organ.

This is not to say that international law has no place in the contemporary procedures of legitimization. States do occasionally resort, and even more frequently propose to resort, to the International Court of Justice or to *ad hoc* arbitral tribunals, and still more often they invoke legal arguments in justification of their positions or denunciation of those of their opponents. One might argue that states should rely predominantly or exclusively upon judicial interpretation of international law for the handling of issues concerning legitimacy, and one might expect that, in a more settled period of international relations, a heavier reliance upon adjudication might develop. But my present concern is with what *is*, not with what should be or might be, and it is a fact of present-day international life that, for whatever reasons of whatever validity, statesmen exhibit a definite preference for a political rather than a legal process of legitimization.

The explanation lies partly in the fact that the legitimacy of international law is widely challenged, that is, there is a defective consensus concerning the acceptability of the standards of legitimacy incorporated in the law. Moreover, the International Court is inhibited in the development of a more prominent role in the legitimizing process by the fact that it can assume jurisdiction in a case only with the consent of both sides, given *ad hoc* or by previous acceptance of the Optional Clause of its Statute, while international political organs are not restricted in this way. More broadly, it must simply be said that this is a highly politicized era, not a legalistic one. Collective legitimization has developed, for better or for worse, as essentially a political function, sought for political reasons, exercised by political organs through the operation of a political process, and productive of political results.

Even when states resort to the International Court of Justice, they often appear to seek a judicial contribution to the success of their cause in the political forum, rather than to express a preference for the legal over the political process of legitimization. Thus, the request for an advisory opinion concerning certain aspects of the United Nations financial crisis, addressed to the International Court in 1961, was designed to strengthen the case for a reassertion by the General Assembly of its competence to assess members for support of peace-keeping operations. Somewhat similarly, the South-West Africa Case, brought before the Court in 1960, was undoubtedly initiated by Ethiopia and Liberia with the hope of obtaining judicial support for an intensified prosecution of South Africa in the General Assembly. The use of the Court in these instances clearly reflects the intention to pursue the issue of legitimacy in the political forum, not to transfer it to the judicial forum. Moreover, the Court's ruling in favor of South Africa in the latter case can be expected to stimulate many states to respond that the South African position, while possibly legal, is certainly not legitimate.

The function of collective legitimization is not, in principle, reserved exclusively to the United Nations. The United States has placed considerable reliance upon the Organization of American States as an instrument for justifying its policy in various cases involving Latin American states, and the anticolonial bloc has used special conferences, beginning with the Bandung Conference of 1955, to proclaim the illegitimacy of continued colonial rule. However, the prominence of the United Nations in the pattern of international organization and its status as an institution approximating universality give it obvious advantages for playing the role of custodian of the seals of international approval and disapproval. While the voice of the United Nations may not be the authentic voice of mankind, it is clearly the best available facsimile thereof, and statesmen have by general consent treated the United Nations as the most impressive and authoritative instrument for the expression of a global version of the general will. The notion that the United Nations gives expression to "world public opinion" is largely a myth, propagated by the winners of diplomatic battles in the organization in order to enhance the significance of their victories. It would be more accurate to say that the judgments of the organization represent the preponderant opinion of the foreign offices and other participants in the management of the foreign affairs of the governments of member states. However, the issue of what the United

Nations actually represents is less important than the fact that the function of collective legitimization has been assigned primarily to that organization.

This function has been given relatively little attention in analyses of the political role of the United Nations. Most studies have tended to focus upon the operational functions of the organization—its programs, interventions, and peace-keeping ventures. Our action-oriented generation has concentrated on the question of what the United Nations can and cannot *do,* on the issue of its executive capacity rather than its verbal performance. When forced to pessimistic conclusions regarding the possibilities of United Nations action, the typical analyst or editorialist falls back upon the dismal assertion that the organization is in danger of being reduced to a mere debating chamber, a contemptible talkshop. Given this negative attitude toward the verbal function, it is small wonder that serious efforts to analyze its significance have been rare. When such efforts have been made, they have usually focused upon the concept of multilateral diplomacy, or that of law-making by multilateral processes. In the case of the former emphasis, the function relating to collective legitimization has been too readily deplored to be seriously explored; it tends to be summarily dismissed as a propagandistic abuse, an activity inimical to meaningful negotiation and alien to genuine diplomacy, multilateral or otherwise. The emphasis upon law-making is closer to the point, but it, nevertheless, misses the central point that the legitimizing function performed by United Nations organs is less a matter of purporting either to apply or to revise the law than of affixing the stamp of political approval or disapproval.

Collective legitimization is an aspect of the verbal rather than the executive functioning of the United Nations, and in some sense it is a result of the organization's incapacity for decisive intervention in and control of international relations. One might argue that the United Nations has resorted to saying "Thou should" because it is in no position to say "Thou shalt," and to saying "Thou may" because it cannot say "Thou must." It authorizes and endorses in compensation for its inability to effectuate commands, and it condemns and deplores in compensation for its inability to prohibit and prevent. However, the mood expressed in a *New York Times* editorial which, noting the danger that financial difficulties would prevent the United Nations from undertaking further peace-keeping operations, warned that "The end result would be abandonment of its Charter obligation to enforce peace and suppress aggression and a consequent slump into the status of a debating society,"[1] is neither realistic nor conducive to a perceptive appraisal of the actual and potential capabilities of the organization. It reflects an exaggerated conception of what the United Nations might have been; surely, no one who had consulted the Charter and the expectations of its framers in preference to his own hopes and ideals could ever have believed that the United

[1] *The New York Times,* September 16, 1963, p. 34.

International Cooperation

Nations promised to be a dependable agency for enforcing peace and suppressing aggression in an era of great power division. Even more, it reflects an exaggerated contempt for international debating societies and a disinclination to examine the question of what it is possible for the United Nations to do when it cannot do the impossible.

If we can learn to judge the United Nations less in terms of its failure to attain the ideals that we postulate and more in terms of its success in responding to the realities that the world presents, we shall be in a better position to analyze its development. Approaching the organization in this spirit, we find that its debating society aspect is not to be deplored and dismissed as evidence of a "slump" but that it deserves to be examined for evidence of the functional adaptation and innovation that it may represent. My thesis is that the function of collective legitimization is one of the most significant elements in the pattern of political activity that the United Nations has evolved in response to the set of limitations and possibilities posed by the political realities of our time.

The development of this function has not been, in any meaningful sense, *undertaken* by the United Nations, conceived as an independent institutional actor upon the global stage. Rather, it has been thrust upon the organization by member states. Collective legitimization is an answer, not to the question of what the United Nations can *do,* but to the question of how it can be *used.*

Statesmen have been more perceptive than scholars in recognizing and appreciating the significance of this potentiality for utilization of the organization. They have persistently, and increasingly, regarded the United Nations as an agency capable of bestowing politically weighty approval and disapproval upon their projects and policies. The General Assembly and, to a lesser degree, the Security Council have been used for this purpose. The debates within, and negotiations around, these political organs have largely concerned the adoption or rejection of resolutions designed to proclaim the legitimacy or the illegitimacy of positions or actions taken by states. Governments have exerted themselves strenuously to promote the passage of resolutions favorable to their cause and the defeat of unfavorable resolutions. In reverse, they have attempted to block resolutions giving approval, and to advance those asserting disapproval, of their opponents' positions.

The scale of values developed by members of the United Nations may be represented schematically by the following device, in which States A and B are assumed to be engaged in a dispute:

1) Approval of A's position
2) Disapproval of B's position
3) Acquiescence in A's position
4) Acquiescence in B's position
5) Disapproval of A's position
6) Approval of B's position

In this scheme, A's preferences would run in descending order from the top of the list, and B's from the bottom of the list. Parliamentary battles over the endorsement, the acceptance, and the condemnation of positions taken by states are a standard feature of the proceedings of the United Nations.

One may question whether proclamations of approval or disapproval by organs of the United Nations, deficient as they typically are in both formal legal significance and effective supportive power, are really important. The answer is that statesmen, by so obviously attaching importance to them, have made them important. Artificial or not, the value of acts of legitimization by the United Nations has been established by the intense demand for them. One may question whether great importance should be attributed to such acts, and contend that the political organs of the United Nations are inappropriately cast as dispensers of legitimacy. But a fact is no less a fact for being deplored, and it *is* a fact that governments have tended more and more to treat those organs as agencies of legitimization.

I do not mean to suggest that states are willing to accept in principle, or to follow in consistent practice, the proposition that the collective judgment of the General Assembly or any other international body is decisive. While states vary in the degree to which they display respect for the function of collective legitimization, this variation appears to reflect differences in experience and expectation rather than in commitment to the principle of the validity of collective evaluation. Any state can be expected to assert the validity of acts of legitimization that support its interests and to deny that acts contrary to its interests are worthy of respect. However, the vigorous effort that states customarily make to prevent the passage of formal denunciations of their positions or policies indicates that they have respect for the significance, if not for the validity, of adverse judgments by international organs. While states may act in violation of General Assembly resolutions, they evidently prefer not to do so, or to appear not to do so, on the ground that collective approbation is an important asset, and collective disapprobation a significant liability, in international relations. A state may hesitate to pursue a policy that has engendered the formal disapproval of the Assembly, not because it is prepared to give the will of that organ priority over its national interest, but because it believes that the adverse judgment of the Assembly makes the pursuit of that policy disadvantageous to the national interest. This is simply to say that statesmen take collective legitimacy seriously as a factor in international politics; the opinions and attitudes of other states, manifested through the parliamentary mechanism of the United Nations, must be taken into account in the conduct of foreign policy.

Clearly, statesmen do not attach identical importance to all judgments of legitimacy pronounced by political organs of the United Nations, but weight the significance of resolutions according to the size and composition of the majorities supporting them and the forcefulness of the language in which they are couched. This variation in the impressiveness of formal resolutions was anticipated in the Charter provisions requiring a two-thirds majority for decisions on important questions in the General Assembly (Article 18, paragraph 2), and unanimity of the permanent members of the Security Council in decisions on non-procedural matters in that body (Article 27, paragraph 3). In practice, it is evident that a Security Council resolution supported by all the permanent members is taken more seriously than one on which three of them abstain, that the support or opposition of India is treated as more significant than that of Iceland in evaluating a resolution of the General Assembly, and that a unanimous decision of the latter body deserves and receives more attention than a narrowly passed resolution. Moreover, a clear and firm act of approval or disapproval carries more weight than a vague and ambiguous pronouncement, and a series of resolutions pointing consistently in the same direction is more impressive than an isolated case. While states value even narrow parliamentary victories, achieved by garnering votes wherever they may be found and diluting the language of resolutions as much as may be necessary, they obviously recognize that the most convincing legitimization is provided by the cumulative impact of repeated and unambiguous endorsements of their positions, supported by massive majorities that include the bulk of the most important and most influential states.

Some Instances of Collective Legitimization

The United Nations has been heavily involved in matters relating to the question of the ratification and solidification of the status claimed, as distinguished from the policies followed, by political entities. Generally, this can be subsumed under the heading of membership business; admission to, or seating in, the organization has tended to take on the political meaning, if not the legal implication, of collective recognition. New states have been inclined to regard the grant of membership as the definitive acknowledgment of their independence. Non-admission of the segments of divided states appears to have been motivated in part by the conviction that admission would somehow sanctify existing divisions, thereby diminishing the prospects for future reunification. West Germany, for instance, has been particularly sensitive to the danger that East German membership would have the effect of legitimizing, and, thus, helping to perpetuate, the division of Germany. The continued acceptance of the Chinese Nationalist regime, and rejection of the Peking regime, has been championed as a device for strengthening the hold of the former upon Taiwan and denying to the latter the advantage of an important international status symbol. The prompt admission of Israel to the United Nations was clearly regarded, by both friends and foes of the new state, as a major contribution to its capacity to survive in a hostile neighborhood. The issue of conferment of status arose, in a different way, when Malaysia was elected to a Security Council seat by the General Assembly. Indonesia's subsequent withdrawal from the organization, ostensibly in protest against that action, can be interpreted as a tribute to the potency of collective legitimization, for Indonesia evidently felt that the United Nations had given an intolerably valuable boost to Malaysia's international stock.

A major campaign has been waged in the United Nations to delegitimize colonialism, to invalidate the claim of colonial powers to legitimate possession of overseas territories—in short, to revoke their sovereignty over colonies. This movement culminated in the overwhelming adoption by the General Assembly of sweeping anticolonial declarations in 1960 and subsequently. The implication of this anticolonial triumph became clear in late 1961, when India was cited before the Security Council for its invasion of Goa.[2] India's defense was, in essence, the assertion that the process of collective legitimization had operated to deprive Portugal of any claim to sovereignty over Goa and, thus, of any right to protest the invasion—which, by virtue of the same process, had become an act of liberation, terminating Portugal's illegal occupation of Goa.

This case illustrates the proximity of the political and the legal aspects which is frequently implicit and occasionally explicit in the operation of the process of collective legitimization. India was accused in legal terms, and it responded in similar vein. The rejoinder by and on behalf of India proclaimed, in effect, that an accumulation of multilateral denunciations of colonialism had effectively abrogated the legal right of European states to rule non-European territories; these acts had created a new law, under which colonialism was invalid. Despite this exchange of legal arguments, it appears that India's real concern was not so much to clear itself legally as to vindicate itself politically. It regarded the political approval or acquiescence of the United Nations as a more important consideration than any legal judgment. In a basic sense, India won the case. Although it obtained no formal endorsement of its position, it carried through its conquest of Goa without incurring formal condemnation, and its Western critics, by declining to take the issue to the Assembly, conceded that they could not expect to win, in that organ, a political verdict unfavorable to India. Obviously, the doctrine of the invalidity of colonial sovereignty has not achieved universal support, and its claim to legal status is most tenuous. But that is beside the point, it has been established by the political process of collective legitimization, and while lawyers are free to brush it aside, statesmen are bound to take it into account as one of the facts of international political life. If the doctrine is illegal, its supporters would claim that this only convicts the law of illegitimacy. In this respect at least, they attach greater weight to the political consensus of the Assembly than to the established provisions of international law. Thus, in one of its aspects, collective legitimacy represents a political revolt against international law.

It should be noted that ex-colonial states have not confined themselves to using the United Nations for legitimization of the campaign for definitive liquidation of the colonial system. In the economic sphere, they have undertaken, in concert with other underdeveloped countries, to use the

[2] See pp. 59–61, above.

organization to secure the establishment and general acceptance of the doctrine that they have a right to receive, and advanced states have a duty to provide, assistance in promoting economic development. Toward the same end, they have invoked the support of the organization for policies designed to free themselves from obligations and arrangements that they regard as exploitative and inimical to economic progress, including foreign ownership or control of their basic natural resources. In an era of rising economic expectations, intensive effort on the part of many new states to establish solid economic foundations for their national structures, and extreme sensitivity to vestiges of the old system of colonial domination, the legitimizing function of the United Nations has had particular significance for the realm of economic policy.

The Goa case is by no means the only one in which the use of military force, either in overt invasions or in more subtle interventions, has been at issue. The United Nations was used to characterize as aggression North Korea's attack upon South Korea in 1950, and, subsequently, Communist China's collaboration in the assault; conversely, the United States sought and won endorsement of a collective military response and gave convincing evidence throughout the Korean War of its high valuation of the United Nations stamp of legitimacy. In the Suez crisis of 1956, the adverse judgment of the Assembly was invoked against the attackers of Egypt, as it was also against Soviet intervention to suppress the Hungarian revolt. In the Congo crisis of 1960, the function of collective legitimization was performed, negatively with respect to Belgian intervention, Katangese secessionist efforts, and unilateral Soviet intrusions, and positively with respect to interventionists organized under United Nations auspices.

The United States, like India in the Goa case, has in some instances profited from collective legitimization in its minimal form: United Nations acquiescence or avoidance of United Nations condemnation. In some of these cases, the United States has pioneered in the development of the strategy of involving a regional organization in the process. When the United States became involved in the overthrow of the Guatemalan government in 1954, it vigorously asserted the claim that the United Nations should disqualify itself from considering the case, in favor of the Organization of American States. This tactic, which clearly reflected American respect for the potency of United Nations disapprobation, was practically, though not technically, successful. In the Cuban crisis of 1962, the United States altered its strategy, opting to combine the functioning of the Organization of American States and the United Nations rather than to set them off against each other. On this occasion, the American scheme, successfully executed, was to secure the legitimizing support of the regional organization, and then to use this asset in the effort to obtain the approval, or avoid the disapproval, of the Security Council with respect to the measures taken against Soviet involvement in Cuba.

More recently, the United States has been conspicuously reluctant to press the United Nations for formal consideration of the situation in South Vietnam, in which American forces have become heavily engaged. This restraint has no doubt derived from lack of confidence that a United Nations organ would endorse the claim of the United States that its military commitment constitutes a legitimate counter-intervention against illegitimate intrusions by Communist states. Policy makers in Washington have evidently given greater weight to the risk of an adverse judgment than to the hope of obtaining a favorable verdict. The implication is not that the American cause is illegitimate, but that political calculations have suggested that it might be branded as illegitimate—and not that the United States has denigrated the value of collective legitimization, but that it has dreaded the effect of possible collective delegitimization. When, in early 1966, the United States did move to place the Vietnam issue before the Security Council, it evidently sought assistance in promoting a negotiated settlement rather than a judgment on the merits of its position. However, the fact that the Soviet Union opposed this move suggests the possibility that Soviet leaders believed that the United States was seeking, and might obtain, United Nations endorsement of its stand in Vietnam.

This account of selected instances in which the United Nations has been involved in the process of collective legitimization suggests that there is great variation in the effectiveness of the positions taken by the organization. It is seldom possible to make confident estimates of the degree of influence upon state behavior exerted by United Nations resolutions, although the intensity of the concern exhibited by states about the outcome of votes in the organization indicates that the seal of approval and the stigma of disapproval are taken seriously.

There is also room for disagreement and uncertainty concerning the merits and demerits of collective legitimization. The entrusting of this function to such an organization as the United Nations is pregnant with both valuable and dangerous possibilities, as the cases discussed may suggest. The endorsement of a United Nations organ can strengthen a good cause, but it can also give aid and comfort to a bad cause—and we can have no guarantee that international political institutions, any more than national ones, will distribute their largess of legitimacy in accordance with the dictates of justice or wisdom. Habitual utilization of the United Nations as an agency for pronouncing on the international acceptability of national policies and positions may inspire statesmen to behave with moderation and circumspection; their concern about the outcome of deliberations by the organization may stimulate them to make compromises designed to improve their chances of securing collective approval or avoiding collective disapproval. On the other hand, this use of the United Nations may promote its exploitation as an arena within which propaganda victories are sought, to the detriment of its role in promoting diplomatic settlements. Collective legitimization may stimulate legal changes that will make international law more worthy of respect and more likely to be respected, but it may also encourage behavior based upon calculation of what the political situation will permit rather than upon consideration of what the principles of order require. In short, the exercise of the function of collective legitimization may be for better or for worse, whether evaluated in terms of its effect upon the interests of a particular state or upon the prospects for a stable and orderly world. The crucial point is that, for better or for worse, the development of the United Nations as custodian of collective legitimacy is an important political phenomenon of our time.

Non-resolution Consequences of the United Nations and Their Effect on International Conflict

C H A P T E R   F I F T E E N

Chadwick F. Alger

Reprinted by permission of the publishers from the *Journal of Conflict Resolution,* Vol. 5 (June, 1961), 128–45. Mr. Alger is Professor of Political Science at Northwestern University.

I. Introduction

Secretary-General Hammarskjold has, on a number of occasions, admonished us to broaden our scope of inquiry when assessing the influence of the United Nations on international relations. For example, in the introduction to his Fourteenth Annual Report to the General Assembly in August, 1959, he declares that there is a tendency to overestimate the significance of votes on General Assembly resolutions in comparison to other consequences of Assembly meetings:

> ...whatever legal standing the Charter may provide for the results of the votes, the significance of these results requires further analysis before a political evaluation is possible. This observation applies to the composition of majorities and minorities as well as to the substance of the resolutions. These resolutions often reflect only part of what has, in fact, emerged from the deliberations and what, therefore, is likely to remain as an active element in future developments [9, p. 10].

It is the purpose of this article to discuss some potential non-resolution[1] consequences of the United Nations—in particular, the General Assembly. It is also a goal of this article to show how these non-resolution consequences may significantly affect international conflict.

In very general terms this discussion will assess, in an exploratory way, how the United Nations has altered patterns of communication among nations, providing new routes of contact under new conditions; how it has had an impact on national policy; and how it has altered the career patterns and possibly the future behavior of participating individuals.

The following questions reveal more specifically the areas of concern:

1. What effect does the need to defend publicly national policy in an international organization have upon the prior formulation of that policy?
2. How does experience in international organizations affect the attitudes of the participants (temporary delegates and members of permanent missions) when they move on to other national roles?
3. What is the effect of the availability of neutral ground for inter-nation contact?

This paper is based on field work at the United Nations in 1958 and 1959 which was supported by funds from the Carnegie Corporation in New York. Helpful criticism of an earlier draft was received from Harold Guetzkow and James A. Robinson of Northwestern University, William A. Scott of the University of Colorado, Keith S. Petersen of the University of Arkansas, and several United Nations diplomats who will remain anonymous.

[1] Resolution here refers to resolutions passed by United Nations bodies; it is not used in the sense of conflict resolution.

4. How do the processes of "parliamentary diplomacy" produce outcomes different from traditional diplomatic practice?

5. What effect does the automatic participation of mediators (secretariat and national delegations) have on the outcome of conflicts—in day-to-day interaction as well as on extraordinary occasions?

6. What is the consequence of increasing the number of nations actively involved in a particular problem?

7. What is the effect of creating an international center where press and other private organizations have new and different kinds of access to officials and to each other?

8. What is the significance of the new sources and kinds of information that members of international organizations obtain?

9. What is the significance of opportunities that international organizations provide for increased informal contact among diplomats?

Although this paper will not be organized in terms of these questions, all will be dealt with to some degree in the discussion that follows. First, however, it might be illuminating to ask why only vague and inferential responses can be given to such important questions. A fundamental reason is the tendency to study political organizations, national as well as international, mainly in terms of their accomplishment of their explicit goals through the explicit mechanisms established for this purpose. In the case of the United Nations, this means that there is concentration on the passage or defeat of resolutions in public meetings and on extraordinary mediation attempts called for by these resolutions. However, this type of activity does not produce the only, nor necessarily the most important, impact that the organization has on relations among members. The tendency to focus upon explicit organizational goals and mechanisms for their attainment is accompanied by a tendency to attribute United Nations influence on the course of events only in cases where a problem is carried through to resolution within United Nations jurisdiction. Thereby we sometimes may miss the impact of the United Nations upon problems that at some point become the subject of United Nations concern but are not finally resolved within its jurisdiction. What, for example, was the effect of yearly United Nations debates on Cyprus on the eventual settlement elsewhere of the dispute? Would the United States-Soviet negotiations in Geneva on nuclear testing have taken place without prior debate on the question in the United Nations and without the pressure for test cessation brought by other nations on American and Soviet delegations during this debate? It is quite clear that the kind of international system in which the United Nations operates has prevented the resolution of such problems within a multilateral organization. But it is contended here that scholars have neglected the study of how multilateral organizations affect the broader international system in which they operate even when problems are not resolved within their walls.

The neglect of non-resolution consequences is, of course, not a limitation of research on international organizations alone.[2] What is known, for

2 The reader may have detected a similarity between Robert K. Merton's "latent functions" and "non-resolution consequences" (14, pp. 19–84). Although his analysis

International Cooperation

example, of the role of the United States Congress aside from its performance of its legislative function? How significant is the United States Congress as a nationwide communications network for local leaders? What is the effect of congressional participation upon congressmen and eventually upon local policy preferences? It may be, however, that the customary perspective in the assessment of the effects of political institutions overlooks matters of more significance in the case of organizations like the United Nations than in the case of bodies like the United States Congress. The Congress is a coercive body which, in most instances of member conflict, insures that minorities comply with the measures passed by majorities. The General Assembly of the United Nations, increasingly the most significant body in the United Nations, is not coercive. The General Assembly is a non-coercive body made up of autonomous subunits. Its resolutions are only recommendations and cannot force minority compliance. Perhaps significant aspects of the General Assembly are being neglected by testing it against a model provided by coercive bodies. New ways may be needed for looking at this type of institution.

Lacking satisfaction with an evaluation of the impact of the General Assembly on world affairs solely on the basis of the resolutions it passes, what raw material is available for making an evaluation broader in scope? A very simple approach will be taken. What does the observer of United Nations Headquarters during a General Assembly session see? The direct observation of the behavior of persons involved in General Assembly activity may provide leads for probing the non-resolution consequences of their behavior. Some of the readily observable aspects of the General Assembly will be described very briefly and then the significance of these characteristics for international relations in general and for international conflict in particular will be examined.

Before proceeding it might be prudent to anticipate the criticism of those readers who are very familiar with the General Assembly and feel that some of what follows is a description of the mundane and obvious. In the first place, some of these things are not as well known to those who have not had the opportunity to observe the General Assembly over a period of time as more knowledgeable scholars sometimes assume. Second, the task of the scholar is not to describe and explain what is not obvious, but the significant. Particularly in the social sciences, where certain fundamental aspects of human behavior are very familiar to the human participant and observer, there is a tendency to focus on the unique and dramatic instead of on patterns of behavior that are significant. The description of the "obvious" characteristics of the international community that the General Assembly brings into being may provide the raw materials for explaining significant effects of this community on international relations.

---

of manifest and latent functions offered fruitful provocation, the term "non-resolution consequences" more precisely indicates the phenomena with which this paper is concerned.

II. Some General Characteristics of the Assembly

The scholar who intensively observes the General Assembly for the first time is impressed by the number of participants, the intensity of their experiences, the variety of situations in which they interact, the size of the agenda debated, and the access to the delegates that is afforded external persons. The contrast between the General Assembly seen first-hand and impressions obtained from most of the literature is striking. The literature leaves an image of the General Assembly Hall with the delegations of eighty-two[3] nations, each occupying ten seats, neatly arranged in rows behind signs designating their countries. Even when committees and less public activities are mentioned, they are treated only very briefly. The Assembly of the observer, however, is a complex international community which includes approximately 1,400 national officials, portions of the some 3,000 members of the Secretariat, and hundreds of private persons: press, members of non-governmental organizations, and others interested in influencing or talking with delegates. Approximately 500 of the national officials are members of permanent missions to the United Nations, the other 900 come only for the Assembly. They come from other diplomatic posts, home government posts, and even private life. The agenda items which they consider in each session have numbered from 56 to 77 items (16, p. 234). The items which they discuss that are not on the agenda stir the imagination and must be many times that of the formal agenda.

The complexity and variety of an Assembly session is attributable largely to the fact that it is in reality composed of the simultaneous meeting of seven "little assemblies" in which most of the work is done. These bodies are the seven committees of the General Assembly: two political committees, and one each for economic and financial, social and humanitarian, administrative and budgetary, trusteeship and non-self-governing territories, and legal affairs. Each member of the United Nations is represented on all of these committees, with a number of nations having two or more delegates present at meetings of some commitees. This makes it impossible for permanent missions of member states to participate in the Assembly without, on the average, almost tripling their complement.

These committees usually meet twice a day, from 10:30 a.m. to approximately 1:00 p.m. and from 3:00 p.m. to about 6:00 p.m. Occasionally there are night sessions, especially toward the end of the three months. As resolutions are passed by the committees they are brought before a plenary session of the General Assembly, a few at a time. But these plenary sessions occupy a relatively small portion of the total time spent in formal meetings. Even the plenary, when it meets to pass on committee resolutions, is often a reconstitution of the committees one at a time. For

---

[3] This paper was completed in March, 1960, before the 1960 expansion of the United Nations to ninety-nine members.

example, after the plenary deals with trusteeship items there may be a period of commotion while trusteeship committee members leave their plenary seats and return to their committee, and members from another committee take the front row seats of their delegation. In the plenary the same committee members pass again on their work, needing now a two-thirds majority to pass resolutions on important questions rather than the simple majority required in committee.

The observer of the General Assembly is immediately struck by the parliamentary atmosphere. Dean Rusk has coined the term "parliamentary diplomacy" to refer to the proceedings (18). In this environment diplomatic rank is noticeably less a restraint on interaction than is the case in national capitals. Parliamentary roles require that diplomats who are sitting on the same committee approach each other directly even though one is an ambassador and the other is a second secretary. Contacts of Assembly members with the press, non-governmental organizations, and other outsiders are more similar to the external contacts of parliamentarians than to those of the foreign office or embassy official. Outside persons buttonhole a delegate in the corridor, page him in the Delegates' Lounge, or send a note asking for him to come out of a committee meeting, rather than seek an office appointment.

The sessions of the General Assembly are an intense and exhausting experience for the delegates. Their day begins with morning delegation meetings at the office of their country's mission to the United Nations. Then delegates go to the United Nations for morning committee sessions. Between the morning and afternoon sessions, business continues as delegates lunch together in the Delegates' Dining Room or talk in the Delegates' Lounge or at other places in United Nations Headquarters. At lunch and at other times during the day small working parties hammer out the exact wording of resolutions. Meetings of representatives of blocs are required to coordinate the positions of members of these blocs. Following the afternoon session there is usually a reception by one of the delegations, perhaps in the Delegates' Dining Room. Most likely more than one party is being held and the delegate must divide time between them. Many delegates must then return to their mission and write up the day's activities, prepare for the next day, and send cables home on important matters so that new instructions may be sent back before the delegation meeting the next morning. With what time remains, an attempt must be made to read the extensive United Nations documentation on the matters being debated. As a result, the working day for many delegates extends to nine or ten o'clock in the evening. For a large number the only respite from Assembly duties comes on the weekends.

These brief descriptive comments could, of course, be considerably extended. However, it is only intended here to describe enough to make the reader who has not observed the Assembly cognizant of the kind of evidence that stimulates an inquiry into the non-resolution consequences of this body. Does this virtually continuous interaction between representatives of most of the nations of the world for extended periods of

Non-resolution Consequences of the United Nations

time have significant consequences beyond the resolutions it produces? It is likely that most scholars and laymen with a reasonable amount of knowledge about the United Nations would say "Yes." But our knowledge about these consequences does not go much beyond the assertion that "When they're debating they're not shooting," and the assumption that "it's useful to keep the communications channels open." What kind of debate or other behavior provides an alternative to violence that is considered satisfactory by conflicting parties? What particular kinds of communications channels are most useful for the kinds of ends that are pursued through the creation of international organizations? These questions lie under the clichés and we do not possess the knowledge that would enable us to answer them.

III. Some Non-Resolution Consequences of the Assembly

Six non-resolution consequences of the General Assembly have been selected for discussion here. They will be presented in the following order: (1) The impact of Assembly experience on participating national civil servants and nationals from other occupations; (2) The development of personal friendships among delegates across national lines; (3) The accentuation by the specialized committees of expert in contrast to purely political factors; (4) The formation of cooperating groups of nations that do not conform to normal political alignments; (5) The extension of the active interest of participating nations to additional geographic areas and to a broader range of international problems; (6) The new information and new sources of information that become available to participants. These factors affect the international system outside the General Assembly and also affect subsequent international relations within the General Assembly, a part of the system.

1. IMPACT OF ASSEMBLY EXPERIENCE ON DELEGATES.

The additional personnel that come to the United Nations for the General Assembly come from other overseas posts, foreign offices, other government departments, parliaments, and private life. For three months they are separated from their normal environment and have what is for many a quite intensive experience that places them in an extraordinarily different communications network. For some this experience is repeated for several years in succession. From posts in which most viewpoints on international relations that are encountered are from the perspective of one nation, they come to a community where they are constantly subjected to many perspectives. In addition, they are in the company of many people, members of the secretariat and others, who look at the system as a whole rather than from the perspective of one nation.

The parliamentary framework of the General Assembly provides an atmosphere that is quite different from that to which most of the delegates

276

are accustomed, since most of them are governmental bureaucrats. For these bureaucrats to become delegates requires that they move away from a rather stationary existence behind a desk that provides, if not isolation, considerable restraints on the access to them by persons not in their own bureaucracy. But in the Assembly, where they become mobile delegates operating most of each day away from a protective bureaucratic shell, they are directly accessible to other delegates. As has already been indicated, the lobbyist, journalist, and scholar can approach them directly as they pass from meeting hall to lounge, to dining room, and back to meeting hall in the relatively open society of the General Assembly. Although the extent of this non-delegate contact may not be great for some delegates, there is little doubt that the sources of intellectual stimulation of most delegates greatly extends that provided by the bureaucrat's incoming box and appointment calendar.

It may also be significant that delegates who participate in the General Assembly return to their normal posts with first-hand knowledge of United Nations procedures. They will be more competent to use these procedures intelligently. In the General Assembly, parliamentary diplomacy has developed into a phenomenon quite different from traditional bilateral diplomacy and is more complex than it was in the smaller League of Nations. Through participation in the General Assembly many national officials are learning parliamentary diplomacy through personal experience. This suggests the hypothesis that those who have mastered this particular kind of procedure for policy implementation are more likely to use it in the future than those who find such procedures unknown, unintelligible, and highly unpredictable.[4] This would include not only temporary delegates but permanent mission officials as well, most of whom move on to other diplomatic posts after a few years' service at the United Nations.

2. FRIENDSHIPS ACROSS NATIONAL BOUNDARIES

The informality of social relations among the delegates impresses the observer who watches them in the corridors, lounges, restaurants, and meeting rooms of the United Nations. This informality may partially be attributed to the large number of persons involved. As hundreds of delegates surge into the Delegates' Lounge, the dining room, and the cafeteria following committee sessions, the social restraints associated with traditional diplomatic interchange give way to more informal patterns of behavior. Events such as the concert (followed by dancing and dinner) given by the Secretary-General and the President of the General Assembly

[4] In an attempt to assess the impact of Assembly experiences on delegates, the writer interviewed delegates to the Fourteenth General Assembly who had not served before. Delegates from thirty countries were interviewed both before and near the end of the Assembly. These data are now being analyzed. In another United Nations field study for Northwestern's International Relations Program, Gary Best studied the difference between diplomacy conducted at the site of an international organization and diplomacy in a national capital. Permanent Mission personnel from all member nations were interviewed in this study (2).

Non-resolution Consequences of the United Nations

in the 1958 session has an atmosphere of informality unexpected for such occasions. The formal attire of the perhaps two thousand persons in attendance was not matched by their informal conduct as they stood in line for Scotch and champagne, attempted to dance on the crowded dance floor, queued up for the buffet dinner, and then searched for a table at which to eat—some resigning themselves to standing up. And as the evening drew to a close there was another line to be faced as delegates obtained their coats from the check room.

In addition to the role of numbers, social interaction among delegates is encouraged by the physical environment offered by the United Nations Headquarters buildings. When one is enmeshed in this environment in the midst of the delegates he is tempted to rank the architect of the United Nations buildings along with the writers of the Charter in importance. The intensity of interaction of members of the General Assembly is heightened by the proximity of all of the arenas of delegate activity while they are on the United Nations premises. The General Assembly Hall, committee rooms, dining room, and lounge are all close to each other. A relatively few hallways connect the main centers of activity and delegates pass and re-pass each other frequently as they go about their tasks. One inhabitant of this system who desires to see another member on a particular day need not make a formal appointment nor look for him very energetically, for he will encounter him a number of times during the day.

Social interaction among the delegates is also encouraged by delegation receptions, with each delegation holding at least one and usually two receptions during the Assembly session. The uniformed attendant, calling out the names of the guests as they arrive, is reminiscent of the diplomatic heritage of the Assembly. Each national delegation to the Assembly must perform the representational functions of a foreign embassy as well as play parliamentary aspects of its role. It is perhaps diplomatic tradition that determines the nature of other social functions such as concerts in the General Assembly Hall and occasional plays and other cultural events. All of these occasions add to the wide variety of situations in which members of the General Assembly encounter each other.

The sustained interaction of the delegates as well as the variety of the occasions on which they confront each other provides opportunities for the development of friendships across national boundaries that surpass those of normal diplomatic intercourse. As a result, delegates have networks of personal friends on other delegations. These networks provide opportunities for inter-nation communication that are more flexible than formal channels. The maintenance of these friendships places certain obligations on delegates, such as alerting friends to changes in policy or gradually adjusting them to change. Two United Nations delegates have themselves described the role of personal friendships:

Seldom is any vote changed by personal relations because persons, unless very senior, have little influence over national policies. It is possible however to foster a better understanding and appreciation of national positions as a result of social con-

International Cooperation

tacts and sometimes to affect subsequent formal exchanges and in the long run voting patterns.... In many eyes the personal relationships established at the United Nations have as much, if not greater, importance than the formal decisions which are reached [8, pp. 39 and 47].

3. PARTICIPATION OF EXPERTS

One of the factors that contributes to the intensity of personal friendships is the camaraderie that develops among groups of delegates who are experts in the same field. Since most delegates spend their time on one committee that is handling one kind of issue, it is advantageous to nations to assign delegates to these committees who are experts in the subject matter being discussed. It is also the case that delegates assigned to these committees without previous claim of expert knowledge become experts, at least in the context of their own delegations, on the matters being considered. In addition to frequent similarities of professional training, the experts on a particular committee spend long hours together in their committee, giving them a common fund of knowledge and shared experience. For those who return to the same committee for several years common bonds are intensified. These bonds facilitate the work of the committees and at times become so pronounced as to create rivalry between committees.

Thus, it is hypothesized that the specialized committees not only create a need for experts in the conduct of Assembly business but also serve as a training ground for additional experts and reinforce the dedication of experts to the norms of their profession. A corollary of this hypothesis is that delegation positions in the Assembly and recommendations to home governments are affected by the professional norms of participating experts in international law, human rights, international economics, and so on.

4. SHIFTING MAJORITIES

One important aspect of the perspective of this analysis is that it probes below the level of national behavior in international organizations to the individual level. It has been suggested that it makes a difference who the individuals that participate are and that the effects of participation upon these individuals are important. Furthermore, it is important in the General Assembly that the simultaneous consideration of a number of issues requires nations to play a number of roles simultaneously. Coordination of the seven committee voices of a national delegation is not always easy, particularly since different issues often require cooperation with a different set of allies. It is contended that the variety of voting alignments across committees in the General Assembly introduces new elements into diplomacy within the United Nations and eventually outside as well.

In the political committees, the United States and the Soviet Union are the main protagonists, with their political allies aligning on the appro-

Non-resolution Consequences of the United Nations

priate side and primarily some Afro-Asian nations playing a mediating role. NATO, the Warsaw Pact, SEATO, the Central Treaty Organization, OAS, and a scattering of bilateral treaties mirror basic alignments on key political questions. But in the economic committee, it is the haves against the have-nots, with the Latin Americans joining the Afro-Asians in a drive for an increase in multilateral economic programs. Often the Soviet Union votes with this group as does the Netherlands and Norway of the NATO bloc. On the social and humanitarian committee, Afro-Asian Moslems and European and Latin American Catholics cooperate on questions relating to birth control. On the trusteeship and non-self-governing territories committee the colonial nations and the newly independent countries are the main protagonists. On a matter before the legal committee related to ocean shipping, the maritime nations are lined up against non-maritime members. Finally, on the budgetary committee the lines of conflict are sometimes drawn with virtually all member nations on one side and the Secretariat on the other, as the committee assumes the typical parliamentary attitude toward the expenditures of executive officials.

Thus as one moves from committee to committee and issue to issue, a variety of alliances is encountered. It is contended that the General Assembly, because of its varied agenda, provides opportunity for and stimulus for cooperative effort that often runs in opposition to political alignments based on organizations other than the United Nations. This cooperative effort opens up new lines of communications. It requires joint effort not only in the public sessions of committees but also in small working parties which negotiate final wordings of resolutions and in bilateral conversations at the United Nations and perhaps also in national capitals. These lines of communication can then be used for other purposes. These alignments and new communications routes become elements in subsequent diplomacy in the United Nations and in diplomacy conducted outside the United Nations.

5. EXPANSION OF NATION CONCERN

The scope of the agenda of the General Assembly also has the effect of expanding the area of concern of participant nations. Participation in deliberations on an average of over seventy agenda items causes each nation to extend, in terms of both geography and subject matter, the range of items with which its diplomacy is directly involved. Most countries vote on almost all of these items and this requires that most of them take positions on matters that they would not have had to take stands on otherwise. It also requires public assertion of positions which might otherwise have been taken in private. Furthermore, private positions must usually be changed—if not in principle at least in emphasis and perhaps in explanation of motives—before they are made public.

It is hypothesized that this expansion of nation concern, along with the extension of the requirements for public declaration of policy, affects

International Cooperation

policy positions already held. When a nation is required to play a role in an agenda of items that covers the world, it assumes obligations that modify roles played in narrower arenas. For example, the extended participation in world affairs that the United Nations requires of the newly independent nations may be very important. After decades of foreign rule, in the first years of independence nations are inclined to be self-centered, to self-consciously assert their independence in relations with other nations and to assume little responsibility for the state of the international system as a whole. The addition of so many independent units to the international system which is now taking place could heighten instability. The fact that United Nations participation prevents the isolation of these nations and extends their responsibilities may be diminishing the instabilities that they create in international affairs.

6. AVAILABILITY OF NEW INFORMATION

The public debates in the General Assembly and private discussions as well provide member nations with a large volume of information on international affairs. For at least some of the smaller nations, the volume of reports sent home from their United Nations mission is greater than that from any other foreign post. Statements by participants on their nation's policy and its underlying rationale comprise a substantial portion of the voluminous documentation of the United Nations. In the "general debate" that opens the annual sessions of the General Assembly, virtually every nation of the world declares its position on what it considers to be the most important international questions. In the course of committee debate most nations participate in the "general debates" on each of the some seventy items on the agenda. Following each vote in the committees a number of nations feel the need to explain their votes. Then, when each item comes to the plenary session, nations that feel the most strongly about it may again take the opportunity to explain their positions.

In addition, there are, of course, constant explanations of positions in discussion by delegates outside the committee and plenary sessions. During the variety of occasions for delegate interaction there is considerable opportunity for detailed explanation of national positions and reasons for maintaining them. This not only includes occasions when delegates can take the initiative in making the policy of their government clear, but also occasions in which delegates can acquire information. In such cases the United Nations environment may be quite important. Much opportunity is offered for a delegate himself, or through a friendly delegate, to get information without betraying the significance of the discussion of the matter. For this reason it is hypothesized that much information is available at the United Nations with virtually no cost. Information may be obtained without revealing explicit intentions or interests to the degree that this is required to cross the more restrictive barriers of diplomacy in a national capital. A diplomat from a European

Non-resolution Consequences of the United Nations

country who has been at the United Nations for several years told the writer: "On the whole, this is probably the best place in the world to pick up information on other governments."

In addition, the Secretariat and special committees and visiting missions of the General Assembly collect and distribute reports on a great number of international problems. These reports, along with records of Assembly debates and other documents, provide voluminous documentation that covers virtually all international problems. To an extent never the case heretofore, a common body of documentation available to all defines the nature of major problems, supplies extensive documentation on positions of conflicting parties, and furnishes detailed background information. This documentation is, of course, more important to some nations than it is to others. For smaller nations and nations not directly involved in some issues, United Nations information sources may provide virtually all of the data on which national positions are based. This suggests the hypothesis that the growth in dependence on documentation shared by all tends to give nations a more similar view of the world.

IV. Non-Resolution Consequences of the General Assembly and International Conflict

Are these non-resolution consequences of the General Assembly intriguing but inconsequential by-products of international relations in this community? Or do they have significance for important problems in international relations? An attempt will now be made to demonstrate that non-resolution consequences of the kind just discussed are potentially significant for what is with considerable unanimity cited as the most important problem in international relations and also as *the* problem of our age: international conflict. The primary purpose for this exploratory exposition is to show that research on non-resolution consequences is not only justified but urgently needed. In decisions so crucial as those involved in the creation of and participation in international organizations, it is not prudent for men to know only vaguely the consequences of their acts when more precise knowledge is obtainable.

To ask the relationship between the non-resolution consequences of the General Assembly and international conflict is to ask a question that international organization scholars have not attempted to answer, except by occasional impressionistic and anecdotal accounts. This does not mean, however, that the scholar who attempts to answer this question must start from scratch. There is knowledge in the social sciences—in the literature on organizations, communications, and conflict, for example —which is useful. Possibly because the study of international organizations has become primarily the domain of political scientists, we are inclined to look at these organizations only as particular kinds of political institutions. But human behavior in international organizations is also a special case, for example, of organizational behavior, communication, and social conflict. Knowledge from these areas of social science can be usefully applied in the study of international organizations along with knowledge gained from the traditional foci of the political scientist. In the exploration of the potential relationship between the non-resolution consequences of the General Assembly and international conflict that follows, knowledge is drawn from outside the international relations area whenever possible.

The ensuing discussion indicates five kinds of ways in which the non-resolution consequences already described may have an effect on international conflict. (1) Change in the traditional patterns of inter-nation communication may affect conflict. Particularly relevant here are the changes in these patterns that personal friendships, extended national interest, and the effects of Assembly experience on delegates bring. (2) There may be a relationship between conflict and new kinds of information that the Assembly makes available. It is asserted that relationship occurs because of the greater predictability of the behavior of other nations that this information allows. (3) The third and fourth examples discuss how Assembly participation places both the nation and the individual in a more varied set of roles than before that may bind each to a larger community. In the case of the nation, the new kinds of alignments that Assembly activity brings and extended national interest are important. (4) In the case of individuals cross-pressures are encouraged by the involvement of professional norms and personal friendships. (5) Finally, the possibility is discussed that conflict in the Assembly may itself be a non-resolution consequence that substitutes for conflict elsewhere.

1. THE CHANNELING OF INFORMATION

When relations among nations are looked at as a communications system, sharp differences are discerned between the part of this system that is within an organization such as the General Assembly and that which is conducted through more traditional channels. Bilateral communications outside an international organization are conducted through the elaborate and, for the most part, extremely formal mechanisms of diplomacy. The restraints that diplomatic practices have placed on inter-nation communication have helped not only to create conditions in which there are significant areas of national ignorance about the policies and intentions of other nations, but the cost of obtaining information to eliminate ignorance has often been high. Formal requests for information may betray ignorance, reveal intentions, or expose areas of concern. These costs must be weighed against the value of the information—if it is even available. Within the General Assembly, however, a portion of the restraints on inter-nation communication are eliminated. The sustained social interaction in a variety of kinds of situations, in the context of

Non-resolution Consequences of the United Nations

a common institution, stimulated by such elements as personal friendships and camaraderie of experts, breaks down these restraints.

Do the new kinds of communications opportunities that the General Assembly permits have any relationship to international conflict? James March and Herbert Simon, in their recent volume summarizing the literature on organizational behavior, suggest that there is a body of knowledge that will give some insight on this question. Studies of organizations have indicated that "the greater the channeling of information-processing, the greater the differentiation of perceptions within the organization" (15, p. 128). By channeling of information they mean limiting the number of organization members to whom any given bit of information is transmitted. Related to the proposition on the channeling of information is another which indicates its relevance to our discussion. It states that differences in the perception of reality are one of the major factors contributing to intergroup conflict (15, p. 121).

The converse of the March and Simon propositions offer stimulating hypotheses when applied to the General Assembly. It is hypothesized that the community of diplomats in New York, largely because of their participation in the General Assembly, is an element in the international communications system where the circulation of information is more diffuse and the patterns of its distribution more complex than in the remainder of the system. Therefore it is further hypothesized that the General Assembly tends to give officials who participate in it a more similar perception of reality than they have before they participate. The information that these persons supply to the remainder of the international system when they report home and when they move on to other posts tends to give all member nations a more similar perception of reality. Thus, as a network of communications routes that supplement and sometimes by-pass traditional diplomatic patterns of communication, the General Assembly tends to lessen the intensity of conflict by causing member nations to have more similar perceptions of the world.

2. PREDICTABILITY

As a consequence of the opportunities that the General Assembly provides for the relaxation of the communications restraints of traditional diplomacy and because of the new information available in the Assembly, it is hypothesized that participating nations know more about the capabilities and intentions of other participating nations than they would without this institution. In other words, it is contended that an organization such as the General Assembly makes the world more predictable for its members. Is there a relationship between predictability and conflict? Robin M. Williams, Jr., in a work on conflict among ethnic, religious, and racial groups in the United States, suggests that "disruption of stable expectations of interpersonal conduct tends to be productive of intergroup conflict" (20, p. 57). Karl Deutsch has asserted the importance of predictability in the development of an international community as

284

follows: "Insofar as members of a stable political community must be able to expect more or less dependable interlocking, interchanging, or at least compatible behavior from each other, they must be able, at least to that extent, to predict one another's actions" (6, p. 53).

The General Assembly may not only make the world more predictable to its members as a result of opening new routes for communication and creating an environment in which nations must give extensive explanations of their policies. This extensive requirement that nations explain policies publicly may tend to make these policies more stable. Conformity with predetermined plans should be greater after these plans have been revealed publicly before most nations of the world than when dissemination has been more restricted. This would seem to be particularly true if these plans have become the basis for multilateral action within the United Nations. The reader may have noted that this is the reverse of a proposition often found in international organization literature which asserts that public debate in bodies such as the General Assembly may intensify conflict by making positions more rigid and thereby eliminating the competence of conflicting parties to compromise. But the importance of predictability to conflict suggests that public commitment may not always be a deterrent to conflict reduction. It would be valuable to know more about the conditions under which each of these seemingly contrary propositions holds true.

3. OVERLAPPING CONFLICT SYSTEMS

This discussion has emphasized ways in which General Assembly processes may tend to diminish the intensity of some international conflicts. It is true, of course, that at times participation intensifies conflict between parties. In some cases, however, there may be potential beneficial effects for the stability of the system as a whole when conflict between traditional allies is intensified as a result of their being required to take a public stand on an issue on which they disagree; this may tend to relax, to some degree, tension between traditional foes who might then find themselves on the same side of an issue. For example, debate on colonial problems sometimes intensifies conflict between NATO allies when some members of NATO find themselves unable to support their allies on colonial issues. This conflict is accompanied by cooperative effort by some NATO members with nations who oppose them on other issues.

The literature on conflict often refers to the salutary effect of overlapping conflicts that in a sense tend to cancel each other out. Edward A. Ross, a sociologist writing several decades ago, described this process:

> Every species of social conflict interferes with every other species in society...
> save only when lines of cleavage coincide; in which case they reinforce one another....
> A society, therefore, which is ridden by a dozen oppositions along lines running in
> every direction may actually be in less danger of being torn with violence or falling
> to pieces than one split just along one line. For each cleavage contributes to narrow

285

the cross clefts, so that one might say that *society is sewn together* by its inner conflicts [17, p. 164–5, author's emphasis].

A mechanism whereby a "society is sewn together" by its conflicts is that of multiple group affiliations of its members which add an element of interdependence to the relations of conflicting groups. The committees of the General Assembly may be looked upon as multiple group affiliations required of the national delegations of the Assembly. Political allies find themselves at cross-purposes in economic and trusteeship committees and political enemies may at times be surprised to discover that they are allies on other issues. In the 1958 Assembly, for example, a resolution was passed urging the establishment of an international capital development fund in which the alignment was basically most NATO nations and a few more developed members of the British Commonwealth against the rest of the world. This was a significant departure from the usual alignment of the Latin American nations and others with the United States on political issues.

Multiple group affiliations bring cross-pressures that tend to restrain the pursuit of the goals of any one affiliation. It has been noted, for example, that workers in so-called "isolated" industries, such as miners, sailors, fishermen, lumbermen, and sheep-tenders, tend to back political extremists. This is believed to be caused by the fact that members of these groups do not have the multiple affiliations that integrate other members of society into the broader community (12 pp. 95–6). Does the broader scope of participation that the General Assembly requires of nations serve to integrate them into a wider community and thereby modify extremist tendencies of nations formerly more isolated?

As an example we might ask whether there is any indication that the Soviet Union is to some extent integrated into the United Nations community by its multiple committee participation. Thomas Hovet, in a study of bloc voting in the General Assembly, has compiled figures that are useful. In roll call votes that Hovet classifies "collective measures, regulation of armaments, etc.," the Soviets have voted with the majority only 18.4 per cent of the time. On resolutions devoted to human rights and self-determination, however, they have voted with the majority on 50 per cent and 45 per cent of the roll call votes, respectively. As a result of these percentages, and others less high, the Soviets have an over-all concurrence with majorities of 39.1 per cent (10, p. 68–70). Although the Soviet Union and its allies are, to a considerable degree, isolated from the remainder of the United Nations community, we hypothesize that the overlapping system of conflicts tends to integrate them into this community. Sharing voting victories on some items makes the Assembly seem less like an institution devised solely for the frustration of Soviet ambitions and makes success in additional areas seem more feasible and worth striving for through parliamentary means. And communication is easier with delegates who, on occasion, are on your side than with delegates who constantly oppose you.

286

As indicated earlier, study of nation participation in international organizations has rarely probed below the nation as a unit of analysis. Simultaneous with the widely held belief that individuals can change the ultimate fate of nations very little, there is the assumption that decisions of importance are made in foreign offices—delegates in international organizations being merely agents for the implementation of these decisions. United Nations delegates do, nonetheless, have a role in shaping policies that they advocate for their governments. In some cases delegates operate under general instructions with the freedom to design specific policies within this framework. However, whether the delegate's instructions be general or specific, the competence of delegates in pursuing national objectives in international bodies determines the kinds of choices that foreign office officials will have available in forming future policy. Furthermore, the delegate in an international organization selects and arranges information that is sent to the foreign office and often makes policy recommendations. The information and recommendations supplied by delegates may play a prominent role in the development of instructions that are sent back to the delegate.

Assuming that the individual delegate does have a role in the development of his nation's policies makes the effect of the General Assembly environment on delegates of some interest. Does the fact that the General Assembly to some degree consists of small international communities of experts and that personal friendships across national boundaries are encouraged have effects that are related to the role of the Assembly in international conflict? The literature on social conflict tells us that the introduction of personal factors in social relations tempers conflict. Lewis Coser, for example, suggests that the "elimination of the personal element tends to make conflict sharper, in the absence of modifying elements which personal factors would normally introduce" (5, p. 118). This is a special case of the so-called cross-pressure hypothesis that has found its way into political studies in surveys of voting behavior (1, p. 283; 3, p. 183). Persons who have opposing forces acting on them that engender internal conflict and indecision in voting situations have been found to be less strongly committed politically. It is not our suggestion, of course, that the cross-pressures brought to bear on General Assembly delegates will necessarily cause them to change votes or do about-faces on policy choices. The development and maintenance of personal friendships and the norms of fellow experts may, however, alter the way in which delegates perceive situations, determine the types of contacts and sources of information available to them, and eventually affect the picture of the situation that they relay home. It is hypothesized that the development of personal friendships tends to temper the intensity of conflict which delegates feel exists between their nation and nations with whose delegates they develop friendships. Devotion by delegates to the norms of their fellow experts on Assembly committees may produce the same effect. Those who bemoan the existence of intercommittee rivalry should not overlook the fact that it is likely caused by inter-nation cooperation!

5. GENERAL ASSEMBLY CONFLICT AS A SUBSTITUTE FOR VIOLENCE

There is a tendency to consider all conflict as negative in its consequences. Such a perspective may prevent the perception of transformations in conflict that are taking place. It has already been indicated that conflicts among members of a subsystem may make the over-all system more stable if they tend to criss-cross a bipolar cleavage that is threatening stability. It is also possible that conflict in one form may serve as a substitute for a more violent variety.

Lewis Coser's book, *The Functions of Social Conflict,* offers a stimulating analysis of the potential positive values of conflict. In discussing the valuable information which conflict allows the antagonists to obtain about each other, Coser asserts:

> Conflict consists in a test of power between antagonistic parties. Accommodation between them is possible only if each is aware of the relative strength of both parties. However, paradoxical as it may seem, such knowledge can most frequently be attained only through conflict, since other mechanisms for testing the respective strength of antagonists seem to be unavailable [5, p. 137].

Earlier Coser tells us that "if alternative means are not available or are believed to be unavailable, the only way to a reappraisal of the contending parties' power is to use the 'weapon of last resort' " (5, p. 136). Does the General Assembly at times provide a suitable alternative means for appraisal of relative strength that may make the resort to "weapons of last resort" unnecessary? It may be seen that the process here is somewhat akin to that earlier described wherein the Assembly contributes to predictability by providing more reliable information on the capabilities and intentions of opponents in conflict. But an element is added; in this instance we ask whether Assembly action might provide a substitute for other kinds of action.

Inis Claude seems to suggest that the General Assembly and the Trusteeship Council of the United Nations may be serving as arenas of final conflict over colonial questions. He reports that the most significant thing about the role of the United Nations in colonial affairs is not that it "has become the registrar of the triumphant surge of dynamic anti-colonialism, but rather that it has become the scene of conflict, the prize ring within which the battle over the future of colonialism has been fought" (4, p. 361). In some quarters, United Nations efforts in colonial questions are judged a failure because all members are not speaking with one voice in the solution of these problems. But this conflict might be enacted in a more violent way were United Nations councils not available as a battle-ground. Are battles of parliamentary diplomacy

288

substitutes for more violent battles elsewhere? It is imperative that we know much more than we do about instances in which this is the case. It is not necessarily true that an Assembly that does not reach agreements on major conflicts has been a total loss. It is crucial that we learn under what kinds of conditions conflict is amenable to transformation from violent conflict to a conflict of parliamentary diplomacy.

V. Conclusion

Some non-resolution consequences of the General Assembly have been discussed with the purpose of providing direction for research that will give more complete understanding of the effect of the United Nations and other international organizations on relations among nations. It has been asserted that perceptivity to such effects may be intensified by looking at these organizations in the context of the entire international system rather than looking at them as complete systems in and of themselves. It has also been suggested that one is more perceptive to the non-resolution consequences of the General Assembly if he recognizes the fact that nations may not be the only units whose Assembly participation merits analysis. It may be significant that each nation is playing a role in seven committees simultaneously. And aspects of the behavior of individual delegates may merit consideration.

In assessing the relationship between the non-resolution consequences of the Assembly and international conflict, literature outside political science and outside international relations has been cited. This was done to show the relevance of bodies of knowledge from other areas of human behavior to the study of international organizations. The intellectual barriers that surround academic departments have cut off this study from resources outside its home base—political science. Indeed, it is only recently that the main stream of political science has begun to affect the study of international organizations. If the great gain of the past decade has been a more general recognition that there is politics in international organizations, perhaps the advance of the coming years will be the acknowledgment that people are to be found there as well.

There seem to be significant patterns of interaction in the United Nations about which we as yet know very little. These patterns were not devised by those who built the organization at San Francisco, and the writer believes that in many cases they have not been implementations of conscious planning. Often they have been the products, it would seem, of widely scattered individual decisions. They have been born out of the daily agony of individual practitioners trying to stave off cataclysm by accomplishing the seemingly impossible. Often the practitioners are so busy with their individual acts that they do not see the over-all patterns. And sometimes when they do see them they do not have time to contemplate their significance. It is up to the social scientist, building on the insights that the practitioner can give, to discern their significance in terms of their effects on international relations and the relationship of these effects to the long-range goals of international organizations.

Up to the present time, the underlying patterns have been neglected because scholars and practitioners have tended to concentrate on the explicit organizational mechanisms for conflict resolution. Changes in the basic interaction process that international organizations may effect have been overlooked. It remains to be seen whether changes have been effected that are measurable, but we may be stumbling into unplanned consequences of organizational building that equal in importance those that are planned. Ernst Haas has concluded, as a result of his study of the European Coal and Steel Community, that international "institutions are crucial causative links in the chain of integration" (7, p. 450). They not only handle their explicitly assigned tasks but become the causes of other new factors that affect relations among their members. Haas reports that "our European lesson drives home the potential role of institutional forces in rechanneling and realigning previous group loyalties and expectations" (7, p. 457).

Furthermore, international organizations may spur integration in a given system through making the relationships between units in the system more complicated. This may occur by the initiation of new kinds of cooperative efforts among nations that run contrary to normal political alignments, the involvement of some nations in problems that they would have ignored were they not required to act in the organization, the establishment of new channels of cooperation for governmental experts, and the establishment of new and more intense friendships among officials across national boundaries.

The creation of international organizations may thus have a two-level effect: one effect being the organization's success at attaining goals for which it is established and the other being basic changes in the international system in which it is established. A closer study of the latter may be a requisite for making international organizations more effective in the achievement of explicit goals. For example, advocates of revision of the United Nations Charter might well look at their proposals not only as revisions of Charter mechanisms but also as revisions of basic patterns of inter-nation relations. Those who voice a desire for more orderly and neatly organized General Assembly processes might also give careful consideration to the potential effects of their proposals. What would be the effects of cutting the size of the General Assembly Committees? What would be the impact of reducing the number of items on the agenda? On the other hand, more sophisticated knowledge about the non-resolution consequences of the Assembly might show opportunities for changes in procedures that could have effects as significant as Charter revision but that require neither Charter revision nor seem threatening to those sensitive to inroads on national sovereignty.

In the introduction to his Fourteenth Annual Report to the General Assembly, Secretary-General Hammarskjold made two recommendations for changed procedures. He asked for regular meetings of the Security

Council in executive session and for the development of international economic policies in short special meetings at the ministerial level, within or under the aegis of the Economic and Social Council. How prepared are international organization scholars to predict the consequences of such innovations? Such predictions cannot be made from the data ordinarily used for international organization research: verbatim records of meetings, resolutions, handouts to the press, and journalistic accounts. These documents are only partial reflections of the consequences of the operation of political institutions. If he is to contribute anything to questions such as these beyond what the insightful practitioner and journalist can offer, the political scientist must collect other types of data and include them in his analysis. Scholars of international organizations have hardly begun the work which could enable them to provide knowledge beyond that which practitioners and journalists can supply. Under the existing documentary material above the surface, lies an iceberg of unknown dimensions. Here may be unanticipated consequences of international organizational building which could make these organizations self-destructive. On the other hand, there may be elements which could be utilized to advantage.

References

1. Berelson, Bernard R., Lazarsfeld, Paul, and McPhee, William N. *Voting.* Chicago: University of Chicago Press, 1954.
2. Best, Gary. "Diplomacy in the United Nations." Doctoral thesis, Northwestern University, 1960.
3. Campbell, Angus, Gurin, Gerald, and Miller, Warren E. *The Voter Decides.* Evanston, Ill.: Row, Peterson and Co., 1954.
4. Claude, Inis L., Jr. *Swords into Plowshares.* New York: Random House, 1956.
5. Coser, Lewis. *The Functions of Social Conflict.* Glencoe, Ill.: Free Press, 1956.
6. Deutsch, Karl. *Political Community at the International Level.* Doubleday Short Studies in Political Science, No. 1, Garden City, N.Y.: Doubleday, 1954.
7. Haas, Ernst. "The challenge of regionalism," *International Organization,* 12 (1958), 440–58.
8. Hadwen, John, and Kaufmann, Johan. *How United Nations Decisions are Made.* New York, 1958. (Mimeographed document prepared by two United Nations delegates.) Revision published, Leyden, Netherlands: A. W. Sijthoff, 1960.
9. Hammarskjold, Dag. "Introduction to fourteenth annual report to the General Assembly on the work of the Organization from June 16, 1958 to June 15, 1959," *United Nations Review,* 6 (1959), 8–18.
10. Hovet, Thomas, Jr. *Bloc Politics in the United Nations.* Cambridge, Mass.: Harvard University Press, 1960.
11. Jessup, Philip. *Parliamentary Diplomacy, An Examination of the Legal*

Quality of the Rules of Procedure of Organs of the United Nations. Leyden, Netherlands: A. W. Sijthoff, 1957.

12. Lipset, Seymour Martin. "Some social requisites of democracy: economic development and political legitimacy," *American Political Science Review,* 53 (1959), 69–105.

13. Mack, Raymond W., and Snyder, Richard C. "The analysis of social conflict—an overview and synthesis," *The Journal of Conflict Resolution,* 1 (1957), 212–47.

14. Merton, Robert K. "Manifest and latent functions," *Social Theory and Social Structure.* Glencoe, Ill.: Free Press, 1957.

15. March, James, and Simon, Herbert, with Guetzkow, Harold. *Organizations.* New York: John Wiley and Sons, 1958.

16. Petersen, Keith S. "The agendas of the United Nations General Assembly: A content analysis," *Southwestern Social Science Quarterly* (December, 1958), 232–41.

17. Ross, Edward Alsworth. *The Principles of Sociology.* New York: Century Co., 1920.

18. Rusk, Dean. "Parliamentary diplomacy—debate versus negotiation," *World Affairs Interpreter,* 26, No. 2 (Summer, 1955).

19. Simmel, Georg. *Conflict and the Web of Group Affiliation.* Glencoe, Ill.: Free Press, 1955.

20. Williams, Robin. *The Reduction of Intergroup Tensions.* New York: Social Science Research Council, 1947.

Discovering

Voting Groups

in the

United Nations

C H A P T E R   S I X T E E N

Bruce M. Russett

Reprinted with permission of the publisher, the American Political Science Association, from *The American Political Science Review,* Vol. 60, No. 2 (June, 1966) 327–39. Mr. Russett is Professor of Political Science at Yale University.

I. An Inductive Approach to Voting Patterns

The discussion of voting groups or blocs within the United Nations General Assembly has long been a popular pastime. It is, of course, merely a special case of a wider concern with groups and coalitions in all aspects of international politics. With the apparent loosening of the early postwar bipolarity it is increasingly important to discern the number, composition, and relative strength of whatever coalitions of nations may emerge from the present seemingly transitional period.

Voting groups in the General Assembly provide a relevant datum, though hardly the only one, for an effort to identify these groups. The United Nations gives no perfect image of broader international politics; due to the one-nation one-vote principle and to the fact that it is not a world government with authority to enforce its decisions, power relationships within the Assembly are not the same as in other arenas, such as functional or geographic ones. It might well be argued that because of the majority-rule principle the smaller and poorer states have an incentive to band together in the UN that they do not have elsewhere. Thus the discovery of a "bloc" of underdeveloped countries in the UN proves nothing about the cohesion of that "bloc" in other contexts. Yet votes in the General Assembly do provide a unique set of data where many national governments commit themselves simultaneously and publicly on a wide variety of major issues. The range of issues includes almost everything of major worldwide concern; even policy positions on parochial or regional questions (the intrabloc relations of Communist states, for instance) can often be inferred from the nations' votes on other issues. However warped or distorted an image of general world politics the General Assembly may convey, it remains one of our best sources of replicable information policy positions for its 100-plus members.

An interest in voting groups may have a number of payoffs. From a frankly manipulative point of view, it may give information which can assist American policy-makers to increase their gains in the UN political process. Of more scientific interest, it can tell us about blocs and coalitions in ways that can be related to broader theories about parliamentary behavior. And finally it can indeed give some, admittedly imperfect, informa-

This research was begun under a Junior Faculty Fellowship from Yale University. It has also been supported by the Yale Political Data Program under a grant from the National Science Foundation, and by the Mental Health Research Institute of the University of Michigan.

tion about the nature—such as bipolar or multipolar—of the emerging international system.

The last concern must proceed from an inductive approach to the identification of voting groups, and so, for most purposes, should the second. That is, if one is asking how many such groups there are, the advance specification of certain aggregates, such as caucusing groups (Commonwealth, Communist, Afro-Asian) is a very roundabout way to get the answer. True, there is a tendency for caucusing groups to be more cohesive than any set of states picked purely at random, but the association between caucusing group membership and voting identity is very rough, as Thomas Hovet has so compellingly demonstrated.[1] Furthermore, by dealing only with pre-selected groups one could easily conclude, for example, that disagreement and conflict within the Afro-Asian group is extremely high, but not even notice some sub-groups, including some which do not formally caucus together, that nevertheless show very high agreement. Or one might ignore the cohesion of an aggregate of states (such as those of the North Atlantic area) which includes both one or more caucusing groups and a number of countries that are not in any caucusing group.

Most of the published studies to date have been directed to measuring the cohesion of caucusing, geographic, or other pre-selected groups.[2] One major exception is Leroy Rieselbach's article, which introduces an inductive method of bloc analysis.[3] He constructs a table showing the percentage of votes on which each of a large number of pairs of countries agree, and arranges the table in such a way as to indicate cohesion, with lines drawn around any group of countries achieving a given level of agreement. In the article he illustrates this method for selected countries, those in Latin America, but it becomes extremely awkward for a body as large as the entire Assembly in recent years (over 110 members). In such a large table (each of 110 countries' scores with every other nation) it is very difficult to be sure one has found all the "blocs" that meet one's criterion.[4] Rieselbach also illustrates an approach using Guttman scaling, but it can only find groups who vote together on a particular set of issues (cold war, colonial self-determination, etc.). We shall discuss this aspect below. In many ways it is a major improvement over studies which attempt to find groups when lumping all issues together, for coalitions on

---

[1] Thomas Hovet, Jr., *Bloc Politics in the United Nations* (Cambridge: Harvard University Press, 1960).

[2] *Ibid.*, and Thomas Hovet, *Africa in the United Nations* (Evanston, Illinois: Northwestern University Press, 1963). See also M. Margaret Ball, "Bloc Voting in the General Assembly," *International Organization*, 5 (1951), 3–31, Robert E. Riggs, *Politics in the United Nations* (Champaign: University of Illinois Press, 1958); and Hayward R. Alker, Jr., and Bruce M. Russett, *World Politics in the General Assembly* (New Haven, Conn.: Yale University Press, 1965), ch. 12.

[3] "Quantitative Techniques for Studying Voting Behavior in the UN General Assembly," *International Organization*, 14 (1960), 291–306.

[4] Even in Rieselbach's Table 2 of Latin American countries there would seem to be one other group (Uruguay, Costa Rica, Paraguay, Honduras, Peru) that meets his criteria (five countries, 80 per cent agreement) for a bloc.

Discovering Voting Groups in the United Nations

cold war issues are *not* identical with those on self-determination. Yet the inability to employ it simultaneously, when one wishes, to more than one issue is a limitation.

Arend Lijphart has with great force pointed out the overwhelming concentration of interest in the previous literature on analyzing pre-selected groups, and to counter it offers an ingenious inductive method which he illustrates for states in the 11th through 13th Sessions.[5] It again depends upon a version of an index of the percentage of times two states' voting positions agree, modified to account for the abstentions which are rather common in the General Assembly. He employs a graphic method of presentation (vaguely reminiscent of spider webs) that is superior to the tabular one but nevertheless becomes quite difficult to interpret for a body the size of the current Assembly. Furthermore, it can only identify those pairs or groups of states which achieve or exceed a particular *level* of agreement (in his illustration, 87.5 per cent), and is not an economical method for showing the *degrees* of agreement which may exist among all states.

Thus no fully satisfactory method for the identification of voting groups has yet appeared in the international organization literature. What is required is a technique which is *inductive,* given to a means of presentation which is readily *interpretable,* which shows *gradations* in agreement among nations (not just whether or not they exceed a particular level of agreement), which reliably *identifies all the groupings,* and which can be applied either to a *selected* set of issues or to *all* roll-call votes of a Session.

I believe that factor analysis, and more specifically a particular application of factor analysis, the so-called "Q-technique," is such a method. Originally developed by psychologists, during the past several years factor analysis has been employed sufficiently widely by political scientists that it probably requires no detailed introduction or justification to most readers, though its application to the United Nations has so far been limited.[6] In the most common employment of factor analysis every variable is correlated with every other variable, using the product-moment correlation coefficient. Factor analysis is then a data-reduction technique, as those variables which show high correlations among themselves and very low correlation with other variables are interpreted as pointing to a single underlying dimension, or *factor.* The factors themselves are uncorrelated with each other. Thus in Alker's initial application of the technique to UN voting patterns it was found that certain roll-calls (e.g., in 1961 on South Africa, Angola, Rhodesia, Ruanda-Urundi, trade, and economic aid) had similar voting alignments that pointed to an

[5] "The Analysis of Bloc Voting in the General Assembly," *The American Political Science Review,* 57 (1963), 902–917.

[6] Hayward R. Alker, Jr. "Dimensions of Conflict in the General Assembly," *The American Political Science Review,* 58 (1964), 642–657 and Alker and Russett, *op. cit.* A much more detailed discussion of how factor analysis is employed can be found in chapter 2 of the latter. As yet unpublished analyses of UN votes have been performed by George Chacko, Rudolph Rummel, Raymond Tanter, Charles Wrigley, and others.

underlying "self-determination" issue. These voting alignments were unrelated to those on such issues as Cuba, Hungary, Tibet, and disarmament, which were like each other and pointed to a different underlying issue (the cold war).[7] In this application each roll-call vote was a variable, with each "actor" (country) serving as an item or observation.

The versatility of factor analysis, however, suggests an alternative use. It can just as readily be used to find similar *actors* (test takers, legislators, nations) as similar *variables* (questions on a psychological test, roll-call votes). If, for example, one began with a table (matrix) where each country was a row and each column a roll-call, one could simply turn the table 90 degrees so that, in effect, the countries became variables and the roll-calls became observations. When the matrix is then factor-analyzed in this fashion the correlations identify *countries* with similar voting patterns and the factors point to voting groups or blocs. This procedure is usually designated "Q-analysis" to distinguish it from the somewhat more common technique mentioned first (R-analysis).[8] To repeat, the procedure is inductive in that it involves no prior specification of the groups to be looked for, nor is even the number of such groups specified in advance.

II. Cohesive Voting Groups: A Q-Analysis of the 18th Session

We shall illustrate the technique with an analysis of roll-call votes in the 18th Session, beginning in the autumn of 1963, and in the process be able to make some useful substantive points about the nature of politics in the Assembly. Because of the United States vs. Russia and France controversy over dues there was only a single recorded vote in the 19th (1964) Session, so these are the most recent data available or likely to become so until the *Official Records* of the 20th (1965) Session are published sometime in 1967.

Our data consist of all 66-roll-call votes, both plenary and committee, except those which are virtually unanimous (defined here as more than 90 per cent of those voting taking one side—usually in favor).[9] This restriction is necessary because the product-moment correlation coefficient

---

[7] Alker, *op. cit.*

[8] Although it has been used rather frequently in other disciplines, to my knowledge the only application in comparative or international politics is a paper by Arthur S. Banks and Phillip Gregg, "Grouping Political Systems: Q-Factor Analysis of *A Cross-Polity Survey*," *American Behavioral Scientist*, 9, 3 (November, 1965), 3–6. An application to the Kansas state legislature can be found in John Grumm, "A Factor Analysis of Legislative Behavior," *Midwest Journal of Political Science*, 7 (1963), 336–356. It is worth noting that in his pioneer study of voting blocs in the United States Congress David Truman discusses the difficulty of finding blocs in a large matrix and suggests factor analysis as a method possibly superior to his own; *The Congressional Party* (New York: John Wiley and Sons, 1959), p. 329.

[9] Committee votes often preview later plenary ones, but more frequently there is no plenary roll-call vote repeating one in committee. Even when the same paragraph or resolution does come up again the alignments usually shift somewhat; there are no duplicates in the following analysis.

Discovering Voting Groups in the United Nations

is seriously distorted by a distribution more lopsided than 90–10. The omission might result in the hiding of any very small group that was consistently in the minority, but is not likely to be important because typically such very lopsided votes account for less than 10 per cent of all those in a Session. In practice the only real possibility of a group whose cohesion and isolation might be understated is the handful of states (Portugal, Spain, South Africa, France, Belgium, sometimes the United Kingdom) which are so out of step with the Assembly majority on African colonial issues. As we shall see below, Portugal and Spain do actually cluster together anyway, and South Africa is not even included in the analysis because of high absenteeism. This example, however, constitutes a warning against processing the data too mechanically without a careful inspection of the *Records*.

On every vote each state was coded either 2 (affirmative) 1 (abstain) or 0 (negative). Absenteeism is rather frequent in the Assembly, however, and posed something of a problem. In a few cases a country, though absent, later officially recorded its position. I listed it as if it had so voted. Also, in some cases an absence is clearly intended to demonstrate opposition to the resolution, or a conviction that the Assembly is overstepping the bounds of its authority in considering the issue. The United Kingdom found itself in such a position over several votes on Southern Rhodesia in the 18th Session. In those cases I recorded the absence as a negative vote. Both of these procedures are in conformity with the practice of earlier researches.[10]

The remaining absences are in general concentrated on a few countries, often those with small delegations. While it would sometimes be possible to estimate an absent nation's voting position from the votes of other states in its geographical area or caucusing group, in our inductive search for voting groups such a procedure would prejudice the results and would not be admissible. Instead I chose to equate an absence with abstention. In many instances an absence does in fact mean abstention, but by no means always, and when it does not the result is to incorporate a degree of imprecision in the analysis. The average absenteeism for the Assembly is about 12 per cent, and for the vast majority of states less than 25 per cent. Since the equation of absence with abstention actually assigns a state to a middle position on our three-point scale, and since it is sometimes the correct interpretation anyway, this treatment of absences will not seriously distort the voting position of all countries with 25 per cent for fewer absences—their scores on the factors below are not affected by more than about 8 per cent. For those countries (11 in the 18th Session) with greater absenteeism the distortion is potentially more serious, and they are marked with a † symbol to indicate that their positions should be treated with some caution. Four other states (Dominican Republic, Honduras, Luxembourg, and South Africa) were absent more than 40 per cent of the time and so were excluded entirely

10 Lijphart, *op. cit.*, and Alker and Russett, *op. cit.*

from the analysis. Kenya and Zanzibar, admitted well after the Session was under way, were also omitted.

Table 1 presents the factor "loadings" of every country on each of the six meaningful factors which emerge from the analysis. Each factor identifies a group of countries whose voting patterns are very similar, and the loadings are product-moment correlation coefficients of a country's voting pattern with the underlying factor. The highest loadings or correlations identify those countries with the "purest" pattern, those whose voting is most fully described by the factor. Labelling the factors is always somewhat arbitrary, but in most cases the descriptive label should be appropriate. The percentages at the head of each column indicate the percentage of the total variation (variance) among all 107 countries that is explained (accounted for) by the factor. All loadings of .50 or greater have been underlined for emphasis, as loadings in the .40's are underscored with dashed lines. Squaring the correlation coefficient provides a means of discovering the amount of the country's total variance which is accounted for by the underlying factor. Thus it is reasonable largely to ignore correlations below .40 since the factor in question accounts for less than a sixth of the variance. The countries are listed in descending order of their loadings on the factor which best "explains" their voting pattern. Countries with no loading above .49 (and thus for whom no one factor "explains" as much as one-fourth of their voting variance) seemed best left "unclassifiable." In factor analytic terms the table presents the orthogonal solution, which means that the factors are uncorrelated with each other.[11]

I have labelled the first factor "Western Community" in an attempt to indicate the predominance of European and European-settled states among those with high loadings. "Western Community" in this context must be interpreted as a cultural and not just a geographical phenomenon, including the white Commonwealth. This relationship is indicated by the fact that of 35 UN members either physically located in Europe or whose population is predominantly of European origin (Argentina, Australia, Canada, Costa Rica, Cyprus, New Zealand, Uruguay, and United States), 22 have loadings of .50 or greater on the second factor. This works out to a fairly low correlation coefficient of .35. Each of the top 15 loadings, however, is held by such a country.

Note also the high loadings of Japan and (nationalist) China on this factor. Japan's basic foreign policy has become quite well integrated with those of her North Atlantic associates in recent years, and is so

11 In Tables 1 and 2 I present the factors as rotated according to the varimax technique. Unities were inserted in the principal diagonal of the correlation matrix. "Rotating" the original factors to "simple structure" maximizes the number of both very high and very low loadings, thus making interpretation easier. Each factor has an "eigen value" which expresses the amount of variance in the entire table that it accounts for. The eigen value, when divided by the total number of variables (countries), gives the *percentage* of variance accounted for by the factor. All 15 factors with eigen values greater than one were rotated. Nine factors which had no more than one loading as high as .50 are omitted from the table.

Discovering Voting Groups in the United Nations

TABLE 1   UNITED NATIONS GROUPINGS IN 1963

Nation	Factor 1 "Western Community" 23%	Factor 2 "Brazzaville Africans" 17%	Factor 3 "Afro-Asians" 16%	Factor 4 "Communist Bloc" 11%	Factor 5 "Conservative Arabs" 4%	Factor 6 "Iberia" 2%
"Western Community"						
Denmark	.90	.12	−.02	−.27	−.01	−.17
Norway	.89	.10	−.03	−.23	−.11	−.04
Sweden	.89	.09	−.03	−.25	−.12	−.09
Finland	.88	.06	.03	−.22	−.04	−.10
Austria	.87	.20	.00	−.17	−.10	−.01
Ireland	.86	.15	−.08	−.25	.16	−.03
Turkey	.83	.18	−.10	−.33	−.04	.23
Australia	.82	.10	−.15	−.38	.01	.10
Belgium	.82	.13	−.15	−.44	−.07	.15
New Zealand	.82	.17	−.14	−.27	.07	.05
Iceland	.82	.14	−.05	−.22	.14	−.20
United States	.81	.07	.23	−.27	.09	.23
Italy	.81	.12	−.12	−.37	.14	.11
Canada	.80	.09	−.15	−.44	−.02	.17
Netherlands	.80	.05	−.11	−.46	.03	.09
Japan	.76	.23	−.11	−.33	.31	.06
China	.75	.40	−.01	−.11	.07	.09
United Kingdom	.72	−.16	−.22	−.46	.07	.09
Greece	.71	.23	−.21	−.29	−.03	.15
*Venezuela	.70	.52	−.01	−.07	.13	−.02
*Argentina	.70	.49	−.04	−.10	.12	.09
*Guatemala	.65	.52	.07	−.17	.09	−.05
*Panama	.63	.51	.05	.08	.09	.05
*Colombia	.62	.52	.15	.08	.16	.09
*Ecuador	.62	.50	−.05	−.06	.32	.05
Iran	.61	.38	−.01	−.04	.33	−.04
*Costa Rica	.61	.61	.09	.11	.11	.05
*Mexico	.61	.52	.11	.01	.39	−.07
*Thailand	.60	.52	.05	−.02	.15	.14
*Jamaica	.59	.51	.03	.06	.32	−.19
†El Salvador	.59	.36	.00	−.29	.29	.34
France	.59	.01	−.48	−.02	−.23	.27
*Chile	.58	.52	.28	−.08	.18	.05
*Brazil	.56	.43	.01	−.04	.10	.05
*Peru	.56	.49	.03	.02	.17	.34
*Malaysia	.55	.55	.21	.06	.43	.03
†Nicaragua	.55	.38	.09	−.32	.02	.17
*Paraguay	.53	.47	.00	−.20	.19	.18
"Brazzaville Africans"						
Chad	.12	.87	.17	.01	−.03	.06
Cameroun	.20	.79	.29	−.08	−.08	−.06
†Gabon	.20	.79	.23	.08	.06	.04
Central African Rep.	.17	.78	.03	.01	−.09	.10
Niger	.02	.78	.34	−.03	.04	.14

* Moderately high loadings on Factors 1 and 2.
† More than 25% absenteeism (but less than 40%); absent equated with abstain.

TABLE 1　(*Continued*)

Nation	Factor 1 "Western Community" 23%	Factor 2 "Brazzaville Africans" 17%	Factor 3 "Afro-Asians" 16%	Factor 4 "Communist Bloc" 11%	Factor 5 "Conservative Arabs" 4%	Factor 6 "Iberia" 2%
Congo (B)	.07	.77	.28	.08	− .09	− .00
Rwanda	.23	.76	.16	− .09	.05	− .20
†Haiti	.16	.74	− .06	.00	.01	.10
Ivory Coast	.08	.73	.35	− .04	.27	− .04
Upper Volta	− .09	.73	.37	.05	− .12	− .06
Congo (L)	.22	.72	.22	.01	.01	− .17
*Cyprus	.52	.71	.04	− .06	.08	.01
Dahomey	.07	.70	.32	− .03	.05	− .11
†Bolivia	.37	.68	.10	− .15	.14	.01
Senegal	.12	.68	.26	.19	.19	.15
Uruguay	.35	.68	.11	.08	.23	.04
*Philippines	.49	.63	.09	− .05	.26	.03
Madagascar	.39	.62	.05	− .14	.32	− .09
Sierra Leone	.05	.62	.41	− .01	− .02	− .09
Liberia	.41	.62	.09	− .14	.32	− .17
Togo	.09	.62	.49	− .02	.23	− .01
*Israel	.43	.53	− .04	− .18	.04	− .31
Mauretania	.08	.53	.38	.18	.49	.00
*Pakistan	.50	.51	.21	.01	.09	− .09
"Afro-Asians"						
Ghana	− .09	.14	.88	.17	− .11	− .04
Afghanistan	− .15	.15	.84	.23	− .00	.06
Indonesia	− .17	.08	.82	.13	− .19	.12
Egypt	− .09	.07	.82	.30	.06	.06
Syria	− .05	.09	.82	.30	.04	.07
Ethiopia	− .02	.11	.82	.18	.00	− .14
Yugoslavia	− .18	.15	.80	.29	− .03	.02
India	.12	.19	.75	.02	.31	− .07
Algeria	− .22	.16	.74	.40	.09	.02
Nigeria	.01	.26	.74	− .13	.04	.25
Iraq	− .24	.15	.73	.30	.25	− .04
Tunisia	− .02	.25	.73	.13	− .01	− .07
†Burma	.05	.13	.72	.24	− .06	.08
Cambodia	− .13	.13	.72	.31	.03	− .03
Tanganyika	− .18	.33	.67	.22	.10	− .16
Guinea	− .13	.29	.67	.32	.09	.05
Mali	− .25	.09	.65	.42	.27	− .11
Ceylon	.02	.19	.65	.21	.05	− .02
Sudan	.00	.24	.60	.24	.05	− .09
Kuwait	.14	.29	.58	.24	.47	− .06
Morocco	− .15	.13	.58	.35	.40	− .06
†Somalia	− .04	.22	.55	.11	.08	− .27
†Uganda	− .02	.32	.55	.27	.06	.03
†Yemen	− .02	.24	.53	.32	.04	− .13
"Communist Bloc"						
Czechoslovakia	− .42	− .04	.28	.85	− .02	− .02
U.S.S.R.	− .42	− .04	.28	.85	− .02	− .02

TABLE 1   *(Continued)*

Nation	Factor 1 "Western Community" 23%	Factor 2 "Brazzaville Africans" 17%	Factor 3 "Afro-Asians" 16%	Factor 4 "Communist Bloc" 11%	Factor 5 "Conservative Arabs" 4%	Factor 6 "Iberia" 2%
Bulgaria	−.41	−.05	.29	.85	−.03	−.02
Byelorussia	−.42	−.05	.29	.85	.07	−.06
Poland	−.42	−.05	.29	.85	.07	−.06
Cuba	−.36	.00	.28	.85	−.07	−.02
Romania	−.39	−.05	.32	.84	−.02	.02
Ukraine	−.45	−.02	.28	.83	−.04	−.03
Hungary	−.40	−.07	.27	.83	.16	−.08
Mongolia	−.42	−.06	.29	.82	.16	−.10
Albania	−.27	.01	.49	.59	−.05	−.07
		"Conservative Arabs"				
Lebanon	.09	.16	.46	.08	.66	.10
Jordan	.17	.34	.46	.25	.58	−.03
Libya	.21	.44	.45	.01	.54	−.05
		"Iberia"				
Portugal	.23	−.25	−.06	−.44	−.08	.68
Spain	.52	.13	−.11	−.26	.09	.66
		Unclassifiable				
Burundi	.14	.30	.48	.19	−.09	−.17
†Laos	.26	.19	.40	.07	.27	.04
Nepal	.14	.36	.47	−.06	.04	−.01
†Saudi Arabia	.22	.14	.39	.32	.18	.15
Trinidad & Tobago	.42	.41	.18	.06	.07	−.03

perceived by Afro-Asian observers.[12] Nationalist China is of course heavily dependent upon United States military and diplomatic support. This leads to another observation about the factor: among those with .50 or higher loadings are 33 of the 38 UN members who have a formal military alliance with the United States (including the United States itself and counting Iran). Such a close association produces a correlation of .79. France is by far the lowest of all NATO allies on this factor, with also a strong *negative* leading on the Afro-Asian factor (number three).

The second factor is named "Brazzaville Africans," though the name is far from perfect and a number of non-African states also correlate with it. The six highest loadings, and 14 above .50 in all, are possessed by countries which were members of the former Brazzaville caucusing group, of whom all but the Congo (Leopoldville) were ex-French colonies. Both the Brazzaville and Casablanca groupings had been formally dissolved by the 18th (1963) Session, ostensibly in the interest of pro-

[12] Cf. Saburo Okita, "Japan and the Developing Nations," *Contemporary Japan*, 28, 2 (1965), 1–14.

moting African unity, but the essential differences in voting patterns seem still to persist. Note also the high loadings of Haiti (Negro, very underdeveloped) and of several Asian and Latin American states. Previous studies have noted that the Brazzaville states tend to be less anti-Western on cold war issues than the Afro-Asian "neutralists," but more so, and especially on colonial questions, than the typical Latin American state. This second factor then picks out, in addition to the Brazzaville Africans, both several of the more pro-Western Asians (Philippines and Pakistan, plus Israel) and a number of Latin Americans who are rather to the "east" of their caucusing group (Uruguay and Bolivia, for example). The first two factors together account for 40 per cent of the total roll-call variance, and indicate most of the states which can generally be expected to take the Western position on most cold war issues.

The third factor quite clearly picks out those Asians and Africans sometimes identified by the term Afro-Asian neutralists. More often than not they vote with the Soviet Union on both cold-war and colonial questions. They include such long-time leaders of this group as Egypt, India, and Indonesia, most of the Arab countries, Yugoslavia, and a number of African states, especially (but not only) those with rother leftist governments which belonged to the former "Casablanca" caucusing group. And while these are (except for Yugoslavia) non-Communist governments, of 24 UN members outside of the Sino-Soviet bloc known to have received economic and/or military aid from China, the U.S.S.R., or Eastern Europe by mid-1962, 19 have loadings of at least .50 with this third factor. Using all 96 non-Soviet bloc governments in this table, and simple receipt or non-receipt of Sino-Soviet aid as the variable, this produces a correlation (r) of .72. All of the top nine countries on this factor received such aid.

Not surprisingly, the Soviet bloc accounts for the other major factor. Only Communist states load heavily on this factor—though Yugoslavia emphatically does not and belongs with Factor 3. Cuba and Mongolia are virtually indistinguishable from the European members of the bloc. But one important evidence of the crack in what had in previous years been a solid voting alignment is the behavior of Albania. Since the defection of Yugoslavia in 1948 this is the first time that any study of the United Nations has shown a noticeable deviation by a Communist nation. Albania's loading on the factor is a mere .59, and if we return to the original votes from which the factor analysis is derived, Albania's voting pattern correlates but .75 with those of other Soviet "bloc" states. That is, voting by the U.S.S.R. "accounts for" little more than half the variance in Albania's behavior in the Assembly.

Finally, there are two minor factors, each accounting for but four and two per cent of the total variance. Factor 5 has three countries loading highly on it: Lebanon, Jordan, and Libya. The name "Conservative Arabs" seems appropriate, for all are non-revolutionary regimes; in cold-war politics these states vote relatively often with the Western powers, and each has received substantial foreign aid from the United

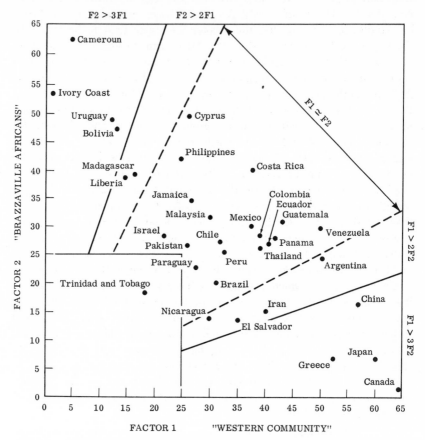

FIGURE 1   *"Latin American" grouping as identified by moderate loadings on Factors 1 and 2.*

States. Factor 6 picks out Portugal and Spain only; the label "Iberia" is obvious.

Most commonly in a factor analysis of this sort the factors can with relative ease be used to identify "groups" of variables (in this case nations). This is true for four of our six factors, but not for two others. Many of the countries loading either on Factors 1 or 2 (called "Western Community" and "Brazzaville Africans") actually show fairly high loadings on *both* factors, so that they cannot unequivocally be identified with either. The majority of states with loadings between .50 and .70 on either factor share this property. In such circumstances it is often useful to make a scattergram and plot the positions of the countries in question on the two competing factors. Figure 1 is a graph where the vertical axis represents the percentage of variance (simply 100 times the factor loading squared) accounted for by Factor 2, and the horizontal axis the percentage explained by Factor 1. All countries with loadings of .40 or higher on *both* factors are represented, as well as a couple of others for reference.

In some instances one factor accounts for three or more times as much of a country's variance as does the other, and when this happens there is little question as to where the nation should be grouped. This applies, for example, to Uruguay and Bolivia, for whom Factor 2 accounts for almost 50 per cent of the variance and Factor 1 less than 15 per cent. Any country which occupies a position either between the vertical axis and the sloping solid line to its right, or between the horizontal axis and the sloping solid line above it, has this variance ratio of more than three to one. The sloping dashed lines to the right and above the solid ones respectively mark the gray area where the variance ratio is over two to one. Although the countries occupying this space are distinctly more marginal than one lying closer to the axes, it is probably not unreasonable still to assign them as weak members of the group whose factor accounts for more than twice as much variance as any other. Most clearly it seems appropriate to think of Liberia and Madagascar with the "Brazzaville" countries. And for any state which has less then 25 per cent of its variance accounted for by any factor (e.g., Trinidad & Tobago) we have little choice but to term it "unclassifiable." The square in the lower left marks out this area of the diagram.

But for the countries where the percentage of variance explained by the most powerful factor is less than twice that of the next most important factor, it may be misleading to label them as belonging with either of the groups for which the factor is named. This is especially so in the situation illustrated in the above figure, where no less than 18 states occupy the area between the two dashed lines. Here we must speak of yet another voting group, which we can label "Latin America." Twelve of these nations are physically located in the Western Hemisphere. With Honduras and the Dominican Republic excluded from our analysis for excessive absenteeism, only Haiti, Bolivia, Uruguay, Cuba, Trinidad & Tobago (in the lower left box), El Salvador, Argentina, and Nicaragua do not fall into this area. And the latter two are extremely marginal. Those 20 countries (including Argentina and Nicaragua) have been marked with an asterisk in Table 1 and should be considered as comprising a separate group. A number of pro-Western Asian states— Malaysia, Thailand, Pakistan, Philippines, and Israel—have quite similar voting patterns.

III. Groups and Super-Issues

The influences affecting these groupings are not unique or substantially peculiar to the 18th Session. By and large the issues voted upon in the Assembly during the Session closely resemble those that prevailed earlier. It has been shown through factor analyses with *issues as variables*

(R-analysis) that three major issue dimensions or "super-issues" can be identified in each of four different Sessions spread over virtually the entire history of the United Nations.[13] They have been characterized as "cold war," "colonial self-determination," and "supranationalism" issues, and among them they regularly accounted for more than half the total variance in all roll-call voting. Two other super-issues, concerned with problems of intervention in southern Africa and of Palestine, were found in three of the four Sessions. The four or five factors appearing in any Session always accounted for between 59 and 70 per cent of the total variance in that Session.

A similar analysis of the 18th (1963) Session (using the roll-call data described earlier in this paper) showed these same five factors appearing and accounting for two-thirds of all the roll-call variance. Most prominent was the cold-war issue, accounting for 21 per cent of the variance and characterized by votes on such specific matters as the seating of Communist China and the role of the United Nations in Korea—both topics which have long exemplified the cold-war issue in the Assembly. A new matter, in form at least, concerned a resolution about extended participation in general multilateral treaties concluded under the League of Nations. Disagreement arose over whether all nations should be eligible, or merely those which were members of the United Nations and its specialized agencies. Since the latter formula would exclude mainland China and East Germany but include West Germany (which is a member of several specialized agencies), it is not surprising that the issue was perceived and voted upon in much the same way as the more familiar cold-war issues. Another set of roll-calls loading highly on this super-issue came from discussing item A/5671, a resolution on "Consideration of Principles of International Law Concerning Friendly Relations and Cooperation Among States." One section which called for the establishment of an international center of inquiry and fact-finding for the peaceful settlement of disputes was opposed by the Soviet Union and its allies.[14]

A second super-issue, accounting for 19 per cent of the variance, concerned such familiar problems as Southern Rhodesia, South West Africa. With the dismemberment of the great overseas empires there are formerly turned up on the self-determination factor or on the southern Africa one; here the super-issue can quite clearly be identified as southern Africa. With the dismemberment of the great overseas empires there are hardly any other concrete colonialism questions. A similar though less

---

[13] Alker and Russett, *op. cit.*

[14] In all there were nine factors with eigen values greater than one, accounting for 75 per cent of the total variance. I list here only those roll-calls which correlated at least .71 with the underlying factor, and thus more than half of whose variance can be accounted for by the factor. More detailed information on the resolutions can be found in the "Summary of Activities" of the General Assembly in *International Organization,* 18, 2 (1964), 313–467 and of course in the *Official Records* themselves. *International Conciliation,* No. 544 (September 1963) discusses the issues before their consideration by the Assembly.

International Cooperation

thorough convergence occurred in 1961.[15] What remains of any separate self-determination issue may perhaps be found in a small factor identified in only two roll-calls and accounting for but 4 per cent of the variance. A section on granting independence to colonial peoples and countries was inserted in the "Draft Declaration on the Elimination of All Forms of Racial Discrimination." The United Kingdom and some Western Europeans tried to have the section deleted, with the argument that it was irrelevant to the Declaration.

The other major super-issue, accounting for 18 per cent of the variance, is related to what has in previous years been called "supranationalism," composed of votes affecting the retention or expansion of the Organization's powers, especially its peacekeeping forces. As in earlier years votes on the United Nations' role in the Congo and UNEF in the Middle East loaded highly on it, as did a number of roll-calls about the proposed expansion and new composition of ECOSOC and the Security Council. While nations' votes on this dimension surely are not solely the product of their preference for or opposition to a stronger and more effective UN, this question is nevertheless a common thread through all these roll-calls. Finally, there was a factor composed primarily of two votes on the status of Palestine refugees and accounting for 4 per cent of the variance.

Thus the basic issues and alignments underlying the groupings in the 18th Session are familiar ones. But in the process of identifying them we are reminded of the distinct and uncorrelated nature of these super-issues; knowing a nation's position on one dimension provides no information by which we can predict its position on another. Because no two of these issue-dimensions or issue-areas[16] together account for more than 40 per cent of all members' voting variance, we must reject one- or two-dimensional representations as *general* interpretations of group voting, for which we used the Q-analysis approach instead. Nevertheless we return to the point raised by Lijphart and Rieselbach: for many purposes we want to distinguish behavior on one super-issue from that on another, and to see how voting on a particular issue-dimension is related to other behavioral or environmental influences.

One procedure has been to compute countries' factor scores on each of the major factors or super-issues from the R-analysis, and then to correlate those factor scores with caucusing or other group memberships and with ecological variables such as national per capita income, foreign aid receipts, or racial composition.[17] The factor score summarizes a nation's voting behavior, especially on those roll-calls which load heavily on the factor in question. It is computed according to an equation which weights each roll-call roughly according to its correlation with the factor, so that the roll-calls which are best accounted for by the factor make the

15 See Table 2 in Alker, *op. cit.*
16 Cf. James Rosenau, "The Functioning of International Systems," *Background,* 7, 3, (1963), 111–117, for an illuminating discussion of issue-areas in national politics.
17 As was done in Alker, *op. cit.,* and Alker and Russett, *op. cit.*

Discovering Voting Groups in the United Nations

greatest contribution to the factor score. Thus a country which voted affirmatively (coded as two) on virtually all successful roll-calls that loaded heavily on, say, the cold-war factor would have a high factor score and a state regularly voting negatively (coded zero) would have a very low one. Because the original factors are uncorrelated with each other the consequent factor scores will also be uncorrelated. These factor scores, serving as summary indices of national behavior on the major super-issues before the Assembly, can then be correlated with national factor loadings from the Q-analysis. Thus we can discover the basic issue-dimensions which distinguish our inductively identified "groupings" of countries. Table 2 gives the correlation of nations' factor scores on each of the three important super-issues (cold war, southern Africa, and supranationalism) with their factor loadings on each of the six factors from the Q-analysis.

From this we can quickly obtain a thumbnail sketch to characterize the behavior of each inductively derived "group" of countries. The Afro-Asians, for example, are pro-Soviet on cold-war issues, or at least they share with the Soviets an opposition to Western use of the UN for cold-war purposes, and are quite anti-colonial about the problems of southern Africa.[18] But they generally favor initiatives, such as those concerning the role of ONUC in the Congo and expanding the Security Council and ECOSOC, which comprise the "supranationalism" dimension and which the Soviet Union vigorously opposed in 1963. It is on these issues that they oppose the Communists and on which Yugoslavia (rather favorable to strengthening the UN in these contexts) is distinguishable from the other Communist states of Eastern Europe. Similarly, the Brazzaville countries more or less share the Afro-Asians' position on southern Africa and supranationalism but are fairly pro-Western on cold-war questions, The Western Community countries generally vote in favor of those supranationalist initiatives that actually come to a roll call, and while moderately unsympathetic with the Assembly's basic position on intervention in Africa are nowhere nearly as isolated as are the lonely Iberians.

It is tempting to refer to some of our groups by more explicitly political labels. The "Brazzaville Africans," for instance, are not well named since they include Latin Americans, Asians, and other Africans as well. Possibly one might want to call them simply "pro-Western underdeveloped states." But we must ascetically refrain from plucking that apple. A word like "pro-Western" demands a unidimensional set of issues which does not exist. Each group's substantive position can be

---

[18] The fact that the Afro-Asians correlate more highly than do the Communists with the "cold-war" factor indicates that the latter is a slightly misleading label. There are some roll-call votes, such as those about the role of the UN in reunifying and rehabilitating Korea or establishing a fact-finding commission for the peaceful settlement of disputes, which have substantial "supranational" loadings and overtones. On these votes the Afro-Asians and Communists often part company, at least to the degree of an abstention. Putting a descriptive label on a factor is always a somewhat tentative exercise, which is why I have here enclosed the labels in quotation marks.

International Cooperation

National Groupings	"Cold War"	"Intervention in Africa"	"Supra-nationalism"
"Western Community"	.79	−.33	.38
"Brazzaville Africans"	.47	.45	.36
"Afro-Asians"	−.82	.43	.17
"Communists"	−.56	.45	−.64
"Conservative Arabs"	.11	.26	.16
"Iberia"	.10	−.74	−.06

spotted only with reference to all *three* of the major issue-dimensions. Imagine a cube defined by three axes—left to right: cold war, with the "West" at the left and the Communists on the right; vertical: intervention in Africa, with the colonial powers at the top and the ex-colonies at the bottom; depth: supranationalism, with those favoring a stronger UN at the front and their opponents behind. These three axes can be thought of as dividing the whole cube into eight subcubes, and each of the major groups falls into a different subcube. The Western Community states belong in the upper left front cube, and the Communists are more or less polar opposites in the lower right rear segment. But the other two groups do *not* fall between the two poles; rather they are off to one side or the other of the shortest-distance-between-two-points lines. The Afro-Asians are lower right but front, and the Brazzaville nations lower front but left. Such a picture implies a multipolar pattern of cross-pressures and shifting coalitions that can mitigate international conflict.

In describing the correlations of the issue factor scores with the "grouping" loadings we of course are only ascertaining the typical voting positions of a group, especially those countries loading heavily on the R-factor. Any individual member may differ from the group pattern, as for example the United States is more "supranationalist" than are most states with equally high loadings on the Western Community factor. Except for establishing very general limits from the group, the behavior of a particular country can be determined only by a check of its own factor scores.

IV. Voting Groups and General Assembly Politics

In the Q-analysis we found that an inductive procedure identified six factors, and through them seven voting groups, in the Assembly. The six factors together accounted for 73 per cent of all the countries' variance. Thus the political process is relatively structured and subject to description by a small number of alignments. Yet the groups resembled only to a limited degree those which would be discovered from a list of geographi-

Discovering Voting Groups in the United Nations

cal or caucusing groups alone. While geographical labels have sometimes been used they are very approximate and neither inclusive nor exclusive (e.g., "Brazzaville Africans"). Of our inductively-derived groups only the "Communists" closely resembled a caucusing group in terms both of who was included and who excluded.

In contrast to the mere evidence of caucusing groups the Q-analysis reveals other politically based groupings as follows:

1. The members of the Scandinavian caucusing group do indeed agree almost entirely among themselves in this Session, but Ireland and Austria differ from them in no significant way.

2. Analysis of the Latin American caucusing group would find a moderate element of cohesion, but entirely miss the very high similarity of Israel and several pro-Western Asians to the Latin voting pattern.

3. If the examination were based on caucusing groups extant in 1963, it would also not uncover the great consensus remaining within the officially disbanded Brazzaville and Casablanca groups.

4. The convergence of interest among the North Atlantic countries would not be found by examining any formal caucusing group.

The use of an inductive procedure also permits us to make some more general statements about politics in the Assembly. A simplified East-West-Neutral categorization which has characterized so much journalistic and even scholarly analysis of the world organization is utterly misleading. In terms of the states' behavior, five major groups (on four factors) emerge, in addition to two small groups and a few marginal countries. It should be emphasized that the identification of these groups depends upon their final behavior in the vote, not upon tacit or explicit bargaining among diverse log-rolling coalitions which may exchange promises of support before the vote. It might be supposed, for instance, that one set of countries might offer its support to another set on cold-war issues, in response to the other's votes on a self-determination roll-call. While this kind of bargaining undoubtedly does occur, an analysis of voting patterns alone would not find it since both sets of countries would *vote* identically, whatever their reasons for doing so. But a number of groups in the General Assembly retain their distinctiveness in the actual balloting. Two or more groups must combine to make a majority, and majorities on each of the different super-issues are composed differently. Comparisons with politics within national parliamentary assemblies may provide many fruitful insights and hypotheses, but the multiparty pattern of shifting coalitions that was approximated in the French Third and Fourth Republic may provide a closer analogy than will the aggregation of multiple interests within two stable parties as in Britain or even the United States.

Finally, there is reason to believe that this multi-group phenomenon is not especially new. It existed both before the well-known conflicts within NATO and the Communist countries became evident, and largely before the admission of most of the new states. I conducted a similar Q-analysis of voters in the 1952 and 1957 Sessions, to be reported upon

310

more fully elsewhere.[19] By the same criteria employed here the 1952 analysis found four groups, and the 1957 analysis uncovered eight, though four were quite small. Therefore the discovery of but five large groups and two small ones in 1963 comes as something of a surprise, especially since the 1952 and 1957 analyses were performed on only 57 and 81 countries respectively. The expansion of Assembly membership (to 107 for purposes of this analysis) has in fact outpaced the differentiation of new voting groups. Nor has their composition altered radically. Except for the emergence of the "Brazzaville" group and a certain greater differentiation between most other Afro-Asians and a somewhat pro-Western minority, the changes over the three Sessions have not been great. Recent discoveries of a complex pattern of relationships in the General Assembly not only identify new reality but also show some lag between reality and our perception of it.

[19] Bruce M. Russett, *International Regions and the International System* (Chicago: Rand McNally, 1967).

Discovering Voting Groups in the United Nations

System and

Process in the

Labor

International

Organization:

A Statistical Afterthought

C H A P T E R   S E V E N T E E N

Ernst B. Haas

Reprinted with the permission of the editors from *World Politics*, Vol. 14 (January, 1962), 322–52. Mr. Haas is Professor of Political Science at the University of California at Berkeley.

It is perhaps surprising that statistical efforts to study political systems have been so slow in making an appearance in the field of international organization. Since the tedium of counting can easily enough be overcome by an externally financed and judicious delegation of authority, even this obstacle should not longer be serious. A more vital question involves the legitimate use to which such statistical exercises might be put. Certainly, counting for the sake of accumulating numerical aggregates, with or without sophisticated manipulation, is a useless enterprise; it can be justified only if the work contributes clarity of demonstration and economy of effort, not otherwise attainable, to an intellectual problem. Even though I shall present some counting techniques applied in a study of the International Labor Organization (ILO) and shall seek to justify their use on this basis, I am by no means convinced that statistical devices found appropriate in other social science contexts should be imitated slavishly in the study of international organization. Roll-call voting studies are admirable devices for determining the waxing and waning of bloc cohesion; but if we are trying to predict the policy position of a state in an international organization, it is far less certain that the Guttman Scale contributes either economy of effort or clarity of demonstration that cannot be obtained by conventional means.[1] The purpose of this article is the demonstration of what may be useful techniques. It is not my aim to extract all possible conclusions from the illustrative data, or to write a full analysis of the ILO.

I. The Environment of International Systems

One strong argument for a judicious amount of quantification in the study of international organizations stems from the increasing use of systems

Without the devoted statistical assistance of Kurt Vogel and Hildegarde Haas the completion of this article would have been impossible. I am also indebted to the Rockefeller Foundation, the Social Science Research Council, and the Institute of International Studies of the University of California (Berkeley) for financial assistance at various times, and to Herbert McClosky for criticism and advice.

[1] See the pioneering article by Leroy N. Rieselbach, "Quantitative Techniques for Studying Voting Behavior in the UN General Assembly," *International Organization*, XIV (Spring 1960), pp. 291–306. The author makes a very convincing case for the use of the Rice Index of Cohesion and a less plausible one for the Guttman Scale, since the predictive possibilities of scalar regularities are so limited as to make unprofitable the burden of establishing them. For other applications of a modified Rice Scale, see my *Consensus Formation in the Council of Europe*, Berkeley, Calif., 1960; and Ernst B. Haas and Peter H. Merkl, "Parliamentarians Against Ministers: The Case of WEU," *International Organization*, XIV (Winter 1960), pp. 37–59.

System and Process in the International Labor Organization

theory. Whether we favor the analytical use of purely heuristic types of systems or the more earthbound variety associated with historical sociology, the fact remains that incisive treatment demands the operational definition of boundaries. Systems that are coterminous with the sum total of international phenomena are merely a further contribution to obfuscation; hence the understandable concern of systems theorists with boundary-maintenance, even at the cost of reifying the system. In any event, a meaningful system also presupposes an "environment."[2] This notion has been responsible for a great deal of difficulty in delineation; however, without an attempt at spelling out the setting in which a given international organization must function, theorizing about the "system" represented by a given organization or group of organizations must remain vague.

It may well be argued, for example, that the ILO represents a system in which governments, employers, and workers—each forming an international sub-system with great functional specificity—influence one another in a regular fashion so as to "put out" a body of norms, the international labor conventions and recommendations. Now it would be most tempting to develop a systemic theory of international social legislation on this basis, but such a temptation must be resolutely resisted unless we specify the social and economic setting in which the actors conduct themselves. This is the purpose of specifying the "environment" in which international labor conventions originate, as shown in Table 1. The table was compiled by determining from the records of each International Labor Conference the identity of the states represented and assigning to each state a characterization on the basis of standard political and economic information available.

The headings referring to location and political alignment are self-explanatory, but the remainder of the categories are not. "Democracy" is considered to be the applicable political characterization of a state if there are agreed and regularly observed rules for peaceful change, if voluntary participation in politics on the basis of associational interest groups prevails, if free choice among two or more political parties is possible, and the rule of law is observed. A state is considered an "oligarchy" if there are no regularly observed rules of peaceful change, continuous participation in politics is limited to a small group of literate and/or wealthy citizens, the political scene is dominated by such institutional interest groups as the army, church, or bureaucracy, and if there is no consistent and reliable rule of law. Examples of oligarchical government are provided by contemporary Nicaragua, Peru, Thailand, and Morocco. States are characterized as "totalitarian," finally, if political leadership is monopolized by one group or party, peaceful change is possi-

---

[2] See David Easton, "An Approach to the Analysis of Political Systems," *World Politics*, IX (April 1957), pp. 383–400; Charles McClelland, "Systems and History in International Relations: Some Perspectives for Empirical Research and Theory," *General Systems Yearbook*, III (1958), pp. 222–34; and McClelland, "The Function of Theory in International Relations," mimeographed paper prepared for the Symposium on the Place of Theory in the Conduct and Study of International Relations, University of Michigan, Ann Arbor, May 1960.

International Cooperation

TABLE 1 THE ENVIRONMENT OF INTERNATIONAL LABOR LEGISLATION AS MEASURED BY CHARACTERISTICS OF STATES PARTICIPATING IN SELECTED INTERNATIONAL LABOR CONFERENCES (IN PER CENT)

	States Participating in Conferences								
	1920	1925	1930	1935	1939	1945	1950	1955	1958
Location									
Europe	67	61	54	55	46	45	39	40	39
North America	4	2	2	4	4	5	5	3	3
Latin America	15	25	27	20	28	29	20	23	23
Australasia	4	2	4	4	4	5	5	3	3
Asia	10	7	9	12	13	10	27	24	21
Africa	0	3	4	5	5	6	4	7	11
Political System									
Democracy	70	55	46	39	42	57	64	55	51
Oligarchy	30	41	46	43	47	33	27	26	24
Totalitarian	0	4	8	18	11	10	10	19	25
Economic Development									
Mature Industrial	22	16	15	16	19	19	20	21	22
Rapidly industrializing	26	20	19	29	26	31	25	26	24
Mature agricultural	22	18	17	12	14	12	11	10	7
Underdeveloped	30	46	49	43	41	38	44	43	47
Economic Institutions									
Free enterprise	81	82	81	63	63	48	41	48	51
Social welfare	19	11	13	27	35	40	50	35	31
Communist	0	0	0	0	0	2	0	11	14
Corporatist	0	7	6	10	2	10	10	6	4
Political Alignment									
West				22	33		73	63	64
Totalitarian				14	5		0	10	13
Neutral				64	62		27	27	23
Number of states participating	27	44	48	49	43	42	44	62	72

ble within that group alone and not within any other actual or potential groups, mass participation in politics is compulsory and without choice of program or party, and the rule of law exists only within the limits of loyalty to the party and its programs. Apart from the Communist states, contemporary Guinea, Cuba, and possibly the former United Arab Republic fall into this pattern.

A word of clarification must be added with respect to our "oligarchies." I have grouped together political systems on the basis of their prevailing structures *in action* and have ignored the more or less sincere declared intentions of their leaders. Edward Shils, by contrast, distinguishes "tutelary democracies," "modernizing oligarchies," "totalitarian oligarchies," and "traditional oligarchies."[3] On the basis of their actual

[3] As cited in Gabriel A. Almond and James S. Coleman (eds.), *The Politics of the Developing Areas,* Princeton, N.J., 1960, pp. 53–54. Shils's categories are applied to the classification of some fifty new nations by Coleman in *ibid.,* pp. 561–76. The apologies and caveats accompanying the classification convinced me that a less ambitious scheme which focuses on immediate structural features to the detriment of declared policy objectives is preferable for spelling out the environment of international

System and Process in the International Labor Organization

conduct, tutelary democracies are either real democracies (India) or approach totalitarianism (Ghana). Totalitarian obligarchies are merely totalitarian systems prevented by an imperfect technology or lack of social mobilization from approaching the Nazi or Soviet prototype, distinctly a short-run factor. While there is a real difference between a traditional and a modernizing oligarchy (e.g., Bolivia before and after the 1952 revolution), the difference resides mainly in the intentions of the oligarchs and not necessarily in the structure of politics; and intentions, as Latin America amply demonstrates, are subject to drastic change. Since we are concerned with establishing the political environment of International Labor Conferences at specific points in time, a purely structural classification is to be preferred.

In categorizing stages of economic development, the overwhelming influence of W. W. Rostow hardly requires acknowledgment.[4] A "mature industrialized state" is characterized by a high or medium per capita GNP, a continuing high rate of investment, a preponderance of manufacturing in the total economy, and high technological inventiveness and adaptability. Examples are furnished by the United States, the Soviet Union, France, and Japan. A "rapidly industrializing state" possesses a medium or low per capita GNP, a very high rate of investment, a marked tendency to create new manufacturing facilities and to de-emphasize agriculture relative to industry, a managerial and administrative eagerness to adopt new techniques, and the likelihood of just having reached or having nearly reached "take-off." Such conditions are found in Argentina, India, Australia, and South Africa. A "mature agricultural state" is characterized by a medium or high per capita GNP, a preponderance in the total economy of scientific and mechanized agriculture for export, high technological and managerial adaptability, and a rate of investment adequate to maintaining the position achieved. Such attributes may be found in Uruguay, Denmark, and New Zealand. An economy is "underdeveloped" if per capita GNP is low or stagnant at a medium level, if there is very little or no capital investment, if there is little managerial or technological capacity or interest in acquiring it, and if the agricultural and / or mining sector is predominant and marked by low capital input. Greece, Guinea, Haiti, Pakistan, and Peru exhibit these attributes.

Economic institutions are increasingly mixed, which makes the following categories more arbitrary than would be desirable if there were not such a crying need for some kind of typology. A "free enterprise economy" prevails if the government, directly or indirectly, does not

organizations. However, in the devising of typologies, the necessity for distinguishing between structural elements, seen at a fixed point in time, and dynamic political motivations among elites by no means negates the desirability of classifying motivations. While it would be tempting to argue that a certain quantity of "inputs" into ILO, deriving from strong social welfare and modernizing commitments on the part of political elites, results in an "output" of a specific type of international convention, the history of ILO and the record of the members in ratifying conventions fail to establish such a connection. See my subsequent discussion of "coverage."

[4] *The Stages of Economic Growth: A Non-Communist Manifesto,* Cambridge, Eng., 1960.

International Cooperation

participate consistently in the growth of the economy, if there is no general interest in extensive social legislation, and if businessmen and farmers are expected to adjust to market forces. Contemporary instances of this orientation may be found in Colombia, Honduras, Tunisia, Laos, and Japan. A "social welfare economy," however, prevails wherever the government seeks somehow to manipulate economic growth, where there is a general commitment to social legislation, and where businessmen and farmers are deliberately cushioned against certain market forces. This type of economic orientation includes the so-called "mixed economies" as well as systems, such as the American, that are free enterprise-oriented largely at the level of slogans. It would encompass, for instance, Belgium, Chile, Australia, India, and Mexico. A "Communist" economic system is characterized by the state's ownership and management of all major means of production, even if technically this be labeled "state capitalism." Finally, a "corporatist economy" prevails if business and labor groups, though permitted to exist, may influence economic life only through the medium of government-manipulated institutions, and if free market forces are not permitted unrestrained scope in order to realize some doctrine of social harmony. Such conditions now exist in Portugal and Viet Nam, and did so in the United Arab Republic, with Spain constituting a marginal case, perhaps closer to free enterprise.

The environmental changes documented in the case of ILO, considered as a system, would have to take a slightly different form if applied to other international organizations. In the case of FAO, a similar survey might include rubrics for a state's share in the international commodity market, the caloric intake of its citizens, per capita agricultural productivity. A UNESCO study might wish to tabulate literacy rates and the availability of primary school facilities per capita. A WHO "environment" would have to include the number of hospital beds, medical personnel, and inoculations per head of population.

Compared with some other current suggestions for classifying the international environment, the scheme here proposed possesses some virtues and drawbacks. One such scheme, proposed by Karl Deutsch, makes possible the construction for each country of a "profile" expressed in code numbers based on summarizing 75 categories.[5] One set of categories—the "measurement profile"—rates each country on the basis of factors relating to the degree of social mobilization and economic development. It is purely quantitative and calls for no evaluative judgment on the part of the student. It covers, in much greater detail, the same ground as my "economic development" category. A second set of categories— called "rating profiles"—does involve some qualitative judgment since it includes factors on the degree of political democracy, political stability,

5 Karl W. Deutsch, "Toward an Inventory of Basic Trends and Patterns in Comparative and International Politics," *American Political Science Review,* LIV (March 1960), esp. pp. 40–44. Measurement profile statistics for African, Asian, and Latin American countries can be found in Almond and Coleman, eds., *op. cit.,* pp. 579–82.

degree of Westernization, and social homogeneity. These rating profiles establish sub-categories for the larger rubrics included under my heading of "political system." Now the Deutsch typology is clearly superior to the one I used in working with ILO materials in the degree of detailed precision that it facilitates. It is also more cumbersome to manage and, in a sense, redundant, since it tabulates data that we already know to be predictably correlated. Some of the rating profile categories can be subsumed under one another and others are often irrelevant to a larger typological effort. Simplicity and economy, however, are the only major arguments that I can muster on behalf of my own procedure. The same kind of results could be achieved with Deutsch's technique, for his larger aim is applicable to the study of system and process in international organizations: "We are thus trying to form three sets of types: types of states (such as small Scandinavian democracies, or middle-sized Asian traditionalistic authoritarian regimes); types of situations (such as a severe business depression or a rapid growth of towns and industries); and a typical behavior when a typical state and a typical situation meet (such as increasing government intervention under constitutional auspices in Scandinavian countries during depression years, or increasing political instability in traditionalistic authoritarian governments under the impact of rapid industrialization."[6] Since, however, the present purpose is the correlation of this tripartite meeting of types with the systemic development of the ILO, certain categories can well be omitted and the whole procedure simplified without major loss of precision. Nor does the application of any such method obviate the eventual making of qualitative judgments by the student.

A slightly different approach dominates the typology employed by Coleman.[7] New nations are here classified with reference to testing Lipset's proposition that political competitiveness and economic development are positively correlated.[8] Concern with this proposition prompted the adoption of a threefold scheme for classifying political systems, using the terms "competitive," "semi-competitive," and "authoritarian" structures. While "competitive" approximates my definition of "democratic," the remaining terms beg more questions than they answer. Guinea, Panama, Mexico, Tunisia, and Thailand—for all their differences—emerge as semi-competitive political systems possessing a "mixed" degree of political modernity. No allowance is made for the difference between a totalitarian system and a mildly authoritarian one, such as is found in most oligarchies, modern and traditional. The usefulness of these categories is scarcely enhanced by their failure clearly to support or rebut Lipset's proposition; but their lack of precision makes them unsuitable for a description of the international environment.

6 Deutsch, *op. cit.,* p. 35.
7 Almond and Coleman, eds., *op. cit.,* concluding chapter entitled "The Political Systems of the Developing Areas," especially pp. 532–44.
8 Seymour M. Lipset, "Some Social Requisites of Democracy: Economic Development and Political Legitimacy," *American Political Science Review,* LIII (March 1959), pp. 69–105.

International Cooperation

Provisionally, then, the interest of both economy and clarity seems adequately served by the eleven categories I employed. Indeed, their major virtue is the possibility of applying them to countries of which we have relatively little empirical knowledge—too little for profound and comprehensive classifications of all structural and functional attributes, but enough for purposes of placing them in a systematic pattern relating to international organizations.

II. The Concept of "Coverage"

One of the chief claims of functional international organizations is their asserted impact on economic and social standards in member states. Technical assistance, of course, occupies the chief operational role here. But the use of multipartite conventions as a method for setting universally applicable standards remains a weapon in the armory of international organizations. This is especially interesting for studies of international integration because it facilitates quantitative assessments of the degree of success achieved. Naturally, this technique tells us nothing of the far more important problems involved in the actual implementation of such conventions; but at least it affords a ready tool for counting and classifying the declared willingness of governments to apply universal standards of welfare to their citizens.

The concept of "coverage" is a statistical device for arriving at conclusions as to what kinds of political and economic systems show an interest in adopting international conventions. The "coverage" of a given kind of convention is computed by counting the *actual* ratifications and stating them as a percentage of *possible* ratifications for all member states in each category of political system, economic development, and economic institutions used in the discussion of the "environment." The situation in the field of international labor conventions, in 1960, is presented on Tables 2a-2e.

The very unequal incidence of the conventions jumps to the eye. One of the useful features of the coverage concept is its ability to lend precision to general statements made by the ILO on behalf of its standard-setting activities. One recent official claim asserts: "Up to 1 October 1959, 77 States had deposited 1,925 ratifications. As was to be expected, there are great variations in the number of ratifications received from the various countries....What is perhaps more surprising is the relatively high proportion of ratifications by countries outside Europe.... These figures tend to indicate that ILO standards are considered useful and applicable by many countries in the earlier stages of economic and social development."[9] This is precisely what the figures do *not* show when presented within the confines of the concept of coverage. What they tend to show is that some countries that are rapidly industrializing are

[9] International Labour Office, *International Labour Standards*, Geneva, 1960, pp. 12–13.

TABLES 2A-2C   COVERAGE OF ILO CONVENTION IN 1960

COVERAGE: The relation of actual ratifications to possible ratifications of ILO Conventions for all member states belonging to specific political and economic categories, expressed in per cent. The computation excludes conventions not yet in force.

D—Democracy	OI—Mature industrial state	CM—Communist economy
O—Oligarchy	RI—Rapidly industrializing	CP—Corporatist economy
T—Totalitarianism	MA—Mature agricultural	
	U—Underdeveloped	
	FE—Free enterprise economy	
	S—Social welfare economy	

TABLE 2A   COVERAGE OF SELECTED ILO CONVENTIONS

		Political System			Economic Development					Economic Institutions			
	Total	D	O	T	OI	RI	MA	U	FE	S	CM	CP	Important non-ratifying states
Category of convention COVERAGE	83	37	25	21	16	18	6	43	41	27	12	3	
Administration of labor legislation (26, 34, 63, 81, 94, 95, 99)	30	42	15	27	37	41	36	22	22	47	25	33	Rat. less than 3 conv.: Canada, China, India, Japan, US, USSR
Occupational hazards (13, 62)	28	36	14	33	37	41	33	17	13	37	46	16	Canada, China, India, Japan, UK, US, USSR

Freedom of association (11, 87, 98)	55	66	33	63	70	70	72	41	39	69	91	33	Canada, India, US
Underground work, women (45)	61	73	44	67	69	83	50	54	59	77	50	67	Bolivia, Canada, Ukraine, US, USSR
Anti-discrimination (100, 111)	27	26	16	43	25	44	25	20	16	30	50	50	Canada, Japan, Netherlands, Sweden, Switzerland, US, USSR
Social security (2, 3, 12, 17, 18, 19, 24, 25, 35, 36, 37, 38, 39, 40, 42, 44, 48, 102, 103)	22	29	10	76	33	36	28	12	13	34	33	15	Rat. less than 9 conv.: Brazil, Canada, China, India, Japan, US, USSR
Minimum age protection of young (5, 6, 10, 33, 59, 60, 77, 78, 79, 90)	25	26	12	37	35	39	40	15	14	30	54	10	Rat. less than 4 conv.: Belgium, Brazil, Canada, China, France, Germany, India, Japan, Sweden, UK, US. Not rat. conv. 29: Bolivia, China, Ethiopia, Guatemala, Panama, Paraguay, S. Africa, US
Forced labor (29, 105)	56	64	44	59	59	67	50	52	46	71	58	83	Not rat. conv. 105: Belgium, Bolivia, Brazil, Czech., Ecuador, Ethiopia, France, Hungary, India, Japan, Liberia, Panama, Paraguay, Peru, Rumania, Spain, US, USSR
Hours and vacations (1, 4, 14, 20, 30, 41, 47, 52, 67, 89, 101, 106)	24	27	15	29	21	35	30	20	17	30	32	39	Rat. less than 5 conv.: Brazil, Canada, China, Germany, India, Japan, UK, US, USSR

TABLE 2B COVERAGE OF CONVENTIONS DEALING WITH NON-METROPOLITAN TERRITORIES

	Total	NUMBER OF MEMBER STATES WITH NON-METROPOLITAN TERRITORIES											
		D	*O*	*T*	*OI*	*RI*	*MA*	*U*	*FE*	*S*	*CM*	*CP*	
	12	9	0	3	5	3	2	2	2	9	0	1	
		COVERAGE											*Important non-ratifying states*
Non-metropolitan territories, etc. (50, 64, 65, 82, 84, 85, 104)	24*	35	—	5	43	5	43	7	0	35	—	14	Rat. less than 4 conv.: Australia, Denmark, France, Italy, Netherlands, Portugal, S. Africa, Spain, US

* Excluding 15 ratifications by member states having no responsibility for indigenous populations in the "non-metropolitan territory" sense.

TABLE 2C COVERAGE OF MARITIME CONVENTIONS

	Total	NUMBER OF MEMBER STATES WITH A MERCHANT MARINE											
		D	*O*	*T*	*OI*	*RI*	*MA*	*U*	*FE*	*S*	*CM*	*CP*	
	50	33	7	10	11	17	5	17	21	23	4	2	
		COVERAGE											*Important non-ratifying states*
Maritime conventions (7, 8, 9, 15, 16, 22, 23, 27, 32, 53, 54, 55, 56, 57, 58, 68, 69, 72, 73, 74, 76, 92, 93, 108)	29*	34	8	28	44	32	34	14	20	35	43	13	Rat. less than 9 conv.: Canada, Colombia, Germany, Greece, Honduras, India, Indonesia, Japan, Liberia, Panama, Philippines, Portugal, Spain, Sweden, US, USSR

* Excluding 72 ratifications by member states having no or negligible merchant marines, according to *UN Statistical Yearbook*, 1959, p. 338.

| | NUMBER OF MEMBER STATES EMPLOYING TRIBAL AND PLANTATION LABOR | | | | |
	Total	Africa	Latin America	Asia	Colonial Powers
	57	11	19	16	11
			COVERAGE		
Tribal and plantation labor (107, 110)	15	14	24	6	5

TABLE 2E   DISTRIBUTION OF COVERAGE CHARACTERISTICS AMONG ILO MEMBER STATES, 1960

| Characteristics | Member States | |
	Number	Per Cent
Oligarchy, underdeveloped, free enterprise	23	27.7
Democracy, old industrialized, social welfare	10	12.0
Democracy, underdeveloped, free enterprise	8	9.6
Democracy, rapidly industrializing, social welfare	7	8.4
Totalitarian, new industrialized, Communist	6	7.2
Democracy, mature agricultural, social welfare	5	6.0
Totalitarian, old industrialized, Communist	4	4.8
Totalitarian, underdeveloped, social welfare	3	3.6
Democracy, rapidly industrializing, free enterprise	3	3.6
Totalitarian, underdeveloped, corporatist	3	3.6
Totalitarian, underdeveloped, free enterprise	2	2.4
Totalitarian, underdeveloped, Communist	2	2.4
Democracy, underdeveloped, social welfare	2	2.4
Democracy, old industrialized, free enterprise	2	2.4
Oligarchy, rapidly industrializing, free enterprise	1	1.3
Totalitarian, rapidly industrializing, free enterprise	1	1.3
Oligarchy, underdeveloped, social welfare	1	1.3
Total	83	100.0
Underdeveloped, free enterprise	32	74.4
Underdeveloped, social welfare	6	14.0
Underdeveloped, Communist	2	4.6
Underdeveloped, corporatist	3	7.0
Total	43	100.0
Democracy, free enterprise	13	35.0
Democracy, social welfare	24	65.0
Total	37	100.0
Rapidly industrializing, free enterprise	5	27.8
Rapidly industrializing, social welfare	7	38.9
Rapidly industrializing, Communist	6	33.3
Total	18	100.0

interested in the International Labor Code. But the bulk of under-developed countries, especially if they are also free enterprise-oriented, display no such fervor. Among the many points giving rise to comment about the possibility of refining gross claims on ratifications, let us single out just one more. Communist-totalitarian countries show excellent coverage for the conventions in the field of human and trade union rights. What is known about their practices in this field—as, indeed,

System and Process in the International Labor Organization

revealed by another aspect of ILO activity—plainly demonstrates the caution with which aggregate ratification statistics have to be treated if they are to be used as an index of international integration.

Coverage, as a refinement in the study of the impact of international conventions, also has an economic dimension. In the words of another official ILO statement: "The international minimum standards that the Code provides...cannot be imposed upon the world. But so wide has been their acceptance that upon the Code has been constructed a vast international network of binding mutual obligations among countries.... [Even though a variety of factors has prevented the even and general ratification of conventions] nevertheless, the Code has achieved a notable measure of success in improving working and living standards in many countries. In doing so, it has been effective in achieving one of the ILO's principal original aims—that of preventing cut-throat competition among countries at the expense of living standards. For an examination of the record of ratifications will show that there is a tendency for competing countries to ratify the same Conventions. Thus social standards in rival countries tend to be equalized, to the benefit both of the workers and the employers."[10] This is the old argument that international labor conventions tend to equalize conditions of competition

TABLE 3   REGIONAL INCIDENCE OF ILO CONVENTIONS

Category of Convention	OAS	EEC	EFTA	NATO	Arab League
Occupational hazards (13, 62)	24	67	29	33	19
Freedom of association (11, 87, 98)	48	89	76	75	37
Anti-discrimination (100, 111)	29	33	43	33	25
Social security (2, 3, 12, 17, 18, 19, 24, 25, 35, 36, 37, 38, 39, 40, 42, 44, 48, 102, 103)	21	51	37	33	13
Hours and vacations (1, 4, 14, 20, 30, 41, 47, 52, 67, 89, 101, 106)	24	31	24	22	14
Administration of labor legislation (26, 34, 63, 81, 94, 95, 99)	29	57	49	41	14
Minimum age and protection of the young (5, 6, 10, 33, 59, 60, 77, 78, 79, 90)	25	55	23	29	5

(The figures show the relation of actual ratifications to possible ratifications for all the members of a given regional organization, expressed in per cent.)

10 International Labour Office, *Lasting Peace the ILO Way,* Geneva, 1951, pp. 60–62.

International Cooperation

among industrialized countries as well as among developing and mature economies, thus permitting progress without damage to labor welfare. The ratification statistics simply do *not* bear out this conclusion. Differences in coverage between mature and underdeveloped countries are obvious. What is more important, however, is the highly *uneven* incidence of conventions in specific fields among the countries most concerned in terms of their economic structure.

A final virtue of the coverage concept may be stressed. It is sometimes argued that economic and political integration among sovereign states proceeds most smoothly when their populations enjoy essentially similar social benefits—i.e., when a substantial measure of identity in economic infrastructure already exists. Table 3 provides the coverage statistics for five contemporary regional groupings. If there is any merit in the argument stressing pre-existing uniformity, the coverage concept permits a measure of projection with respect to the chances of achieving fuller integration in these regions.[11]

III. National Solidarity and the Logic of Pluralism

The claim of the ILO to uniqueness in the array of modern international organizations rests on its tripartite structure; ILO is not merely another intergovernmental agency but provides for the full voting participation of representatives of national trade unions and employer organizations alongside the spokesmen of their governments. In theory, at least, these interest-group representatives are selected irrespective of their support of the national government, on the basis of the "most representative organization" formula. If the theory corresponds to the facts, the logic of pluralism—at least as it operates in industrialized countries permitting freedom of association—may be expected to work itself out in such a way that union and employer representatives carry over into the international arena their claims against the national government. In doing so they would weaken the appeal of the national state as the exclusive font of loyalty, as the high altar from which alone the indulgences of economic advantage are dispensed. On the other hand, if cohesion among the delegates of a given nation tends to prevail, the international forum merely provides another opportunity for the clamor of rival claims to be heard, with the nation-state continuing to be the only analytically legitimate criterion of classification. Table 4 presents the statistics for making a judgment on this issue.

National delegations to International Labor Conferences consist of four individuals: two representatives of the government, and one each for the major trade union and the major employer association. An index labeled "percentage of dissent" was constructed by using all roll-call votes taken between 1919 and 1958 at the first forty-two sessions

[11] For an elaboration of this argument and other statistical means for dealing with it, see Deutsch, *op. cit.*, pp. 46–48.

System and Process in the International Labor Organization

TABLE 4 COHESION OF NATIONAL DELEGATIONS IN THE INTERNATIONAL LABOR CONFERENCE, 1919–1958

	Country	Per Cent of Dissent 1919–29	Per Cent of Dissent 1930–44	Per Cent of Dissent 1945–58
Employers	Afghanistan	—	0	0
Labor		—	0	0
Employers	Albania	0	0	0
Labor		0	0	0
Employers	Argentina	25	12.3	18.4
Labor		12	21.5	6.4
Employers	Australia	15.9	32.1	46.2
Labor		36.4	12.5	21.5
Employers	Austria	23.8	24.8	58.3
Labor		20	27.8	20.8
Employers	Belgium	45.4	66.7	55.8
Labor		16.9	17.9	11
Employers	Bolivia	—	0	0
Labor		—	0	0
Employers	Brazil	3.1	33.3	20.2
Labor		7.1	11.8	15.6
Employers	Bulgaria	24.5	29	0
Labor		9.2	5.8	1.4
Employers	Burma	—	—	34.5
Labor		—	—	5.2
Employers	Byelorussia	—	—	0
Labor		—	—	0
Employers	Canada	38.7	46.4	49.3
Labor		24.4	20.2	22.5
Employers	Ceylon	—	—	53.8
Labor		—	—	12.8
Employers	Chile	0.8	2.9	19.3
Labor		4.1	4.9	14.7
Employers	China	1.5	33.7	35.6
Labor		1.5	9.5	7.9
Employers	Colombia	0	0	9.3
Labor		0	0	8
Employers	Costa Rica	—	0	33.6
Labor		—	0	0
Employers	Cuba	19.1	15.1	26.9
Labor		12.4	10.1	8.4
Employers	Czechoslovakia	34.5	45.6	0
Labor		10.3	7.9	1
Employers	Denmark	44.9	71.3	55.2
Labor		16.1	6.1	19
Employers	Dominican Republic	0	0	13.9
Labor		0	0	8.9
Employers	Ecuador	0	0	0
Labor		0	0	1.8
Employers	Egypt	—	0	18.5
Labor		—	0	4.3
Employers	El Salvador	0	—	25
Labor		0	—	9.1
Employers	Esthonia	30.2	21.3	—
Labor		11.4	47.5	—
Employers	Ethiopia	—	0	—
Labor		—	0	—
Employers	Finland	29.4	39.1	71.9
Labor		15.6	36.5	11.4
Employers	France	40.1	46.2	52.3
Labor		13.8	13.2	11.7
Employers	Germany	40.5	24.2	36.3
Labor		13.8	36.4	21.3
Employers	Ghana	—	—	50
Labor		—	—	16.7
Employers	Gt. Britain	24	29.2	52.9
Labor		32.6	50	20.7
Employers	Greece	28.1	30	40.9
Labor		14.1	17.1	18.2
Employers	Guatemala	2.8	0	3.5
Labor		2.8	0	7
Employers	Haiti	0	0	0
Labor		0	0	1.9
Employers	Honduras	—	—	4.2
Labor		—	—	0
Employers	Hungary	7.8	16	5.7
Labor		21.8	30	1.9
Employers	Iceland	—	—	13.9
Labor		—	—	2.8
Employers	India	20.6	8.5	34.7
Labor		40.2	74.6	10.5
Employers	Indonesia	—	—	23.8
Labor		—	—	3.2
Employers	Iran	0	0	47.8
Labor		0	0	23.9
Employers	Iraq	—	—	14.9
Labor		—	—	6
Employers	Ireland	23.2	43.1	51.9
Labor		16.1	24.1	14.8

TABLE 4 (*Continued*)

	Country	Per Cent of Dissent 1919–29	1930–44	1945–58
Employers	Israel	—	—	45
Labor		—	—	8.8
Employers	Italy	23.9	11.4	44.4
Labor		7.7	4.3	10.5
Employers	Japan	25.5	7.5	42
Labor		36.4	62.1	37.7
Employers	Jordan	—	—	0
Labor		—	—	0
Employers	Latvia	44.9	22.8	—
Labor		4.5	6.3	—
Employers	Lebanon	—	—	21.9
Labor		—	—	9.4
Employers	Liberia	9.1	0	32.9
Labor		0	0	15.7
Employers	Libya	—	—	12.2
Labor		—	—	8.2
Employers	Lithuania	0	4.7	—
Labor		0	0	—
Employers	Luxembourg	5	51	50
Labor		20	16.7	6.4
Employers	Malaya	—	—	66.7
Labor		—	—	33.3
Employers	Mexico	—	35.5	20
Labor		—	2.1	3.5
Employers	Morocco	—	—	19.4
Labor		—	—	13.9

	Country	Per Cent of Dissent 1919–29	1930–44	1945–58
Employers	Netherlands	26.1	39.1	50
Labor		15.2	40.5	19.2
Employers	New Zealand	—	76.1	52.9
Labor		—	13	17.6
Employers	Nicaragua	0	0	—
Labor		0	0	—
Employers	Norway	14.3	57.4	57.4
Labor		14.3	1.7	12.3
Employers	Pakistan	—	—	34.6
Labor		—	—	17.3
Employers	Panama	0	0	4
Labor		0	0	6
Employers	Paraguay	0	—	—
Labor		0	—	—
Employers	Peru	9.7	0	10.3
Labor		6.5	0	2.8
Employers	Philippines	—	—	8.7
Labor		—	—	7.6
Employers	Poland	35.1	43.6	4.7
Labor		13.7	24.5	1.6
Employers	Portugal	14.8	14.9	32.3
Labor		20.4	31.9	16.2
Employers	Rumania	15	11.3	0
Labor		7.1	22.5	0
Employers	S. Africa	22.6	36	25.6
Labor		25.8	28	25.6

	Country	Per Cent of Dissent 1919–29	1930–44	1945–58
Employers	Spain	37.6	42.1	30.4
Labor		18	6.1	15.2
Employers	Sudan	—	—	8.7
Labor		—	—	8.7
Employers	Sweden	50.8	52.4	66.9
Labor		17	15.2	10.2
Employers	Switzerland	25.6	35	49.4
Labor		34.4	47	30.3
Employers	Syria	—	—	12
Labor		—	—	0
Employers	Thailand	0	0	20.5
Labor		0	0	0
Employers	Tunisia	—	—	27.9
Labor		—	—	16.3
Employers	Turkey	—	0	29.5
Labor		—	0	5.4
Employers	Ukraine	—	—	1.6
Labor		—	—	1.6
Employers	Uruguay	0	0	39.4
Labor		7.9	4.2	11.7
Employers	Venezuela	4.5	7.9	37.3
Labor		2.2	0	6.8
Employers	Viet Nam	—	—	24.6
Labor		—	—	8.7
Employers	Yugoslavia	26.9	28.7	2.1
Labor		18.7	31	1

of the International Labor Conference. Our "sample" was then made up of the entire "population" of 416 votes, "record votes" that permitted the identification of the voter. For each country the total number of votes was counted in which government delegates participated, excluding the few occasions on which the two government delegates opposed one another. Then the number of instances was counted in which labor and/or employer delegates from the same country voted differently from the government representatives Abstentions by interest-group delegates were counted as dissenting votes whenever the government representatives did not abstain; conversely, affirmative or negative votes by the interest-group delegates were counted as dissenting whenever the government abstained. Total disagreement with the government yields a figure of 100 per cent; total agreement results in a score of 0 per cent. The same technique may be used for judging the influence of a given state in intergovernmental organizations of the standard variety.[12]

Broadly speaking, Table 4 furnishes data which give substance to the claim of the ILO that workers and employers act in the capacity of representatives of their groups at home and not as yes-men for their governments. This trend is most obvious in the older industrialized countries with traditions of voluntary group organization of a functionally specific character. But it is curious that the figures for such countries as Australia, Austria, Canada, Finland, Yugoslavia, Latvia, Ireland, and Greece indicate that group dissent was the rule *before* industrialization was fully established. A feeling of group autonomy clearly antedates the realization of the modal type of democratic industrial society. On the other hand, the figures for most of the Latin American countries show no such autonomy until the most recent period. Compared with voting patterns in non-industrial countries that gained their independence since 1945, this Latin American pattern is curiously oligarchical. Ghana, Pakistan, and Ceylon are hardly more industrialized and modern than El Salvador and Costa Rica, yet they show vigorous group dissent. The degree of industrialization thus does not seem to be the chief factor associated with the growth of pluralist self-consciousness at the international level.

Nor is the degree of repressiveness of the national government a certain criterion for predicting the independence of interest group representatives. While the voting pattern in the Soviet orbit is eloquently simple, Spain, Portugal, the Dominican Republic, Poland under the regime of the colonels, Japan during the 1930's, and even Fascist Italy show surprising amounts of dissent. Granting that these dissenting votes may have been symbolic demonstrations of opposition rather than genuine measures for influencing national social legislation, they indicate that the character of the political system at home (except in the Communist case) *cannot* be used as a factor for specifying the degree of national

12 See Robert E. Riggs, *Politics in the United Nations*, Urbana, Ill., 1958; Thomas Hovet, Jr., *Bloc Politics in the United Nations*, Cambridge, Mass., 1960.

International Cooperation

unity in international meetings. The only major positive virtue of this technique of counting, therefore, is the verification of the ILO's claim to having undermined the unity of national delegations. However, whether the implied growth of pluralism at the international level brings with it consequences transforming the national state and making for international integration is a question that cannot be dealt with on the basis of this technique.

IV. International Solidarity and the Logic of Pluralism

We can, however, measure the cohesion of the organized international groups in the International Labor Conference as well as the solidarity diplayed by unorganized clusters of delegates within them. Together with the measure of national disintegration discussed above, the reality of the collective will of international functional groups can be statistically sketched. Obviously this technique will provide no clues as to the causes for cohesion or the lack of it, nor provide any insight into the consequences of such a condition. Both of these questions are much more vital in the study of international organization than the mere establishment of the fact of cohesion, but the establishment of the fact—if fact it is—remains a necessary precondition.

Among the questions relating to the processes of international organizations in the context of world politics, facts concerning group cohesion may shed light on some or all of the following:

(1) Does a pluralistic institutional framework bring with it increasing value-sharing among the employers, workers, and government officials represented?

(2) Is intra-group cohesion more readily achieved with respect to substantive or procedural issues? My study of the Council of Europe suggests that procedural issues are more important in this context, a conclusion which may not be borne out by the ILO data.

(3) Do voting patterns in functional international organizations permitting the participation of non-governmental professional groups bear out Mitrany's assertion that political issues can be separated from functional preoccupations, thus producing harmony along group lines?[13]

(4) Are regionally, ideologically, culturally, or politically distinct sub-groups among the representatives of workers, employers, and governments more or less united than the group as a whole? If they are less united, does the lack of cohesion correspond to major world political divisions, thus seemingly invalidating Mitrany?

The index I use in the study of group cohesion is called "deviation

[13] For the most complete statement of the functional argument, see David Mitrany, *A Working Peace System*, London, Royal Institute of International Affairs, 1943. For a succinct summary and critique of Mitrany's assumptions, see Inis L. Claude, Jr., *Swords into Plowshares*, New York, 1959, ch. 16.

from unanimity," an adaptation of the Rice Scale to the study of international assemblies. It is computed in the following manner: the total number of votes cast, or the number of votes on specific issues, is counted for a predetermined period; voters are identified by nationality and affiliation with one of the three organized ILO Groups (Governments, Employers, Workers). We then count the number of times each delegate voted with the majority (or minority) in his Group. The frequency of identification with the minority will then be specified as the percentage of the minority vote of the total vote. For this purpose it is immaterial whether the delegate whose votes are being counted voted "yes," "no," or abstained. The only concern is his identification with the minority or the majority. If the Group splits into three divisions on a vote, as happens frequently, the "majority" is the division that includes the largest number of members voting, and the "minority" is the sum of the two remaining divisions. This occasionally results in the "minority's" outnumbering the "majority." A deviation from unanimity of 50 per cent indicates a complete splitting of the Group; a score of 0 per cent signifies complete unity.

We are entitled to speak of a "group" when it is no longer empirically necessary to establish its existence: in the case of the three ILO Groups, the fact of institutional existence, complete with officers, secretariats, and rules of procedure, has prevailed since 1919. It is otherwise with the regional clusters for which the index was also computed. These have no institutional existence, and it is not even definitely known that all the individuals counted in this context caucus regularly. The computation was made merely in order to discover whether possible geographical or ideological ties among these individuals result in *ad hoc* patterns of cohesion. Tables 5, 6, and 7 give the results for all roll-call votes which occurred in the International Labor Conference, considered together, whereas Tables 8 through 19 specify voting cohesion for each of the three Groups as it applies to specific issues before the Conference.

The Government Group (Table 5) differs from the others in that it functions essentially for procedural purposes only. Governments are not united outside the ILO by any kind of permanent organization, whereas workers and employers are. The governments make no attempt to arrive at common policy positions vis-à-vis the other Groups on matters of substance. Their primary concern is to make common policy in matters relating to the election of the government members of ILO organs and committees and with respect to budget, personnel, and credentials. The table suggests that in an organization thrown open to the pluralist dynamic, in a context in which major political quarrels do not always dominate business, a "group" of governments is an anomaly in the sense that it does not collectively join or oppose the other Groups. Aggregate figures on group cohesion show no trend of any kind, with solidarity waxing and waning from session to session, depending on the agenda. The only approximation to a trend stands revealed in the sharp decline in group cohesion that followed the re-entry of the Soviet Union into

330

the ILO in 1954.[14] From that point on, issues of economic development, colonial freedom, and the standardization of workers' rights increasingly were debated within the aura of the Cold War, with obvious disintegrative consequences.

The regional computations suggest a somewhat different trend. Before World War II only two putative regional groupings are apparent, Latin America and the Commonwealth. Both show internal cohesion in excess of that of the Government Group after the mid-1920's for reasons probably relating to the deterioration of world commodity prices and concern with stabilization during the depression years. Internal cohesion among Western European, Eastern European, and Asian-African government representatives was frequently less than for the Government Group as a whole, suggesting a minimum of internal compromise, consultation, and mutual responsiveness in two of the very regions which after 1945 made the most rapid strides toward internal integration. During the postwar years, the influence of the Cold War is striking in undermining the regional clusters and their possible bases for internal unity. The Western governments are only very slightly more united than the Group as a whole, whether they are considered as neutrals in the Cold War or as NATO members. The habits of unity developed in regional organizations were *not* carried over into the different functional context that ILO represents. While the Soviet bloc is truly monolithic after the Czech coup, cohesion among Latin American governments declined after the war despite the gradual solidification of the inter-American system. The Afro-Asian governments, for purposes of computation, were divided into two hypothetical groups: countries somehow allied with Western nations and those which profess a self-conscious neutralism. The pro-Western group is shown to be a pure abstraction, possessing no reality so far as voting behavior is concerned. While the neutrals are somewhat more cohesive than the Government Group as a whole, they are also clearly the least united regional cluster in the International Labor Conference, apparently severely buffeted by the winds blowing from Washington and Moscow.

Table 6 shows that the Employer Group is slightly more cohesive than the governments and that its global unity deteriorated sharply over the years. At the same time, however, the regional patterns indicate an altogether different trend. The Afro-Asian employers disagree more with each other as the Soviet challenge intensifies; Latin American employers oscillate sharply and apparently without pattern. The employers in the NATO countries clearly have increased their internal cohesion as compared with the pre-1945 pattern, but their colleagues from neutral European countries seem as ambivalent as the Asian employers as the Cold War atmosphere of discussions in the ILO becomes a regular feature.

Workers in the ILO display an altogether different behavior pattern.

14 For an exhaustive and balanced evaluation of the consequences of the Soviet reutrn to the ILO, see Harold K. Jacobson, "The USSR and ILO," *International Organization*, XIV (Summer 1960), pp. 402–28.

System and Process in the International Labor Organization

	Session	Western Europe	Eastern Europe	Asia-Africa	Latin America	Common-wealth	Government Group
1919	1	17.5	10.5	9.1	9.9	4.2	18.3
1920	2	17.5	3.1	16.1	6.9	10.9	17.5
1921	3	15.2	12.7	13.2	9.6	15.9	16.8
1922	4	10.5	3.9	20	0	14.3	9.2
1923	5	12.8	8.4	14.3	5.9	0	10.8
1924	6	12.4	3.7	4.7	2.5	20	9.2
1925	7	23.9	3.8	11.1	5.9	12.6	9.5
1926	8	11.2	9.6	0	0	20	14.2
1926	9	14.2	2.9	15.4	5.7	12.1	12.2
1927	10	18.4	5.9	12.9	7.6	9.4	17.6
1928	11	0	6.6	0	0	5.9	1.9
1929	12	8.6	6.5	1.9	8.4	4.9	10.0
1929	13	3.1	0	0	0	0	1.4
1930	14	9.8	11.1	6	4.3	7.1	10.0
1931	15	7.5	11.7	0	10.4	0	10.7
1932	16	9.9	7.4	18.5	6	0	11.8
1933	17	5.9	3.6	0	12	2.9	6.5
1934	18	18.2	18.3	22.8	4.5	0	17.4
1935	19	25.1	17.9	32.1	5.2	8.6	22.5
1936	20	23.4	16	26.1	1.4	8.5	17.8
1936	21	14.7	6.3	25.6	0	4.8	14.5
1937	23	17.6	7.6	11.6	0	4.3	12.1
1938	24	0	1.3	0	0	0	0.3
1939	25	0	0	16.4	0	0	2.8
1944	26	5.9	0	8.3	0	0	2.7

		West	Western Neutrals	Soviet Bloc	Latin America	Afro-Asian Neutrals	Afro-Asian Westerns	
1945	27	0	0	0	0	0	0	0
1946	28	12.6	2.6	0	14.7	9.1	0	16.0
1946	29	21.1	11.1	0	15.8	20	0	26.6
1947	30	12.8	10.5	6.7	10.3	0	0	13.5
1948	31	9.2	6.9	0	9.4	5.9	4.3	9.4
1949	32	1.7	0	1.5	4.8	0	0	5.3
1950	33	0	7.4	—	0	0	10.5	2.0
1951	34	7.7	7.8	0	0	6.9	7.3	8.1
1952	35	7.5	2.4	0	3	16.9	7.1	8.3
1953	36	14.1	12.9	0	6.8	18.8	4.3	17.1
1954	37	16	13.8	0	11	9.1	21.1	21.9
1955	38	9	11	0	8.8	7.1	8.8	18.5
1956	39	19	30.9	0	11.6	18.9	28.9	28.7
1957	40	23.5	22	1.6	13.7	11.6	30.1	24.6
1958	41	18	10.8	0	18.9	12.9	23.7	15.1
1958	42	16.2	27	0	15.3	25.3	24.2	30.9

	Session	Western Europe	Eastern Europe	Asia-Africa	Latin America	Common-wealth	Employer Group
1919	1	21.9	15.4	5	10.8	6.7	21.6
1920	2	16.3	6.7	0	0	0	10.4
1921	3	11.2	12.4	10	—	6.8	16.3
1922	4	12.5	6.7	0	—	0	9.3
1923	5	3.2	3.6	0	—	11.1	3.7
1924	6	4.5	0	0	0	9.1	5.8
1925	7	3.9	4.5	0	3.5	2	5.5
1926	8	9.8	0	12.5	0	9.1	10.4
1926	9	3.7	3.4	8.7	9.7	0	7.1
1927	10	10.3	5.4	15.4	3.6	0	14.1
1928	11	9.8	2.9	0	15.4	9.1	8.6
1929	12	5.4	2.9	4.2	5.3	3.7	5.2
1929	13	9.1	6.7	0	—	0	6.6
1930	14	6	4.8	2.9	0	6.9	6.8
1931	15	4.3	3.8	11.1	0	0	5.7
1932	16	2.8	0	0	0	0	1.4
1933	17	12.6	12.2	20	12	2.8	18.1
1934	18	10.7	7.7	0	0	0	11.5
1935	19	7.7	0.7	0	2.6	7.3	6.5
1936	20	5.3	0	2.9	3.8	0	3.5
1936	21	16.7	30.5	14.3	—	15.4	23.6
1937	23	3.3	15.2	3.8	26.3	3	10.8
1938	24	5.7	0	0	0	0	4.6
1939	25	0	0	0	15	0	10.5
1944	26	25	0	0	16.7	25	36.4

		West	Western Neutrals	Soviet Bloc	Latin America	Afro-Asian Neutrals	Afro-Asian Westerns	
1945	27	0	0	0	0	0	0	0
1946	28	10.9	2	6.3	17.8	—	0	14.8
1946	29	16.2	0	0	18.8	0	0	16.7
1947	30	3.8	0	25	25	0	0	8.7
1948	31	1.6	0	0	22.2	16.7	20	11.1
1949	32	8.1	4.7	2.3	0	0	7.4	19.3
1950	33	0	0	—	27.3	0	0	11.0
1951	34	2.1	15.9	0	25.5	9.1	15.2	19.4
1952	35	4	19.6	0	26.5	9.4	3.1	19.5
1953	36	3.5	21.7	0	0	14.3	4.2	16.0
1954	37	1.7	14	0	1.9	15.2	8.5	18.7
1955	38	3.1	11.6	0	8.2	16.7	6	16.5
1956	39	4.8	12.5	0	8.1	15.9	21.5	27.7
1957	40	6.8	12.2	3	9.3	24.6	15.9	25.0
1958	41	8.3	17.4	0	25	37.5	15.4	16.0
1958	42	9.8	8.7	0	14.4	29.6	15.9	26.7

	Session	Western Europe	Eastern Europe	Asia-Africa	Latin America	Common-wealth	Worker Group
1919	1	5.3	4.3	6.3	2.2	6.9	8.4
1920	2	3.2	0	6.7	0	0	3.8
1921	3	0.3	0.7	0	—	1.9	0.5
1922	4	0	0	16.7	—	0	3.4
1923	5	5	7.4	0	—	0	4.8
1924	6	0	2	0	9.1	0	1.2
1925	7	0.8	0	0	0	0	0.4
1926	8	1.9	0	0	0	0	0.9
1926	9	1.6	1.4	0	0	0	1.1
1927	10	2	0	9.1	4.8	0	2.5
1928	11	0	2.3	0	0	0	0.7
1929	12	0	0	0	2.3	0	0.3
1929	13	1.5	0	0	—	0	0.7
1930	14	1.8	2.4	0	0	1.7	1.6
1931	15	1.4	0	0	3.3	0	1.1
1932	16	2.1	0	0	0	0	1.1
1933	17	1.4	0	0	0	0	0.6
1934	18	0	0	0	0	0	0
1935	19	1.6	1.6	0	0	0	1.1
1936	20	0	0	0	0	0	0
1936	21	0	0	0	—	0	2.9
1937	23	0.7	2.9	0	0	0	1.1
1938	24	0	0	0	0	0	0
1939	25	0	0	0	3.1	0	1.0
1944	26	0	0	0	0	0	0

		West	Western Neutrals	Soviet Bloc	Latin America	Afro-Asian Neutrals	Afro-Asian Westerns	
1945	27	0	0	0	0	0	0	0
1946	28	4.1	0	0	6.5	0	0	5.5
1946	29	2.1	14.3	0	8	0	0	12.1
1947	30	5.4	7.1	—	8	0	16.7	6.7
1948	31	1.6	6.2	0	2.7	1.7	0	2.9
1949	32	0.5	0	2.3	1.2	0	0	4.4
1950	33	0	0	—	0	0	0	0
1951	34	0	1.6	0	1.3	0	0	1.4
1952	35	1.4	5.9	0	4.5	8.1	2	4.4
1953	36	9.3	9.1	0	4.2	16.7	7.7	11.2
1954	37	11.9	15.9	0	5.6	6.1	25	26.4
1955	38	5.8	14	0	6.5	0	11.6	20.6
1956	39	19.6	27	0	21.5	6.5	26.9	32.0
1957	40	10.4	20.6	1	10.5	6.6	15.5	19.5
1958	41	0	0	0	6.3	8.3	7.7	2.1
1958	42	4.7	8.9	0	8.2	12.5	21.8	20.6

TABLE 8 ILO CONVENTIONS: VOTING COHESION OF GOVERNMENT GROUP, AND OF REGIONAL CLUSTERS IN THE GROUP, 1919-1958

(DEVIATION FROM UNANIMITY IN PER CENT)

	1919–1929 Session 1–13	1930–1944 Session 14–26		1945–1958 Session 27–42
Governments	12.4	17.3	Governments	14.5
Western Europe	13.1	18.6	West	13.5
Eastern Europe	4.8	15.6	Western Neutrals	8.6
Asia-Africa	12	21.6	Soviet Bloc	0.8
Latin America	5.2	5.3	Latin America	10.1
Commonwealth	9.9	2.7	Afro-Asian Neutrals	9.2
			Afro-Asian Westerns	9.8

TABLE 9 ILO CONVENTIONS: VOTING COHESION OF EMPLOYER GROUP, AND OF REGIONAL CLUSTERS IN THE GROUP, 1919-1958

(DEVIATION FROM UNANIMITY IN PER CENT)

	1919–1929 Session 1–13	1930–1944 Session 14–26		1945–1958 Session 27–42
Employers	8.7	10.5	Employers	22.3
Western Europe	7.9	8.2	West	9.5
Eastern Europe	4.2	7.7	Western Neutrals	10.2
Asia-Africa	5.5	4.5	Soviet Bloc	2.3
Latin America	6.3	8.1	Latin America	22
Commonwealth	1	2.7	Afro-Asian Neutrals	19.5
			Afro-Asian Westerns	12.9

TABLE 10 ILO CONVENTIONS: VOTING COHESION OF WORKER GROUP, AND OF REGIONAL CLUSTERS IN THE GROUP, 1919-1958

(DEVIATION FROM UNANIMITY IN PER CENT)

	1919–1929 Session 1–13	1930–1944 Session 14–26		1945–1958 Session 27–42
Workers	1.3	0.5	Workers	4.1
Western Europe	1.4	0.3	West	2.1
Eastern Europe	0.3	0	Western Neutrals	1.4
Asia-Africa	0.9	0	Soviet Bloc	0.8
Latin America	0	0.5	Latin America	3
Commonwealth	1.5	0	Afro-Asian Neutrals	2.8
			Afro-Asian Westerns	1.7

System and Process in the International Labor Organization

TABLE 11 ILO RECOMMENDATIONS: VOTING COHESION OF GOVERNMENT GROUP, AND OF REGIONAL CLUSTERS IN THE GROUP, 1919-1958

(DEVIATION FROM UNANIMITY IN PER CENT)

	1919–1929 Session 1–13	1930–1944 Session 14–26		1945–1958 Session 27–42
Governments	9.5	2.3	Governments	9.7
Western Europe	8.2	2.2	West	8.4
Eastern Europe	8.1	1.3	Western Neutrals	6.9
Asia-Africa	9.3	11.1	Soviet Bloc	0.9
Latin America	5.3	0	Latin America	7.4
Commonwealth	7.5	6.3	Afro-Asian Neutrals	5.9
			Afro-Asian Westerns	13.7

TABLE 12 ILO RECOMMENDATIONS: VOTING COHESION OF EMPLOYER GROUP, AND OF REGIONAL CLUSTERS IN THE GROUP, 1919-1958

(DEVIATION FROM UNANIMITY IN PER CENT)

	1919–1929 Session 1–13	1930–1944 Session 14–26		1945–1958 Session 27–42
Employers	15.5	16.6	Employers	23.2
Western Europe	12.9	9.6	West	8.1
Eastern Europe	9.2	12.2	Western Neutrals	12.6
Asia-Africa	7.4	0	Soviet Bloc	0
Latin America	11.9	0	Latin America	17.2
Commonwealth	5.2	9.7	Afro-Asian Neutrals	16.4
			Afro-Asian Westerns	15.5

TABLE 13 ILO RECOMMENDATIONS: VOTING COHESION OF WORKER GROUP, AND OF REGIONAL CLUSTERS IN THE GROUP, 1919-1958

(DEVIATION FROM UNANIMITY IN PER CENT)

	1919–1929 Session 1–13	1930–1944 Session 14–26		1945–1958 Session 27–42
Workers	0.6	0	Workers	9.1
Western Europe	0.9	0	West	5.4
Eastern Europe	0.5	0	Western Neutrals	6.9
Asia-Africa	0	0	Soviet Bloc	0
Latin America	0	0	Latin America	7.6
Commonwealth	0	0	Afro-Asian Neutrals	4.1
			Afro-Asian Westerns	10.7

TABLE 14   AGENDA OF ILO CONFERENCE : VOTING COHESION OF GOVERNMENT GROUP, AND OF REGIONAL CLUSTERS IN THE GROUP, 1919-1958

(DEVIATION FROM UNANIMITY IN PER CENT)

	1919–1929 Session 1–13	1930–1944 Session 14–26		1945–1958 Session 27–42
Governments	15	4.5	Governments	22.7
Western Europe	15.5	3.7	West	11
Eastern Europe	7.5	2.7	Western Neutrals	17
Asia-Africa	2.7	15.4	Soviet Bloc	0
Latin America	7.9	1.6	Latin America	9.1
Commonwealth	24	3.4	Afro-Asian Neutrals	16.7
			Afro-Asian Westerns	21.3

TABLE 15   AGENDA OF ILO CONFERENCE : VOTING COHESION OF EMPLOYER GROUP, AND OF REGIONAL CLUSTERS IN THE GROUP, 1919-1958

(DEVIATION FROM UNANIMITY IN PER CENT)

	1919–1929 Session 1–13	1930–1944 Session 14–26		1945–1958 Session 27–42
Employers	12.5	8.5	Employers	15.8
Western Europe	14.6	7.8	West	2.2
Eastern Europe	7.1	3.9	Western Neutrals	10.1
Asia-Africa	0	5.3	Soviet Bloc	0
Latin America	0	10.7	Latin America	9.1
Commonwealth	10	6.7	Afro-Asian Neutrals	11.1
			Afro-Asian Westerns	8.3

TABLE 16   AGENDA OF ILO CONFERENCE : VOTING COHESION OF WORKER GROUP, AND OF REGIONAL CLUSTERS IN THE GROUP, 1919-1958

(DEVIATION FROM UNANIMITY IN PER CENT)

	1919–1929 Session 1–13	1930–1944 Session 14–26		1945–1958 Session 27–42
Workers	0.5	0	Workers	15.2
Western Europe	0	0	West	5.3
Eastern Europe	0.9	0	Western Neutrals	8
Asia-Africa	0	0	Soviet Bloc	0
Latin America	0	0	Latin America	9.7
Commonwealth	0	0	Afro-Asian Neutrals	2.3
			Afro-Asian Westerns	13.4

System and Process in the International Labor Organization

TABLE 17 SEATING OF DELEGATIONS IN ILO CONFERENCE: VOTING COHESION OF GOVERNMENT GROUP, AND OF REGIONAL CLUSTERS IN THE GROUP, 1919-1958 (DEVIATION FROM UNANIMITY IN PER CENT)

	1919–1929 Session 1–13	1930–1944 Session 14–26		1945–1958 Session 27–42
Governments	3.3	1	Governments	28
Western Europe	4.2	1.6	West	18.4
Eastern Europe	0.5	1.4	Western Neutrals	24.5
Asia-Africa	0	0	Soviet Bloc	0
Latin America	3.1	0	Latin America	12.6
Commonwealth	12.8	0	Afro-Asian Neutrals	18.7
			Afro-Asian Westerns	27

TABLE 18 SEATING OF DELEGATIONS IN ILO CONFERENCE: VOTING COHESION OF EMPLOYER GROUP, AND OF REGIONAL CLUSTERS IN THE GROUP, 1919-1958 (DEVIATION FROM UNANIMITY IN PER CENT)

	1919–1929 Session 1–13	1930–1944 Session 14–26		1945–1958 Session 27–42
Employers	2	0.4	Employers	20.8
Western Europe	0.6	0	West	0.8
Eastern Europe	1.3	1.5	Western Neutrals	12.7
Asia-Africa	4.2	0	Soviet Bloc	0
Latin America	0	0	Latin America	5.7
Commonwealth	11.1	0	Afro-Asian Neutrals	16.7
			Afro-Asian Westerns	14.7

TABLE 19 SEATING OF DELEGATIONS IN ILO CONFERENCE: VOTING COHESION OF WORKER GROUP, AND OF REGIONAL CLUSTERS IN THE GROUP, 1919-1958 (DEVIATION FROM UNANIMITY IN PER CENT)

	1919–1929 Session 1–13	1930–1944 Session 14–26		1945–1958 Session 27–42
Workers	2.5	7.8	Workers	31.7
Western Europe	2.5	8.8	West	14.2
Eastern Europe	2.4	13.1	Western Neutrals	22.3
Asia-Africa	0	0	Soviet Bloc	0
Latin America	3.5	3.7	Latin America	15
Commonwealth	0	0	Afro-Asian Neutrals	6
			Afro-Asian Westerns	31.3

Before the onset of the ideological conflict in the postwar world, they approached something resembling international working-class solidarity with almost perfect internal cohesion, made possible in part by the near-monopoly of the International Federation of Trade Unions in claiming the affiliation of worker delegates. The postwar division of the world trade-union movement decreased the solidarity of the Worker Group. With the exception of the Soviet bloc delegates, all the regional clusters show evidence of internal strain, but the degree of cohesion within each putative group is still greater than the Group's overall consensus, which seems to have deteriorated irretrievably since the war. The Cold War has brought about the disappearance of global working-class solidarity, but it has also furnished a visible impetus toward the regionalization of trade union interests and loyalties.

Tables 8 through 19 attempt to break down the trends suggested by the gross voting statistics with respect to specific issues that recur in the life of the ILO.[15] With respect to the Government Group (Tables 8, 11, 14, 17), they demonstrate that what appears in the gross statistics as an absence of trend really amounts to a sharp deterioration of consensus since 1945 when applied to controversy on the credentials of delegates and the agenda of the Conference. As regards conventions and recommendations, however, the postwar lack of consensus is no greater than similar disunity during the interwar period. With the perhaps not wholly unexpected exception of the Soviet bloc, the regional clusters show no marked trends. Internal dissent was always most marked on the matter of labor conventions and continues to be so, whereas the less controversial matter of recommendations predictably produced less disunity within the Group as a whole and within the regional clusters. Again, the Cold War clearly produced a decline in intra-group cohesion in the matter of seating delegations whose credentials were challenged. In short, a breakdown of votes by subject matter contains no suggestion that regional groupings among governments have solidified over the years.

The Employer Group grew less cohesive over the years on each of the four issues isolated for study, thus scarcely supporting any kind of argument that the logic of pluralism has worked in the direction of active international value-sharing among industrialists (Tables 9, 12, 15, 18). There is no trace of any managerial common front, or of any ideology. Clearly, the fact that employers freely oppose their own government delegates hardly implies that they then seek to advance their professional interest at the international level by uniting tactically and

[15] The same 416 roll-call votes that were used as our data thus far were broken down as follows in terms of specific issues:

International Labor Conventions	177 votes	(Tables 8, 9, 10)
International Labor Recommendations	78 votes	(Tables 11, 12, 13)
Agenda	49 votes	(Tables 14, 15, 16)
Credentials of Delegates to International Labor Conference	48 votes	(Tables 17, 18, 19)
Others	64 votes	(not computed separately)

ideologically. With the exception of the Soviet bloc "employers," the regional groupings display exactly the same tendency as the entire Group toward disunity with respect to the major substantive issues, conventions, and recommendations. However, this is not true for the employers from NATO countries: these show a consistent tendency toward greater mutual support on the issue of excluding Communist bloc employers from the ILO and on keeping the Conference agenda small, without at the same time seeming to achieve unity on substantive questions. Small comfort is afforded by the fact that regional solidarity in general is somewhat greater than overall unity. The differences are small except in the case of the Western employers after 1945. The Cold War, through the medium of the ILO forum, has contributed to shattering any semblance of global consensus among non-Communist employers; it has merely brought about a hardening of differences in pitting the Western employers against their colleagues from elsewhere as well as against the workers.

The disintegration of Group consensus is most marked in the case of the workers (Tables 10, 13, 16, 19). It applies to all types of issues, though unity remains strongest in the case of labor conventions. Neutrals and Western-allied, Latin American, and NATO members show more internal dissent on the issue of recommendations than was true before 1945; in part, at least, this reflects differences over the degree of militancy thought desirable, with many union delegates voting against recommendations because they preferred conventions. In the instance of the Conference agenda (Table 16), perfect unanimity before the war has given rise to internal differences at the regional and the global levels, reflecting in part uncertainty over the desirability of including items relating to the Cold War and the colonial struggle. And the question of credentials (Table 19) has occasioned the greatest differences of opinion at all levels. The sharp clashes within the regional groupings reflect the uncertainty among national unions over the desirability of accepting without question the delegates of totalitarian nations. Universality as the dominant argument rivals the concern over ideological purity in the selection of delegations. The voting trends merely indicate that the labor movement has not achieved internal unity on this issue, despite the existence of a forum that provides institutional scope to the integrative dynamic of pluralism.

Numerous other conclusions and suggestions could be culled from these statistical compilations. To exploit them all fully is not the purpose of this article. The voting tables provide interesting hints as to trends, and they provide clear and economic means for demonstrating the degree of integration achieved by the groups being studied. As such, they prove again that statements of process derived from a purely legal and structural rendering of international organizations are to be mistrusted, for the close integration of employers and workers, respectively, expected by the early commentators on the ILO simply has not come about. They also prove that glowing statements by international officials concerning the same trend are frequently based on hope rather than on fact. Functionalism and pluralism at the international level remain interesting phenomena, potentially capable of transforming the international environment; but the nature of the transformation will not consist of a simple re-enactment of the modal collective-bargaining situation at the global level.

THE WORLD COMMUNITY: THE INTEGRATED INTERNATIONAL SYSTEM

Finally, international relations can be studied as a system of action. We shift from looking at different aspects of the construction of the international political system to consider the system as a whole. Systems of human action are the continuing patterns of behavior that seem at the same time to describe the relationship among actors in a group and to make that relationship possible. These clustered human interactions look as if they serve their actors in certain broad ways; they can be described in terms of certain sorts of functions that must be carried out if group interaction is to have any reality. These "functional imperatives" are not tasks which people must assume

343

knowingly. Only rarely do people deliberately try to differentiate their group from other groups, to further group goals, to preserve inner harmony for the group, or to build up individual commitment to the group. Yet if individual acts do not add up to pattern maintenance, goal attainment, adaptation, and integration, soon there will be nothing that can be called a group. A crucial part of the system is the institutional machinery that coordinates individual behavior into the functional imperatives the system consists of and relies on. In national or subnational systems the institutions vary from police forces and legislatures to infant training and magic.

There is considerable disagreement among scholars about what are, in fact, the minimum functional requirements of a human system of action. The international system seems to lack most of them, or at any rate not to have the necessary institutions. Still, it seems as if, by definition, a system must have enough integration to resolve its internal conflicts without destroying itself. The international system may be what has been called a "segmental system," one with just enough fragile integration not to fall apart completely. This, however, implies a strong likelihood of disintegration of the system. Theoretically destruction of a system of action need not mean for its actors anything more than a change in their behavior. They would merely drop one set of interactions. But the members of the international system cannot discard their interactions, since their separate identity depends on it. Destruction of the system seems to imply destruction of its members. This would be what a world state—or a world holocaust—would mean. Hence the interest in trying to describe, predict, and, hopefully, influence at least the integrative aspect of the international system.

If we were to think of international relations as taking place within a nation, the international system would look anarchic. International relations are, in fact, characterized by the sort of violence that, within a nation, indicates the breakdown of order. If the international scene were no more than the conflicting acts of the separate nations, the only adequate policy for each state would be the search for national advantage, with the knowledge that there was no security in any relationship. The continuing avoidance of a nuclear world war, however, suggests that appearances of world disorder are misleading. In his "World Politics as a Primitive Political System," Roger Masters suggests that the international system is condemned because it is compared to an inaccurate idea of the national system. As modern anthropology has shown, even the most "advanced" national system has only a partial reign of order, while the most "primitive" and "unstructured" societies are usually able to handle internal conflict. Primitive institutions do not usually have identifiable meeting places and designated personnel with clearly defined roles. In spite of this informality (which also characterizes many aspects of more sophisticated systems), primitive institutions are able to keep conflict within tolerable bounds. Masters suggests that the international system may well use analagous techniques for avoiding self-

The World Community

destruction. He gives both a new line of comparative description and the beginnings of a new set of policy recommendations.

Masters's piece puts the international system into the context of the comparative study of political systems, drawing the comparison between developing pre-national systems and the, perhaps, equally primitive international one. The next two articles, by Karl Deutsch and by Ronald Inglehart, compare the world system to post-national or supranational systems. The actors in the international system exist within nations and channel most of their international behavior through the nations. This is one reason why it is difficult to compare the international system with national systems. Comparisons must become so abstract that they are often not much more than metaphors. But supranational systems like the organizations of united Europe developed out of nations; they can be used as limited examples of systems of action with more than national scope. Theorists of international integration have, in fact, studied postwar Europe with great care. There they can see integration developing until war has become unthinkable, and there is movement towards shared institutions and attitudes. Deutsch has pioneered in the search for quantitative indicators and predictors of integration. His piece, "Integration and Arms Control in the European Political Environment," is an account of a recent massive study of a number of aspects of European integration, including prospects for agreement on the control of armaments. Deutsch and his many associates plotted elite and mass attitudes through interviews, content analysis of editorials in elite newspapers, and opinion polls. They correlated this material with indicators of transactions across national boundaries. These transactions—which include trade, communication by mail and telephone, and movement of people such as tourists and students—are both necessary conditions for and indicators of an increase in integration among nations. This study can be compared to Merritt's work on nation-building in the Thirteen Colonies (Part One, Chapter 2); the theoretical basis is the same. Deutsch reports that the increase in integration in Europe seems to have reached a stopping point. The elites and the masses alike seem to set definite limits on how far they are willing to support a merging of national functions and identities. Deutsch concludes that there is unlikely to be much movement towards continental integration, and he sees pessimistic implications for integration of the international system as a whole.

The technique of Deutsch's study is what he calls elsewhere the "confrontation of data streams." This is the attempt to bring to bear simultaneously on a problem as many approaches as possible. There is some stress on the quantitative techniques, which are felt to be most useful if used together and in conjunction with more qualitative methods. In "An End to European Integration?" Ronald Inglehart picks one narrow technique and one small strand of the study of international integration. He focuses on the attitudes of European elites, separating them carefully by country and age. Acts tending to create an international system can always be either promoted or hindered by national leaders who, for instance, may prevent travel abroad or further student exchanges. Given Deutsch's demonstration that the rate of increase of international transactions is slowing in Europe, the attitudes of the elites may be even more important. Inglehart shows that people who grow up in circumstances of international integration are markedly more favorable to such integration than those who encounter it only late in life. At the key time—fifteen or twenty years from now—the current leaders, who show at most a doctrinaire approval of integration, will have been succeeded by leaders whose formative years were spent in the postwar heyday of European unity. For ideological or political reasons, then, integration can be expected to take a spurt forward not predictable by the patterns of aggregate transaction data alone.

Finally, by way of some very sophisticated theorizing we approach the international system itself. Morton Kaplan writes of nations as they are and international systems as they may be. He describes the only patterns of international behavior that seem likely to be able to last any length of time. These are the relatively stable patterns that are logically possible. They are described in terms of what the participating nations are like and what rules of behavior they give the appearance of following. Kaplan maps out six major patterns. Their names are intended to remind us of the central behavioral characteristics of the systems: the balance of power system, the loose bipolar system, the tight bipolar system, the universal system, the hierarchical system, and the unit veto system. Only two of these systems correspond much to anything that has existed historically. Kaplan's "balance of power" is a highly abstract version of the international politics of nineteenth century Europe, and his loose bipolar system approximates the world of today. But Kaplan is not attempting to describe reality except in respect to the sorts of possible relationships between international behavior and international structure. He aspires to predict only what sorts of changes in a system would lead to what other system, and in what way. Surprisingly enough, this very abstract analysis has policy implications that Kaplan has made explicit in some of his other writings. We may eventually be able to say of a given kind of international system that it is more or less stable than another, and we can describe the sort of national behavior that comprises movement from this to another system. This gives indications, for example, of the kinds of acts a major power in a loose bipolar system should avoid if it wants to avoid transformation of the system to a unit veto one. Translated into policy terms, this is what the United States should do to help avoid nuclear proliferation. Kaplan's theory still has only limited predictive power. But in the article reprinted here we can see the potentialities it holds for the study of actual conditions, for Kaplan relates his models to specific historical situations to show something of the range of conditions covered by his abstractions.

Kaplan's "system analysis" is deliberately abstract and general. Yet it shows the importance of the behavior of individual human beings,

The World Community

for theirs are the acts that his rules and systems are abstracted from. Individuals set the parameters of the system. To use Kaplan's terms, we are the units who create a hierarchy or wield a veto. And this is why international relations is studied as the political behavior whose result is the international political system.

World
Politics
as a Primitive
Political
System

Roger D. Masters

Reprinted with the permission of the editors from *World Politics*, Vol. 16 (July, 1964), 595–619. Mr. Masters is Associate Professor of Government at Dartmouth College.

I. Reasons for Comparing Primitive and International Politics

Many primitive peoples have political systems which are very much like the international political system. If the characterization of world politics as mere "anarchy" is an exaggeration, surely anarchy moderated or inhibited by a balance of power is a fairly accurate description of the rivalry between sovereign nation-states. The Nuer, a primitive African people, have been described as living in an "ordered anarchy" which depends on a "balanced opposition of political segments."[1] It is commonplace to describe the international system as lacking a government, so that "might makes right." "In Nuerland legislative, judicial and executive functions are not invested in any persons or councils"; hence, throughout the society, "the club and the spear are the sanctions of rights."[2]

To be sure, politics among the Nuer—or any other primitive people—is not identical to world politics, but however important the differences may be, a number of writers have suggested the possibility of comparing the two kinds of political systems.[3] Curiously enough, however, there has been virtually no effort to elaborate these similarities comprehensively from a theoretical point of view.[4]

It should be noted in passing that there are three more general reasons for comparing primitive and international political systems. An attempt to bridge the gap between political science and anthropology

The author's research has been undertaken with the assistance of a grant from the Stimson Fund, Yale University.

[1] E. E. Evans-Pritchard, *The Nuer* (Oxford 1940), 181; *idem,* "The Nuer of the Southern Sudan," in M. Fortes and E. E. Evans-Pritchard, eds., *African Political Systems* (London 1940), 293.

[2] Evans-Pritchard, *The Nuer,* 162, 169. Cf. R. F. Barton, "Ifugao Law," *University of California Publications in American Archaeology and Ethnology,* xv (February 1915), 15.

[3] E.g., Hans Morgenthau, *Politics Among Nations* (1st edn., New York 1953), 221; George Modelski, "Agraria and Industria: Two Models of the International System," in Klaus Knorr and Sidney Verba, eds., *The International System* (Princeton 1961), 125–26; and David Easton, "Political Anthropology," in Bernard J. Siegel, ed., *Biennial Review of Anthropology 1959* (Stanford 1959), 235–36. At least one anthropologist was aware of the analogy: see R. F. Barton, *The Half-Way Sun* (New York 1930), 109–10; *idem, The Kalingas* (Chicago 1949), 101; and *idem,* "Ifugao Law," 100, 103. In his introduction to *The Kalingas,* E. A. Hoebel wrote: "International law is primitive law on a world scale" (p. 5). Cf. Hoebel's *The Law of Primitive Man* (Cambridge, Mass., 1954), 125–26, 318, 321, 330–33.

[4] Since this study was undertaken, an article has been published that marks a first step in this direction. See Chadwick F. Alger, "Comparison of Intranational and International Politics," *American Political Science Review,* LVII (June 1963), 414–19.

The World Community

has merits because such cross-disciplinary endeavors may free one from unnecessarily narrow assumptions which often dominate research in a given field. This is particularly true with respect to political anthropology, since the political aspects of primitive society have often been only imperfectly analyzed.[5]

Secondly, it may not be amiss to point out that long before anthropology was established as a discipline, political philosophers analyzed the social and political antecedents of existing states and governments.[6] The idea of a "state of nature," in which men lived before the establishment of governments, plays an important role in the history of political philosophy. Although recent students of primitive society have argued that "the theories of political philosophers" are "of little scientific value,"[7] the existence of a tradition which considered the "state of nature" as relevant to any political theory may indicate that political scientists should consider primitive politics more fully than they now do.

This general point is of specific importance for the theory of international politics because it can be said that the modern theory of international relations took the notion of a "state of nature" as its model.[8] Since anthropologists have asserted that such a "state of nature" never existed, consideration of the empirical and theoretical relevance of the concept may well be in order; not the least of the advantages of a comparison between primitive and international politics would be a fuller understanding of the relevance of modern political philosophy to a theory of world politics.[9]

Finally, as Ragnar Numelin has shown, "international relations" (or its analog) exists among uncivilized peoples; the "discovery" of diplomacy cannot be attributed, as it customarily is, to the "historical" cultures of the Mediterranean or Orient.[10] Thus any exhaustive theory

[5] In 1940, A. R. Radcliffe-Brown said: "The comparative study of political institutions, with special reference to the simpler societies, is an important branch of social anthropology which has not yet received the attention it deserves" (Preface, in Fortes and Evans-Pritchard, eds., *African Political Systems,* xi). More recently, David Easton has written: "Such a subfield [as political anthropology] does not yet exist" ("Political Anthropology," 210).

[6] E.g., Montaigne, *Essays,* I, xxiii ("Of Custom, and that We Should Not Easily Change a Law Received"), and I, xxxi ("Of Cannibals"); Rousseau, *Second Discourse,* esp. First Part and notes c-q; and Locke, *Second Treatise of Civil Government,* esp. chaps. 2 and 3.

[7] Fortes and Evans-Pritchard, *African Political Systems,* 4. See also Henry Sumner Maine's sharp criticism of Rousseau's conception of the "state of nature" in *Ancient Law* (New York 1874), 84–88, 299.

[8] On the relations between the concept of a "state of nature" and the prevailing theory of politics among sovereign states, see Kenneth N. Waltz, *Man, the State, and War* (New York 1959), esp. chaps. 6–8; and Richard H. Cox, *Locke on War and Peace* (Oxford 1960), esp. chap. 4.

[9] Cf. Kenneth N. Waltz, "Political Philosophy and the Study of International Relations," in William T. R. Fox, ed., *Theoretical Aspects of International Relations* (Notre Dame, Ind., 1959), 51–68; and Arnold Wolfers, "Political Theory and International Relations," in Arnold Wolfers and Laurence W. Martin, eds., *The Anglo-American Tradition in Foreign Affairs* (New Haven 1956), esp. xi–xiii.

[10] Ragnar Numelin, *The Beginnings of Diplomacy* (New York 1950), 125 *et passim.*

World Politics as a Primitive Political System

of world politics would have to comprehened the rivalry, warfare, and diplomacy of primitive peoples as genuine examples of "international politics."

II. Similarities Between Primitive and International Politics

At the outset, four elements common to politics within a number of primitive societies and international relations deserve mention: first, the absence of a formal government with power to judge and punish violations of law; second, the use of violence and "self-help" by the members of the system to achieve their objectives and enforce obligations; third, the derivation of law and moral obligations either from custom or from explicit, particular bargaining relationships (i.e., the absence of a formal legislative body operating on the basis of—and making— general rules); and fourth, a predominant organizational principle which establishes political units serving many functions in the overall social system.

The first three of these similarities between primitive and international politics are relatively self-evident when one considers those primitive societies which lack fully developed governments. The fourth, however, may not be as clear. In certain primitive societies, territorial political units are largely defined, especially in the eyes of their members, in terms of kinship groups which are reckoned either "unilaterally" (i.e., groups such as the "lineage," in which descent is in either the male or female line from a common ancestor), or "bilaterally" (i.e., the family group includes relatives of both mother and father, as in modern "Western" society).[11] Different combinations or divisions of these groups, on a territorial basis, often provide the basic structure of the entire political system.

Although it is not normally noted, the international system of sovereign states is also organized largely on the basis of a single principle. In this case, the principle is that of "territorial sovereignty"—i.e., the conception that sovereignty "is always associated with the proprietorship of a limited portion of the earth's surface, and the 'sovereigns' *inter se* are to be deemed not *paramount,* but *absolute* owners of the state's territory."[12] This ultimate authority can, of course, be divided, as it is in federal states, but so, too, with the lineage principle in some primitive systems which are divided into different levels of units.[13]

---

11 See Fortes and Evans-Pritchard, *African Political Systems,* 11; and Barton, "Ifugao Law," 92–94, 110. Carl Landé, in a stimulating unpublished paper entitled "Kinship and Politics in Pre-Modern and Non-Western Societies," has emphasized the different effects of these two types of kinship groups.

12 Maine, *Ancient Law,* 99 (original italics).

13 The foregoing comparison may appear to come strikingly close to the formulations of Maine (*ibid.,* 124–25) and Lewis H. Morgan (*Ancient Society* [New York 1877], 6–7)—formulations which have been criticized in recent years by anthropologists. See I. Schapera, *Government and Politics in Tribal Societies* (London 1956),

The World Community

In primitive societies like the Nuer, lineage or kinship groups perform a wide variety of functions, so that it is not possible to point to a specific action and define it as "political";[14] rather, there is a political element in many actions which simultaneously serve other purposes. This characteristic has been described in recent sociological literature as the "functional diffuseness" of traditional social structures.[15] The conception of "diffuseness" is thus opposed to "functional specificity" (i.e., the organization of a special group or institution to perform a given activity or function), which is supposed to prevail in all modern societies.

An extreme example of this usage is found in Riggs's polar conceptions of a "fused" system, in which "a single structure performs all the necessary functions," and a "refracted society," in which, "for every function, a corresponding structure exists."[16] Riggs argues that traditional agrarian societies are "fused," whereas modern industrialized societies are "refracted." While such a distinction may indicate an important tendency, it is a radical exaggeration to imply that in modern political systems "for every function, a corresponding structure exists." The political unit of the modern state system has a "fused" character which parallels the "diffuse" role of kindship groups in primitive societies like the Nuer.[17] Moreover, just as an industrial civilization does not presuppose a perfectly "refracted" society, traditional societies are rarely totally "fused."[18]

Up to this point we have tried to show two things: first, that there is a striking similarity between some primitive political systems and

2–5. Despite the inadequacies of the conceptions of Maine and Morgan, especially with reference to their presumption of progress in human development, some distinction between primitive or traditional society, in which kinship and personal "status" play a predominant role, and modern territorial states, based on citizenship and contract, is today accepted by many social scientists. Indeed, it is paradoxical that while anthropologists have been attacking the Maine-Morgan dichotomy (by showing that all societies have a territorial element), sociologists and political scientists have been adopting the distinction from the works of Tönnies, Weber, Parsons, or Levy. E.g., see Fred W. Riggs, "Agraria and Industria—Toward a Typology of Comparative Administration," in William J. Siffin, ed., *Toward the Comparative Study of Public Administration* (Bloomington 1959), 28–30, III.

14 E.g., according to Evans-Pritchard, "We do not therefore say that a man is acting politically or otherwise, but that between local groups there are relations of a structural order that can be called political" (*The Nuer*, 264–65).

15 See Talcott Parsons, *The Social System* (Glencoe, Ill., 1951), 65–67.

16 Fred W. Riggs, "International Relations as a Prismatic System," in Knorr and Verba, eds., *The International System*, 149. Cf. Modelski, "Agraria and Industria," in *ibid.*, for a stimulating adaptation of Riggs's concepts.

17 To be sure, it is easier to specify what actions are "political" in the twentieth-century world than it was for Evans-Pritchard among the Nuer. Nonetheless, as Karl Deutsch has remarked, the nation-state is itself "functionally diffuse," performing an extraordinary range of economic, social, and political functions. See "Towards Western European Integration: An Interim Assessment," *Journal of International Affairs*, XVI (1962), 95–96. Cf. Gabriel A. Almond, "Introduction," in Gabriel A. Almond and James S. Coleman, eds., *The Politics of the Developing Areas* (Princeton 1960), 11, 63.

18 It is simply incorrect to assert that nonliterate peoples, however traditionally minded, were incapable of developing "functionally specific roles," "achievement norms of recruitment," or the "state" as a formal organization; each of these attri-

World Politics as a Primitive Political System

the modern international system; and second, that one element of this similarity is the "functional diffuseness" of political units in both types of system. If this is so, one cannot employ the polar opposites of "primitive" and "modern" or "functionally diffuse" and "functionally specific" as the basis of a comparative analysis of primitive political systems. Because primitive political systems vary enormously, one must explicitly distinguish the particular *kind* of primitive society which is supposed to present the greatest similarity to world politics.

In order to compare primitive and international politics, therefore, one needs a classification which distinguishes primitive societies in terms of their political structure. Although the typologies of primitive political systems hitherto developed by anthropologists have been imperfect, it will be useful to accept provisionally the distinction between primitive peoples which have developed some form of governmental institutions and those which have generally been called "stateless societies."[19]

The following comparison will focus on primitive societies that lack formal governments. Such systems may be described as having "diffuse leadership," since individuals or groups have influence without formally institutionalized coercive authority. There may be a "titular chief" in these societies, but such an individual, even together with other influential men, does not act as a ruler. Since the modern world, as a political system, shares this structural characteristic of "statelessness," a résumé of political life in primitive stateless societies will show the utility of comparing them to the international political system.

III. "Self-Help" and Violence in Primitive Stateless Societies

In stateless systems, disputes cannot be referred to an impartial government backed by a police force. The characteristic pattern of responding to criminal or civil wrongs is "self-help": the individual or group which feels injured considers himself or itself legitimately responsible for punishing a crime or penalizing a tort. Self-help in these circumstances involves two stages which appear to be directly comparable to the functions of adjudication and enforcement in modern legal systems. In either system, first it is necessary to determine that a wrong has occurred and that a

---

butes, so readily described as "modern," can be found in societies which must be described as "primitive." For an example, see S. F. Nadel, *A Black Byzantium: The Kingdom of the Nupe in Nigeria* (London 1942). Cf. Riggs, "Agraria and Industria," 28. While some anthropologists would argue that primitive bands, such as those of the Australian aborigines and African bushmen, are an exception, others would suggest that there are some "functionally specific" roles even in these societies.

[19] See Fortes and Evans-Pritchard, *African Political Systems*, 5–23; John Middleton and David Tait, eds., *Tribes Without Rulers* (London 1958), 1–3; Lucy Mair, *Primitive Government* (Baltimore 1962), Part 1; Schapera, *Government and Politics*, 63–64, 208–14; and Robert Lowie, *Social Organization* (New York 1948), chap. 14. For a critique of the categories used by anthropologists, see Easton, "Political Anthropology," 210–26.

The World Community

particular individual or group will be punished in a particular way; second, the punishment or penalty for that wrong must be enforced or implemented.

In the simplest primitive societies, both stages are accomplished by the individual or family that has been wronged. For example, when a kinship group discovers that one of its members has been murdered, the guilty individual and his kinship group will be identified and a retaliatory killing (or other punishment) will be inflicted by the wronged group. As Barton indicated in his study of Philippine headhunters, such self-enforcement of legal penalties[20] raises a crucial problem among stateless primitive peoples. The kinship group which enforces the *lex talionis* by killing a murderer or one of his kin sees this act as not only necessary, but also legitimate. Although unrelated bystanders may accept this interpretation, since retaliatory killing is customary, the kinship group which is penalized may not consider the retaliation to be a legitimate punishment.[21] When this occurs, there is often a tendency for crime and punishment to "escalate" into a more or less permanent relation of "feud" between the kinship groups involved.[22]

In feuds, violence usually takes the form of sporadic surprise attacks by individuals or small groups. Hence a condition of feud should not be equated too completely with what we call "war",[23] rather, it is a condition of rivalry in which intermittent violence and aggression (e.g., seizure of property or person as well as retaliatory killing) appear legitimate to those who attack, and illegitimate to the victims. The similarity of this "state of feud" and a Hobbesian "state of nature" is obvious, with the important difference that kinship groups are often involved, instead of isolated individuals.

Although the notion of modern warfare cannot be accurately applied to all primitive intergroup fighting, primitive violence sometimes approximates a civilized war. The gradations of conflict arising out of self-help have been clarified by Tait and Middleton, who suggest that primitive feuds and wars be distinguished because only in the latter is

[20] It must be emphasized that the retaliation is *legal*, being sanctioned by customary law (or, in Weber's terms, "traditional legitimacy"). Cf. Mair, *Primitive Government*, 16–19; and A. R. Radcliffe-Brown, *Structure and Function in Prmitive Society* (Glencoe, Ill., 1952), chap. 12.

[21] See Barton, *The Kalingas*, 231. Note the parallel tendency in world politics: "One state's aggression is always another state's 'legitimate use of force to defend vital national interests'" (Inis L. Claude, Jr., "United Nations Use of Military Force," *Journal of Conflict Resolution,* vii [June 1963], 119).

[22] Cf. Barton, *The Half-Way Sun*, chaps. 5 and 6. In some situations, however, a group may refrain from counterretaliation, either because the kinsman who was punished was offensive to his own kin or because the group lacks the power to react. As Carl Landé has pointed out to me, the principles of "an eye for an eye" and "might makes right" may, and often do, conflict in the operation of both primitive and international political systems.

[23] Numelin argues that organized, continuous warfare of the type known to civilized man is practically unknown among primitive peoples (*The Beginnings of Diplomacy*, chap. 2). Cf. Schapera, *Government and Politics,* 215, 219; and Melville J. Herskovits, *Cultural Anthropology* (New York 1955), 207–8.

World Politics as a Primitive Political System

there no obligation to attempt to settle the dispute.[24] They argue that within a restricted range (which varies from one primitive society to another) the more or less permanent condition of feud rivalry is rendered unlikely, if not impossible, by the existence of close kinship ties and relationships of "administrative organization."

At this level there may be a duel or the requirement that ritual acts of atonement be performed, but prolonged group rivalry is unlikely since the individuals concerned are all members of a single "nuclear group" (which is, normally, a local community, a kinship group, or both). Within such a local or family unit, disputes culminating in violence are not self-perpetuating; as in modern states, a punishment or penalty "atones" for a crime and thereby completes the legal case.[25]

Outside of this range, punishment does not terminate the rivalry arising out of a dispute; although retaliatory violence tends to be self-perpetuating, Tait and Middleton suggest that there is a zone in which violence can be described as a feud because the opposed groups recognize an obligation to settle their dispute. In this range of social interaction there are normally procedures for arriving at a settlement. Hence, among the Nuer, the "leopard-skin chief" holds an office which serves the function of settling feuds on the basis of compensation.[26] The "go-between" among the Ifugao serves a similar function.[27]

This does not mean that such means of settling the feud are always successful, nor that the settlement is in fact permanent. On the contrary, Evans-Pritchard concludes: "Though the chief admonishes the relatives of the dead man at the ceremonies of settlement that the feud is ended and must not be renewed, Nuer know that 'a feud never ends'... There is no frequent fighting or continuous unabated hostility, but the sore rankles and the feud, though formally concluded, may at any time break out again."[28] Hence the settlement of a feud amounts to a truce—one might say a treaty, given the impermanence of similar

---

[24] "Introduction," *Tribes Without Rulers*, 20–22. Cf. Radcliffe-Brown, *African Political Systems*, xx. A similar though not identical distinction is made by Barton, "Ifugao Law," 77–78. Kinds of violence in primitive society could also be distinguished in terms of the extent to which groups act as corporate units and the degree to which violence is continuous. In this sense, a true "war" would consist of more or less continuous hostilities between corporate groups, whereas "feuds," in the purest case, would be intermittent conflicts between individuals (albeit with the support of kinship groups). Although such an approach would take into consideration the fundamental issue raised by Rousseau's criticism of Hobbes's concept of a "state of war" (see *L'Etat de guerre*, in C. E. Vaughan, ed., *The Political Writings of Rousseau* [2 vols., Cambridge, Eng., 1915], 1, 293–307), it raises theoretical questions which require a more exhaustive analysis than is here possible. For the present, therefore, it is useful to accept provisionally the distinction between feud and war as elaborated by anthropologists.

[25] Tait and Middleton, *Tribes Without Rulers*, 19–20. See Barton, "Ifugao Law," 14–15, and the example, 120–21.

[26] Evans-Pritchard, *The Nuer*, 152–54.

[27] Barton, *The Half-Way Sun*, 109–10, and the example described on 70ff.

[28] *The Nuer*, 155. Cf. Barton, "Ifugao Law," 75; "Once started, a blood feud was well-nigh eternal (unless ended by a fusion of the families by means of marriage)."

The World Community

settlements in international politics—between rival groups. Such a settlement may occur because feuding segments need to cooperate on other matters, but it cannot unite them into a harmonious unit without further steps, such as a marriage between the feuding families.[29]

Tait and Middleton use the term "jural community" to describe the unit within which disputes take the form of feuds to be settled by an established procedure.[30] Violence on this level tends to be limited in a way which presents very revealing similarities to procedures in international affairs: as with "limited war," there is a restriction on the means of violence used and the ends sought, and like some interstate treaties, each rival group is willing to end violence (if only temporarily) because of the need to cooperate with its rivals. Hence the settlement of a feud does not ordinarily preclude the recurrence of violence; as in international treaties, the parties are their own judges of the maintenance of the conditions of the peaceful settlement.[31]

The feuding condition is thus a relationship between rival groups in which violence is a latent but ever-present threat should disputes arise. War, as defined by Tait and Middleton, is a more extreme form of competition, since there is no obligation to settle conflict, however temporarily. Among many peoples with leaders instead of rulers and governments, a distinction is made between those groups with whom violence is limited to feuding and those with whom there is a continuous condition of war. A given group is not bound by common procedures of dispute settlement with foreigners or with individuals from different parts (or "jural communities") of the same nation. For example, whereas conflicting groups from the same Nuer tribe could only be in a state of feud, individuals or groups from different Nuer tribes are always in a potential state of war with each other. When spatially or culturally distant groups are involved, violence is likely to emerge at any time, even in the absence of a formal dispute.[32]

Among stateless primitive peoples, therefore, social distance (which is highly correlated with geographical distance) decreases the likelihood that violence, should it occur, will be limited.[33] This spatial distinction between those who are "far" and those who are "near" tends to produce

29 See the example in Barton, *The Half-Way Sun,* 115.

30 "The jural community...is the widest grouping within which there are a moral obligation and a means ultimately to settle disputes peaceably" (*Tribes Without Rulers,* 9).

31 Cf. the rarity of the emergence of what has been called a "security community" in international politics. Karl Deutsch *et al., Political Community and the North Atlantic Area* (Princeton 1957), chap. 1.

32 Evans-Pritchard, *The Nuer.* 121–22. Cf. Lewis H. Morgan, *League of the Iroquois* (Rochester 1851), 73.

33 The conquest of physical space by modern technology has altered the character of "social distance" without destroying it. Today differences in the kind of political regime tend to have effects similar to those of geographical distance between primitive tribes; because of their political principles, Communist regimes are those farthest from the United States even when they are close to us in miles. Cf. the concepts of "structural distance" (Evans-Pritchard, *The Nuer,* 113ff.) and "social distance" (Emory S. Bogardus, *Sociology* [4th edn., New York 1954], 535–36).

World Politics as a Primitive Political System

a series of concentric zones around each group in many primitive worlds.[34] Where such zones have been found, the specific boundaries of each region are often unclear. Thus there is considerable evidence that, for a member of many primitive societies without a government, the group or "political community" to which allegiance is owed varies, depending on the dispute in question.[35]

This characteristic is related to one of the fundamental differences between many primitive political systems and world politics—namely, the fusion of various levels of social intercourse which we are accustomed to distinguish. In modern life, one can speak of a distinction between the level of a society (normally organized as a nation-state), that of a local community, and that of a family. For the primitive, the family or kinship group may include all residents of a locality; even if it does not, the kinship group or locality will tend to have many of the functions of a modern society without having either the political structure or the unique claim to allegiance of the modern state. As a consequence, parallels drawn between primitive political systems and international politics, however useful they may be in other respects, must take into consideration differences in the scope and powers of units in the two kinds of systems.[36]

Despite these differences, however, there are some striking similarities between primitive stateless societies and international political systems with respect to the role of violence in intergroup conflict. In both, there is a range of social relationships which is relatively exempt from self-perpetuating violence; within the "nuclear groups" composing both systems, the procedures for settling disputes or atoning for crimes are terminal, at least in principle. In both types of systems, intermittent, violent conflict between nuclear groups can be temporarily settled without removing the potentiality of further attacks. Violence is justified in the eyes of the aggressive group because the legal system permits self-help as a means of enforcing one's rights. Since the punished group denies this justification, there is a tendency for a conflict to erupt into an exchange of hostilities, a tendency which is restrained between those groups which consider themselves to be similar or "near" each other. These similarities indicate that the analogy between primitive political systems without governments and international politics is not merely

[34] See the similar diagrams in Barton, *The Half-Way Sun,* 114, and Evans-Pritchard, *The Nuer,* 114. Note that Barton distinguishes a "neutral zone" between the "home region' and the zone of feuding.

[35] See Mair, *Primitive Government,* 46–48, 104–6.

[36] The problem of units anl levels of analysis has had surprisingly little attention in recent theorizing on international politics. For exceptions, see Karl Deutsch, *Political Community at the International Level* (Garden City, N.Y., 1954); Waltz, *Man, the State, and War*; and J. David Singer, "The Level-of-Analysis Problem in International Relations," in Knorr and Verba, eds., *The International System,* 77–92. Of particular importance is the relationship between a cultural community or "people" and organized "political communities." Cf. Gabriel A. Almond, "Comparative Political Systems," *Journal of Politics,* xviii (August 1956), 393–408.

The World Community

fanciful; both appear to belong to a general class of political systems in which self-help or violence is an accepted and legitimate mode of procedure.

IV. Order in Primitive Stateless Societies

In discussing the characteristics of violence in primitive societies which lack rulers, there has been an emphasis on the competitive relationship of opposed groups. When seen in this light, primitive society may seem to be a barely controlled anarchy in which security of life and limb is scarcely to be expected. Since this impression is inaccurate, it is of the greatest importance to emphasize the variety of political functions performed in primitive stateless societies.

Even if one disputes Barton's estimate that the life of the Philippine headhunter was more secure than that of a citizen in modern societies, it is undoubtedly true that, as he says, "a people having no vestige of constituted authority and therefore living in literal anarchy, [can] dwell in comparative peace and security of life and property."[37] Whatever the logical merits of Hobbes's conception of a "state of nature," it does not seem to follow, at least among primitive peoples, that the anarchy of social life without a government produces a violent war of all against all. Quite the contrary, it would appear that violence in such primitive societies often serves the function of maintaining law and order according to customary procedures.

The pacific functions of self-help can be clearly seen if one considers the circumstances in which violence does *not* arise out of conflict in a stateless primitive system. In the simplest of such societies, the necessities of cooperation tend to preclude violence within the family and locality, while the limitations of technology tend to restrict social intercourse to these relatively narrow groups; hence, among the technologically least developed primitives, feuding relations are rare and wars virtually unknown. In this kind of system, self-help and retaliation function effectively as the only forcible means for punishing crimes because social opprobrium is, in itself, a strong punishment.[38]

Among primitive peoples with a more complex stateless system, such as the Ifugao studied by Barton, there are many occasions for feuding or warfare, but actual violence does not arise out of every dispute. The limitation of violence between potentially feuding groups is related to

[37] Barton, "Ifugao Law," 6. Barton calculated the annual death rate from head-hunting at 2 per 1000 during a period of "abnormally high" activity (*The Half-Way Sun*, 200). In the United States, accidental deaths from all causes during 1963 were at the rate of 5.3 per 1000.
[38] E.g., A. R. [Radcliffe-] Brown, *The Andaman Islanders* (Cambridge, Eng., 1922), 48–52, 84–87.

the institutions which serve the function of settling feuds. The Ifugao "go-between" not only acts as a mediator in feuds which have caused deaths on either side, but also acts prior to the eruption of violence in an effort to prevent such killings. In negotiating disputes which have not yet led to killing, he emphasizes at every stage the dangers implicit in open feuding; by describing these dangers in detail, the "go-between" (with the backing of his own family and the local community at large) attempts to deter an attack by either of the opposed families.

Institutionalized pressures to prevent the outbreak of violence also occur within the rival groups themselves. Thus, while the closest relatives of an offended individual may insist on the need for killing as a punishment for such wrongs as adultery, sorcery, or refusal to pay debts, more wealthy relations (who, according to Ifugao custom, may be more vulnerable to counterretaliation than the killer should a feud occur) frequently counsel moderation.[39] Since retaliation is an action decided upon by the family as a unit, and since feuds are difficult to settle, "the accuser is usually not overanxious to kill the accused."[40]

Whether originating with a "go-between" or a member of a wronged group, advice that open feuding be avoided, or at least limited, is characteristic of a phenomenon which has recently received extensive attention in foreign affairs—namely, deterrence. Although it has sometimes been assumed that deterrence requires a rational calculation of the consequences of an attack, deterrence and self-help among primitive peoples do not presuppose a conscious strategic calculation of the type formalized by game theorists.[41] Thus the possibility of violent counterretaliation may, in itself and without further calculation, stabilize rivalries and limit conflicts when there is no governmental arbiter to enforce law and order.

In order to avoid an overemphasis on either the stability produced by deterrence or the violence resulting from self-help, it will be useful to view both as necessarily related consequences of a political system which lacks authoritative governmental institutions. In political regimes of this kind, self-help and deterrence have the function of regulating bargaining between opposed groups, but they also serve as a means of organizing social intercourse in a predictable fashion. This latter function is especially important, though it tends to be overlooked in analyses of deterrence from the standpoint of a theory of strategy.

Retaliation by an offended group, both as a means of deterring wrongs and as a method of punishment, can therefore be studied in terms of its social consequences. As Barton points out with reference to

---

[39] On the characteristics of self-help and retaliation among the Ifugao, see Barton, *The Half-Way Sun,* chaps. 3, 5, and 6; and "Ifugao Law," 75–87, 92–95, 99–109.
[40] *Ibid.,* 95. Compare the Cuban crisis of October 1962.
[41] Sophisticated students of strategy have never assumed, of course, that rivals can deter each other only if their calculations are formulated in terms of game theory. Cf. Thomas Schelling's analogy of deterring a child, *The Strategy of Conflict* (Cambridge, Mass., 1960), 11. Nonetheless, popular analyses often assert that deterrence implies—and requires—rational calculation on both sides. E.g., Seymour Melman, *The Peace Race* (New York 1961), 22.

headhunting, these consequences are multiple, and are sometimes not consciously perceived by those concerned.[42] Consciously, retaliation is a means of maintaining the well-being of an offended group and of responding to a specific wrong. Unintentionally or unconsciously, self-help serves to preserve and unite a group which has been threatened by another, to fix responsibility for wrongs, and thus to maintain a legal order. For a specific individual who executes retaliation, the dangerous exploits required for self-help may consciously be a means of gaining glory and influence as well as a means of preserving his legal rights.[43] Since all of these functions have analogies in the self-help conducted by sovereign nation-states, it would be unwise to see in retaliation and deterrence merely a means of maximizing the advantage gained by one of two or more rivals.

The essential character of both self-help and deterrence in primitive society is thus political in the broadest sense: when there is no government, retaliation and the threat of violence serve to unite social groups and maintain legal or moral criteria of right and wrong. This use of might to make right seems repugnant to civilized men, for it has been largely (though not completely) superseded within modern society; nonetheless, such a procedure is consonant with a particular kind of social order and cannot be dismissed as having been surpassed with the formation of the first political society. Primitive legal procedures may largely be confined to the international political system today, but on this level the uncivilized notions of self-help and retaliation continue to play a decisive role.[44]

Indeed, the example of primitive societies which have successfully developed governmental institutions shows how difficult it is to substitute hierarchical legal procedures for self-help. Even among peoples like the Alur, who are ruled by chiefs, a significant category of wrongs are punished, at least in the first instance, by retaliation on the part of the offended group.[45] Only if the consequences of retaliation and counter-retaliation threaten the security of innocent bystanders do the chiefs intervene, making the conflict a matter of "public law" punishable by an authority acting in the name of the tribe as a whole. In this eventuality, punishment may be meted out impartially to both parties to a feud; the creation of specifically governmental institutions represents a departure from the principle of self-help, and requires a minimal awareness that there is an organized community at a higher level than that of the contending groups.[46]

---

[42] For the distinction between latent and manifest functions which is here implied, see Marion J. Levy, Jr., *The Structure of Society* (Princeton 1952), 83–85. Cf. Barton, *The Half-Way Sun*, 196–97.

[43] *Ibid.* Barton also notes that headhunting served the latent function of providing "relief from the monotony of daily life."

[44] Cf. Aristotle, *Nicomachean Ethics,* V.1130b30–1134a15.

[45] Aidan W. Southall, *Alur Society* (Cambridge, Eng., n.d.), 144. See also 122–36, 160–65.

[46] *Ibid.*, 144–46, 234, 237–39.

V. International Politics as a Primitive, Stateless System

The foregoing analysis has attempted to show how self-help, retaliation, and deterrence can be viewed as a characteristically primitive approach to law and order. Through this focus on stateless primitive peoples, the reliance upon self-help and deterrence in international relations appears to be evidence that the world forms a political system that is in many respects similar to primitive systems. Although it is often argued that international law and politics are *sui generis*,[47] the utility of a comparison between international affairs and stateless primitive societies is shown by two characteristic similarities: first, the relation of law to violence as a means of organizing a coherent social system; and second, the relationship of custom to rivalry and bargaining as means of making and applying known rules.[48]

Although it is fashionable to describe international relations as a lawless anarchy,[49] and to admit that international law exists only on condition that it be called "weak" law,[50] these habitual opinions must be questioned. It is true that the international system permits and even sanctions a considerable amount of violence and bloodshed; but, as has been seen, there is a class of stateless political systems which have this characteristic because they depend upon self-help for the enforcement of law. In such systems law and violence are related in a way that is quite different from the internal political order under which civilized man is accustomed to live; if we speak of international "anarchy," it would be well to bear in mind that it is an "ordered anarchy."

To prove that international law is not necessarily "weak," one need only consider the functions of law in a political system. Hoffmann has suggested that any legal order has three functions: it should produce "security," "satisfaction," and "flexibility."[51] According to these criteria, a legal system dependent upon the self-enforcement of rights by auton-

---

[47] E.g., Stanley Hoffmann, "International Systems and International Law," in Knorr and Verba, eds., *The International System,* 205.

[48] The second of these characteristics is concerned, speaking crudely, with the relationship between what Almond has called the "political functions" of rule-making, rule application, and interest articulation, while the first corresponds roughly to his functions of interest aggregation and rule adjudication. The last of these functions, in a stateless system, should really be spoken of as rule enforcement, for obvious reasons. Cf. "Introduction," in Almond and Coleman, eds., *The Politics of the Developing Areas,* 17; and see note 82 below.

[49] Cf. Waltz, *Man, the State, and War,* chaps. 6 and 7. While the present essay is in complete agreement with Waltz's major theme (i.e., that war is a necessary consequence of the state system, since "in anarchy there is no automatic harmony"), his emphasis on the problem of war tends to understate the elements of legality and order in world politics.

[50] E.g., Hoffmann, "International Systems and International Law," 206–7.

[51] *Ibid.,* 212.

omous groups (be they families or nation-states) is "strong" in all three respects.

Most obviously, "flexibility" is assured in a system which recognizes any change in power; to the extent that might makes right, changes in might produce changes in right. It may be somewhat less evident that international law produces a "satisfactory" solution for disputes, yet this is on the whole true because of the admitted impossibility of reversing the verdict of brute force.[52] And, finally, the stateless international system even produces a modicum of security, most especially through deterrence based upon a mutual recognition that rival nations will both be harmed (if not destroyed) by the use of their legitimate right to self-help. In this respect it is worth emphasizing that the nuclear age, with its awesome potentialities for destruction, has also seen a corresponding increase in the unwillingness of powerful nation-states to resort to overt war.[53]

To reveal more clearly the orderly (if violent) aspects of a stateless international system, several elements of the relationship between force and law need to be spelled out in greater detail. As in primitive stateless societies, not only does violence erupt intermittently from a continuing condition of potential feud or war between autonomous groups; cooperation also occurs sporadically. While such cooperation is sometimes limited to actions which prepare for or prosecute warfare (as in most alliances), the members of the interstate system have also been capable of making mutually binding cooperative decisions in *ad hoc* multilateral conferences.[54] The Concert of Europe provides a more institutionalized example of such intermittent structures, which act as a kind of temporary "government" while preserving the sovereignty of the major states in the international system.[55]

This type of cooperative decision-making, subject to veto by a participating state, must be seen as a feasible—if obviously limited—method of procedure; it is present not only in *ad hoc* bilateral or multilateral meetings, but also in the continuously functioning international

[52] Although the "satisfaction" with defeat in war may be of short duration, this is not a necessary consequence of military defeat (as the pro-Western attitude of West Germany and Japan after World War II indicates). The limited durability of "satisfactory" settlements will be discussed below.

[53] Since World War II there have been numerous international incidents which, under prenuclear conditions, would probably have resulted in open warfare. Cf. Herman Kahn, "The Arms Race and Some of Its Hazards," in Donald G. Brennan, ed., *Arms Control, Disarmament, and National Security* (New York 1961), 93ff. On the security offered by the "impermeable" nation-state before the development of nuclear weapons, see John H. Herz, *International Politics in the Atomic Age* (New York 1959), Part 1.

[54] Most notably, of course, in peace conferences terminating major wars.

[55] On the Concert of Europe, see Richard N. Rosecrance, *Action and Reaction in World Politics* (Boston 1963), chap. 4, and the references there cited. Compare the specialized, intermittent political agencies in many stateless primitive societies: Robert H. Lowie, "Some Aspects of Political Organization Among American Aborigines," *Journal of the Royal Anthropological Institute*, LXXVII (1948), 17–18; and Radcliffe-Brown, *African Political Systems*, xix.

World Politics as a Primitive Political System

organizations (the League of Nations and the UN) which have been developed in this century.[56] It should also be noted that the emergence of so-called "functional" organizations represents a trend toward continuously functioning institutions capable of limited but very real cooperation in the international political system.[57]

The limitations as well as the importance of both violence and cooperation in world politics must therefore be equally emphasized in any total assessment of the international system. In so doing, the comparison with stateless primitive peoples serves the useful purpose of identifying the characteristic properties of a political system in which law is sanctioned by self-help. As among the primitives, retaliation is an acceptable means of righting a wrong, though it is true that civilized nations regard strict retaliation—"an eye for an eye"—as a more extreme recourse than do savage peoples.[58] As among stateless primitives, neutrality is possible, and non-involved groups often attempt to mediate conflict and induce rivals to cease fighting. As among stateless primitives, finally, the very possibility that conflict may escalate serves to deter violence on some occasions.[59] Hence the relation of law to force in the multistate system, like the "ordered anarchy" of primitive societies without governments, is derived from the lack of authoritative political institutions.

When we turn more directly to the decision-making process—the second characteristic mentioned above—it may be recalled that in many primitive political systems, especially those lacking governmental institutions, custom and bargaining are related in a crucial way, since they are the only methods for establishing enforceable rules. The same can be said of the international political system, for it too lacks an authoritative legislature or an all-powerful executive. International law can be said to be created in two major ways: a practice or rule either becomes a custom, having been followed for a considerable time, or it is adopted by mutual consent, as binding specific groups under particular circumstances. While the second of these legislative methods is relatively unambiguous to the extent that it produces formal treaties and agreements, the first produces

[56] Note the similarity between the Iroquois Confederacy, which could act as a unit only if a decision was unanimous, and the UN Security Council. See Morgan, *League of the Iroquois,* 111–14; and Inis L. Claude, Jr., *Swords into Plowshares* (2nd edn., New York 1959), chap. 8.

[57] Cf. the limited but continuous role of the *pangats* and "pact-holders" among the Kalinga, which Barton contrasts with the intermittent action of the Ifugao "go-betweens" and "trading partners" (*The Kalingas,* 144–46). On the question of the "continuity" or "contingency" of political structures, see Easton, "Political Anthropology," 235–38, 245–46.

[58] Henry S. Maine, *International Law* (New York 1888), 174–75. Primitive peoples do not always exact strict retaliation, however; the institution of a "weregild" or payment in lieu of retaliation is paralleled in international politics by reparations and other penalties exacted in the negotiation of peace treaties. Also, compare Morton A. Kaplan, "The Strategy of Limited Retaliation," Policy Memorandum No. 19 (Princeton, Center of International Studies, 1959), and, more generally, recent strategic discussions of "graduated deterrence"—e.g., Henry A. Kissinger, *The Necessity for Choice* (New York 1961), 65–70.

[59] Cf. Schelling, *The Strategy of Conflict,* chap. 8.

The World Community

customary law slowly and imperceptibly, so that in periods of rapid change one may wonder if any such law really exists. Over time, nonetheless, specific legal rules have been adopted and accepted as valid by the nation-states composing the modern international system.[60]

At any moment of time, international law seems to be chaotic and uncertain; "double standards" often appear to bind weak or law-abiding states, while permitting the ruthless or strong to satisfy their demands with impunity.[61] But when a longer-range view is taken and the world is considered as a stateless political system in which self-help is a legitimate means of legal procedure, disputes over the content of international law (like disputes over the legitimacy of each killing in a primitive feud) become a predictable consequence of the system's structure. As the world is now organized, international law almost requires conflict concerning the substantive provisions relating to a given dispute, and warfare is a legal means of bargaining prior to the conclusion of more or less temporary settlements.[62]

One peculiar characteristic of laws in a stateless political system is thus the legitimization of dispute concerning the application of legal rights to particular circumstances. While it is usual in this context to emphasize the relationship of force to law (by pointing out that "might makes right" in anarchy), the frequency and necessity of disputes over the substance of rights have another consequence: the primacy of political rivalry. Within a society with a government, men whose interests conflict must channel their demands through a specific institutional structure,

60 On the character of international law and its sources, see James L. Brierly, *The Law of Nations* (4th edn., London 1949), 1–91, 229–36; Percy E. Corbett, *Law and Society in the Relations of States* (New York 1951, 3–52); and Morton A. Kaplan and Nicholas de B. Katzenbach, *The Political Foundations of International Law* (New York 1961), chap. 9. Some observers of international relations, following John Austin's legal theory, have doubted that a system without a single sovereign authority could have "true" law. For a criticism of this application of Austin's view, see Maine, *International Law*, 47–51.

61 William Foltz has pointed out to me that there is also a parallel "reverse double standard" in both primitive and international systems; weak and unimportant groups are often permitted actions which major groups would not commit (or which would be strongly criticized if committed). Many primitive systems allow inferior lineages or castes wider latitude in many forms of conduct (dishonesty, petty thievery, public defamation, etc.) than is permitted major lineages or castes. As long as the stability of the system or the vital interests of a major group are not threatened, such behavior may be a useful safety valve. The behavior of so-called "nonaligned" states in the UN General Assembly offers an obvious parallel.

62 From the point of view of a systematic analysis, law need not be a "good." Indeed, law need not produce peaceful "order," though as civilized men we infer from our political experience that this *should* be so. Hence authorities on international law often feel compelled to go beyond mere restatements of accepted legal principles; the international law texts, long an important method of codifying customary international law, are frequently animated by a desire for reform. Cf. Maine, *International Law*, Lectures 1, xii, *et passim*. Unlike the sphere of domestic politics, in which relativism sometimes seems tenable to scholars, international law and politics are difficult to treat in a wholly positivist fashion without thereby accepting as justifiable a condition of legal self-help and war which civilized men tend to reject as barbarous, if not unjust. Hence world politics is perhaps *the* area in which it is most evident that satisfactory political theory cannot divorce objectivity (and especially freedom from partisanship) from the quest for standards of justice.

World Politics as a Primitive Political System

ultimately recognizing (in principle) the legitimacy of political attitudes which have been sanctioned by governmental decision.[63]

In international politics, this relatively terminal character of intra-state political decisions is often lacking; the policies of one's rivals need not be legitimized even by victory in warfare. In a sense, therefore, might does *not* make right in international politics (as, indeed, the French insisted after 1871 and the Germans after 1918). Like primitive feuds, international disputes are only temporarily settled; a settlement which precludes the possibility of further conflict is rare.[64] This means that political differences, and the interests upon which these differences are based, are often more visible in world politics than in intra-state politics. Conflicting demands for the satisfaction of the desires of one's own group—politics and rivalry—are therefore the prime factors in international relations.[65]

This primacy of political conflict in world affairs is especially important because of a further similarity between primitive and international politics. Just as some stateless primitive societies are differentiated into spatial "zones" of increasing opposition, so the world can be divided into areas which are politically "far" from each other.[66] Here again, a characteristic of world politics which often appears to be *sui generis* can be understood more broadly in the context of a comparison between primitive and international politics.

VI. Some Differences Between Primitive and International Political Systems

In arguing that stateless primitive political systems resemble the international political system in many ways, the search for analogies should not obscure the massive differences which must have been only too easily noticed by the reader. By specifying some of these differences, however, it will be possible to distinguish those aspects in which world politics is unique from those that are due to the absence of a formally constituted world government. In particular, there are two general differences between primitive and international politics which will make it easier to see the limits of the structural similarity between the two. It will be

[63] But note that, even in domestic politics, the legitimacy of governmental decisions may be challenged by those who are willing to be "bellicose." Cf. Bertrand de Jouvenel, *The Pure Theory of Politics* (New Haven 1963), 180ff.

[64] For the prerequisites for these rare cases, see the study cited in note 31. Note the function of "marriage" (between representatives of rival kinship groups in primitive societies and between ruling families in the earlier period of the modern state system) as a means of formalizing such a settlement.

[65] Cf. the "principle of political primacy" emphasized by Robert E. Osgood, *Limited War* (Chicago 1957), 13–15.

[66] "Blocs" and regional systems are, of course, ready examples. On the relationship between the global system and regional systems in international politics, see George Liska, *Nations in Alliance* (Baltimore 1962), 19–20, 22–24, 259–62.

The World Community

necessary to consider, first, the role of political culture, and second, the impact of change.

Although it is usually assumed that the beliefs, manners, and customs of nonliterate peoples are homogeneous, many primitive societies are composed of heterogeneous ethnic stocks; indeed, such heterogeneity is particularly important, for it appears to be related to the emergence of governmental institutions, at least among many African peoples.[67] Nonetheless, there is a marked tendency toward cultural homogeneity in primitive stateless societies, since most individuals accept without question the established way of life.[68] Although the application of traditional rules to specific cases may be and frequently is disputed, the relative stability of culture limits the kinds of change occurring in most primitive systems.[69]

In contrast, the international political system currently includes radically different political cultures. As Almond has shown, national political systems which face the task of integrating different political cultures are subject to strains that are absent in more homogeneous societies; *a fortiori,* this problem is even greater in a system which permits many antagonistic political cultures to organize themselves into autonomous nation-states.[70] In general, therefore, it could be argued that self-help and structural decentralization tend to produce a greater degree of instability in world politics than in most primitive stateless societies.[71]

An additional feature compounds this problem. The historical development of Western civilization, as it has increased man's control over nature and spread the effects of modern science throughout the world, has produced particularly sharp differences between political cultures, at the same time that it has brought these cultures into closer contact than was possible before the advent of modern technology. And, simultaneously with this intensification of the contact between different cultures, it has become apparent that technologically advanced societies are capable of what seems to be virtually infinite material progress, so that the most powerful nations can continuously increase their technological superiority over "backward" or "underdeveloped" states.

The main consequence of the interaction of modern, scientific technology upon cultural differences has been extraordinarily rapid change in world politics, of which the great increase in the number of nation-states is but the most superficial index.[72] The stateless structure of a

[67] See Schapera, *Government and Politics,* 124–25; and Mair, *Primitive Government,* chap. 5.

[68] Cf. Fortes and Evans-Pritchard, *African Political Systems,* 9–10.

[69] Hence there may be disputes concerning the power and influence of opposed groups, but these conflicts are rarely ideological in character.

[70] See Almond, "Comparative Political Systems," 400–2. Cf. the importance of the nationality problem in the USSR.

[71] Note, however, that many primitive societies are not as stable and unchanging as is often believed. E.g., see Southall, *Alur Society,* 224–27, 236, *et passim*; and J. A. Barnes, *Politics in a Changing Society* (London 1954), chap. 2.

[72] On the distinction between "stable" and "revolutionary" international systems, see Hoffmann, "International Systems and International Law," 208–11. Hoffmann

primitive political system may be tolerably stable, despite the reliance upon self-help in legal enforcement; a similar structure, in the changing context of international politics, may well lead to chaos. Even in a primitive world, the contact of a more "advanced" people with a society without governmental institutions has often produced a rapid domination of the latter by the former.[73] It is all the more to be expected, therefore, that the present structure of the international system is essentially transitional, and that quite considerable changes must be expected in the next century.

VII. Conclusion: Directions for Research

The reader may well wonder, at this point, whether the foregoing analysis has any theoretical significance: can the contrast between primitive stateless societies and the interstate system provide any substantive insights otherwise missed by students of world politics? The relative novelty of the comparison here proposed is not, in itself, sufficient justification of the endeavor. Almost eighty years ago, Henry Sumner Maine saw this parallel when he remarked: "Ancient jurisprudence, if perhaps a deceptive comparison may be employed, may be likened to international Law, filling nothing, as it were, except the interstices between the great groups which are the atoms of society."[74] While the parallels noted above may be nothing but a "deceptive comparison," Maine's formulation itself suggests the important element of similarity which promises to clarify our understanding of world politics.

Although both primitive and international politics can take place in "the interstices between the great groups which are the atoms of society," the "groups" which are "atoms" are not always the same. While this has obviously been true in international affairs at different times and places, it is no less so in primitive societies. As a result, there are an immense variety of types of primitive political systems, just as there have been widely different international political systems.

The question, then, is whether there are different patterns of groups—or different political structures—which can be identified as typical alternatives among primitive peoples; if this is the case, then perhaps the types of primitive political systems have similarities to the possible types of international political systems.

To date, there have been two major approaches to the construction of typologies of international systems: on the one hand, models of the

---

suggests that three variables determine the stability or instability of an international system: (1) "the basic structure of the world," (2) "the technology of conflict," and (3) "the units' purposes" (*ibid.*, 207–8). In the present essay, emphasis is placed on the first of these variables—see below, section VII.

73 Southall, *Alur Society*, 229–34.

74 *Ancient Law*, 161.

international system have been defined in terms of behavioral rules,[75] and on the other, types of international systems have been distinguished on the basis of historical evidence.[76] Without entering into methodological discussion, it can be wondered whether both of these approaches have shortcomings: the former tends to be *ad hoc,* and the latter to be restricted to the periods one studies.[77] Given the orientation of recent theoretical efforts in political science, the construction of a structural typology of political systems would seem to be a useful supplement to other approaches.[78]

Because such a typology appears to derive from "structural-functional" theory, developed especially by some British anthropologists,[79] it would be well to specify more precisely what is meant by "structure," and why it is emphasized rather than "function." As Marion J. Levy, Jr., has suggested, the term "structure," in its most general sense, "means a pattern, i.e., an observable uniformity, of action or operation."[80] Levy adds: "Functions refer to what is done, and structure refers to how (including in the meaning of 'how' the concept 'by what') what is done is done. One refers to the results of actions (or empirical phenomena in general), and the other to the forms or patterns of action (or empirical phenomena in general). . . . The same empirical phenomenon may be an example of either a function or a structure, depending upon the point from which it is viewed. . . . An interest in the results of operation of a unit focuses attention on the concept of function. An interest in the patterns of operation focuses attention on structure. An interest in the results of operation of a unit and the implications of those results focuses attention on both function and structure since the implications that can be studied scientifically lie in their effects on observable uniformities."[81] As is evident, from the point of view of sociological theory it is impossible to develop a general theory which emphasizes solely either "structure" or "function." Nonetheless there are good reasons for suggesting that a structural typology precede refined "functional" analysis.

This advantage can best be shown by referring to Alger's analysis of

[75] The most well-known example of this approach is, of course, Morton A. Kaplan's *System and Process in International Politics* (New York 1957), chap. 2.

[76] See Hoffmann, "International Systems and International Law," 215–33; and Rosecrance, *Action and Reaction in World Politics,* esp. Part II.

[77] Cf. *ibid.,* chap. 1, and Stanley Hoffmann, ed., *Contemporary Theory in International Relations* (Englewood Cliffs, N.J., 1960), 40–50, 174–84.

[78] It seems, for example, that the distinction between stateless systems and fully developed states is insufficient because it ignores an intermediary type which Southall called "pyramidal" or "segmentary states." In such systems, of which feudalism is but one example, there are a multiplicity of levels of authority, the most comprehensive of which is "paramount" without being "sovereign." See Southall, *Alur Society,* 241–60; and Barnes, *Politics in a Changing Society,* 47–53. Further development of the conception of such pyramidal systems and its application to world politics will be attempted in subsequent publications.

[79] E.g., see Radcliffe-Brown, *Structure and Function in Primitive Society,* esp. Introduction and chap. 10.

[80] Levy, *The Structure of Society,* 57.

[81] *Ibid.,* 60–62.

World Politics as a Primitive Political System

the similarities between intranational and international politics. Although Alger suggests that Almond's list of political functions is useful for such a comparison,[82] when he turns to the parallel between primitive and international politics, he emphasizes three factors, derived from Easton's work, which are ultimately structural in character: namely, the differentiation of political roles and the contingency or continuity of their operation, the specialization of roles which control physical force, and the character of overlapping memberships.

The reason why Almond's political functions are not immediately useful in comparing primitive and international politics is not hard to see. As Alger remarked, "A headman of a primitive society may perform intermittently as interest articulator, aggregator, and rule-maker."[83] If Almond's functions are not performed by specialized individuals in many primitive societies, concentration on these functions may only emphasize the "diffuseness" of roles, without indicating the different patterns which emerge in different primitive systems. It is necessary to see in what kinds of situations different individuals act in different ways; functional categories derived from "modern" complex political systems may be simply inappropriate for the study of primitive societies.[84]

As Almond himself was at pains to point out, "The functional categories which one employs have to be adapted to the particular aspect of the political system with which one is concerned."[85] Since a comparison of primitive and international political systems must identify the "particular aspects" of each type of system which are analogous, the use of functional categories would seem to be unpromising at the outset. In contrast, the use of a structural typology of political systems, if it proves possible to define kinds of political structures which exist in *both* primitive and international politics, has a double advantage; this approach should permit one to see not only the similarities between systems, but also the sources of the differences between modern international politics and primitive political systems.[86]

[82] Alger emphasizes the similarities between international politics and the internal politics of both developing nations and primitive societies ("Comparison of Intranational and International Politics," 410–19). He suggests that the "input functions" ("political socialization and recruitment, interest articulation, interest aggregation, and political communication") are more relevant than the "output functions" ("rule-making, rule application, and rule adjudication"). Cf. Almond and Coleman, eds., *The Politics of the Developing Areas,* 16–17; and note 48 above.

[83] Alger, "Comparison of Intranational and International Politics," 412. Cf. Almond and Coleman, eds., 19.

[84] An additional critique which might be made is that the Almond functions imply a political teleology: since traditional, "diffuse" systems tend to be replaced by modern, "functionally specific" ones, analysis may be oriented toward finding those activities which favor the trend toward "modernity." Cf. Almond and Coleman, eds., 16–17. However minor the danger of this implication in the analysis of developing nations, it would certainly be erroneous in international politics, since we have no reason to believe that present tendencies will produce a world government in which Almond's political functions have been specialized.

[85] *Ibid.,* 16.

[86] In addition, an emphasis on structure should permit one to handle more explicitly the troublesome problem of defining the "actors" in the international system.

The World Community

Finally, it should be pointed out that research in this direction, while it appears to utilize recent theoretical approaches derived from anthropology, sociology, and behavioral political science, is not divorced from the problems posed by traditional political philosophy. By emphasizing the existence of a class of social systems in which no formally instituted governments are established, the relevance of the notion of a "state of nature" to international politics can be shown to be more than a mere by-product of "normative" theories developed by political philosophers.

At the same time, however, since the apparent "anarchy" of a "state of nature" is found in primitive societies, analysis of the various kinds of primitive political structures suggests that some of the implications of the "state of nature" doctrine in political philosophy are questionable. In particular, the phenomenon of stateless societies implies that even if one can speak of a "state of nature," such a condition cannot be used to prove that man is by nature an asocial being; as a result, the "state of nature" (whether in primitive or international politics) need not be considered the *natural* human condition, as opposed to the purely *conventional* political community or state. Hence the comparison of international and intranational politics—and, more specifically, the analysis of similarities between primitive and world politics—among other things leads us to a reassessment of the sufficiency of the theory of politics established by Hobbes and elaborated by Locke, Rousseau, and Kant.[87]

Cf. Arnold Wolfers, "The Actors in International Politics," *Discord and Collaboration* (Baltimore 1962), 3–24. Alger seems to adopt the so-called "individuals-as-actors" approach, which raises some severe methodological problems; for example, he suggests (in applying Easton's work) that "international systems would tend to be distributed toward the contingent end of the continuum" which ranges from "contingent" to "continuous." This is a questionable conclusion if one considers that not only international organizations, but specific roles within national governments (e.g., "foreign minister"), function continuously in the modern state system. Cf. Alger, "Comparison of Intranational and International Politics," esp. 416, with the discussion above, p. 610. As Wolfers concluded: "While it would be dangerous for theorists to divert their primary attention from the nation-state and multistate systems which continue to occupy most of the stage of contemporary world politics, theory remains inadequate if it is unable to include such phenomena as overlapping authorities, split loyalties, and divided sovereignty, which were pre-eminent characteristics of medieval actors" ("Actors in International Politics," 24). The structural approach proposed here seems best suited to satisfy the theoretical requirements suggested by Wolfers.

[87] For a sophisticated attempt to show the continuing relevance of the philosophy of Rousseau as the basis of a theory of international politics, see Stanley Hoffmann, "Rousseau on War and Peace," *American Political Science Review*, LVII (June 1963), 317–33. Cf. Kenneth J. Waltz, "Kant, Liberalism, and War," *ibid.*, LVI (June 1962), 331–40.

World Politics as a Primitive Political System

Integration and Arms Control in the European Political Environment:
A Summary Report

Karl W. Deutsch

Reprinted with permission of the publisher, The American Political Science Association, from *The American Political Science Review*, Vol. 60, No. 2 (June, 1966) 354–65. Mr. Deutsch is Professor of Government at Harvard University.

I. The Aims and Conduct of the Study

At the heart of our research was a single basic question: What arms control and disarmament measures might be acceptable to Europeans in 1966, in 1971, and in 1976? And differently put: What would be Europe's attitude in those years either to arms competition or to arms control, and what particular policies would be most popular or least popular in Europe in this respect?

This basic question implied four more detailed questions. The first: What is Europe now, in 1966, and where is it going for the 1971 to 1976 period? Is it going to be a Europe of nation-states with only marginal common functional arrangements on matters not central in importance to the concerns of its citizens? Or will it be to some extent substantially integrated, with some major policy decisions made by common institutions? Or will it be a common body politic, speaking with a single voice and developing common institutions for a wide range of decisions?

Second: Do Europeans in general approve or disapprove of arms control? Do they welcome the relaxation of tensions between America and Russia and between the East and West, or do they fear such relaxation?

Third: What specific arms control measures are likely to be most acceptable to Europeans, and which arms control measures are likely to be least acceptable?

And fourth: What are the strength, location, and time aspects of

The findings reported in this paper are based on a study carried out in 1963–1965 at Yale University, and in Western Europe, under the research direction of the author and the administrative direction of Richard L. Merritt. The chief investigators were Karl W. Deutsch, Richard L. Merritt, J. Zvi Namenwirth, and Bruce M. Russett at Yale, together with Lewis J. Edinger of Washington University, St. Louis, and Roy C. Macridis of Brandeis University. Other collaborators included Bernard Brown, Gerald Braunthal, Peter Merkl, Eugene McCreary, Henry C. Galant, Donald Puchala, Ellen Pirro and Carolyn Cooper. Valuable criticism, advice and information were received at various stages from Henry W. Ehrmann, Morton Gorden, Stanley Hoffmann, Daniel Lerner, Erwin Scheuch, Adolf Sturmthal, and others. The responsibility for all weaknesses of the present summary remains, of course, my own.

Research utilized in this article was supported in part by the United States Arms Control and Disarmament Agency. Any judgments or opinions expressed in the article are those of the author and do not necessarily reflect the views of the United States Arms Control and Disarmament Agency or any other department or agency of the United States Government.

Fuller versions of the findings are published in two books: *France, Germany and the Western Alliance* by Karl W. Deutsch, Lewis J. Edinger, Roy C. Macridis, and Richard L. Merritt (New York, Scribners, 1967) and *Arms Control and Atlantic Unity* by Karl W. Deutsch (New York, Wiley, 1967).

Integration and Arms Control

political support for specific policies, such as the policies of France and its President de Gaulle vis-à-vis the NATO Alliance and the United States? What is the European attitude to the nuclear striking force of France, the *force de frappe,* and the proposals that other European countries should also have national nuclear striking forces? What is the attitude of Europeans, both in Germany and elsewhere, to the idea of nuclear weapons for Germany, either directly, for instance through purchase by the German Government for the German military establishment, or through the abrogation of the Paris Agreements of 1954 and therefore eventually through the German manufacture of nuclear weapons? And what is the attitude of Europeans to a multi-lateral nuclear force, either limited to European countries alone or including the United States?

To attempt to answer such questions requires a combination of evidence and judgment. The diagnosis of a physician, the verdict of a judge, and the judgment of a political scientist or analyst all are made in the light of many considerations, not all of which can be made fully explicit. A doctor who has seen many sick people, a judge who has listened to many plausible but not always trustworthy witnesses, a political scientist who has gained some experience in his professional work as to how deceptive evidence can be—each of these is likely to do better in his appraisal of reality than one who only looks at mere statistics and interview reports.

Nevertheless, though it must be interpreted with judgment, evidence speaks with its own voice and deserves to be taken seriously in its own right. We tried to develop five lines of mutually independent evidence. The first was evidence from elite interviews of 147 French and 173 West German leaders.

We also surveyed relevant mass opinion polls, going back for about fifteen years. In many cases the same question had been asked every year of samples of voters ranging from between one thousand and two thousand respondents. On many questions it was possible to compare how mass opinion had changed over time, and how it agreed with or differed from elite views in the early 1960's.

Another source of evidence was a survey of arms control and disarmament proposals which were specifically focused on Europe. This permitted us to trace the growth and decline of interest in this particular approach to arms control, in contrast either to the rejection of all arms control, or else—more realistically—to the shift of interest to more nearly worldwide approaches to arms control and disarmament, as in the 1963 nuclear test ban treaty.

We also carried on two content analysis projects. In one, a large number of newspapers and periodicals in four countries (France, West Germany, Great Britain and the United States) were examined for editorial responses to ten major arms control events by coders using their own judgment and "hand-coding" techniques. The other project studied in greater depth the editorials on European integration in four leading newspapers in France, West Germany, Great Britain and the United States by computer or machine content analysis.

374

Finally, we collected and analyzed a large number of aggregative data about actual behavior. What is happening, not to editorials about trade, but to actual trade? What is happening, not to speeches about universities, but to the numbers of young Germans and young Frenchmen actually crossing the border to study in the other country? What is happening to travel? What is happening to migration? What is happening to the exchange of mail? These data were available from the statistics published by the countries concerned or by various international organizations, and they did tell us whether these transactions had increased or declined, relative to other transactions or to the same transactions in other years or with other countries.

Using all these five streams of evidence, we then tried to make our judgments. A few of the points that came out of the combined use of the five types of evidence can be briefly summarized.

II. The Halting of European Integration Since the Mid-1950's

The first point to emerge was this: European integration has slowed since the mid-1950's, and has stopped or reached a plateau since 1957–58. An analysis of trade data, going back as far as 1890, suggests that in the 1957–58 period Europe reached the highest level of structural integration it has ever had. Most of this high level was reached by 1954, but there were slow advances to 1957–58. Europe now is much more highly integrated than it was between the wars or before World War I, but from about 1957–58 on there have been no further gains. The absolute increases after 1958 in trade, travel, postal correspondence and the exchange of students are accountable for from the effects of prosperity and the general increase in the level of these activities. There have been no increases in integration in regard to all these transactions beyond what one would expect from mere random probability and the increase in prosperity in the countries concerned.

The spectacular development of formal European treaties and institutions since the mid-1950's has not been matched by any corresponding deeper integration of actual behavior.

As far as they go, the transaction data do not suggest that any substantial increase in European integration should be expected by 1970 or 1975, even among the Six, if there should be a mere continuation of the practices and methods of the 1950's and the early 1960's. The expectable pattern for the next ten years, as suggested by a study of the trends in European transactions from 1928 to 1963, is toward a Europe of national states, linked by marked but moderate preferences for mutual transactions, with little growth—and possibly some decline—in the intensity of those preferences as expressed in actual behavior of the populations and business communities of the European countries.

The foregoing observations apply with particular strength to France. France alone of the EEC countries has retreated in part from foreign trade.

It has now a much lower proportion of foreign trade to gross national product—28 per cent in 1963—than it had in 1928, when the same proportion stood at 46 per cent. France thus has retained a greater amount of national self-preoccupation, and it has accepted in its actions somewhat less of the limited European integration than have Germany, Italy and the Benelux countries.

A different line of analysis of economic data suggests, on the basis of provisional computations, that Western Europe now has traversed about one half of the way toward structural economic integration and that perhaps another 40 years might be needed, at rates of progress from 1913 to 1955, to complete the process.[1] In any case, the pace of actual progress seems much slower than the pace of such legal and theoretical timetables as those in the formal treaties of integration. Difficulties in implementing these timetables in 1966 and thereafter may be in part inherent in this underlying situation.

III. The Decline of Interest in General Designs for European Unification

1. THE EVIDENCE OF THE ELITE PRESS

The impression of a halt in the growth of integrative sentiment in Europe is confirmed by the evidence of content analysis of "prestige" newspapers. For the years 1953 and 1963, *Le Monde,* the *Frankfurter Allgemeine Zeitung, The Times of London,* and *The New York Times,* were selected as the most representative elite newspapers of France, West Germany, Great Britain and the United States, respectively. In these papers, all editorials dealing with European or Atlantic integration or European politics in general were identified, and a sample of 200 editorials was chosen by appropriate procedures. This sample was then subjected to intensive content analysis by computer. The main changes found in the relevant editorials of each elite paper from 1953 to 1963 were as follows:

Interest in Atlantic Alliance, with military emphasis, and seen against the background of a bipolar world, has declined markedly in all three European papers. This decline is moderate but clear in the London *Times*. It is greater in the *Frankfurter Allgemeine Zeitung;* and it is greatest in *Le Monde.* All three European papers have moved toward greater concern for primarily European integration, seen in economic terms, and against the background of an increasingly multi-polar world. Only *The New York Times* has not shared in this trend. Its editorials alone intensified their Atlantic and military emphasis and their view of the world as a continuing bipolar power system.

There has been a general decline in the attention of all four papers to any general political or legal designs for a unified Europe, and a corresponding shift to greater concern with concrete difficulties of European

---

[1] This 40 years period is suggested by unpublished provisional results of research by Robert Schaefer, Yale University, 1965–1966.

integration or cooperation in regard to such matters as agriculture. In 1963, only *The New York Times* still maintained a reduced but still marked preponderance of interest in idealized political or legal designs for a unified Europe.

The concern with domestic French and German controversies, as opposed to any attention given to the requirements and costs of supranational alliances, remained unchanged in all four papers over the ten-year period. According to some theories of political integration, such concern with domestic controversies should have been expected to decline, and the interest in the needs of supranational alliances to increase, if there had been major progress toward supranational integration during that decade. No evidence of such a shift was found.

In all four papers, concern increased from 1953 to 1963 in regard to United States pressure for the extension of the powers of supranational organizations, particularly within an Atlantic framework. By 1963, supranational integration had become more closely identified with United States initiatives and pressures. On this issue *The New York Times* alone among the four papers shifted from an attitude of moderate but marked concern for American initiatives and pressures for European unification in 1953 to a so much stronger emphasis in 1963 that in regard to this issue, in the latter year, it seemed to be living in a different world from that of the European papers.

The chief form of United States activism, as discussed in these editorials, referred to American efforts to merge military and economic supranational instrumentalities in Europe or in the Atlantic area. Such a linkage between economic and military policies, however, appeared in 1963 as a theme chiefly created by American speakers and writers, with no substantial support in any of the European papers we studied.

References to arms control and disarmament were so rare in the editorials on European politics and integration, as studied in all four papers, that no statistical analysis could be undertaken in regard to these topics. These problems were not seen, it appears, in the context of European unity and general European politics.

2. THE EVIDENCE OF MASS OPINION

A considerable number of French and German public opinion polls from the years 1952–1962 were analyzed for the purpose of making comparisons between the two countries as well as comparisons of political attitudes among different groups, and comparisons with a smaller number of comparable polls from Italy and Britain. Methods used included the charting of time trends with the help of graphs, and factor analysis with the aid of computers. From these analyses several tentative findings emerged:

There was persistently greater elite and mass attention to national concerns rather than European. Large samples of Germans were asked year after year by German interviewers: "What is the most important task before our country?" In the spring of 1965, 51 per cent said "national

377

reunification," while only 3 per cent said "European union." National interests outpolled European interests fifteen to one for the top spot of attention—and had done much the same for more than a decade.

Throughout the period 1954–1962, the difference between French and German mass opinion tended to be larger than those between opinion in either of these countries and that in Italy or Britain, or between British and Italian attitudes.

Friendly feelings in French mass opinion about Germany and in German mass opinion about France increased substantially to roughly one-half of the Germans and Frenchmen polled in 1963–64. Feelings of mutual trust increased much less, to about one-fifth of the respondents in each country. Answers in the mid-1950's to the specific question "Which country would you trust as an ally in case of war?" showed markedly greater trust of France and Germany in Britain, and still greater trust in the United States than they showed between those two continental countries.

Questions in the mid-1950's about the Western alliance in peacetime, and about the same alliance in case of war, revealed very marked decreases in its support by French and German mass opinion for the latter and more serious eventuality, but stability or even a slight increase in the British popular commitment.

Nevertheless, factor analysis of many French and German opinion poll results between 1954 and 1962 indicated a marked increase in the similarity of underlying images between the two countries, as expressed by the amount of observed opinion variation that could be accounted for by factors common to opinion in both countries. In particular, there was a marked increase between 1954 and 1962 in the importance of an image of a United Europe in both French and German opinion. Most of this increase occurred between 1957 and 1962. During the same years, there occurred a marked decline in the perception of any military threat and of the danger of nuclear war. Increased relevance of European unity thus appeared quite compatible with a decreased sense of military danger.

The increased similarity of French and German perceptions in 1962, as compared to 1957 and 1954, was not matched, however, by any net increase in the similarity of French and German political values. Although Frenchmen and Germans had come to agree to an increased extent on what they saw in the world around them, they continued to disagree on what they liked.

The strongest difference between French and German mass opinion in the analysis of these surveys was found in the area of international politics. Germans had a clearly favorable image of the Western alliance and a clearly unfavorable one of the Soviet Union, while the French attitude towards symbols of Western unity was negative in 1962, and their anti-Russian posture was conditional and reserved. French popular opinion became increasingly pessimistic about NATO from 1957 to 1961, and in the confrontations of 1962 it continued to blame the United States for world insecurity, while being divided in blaming the Russians for recklessness. German mass opinion, however, saw United States policy as directed toward world security, and saw the Russians as acting recklessly. Generally, German mass opinion was markedly pro-American, while the French majority was so only with reservations, and a sizeable minority gave outright anti-American responses.

Only in regard to accepting European unity, at least in general terms, Frenchmen and Germans agreed to a greater extent in 1962 than they had done in earlier years. Even here, however, on the specific questions of European political unity and federation, French mass opinion remained significantly less "European" than its German counterpart.

The overall impression from the analysis of the trend of French and German mass opinion data from 1954 to 1962 is that of opinion halting or hestitating at a threshold. There is a consensus that European unity is a good thing, and that some steps should be taken to maintain and strengthen what European unity there is, and to go somewhat further in that direction. There seems to be no clear image in mass opinion as to what these steps should be, or how far they should go, nor is there any sense of urgency about them.

There is thus now in European mass opinion a latent clash between the continuing acceptance of the reality of the nation-state and the newly accepted image of some vague sort of European unity. The ensemble of these present public moods may facilitate general expression of good will, combined with policies of temporizing, caution, national consolidation, and only gradual and sectoral advance toward somewhat greater European integration.

3. THE EVIDENCE OF ELITE INTERVIEWS, 1964

Since the results of the elite interviews conducted in the summer of 1964 with 147 French and 173 West German respondents are discussed at considerable length elsewhere, only a few major points will be summarized here.[2]

PERSISTENT NATIONALISM WITH MAJOR CLEAVAGES: THE DIVIDED ELITES OF FRANCE

French elite responses show the continuing strength of self-assertive nationalism. Nearly seven-eighths of the respondents see current French policies as increasingly nationalistic, and nearly three-quarters see the world as an increasingly multi-polar power system, replacing the earlier bipolar United States-Soviet predominance. Three-fifths definitely approve this new trend, and a majority assert a "manifest destiny" for France.

[2] Percentages given in this summary are based on all respondents, including those who said "don't know," as well as those who did not comment on the particular question, *if* this category amounted to no more than 5 per cent of the total. If a larger proportion did not touch on a particular question, the percentages given refer only to the "articulate" respondents, that is, to those who did make a comment, even if they only professed themselves to be undecided or uninformed. In this latter case, the actual number of articulate respondents on the question is indicated.

Integration and Arms Control

There is overwhelming French elite consensus on not trusting Germany beyond a very limited extent. This was expressed in many ways throughout most of the interviews. Only 7 per cent of 136 articulate French leaders are willing to trust the German Federal Republic "a great deal." Of the 109 French leaders who express their views on German reunification, only 7 per cent favor it unconditionally, and of the 77 French leaders who comment on its security aspects, 58 per cent consider it a threat to French security.

On many issues, outright nationalist views command only strong minority support. A plurality of nearly one-half flatly deny that Europe will be unified within the next ten years; and 41 per cent choose national predominance as their preferred form of European integration, as against 43 per cent who want supranational influences to predominate. Only 30 per cent endorse an independent national foreign policy for France, while 70 per cent prefer a policy of alliances.

Efforts toward some further limitations on national sovereignty are favored, at least conditionally, by 83 per cent of French leaders, and definitely so by 45 per cent, with only 14 per cent even conditionally opposed. French elite consensus seems more favorable to at least some limited further steps toward supranational collaboration than have been the recent policies of President de Gaulle. During the next few years, such limited steps might well be undertaken with elite support by himself or his successors.

The basic pattern of national self-assertion and of French elite preferences and expectations, however, seems likely to persist. Current (i.e., relatively stressful) French policies toward the United States and NATO are most often mentioned (29 per cent) as likely to continue after President de Gaulle.

French domestic cleavages, too, seem certain to persist. Less than one-fifth of our respondents turn out to be clearcut Gaullists. While a majority expect that the Fourth Republic will not be restored, and that some institutions of the Fifth Republic will survive de Gaulle, there is no agreement on just which features will survive. The hopes for a more pragmatic and consensual "new politics" in France have not materialized.

An analysis of elite age groups indicates no major changes over the next ten years. Typically, age accounts for less than 5 per cent of the variance in the answers found. Within these limits, the "middle elites"— those in their fifties and hence the generation of the 1930's and World War II—tend to differ from both their elders and juniors, who in turn often resemble each other. This middle elite group is somewhat more nationalistic and more closely identified with the deGaulle regime.

The junior elite—those under 50—are more internationalist, more in favor of alliances, and still more opposed to an independent foreign policy for France. A moderate shift toward a somewhat more internationalist foreign policy might be supported by this generation, once its members win full power in the 1970's, but the essential features of French politics are likely to remain.

The World Community

French elite members themselves do not expect to change their minds. An above-average degree of closure of thinking is reported for 70 per cent of the respondents, and only 1 per cent feel that the policies proposed by them for defending the French national interest might become impractical in the future.

A brief follow-up survey was taken among the same group of respondents in December, 1964, after Khrushchev's fall, President Johnson's re-election, and the Chinese nuclear explosion. It elicited about 60 per cent usable responses and confirmed the stability of French attitudes expressed in mid-1964.

STRENGTHENED NATIONAL CONSENSUS AND GREATER READINESS FOR SURPRANATIONAL STEPS: THE INTEGRATED ELITES OF THE GERMAN FEDERAL REPUBLIC

Elite consensus of definite satisfaction with the present West German regime and basic policies includes nearly three-quarters of West German respondents. Adding those indicating moderate satisfaction brings total elite support for the basic GFR regime to 93 per cent. This support extends solidly across all groupings of age, class, occupation, major party and past political record.

In contrast to their more detached or alienated French counterparts, large majorities of West German elite members see themselves as influential in the policies of their own country and appear more likely to identify with them. As recorded by interviewers, 73 per cent of German respondents indicate that they think they have more than average influence in domestic affairs, and 66 per cent do so in regard to foreign policy, in contrast to only 33 per cent and 18 per cent, respectively, among the French.

The foreign policy of the German Federal Republic is definitely supported by 55 per cent of the West German leaders, in contrast to France, whose current foreign policy is clearly supported by only 33 per cent of French elite respondents. West German support for "all features" of current foreign policy, and particularly for the alliance with the United States, is expected to continue beyond Chancellor Erhard's term of office.

West German leaders are in overwhelming agreement on their country's need for allies: 93 per cent see alliances and international instrumentalities as the best means for defending the national interest of their country. Only 7 per cent name national instrumentalities, and only 6 per cent favor an independent national policy. Enduring common interests with the United States are stressed by 72 per cent, and 71 per cent favor policies aiming at further reductions in national sovereignty.

In contrast to France, two-thirds of the West German leaders continue to see the world as a bipolar power system, dominated by the United States and the Soviet Union, and they believe that it will remain so. Among the French leaders, on the contrary, nearly three-quarters see an increasingly multi-polar world around them. Faith in a continuing bipolar world is somewhat weaker among West German politicians (58 per cent), and it is shared only by a minority of German civil servants (44 per cent).

There is less agreement among German leaders as to just how far these internationalist policies will go, or ought to go. A strong plurality —46 per cent—expect European integration to be achieved within the next ten years, while 35 per cent consider this unlikely. A predominantly supranational form of European union—if it should come to pass—is chosen by a bare majority of the respondents, but 45 per cent prefer "confederation" or arrangements implying the clearcut predominance of nation-states. In France, only 19 per cent expect European union within 10 years, while 49 per cent explicitly do not; and 56 per cent of responses prefer confederation or national predominance.

Not unconnected, perhaps, with the increased strength of the West German army, German elite support for the 1954 project of a European Defense Community of conventional forces changed by 1964 to definite opposition by a plurality, 44 per cent, against only 35 per cent in clear support. In France, a much smaller trend seems to have gone in the opposite direction; 23 per cent of the French leaders now definitely favor EDC, and only 18 per cent clearly oppose it.

CONTRASTING FRENCH AND WEST GERMAN VIEWS OF FUTURE CHANGES

French response patterns generally indicate that the Fifth Republic is not perceived as deeply rooted, and that many pre-de Gaulle institutions and forces—such as the old political parties—may be expected to reassert themselves after President de Gaulle's departure from political activity. French leaders thus expect short-run changes after de Gaulle, restoring a considerable measure of long-run continuity in society and politics.

German leaders, on the contrary, expect the trends of change, initiated by the Bonn Republic, to continue beyond Chancellor Erhard's tenure of office, and in their large majority they expect no return or revival of any of the pre-Bonn political forces or practices from the Nazi or the Weimar period. As many as 86 per cent of articulate respondents consider Nazism dead; 73 per cent see the possibility of a Social Democratic government within the next 10 years, and 40 per cent consider it likely, but in any case a majority feels sure that it would make very little difference to domestic or foreign policies, except at most in regard to personnel recruitment.

French and German elite expectations differ strongly in regard to German reunification, as well as to European union. Of the 173 German leaders in our sample, only 9 do not comment on this point, while over one-third of the French do not. Among articulate German respondents, 20 per cent definitely expect reunification to take place within the next 25 years, but only 2 per cent among the articulate French do so. Another

38 per cent of the Germans have at least conditional hopes for reunification within the next quarter century, but only 11 per cent of the French agree with them; and 83 per cent of the Frenchmen commenting consider German reunification as at least unlikely within that period.[3]

As to European unification, a plurality of 46 per cent among the 158 articulate German elite members see it as likely to succeed within the next 10 years, or at least to make substantial progress, but only 19 per cent among the 141 articulate French leaders share this view. By contrast, no success of, nor any substantial progress toward, European union within the next 10 years is expected by 35 per cent of the articulate German leaders but by as many as 49 per cent among the French.

ATLANTIC ALLIANCE AND EUROPEAN ASPIRATIONS: FRENCH AND GERMAN LINKAGES AND CLASHES

French and German leaders agree—90 per cent in Germany and 72 per cent in France—that the ultimate military security of their countries depends "completely" or "in large measure" upon the deterrent force of the United States. Most German respondents use the stronger, and most Frenchmen the more cautious, wording. Large majorities of elite respondents—79 per cent in Germany and 65 per cent in France—feel sure that the United States is unlikely to abandon its commitments to the defense of Western Europe. Even larger majorities in both countries defer to long-run common interests, linking their nations with the United States.

There is also agreement among 65 per cent of the German and 62 per cent of the French elite respondents that NATO can be relied upon completely or to a considerable extent. The stronger alternative is more popular in Germany, and the weaker one in France. Minorities of 18 per cent of the German and 30 per cent of the French leaders, however, prefer to rely on NATO only "to a limited extent" or not at all.

Large majorities—68 per cent in Germany and 63 per cent in France —agree that Britain ought to be included in an integrated Europe. A majority of 52 per cent in France stress long-term common interests with Britain, but only 28 per cent do so in Germany.

The same elite proportion of 28 per cent in Germany stress common long-term interests with France, and 37 per cent in France feel they share common long-run interests with Germany. In addition, common interests with the other five EEC members, including Germany and France, respectively, are emphasized by 88 per cent of the French and 35 per cent of the German elite members.

The result is somewhat paradoxical but in line with other evidence. Majorities of French and German leaders see their countries as linked by long-run political and military interests more strongly to the United States—and in the second place to Britain—than they are linked to one another. Any weakening of French ties to the United States thus might weaken the German-French relationship. In distinction from the views

[3] For French preferences in regard to German reunification, see p. 380 above.

Integration and Arms Control

of President de Gaulle, the majority of French elite respondents prefer to keep strong these links to the United States, if this could be done on terms nearer to political equality.

French aspirations to a greater measure of equality divide many French and German views on NATO. Among articulate French leaders, 78 per cent favor NATO reforms in this direction, and only 2 per cent say no reforms are needed. Among their German counterparts, only 47 per cent desire such reforms, and 38 per cent consider all NATO reforms unnecessary.

When asked to choose between policies of strengthening mainly European institutions, such as EEC, and strengthening NATO, 40 per cent of the 124 articulate French respondents prefer EEC, against only 4 per cent who favor NATO. The 141 articulate Germans are split more evenly, with 15 per cent picking EEC and 11 per cent choosing NATO, but a 72 per cent majority refuses to choose and insists on supporting both—a middle way favored also by a French plurality of 49 per cent. Major attempts, by President de Gaulle or any successor, to put in a forced choice "Europeanism" against "Atlanticism" are thus likely to run into strong elite opposition in both countries.

Despite this reluctance of French and, even more, of German leaders to choose between Atlantic and European alignments, it seems from many subtle indications that the latter had come to command by 1964 much the larger share of elite imagination and emotional involvement. The vision of a rich, multidimensioned and growing Atlantic Community has faded.

DIFFERENTIATED FRENCH AND WEST GERMAN VIEWS OF COLD WAR PROBLEMS AND INTERNATIONAL RELAXATION

French and German elite members strongly agree in seeing in Communist states and activities the greatest threat to the security of their countries, and in opposing the withdrawals of troops or nuclear weapons from Central Europe. The neutralization of Central Europe is definitely opposed by 69 per cent of the 166 German elite members who express their views, but only by a plurality of 38 per cent of the 71 Frenchmen who did so.

Despite the perception of a Communist threat, European integration is seen as primarily nonmilitary in purpose. Strengthening the West against communism is seen as the purpose of European integration by only 19 per cent of the French and 10 per cent of the German respondents, while 45 per cent of the French and 67 per cent of the Germans emphasize economic and cultural purposes.

There is near-record consensus among both French and German leaders that in the next few years relations between their nations and "the countries of Eastern Europe" will become more cordial. No fewer than 99 per cent among the 118 articulate French respondents say so, and so do 83 per cent of the 162 articulate German leaders.

There is much less support, however, for the familiar proposals to

The World Community

relax international tensions by formally recognizing either the division or the current boundaries of Germany. Of the former measure, only 25 per cent of 153 articulate Germans and 18 per cent of 55 articulate French leaders think that it might ease international tensions. Recognition of the Oder-Neisse boundary with Poland is seen as probably helpful in easing such tensions by a majority of 52 per cent of the 155 articulate Germans, but only by a plurality of 42 per cent among the 52 French leaders who commented on this matter.

Altogether, French and German leaders produce parallel majorities on six out of ten questions relating to the Cold War complex, but in most cases they differ even there in regard to saliency and perhaps in underlying expectations. A majority of German respondents favor a partial continuation of the "hard line" policies of Cold War days, in the hope that these will ultimately lead to success or to desirable changes in the bipolar struggle; the French leaders seem to back the same policies with much greater detachment, in the expectation that they might best preserve the German status quo in a multi-polar world.

It is against this background of manifest and latent differences in French and German views that current and prospective French and German responses to arms control and disarmament proposals have to be appraised.

IV. Attitudes Toward Arms Control

1. THE ATTITUDES OF THE EUROPEAN PRESS

The machine content analysis of 1953 and 1963 editorials, reported in a preceeding section, was limited to four elite papers and to editorials dealing with European or Atlantic integration. To supplement it, another content analysis operation was carried out on a larger number of newspapers and periodicals from the same four countries, but focusing this time upon editorial responses to specific proposals or events relevant to disarmament or arms control. For this purpose, a list was compiled of ten such major proposals or events, with the first five items spanning the years from the Baruch Plan of 1946 to the Rapacki Plan of 1957, and the second five items, the years from Khrushchev's speech in 1959 to the nuclear test-ban in 1963. For editorial comments on these ten events, 97 newspapers and periodicals were searched, 35 American, 29 British, 16 French and 17 German. A total of 655 issues were consulted for the relevant periods, and 370 editorials were found and analyzed.

Within the selected periods, following major disarmament-related proposals or events, the general issue of disarmament and arms control was perceived as fairly salient. Over the entire period 1946–1963, editorial responses were found in an average of 58 per cent of the journal issues examined for the four countries. The general attitude toward efforts at disarmament or arms control was overwhelmingly friendly, with 63 per cent of all mentions favorable.

Over time, interest in arms control and disarmament rose substantially in all four countries, from an average of 43 per cent during 1946–57 to 70 per cent for the years 1959–63.

Specific arms control proposals were treated most often as serious and sincere, despite a minority current of comments labeling many of them as unrealistic or as propaganda. The emotional attitudes toward specific proposals, however, were fairly evenly divided; they were almost as likely to be negative as positive or neutral.

Among the four countries, most attention to arms control problems was paid by the press of the German Federal Republic (77 per cent) and of France (61 per cent), followed by that of the United Kingdom (48 per cent) and the United States (45 per cent). To the extent that these differences reflect reader interest rather than the accidents of our very crude sample selection, they may indicate the existence of a significant reservoir of public interest in disarmament and arms control in Germany and France.

As targets of attention, Russia, the United States, and France were the countries whose names and comments received most attention over the period as a whole, accounting for about two-thirds of all national comments reported. They were followed by Britain, Red China (and other Asian Communist countries), and West Germany.

Emotional attitudes toward nations varied. Toward the United States they were about 30 per cent friendly and 60 per cent neutral. Toward the Soviet Union they were most often negative (56 per cent) or else neutral (34 per cent). Toward Great Britain they were almost as often friendly (41 per cent) as neutral (44 per cent). Toward France and Germany they were predominantly neutral.

There was a frequent tendency in the press of the United States, France, and Great Britain, respectively, to pay most attention to the proposals of its own government, and less attention to the proposals or moves of other countries. Although there were some exceptions to this— the German press paid a great deal of worried attention to many moves by other countries—the evidence confirms the familiar picture of the national press of each country conducting often a kind of national monologue rather than genuine cross-national communication within the Western alliance.

2. THE DECLINE OF SPECIFIC PROPOSALS FOR ARMS CONTROL IN EUROPE, 1960-1964

A survey was made of 64 proposals made between 1947 and 1964 from the United States, the Soviet Union, Britain, France, West Germany, and Poland, for arms control or disarmament in Europe. They included both official proposals and major public suggestions made by political leaders, parties, or respected writers. Its findings are subject to the limitations that only proposals specifically focused on Europe were considered, that repetitions or minor variations of old proposals were excluded, and that some proposals may have been overlooked, but it seems likely that all salient Europe-centered proposals were included. The survey shows:

(1) French interest in arms control has been much lower than that of any other major country. During the 18 years covered, there were only four French proposals, two of which were made in 1959 by political leaders out of office, Pierre Mendès-France and Jules Moch. No official French proposals were found after 1956, and no significant French proposals from any source after 1959.

(2) In rank order of frequency, proposals came most often from the Soviet Union (18), and the United States (14), followed by Britain (11), the German Federal Republic (10), Poland (7), and France (4).

(3) Over three-fifths of the proposals for Europe made by government spokesmen of some kind, and nearly nine-tenths of the proposals from opposition leaders or private persons, came in the five-year period from 1955 to 1959. During this peak period, official Western and East bloc proposals were equally frequent. From 1960 onward, official proposals from the United States for European arms control diminished; Britain and West Germany made no such proposals at all, and by the criteria of relevance used for this report they contributed only one unofficial proposal apiece, and France contributed nothing at all. However, the East bloc countries (i.e., the U.S.S.R. and Poland) continued in 1961–64 to make proposals for Europe at nearly the same rate as in 1955–59, with a somewhat larger share of proposals coming from Poland.

This undiminished East bloc activity might have the possible effect of pre-empting some of the role of champions of European disarmament for the East bloc countries, but also of associating to some extent in the minds of West European elite members the entire topic of arms control with East bloc propaganda, so as to reinforce the partial withdrawal of West European elite interest from this topic. If Europe-centered United States proposals should again become salient and frequent, Western European elite interests might again increase.

The shift, however, in United States interest to more nearly worldwide approaches to arms control and disarmament, such as the 1963 nuclear test-ban treaty, accords well with the preferences of the French and German elite members, most of whom favor further worldwide arms control arrangements of this kind but many of whom express misgivings about narrowly regional arms control arrangements for Central Europe alone, which they fear might leave the area unprotected in a world of military pressures.

3. THE COMMON FEAR OF NUCLEAR PROLIFERATION AND THE GENERAL SUPPORT FOR DISARMAMENT AND ARMS CONTROL

There are clear indications of anti-Communism, and of "tough-mindedness" in regard to disarmament, among majorities of both French and German elite respondents. Inspection arrangements are demanded or desired as part of any East-West arms control agreement by 78 per cent of the articulate German elite members, but only by 38 per cent of the corresponding group in France.

Within this context however, support for arms control and disarmament produces a striking number of strong and parallel majorities among French and German elites. Efforts to stop the proliferation of nuclear weapons "to countries that do not now possess them" are supported by articulate majorities of 78 per cent in France and 90 per cent in Germany. Discussions of disarmament are favored by 69 per cent of the articulate French respondents and 76 per cent of their German counterparts; 20 per cent among the French supporters of disarmament discussions say, however, that the idea is utopian but worth discussing anyway. Some plan for arms control is endorsed by 66 per cent of French and 61 per cent of German responses, and only 17 and 30 per cent, respectively, do not favor any plans. The 1963 American-British-Soviet nuclear test-ban treaty—which France has not joined—is endorsed by a French plurality of only 46 per cent, but by a strong German majority of 84 per cent.

Further arms control and disarmament agreements are definitely backed by 52 per cent of the 134 French and by 84 per cent of the 165 German respondents who comment on the matter. Even if their own countries should not be consulted about future arms control agreements, 55 per cent of the 129 articulate French respondents and 65 per cent of the corresponding 152 Germans still are willing to support them. (German mass opinion in mid-1954 took the same view by a majority of 77 per cent of all those envisaging this possibility, or by a plurality of 44 per cent.)

4. THE LACK OF POPULAR SUPPORT FOR NATIONAL NUCLEAR DETERRENTS AND MLF PROPOSALS

The idea of a national nuclear deterrent is unpopular among the elites in France, where it is official government policy and still more unpopular among the elites of Germany, where it sometimes has been described— by outside observers—as a possible latent aspiration. In fact, it seems to be not even that. A national nuclear deterrent is rejected as unnecessary for national prestige or national independence, and as not credible to the nation's enemies, by majorities ranging between 54 and 63 per cent in France, and 64 and 94 per cent in Germany.

France's current national *force de frappe* is not expected to survive President de Gaulle. Only 22 per cent of all French respondents expect it to be kept and strengthened, while 49 per cent expect it to be turned into a European institution, and another 6 per cent expect it to be abandoned.

Although clear majorities reject the main arguments in favor of a national nuclear deterrent, French respondents are exactly divided between 46 per cent who feel that such a deterrent still is worth its cost, and the same proportion who feel that it is not.

There is no such division in West Germany, where the thrifty rejection of a national nuclear deterrent as not worth its cost is backed by a landslide majority of 95 per cent of the 163 German respondents com-

388

menting on this point. This German majority is so large as to swamp all differences among age or interest groups.

These German elite data tend to disconfirm the notion of a supposedly strong German desire for national nuclear weapons—a desire which would have to be bought off or headed off by offering the German Federal Republic some share in a supranational nuclear weapons system. So far as our evidence goes there is no such German desire for national nuclear weapons at this time.

A multilateral nuclear force under NATO is clearly favored only by 18 per cent, and clearly opposed by 27 per cent of the 100 French respondents who comment on this proposal. In Germany, where practically all respondents comment, the same proposal divides the elites exactly, with 34 per cent clearly in favor and 34 per cent definitely opposed. This last division contrasts sharply with the usual propensity for strong elite consensus in the Bonn Republic.

A European multilateral nuclear force, independent of NATO, would be somewhat more popular among elites in France, where a plurality of 40 per cent of 134 respondents clearly favors it, with only 12 per cent clearly opposed, but it would be much less popular in Germany, where no more than 6 per cent of 168 respondents back the project, while a solid 80 per cent express their opposition.

If a multilateral nuclear force within NATO should come into existence, only 16 per cent of the 102 French respondents to this question would definitely wish their country to participate, but another 43 per cent might agree to such a course under certain conditions. Among the 160 German respondents to the same question these proportions are reversed: 58 per cent clearly favor participation in such a NATO development, with another 13 per cent supporting it conditionally; and only 17 per cent definitely oppose it.

The proportions of the various responses to these and related questions confirm an impression from our interviews: there is no substantial German pressure for an MLF, but rather a willingness to go along with such a scheme, if Germany's ally, the United States, should insist on it.

The pattern of responses to this entire complex of questions suggests that neither French nor German elites are pressing strongly at this time for nuclear weapons, either national or collective. Rather, the issues of the national deterrent and the MLF tend to evoke opposition or division. This contrasts with the high majorities in both countries in favor of arms control.

The evidence of the elite survey, as far as it goes, accords well with the data from mass opinion polls and the other types of evidence examined in this study. All of this evidence is limited and incomplete, and must be appraised with judgment. At the same time it should be borne in mind that none of the evidence we have found, in terms of differences among age groups or of trends over time, points to the likelihood of any drastic changes in the next few years due to any autonomously developing changes in the French or West German political system.

V. Conclusions

The lines of evidence pursued in our inquiry tend to converge. Although there are minor differences, the weight of evidence points to several major conclusions.

1. THE STRENGTH OF NATIONALISM

The movement toward structural European unification since 1957 has been largely halted or very much slowed down. The next decade of European politics is likely to be dominated by the politics of nation-states, and not by any supranational European institutions.

Within France, and within Germany, the various elite groups generally are closer in their attitudes to each other, and to the mass opinion of their own country, than they are to the opinion of their counterparts in the other country. Nationality continues to be a far stronger determinant —or indicator—of political attitudes than do class, age, occupation, religion, party affiliation, and even, for most respondents, ideology.

A provisional factor analysis of our elite survey data confirms this finding. Its results suggest that nationalty seems to be between two and ten times as powerful as any one cross-national factor, such as religion, occupation, socialist party affiliation, in accounting for the distribution of responses.

To restore now to the movement toward European unification the vigor and the momentum of the years 1947–1955 would require much larger efforts on the part of Europeans and of the United States than seem to be contemplated now in any quarter of authority. In terms of politics, it would require a visible increase in the share of American attention fixed on Europe rather than on Asia.

2. THE DESIRE FOR ALLIANCES AND NEAR-EQUALITY

Alliances, particularly with the United States, and limited steps toward additional supranational arrangements and institutions are popular among elites and acceptable to mass opinion. National isolationism is being rejected, but increasing national equality—or perhaps a share in great power privilege—is being demanded, particularly by the elites of France.

3. THE DESIRE FOR WIDER ARMS CONTROL AND DISARMAMENT

There is striking consensus in France and Germany on the desirability of arms control and disarmament on a more than local or regional scale, and including further direct agreements between the United States and the Soviet Union. There is particularly strong consensus on the desirability

The World Community

of halting the spread of nuclear weapons to nations which do not now possess them.

4. THE LACK OF ANY STRONG GERMAN DEMAND FOR NUCLEAR WEAPONS

There is strong opposition in Germany to the acquisition of national nuclear weapons, and there is no strong positive desire for any German share in a nuclear weapons system through some multilateral arrangement, such as the MLF project; and there is overwhelming and deep-rooted French hostility to any idea of a German national nuclear weapon, or to a substantial German share in a multilateral nuclear weapons system.

5. THE POSSIBLE EUROPEAN SUPPORT FOR A NUCLEAR NON-PROLIFERATION TREATY

Under these conditions of European politics, the most nearly acceptable approach to arms control and disarmament might be an international agreement limiting the possession of nuclear weapons to those five powers now possessing them: the United States, Britain, France, the Soviet Union, and Communist China.

These five are the governments in control of the five countries whose special importance is recognized in the United Nations Charter by giving them the status of Permanent Members of the United Nations Security Council. The legal status of Communist China is currently blocked in this respect, but her acquisition of a nuclear device has been tacitly tolerated by all other nuclear powers; and an explicit or tacit nuclear *modus vivendi* with Communist China does not seem unacceptable to European leaders.

Even without an agreement with China, an anti-proliferation agreement and extended nuclear test-ban among the "Big Four"—United States, the United Kingdom, France, and the Soviet Union—might prove feasible, and might pave the way to further steps to arms control. Such an approach might meet some of the French desire for a full and genuine share in international leadership, and our data suggest that such an acccommodation of French desires on the part of the United States and Britain would be acceptable to the majority of the West German leaders.

6. PROSPECTS

The picture emerging from this study is complex but not without hope. At moments of crisis the main ties of Western unity will be to Washington rather than among the European countries. For the next decade at least, national political issues will predominate over supranational ones in both France and West Germany. Viable alliances during this period will have to be concluded on specific matters, among sovereign powers, and on a footing of equality, particularly in regard to France. Greater unity of action, as well as deeper emotional ties in Western Europe, are growing very slowly. In terms of European unification, we may expect after 1975

Integration and Arms Control

a possible resumption of the advances of the 1950's, but not much earlier. Until then we can expect to hold the present plateau and improve it slightly.

Western Europeans on the whole, if French and German leaders are representative of their opinions, now favor worldwide measures of arms control. They favor particularly the relaxation of tensions between the great powers, extensions of the ban on nuclear testing, and measures against the proliferation of nuclear weapons to any countries not now possessing them. They favor all these policies, however, only provided that they can keep the American alliance and the American nuclear shield. Within this very wide range of policies acceptable to Europeans, the United States at this time has a remarkably wide range of discretion and perhaps an unparalleled opportunity for leadership.

Opportunities can be used or lost, together with the work of years of preparation. Once lost, they may be gone, or recoverable only at a great sacrifice. The value of the present American opportunities for leadership to European unity and worldwide arms control must be weighed carefully in the balance against the attractions of any policy of predominant or unlimited United States commitments on the continent of Asia.

The World Community

An End
to European
Integration?

C H A P T E R   T W E N T Y

Ronald Inglehart

Reprinted with permission of the publisher, The American Political Science Association, from *The American Political Science Review,* Vol. 61, No. 1 (March, 1967), 91–105. Mr. Inglehart is Associate Professor of Political Science at the University of Michigan.

"European Integration has slowed since the mid–1950's, and has stopped or reached a plateau since 1957–58."[1] This is Karl Deutsch's first major conclusion in a recent summary report of findings from a study which he and a number of colleagues have been executing over the past few years.[2] The study appears to be one of the most ambitious and interesting political research projects undertaken in recent years; its findings should be widely useful. In reaching this conclusion, Deutsch's interpretation is not merely that integration has stopped in the relatively narrow realm of formal government decisions; on the contrary, he contends that the process has come to a halt in the "European political environment" as a whole.

Deutsch bases his case on an analysis of trade flows and other transactions, content analysis of the elite press, public opinion surveys and elite interviews. An examination of much the same data, in connection with a study of political socialization in Western Europe, has led me to a radically different conclusion. Far from finding a stagnation of integrative processes since 1958, I would argue that, in some respects, European integration may have moved into full gear only *since* 1958. In this article I will first present some new evidence concerning attitudes among the younger generation in The Netherlands, France, West Germany and Great Britain; I will then review Deutsch's findings in this context.

I. Attitudes Among Western European Youth

I hypothesize that important changes in political socialization may have been taking place in recent years, as a result of the postwar European movement, the increases in trade, exchange of persons, and the erection

I wish to thank Samuel Barnes, M. Kent Jennings, Warren Miller and David Segal for their valuable criticisms of an earlier draft of this article. I am also grateful to Karl Deutsch for generously giving access to research reports from his study. The interpretations reached here are, of course, my own.

[1] "Integration and Arms Control in the European Political Environment," See Chap. 19 of this book, page 372. Deutsch's collaborators are listed in a footnote on p. 373. The same footnote indicates that fuller versions of the findings have been published in two books.

[2] Deutsch does not seem to be alone in taking this general view. Sen. Frank Church suggests that "European sentiment may have shifted toward a different arrangement, that what might have been achieved in the vision of such men as Jean Monnet when Europe lay prostrate after the war may no longer represent a practical possibility," see "U.S. Policy and the New Europe," *Foreign Affairs,* 45 (1966), p. 52.

of European institutions. If this is the case, we might expect to find differences between adults and youth in their orientations toward European integration. To test this hypothesis, I made a secondary analysis of two cross-national studies of adult attitudes, made in 1962 and 1963. I will compare these data with material which I collected in 1964 and 1965 through surveys of the school populations of France, The Netherlands, West Germany and England.[3] My sampling technique consisted of selecting several schools in each country which were considered representative of the important social and economic groups, on consultation with educational authorities in the respective countries. Self-administered questionnaires were given to all members of specific classes in these schools, under the supervision of a teacher.[4] The questionnaires incorporated a number of items from the two adult surveys just mentioned. The data indicate that a gap does exist between adults and youth in relative degree of "Europeanness."

In response to the question, "To what extent are you in favor of, or opposed to, the efforts being made to unify Europe?" adults compared with youth (ages 13–19) as follows:

TABLE 1   OVERALL PERCENTAGE "STRONGLY FOR" OR "FOR" EUROPEAN UNIFICATION

	Netherlands	France	Germany	Britain
Adults 1962	87%	72%	81%	(65%)[5]
Youth 1964–65	95	93	95	72

Among youth of the three European Community countries, this is about as near to a unanimous verdict as one is likely to come in survey research. The response is overwhelmingly favorable to European unification by a majority which swamps all differences of social class, sex, religion, etc.

[3] The data collection was supported by a Fulbright grant, with additional aid from the Dutch Ministry of Education. The analysis has been supported by a National Science Foundation Cooperative Fellowship.

[4] Total numbers of questionnaires obtained are as follows: France: 700; The Netherlands: 3,100; West Germany: 700; England: 500. Each social type is not included in proportion to its occurrence in the overall population. In order to correct for this fact, I will base my comparisons on samples which are weighted to compensate for the relative shortage of working-class students. I weighted our SES groups according to the proportions of manual to non-manual occupations indicated in the adult surveys (approx. 2:1). My estimates, therefore, can only be regarded as a spot check on the overall distribution of attitudes. I resorted to this approach because funds did not permit obtaining a probability sample, and no alternative data were available. In a more extensive analysis, I examine other factors which seem to influence support for European integration, and attempt to control for them also. See Ronald Inglehart, *The Socialization of "Europeans"* (unpublished Ph.D. dissertation, University of Chicago, 1967).

[5] In the three most recent surveys in which this question was asked of British adults (1955, 56, and 57) the percentage favorable ranged from 64% to 66%.

An End to European Integration?

Among adults in these three countries, a substantial degree of hesitation exists, especially in France; it virtually vanishes among the younger generation. English youth is far from unanimity, but does give a fairly solid majority in support.

The foregoing question merely indicates support or opposition to European "unification" as a general idea. What happens when we pin our respondents down to specific measures? A series of questions was asked concerning concrete proposals for European integration. We find that the favorable percentage declines in every case; a strong majority gives lip service, at least, to the general idea of "unification" but is less emphatically in favor of given specific proposals. A factor analysis of our secondary school data revealed that a number of these responses clustered together, evidently indicating a "Europeanness" dimension. Using the four highest-loading items which are common to both surveys, let us compare the responses of youth with those of adults in 1963:

TABLE 2   PERCENTAGE "FOR" FOUR PROPOSALS: ADULTS V. YOUTH

	Netherlands	France	Germany	Britain
1. "Abolish Tariffs?"				
Adults	79%	72%	71%	70%
Youth	87	83	89	74
2. "Free Movement of Labor and Businesses?"				
Adults	76	57	64	52
Youth	64	65	75	65
3. "Common Foreign Policy"				
Adults	67	50	60	41
Youth	80	71	74	56
4. "Use 'Our' Taxes to Aid Poorer European Countries?"				
Adults	70	43	52	63
Youth	82	68	72	57

TABLE 3   AVERAGE PERCENTAGE "FOR" FOUR MEASURES

	Netherlands	France	Germany	Britain
Adults	73%	56%	62%	57%
Youth	78	72	78	63
Difference	+5	+16	+16	+6
Normalized Difference[6]	19	36	42	14

The Netherlands (in which the adult population already displayed a relatively high level of support for European integration) shows a relatively

6 Normalized according to the Effectiveness Index described by Carl I. Hovland *et al.* "A Baseline for Measurement of Percentage Change" in Paul F. Lazarsfeld and Morris Rosenberg, *The Language of Social Research* (Glencoe, 1955), pp. 77–82.

The World Community

small age group difference; but over the four measures, our samples of French and German youth show pronounced increases in Europeanness relative to the adults in those countries. English youth lag behind here, as in our other comparison, although there is an indication of some increase in Europeanness relative to the adult population of Britain.[7] Striking as these generational differences are, they become even more interesting when we break down the adult responses according to age group:

TABLE 4   AVERAGE PERCENTAGE "FOR" FOUR MEASURES, BY AGE GROUP

Age Groups	Netherlands	France	Germany	Britain
55 and over	70%	47%	52%	49%
40–50	73	58	63	57
30–39	71	59	64	61
21–29	72	58	67	60
16–19 (youth sample)	77	72	78	63

In the Netherlands, the most notable feature of this pattern is its stability among different age groups. Dutch youth are more European than the oldest adult group (55 and over), but the difference is one of only 7 percentage points: an average of 77% "For" among the teenagers, as compared with 70% among the oldest group. The gap between the "55 and over" Germans and the teen-age Germans is much larger: fully 26 percentage points separate the two groups, building from a base of 52%. This seems to confirm other findings of striking differences among age groups reported for that country. One hears less talk of a "generations conflict" in France, yet in regard to the European issue, my data indicate that among the French there is almost as great a change from middle-agers to teen-agers as in the case of Germany: an increase of 25 percentage points in over-all support of the four European integration measures. The increase from oldest to youngest age group in England is intermediate: 14 percentage points.

While the average levels of support for these concrete proposals are considerably below the landslide approval of European "unification," we might tentatively draw the conclusion that the youngest generation in each of these countries is significantly more favorable to European integration than the group 55 and over—the age group which now holds most top-level positions of political power in these countries. Two relative dis-

7 Does this imply that youth is more cosmopolitan than adults as a general rule? Not necessarily. The example of the Hitler youth might be cited as an indication that the reverse relationship is also possible. My interpretation is simply that, because of the specific influences present in their early socialization, this *particular* crop of youth has been oriented in a more European and less nationalistic direction than preceding age cohorts.

An End to European Integration?

continuities are particularly interesting in the age-group pattern: first, we notice that in France, Germany and Britain, the "over 55" group is markedly less European than the group immediately bordering it: there is a sharp drop of 8 to 11 percentage points. On the other hand, we find no sizeable gap between the oldest *Dutch* group and the next younger group, in regard to Europeanness. Indeed, the "over 55" group in that country is within 2 points of the "21–29" group. This contrast between Dutch stability and the rather sharp changes in the age group patterns of her neighbors cannot readily be interpreted in terms of a life cycle explanation and it leads us to a very interesting alternative interpretation.

The age group which was 55 and older in 1963 was at least 10 years old at the end of World War I. These individuals were exposed to the period of intense nationalism which preceded that war, and to the powerful fears and suspicions the war aroused during a relatively impressionable stage of life. Alone among these four countries, Holland did not participate in World War I—nor was she deeply involved in the preceding great-power rivalries. If one's concept of nationality tends to be established early in life,[8] then the sharp decline in Europeanness which we find among this age group in each country *except* the Netherlands might be attributed to a residue from experiences in childhood and youth. It seems plausible that the effect of a major war on one's feelings of trust and kinship with the "enemy" people (e.g., the French toward the Germans) is strongly negative.

The "over 55" group in France, Germany and Britain had a powerful dose of the influences of World War I in its early years: the corresponding group in Holland was much less affected by them. And the next younger group (this time in all four countries) also shows less of the effect which we might attribute to that period: the median year of birth for this group is 1916. The oldest members of the younger group would have had some exposure to World War I (and their Europeanness would be lessened accordingly); but to a large extent this group was too young to be directly aware of World War I, and had reached adulthood before the outbreak of World War II. Karl Deutsch reports a phenomenon which seems to fit in with this interpretation. Drawing on data from a series of elite interviews in France, he reports:

Typically, age accounts for less than 5 per cent of the variance in the answers found. Within these limits, the "middle elites"—those in their fifties and hence the generation of the 1930's and World War II—tend to differ from both their elders and juniors, who in turn often resemble each other. This middle elite group is somewhat more nationalistic and more closely identified with the de Gaulle regime. The junior elite—

8 See, for example, Jean Piaget, "Le developpement chez l'enfant de l'idée de patrie et de relations avec l'étranger," *Bulletin Internationale de Science Sociale,* UNESCO, 1961, pp. 3, 605, 621. Piaget concludes that the concept of nationality is fully developed by age 14. Cf. Robert Hess, Judith Torney and David Jackson, *The Development of Basic Attitudes and Values Toward Government, Part I* (Chicago, 1965), p. 380; and Gustav Jahoda, "Children's Ideas about Country and Nationality" *British Journal of Educational Psychology,* June, 1963.

The World Community

those under 50—are more internationalistic, more in favor of alliances, and still more opposed to an independent foreign policy for France.[9]

While Deutsch refers to the relatively nationalistic group as "the generation of the 1930's and World War II," they might also be described as "the generation of World War I": in their fifties in 1964 (the time of the interviews), the Great War was probably felt as *the* important event of their childhood. They were 4 to 14 years old at the War's end. The next younger group was unaware of the war, while most of the older group had already passed through their most important years of political socialization by that time.

Moving down the age group tables, we notice little further increase in Europeanness among the adult population. This would be surprising if we were to work on the assumption that younger people are naturally more open to new ideas (a favorite assumption of intuitive life-cycle interpretations). Again we would attribute this peculiarity to the psyhcological residue of a major event—in this case, World War II. The median year of birth of the youngest adult group is 1938: by 1945, its members were 3 to 11 years old, and had experienced blitz, occupation, and devastation during the most impressionable years of life. The "European" atmosphere of the postwar years should *also* have made a relatively great impact on this youngest adult group—but apparently not enough to make them significantly more European than the older adult groups.

Except for the oldest group, none of the age groups discussed so far is a "pure" category from the standpoint of historical experiences. To some extent they overlap, containing individuals who were socialized during periods which we would consider optimal (from the standpoint of developing Europeanness) as well as individuals who were exposed to powerful negative influences during the years of childhood and early youth. The youngest group of all (those in the 16 to 19-year-old category) do constitute a "pure" group in this sense. All of these individuals were born in 1945 or later; they have gained their first political perceptions in a world where European organization seems natural and right, and nationalism seems archaic and dangerous. It is among this youngest group that we find (as we did with the oldest group) a relatively great discontinuity from the level of Europeanness of the adjacent group. This discontinuity is most marked in France and Germany; it exists also in the Netherlands; but it is very slight in England. The latter finding may be highly significant. I conclude that at least two elements are necessary for the establishment of a strong sense of Europeanness:

1. The absence of divisive memories (but this is not enough in itself).
2. A sense of positive participation in substantial common activities. Britain has not participated in the institutions of the European Community. Youth in the other three countries, however, have grown up with some awareness of a common endeavor, and this may explain, at least in part, their greater degree of backing for European integration measures.

[9] Deutsch, "Arms Control," *op. cit.*, p. 380.

An End to European Integration?

II. Age, Cohort and Historical Period

Projecting from the foregoing data, we might anticipate that the current generation of youth in these countries will manifest a relatively "European" outlook when they become adults, because this accords with conditions obtaining at that point in time when their basic political orientations were instilled. At this point, let me introduce an hypothesis which will make more explicit the relationship which I believe exists between certain distinctive aspects of the attitudes of a given age cohort and the period in which the group received its early socialization. The central element in this hypothesis is something which we might call "structural inertia" in concept formation. Taking this view, we would regard the socialization process as one in which perceptions become ordered into increasingly complex conceptual structures. Only a few of the infant's earliest perceptions—those related to basic needs—will give rise to subjectively important symbols. Most other stimuli will be disregarded as "noise." Subsequent perceptions which are regularly associated with these symbols may take on a derivative importance; these will tend to become relatively permanent, to the extent that a relatively large number of perceptions are associated together around a given basic symbol. To change a central part of the system would require a disassembly and reintegration of the whole structure. Accordingly, adult learning has been contrasted with infant learning as the "recombination of a smaller number of larger subassemblies of memories or habits. . . ."[10] When one has reached adulthood, only a very important event, making a deep and continuing impact on the individual's life, would justify the cost of such a conceptual reorganization.

My expectation on the basis of this hypothesis, is that the full impact of the postwar European movement has not yet manifested itself among the adult population. I would anticipate a time lag between certain types of major political outputs and the resulting feedback into the political system, because of the gap in time between the early political socialization of individuals,[11] and the point at which they become politically relevant. We might diagram the basis of this time lag as in Figure 1.

A major event (war, or the establishment of new political institutions, let us say) occurs at time X—during the adult years of generation "1," bringing about a relatively superficial attitudinal change in that generation. It has occurred during the late childhood of generation "2" and influences the basic political orientation of that age group. Its political feed-back, however, may not be felt until time Y, when that generation "surfaces" into political relevance. (This point is arbitrarily indicated as age 21.) Such a time-lag effect would only be expected to operate in connection with relatively early-established and persisting aspects of political

---

10 D. O. Hebb, cited in Karl Deutsch, *The Nerves of Government* (New York, 1963), p. 16.
11 That is, the socialization which takes place in childhood and youth.

The World Community

socialization. Provisionally, I interpret these data on development of a sense of European political identity according to this model.[12]

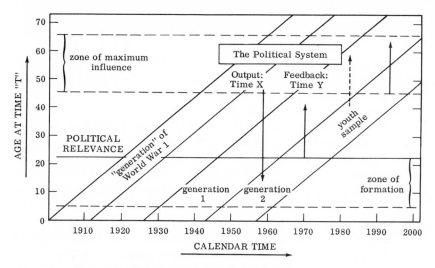

Figure 1   *Time Lag and Attitude Development*

It is, of course, impossible to predict with certainty what attitudes a given age group will express in a decade or two. My interpretation would be far more convincing if I were able to support it with longitudinal data based on national probability samples made at *several* different points in time. This is a goal for further research. On the basis of the evidence we have examined, however, we might infer tentatively that the younger generation has a stronger *tendency* to support the concept of a federal Europe than do older age groups in these countries. The Europeanness

[12] The concept also seems useful for interpreting political activity in other areas —notably Red China. Peking's recent mobilization of teen-agers to enforce conformity on the part of their elders may be linked with differences in the early political socialization of youth as contrasted with the adults. Fragmentary as our evidence is, there seem to be indications of a wide cleavage between the older and the youngest generations in the population at large, regarding their degree of commitment to the Maoist vision for Chinese society. It is probably noteworthy that the current teenage group has received its basic political socialization entirely since 1949, the year of Communist victory on the Mainland. This regime has given intense attention to the indoctrination of a new set of societal values. Apparently, the program of thought reform has not achieved the desired degree of Communist piety through reorientation of adults in the general population. Its efforts have only now begun to reach fruition in the production of a highly-committed age cohort, capable of being used as guardians over less firmly Maoist groups. A parallel to the European phenomenon also seems to exist in the American context; it could be interpreted as due to a differential impact of this country's postwar internationalism on different age cohorts. A nation-wide survey of high school seniors and their parents in 1965 produced evidence of a possible intergenerational shift in the direction of more cosmopolitan political attitudes. Ranking the relative salience which four levels of government had for them (international, national, state and local), fully 65% of the students rated international politics in first or second place; only 42% of the parents did so. See M. Kent Jennings, *Pre-Adult Orientations to Multiple Systems of Government* (paper presented to the Midwest Conference of Political Scientists, Chicago, April 1966).

401

An End to European Integration?

of the youth samples presumably represents a basic orientation, rather than a re-orientation in conformity with current experience.

III. Decay or Stability in Age Group Differences?

We find age group differences, then, as predicted by our model. But will these differences persist? From the perspective of the exceptionally stable American political community (which has experienced a relatively slowly changing political consensus for about a century) one may be tempted to assume that these age-group differences will decay—that by the time the current European youths are old as today's adults, they will hold the same attitudes. To be sure, a life-cycle interpretation may provide a valid explanation for many or most of the age-group differences which have been found in survey research, especially among societies which are not undergoing rapid social change. On the other hand, it is clear that this is not true in *all* cases, even in Western societies.[13]

The relative importance of decay in age group differences probably varies according to at least three sets of circumstances: (1) The type of attitude involved. Preferences in popular music, for example, may be very largely governed by life-cycle factors; political party preference, or matters of even more fundamental self-identification may be much less so. (2) The age at which the given orientation is established. According to our concept of structural inertia, those attitudes which are earliest established should be hardest to change. Orientation toward the political community seems to be established relatively early in life. (3) The causes of the given set of age-group differences: are they attributable to different reactions to the same environmental conditions at different points in the life cycle, or are they due to different conditions of early socialization? If the latter, we might expect decay to be relatively unimportant, particularly if the changed conditions persist.

If Europeanness were a matter of teen-age rebellion, for example, we might be justified in assuming that it would diminish with increasing maturity. Our interviews gave little indication that Europeanness was regarded by youth as a form of rebellion.[14] On the contrary, it seemed

---

[13] There are indications that an age-specific pattern in American political party preferences may be linked to the differential impact which the Great Depression had on different age groups. These differences apparently have not decayed. See Angus Campbell, Philip E. Converse, Warren E. Miller, and Donald E. Stokes, *The American Voter* (New York, 1960), pp. 153–156.

[14] The relative Europeanness of the youth in our samples probably springs from naiveté or adolescent rebellion to only a very limited degree. The fact that they have a relatively pessimistic (and perhaps realistic) view of how long it will take for Europe to become "unified"—and the fact that they have a level of knowledge which compares favorably with that of adults—tends to make an explanation in terms of naiveté somewhat untenable. Our interviews indicated, moreover, that rebellion is not an important theme in connection with European integration. Despite the widespread prevalence of a stereotype of youthful rebellion, the available evidence suggests that it is important only in exceptional individual cases, as far as political views are concerned. See M. Kent Jennings and Richard G. Niemi, *Family Structure and the Trans-*

The World Community

to be generally regarded as an enlightened and highly respectable orientation. Analysis by social status reinforces this impression; far from being a deviant position, "Europeanness" is likely to be found among those of higher status and those who are most integrated into the community. My interpretation links the age group differences which seem to exist regarding Europeanness with the following differences in the conditions of early socialization:

a. Absence of a major intra-European war from the younger individuals' experience.

b. A marked increase in intra-European transactions, with a possible reduction in the psychological distance between the groups concerned.

c. Development of European institutions which perform important functions and are widely regarded as beneficial.

All these factors have distinguished the early socialization of European youth from that of the older generations. Moreover, they continue to operate; we might well argue that their impact is likely to *increase* rather than disappear as the current crop of youth grows older. These do not appear to be transient stimuli, felt only at a certain stage of life, but persisting factors. Although they probably reach their greatest degree of effectiveness in orienting (presumably malleable) children, they may also have some effect in resocializing adults in the same direction. The fact that adult age cohorts appear to have become somewhat more European during their mature years suggests that one might reverse the question about decay, and ask "How much *more* European are these younger people likely to become by the time they are 30 or 40 years old?" By their very nature, our data can not give a conclusive answer to this question (or its reverse). It would be rash, however, to flatly assume that a decay in Europeanness will take place.

IV. Stability of Attitudes Over Time

At this point one might reasonably ask if it is plausible that individuals respond to survey questions such as these because of events in their childhood and youth: just how stable are these attitudes? To deal with this point, let us review the manner in which public support for European integration has varied over a decade's time. During that period, the question about "making efforts toward uniting Europe" has been asked repeatedly in three of the countries included in our survey. The following percentages of adult samples responded that they were "for" these efforts:[15]

mission of Political Values (paper presented at the 1966 annual meeting of the American Political Science Association, New York City, Sept. 6–10). Cf. Eleanor Maccoby et al., "Youth and Political Change," *Public Opinion Quarterly* (Spring 1954), pp. 23–29.

15 1952–57 figures from USIA surveys cited in Donald Puchala, *Western European Attitudes on International Problems, 1952–61* (New Haven, 1964), p. 9; 1962 figures from European Communities Information Service survey cited in *Sondages*, #1, 1963, p. 8.

An End to European Integration?

TABLE 5   PERCENT OF ADULTS "FOR" EFFORTS TO UNITE EUROPE

	Sept. '52	Oct. '54	Feb. '55	Dec. '55	Apr. '56	Oct. '56	June '57	Feb. '62
W. Ger.	70%	82%	73%	69%	79%	82%	79%	81%
Britain	58	78	67	66	65	—	64	—
France	60	63	49	45	53	67	55	72

As we see, support for European integration fluctuates from year to year, even from month to month. Are we justified in attributing variations in Europeanness among different age groups to the effect of events which took place as much as 50 years ago? Despite the manifest fluctuation, there is a certain underlying stability. Although varying proportions of the population favored "efforts toward unifying Europe" at varying times, in every case the German adults gave the highest level of favorable response among these countries; and in five of the six cases where comparative data are available, the British adults ranked second.[16] The levels of support for European unity rise and fall simultaneously in the three countries—perhaps in response to important events in the international environment.

There is also a degree of consistency in response patterns when we break them down according to social categories within these countries. In nearly every case, the upper socioeconomic groups give a stronger favorable response than do the lower groups.[17] Moreover the adherents of certain political parties have consistently been more favorable to uniting Europe than those of other parties. Although the over-all level of support rises and falls, the same social groups (and, I infer, the same individuals) tend to be relatively strong or relatively weak in support for European unification. Certain major events come to mind as plausible causes of this rise and fall: I will make a few conjectures about them.

The first two polls in the above series were made in 1952 and 1954—immediately after the Korean War, formation of the E.C.S.C. and during the efforts to form a European Defense Community. There was, probably, a sense of common danger, and a feeling that European unification was moving ahead successfully. Optimism about the imminence of European unification seems to be associated with expressions of support for Euro-

---

[16] Prior to the establishment of the EEC, British adults were consistently more favorable to European unification than were the French (see Table 4). Participation in a common (and successful) endeavor seems to have brought the French adults about even with British adults in Europeanness, while a reversal of the earlier relationship seems clearly reflected in the outlook of youth in the two countries. States of public opinion apparently can be outputs as well as inputs in relation to government decisions.

[17] The patterns of age group responses cannot readily be compared due to the variety of categories used from survey to survey, and because of the excessive breadth of the categories.

The World Community

pean unification.[18] The collapse of the EDC project (and perhaps a diminishing sense of military danger) had the converse effect—leading to a decline in pro-European sentiment in 1955 and early 1956.[19] Subsequent rises in the level of sentiment supporting European unification might be associated with the impact of the Hungarian revolt and the Suez invasion in late 1956; and with a generally optimistic climate created by the establishment and rapid implementation of the Common Market, by 1962.

The question about "efforts toward unifying Europe" was not asked in the 1963 cross-national survey of adults, but there are strong indications that de Gaulle's veto of British admission to the Common Market dispelled the mood of high expectations, bringing a period of relative pessimism which perhaps persists today. One piece of evidence consists in the fact that there was a sharp drop in levels of support for the four key European integration proposals discussed earlier in this paper. Average levels of support for the four measures declined as follows:

TABLE 6   LEVELS OF SUPPORT FOR INTEGRATION PROPOSALS, 1962-1963

	(Feb.) 1962	(Feb.) 1963
The Netherlands	78.5%	73.0%
West Germany	68.2	61.8
France	58.8	54.4
Great Britain (data not available)		

Between January, 1961 and December, 1965, the percentage of Germans who "expect some day to see the countries of Europe united to constitute a United States of Europe" dropped from 36% to 29%. This decline in optimism was especially marked among people over 45 years of age.[20]

[18] In the factor analysis of responses from youth in the four countries, an item tapping the students' estimates of the length of time which will elapse before Europe is "united" had consistent (although only moderately high) loadings on the "Europeanness" factor; the direction of the relationship was always such as to indicate that an optimistic time estimate was linked with support for integrative measures.

[19] There is an apparent flaw in this timetable: the defeat of EDC in the French legislature came *before* the October, 1954 survey. However, at that time it was widely believed that the London Conference establishing the Western European Union would produce an even greater measure of European unification than would have emerged from the EDC (a union which would, moreover, include Britain). An IFOP survey in October, 1954 found that 52% of the Frenchmen surveyed thought that the London Conference was a move toward European unification, as against 17% who thought it was a simple military alliance. A plurality of the former group felt that W.E.U. would go farther in this direction than EDC. These expectations were, of course, false; they seem to have produced a short-lived bubble of optimism about European unification. See IFOP surveys cited by Jean Stoetzel, "The Evolution of French Opinion" in D. Lerner and R. Aron, *France Defeats EDC* (New York: Praeger, 1957), p. 101.

[20] *Jahrbuch der offentlichen Meinung* (Verlag fur Demoskopie, Allensbach, 1957); and *Informationsdienst,* Institut für Demoskopie, January, 1966, cited in Jacques-René Rabier, *L'Opinion Publique et l'Europe* (Brussels, 1966), p. 19.

An End to European Integration?

Moreover, despite the proverbial optimism of youth, the young people in our samples are much less likely to view European unification as something which will be attained in the near future than were adults in the 1962 samples. In response to the question "Do you believe that Europe will become unified?...If YES, in how long a period of time?" the following responses were obtained:

TABLE 7   EXPECTATIONS OF EUROPEAN UNIFICATION

	NETHERLANDS "Never" or "over 20 yrs."	Within 15 yrs.	FRANCE Over 20 yrs.	Within 15 yrs.	GERMANY Over 20 yrs.	Within 15 yrs.
Adults (1962)	57%	43%	51%	49%	42%	58%
Young (1964–65)	82	18	83	17	78	22

The adults were about evenly split (in 1962) between those who saw European unification as something quite close at hand, and those who felt it would come only in the remote future or never. About four-fifths of the youth in all three countries saw it as something relatively remote (and the stalemate which existed in European politics at the time of their responses made their position seem fairly realistic). We believe that this factor probably acted to deflate the level of support for European integration expressed by the younger people in 1964–65. Nevertheless, despite an apparent realization that European unification had bogged down, the youth in our samples gave a relatively strong measure of support for "European" proposals. This shows up even when we compare their responses in 1964–65 with the adult responses from 1962.[21] Basing our comparison on the same four key proposals described earlier in this paper, average levels of support were as follows:

TABLE 8   AVERAGE PERCENTAGE "FOR" FOUR MEASURES

	Netherlands	France	Germany
Adults—1963	78%	59%	68%
Youth 1964–65	77	72	78

In this comparison, the youth in our Dutch sample are actually slightly

[21] Let me emphasize, however, that in my opinion the comparison with the 1963 adult data is definitely the more appropriate intergenerational comparison. Unfortunately, a different set of age categories was used in coding this adult data, from those which were used with the 1963 adult data; we cannot make direct comparisons between adult groups. These age categories, of course, have a different relationship to periods of socialization than did the previous data.

less European than the adults; I attribute this to a reaction to the veto of British admission (and other lesser events) which intervened between the times when the two surveys were taken. In the other two comparisons, the younger generation is substantially more European than the adult age groups, despite the fact that the outlook in 1964 was decidedly less auspicious that it had been in 1962.

V. Relative Stability of Attitude Among Different Age Groups: The Impact of the de Gaulle Veto

The existence of data from two cross-national surveys of attitudes toward European integration, made within a year of each other but giving responses both before and after the veto of British admission to the Common Market, gives us an opportunity to check the relative stability of support for "Europe" among different groups in the adult population of Western Europe. And some intriguing patterns emerge when we compare responses to nine questions which were asked in both the 1962 and 1963 international surveys.

Over the six EEC countries there is a net decline of slightly more than 6% from 1962 to 1963 in the average level of support for the nine European integration proposals. For the most part, this does not reflect a movement into opposition, but a shift from being "for" to "no answer." The percentage giving no answer increased an average of about 8 points from the first survey to the next, so that the percentage "against" actually *declined* slightly.

The increase in the proportion not answering, from 1962 to 1963, seems to be an emotional response to a discouraging event; it can scarcely be attributed to a decline in knowledge or public interest. On the contrary, during the year intervening between the two surveys, the negotiations for British entry brought forth very extensive coverage of the European integration question by the mass media, and almost certainly increased public interest in the topic. Viewed in this context, the rather large increase in the percentage not answering (which would normally seem paradoxical) makes sense: apparently a number of new converts had been made to the European cause during the course of the negotiations. They were recruited largely from among the previously uninformed—and were the least stable adherents.

The veto of British admission on January 14, 1963, suddenly made the outlook for the cause seem bleak. Reacting to this, many of those who had been "for" Europe were apparently jolted off the bandwagon (especially the newer converts, I hypothesize). They were discouraged, but they did not go so far as to register an opinion *against* European integration, however. Instead, they abstained from answering. This is reflected in the substantial and consistent increase in "no answer" responses in each country. By abstaining, these individuals avoided the psychic pain of acknowledging that they were "for" what appeared to be a losing cause.

An End to European Integration?

In which countries was the shock most keenly felt? Expressed as a percentage of those originally "for" each measure, the average decline for the respective nations was: Germany, 15.0%; Belgium, 13.6%; The Netherlands, 10.4%; France, 6.2%; and Italy, 5.1%. In the 1962 survey, the most European country was The Netherlands, followed closely by Belgium and Germany, with France and Italy lagging behind. To an extent, the most European countries suffered the greatest decline from one survey to the next (which I will refer to as "fall-out").

We might explain this phenomenon as follows: a large share of the population of any nation is more or less apolitical; the consensus favorable to a given measure in such a country will therefore contain a higher proportion of fair-weather friends, who have been only faintly interested in the measure, but indicate that they favor it because it is perceived as widely accepted. If 90% of the population of a country expresses itself as favorable to a given proposition, we may be sure that a good share of them—perhaps 20% or 30% of those favorable—have only the vaguest attachment to the measure.

In this connection, we may note that the French level of support was already relatively low in 1962, apparently fairly near a level where only persons with some genuine conviction would express themselves as favorable to a given proposal for integration. France was thus less vulnerable to a decline in support, as a result of a discouraging event, because sufficient opposition was being voiced within the political culture so that apoliticals were less sure which was the "proper" response.[22]

But when we look at the data more closely, we find that the relative attrition is not simply due to having had a comparatively large proportion of the population giving nominal support; some persisting element of a nation's political culture seems to be equally important. For we find a relative stability in The Netherlands (the most European country in 1962) as compared with Germany. In 1963, the latter country had dropped sharply, to a level below France although still ahead of Italy.[23] By contrast, Holland was still clearly in the lead after the veto. While she did experience considerable decline, it was substantially less than that in Germany. I hypothesized that "fall-out" is caused chiefly by defection of the bandwagon riders; but this group may contain two types of individuals: those whose commitment to a given position is relatively

[22] It may also be speculated that the French were relatively less discouraged by the de Gaulle veto because it was, in a sense "their" veto; it was the French who were keeping the British out, and who could, perhaps, reverse themselves. To the Germans and Dutch, on the other hand, there may have been a greater sense of helplessness. A measure they strongly favored had been defeated by a man over whom they had no political control.

[23] The Italian case is somewhat special. This country had a considerably lower level of political information than did any of the other EEC countries. A rather large "non-mobilized" segment of the Italian population had never pronounced itself as favorable to these measures in the first place, and hence did not fall away from supporting them in the face of the veto. Germany continues to rank ahead of France on the most important European measures in 1963, however (i.e., those loading highest on the Europeanness factor). We eliminate Luxemburg from this analysis because of the small sample size for that country.

The World Community

superficial because they are weakly involved politically, and those whose commitment is unstable because they are expressing agreement with a popular or fashionable trend without its being in harmony with the outlook instilled in their primary political socialization.

Our previous analysis has pointed to The Netherlands as an example of stable internationalism, over the three generations for which we have data. Internationalism has deeper historical roots there than among her neighbors.[24] Non-participation in World War I may be an additional factor which would help to maintain a relatively even pattern among the Dutch adult age groups. This may explain the relatively small degree of "fall-out" in The Netherlands, despite the fact that disappointment there must have been especially sharp in reaction to de Gaulle's veto: Holland was the country which was most keenly in favor of British admission, among the Six.[25]

The relative importance of "fall-out" is greater in Germany. Apparently the German consensus favoring Europe was a particularly vulnerable one, containing a relatively large proportion of persons who were expressing internationalistic views which were not in harmony with their primary attitudes.

To check the validity of this interpretation, let us examine the responses of different age groups within these countries, and the degree to which they shifted from 1962 to 1963. This age group analysis so far has suggested that the adults who received their primary political socialization in the interwar period, and the youth socialized after World War II, are relatively strongly European. According to my interpretation, it is these age groups which have underlying concepts of nationality which are most nearly akin to the currently-expressed Europeanism. I would predict, therefore, that these age groups should show the least "fall-out."[26]

Let me point out that a normal expectation would be that the older group would show less "fall-out" from one year to the next: (1) they would be expected to have a relatively inflexible mentality; (2) they have held their opinions longer, and should be relatively "immunized" to change.[27] My prediction, however, is to the contrary: I hypothesize that the older group has a more nationalistic basic concept of political identity,

[24] She has, for example, favored a free-trade policy ever since the end of the Napoleonic Wars; her interest in international law dates back to Grotius, and was reorganized (and perhaps strengthened) by the location of the World Court in The Hague.

[25] This was true of public opinion, as well as of official Dutch policy. Indeed, an absolute majority of Dutch adults polled immediately after the veto said they would prefer a Common Market with Britain but without France, if it were necessary to choose. See *Sondages,* #1, 1963, p. 108.

[26] I select this 28% of respondents from this age group at random, since there is no finer age-identification available. To the extent that the predicted age-group differences hold true within this 15-year age group, this method will result in under-estimating the age-group contrasts—for I will be including a certain number of cases which dilute the differences between the younger and older halves. This is a fairly close approximation to recoding according to consistent (and more usable) age groups —and despite its imperfection, a fairly striking set of age group contrasts does result.

[27] See *The American Voter, op. cit.,* pp. 161ff.

An End to European Integration?

and that these individuals are consequently more vulnerable to change as the result of a blow to a bandwagon mentality.

A comparison of relative rates of "fall-out" indicates that there is very little difference between the older and the younger groups in The Netherlands—once again reflecting her history of a relative internationalism over the past three generations. Since both groups had about the same inner orientation, Dutchmen of 40 and over suffered just about the same degree of set-back as did the younger Dutch adults. On the other hand, the older Frenchmen and Germans suffered a substantially greater degree of "fall-out" than did their younger compatriots. This suggests that they experienced a greater degree of dissonance between expressed and inner orientation than did the younger group.

Note that the younger German group is more stable in its Europeanism than the younger Dutch group: evidently nationalism in Germany exists mainly among those aged forty and over.[28]

TABLE 9   "FALL-OUT" FROM 1962 TO 1963 BY AGE GROUP, FOUR KEY MEASURES

	Netherlands		France		Germany	
	20–39	40+	20–39	40+	20–30	40+
Abolish Tariff:	−10%	−14%	−5%	−15%	− 5%	−11%
Free Movement Labor, Bus.	+ 8	—	+9	− 1	− 2	− 8
Common Foreign Pol.	−13	− 5	−8	−11	−13	−11
Aid European Countries	−10	− 7	+8	− 1	+ 2	− 1
Average Points of "Fall-Out"	− 6.3	− 6.5	+1	− 7	− 4.5	− 7.8

This analysis suggests that the younger adults (particularly in France and Germany) have a more stable commitment to European integration than do the older adults. Despite the fact that (under favorable conditions) both groups may express approximately the same level of support for "European" proposals, there appear to be fewer bandwagon-riders among the younger group. I attribute this phenomenon to differences in the early socialization of the different age categories.

VI. The Evidence of Other Indicators

Let us return now to the question posed at the start: Has European integration *in general* come to an end? If not, why is it that two analyses (Karl Deutsch's and mine) have come to such opposite conclusions?

Deutsch, of course, does not draw upon political socialization data

[28] This holds true of the younger French group as well; as indicated in the foregoing pages, the situation in that country is not quite comparable with the Dutch and German cases in relation to the veto of British admission.

The World Community

in concluding that European integration has levelled off or come to a halt; not having this material available may have led him to underestimate the degree to which the integrative process has continued. But the difference in results cannot be attributed to this alone. My own analysis relies partly on an assertion that the over-all European political environment is currently favorable to formation of a European outlook, and that it has grown more, not less so since 1958.

In making his argument, Deutsch draws on some imaginative and sophisticated analysis; it is worth reviewing in detail. He bases much of his case on an examination of "structural integration." He states: "An analysis of trade data going back as far as 1890 suggests that in the 1957–58 period Europe reached the highest level of structural integration it ever had." Deutsch argues, in effect, that although the total amount of trade among the members of the European Community has increased since 1958, this fact must be discounted because the rate of increase has been no greater than the general rise of trade and productivity. His interpretation might be debated on a variety of grounds. In the period 1958–62, total trade among the countries of the European Community increased by 73%.[29] At the same time, these countries experienced their most impressive four years of economic growth in modern history[30]— a growth which may have been stimulated in part by the extraordinary increase in Community trade. Are we to discount the importance of the trade increase because of the simultaneous occurrence of economic growth? This line of reasoning by itself would lead us to conclude, for example, that the United States was less than half as "integrated" with Western Europe in 1957 as it was in 1929—at the height of isolationism.[31] America's foreign trade increased substantially during the intervening period but GNP increased even faster.

In regard to the economic sphere, Deutsch's argument is useful, though not compelling.[32] When he shifts the analogy to other spheres, however, his conclusions become dubious, particularly where the psychological dimension of the transaction is crucial. Deutsch states, "The absolute increases after 1958 in trade, travel, postal correspondence and the exchange of students are accountable for from the effects of prosperity

[29] EEC Statistical Office, *Foreign Trade Monthly Statistics,* No. 4, Brussels, 1962, p. 9. This was a considerably higher rate of increase than obtained in the four years preceding 1958, See *Economische Statistiche Bericht, Rotterdam,* Jan. 16, 1964.

[30] OECD *General Statistics 1958–62* (Paris, 1963).

[31] U.S. Department of Commerce, *Historical Statistics of the U.S.* (Washington, D.C., 1960), pp. 550, 552.

[32] As presently constructed, the "index of relative acceptability" of foreign trade may reflect a general tendency for foreign trade to decline in proportion to GNP, as nations become highly industrialized. A primitive extractive economy, selling a few plantation crops or raw materials abroad and importing nearly all manufactured items, will be relatively dependent on foreign trade; a large and advanced industrial economy may be less so. As indicated by the American record, isolationism can accompany the early stage, and internationalism the latter stage. This is not accidental: America's high degree of involvement in world affairs at the present time is not weakened by her high domestic productivity—on the contrary, to a large extent, it is made possible by it.

411

An End to European Integration?

and the general increase in the level of these activities. There have been no increases in integration in regard to all these transactions beyond what one would expect from mere random probability and the increase in prosperity in the countries concerned."[33]

Does the fact that these changes have been accompanied by rising prosperity mean that "integration" has not been taking place?[34] I would argue that the chief significance of these trends lies not in the extent to which they have produced "structural integration" in the sense in which Deutsch defines it, but in the degree to which they reshape the political aspirations of the major groups in the society. For example, are we to regard an increase in the number of students being educated abroad as offset by the fact that there has been an increase in higher education within these countries? On the contrary, there is every reason to believe that both tendencies are contributing to the process of European integration. Virtually every opinion survey from which data are available indicates that a relatively high level of education is associated with a stronger degree of support for European unification.[35] Assume that we were able to demonstrate that increases in the exchange of students and in higher education generally *both* encourage the development of a sense of European citizenship; assume also that these increases in educational activities can be attributed entirely to rising prosperity. We would then have demonstrated the (unsurprising) point that prosperity encourages political integration; we would not have shown that integration is not taking place.

Similarly, let us assume that travel in other EEC countries makes an individual more favorable to European integration; is this effect nullified by travel in other places? The absolute increase in exchange of tourists among EEC countries since 1958 has been very sizeable; the influx of EEC tourists in 1963 compares with that in 1958 as follows: Italy, 176%; France, 348%; Germany, 139%; Belgium-Luxemburg, 138%; The Netherlands, 146%.[36] There are indications that this trend is strongly favorable to the process of European integration.[37] In 1963, over six million German tourists visited Italy (equal to the *total* influx of tourists into the U.S. from all nations that year), a figure which represents one out of every nine Germans. At the same time, there were about three million visitors from France, a million from The Netherlands, two-thirds of a million from Belgium. To be sure, the rate of increase has levelled off in recent years. But this may be because the process is reaching a

---

[33] Deutsch, *op. cit.*

[34] Political "integration" has been defined as the attainment within a territory of a "sense of community"—a belief that common social problems must and can be resolved by a process of "peaceful change"; and of institutions and practices strong enough and widespread enough to assure, for a "long" time, dependable expectations of "peaceful change" among its population. Karl Deutsch *et al., Political Community and the North Atlantic Area,* Princeton, 1957, p. 5.

[35] See, for example, Gallup International, *L'Opinion Publique et l'Europe des Six* (Paris, 1962), pp. 29–32.

[36] Calculated from OECD, *Tourism in Member Countries, 1965* (Paris, 1965); and OECD, *Tourism in Europe, 1959* (Paris, 1959).

[37] See *Sondages* (1963), #1, p. 38; cf. Inglehart, *op. cit.,* Ch. 8.

The World Community

saturation point. Overall, in 1963, and again in 1964, about one out of every twelve citizens from her EEC partner countries visited Italy. This is comparable to the proportion of Americans who visit Florida in a given year.[38]

It is also true that rates of travel to countries outside the European Community have increased markedly since 1958; presumably this should act to encourage integration with those countries as well. But there is no reason to assume that an increase in "Europeanness" can come about only through a relative exclusiveness vis-à-vis the outside world. Conceivably, the two might increase concomitantly. In fact, as we shall see presently, this seems to be the case.

Deutsch's distinction between structural integration and probabilistic integration is useful; but he tends to overstress the former at the expense of the latter. Furthermore, he seems to overlook the possible existence of a threshold effect. Deutsch would, no doubt, agree that the EEC area has already reached a relatively high level of structural integration (his data indicate that, in general, a 70–80% level has been attained). It is quite conceivable that this is a high enough level for political integration to take place, even if further increases in these exchanges do not rise above random probability rates. Deutsch would further probably agree that the development of a sense of community is central to the process of integration.[39] Material on "structural integration" provides a relatively indirect indication as to whether this process is taking place. Nevertheless, although Deutsch himself uncovers a more direct kind of evidence of such crucial changes in orientation, he tends to underplay its importance.

Let me cite some of these cases: he finds that "Friendly feelings in French mass opinion about Germany and in German mass opinion about France increased substantially to roughly one-half of the Germans and Frenchmen polled in 1963–4. Feelings of mutual trust increased much less, to about one-fifth of the respondents in each country."[40] He also finds an increase in agreement on accepting European unity between the two countries since 1958; and that elites in the two countries agree on most major issues—and furthermore, seem to be converging over time. Deutsch states that, "Factor analysis of many French and German opinion poll results between 1954 and 1962 indicated a marked increase in the similarity of underlying images between the two countries. . . . In particular, there was a marked increase. . .in the importance of an image of a United Europe in both French and German opinion. Most of this increase occurred between 1957 and 1962." He then notes that "In regard to accepting European unity, at least in general terms, Frenchmen and Germans agreed to a greater extent in 1962 that they had done in earlier years."[41]

[38] About one in fourteen out-of-state Americans visited Florida in 1961. See Florida Council on Economic Development, *Statistical Abstract of Florida* (Tallahassee, 1962), p. 90.

[39] See his definition, footnote 34.

[40] Deutsch, "Integration and Arms Control," *op. cit.*, p. 378.

[41] *Ibid.*, p. 379.

An End to European Integration?

Deutsch tends to discount this primarily on the basis of three points: first, the people of the two countries trust the U.S. more than each other; and Britain trusts both of them more than they do each other. Here again we encounter in its most explicit form an assumption which also seems to underlie Deutsch's reasoning about "structural integration." It might be legitimate to discount indicators of increased European integration on the ground that these interactions have also risen with regard to the outside world; this could be justified if, and only if, European integration and Atlantic integration (and international integration in general) take place in different psychological directions, one tending to develop at the expense of the other. If "Europeanness" were a traditional form of nationalism, this assumption might be justified. But, in fact, the available evidence indicates that this is not the case: they seem to lie on a common psychological dimension. As an individual is converted to a European (or Atlantic) point of view, he tends to become more favorable to other forms of internationalism as well. An openness to Atlantic unity and toward *rapprochement* with Eastern Europe has characterized the Monnet Europeans for a number of years;[42] this orientation also seems to characterize the pro-Europeans among the general population. My survey of youth in Western Europe found the following correlations between relatively strong support for European federation and for U.S. association with the EEC:[43]

	Netherlands	France	Germany	Britain
$Q =$	$+.38$	$+.70$	$+.58$	$+.51$

The tendency for partisans of European federation to favor world government was generally weaker, but consistently positive:

	Netherlands	France	Germany	Britain
$Q =$	$+.42$	$+.38$	$+.49$	$+.29$

If this is true, the relevant question is whether two given countries are in fact coming to trust each other and agree with each other to a greater extent as time passes. The existence of relatively high levels of trust for the U.S. is certainly interesting but it does not diminish the significance of the increasing levels of trust and agreement on European unification between France and Germany.

Deutsch's second reason for discounting the foregoing evidence is that elites in France and Germany show different levels of support for NATO and arms control proposals. But the process of integration implies a continuing convergence—not necessarily that the integrating partners have reached the same absolute level at a given time.

The third point which Deutsch cites centers on the decline of interest in NATO and in arms control proposals—by governments, in the press, and among the general public. In view of the decline of a sense of threat of Russian invasion, this change in attitude is perfectly comprehensible: the

---

42 See, for example, Declaration of the Action Committee for a United States of Europe, June, 1962.

43 See Ronald Inglehart, *op. cit.*, Ch. 3. I use Yule's Q as a measure of association. Figures are for middle class youth only.

The World Community

problem is less interesting because it seems less important. In the early 1950's, European "unification" was largely manifested in NATO, a military response to a military threat. Today it connotes economic and social integration to a much greater extent, as exemplified by the European Community. Deutsch's elite interview data indicate that at present support for European integration is not dependent on a sense of military threat.[44] Nevertheless, he uses evidence of declining interest in military matters to support his contention that European integration has come to a stop. One might hazard the guess that Deutsch's conclusion may have been unduly influenced by the study of top-level decisionmaking. It is at precisely this level that European integrative activity has been most effectively blocked since 1958 (but even here one cannot overlook such important bits of progress as the agreement to unify the three European Community executive bodies, and the agreement on a common agricultural policy). In broader spheres of European society, I would argue, the process of integration has been going on.

At least a limited amount of reorientation in favor of "Europe" seems to have taken place among the adult population since 1958. But perhaps more important are the changes which seem to characterize the outlook of the generation which has been undergoing formation since the end of World War II, and especially since the creation of the European Communities. There are indications that their Europeanness is more stable than that of older age cohorts, and it seems to persist even under rather adverse conditions. I would argue that this is true because, for them, a European outlook is not a superficial reorientation, but reflects their earliest political perceptions. Before the end of the 1970's, a majority of the voting population in the Common Market countries will consist of people who entered primary school after World War II. It is not inconceivable that the entry into political relevance of new elements will tend to further change the political environment in important ways.

All of the foregoing calls into question the projections which have been made concerning the likelihood of further progress toward erecting the institutional framework for a United States of Europe. At this level, I agree, there has been relatively little progress in the last several years. But there are, after all, certain blocking factors which currently act to prevent much change in this sphere—the most important being the attitude of the present French government.[45] It is dubious whether

44 See Deutsch, "Integration and Arms Control," op. cit., p. 384.

45 Leon Lindberg goes so far as to argue that de Gaulle's boycott of the EEC in 1965–66 does not even represent an attempt to halt the process of integration; it is, rather, a struggle over the form and content of decision-making procedures among actors who accept the European Community system. He presents persuasive evidence that the Common Market has developed such powerful support among economic elite groups that it is now irreversible—and recognized as such by de Gaulle. If Lindberg is correct, this is a highly significant development—and one which, necessarily, must have taken place since 1958. See Leon Lindberg, "Integration as a Source of Stress on the European Community System," *International Organization*, 30 (1966), pp. 233–266.

An End to European Integration?

de Gaulle will remain in power much beyond 1970. Deutsch's evidence indicates that French elites on the whole are a good deal more favorable to European integration than is de Gaulle himself;[46] it therefore seems quite conceivable that with the passing of the General from supreme power, they may be considerably more responsive to the pressures for European political unification than he himself has been.

[46] A plurality of them favor *supranational* European integration (Deutsch, "Arms Control," *op. cit.*, p. 380) ; 72% of French leaders agree that the military security of their country rests upon the deterrent force of the U.S. and "the idea of a national deterrent is unpopular among the elites in France, where it is official government policy." (*Ibid.*, p. 363.) Finally, "a large majority of French leaders (63%) agree that Britain ought to be included in an integrated Europe." (*Ibid.*, p. 360.)

The World Community

Some Problems of International Systems Research

of

International

Systems

Research

C H A P T E R   T W E N T Y - O N E

Morton A. Kaplan

Reprinted with permission of Morton A. Kaplan from *International Political Communities: An Anthology* (Garden City, N.Y.: Doubleday & Company, Inc., 1966), pp. 469–501. Mr. Kaplan is Professor of Political Science at the University of Chicago.

This essay will attempt to provide a brief and non-technical account of some of the theoretical models employed in *System and Process in International Politics,* to indicate some of the problems of a theoretical nature to which these models give rise, and to provide a preliminary account of some research efforts that are intended to test these models. Although these models are not intended to deal with problems of political unification and do not permit a systematic exploration of that subject, the research so far conducted permits an occasional inference with respect to that subject and these will be adumbrated at the end of this paper.

I

A number of theoretical considerations underlie this essay. One is that some pattern of repeatable or characteristic behavior does occur within the international system. Another is that this behavior falls into a pattern because the elements of the pattern are internally consistent and because they satisfy needs that are both international and national in scope. A third is that international patterns of behavior are related, in ways that can be specified, to the characteristics of the entities participating in international politics and to the functions they perform. A fourth is that international behavior can also be related to other factors such as military and economic capability, communication and information, technological change, demographic change, and additional factors long recognized by political scientists.

Just as it is possible to build alternative models of political systems, e.g., democratic or totalitarian, and of family systems, e.g., nuclear families, extended families or monogamous or polygamous families, so it is possible to build different models of international systems. The models can be given an empirical interpretation and the specific propositions of the models can be tested.

The aspiration to state testable propositions in the field of international politics is useful provided some degree of caution is observed concerning the kinds of propositions one proposes to test. For instance, can a theory of international politics yield a prediction of a specific event like the Hungarian revolution of October 1956? The answer probably must be negative. Yet why make such a demand of theory?

Two basic limitations upon prediction in the physical sciences are relevant to this problem. In the first place, the mathematics of complicated interaction problems has not been worked out. For instance, the physical scientist can make accurate predictions based on general formulas with respect to the two-body problem, more complicated and less general predictions with respect to the three-body problem, and only very *ad hoc* predictions concerning larger numbers of bodies. The scientist cannot predict the path of a single molecule of gas in a tank of gas.

In the second place, the physical scientist's predictions are predictions concerning an isolated system. He does not predict that so much gas will be in the tank, that the temperature or pressure of the tank will not be changed by someone, or even that the tank will remain in the experimental room. He predicts what the characteristic behavior of the mass of gas molecules will be if stated conditions of temperature, pressure, etc. hold.

The engineer deals with systems in which many free variables enter. If he acts wisely—for instance, in designing aircraft—he works within the constraints imposed by the laws of physics. But many aspects of exact design stem from experiments in wind tunnels or practical applications of past experiences rather than directly from the laws of physical science.

A theory of international politics normally cannot be expected to predict individual actions, because the interaction problem is too complex and because there are too many free variables. It can be expected, however, to predict characteristic or modal behavior within a particular kind of international system. Moreover, the theory should be able to predict the conditions under which the system will remain stable, the conditions under which it will be transformed, and the kinds of transformations that may be expected to take place.

II

Six alternative models of international systems are presented in this section. These models do not exhaust the possibilities. They are, however, intended to explore the continuum of possibilities. In their present stage of development the models are heuristic. Yet, if they have some degree of adequacy, they may permit a more meaningful organization of existing knowledge and more productive organization of future research. Only two of the models—the "balance of power" system and the loose bipolar system—have historical counterparts.

"BALANCE OF POWER" SYSTEM

The first system to be examined is the "balance of power" international system. Quotation marks are placed around the term to indicate its metaphoric character.

The "balance of power" international system is an international social system that does not have as a component a political sub-system. The

Some Problems of International Systems Research

actors within the system are exclusively national actors, such as France, Germany, and Italy. Five national actors—as a minimum—must fall within the classification "essential national actor"[1] to enable the system to work.

The "balance of power" international system is characterized by the operation of the following essential rules, which constitute the characteristic behavior of the system: (1) increase capabilities, but negotiate rather than fight; (2) fight rather than fail to increase capabilities; (3) stop fighting rather than eliminate an essential actor; (4) oppose any coalition or single actor that tends to assume a position of predominance within the system; (5) constrain actors who subscribe to supranational organizational principles; and (6) permit defeated or constrained essential national actors to re-enter the system as acceptable role partners, or act to bring some previously inessential actor within the essential actor classification. Treat all essential actors as acceptable role partners.

The first two rules of the "balance of power" international system reflect the fact that no political sub-system exists within the international social system. Therefore, essential national actors must rely upon themselves or upon their allies for protection. However, if they are weak, their allies may desert them. Therefore, an essential national actor must ultimately be capable of protecting its own national values. The third essential rule illustrates the fact that other nations are valuable as potential allies. In addition, nationality may set limits on potential expansion.

The fourth and fifth rules give recognition to the fact that a predominant coalition or national actor would constitute a threat to the interests of other national actors. Moreover, if a coalition were to become predominant, then the largest member of that coalition might also become predominant over the lesser members of its own coalition. For this reason, members of a successful coalition may be alienated; they may also be able to bargain for more from the losers than from their own allies.

The sixth rule states that membership in the system is dependent upon only behavior that corresponds with the essential rules or norms of the "balance of power" system. If the number of essential actors is reduced, the "balance of power" international system will become unstable. Therefore, maintaining the number of essential national actors above a critical lower bound is a necessary condition for the stability of the system. This is best done by returning to full membership in the system defeated actors or reformed deviant actors.

Although any particular action or alignment may be the product of "accidents," i.e., of the set of specific conditions producing the action or alignment, including such elements as chance meetings or personality factors, a high correlation between the pattern of national behavior and the essential rules of the international system would represent a confirmation of the predictions of the theory.

[1] The term "essential actor" refers roughly to "major power" as distinguished from "minor power."

Just as any particular molecule of gas in a gas tank may travel in any direction, depending upon accidental bumpings with other molecules, particular actions of national actors may depend upon chance or random conjunctions. Yet, just as the general pattern of behavior of the gas may represent its adjustment to pressure and temperature conditions within the tank, the set of actions of national actors may correspond to the essential rules of the system when the other variables take the appropriate specified values.

By shifting the focus of analysis from the particular event to the type of event, seemingly accidental events may become part of a meaningful pattern. In this way, the historical loses its quality of uniqueness and is translated into the universal language of science.

The number of essential rules cannot be reduced. The failure of any rule to operate will result in the failure of at least one other rule. Moreover, at this level of abstraction, there does not seem to be any other rule that is interrelated with the specified set in this fashion.

Any essential rule of the system is in equilibrium[2] with the remaining rules of the set. This does not imply that particular rules can appear only in one kind of international system. The first two rules, for instance, also apply to bloc leaders in the bipolar system. However, they are necessary to each of the systems and, in their absence, other rules of the two systems will be transformed.

The rules of the system are interdependent. For instance, the failure to restore or to replace defeated essential national actors eventually will interfere with the formation of coalitions capable of constraining deviant national actors or potentially predominant coalitions.

The equilibrium of the set of rules is not a continuous equilibrium but one that results from discrete actions over periods of time. Therefore, the possibility of some change operating to transform the system becomes great if sufficient time is allowed.

Apart from the equilibrium within the set of essential rules, there are two other kinds of equilibrium characteristic of the international system: the equilibrium between the set of essential rules and the other variables of the international system and the equilibrium between the international system and its environment or setting.

If the actors do not manifest the behavior indicated by the rules, the kind and number of actors will change. If the kind or number of actors changes, the behavior called for in the rules cannot be maintained. Some changes in capabilities and information, for instance, may be compatible

---

[2] This kind of equilibrium is not mechanical like the equilibrium of the seesaw, which re-establishes itself mechanically after a disturbance. Instead, it is a "steady state" or homeostatic equilibrium which maintains the stability of selected variables as the consequence of changes in other variables. For instance, the body maintains the temperature of blood in a "steady state" by perspiring in hot weather and by flushing the skin in cold weather. The international system is not simply stable but in Ashby's sense is ultrastable. That is, it acts selectively toward states of its internal variables and rejects those which lead to unstable states. See W. Ross Ashby, *Design for a Brain*, p. 99, New York: John Wiley and Sons, 1952, for a precise treatment of the concept of ultrastability (and also of multistability).

Some Problems of International Systems Research

with the rules of the system, while others may not. If the value of one variable changes—for instance, the capabilities of a given coalition—the system may not maintain itself unless the information of some of the actors changes correspondingly. Otherwise a necessary "counter-balancing" shift in alignment may not take place. Some shifts in the pattern of alliance may be compatible with the rules of the system and others may not.

The rules, in short, are equilibrium rules for the system. This does not, however, imply that the rules will be followed by the actors because they are equilibrium rules, unless an actor has an interest in maintaining the equilibrium of the system. The constraints on the actor must motivate it to behave consonantly with the rules; or, if one or more actors are not so motivated, the others must be motivated to act in a way which forces the deviant actors back to rule-consonant behavior.[3] Thus the rules may be viewed normatively, that is, as describing the behavior which will maintain the equilibrium of the system or as predictive, that is, as predicting that actors will so behave if the other variables of the system and the environment are at their equilibrium settings. If the other variables of the system and the environment are not at their equilibrium settings, deviant behavior is expected.

It is relatively easy to find historical examples illustrating the operation of the "balance of power" system. The European states would have accepted Napoleon had he been willing to play according to the rules of the game.[4] The restoration of the Bourbons permitted the application of rule three. Had this not been possible, the international system would immediately have become unstable. Readmission of France to the international system after restoration fulfilled rule six.

The European concert, so ably described by Mowat, illustrates rule one. The *entente cordiale* illustrates rule four and the history of the eighteenth and nineteenth centuries rule two. Perhaps the best example of rule three, however, can be found in the diplomacy of Bismarck at Sadowa, although his motivation was more complex than the rule alone would indicate. It is not the purpose of this essay to multiply historical illustrations. The reader can make his own survey to determine whether international behavior tended to correspond to these rules during the eighteenth and nineteenth centuries.

The changes in conditions that may make the "balance of power" international system unstable are: the existence of an essential national actor who does not play according to the rules of the game, such as one who acts contrary to the essential rules of the system; in the example discussed, a player who seeks hegemony; failures of information which prevent a national actor from taking the required measures to protect its

---

[3] See Morton Kaplan, Arthur Burns, and Richard Quandt, "Theoretical Analysis of the 'Balance of Power,' " *Behavioral Science,* Vol. V, No. 3, July 1960, pp. 240–52, for an account of why consonant motivation is expected.

[4] It is nevertheless true that since Napoleon threatened the principle of dynastic legitimacy, the system would have been strained. The principle of legitimacy, for quite some time, reduced the suspicions that are natural to a "balance of power" system.

own international position; capability changes that become cumulative and thus increase an initial disparity between the capabilities of essential national actors; conflicts between the prescriptions of different rules under some conditions; difficulties arising from the logistics of the "balancing" process, the small number of essential actors, or an inflexibility of the "balancing" mechanism.

An important condition for stability concerns the number of essential national actors. If there are only three, and if they are relatively equal in capability, the probability that two would combine to eliminate the third is relatively great. Although the two victorious nations would have an interest in limiting the defeat of the third and in restoring it to the system as an acceptable role partner, they might not do so. Since this might not happen, the penalty for being left out of an alliance would be high and even the hazards of being in an alliance relatively great. Even if a nation were in one alliance, it might be left out of the next. Therefore this would be a system in which each victorious nation might attempt to gain as much as it could from the war as a protection against what might happen in the next round. Moreover, each victorious nation would attempt to double-cross the other in order to obtain a differential advantage. There would be a premium upon deceit and dishonesty. On the other hand the addition of some other nations to the system would remove many of the pressures and add to the stability of the system.

Coalitions with many members may thus regard loosely attached members with equanimity. The role of the non-member of the coalition will also be tolerated. When there are a large number of loosely attached actors or non-members of an alliance, any change of alliance or addition to an alliance can be "counter-balanced" by the use of an appropriate reward or by the cognition by some national actor of danger to its national interest.

When, however, there are very few loosely attached or non-member actors, a change in or an addition to an alignment introduces considerable tension into the international system. Under these circumstances, it becomes difficult to make the necessary compensatory adjustments.

For the same reasons, coalition members will have more tolerance for the role of "balancer," i.e., the actor who implements rule four, if the international system has a large number of members and the alignments are fluid. Under these conditions, the "balancer" does not constitute a lethal threat to the coalition against which it "balances." If, however, there are only a few essential actors, the very act of "balancing" may create a permanent "unbalance." In these circumstances the tolerance of the system for the "balancing" role will be slight and the "balance of power" system will become unstable.

Instability may result, although the various national actors have no intention of overthrowing the "balance of power" system. The wars against Poland corresponded to the rule directing the various national actors to increase their capabilities. Since Poland was not an essential national actor, it did not violate the norms of the system to eliminate Poland as an actor. The Polish spoils were divided among the victorious essential national actors. Nevertheless, even this co-operation among the essential national actors had an "unbalancing" effect. Since the acquisitions of the victorious actors could not be equal—unless some exact method were found for weighting geographic, strategic, demographic, industrial, material factors, etc. and determining accurately how the values of these factors would be projected into the future—a differential factor making the system unstable could not easily be avoided.

Even the endeavor to defeat Napoleon and to restrict France to her historic limits had some effects of this kind. This effort, although conforming to rules four, five, and six, also aggrandized Prussia and hence upset the internal equilibrium among the German actors. This episode may have triggered the process which later led to Prussian hegemony within Germany and to German hegemony within Europe. Thus, a dynamic process was set off for which shifts within alignments or coalitions were not able to compensate.

The logistical or environmental possibilities for "balancing" may be decisive in determining whether the "balancing" role within the "balance of power" international system will be filled effectively. For example, even had it so desired, the Soviet Union could not have "balanced" Nazi pressure against Czechoslovakia without territorial access to the zone of potential conflict. In addition, the intervening actors—Poland and Rumania—and possibly also Great Britain and France regarded Soviet intervention as a threat to their national interests. Therefore, they refused to co-operate.

It is possible that a major factor accounting for British success in the "balancing" role in the nineteenth century lay in the fact that Great Britain was predominantly a naval power and had no territorial ambitions on the European continent. These facts increased the tolerance of other national actors for Britain's "balancing" role. As a preponderant maritime power, Great Britain could interfere with the shipping of other powers and could transport its small army; it also was able to use its naval capabilities to dispel invading forces. Even so, Palmerston discovered occasions on which it was difficult to play the "balancing" role either because it was difficult to make effective use of Britain's limited manpower or because other powers displayed little tolerance for the role.

The "balance of power" system has the following consequences. Alliances tend to be specific, of short duration, and to shift according to advantage and not according to ideology (even within war). Wars tend to be limited in objectives. There is a wide range of international law that applies universally within the system. Among the most significant rules of applicable law are those dealing with the rules of war and the doctrine of non-intervention.[5]

[5] For an explication at greater length of the hypothetical relationship between system structure and system of norms, see Morton A. Kaplan, and Nicholas deB. Katzenbach, *The Political Foundations of International Law,* New York: John Wiley and Sons, 1961.

The World Community

The "balance of power" system in its ideal form is a system in which any combination of actors within alliances is possible so long as no alliance gains a marked preponderance in capabilities. The system tends to be maintained by the fact that even should any nation desire to become predominant itself, it must, to protect its own interests, act to prevent any other nation from accomplishing such an objective. Like Adam Smith's "unseen hand" of competition, the international system is policed informally by self-interest, without the necessity of a political sub-system.

The rise of powerful deviant actors, inadequate counter-measures by non-deviant actors,[6] new international ideologies, and the growth of supranational organizations like the Communist bloc with its internationally organized political parties sounded the death knell for the "balance of power" international system.

LOOSE BIPOLAR SYSTEM

In its place, after an initial period of instability, the loose bipolar system appeared. This system differs in many important respects from the "balance of power" system. Supranational actors participate within the international system. These supranational actors may be bloc actors like NATO or the Communist bloc or universal actors like the United Nations. Nearly all national actors belong to the universal actor organization and many—including most of the major national actors—belong to one or the other of the major blocs. Some national actors, however, may be non-members of bloc organizations.

In distinction to the "balance of power" international system, in which the rules applied uniformly to all national actors, the essential rules of the loose bipolar system distinguish, for instance, between the role functions of actors who are members of blocs and those who are not.

In the "balance of power" system, the role of the "balancer" was an integrating role because it prevented any alliance from becoming predominant. In the ideal form of the system, any national actor is qualified to fill that role. In the loose bipolar system, however, the integrating role is a mediatory role. The actor filling it does not join one side or the other but mediates between the contending sides. Therefore, only non-bloc members or universal actor organizations can fill the integrative role in the loose bipolar system.

The functioning of the loose bipolar system depends upon the organizational characteristics of the supranational blocs.[7] If the two blocs are not hierarchically organized, the loose bipolar system tends to resemble the "balance of power" system, except that the shifting of alignments takes place around two fixed points. Such shifting is limited by the func-

---

6 Britain and France violated rules one, two, four, five, and six in the 1930's.

7 Extensional definitions would identify NATO as relatively non-hierarchical and the Communist bloc as mixed hierarchical. If the Communist bloc were to be so integrated that national boundaries and organizational forms were eliminated, it would become fully hierarchical.

tional integration of facilities, since a shift may require the destruction of facilities and the reduction of the capabilities of the shifting national actor. Shifting in alignment tends also to be limited by geographic and other logistic considerations. Nevertheless, the bloc actors constitute relatively loose organizations and the international system itself develops a considerable flexibility.

If one bloc has some hierarchical organizational features and the other is not hierarchically organized, a number of consequences can be expected. The hierarchical or mixed hierarchical bloc will retain its membership, since functional integration will be so great that it would be difficult for satellite members to withdraw or to form viable national entities if they did.[8] The relative permanence of membership in the bloc constitutes a threat to non-members. Therefore, such a bloc is unlikely to attract new members except as a consequence of military absorption or political conquest by a native political party which already had associate membership in the bloc through the medium of an international party organization. The relatively irreversible characteristics of membership in such a bloc constitute a threat to all other national actors, whether associated in a bloc or not.

The non-hierarchical bloc has a looser hold over its members but is more likely to enter into co-operative pacts of one kind or another with non-bloc members. The pressure emanating from the hierarchically organized bloc, however, is likely to force the non-hierarchically organized bloc to integrate its bloc activities more closely and to extend them to other functional areas, or alternatively is likely to weaken and undermine the bloc.

If both blocs subscribe to hierarchical integrating rules, their memberships become rigid and only uncommitted states can, by choosing an alignment, change the existing line-up. Any action of this sort, however, would tend to reduce the flexibility of the international system by eliminating nations not included in blocs. Non-bloc member actors therefore would be more likely to support one or the other of the blocs on specific issues than to support either in general. If both blocs are hierarchically organized, their goals are similar—hierarchical world organization—and incompatible, since only one can succeed in leading such a world system.

With only two major groupings in the bipolar system, any rapid change in military capabilities tends to make this system unstable. For this reason, possession of second-strike nuclear systems by both major blocs is a factor for stability within the system.

The rules of the loose bipolar system follow:

1) All blocs subscribing to hierarchical or mixed hierarchical integrating principles are to eliminate the rival bloc.

2) All blocs subscribing to hierarchical or mixed hierarchical integrating principles are to negotiate rather than to fight, to fight minor wars rather than major wars, and

---

[8] In this connection, it is noteworthy that the Yugoslavs were able to resist the drastic Soviet demands for economic integration. Tito's withdrawal would have been much more difficult—and perhaps impossible—had this not been the case.

The World Community

to fight major wars—under given risk and cost factors—rather than to fail to eliminate the rival bloc.

3) All bloc actors are to increase their capabilities relative to those of the opposing bloc.

4) All bloc actors subscribing to non-hierarchical organizational principles are to negotiate rather than to fight to increase capabilities, to fight minor wars rather than to fail to increase capabilities, but to refrain from initiating major wars for this purpose.

5) All bloc actors are to engage in major wars rather than to permit the rival bloc to attain a position of preponderant strength.

6) All bloc members are to subordinate objectives of the universal actor to the objectives of their bloc in the event of gross conflict between these objectives but to subordinate the objectives of the rival bloc to those of the universal actor.

7) All non-bloc member national actors are to co-ordinate their national objectives with those of the universal actor and to attempt to subordinate the objectives of bloc actors to those of the universal actor.

8) Bloc actors are to attempt to extend the membership of their bloc but to tolerate the non-member position of a given national actor if the alternative is to force that national actor to join the rival bloc or to support its objectives.

9) Non-bloc member national actors are to act to reduce the danger of war between the bloc actors.

10) Non-bloc members are to refuse to support the policies of one bloc actor as against the other except in their roles as members of a universal actor.

11) Universal actors are to reduce the incompatibility between the blocs.

12) Universal actors are to mobilize non-bloc member national actors against cases of gross deviation, e.g., resort to force by a bloc actor. This rule, unless counterbalanced by the other rules, would enable the universal actor to become the prototype of a universal international system.

Unlike the "balance of power" international system, there is a high degree of role differentiation in the loose bipolar system. If any of the roles is pursued to the exclusion of others, the system will be transformed. If one bloc actor eliminates another, the system may be transformed into a hierarchical system. If the universal actor performs its functions too well, the system may be transformed into a universal international system. Other variations are possible.

The consequences of the loose bipolar system are as follows. Alliances tend to be long-term, to be based on permanent and not on shifting interests, and to have ideological components. Wars, except for the fear of nuclears, would tend to be unlimited. However, the fears concerning nuclear escalation are so great that there is, in fact, a greater dampening of war than in the "balance of power" system. Thus, wars tend to be quite limited, and even limited wars are rare. In the field of law, there are fewer restrictions on intervention than in the "balance of power" system and the limitations which do exist stem largely from the fear of escalation. The universal organization is used primarily for mediation and to some extent for war dampening.

TIGHT BIPOLAR SYSTEM

The tight bipolar international system represents a modification of the loose bipolar system in which non-bloc member actors and universal actors

Some Problems of International Systems Research

either disappear entirely or cease to be significant. Unless both blocs are hierarchically organized, however, the system will tend toward instability.

There is no integrative or mediatory role in the tight bipolar system. Therefore there will tend to be a high degree of dysfunctional tension in the system. For this reason, the tight bipolar system will not be a highly stable or well-integrated system.

UNIVERSAL SYSTEM

The universal international system might develop as a consequence of the functioning of a universal actor organization in a loose bipolar system. The universal system as distinguished from those international systems previously discussed, would have a political system as a sub-system of the international social system. However, it is possible that this political system would be of the confederated type, i.e., that it would operate on territorial governments rather than directly on human individuals.

The universal international system would be an integrated and solidary system. Although informal political groupings might take place within the system, conflicts of interest would be settled according to the political rules of the system. Moreover, a body of political officials and administrators would exist whose primary loyalty would be to the international system itself rather than to any territorial sub-system of the international system.

Whether or not the universal international system is a stable system depends upon the extent to which it has direct access to resources and facilities and upon the ratio between its capabilities and the capabilities of the national actors who are members of the system.

HIERARCHICAL SYSTEM

The hierarchical international system may be democratic or authoritarian in form. If it evolves from a universal international system—perhaps because the satisfactions arising from the successful operation of such a universal international system lead to a desire for an even more integrated and solidary international system—it is likely to be a democratic system. If, on the other hand, the hierarchical system is imposed upon unwilling national actors by a victorious or powerful bloc, then the international system is likely to be authoritarian.

The hierarchical system contains a political system. Within it, functional lines of organization are stronger than geographical lines. This highly integrated characteristic of the hierarchical international system makes for greater stability. Functional cross-cutting makes it most difficult to organize successfully against the international system or to withdraw from it. Even if the constitution of the system were to permit such withdrawal, the integration of facilities over time would raise the costs of withdrawal too high.

428

The World Community

Consider a world in which some twenty-odd nations have nuclear systems capable of a not incredible first strike. That is, each nation would have a nuclear system that would not completely reduce enemy forces in a first strike but that might nonetheless reduce the enemy forces so much, if everything went according to plan, that a war begun by a first strike might be contemplated. However, even a successful first strike would then leave a nation launching such an attack, because of its depleted arsenal, quite vulnerable to attack by a third nation—an attack that might not be unlikely either if its own attack had been without provocation or if the other nation were malevolent. In any event, the vulnerability of the attacker to subsequent attack by a third state would tend to inhibit such a first strike except in the most extremely provocative circumstances.

There would be little need for specific alliances in this world. To the extent that alliances did occur, one would expect them to be of a non-ideological nature. Nations might ally themselves in pacts establishing an obligation to retaliate against any "aggressor" who launched a nuclear attack, which exceeded certain specified proportions, against an alliance member.

In this system one does not expect large counter-value[9] or counter-force[10] wars. If nuclear weapons are used at all, they will tend to be used in limited retaliations for purposes of warning or in other strictly limited ways. The wars that do occur will tend to be non-nuclear and limited in geographic area and means of war-fighting. Sub-limited wars will occur more often than actual wars.

The system, however, might seem to have some potentiality for triggering wars or for catalytic wars. That is, if one nation engages in a counter-force attack, this in some views would likely trigger an attack on it by a third state. Or an anonymous attack or accident might catalyze a series of wars. These possibilities cannot be denied, particularly if tensions within the system become high. Nonetheless first strikes and accidental wars are unlikely because credible first-strike forces will not exist and because adequate command and control systems will be available. Thus the nuclear systems will be relatively stable against accidents. An anonymous attack will be a theoretical possibility but not a practicable one unless many nations develop Polaris forces, that is, forces such that an attack cannot be attributed to a particular nation. Even so, it would seem difficult to identify the rational motive for attack in such a world. An anonymous attack would not seem to have any reasonable political motive, since by definition, the aggressor could not identify himself and thus

[9] A counter-value attack is directed against cities or other non-combatant installations that are of social importance.

[10] A counter-force attack is one directed against military installations. The term usually refers to strikes against nuclear installations.

Some Problems of International Systems Research

secure the benefits arising from threats. Numerous nervous rivals would remain, and the attack might very well trigger a holocaust.

Because of the adequacy of nuclear systems and the relative unimportance of alliances, when contrasted with the "balance of power" international system, interventions would not be as ominous as in that system and therefore would not be as strongly interdicted. But since the gains resulting from such interventions would be smaller than in the loose bipolar system, they are unlikely to become characteristic of this system. The danger of escalation, moreover, would tend to limit them. If universal organizations exist in this system, they would act as mediators, as would non-involved states whether nuclear or non-nuclear. In general, though, the universal organization would have fewer and less important functions than in the loose bipolar system. Nations equipped with nuclear forces in the unit veto system will tend to be self-sufficient and to reject outside pressures, even if coming from universal organizations. In particular, the functions of the universal organization dealing with political change will tend to be minimized. This will be reinforced by the disappearance of the colonial question as an important issue in world politics.

The foreign policies of the great nuclear powers will tend to be isolationist. Alliances, as specified, will recede in importance. Hegemonial ambitions will be curbed—primarily by an obvious inability to achieve them. Protective functions will tend to be shifted to "other" shoulders, when aggression does occur, since no "natural" assignment of this function will be possible. (That is, almost any one of the nuclear powers could play the role; there is no particular pressure on any particular nation to assume it.)[11]

One would expect nations such as the Soviet Union and China to be less revolutionary, as the prospects for revolutionary solidarity receded even further, and as the frictions between nuclear powers, regardless of ideology, increased. As a consequence nations such as the United States would have less incentive to resist changes in the status quo.

The domestic corollary of the above would involve publics suspicious of foreign nations, relatively uninterested in the morals of quarrels or in social change external to the nation, and lacking the assurance necessary for an articulated goal-oriented foreign policy.

III

A number of models follow which may be considered either variations of the loose bipolar system or of the unit veto system. The variations will

[11] This is parallel to the situation between the two world wars, when the League of Nations sought to control aggression. The onus of stopping aggression could always be shifted to other shoulders and was not undertaken by any nation or combination of nations until very late in the game. At the time of Korea, on the other hand, in the loose bipolar system, if aggression were to be halted, only the United States was in a position to accomplish this. Thus the fact that the system singled out a particular nation for this role served to reinforce the performance of the role function.

The World Community

occur under conditions that are not consonant with maximum stability for either kind of system. Although perhaps not genuinely equilibrium systems, they correspond with conditions that conceivably might persist for critical periods of time. In this sense they might be considered to have some sort of local stability. They are worth exploration since they indicate some potential lines of development from the existing situation. Indeed the very loose bipolar system is descriptively reasonably close to the existing situation. Still for purposes of model construction we simplify and reduce the number of variables involved. We look for those conditions which make for maximum stability within the limitations of the somewhat destabilizing constraints which we do place on the models. Other variants could easily be constructed.

VERY LOOSE BIPOLAR SYSTEM

This is a model that does not appear in *System and Process*. It has elements of great inherent instability and would not be presented at all, except that it has striking resemblances to contemporary international politics. In the loose bipolar system, the nations playing different roles are not differentiated in terms of history, culture, state of economic development, color, and so forth. In the real world, the uncommitted nations, by and large, are ex-colonies, in particular, ex-colonies of nations belonging to NATO; are in bad economic circumstances; are attempting to modernize and develop; belong, by and large, to the so-called colored races; and possess ideologies that make them hostile to much the NATO bloc stands for. Increased nuclear stability has reduced the fear of central war, except as a consequence of escalation. This has tended to dampen international crises of the classical military kind but has created a shelter for guerrilla and sub-limited wars as well as for rare limited wars in areas where escalation is not likely. The blocs have weakened, although they still exist. Large areas of accord and common interest between the United States and the Soviet Union appear to have arisen. Meanwhile Communist China has appeared to many as a potential threat to the U.S. and the U.S.S.R. There has also been a limited extent of nuclear diffusion.

In this system, the universal organization is used in ways consonant, but not identical, with the revolutionary drives of many of the uncommitted nations. Within the universal organization both blocs will compete for the support of the uncommitted states with respect to the issues of decolonization and of racial equality. In this competition the bloc which, for the most part, supports the status quo will, by and large, be outbid. The conservative bloc will be more effective in those areas in which it can intervene directly or even indirectly, with military force and economic support.

Although the conservative bloc has sufficient support to prevent a rapid shift to the left within the universal organization, the competition for the support of the uncommitted nations will be shifted from the two blocs to a competition between the more and less radical wings of the

431

Some Problems of International Systems Research

revolutionary bloc. The process adumbrated above will likely coincide with the quasi-legitimization of intervention against existing "conservative" governments by revolutionary governments.[12]

This system will be characterized by the search for arms control, for accommodation between the blocs, and by the opposition to bloc policy by important members of both blocs. There will be a fragmentation, or at least weakening, of bloc structures. In the area of law, the rule of non-intervention will be breached even more than in the loose bipolar system. The universal organization will be used primarily to control the path of political change rather than primarily as a mediatory instrument. As a consequence, it is likely to have forced upon it more and more difficult problems that are not unlikely to be beyond the competence of the organization. They will likely involve strong conflicts of interest between the bloc leaders and may reach such a magnitude that the support of the bloc leaders for the universal organization may be called in question. Extreme self-restraint on the part of the bloc leaders will be required if the system is not to become unstable and if, in particular, the universal organization is to remain viable and to continue to perform its mediating functions.

THE DÉTENTE SYSTEM

The "détente system" world assumes that some of the favorable projections as to changes within both the Soviet and American systems occur. Soviet society becomes more open and less aggressive and the U.S. less defensive of the international status quo. Although no responsible, reasonable, and cautious social scientist would predict these changes, it still would be interesting to see if we can picture the kind of system which might occur if these changes did take place. In general, we assume the amelioration of the Soviet system, the domestication of the Chinese system, or at least the inability of the Chinese to create difficulty, and stability in much of the uncommitted world.

This is a world in which the U.S. and the U.S.S.R. are still strongly competitive but in which the competition is not conflictful. Tensions are relaxed and important arms control agreements reached. As a consequence Russia and the U.S. support nuclear forces capable only of mostly finite deterrence and there are portents that the forces are being reduced to those required for minimum deterrence only.

[12] An example of this is given by the announced support for the Congolese rebels by the Egyptian and Algerian governments. According to *The New York Times* of January 2, 1965, after the Security Council's resolution calling for non-intervention in the Congo, the State Department, "believed, for example, that the United Arab Republic and Algeria will no longer be willing to admit that they are shipping arms to the Congolese rebels. The two countries may continue their shipments but at a restricted level that can be kept secret it is believed." This pathetic quotation indicates graphically the extent of the shift involved. (According to *The New York Times* of February 1, 1965, the Algerians announced their support for the rebels and the Egyptians, as a gesture of support to the rebels, asked the Congolese to close their embassy in Cairo.)

The World Community

As a consequence of this "détente system," the internal organization of the two blocs loosens up. Some of the Soviet satellites begin to take occasional positions on foreign policy agreeing with those of the West rather than with the Soviet Union. Fissures within the Western bloc increase. Although most issues tend to find groupings revolving around the Soviet Union and the United States, the alignments have some tendency to differ from issue to issue. And on some issues the U.S. and the U.S.S.R. are in agreement and differ with China or one or more Western states.

The foreign policies of the U.S. and the U.S.S.R. tend to liberal interventionism. Anti-colonialism is carried to completion. The U.S. quits backing oligarchical but anti-Communist states. The Soviet Union learns how to live with non-Communist new nations and ceases its support of national liberation movements within genuinely independent nations. Some difficulties attend Chinese attempts to aid national liberation movements.

In the area of law, non-intervention in the internal affairs of other states is stressed. This is a necessary corollary of the "détente system." Although some of the rules of international law are changed to accord with new values—on the subject of expropriation, for instance—in general the rules of international law are strengthened and enforced. They are extended to outer space and celestial bodies.

The universal organization plays a strong role in the governance of space, celestial bodies, and the polar regions. It aids in the extinguishment of colonialism, in the regulation of arms control measures, and takes a leading role in the dampening of international breaches of the peace.

Breaches of the peace—or even wars—may occur in this system, but they will not involve the U.S. and the U.S.S.R., at least in direct confrontations with each other. Such wars will tend to be local, to be strictly limited in objectives, to involve minor nations, and to be strictly non-nuclear. Where this threatens not to be the case, the U.S. and the U.S.S.R. are likely to co-operate within limits to prevent occurrences that might escalate. And, if they do not co-operate in this endeavor, at least they will not seriously interfere with each other's actions toward this end. They will usually work through the universal organization in these cases.

THE UNSTABLE BLOC SYSTEM

The world of "the unstable bloc system" is a world in which developments contrary to those assumed for the "détente system" world have taken place. This is a world in which tension has increased and in which the U.S. and the U.S.S.R. are highly suspicious of each other. Arms control agreements are minimal in this world. Third area conflicts are extensive. There are local outbreaks of violence. And national liberation movements continue to be a problem. Qualitative developments have made nuclear systems cheaper and easier to acquire.

The nuclear systems of the U.S. and U.S.S.R. vary in strength from mostly finite deterrence to not incredible massive retaliation. Four or five other states have nuclear systems but these are good for minimum deterrence only. All nuclear powers possess strategies calling for limited strategic reprisal under appropriate circumstances. But obviously it is easier and safer for the U.S. and U.S.S.R. to use this strategy, even against each other, and certainly against the small nuclear powers, than it is for the small nuclear powers to use it against each other. It is conceivable— but barely so—and not credible that the small nuclear powers would use limited strategic reprisal against one of the large nuclear powers. The chance is much greater that the small power attempting this would be left to its fate and that the retaliation then applied against it would not trigger off the other large nuclear power than that it would. Thus the deterrent value of such a threat by a small nuclear power—unless led by an apparent madman—would not be great.

Alliance policy in this system is highly dependent upon military capability and policy. If the United States' posture, for instance, is clearly not adequate for deterrence against aggression directed at countries other than the United States, the strains on its alliance during periods of crises might prove insuperable, except in those cases where its allies' capabilities, in addition to its own, might produce the requisite deterrence. One would assume that the Warsaw Pact powers would not be as susceptible to splitting tactics as NATO because of the "organic" political relationships among the members and because of the presence of the Russian army on satellite soil. Although this position is debatable, it is nonetheless plausible.

In general, bloc alignments would be subject to two conflicting pressures. The fact of crisis in a basically bipolar world would give the blocs greater reason for being and greater cohesion. The additional fact, however, that the U.S., or any other nation, might hesitate before inviting nuclear destruction on its own territory provides an opening for nuclear blackmail. That such blackmail might be dangerous and that it is unlikely to be practiced except under conditions of very great provocation does not negate this consideration. Moreover, the threat need not be overt. The fact that it is operative in the situation is enough to help shape expectations, attitudes, and national policies. How the two conflicting pressures factor out depends upon an interplay of considerations difficult to consider in the abstract.

The foreign policies of the U.S. and the U.S.S.R. in this model will tend to be interventionist. They will respond to the basic clash of interests and not to a general concordance of interests as in the "détente system." U.S. policy will tend toward conservatism, that is, toward the support of status quo conservative regimes. Change will tend to be viewed as a threat, despite some plausible arguments to the contrary.[13] There will be a consequent alienation of a considerable portion of the intellectual elite within the U.S. and in the other NATO states. Soviet policy will be oriented toward national liberation movements despite a desire not to "rock the boat" in the dangerous nuclear age. Additional "Hungarys"

[13] For some of these arguments, see "United States Foreign Policy in a Revolutionary Age," in Morton A. Kaplan, ed., *The Revolution in World Politics,* John Wiley and Sons, New York, New York, 1962.

434

may occur, or other events may occur which disillusion Soviet intellectuals. Relations between Russia and China will influence Soviet policy. If, as at present, they are at odds, China will tend to pre-empt the revolutionary position and this might moderate Soviet policy to some extent. But, by assumption, this would not go too far, or we would be back in the "détente system." It is also possible, but not likely, that with the retirement of Khrushchev and after the death of Mao, the two nations become more closely allied. In this latter case, the conflict and tension between the blocs will increase greatly.

Although most breaches of the peace in this system will not involve direct confrontations between the U.S. and the U.S.S.R., such confrontations are not entirely unlikely in this system. Moreover, there is a distinct possibility that nuclear weapons may be used in some limited fashion. If so, the use will probably be of the limited reprisal variety.

The role of the universal organization will be primarily mediatory and adapted to dampening the consequences of outbreaks of violence. Although each bloc will support political changes contrary to the interests of the opposing bloc, the efforts to secure a constitutional majority in the universal organization will generally prove ineffective. The universal organization will not acquire authority over outer space, celestial bodies, and serious arms control measures.

Intervention in the internal affairs of other nations will be rampant in this system and will be limited primarily by the fear of nuclear escalation. This system will not be noted for the growth of international law. If anything, there will be retrogression. Existing standards will erode and will not be replaced by generally agreed-upon norms.

INCOMPLETE NUCLEAR DIFFUSION SYSTEM

We will now consider another variation of the "unstable bloc system." The description of this system is roughly similar to the previously mentioned one, except that fifteen or twenty nations, additional to the U.S. and the U.S.S.R., will have nuclear forces. But these forces will be of the small vulnerable variety. Our analysis will stress only those features of this world that differ from the "unstable bloc system."

The United States and the U.S.S.R. will have nuclear forces that are not capable of first strike but that do give some significant advantage if used first. The smaller nuclear nations will possess what is ordinarily called minimum deterrence. This is similar to the French idea of "tearing an arm off." These forces would, in fact, deter most attacks against the homeland, but not all, and probably not in extremely provocative situations. Their triggering capability would be quite small. And they would be quite vulnerable to surprise attack.

Alliances would be possible between major and minor nuclear powers or among minor nuclear powers. But the former type of alliance would be inhibited by the small state's possession of nuclear arms. Possession would by itself be a sign of independence and distrust. Moreover the large state would fear commitment by the small state's nuclear use. It would desire to insulate itself from a chain of actions that it could not control. And, although a general alliance among most of the small states possessing nuclear forces might create a reasonable deterrent, unless there were exceptional political or cultural circumstances the alliance would be very susceptible to nuclear blackmail and splitting tactics. Otherwise the discussion of the "unstable bloc system" is applicable with respect to alliance conditions.

Although wars in this system would tend to be limited, as in the "unstable bloc system," the degree of tension would be higher also; and the possibility of escalation would be greater. Limited and direct confrontations between the U.S. and the U.S.S.R. might occur in non-European areas. A central confrontation in Europe might also occur, but here the danger of escalation beyond the limited-war category would be very great. And for this reason the factors operating against central confrontation would tend to be very great.

The mediatory functions of the universal organization would be more important than in the "unstable bloc system" world and would tend to be more stressed, although it would also prove more difficult to use them successfully. Outside of mediatory functions the universal organization would have even fewer functions than in the "unstable bloc system" world and would handle them less successfully on the whole.

The legal system would function even more poorly than in the "unstable bloc system" world, and intervention in the internal affairs of other states would be even more extensive. Foreign policy would be as in the "détente system" world, but the conservative interventionist nature of American policy would be even more pronounced. Soviet policy would tend to be more revolutionary. The alienation of some intellectuals would be increased, but the obvious dangers of the situation would also create a counter-current of chauvinism leading to a highly dangerous bifurcation of intellectual opinion within both blocs and within the leading nation of each. Governments and their supporters would lack assurance and might become susceptible to ill-considered actions. There might be a swing between excessive caution and excessive adventurism.

IV

The use of the equilibrium models involves three major problems. The first involves the problem of adjusting a closed model to open reality. The second involves the problem of investigating the consistency and power of the model. The third involves the historical testing of the model. A brief effort will be made to elucidate each of these problems.

ENGINEERING A MODEL

We have first the problem of engineering a model to explain specific historical situations or to prescribe for particular policy problems. This involves adding variables in an *ad hoc* manner and is somewhat similar to the method whereby physicists or other physical scientists are able to use their models for predictive purposes only after specifying the starting states or conditions in which the application is to occur. There are many unresolved problems here and these cannot now be considered.[14] However an example follows. The "balance of power" theory, for instance, predicts that alliances will be short-lived, based on immediate interest, and neglectful of existing or previous alliance status. The rigid alliance systems of the European great nations between 1871 and 1914 and the relatively unlimited nature of the First World War would seem, superficially at least, inconsistent with the prescriptions of the "balance of power" theory. If one recognizes, however, as there is reason to believe Bismarck foresaw, that the seizure of Alsace-Lorraine by Prussia created in France a public opinion that was ineluctably revanchist, this parameter change permits engineering the theory in a way consistent with the developments that followed. As long as Germany was unwilling to return Alsace-Lorraine to France, France would be Germany's enemy. Thus France and Germany became the poles of rigid opposed alliances, as neither would enter the same coalition regardless of other common interests. The chief motivation for limitation in the theoretical system is the need to maintain the existence of other essential actors as potential future allies. However, for the foreseeable future, neither France nor Germany was the potential ally of the other. Consequently neither had any incentive to limit its war aims against the other. Hence, what had been an incentive for limitation became instead a disincentive.

CONSISTENCY OF THE MODELS

The problem of investigating the power and consistency of the models is compounded by the fact that they are based on plausible rather than on necessary reasoning. For instance, the essential rules of the "balance of power" system do not specify the kind of risk one ought to take to add how much of what kinds of capabilities to one's national capabilities. It is not specified how much a nation ought to risk, or under what conditions, to prevent some other nation from being weakened beyond some unspecified point.

A simple model of the "balance of power" system has, as recently as late 1964, been simulated by an associate of the author on a computer at the University of Chicago. In the initial model, the computer makes decisions for five players. (Steps are being taken to generalize the model for three to seven players.) The players, which represent essential national actors, are assigned sizes, military capabilities, attitudes toward risk, attitudes toward foreign imbalance, subjective estimates of military

---

[14] For a general exploration of this problem, see "Problems of Theory Building and Theory Confirmation in International Politics," Morton A. Kaplan, in *The International System, Theoretical Essays*, Klaus Knorr and Sidney Verba, eds., Princeton University Press, Princeton, New Jersey, 1961.

Some Problems of International Systems Research

strengths (which may differ from the objective strengths), and a factor representing eagerness to form coalitions. The machine then can examine the difference which adding or subtracting a player makes—something that cannot be done with the verbal model. Does it really make a difference whether there are six or seven actors in the game? Or seven or eight? Or seven or nine?

How much difference is made in the model by changing the formula for figuring "imbalance" within the system? How much difference is made by changing the ways in which alignments are formed or the rules which determine which state can align with which? How much difference is made by different formulas for figuring battle exchanges? By changing these formulas in sensitivity studies it is possible to gain a considerable amount of significant knowledge about the models

The machine makes decisions for the players on the basis of recursive optimization procedures, which take into account the results over one war cycle. Since alternative formulas for aspects of the procedures have not been tested comparatively, the results so far obtained may be only artifacts. The results nonetheless have some speculative interest. According to the early runs, if the players have a small distaste for foreign imbalance, that is, if they behave like the postulated "balance of power" players, there is a series of limited wars which do not eliminate any of the players. Raising the distaste for foreign imbalance produces peace. Lowering it produces an unstable series of wars in which players are eliminated. If one of the players likes foreign imbalance, it is necessary to raise the distaste of the other players to produce stability. Conceivably stability might be maintained alternatively by employing a recognition factor, in effect, an analogue of rule four of the "balance of power" system, which calls for coalitions against deviant players that strive for hegemony within the system. In the absence of such a recognition factor—and one has not yet been devised for the machine—if one of the players likes imbalance and if the distaste for imbalance of the other players is not increased, one or more of the players will be eliminated. The deviant player who likes imbalance will not be among the eliminated players and thus will have a selective advantage.

It seems plausible, therefore, in the absence of a special recognition factor analogous to rule four, that it would be advantageous, even for players with a distaste for imbalance, to play as if they did have a liking for foreign imbalance. But, in this case, the system would become unstable. And having—or acting as if one had—a liking for imbalance would then create no selective advantage. Security would be lower than if all acted as if they had a distaste for imbalance. Thus, if players with a distaste for imbalance could choose between acting as if their distaste for imbalance were low—or their taste for imbalance high—and concerting against deviant actors by means of some recognition factor, they would likely choose the latter. And if the recognition factor also included punishment for deviancy, as well as concerted action against the deviant player, even

438

players with a taste for imbalance might prefer to act as if they had a distaste for imbalance. However, these sophisticated complications have not yet been worked out on the computer and thus serve only to illustrate how a machine model that optimizes only over one war cycle might still be used to test for strategies that are optimal over the long run.

No effort has yet been made to put more complicated international systems on the computer, for instance, systems similar to the loose bipolar system. It is not yet known how to program for the complicated features of this system and it is not unlikely that more sophisticated computers with more powerful memory systems will be required. In any event, it seems reasonable to learn more about the simpler systems before moving on to more complex systems.

COMPARATIVE INTERNATIONAL HISTORY AND SYSTEMS MODELS

There are also problems connected with the use of historical materials. A number of historical projects are being carried on by members of the Ford International Politics Workshop at the University of Chicago in order to test one or more of the models employed in *System and Process in International Politics*. Each historical system occurs in its specific set of environmental circumstances. In some of the systems, specialized circumstances not even considered in one of the models, although not necessarily inconsistent either with the conditions of the model or the equilibrium of the system, participate in the activity of the system. A case in point is the mercenary system in the Italian city-state system. The mercenaries have an incentive to behave consistently with the essential rules of the system, for instability would undercut their own role in the system. That is, if there were a roll-up, there would no longer be a need for mercenaries within the system. Moreover, mercenaries occasionally did transform themselves into rulers of an Italian city state. This again gave them an incentive to help maintain the system. In a case of this kind, the explanation offered by the theory holds in general, but the explanation of the particular way in which the equilibrium is maintained requires, among other things, an analysis of the interaction of the mercenary system with the Italian system of city states.

In this case, the historical investigation does not really produce a modification of the model. It simply illustrates how in a specialized set of circumstances a quite particular institution was useful in reinforcing equilibrium. If, on the other hand, our investigations were to show that historic "balance of power" systems were stable only when some additional kind or type of actor is operating—not the mercenary system itself, for it is known not to be universal to "balance of power" systems—then one would have to modify the systems model to include this type of variable. This factor might also be built into the computer model to see what its effects are. If the computer model is stable without this factor, one might investigate what alternative changes in the computer model would be needed to make such a factor necessary for stability. In this case, we would be attempting to replicate to some extent what happens in the real world.

Thus there would be a continued process of learning with feedback between historical studies, system theories, and computer models. More-over, the use of a number of historical models should permit empirical comparative studies to be carried out. These conceivably could shed a good deal of light on the problem with which the book in which this essay is included is primarily concerned. For instance, two of the studies in the Workshops deal with the Italian city-state system and the Chinese war-lord system as international systems. One of these systems turned out to be quite stable; the other quite unstable. In one case, what later developed into the Italian nation continued for several hundred years as, in effect, an international system. In the other case, that of China, national unity was quickly achieved.

Although these studies are still in a preliminary state, some of the reasons for the differences may be conjectured. In the case of the Italian city-state system, the five major city states of the system developed within their localized regions in a period when the interaction possibilities between the major centers of military capability were almost nil for logistic reasons and also for capability reasons. The cities expanded first within the county—a unit which had a certain amount of legitimacy. Almost without exception, they had economic advantages over their potential rivals within the county. Beyond the county, but within the local region, expansion occurred so fast that a roll-up took place. Within this regional system, there were many contenders for hegemony. The large numbers involved seem to permit successful hegemonial aspirations. On the other hand, unlike the situation in France or England, there was no monarch sitting at a seat (Paris or London) that had significantly greater capabili-ties than any potential rivals. By the time hegemony had been gained within the localized regions, there were five major city states, the hypothe-sized lower bound for a stable system.

There were counter-indicants. There were rich interactions among the city states, for instance, involving intermarriage among the leading families and consequently dynastic claims inconsistent with stability. The system was disturbed by the existence of Guelph and Ghibelline rivalries which cut across the cities and established factions within the cities that supported alignments rival to those in which the city state participated. Yet, despite these factors and some similarity in language and tradition, the system persisted. The denizens of the cities had a local orientation. The rulers were concerned primarily to preserve their local rule. The surrounding countryside was fought over, and the inhabitants of the countryside wanted only to escape war. They did not particularly care who ruled them, for all rulers governed harshly.

In the case of the Chinese war-lord system the regional roll-ups did not produce as many as five essential actors. There was a putative national

440

government in Peking which did have some kind of a legitimacy. But it was, in fact, controlled by the regional war lord. Among the intellectuals there was a strong degree of nationalism which had no counterpart in the Italian city-state system. The nature of the interrelationships among individuals within the actors and between them was even richer and more complicated than in the Italian system. The major system which included the northern war lords had grown unstable, and its participants had been gravely weakened before the Kuomintang swept up from the south. There was a strong likelihood of hegemony within this system even before the Kuomintang intervened. However, had unification occurred under the war lords, it is likely that a pluralistic system would have emerged, in which local war lords dependent upon the major center of power retained some independent viability. When the Kuomintang forces under Chiang Kai-shek swept northward they attacked a greatly weakened and unstable system at a time when there was much intellectual support for national reunification. Thus, the Chinese war-lord system contrasts sharply with the Italian city-state system and provides some tentative comparisons. On the other hand, the classic Chinese state system, on which we have some scattered and preliminary studies, would seem to provide a closer analogy to the Italian city-state system.

All the studies which the Workshops are carrying out are distinguished from contemporary systems in a very important way. The Italian city-state system is generally considered contemporaneous with the development of the modern bureaucratic state. Yet the Italian city-state system, as the others mentioned, was highly dependent on the personal characteristics of the rulers. The effectiveness of policy was directly related to these ruler characteristics. Also, although this was the period in which the modern state bureaucracies may be said to have had their beginning, these also were as yet highly dependent upon the rulers. Thus these city states did not impede unification by including centers of organization independent of rulers; nor did they provide a continuity which protected existing units when rulers were changed. Since dynastic claims interfered with external rationality in the international politics of the city-state system—something the extensions of the model contra-indicate—and did reduce stability— something the model predicts—this indicates that there was considerable stability in the system. It persisted despite these major disturbances. This indicates that the systemic obstacles to unification must have been exceptionally strong.

Additional studies of the systems type would probably shed much more light on the problems of national and regional unification than these brief contrasts allow. For instance, studies of the formation and disruption of empires might be very useful here. A preliminary study, which is going on in the Workshops, of the breakup of the Alexandrian empire seems to indicate this. There are more actors in this system than in the Chinese war-lord system that evolved from the breakup of the national system under Yuan Shih-kai. The actors are not as closely tied to territory as

441

in the case of the Chinese war lords, with the exception of the Ptolemies in Egypt and they are much less tied to territory than were the lords of the Italian city-state system.

There is a parallel with the Chinese war-lord system, however. The warfare within the system leads to a general weakening and debilitation of the system until an outside power sweeps in and takes over. Interestingly enough, there is also a parallel with the Italian city-state system. The Roman intervention occurred only after invitations from one or more of the Greek states. In the Italian case, the states of the major European system intervene only after local conflicts seem to make advisable to one or more city states the invitation of outside aid. All three systems, of course, are local international systems which exist within a larger international system and this accounts for some of the similarities to each other and for some of the differences from the "balance of power" model. Still the interaction patterns are extremely interesting, and much can be learned concerning the conditions for unification.

The relevance of these conclusions for the future is, of course, still open to question. The existence of extremely large nations external to local systems in the present world and the possession of nuclear weapons by these large nations provide an incentive on the part of these nations to prevent the kind of continual warfare which characterized the three historical systems we have discussed. This is an obvious consequence of the fear of escalation. Whether in the long run guerrilla and sub-limited war will have the same consequences for the local systems as intrasystem warfare had in the past is a question that is not easy to answer. Also, the nations of the international sub-systems in the contemporary world are, in fact, logistically quite separated, as were the Italian city states in the early stages of the Italian city-state system, that is, before five major city-states had developed. Most modern uncommitted states cannot in fact extend themselves with even minimal effectiveness far beyond their present frontiers. They resort to guerrilla or sub-limited war or subversion as a consequence not merely of the nuclear umbrella but also of their inability to engage in other types of warfare. It is not helpful to speculate inordinately upon this problem, however. We do not yet have sufficient studies for genuine comparative analysis, even apart from attempts to answer questions that pertain to the new conditions of our contemporary world.

The World Community